CHILDREN'S LITERATURE

To Bobbi
Enjoy!
warmly
Martha K Ru
10-16-89

CHILDREN'S LITERATURE

An Issues Approach

Second Edition

Masha Kabakow Rudman

University of Massachusetts
at Amherst

Longman

New York & London

Children's Literature: An Issues Approach
Second Edition

Longman Inc., 95 Church St., White Plains, N.Y. 10601
Associated companies, branches, and representatives
throughout the world

Copyright © 1984, by Longman Inc.

Original 1976 edition copyright
© D.C. Heath and Company

Editorial and Design Supervisor: James J. Fields
Interior Designer: Eileen Beirne
Production/Manufacturing: Ferne Y. Kawahara

Library of Congress Cataloging in Publication Data

Rudman, Masna Kabakow.
  Children's literature.

  Includes bibliographies and index.
  1. Children's literature—History and criticism.
2. Children's literature—Bibliography. I. Title.
PN1009.A1R8 1984   011'.62   83-22217
ISBN 0-582-28398-1
ISBN 0-582-28397-3 (pbk.)

Manufactured in the United States of America
Printing: 9 8 7 6 5   Year: 92 91 90 89 88

This book is dedicated to

> *My parents, Gussie and Ben Kabakow*
> *My husband, Sy*
> *My daughters, Rachel, Reva, and Debbie*

Whose encouragement and support nurture me

CONTENTS

FOREWORD

NOT TOO LONG AGO, a friend of mine told me "I love your book *Greyling* and have read it over and over." And while I took my turn to preen and look modest at once, she added, "I changed the ending, of course."

What my erstwhile friend was doing was not just changing the ending. She was joining a long line of censors who, down through the ages, have marked stories for children with their own brand. Francis James Childs, the collector of the Child ballads, called such people the "blind beggar, the nursery maid, and the clerk."

Certainly I can understand the desire to tamper with a tale for morality's sake. But I wish my friend had not told me of her change. After all, the story had not been written in a vacuum, moral or otherwise.

All art is moral, a striving for the light. But unlike earlier moralities which are consistent in their demands on men and women and, hence, artists, the moralities of today are shifting and changing by decades rather than slowly, over centuries. Communications are swift today, the speed of light. And minorities which could previously be ignored are eloquent in their demands for redress, for justice. They are heard and reheard, and they cannot be denied.

Artists are aware, are made aware, of injustices. As individuals in an individual age, they create out of an idiosyncratic sense of what is right. This is not to say that writers and other artists should try to be moralists and create propaganda. Propaganda is bad art. And, so Isaac Bashevis Singer reminds us, "In art, a truth that is boring is not true."

But the best writers write from the heart. As Harlan Ellison, the science fiction writer, has said, "I write what I am. There is no way to create literature."

And if all art is moral, then all art becomes morality. What I write out of my own needs and ideas and ideals becomes a statement. That statement can be accepted or rejected by the reader. If the reader is an adult, the acceptance or rejection is probably a fairly conscious choice.

The child does not read that way. A child reader reads with the heart. And so, if I write for children, I must be aware that children are going to accept what I write with their hearts. My morality becomes their morality. Heart to heart, body to body, blood to blood, a kind of literary eucharist.

The changing of the ending can change the morality of a tale, but it changes the author's intent also. That is not consistent with the idea of literature.

However, there are times when the morality of a book, even a fine literary work, is inconsistent with that of the teacher, the librarian, the parent. The answer then is not to force a change of endings, or the more extreme version of that—burn books. As a teaching device, changing the ending,characters, sex, and so on can be most productive. But arbitrarily changing an ending, without letting the child know that such a thing is happening, is direct censorship and *does* change the author's intent, whether the intent was an overt or covert one.

Dr. Rudman offers many ways in which an educator can help to structure the reading and aid young readers in sorting out conflicting or inconsistent moralities. She does not necessarily throw out a book because its morality is outdated or its characters mouth inhumane statements. Rather, she suggests methods of dealing with these problems within the classroom or home. She does not necessarily recommend a book even though it is correct in its preaching, if preaching is all the book does. She is concerned with human relationships, with understandings, with morality. But she is concerned with literature, too. In a field which is all too often crowded with didactic moralists, Dr. Rudman is literature's champion.

As a writer, I thank Dr. Rudman for that concern. However, I must also point out that what she is offering is the second step in a two-step process. The first step, of course, lies with the authors and illustrators who create the materials with which children dream. We are the myth-makers.

We must write from the heart. Write from the heart and you write your own truth. And if we have changed and grown inside, the truth we write will change and grow, too.

Then the children will be touched. Touch and pass it on. It is the only way.

PREFACE

HOW TO USE THIS BOOK

THIS BOOK IS DESIGNED FOR USE as a reference and a guide to selection of children's books with regard to their appropriateness for the purpose of bibliotherapy as well as a consideration of how issues of a societal and developmental nature are treated.
Each chapter contains:

1. An introduction to, and discussion of, an issue.

2. A section relating particular books to the topic as exemplars of how that issue is handled in children's literature.

3. Suggestions (''Try This'') for activities that teachers or other concerned adults may follow in order to personalize and extend the reading of the chapter.

4. Activities for adults to use with children as an adjunct and extension of their reading.

5. An annotated reference list of sources relating the topic to children and books, and, where possible, a list of organizations providing supplemental materials on the issue at hand.

6. A selected recommended list of children's books pertaining to the topic. The age levels attached to the books are those suggested by the publisher in most cases, but readers are cautioned to use their own judgment on the appropriateness of any book to their intended audience. No book of quality is too simple for any age level. There are, however, books that are too complex or advanced for young children's developmental levels.

Different from the first edition of this text, the annotated books constitute a recommended list. There are too many titles in libraries and bookstores to even attempt to include them all; for the purpose of this edition, books are selected from publishers' catalogs, published annotated bibliographies, and various review journals such as *The School Library Journal, The Bulletin* of the Chicago University Center for

Children's Books, the *Bulletin* of the Council on Interracial Books for Children, *The Horn Book Magazine, Booklist,* specialized compendia of issues-related books (listed with the References at the end of each chapter), and recommendations from colleagues and students.

Some of the books in the lists are out of print. They remain available in libraries, and it is possible that the public will demand their reprinting. Readers would be advised to contact publishers of books that are no longer in the bookstores. Perhaps some of the fine books that have unaccountably been discontinued will gain new life through these efforts.

Prices are not included in the listings; they change so rapidly that they are often out of date upon publication. A listing of publishers' addresses is appended so that readers may contact publishers directly if local bookstores cannot supply the information.

More poetry is included in this edition than in the first one. Readers are invited to send recommendations for new entries to be included in future revisions of this text. This author is an advocate of books and reading. If any titles have been omitted that are appropriate and of high quality, I invite your sending them for my consideration. I welcome comments and suggestions for improvement.

Masha Kabakow Rudman
University of Massachusetts at Amherst

ACKNOWLEDGMENTS

IN AN EFFORT OF THIS MAGNITUDE, spanning many years and thousands of books, a small army of people has been involved. The idea for the text arose from the format of my seminar in children's literature. My students, most of them classroom teachers and librarians, wanted references to consult for a thematic approach to children's books. They also wanted recommendations of books to use with children in order to help them with their emotional and societal needs. It was on their instigation that I wrote the first edition. The response to the book and to an issues approach has sustained me and motivated me to prepare this second edition.

Many people have directly helped me in the preparation of the text. My husband is always my first reader. His comments, from a psychological perspective and as a jargon detector, have aided me. Furthermore, his tolerance of the endless piles of books and papers in every room of our house was a testimony to love and devotion. Jane Yolen's careful and constructive reading of the manuscript was invaluable. Without Kathy Gagne's patient and competent reading, organization, and research, it would have been impossible for me to have completed this revision. Her humor in the face of panic, her gentle but perceptive criticism, and her hours of labor were unmatched.

Research for this text also involved the efforts of a number of students, friends, and professionals in the field. People kept finding new articles and sources they thought I might be interested in reading, and their conversation and suggestions about children's literature in general, and issues specifically, were stimulating and constructive. Particularly helpful in this respect were Sondra Radosh and the entire staff of the Jones Library in Amherst, Rich Morrill and the reference staff of the University of Massachusetts Library, and Pat Drake and Sue Woodfork of the Amherst Public School libraries, Anna Pearce, and Grant McGiffin who also helped in critiquing the manuscript, Sonia Nieto, Rudine Sims, Bernice Hauser, Mary Lee Cox of the New England Resource Center for Children and Families, Debra Morey Smith, Sheila Stackhouse, and all of the students in my children's literature seminars who supplied annotated lists of books. The faculty seminar on children's literature, and William Moebius especially, were active in giving thought-provoking questions and directions to follow.

The specialized libraries of the Children's Book Council and the Council on Interracial Books for Children were enormous aids to my research. Brad Chambers of the Council was particularly generous with materials and information. Publishers, too, were helpful in providing catalogs and review copies.

The mechanical aspects of completing this text involved thousands of hours of typing and checking on accuracy. Credit and heartfelt thanks go to Dianne Kaplan deVries, Constance Bunker, and Robin Silver, as well as Signia Warner, May Thayer, and Joyce Vann and her team of people including Karen Greber and Lisa Kurtz.

My editor, Lane Akers, who has been with this project from its inception, has been infinitely patient and supportive. His knowledge of the educational field and his special competence in the publishing world have been a source of sustenance for me.

To all of these, and to those whom I have not named but who always have been supportive and ready to help, I acknowledge my debt and tender my thanks.

I must add my appreciation too, to the wonderful advent of the computer and its use as a word processor and data-retrieval instrument.

ONE

INTRODUCTION

AS EDUCATORS WE HAVE WITHIN OUR POWER the means to inculcate values, develop skills, influence attitudes, and affect the physical, social, emotional, intellectual, and moral development of today's youth and tomorrow's adults. We accept this responsibility when we become parents, teachers, counselors, librarians, or take any position in which we influence children. We hope that our instruction will produce positive attitudes, values, and behaviors. In order to build a healthy society, we are continuously searching for additional and better means to transmit what we believe is positive and to change what we perceive is wrong.

Schooling should insure the appropriate acquisition of skills in such basic areas as reading, writing, and computation. Skills taught in isolation or placed in meaningless context serve no function; knowing how to read is useless unless one reads. Recognizing this principle, contemporary educators must provide many opportunities for children to practice the basic skills in ways that make sense. They must also entice children into the joy of reading by making available as many interesting, well-written books as they possibly can. Reading aloud, engaging in projects that are related to reading, instituting silent reading times when everyone, including the teacher, reads for pleasure, inviting authors to the classroom, and showing genuine enjoyment in their own reading are but a few of the activities teachers might try.

We also know that society needs responsible decision-makers. There is no magic age when this ability suddenly appears; it must be carefully developed. We should not wait until a child has reached college, high school, or even junior high school; the process should begin as soon as the child begins to reason. Decision-making skills need not be restricted to important, long-range matters; they are practiced whenever choices are available.

When given the opportunity, even preschool children are able to make decisions. They can select what clothing they will wear, what activities they will engage in, and which friends they will play with. Though the extent of their choices may be somewhat limited, they should be encouraged to evaluate the success of their decisions. Questions such as: "How comfortable was that sweater?" "How satisfied were you with your choice of the ice cream rather than the pudding?" "How pleased are you that you chose to visit Timmy today?'' may help them to think about their selections. Young children learn to negotiate with each other over what games to play, what the rules will be, and when to begin and end their game. Not only are their peer-involved choices valid, but also adults usually accept their children's requests for favorite specific gifts for birthdays and special occasions.

Often in kindergarten or first grade, some of these very same children are not considered capable of making responsible choices about their use of time, selection of activity, or preference in literature. In keeping with the philosophy governing some classrooms, they are told when and where to sit and stand, and, sometimes even when to be thirsty and when to have to go to the bathroom. These kinds of schools value conformity over individual decision-making.

The current emphasis in education is on basic skills, individualized instruction and problem solving. The structure of the conventional classroom has changed and continues to change. Means are being sought to enable children to maintain and improve their decision-making and evaluative skills. Students are being encouraged to explore their environment and to extract from it that which is meaningful to them. Reading, one of the most important areas of instruction in the schools, has emerged as a critical tool for the development of the skills of independent and responsible critical thinking and behavior.

In the past, reading programs concentrated on the mechanical aspects of skills. Though concerned publishers and educators attempted to address comprehension and critical reading, the important part of reading instruction was confined to simple decoding, or word calling. Now the more complex and advanced requirements for comprehension are emphasized. Teachers ask fewer ''one-right-answer'' questions and require children to think more deeply about what they read. Children's textbooks have undergone a marked transformation. They are, in general, more colorful, more diverse, and are designed to attract and interest the young reader. More interesting stories are included in their contents. Good teachers consistently use supplemental materials and recognize the importance of a class library.

The field of children's literature has kept pace with the trends in education as a whole. Probably the most widespread method of study is the genre approach, which examines the different literary categories of children's books (e.g., folk tales, poetry, fiction, biography), There are many excellent sources and texts guiding students in this approach, which has the advantage of providing the adult with an overview of the field. The genre approach also attempts to assist the reader in developing a set of literary criteria to use in selecting children's books.

In keeping with contemporary aims of education, directions in publishing for children, and societal needs, this author recommends an additional approach to the study of children's literature. A critical examination of the books in the light of how they treat contemporary social problems and conditions is a valuable adjunct to a literary perspective. Books are important influences on their readers' minds. They can help us when we attempt to construct suitable bases for attitudes and behaviors. A critical, or issues, approach should, therefore, be included in the repertoire of courses and texts available to adult learners.

To assess the effectiveness in literature of issues of social and personal concern, the reader is required first to examine his or her own knowledge, attitudes, and prejudices. Psychologists and sociologists have provided us with excellent advice for handling various problems constructively with children. Family relations, divorce, adoption, sibling rivalry, death, sex, old age, war, special needs, gender roles, different heritages are all potentially volatile and wrenching matters. Books afford us the opportunity to explore and confront these issues with children through a protected vicarious situation.

The practice of bibliotherapy—the use of books to help children solve their personal problems and become aware of societal concerns—has become accepted as an important part of teaching. Librarians and counselors, as well as parents, search for books that mirror a problem they wish to help a child overcome. It is a technique that has been in practice since books were first printed. The ancient library at Thebes bore the inscription: "Healing place of the soul." The word "bibliotherapy" was coined in the 1920s, and accepted immediately by the medical profession. The Menningers used the term to prescribe books for their patients. By the 1940s the practice was taken beyond the medical profession and the notion of corrective therapy and was adopted by teachers and librarians as part of their everyday responses to children's interests and needs. In 1962 Ruth M. Tews edited the first issue of *Library Trends* devoted entirely to the topic of bibliotherapy. Since then many books and articles have been written on the subject. In using bibliotherapy educators do not assume the role of psychologists or physicians, but recognize that children today walk into the classroom with their minds crowded with issues. Teachers, who next to parents spend the most time with young people, need the competence to handle the children's questions and concerns.

Adults who conduct this guidance through books know that to be successful the practice must not be specifically prescriptive or forced. When a book is assigned as medicine, the chances of its being accepted are slim. Rather, if informal strategies are used, then the likelihood of success is enhanced. Book exhibits on a given theme, regular reading aloud by the teacher, other adults, or students, a list of recommended titles posted in an accessible area, and regular conferences between the teacher and child are some of the ingredients contributing to bibliotherapy. The idea is to construct a setting in which children will be attracted to reading about their concerns.

The selected books should be well written and appropriate to the child's developmental level. Teachers and librarians must continuously update their knowledge of what is available in children's books; hundreds of appropriate titles are published each year. Reading the books is not enough; activities, discussion, and more reading should follow the initial reading. Adults must always be sensitive to the children's reactions. In order for the process to be successful, the child reader should be able to identify with the character and action in the book. Then catharsis can take place, and finally, insight. With insight it is to be hoped that the young person will be able to change behavior or attitude and be helped to acquire a healthy perspective.

Today's world makes it incumbent on adults who work with children to have a background and knowledge of as many as possible of the concerns that children have. They should search for more and more books to use as resources to help children deal responsibly with the issues. Children and adults, looking critically at the way these topics are handled, should judge for themselves whether or not the authors are presenting accurate pictures. Those books that attempt to teach lessons should be analyzed for their effectiveness as well as for their intent. But readers should be aware that those books that are not obviously didactic are the most potent. The literary quality of a book is one of the most important factors affecting its impact.

This text examines literature for children from kindergarten through high school. Books for older children have consistently contained issues that relate to life's problems, but until fairly recently books for young children attempted to shield their audience from dissension and dilemmas of social import. That situation has drastically changed over the past two decades. There is almost no topic that is unmentionable in a child's book. Young children are encouraged to read and think about all the issues mentioned in this text, and more.

It is important to remember that even when an issues approach is the chosen mode of looking at a book, a particular issue does not constitute or represent the whole book. Any good work of literature contains many issues, and, above all, must provide either a good story or a well-designed factual presentation. Thus, the death of Charlotte in *Charlotte's Web* helps readers to understand and handle the concept of death. But the book is much more than a discussion and examination of this topic; Charlotte's character is a masterful literary creation. Her grappling with the ferocity of her life as a spider, her friendship with Wilbur, her cleverness, and her perspective on life enrich the experience of reading the book. To say merely that the book is about death would be seriously misleading, and do damage to effective appreciation of the book as a whole.

Sometimes books teach negative lessons without their authors' recognition of the fact. Well-intentioned authors, like all of us, are only human. They project their prejudices and values into their writing. They are limited by their own experiences and the resources to which they have access. They may not consciously err, but no one person can know all of the facts about anything. It is the intent of this text to encourage readers to ask questions about every book they read. Furthermore, this author hopes that, after using this text, readers will acknowlege that every child's book has implications that bear examining. A critical perspective does not mean that the reader should dislike the book or that the book should be withheld. After all, we love our friends and family even when we know their faults. But a reader needs to come to a book with an awareness of its potential for inherent messages.

Criticizing a book is not the same as censoring it. No lover of books condones censorship. School boards and self-appointed watchdogs who demand the withdrawal of books from shelves do damage to the process of education as well as freedom of speech. But critical analysis is necessary to maintain an atmosphere of lively interaction. Proponents of certain viewpoints have the right and obligation to speak out; reader have the right and obligation to accept or reject the arguments. Advocacy groups of all sorts are fervent in their comments about what they consider to be damaging in books. We may approve of and agree with some, and violently oppose the views of others, but to silence any of them would constitute censorship. They do not have the right to ban or burn books; but they may urge, exhort, and publish articles of criticism. If their views spark controversy, so much the better for the health of the children's book industry. We could not do without such helpful book advocates as the Children's Book Council; we also need the gadflies and consciences to hone our awareness.

Children should be taught to become critics too. This fits into an approach to problem solving that is rapidly gaining interest across the country. Schools are incorporating curricula teaching problem-solving strategies. An issues approach to children's literature includes an examination of problem situations in stories. It also fosters the development of those skills defined as critical reading, comprehension, and critical thinking. Many classrooms now integrate the teaching of social studies with reading. Many works of fiction are excellent vehicles for teaching history. It therefore is important for adults working with children to become ever more knowledgeable about the scope and materials of children's literature. This book is designed to serve that function.

Chapters Two through Nine of this text explore specific life issues. They are arranged in approximate developmental order, moving from that which is closest to the child—the family, and ending with the global issue of war.

SUMMARY OF FOLLOWING CHAPTERS

CHAPTER TWO: THE FAMILY

The family is the first social structure. It provides the model for other relationships. The first section of this chapter explores sibling interaction, which is one of the foundations for children's future social behavior. Books in which characters are siblings present a variety of different models of interaction. Parents' behaviors in these books range from destructive and irresponsible to supportive and nurturing. An appreciation of different heritages can be found in these books as well. Sibling relationships also contain implications for gender-role expectations and behaviors. A valuing of cooperative behavior is communicated in a number of the books.

Divorce is the topic of the next section in the chapter. Statistics indicate that divorce is wielding a tremendous impact on many children's lives. Books on the topic of divorce attempt to help young readers recognize that they are not alone and that their problems do have solutions. The amount of fiction and nonfiction about this issue increases steadily. Most books respect the child's perception and communicate that respect. Some books, centering exclusively on the child, ignore the adults' reactions; others help young readers to understand the causes of their parents' dissension. Though lifestyles generally remain somewhat conventional, occasionally a different mode of life is presented to the reader's view.

Adoption and foster care form the next section of Chapter Two. The feelings of adopted children have been more acknowledged in recent years, particularly with the advent of new legislation granting people the right to find out about their birth parents. Many books contain perspectives on this and other questions. Foster children, too, figure in a number of children's books, helping the reader to empathize with their plight.

CHAPTER THREE: SEX

Sex education arouses much controversy among educators and other members of any community. Although everyone agrees that sex education is necessary, the manner, materials, timing, quantity, and setting are all matters for argument. Consequently, many different presentations exist in books. Topics include reproduction, birth, puberty, homosexuality, abortion, and the relationship between sexual activity and love. Although it is more difficult for children to locate and acquire these books than those in any other category, they often manage to share what they do find with each other. Peer education and miseducation on this topic is greater than on any other. Adults must decide if and how they wish to intervene. Books can help with this intervention.

CHAPTER FOUR: GENDER ROLES

The role of the female is one that the public has been discussing actively. Male roles, as well, need to be examined, and perhaps, redefined. Different points of view are emerging. Many annotations and references accompany the text in this and the other chapters. Readers are encouraged to seek out these resources to be able to formulate their own positions. The activities in this chapter are aimed at self-evaluation. The discussion of the books is categorized so that different aspects of gender role expectations and stereotypes are reviewed.

CHAPTER FIVE: HERITAGE

People from any group other than the white middle class once were missing from consideration or even actively distorted in most children's books. That error is slowly being corrected. Now more and more excellent books can be found that include characters representing different heritages in significant roles. Children from other than the dominant culture can now read about themselves. Critical reaction to books dealing with various heritages is by no means uniform. Opinions range from appreciation of good intentions on the part of the author to rejection of any book that is not written by a member of the group discussed in the book. This chapter discusses and presents some criteria for the reader's consideration. It focuses particularly on two heritages, and includes others in a less comprehensive treatment.

The first section of Chapter Five deals with native Americans. It contains a brief history of the United States government's treatment of the native American and also presents some contemporary concerns related to this group today. Different perspectives are shared; suggestions are offered for further study.

The second section probes the treatment of Afro-American characters in children's books. Many books now feature realistic, strong black characters. Black authors have also begun to gain recognition. Books about people from other heritages, such as Hispanics, Asian-Americans, immigrants, and people holding various religious beliefs comprise the rest of this chapter. The intent of Chapter Five is to analyze the literary treatment of these groups and to identify positive approaches to the depiction of different heritages in the literature.

CHAPTER SIX: SPECIAL NEEDS

This chapter deals with children's literature that contains characters who have special needs. It is one of the newest areas of concern in books. The category includes not only those children who are mentally or physically disabled, but also those with emotional problems; those who are substance abusers; children who have themselves been abused; gifted children; and characters who feel, act, or look different from most of their peers (apart from the differences caused by race, country of origin, or sex). Almost any child might fit into one of these categories. This chapter attempts to provide a context for reading about these children, and for using the books in a library or classroom setting.

CHAPTER SEVEN: OLD AGE

Like members of other special populations, old people are subject to stereotyping and misunderstanding. They appear in many children's books, sometimes as three-dimensional characters, sometimes as cardboard devices.

The median age in our country is increasing, and more and more old people are rightfully demanding understanding and recognition. Criteria for appropriate presentation and a description of books containing a variety of old people are included here.

CHAPTER EIGHT: DEATH

Death has received much attention in literature for children. Different religious views, family reactions, problems, and methods of coping are presented in great variety in books, some of which are extremely well written, while others will not last long in readers' memories. Stereotypes are presented and surmounted. Painful situations are experienced. Important questions are brought to the readers' attention. This chapter, in common with the others, suggests activities for both adults and children in order to increase their awareness of the issues presented. It also discusses developmental stages of knowing about death, and the universal reactions to the death of loved ones.

CHAPTER NINE: WAR

As with each of the other issues, war contains complexities beyond a simple discussion of right or wrong. Each war has individual characteristics differentiating it from others, but there are universal factors also to be considered. Books about war range from allegories and satires to realistic, personal accounts. Children's books should be sought that convey the complex aspects of war; consequently, much careful adult guidance is needed in this area. Occasionally books can be found that help the reader become aware of the ambiguous morality and the ambivalent outcomes surrounding this topic. Criteria for analysis of the books are suggested.

CHAPTER TEN: METHODOLOGY

The last chapter describes a methodology for using children's books as materials for a skills approach to the teaching of reading. The reading process, activities for stimulating interest in reading, and practical guidelines for the classroom are contained here.

It is our responsibility to locate resources that help readers build a solid basis for forming opinions and developing attitudes. The more informed people are, the more constructive their behavior can be. Too often, people act out of ignorance. Education is the key to positive action. In this author's opinion, it is the hope of the world.

REFERENCES

BAWDEN, NINA. "Emotional Realism in Books for Young People," *The Horn Book Magazine*, Vol. 56, No. 1, February 1980, pp. 17–33.
Bawden reminds us that emotional realism invites young readers to discover themselves in books. Those books that give an honest accounting of a character's feelings provide the reader with "a little hope and courage for the journey."

BERNSTEIN, JOANNE E. *Books to Help Children Cope with Separation and Loss.* New York: Bowker, 1983. (2nd ed.)
Provides an excellent general psychological background on the issues and experience of any sort of loss in a child's world. Includes comments and annotated entries on death, divorce, desertion, serious illness, war, foster care and adoption, and other loss-related situations. Provides an extensive bibliography of children's books, each one sensitively annotated and critiqued by the author. Four hundred titles have been added to this revised edition.

BISKIN, DONALD, AND HOSKISSON, KENNETH. "Moral Development through Children's Literature," *Elementary School Journal*, Vol. 75, No. 3, December 1974, pp. 153–57.
Describes levels of moral development as identified by Kohlberg. Locates moral issues in several children's books and analyzes them according to their stage. Suggests that books can be used to help develop children's moral awareness.

BRACKEN, JEANNE, AND WIGUTOFF, SHARON. *Books for Today's Children: An Annotated Bibliography of Non-Stereotyped Picture Books.* Old Westbury, New York: Feminist Press, 1979.
Discusses and recommends over 100 books for young children containing positive values. The titles are arranged in lists of highly recommended, recommended, and recommended with some reservation. Otherwise, the books are not placed into categories.

BRACKEN, JEANNE, AND WIGUTOFF, SHARON; WITH BAKER, ILENE. *Books for Today's Young Readers: An Annotated Bibliography of Recommended Eiction for Ages 10–14.* Old Westbury, New York: Feminist Press, 1981.
Descriptions and analyses of books for older readers. Gender, peer friendships, special needs, families in transition, foster care and adoption, and views of old people are some of the categories specified. Very helpful discussion and format.

BUTLER, DOROTHY. *Cushla and Her Books.* 1st American ed. Boston: The Horn Book. 1980.
A beautiful tribute to the effect books and loving attention can have on a child, even when that child is disabled.

CAMPBELL, PATRICIA B., AND WIRTENBERG, JEANA. "How Books Influence Children: What the Research Shows," *Bulletin of the Council on Interracial Books for Children,* Vol. 11, No. 6, 1980, pp. 3–6.
Summarizes studies that indicate that children's attitudes can be affected by what they read. Some studies showed that performance can also be affected by how gender role and heritage are treated in books and texts.

CIANCIOLO, PATRICIA. "Feeling Books Develop Social and Personal Sensitivities," *Elementary English*, Vol. 52, No. 1, January 1975, pp. 37–42.
Confirms the importance of exposing children to books that convey and elicit feelings on the part of the readers. Cianciolo stresses the power of books to influence readers' behavior and attitudes. She describes and discusses several books from this perspective.

CORNETT, CLAUDIA E. AND CHARLES F. *Bibliotherapy: The Right Book at the Right Time*. Bloomington, Indiana: Phi Delta Kappa Educational Foundation, 1980 (A Fastback.)
In a brief but comprehensive booklet, the definition, history, methodology, and rationale for bibliotheraphy are provided. Basic resources and references are also included.

COUNCIL ON INTERRACIAL BOOKS FOR CHILDREN. *Human (and Anti-Human) Values in Children's Books*. New York: Racism and Sexism Resource Center, 1976.
Provides a checklist and analyzes children's books for their treatment of values.

COX, MAHALA. "Children's Literature and Value Theory," *Elementary English*, Vol. 51, No. 3, March 1974, pp. 355–359.
Recommends the addition of values clarification to interpretation of children's books. Presents several books and examples of how to do this.

CULLINAN, BERNICE E. "Reality Reflected in Children's Literature," *Elementary English,* Vol. 51, No. 3, March 1974, pp. 415–419.
Responds to critics of realism in children's books by discussing several high-quality books that are concerned with realistic and social issues. Praises these books and their impact.

DIXON, BOB. *Catching Them Young, Vols. 1 and 2: Sex, Race and Class in Children's Fiction* and *Political Ideas in Children's Fiction*. London: Pluto Press, 1977.
Both books discuss the values presented to children through their literature and analyze several books that convey harmful messages.

DONELSON, KENNETH L. "What to Do When the Censor Comes," *Elementary English*, Vol. 51, No. 3, March 1974, pp. 403–409.
Lists five benefits of reading for young people: enjoyment, objective recognition of one's own problems, provision of vicarious experiences, exposure to diverse value systems, and discovery of the real world.

DREYER, SHARON. *The Bookfinder: A Guide to Children's Literature about the Needs and Problems of Youth Aged 2–15*. Circle Pines, Minn.: American Guidance Service, 1981.
An extensive listing, by subject, author and title, in a split-page format designed for ease of location.

FASSLER, JOAN. *Helping Children Cope: Mastering Stress through Books and Stories*. New York: Free Press, 1978.
Discusses issues of death, separation, hospitalization, illness, lifestyle changes and other potentially stress-causing situations as they are presented in books for children ages four to eight.

GALLAGHER, SISTER MARY. "Trends and Issues in Literature for Young Adults," *Catholic Library World*, October 1982, pp. 116–118.
Provides several sources for book selection, and a reading list for teenagers that address themes of concern to this audience.

GILLIS, RUTH J. *Children's Books for Times of Stress: An Annotated Bibilography.* Bloomington: Indiana University Press, 1978.
Uses seven categories: Emotions, Behavior, Family, Difficult Situation, New Situation, Self Concept, and Friendship. Lists books for children ages three to nine.

HALL, ELVALEAN. *Personal Problems of Children.* Boston: Campbell and Hall, 1970.
A series of pamphlets presenting annotated bibliographies of books to use with children who have different sorts of personal problems.

JALONGO, MARY RENCK. "Bibliotherapy: Literature to Promote Socioemotional Growth," *The Reading Teacher*, Vol. 36, No. 8, April 1983, pp. 796–803.
Describes strategies and process for bibliotherapy in the classroom. Lists some selection criteria and some sources of book suggestions.

_____. "Using Crisis-Oriented Books with Young Children." *Young Children,* Vol. 38, No. 5, July 1983, pp. 29–35.
An informative article providing guidelines for evaluating the use of picture books in bibliotherapy. An excellent list of resources and suggested children's literature included.

JORDAN, JUNE. "Young People: Victims of Realism in Books and in Life," *Wilson Library Bulletin*, Vol. 48, No. 2, October 1973, pp. 142–145.
Discusses realism and its various interpretations in children's books. Pleads for nourishing, constructive reality. Commits herself as a writer to this goal.

KEATING, CHARLOTTE MATTHEWS. *Building Bridges of Understanding between Cultures.* Tucson: Palo Verde Publishing Company, 1971.
A personalized annotated bibliography of books for children dealing with different cultural groups. In general, the annotations are helpful and interesting.

KENISTON, KENNETH. " 'Good Children' (Our Own), 'Bad Children' (Other People's), and the Horrible Work Ethic," *Yale Alumni Magazine*, April 1974, pp. 6–10.
Discusses the American practice of valuing work over almost any other ethic. Analyzes its impact on children. Suggests that our emphasis shift toward humaneness and imagination in addition to productivity. Demonstrates that books contribute to whatever society values.

LARRICK, NANCY. "Divorce, Drugs, Desertion, the Draft: Facing Up to the Realities in Children's Literature," *Publisher's Weekly*, Vol. 201, 21 February 1972, pp. 90–91.
Defends the use of realism in books as helpful to a consideration of children's concerns. Recommends that parents read these books and discuss them with their children. Affirms that "Students of children's literature must be taught to face controversial issues in the books for young readers."

LIVINGSTON, MYRA C. "Children's Literature—in Chaos, a Creative Weapon," *Reading Teacher*, Vol. 27, No. 6, March 1974, pp. 534–539.
Urges individualization in book selection for children. Recommends a constructive blend of fantasy and reality. Recognizes the power of children's books.

LOWRY, HEATH W. "Evaluative Criteria to Be Used as Guides by Writers of Children's Literature," *Elementary English*, Vol. 48, No. 8, December 1971, pp. 922–925.
Presents responses from editors of children's books listing criteria that they use for publishing these books. Concludes that children's books must have the same qualities of excellence as adult books.

MEEGAN, MARY ELLEN. "Bibliotherapeutic Facets in Literature for Children." Unpublished doctoral dissertation, Boston College, 1976.
Finds that good literature contains material for bibliotherapy. Identifies thirty-nine components for enchancing values in literature for second graders.

PERRY, JEAN M. "The Changing Role of the Child in American Society as Reflected in Literature for Children." Unpublished Master's report, Palmer Graduate Library School, Long Island University, Brookville, New York, 1971.
A historical perspective of the changes in children's literature in terms of contemporary social implications. The author contends that these changes reflect society's attitudinal changes toward children. Thirty-three children's books and many adult references are examined and reviewed. The study includes the period from 1900 to 1970.

RIGGS, CORINNE W. *Bibliotherapy: An Annotated Bibliography*. Neward, Delaware: International Reading Association, 1971.
A well-selected list of books, periodicals, and unpublished materials for adults concerned with the therapeutic use of books for children. Annotations are brief but informative.

RUBIN, RHEA J. *Using Bibliotherapy: A Guide to Theory and Practice*. Phoenix: Oryx Press, 1978.
Aimed at the professional who wants a program using books and reading to help clients overcome problems or gain insight into normal developmental concerns. Provides a comprehensive overview of the practice and theories of bibliotherapy.

SCHULTE, EMERITA SCHOER. "Today's Literature for Today's Children," *Elementary English*, Vol. 49, No. 3, March 1972, pp. 355–363.
Recognizes that literature should be directed toward all children, including those who do not enjoy reading. Reviews and recommends a number of books that present reality to minority children. Includes bibliography.

SCHWARTZ, SHEILA. *Teaching Adolescent Literature: A Humanities Approach*. Rochelle Park, New Jersey: Hayden Book Co., 1979.
Chapters are divided into themes such as Minorities, Violence, Teenagers and Sex, Family Life and The Outsider. Recommendations for activities and discussions are included.

SHEPARD, JOHN P. "The Treatment of Characters in Popular Children's Fiction," *Elementary English*, Vol. 39, No. 7, November 1962, pp. 672–676.

Conducted a study demonstrating the negative impact of many children's books. Urges adults to be aware of the subtle implications in children's books and to intervene appropriately.

TUCKER, NICHOLAS, ed. *Suitable for Children? Controversies in Children's Literature.* Edinburgh: Sussex University Press, 1978. Distinguished authors, and critics' essays on the topic of children's literature, including what makes it valuable.

TEWS, RUTH M., ed. "Bibliotherapy," *Library Trends,* Vol. 11, October 1962, pp. 97–228. Several articles describing the practice of bibliotherapy and validating its use outside the medical profession.

TWAY, EILEEN, ed. *Reading Ladders for Human Relations.* 6th ed. Washington, D.C: American Council on Education, 1981 (with National Council of Teachers of English, Urbana, Illinois).
This invaluable resource contains hundreds of annotations of books that can be used to help children better understand themselves, each other, and the world they live in.

ZIMET, SARA GOODMAN. "Teaching Children to Detect Social Bias in Books," *Reading Teacher*, Vol. 36, No. 4, January 1983, pp. 418–421.
Recommends a text analysis procedure to help children uncover stereotypes in books. Enables even very young children to detect bias in language and presentation.

ZIPES, JACK. "Who's Afraid of the Brothers Grimm?" *The Lion and the Unicorn*, Vol. 3, No. 2, Winter 1979–1980, pp. 4–56.
One of several articles that focus on social issues in children's literature. The author analyzes several tales and describes the history, to the present time, of using such tales to socialize the child reader.

•TWO•

FAMILY

FAMILY INTERACTION FORMS THE BASIS for future social relationships. In the past decade there have been some books written about single-parent families and one or two about communal groups, but the preponderance of literature assumes the intact nuclear family. In some cases an extended family situation is presented, but it is usually recognized as something out of the ordinary. Many of the exceptions to the conventional family are used as vehicles for presenting the problems that they generate. Issues pertaining to the family include sibling relations, divorce, the single parent, adoption, and foster care. Models of constructive family behavior as well as dramatic representations of negative situations may be found in the literature for children.

SIBLINGS

Sibling relationships do not constitute a major societal problem, but they are a universal phenomenon, playing an important part in how individuals feel about themselves and how they relate to other people. Sibling interaction often serves as a model for people in relating to friends, new acquaintances, mates, their own children, and to society in general.

Siblings who grow up together learn each other's characteristics in a way that no other people do, and they have little room for pretense. Besides having to share their parents' time, attention, and love, they are forced to share physical space and possessions. They must develop a procedure for living together that will be acceptable most of the time. They can test out behaviors with the relative security of knowing that their siblings probably will not have the option of leaving them forever, as is the case with friends. They can usually rely on getting honest reactions to their behaviors. Parents influence siblings' interactions in the way that they deal with their children. If we are to believe what we read, no one seems to escape the imposition of her or his family placement. It is rare in literature that birth order does not play an important role. The only child is frequently depicted as a lonely, spoiled, self-centered individual who is unable to get along with peers, too adult-oriented, and in general, maladjusted. The expected reactions when we hear that someone is a middle child are fairly well programmed for us. We anticipate that the person is resentful, squeezed, quick-tempered, unvalued, overly sensitive, and unhappy. The youngest is pampered, demanding, and favored. Sometimes we have to remind ourselves that it is possible for us to overcome the effects of our birth order; we are tempted to succumb to these popularly held stereotypes about our own, our siblings', and our children's behaviors.

•TRY THIS

What position do you occupy in birth order in your family? How has this position affected your relationship with your sibling(s)? How did it affect your relationship with your parents when you were growing up? Which of the books in the Bibliography at the end of this chapter most closely approximates your situation? Find someone who occupies the same birth-order position that you do. Share the book with that person to see how your perceptions and experiences match.

Books containing siblings as characters are varied. Some of them deal with the topic of the sibling relationship as the main thrust of the story. Some of them only incidentally include the interaction between siblings within the context of the plot. But whether or not the intent is to look at this issue as a problem or as a model, the young reader, assisted by the helpful adult, can find the type of book needed.

Other factors besides birth order affect a family's interactions. The number of years between children; the sex of the children; the economic, social, and emotional circumstances of the family during the time the children are being reared; the state of each person's health; the physical environment; the influence of peers and schooling—all these are external, but contribute to how members of a family perceive themselves and one another. Children's books offer a wide range of family settings for readers to experience vicariously. Some of the books can be very helpful in assuring children that, contrary to their fears, they and their family are normal.

In the past twenty years authors have represented families as having internal struggles and problems. Permitting siblings to dislike each other, they have portrayed rivalries and unpleasant relationships. In addition, they have continued the tradition of making siblings responsible for one another in times of extreme crisis and have also begun to present useful models for parents and siblings to emulate in normal stress situations.

SUGGESTED CRITERIA

In searching for books adults can use in either a therapeutic or modeling fashion with children, it is wise to seek out those stories that have realistic solutions to problems. Fairy tale endings are not valuable in these cases. If real issues are being presented, their effect is lessened if they come to a happy but unlikely end. A solution that is too pat is also less valuable than one indicating that more thought and time need to be given to the problem. It is far better to suggest that there is no one answer than to present one that is not feasible. For example, the situation of a new baby in the house is usually resolved in life only for short periods of time and needs constant reexamination and additional strategies as both the new arrival and the elder sibling(s) develop. Books that indicate this expectation are useful.

The behavior of the parents is an important element of stories concerned with sibling interaction. Models should be presented wherever possible in which parents behave humanely, responsively, and plausibly. Although no parents are saints, and some are cruel, if the problem in a book is that of a parental desertion, it should be described as arising from the plot, with some rationale indicated. An explanation for characters' behavior always contributes to the quality of a story.

The illustrations in any of these books should attempt to demonstrate the universality of sibling problems. Particularly in nonfiction, different ethnic groups and family styles should be depicted. In any case, stereotypes—both visual and literary—should be avoided. Parental and sibling roles should reflect a realistic pattern, but expectations need not be rigid or stereotypic. Sometimes a middle child is atypical; sometimes the youngest and eldest share characteristics. No matter what the behavior, it should be in the context of the story, rather than imposed on it.

Readers can judge for themselves whether or not any of the siblings is being either unjustly favored or victimized. Sometimes the author purposely describes such a predicament, leading young readers to examine their own reactions to the injustice.

Sibling conflict should not be judged as abnormal. Books can help to provide the context for healthy reactions and interactions on the part of readers. Guilt should not be imposed, particularly since arguments and hostility between siblings is such an expected part of normal development.

Books are most effective when they have literary merit. The best lessons are taught unobtrusively. Too obvious a message damages a story.

DISCUSSION OF CHILDREN'S BOOKS

THE NEW BABY

The elder sibling—particularly when that child has been an only child up to the arrival of the new baby—is the subject of sympathetic concern in many books. It is generally the three-to six-year-old child to whom these books are directed, perhaps because it is these children who react most keenly to the new baby. Some of the books dealing directly with this topic are factual. They are designed to be read to the child in order to give information that will help the child to understand the process. Joan Samson's *Watching the New Baby* is one such book. It is illustrated with photographs that show not only new babies but also their brothers and sisters in pleasant activities. The book attempts to involve the elder sibling in an understanding of the baby's development, so that the child will not resent the baby's behavior. Although a very young child has little capacity for empathy, some of the explanations will probably alleviate anxiety and anger and will help the elder child feel more comfortable as a result of the additional knowledge.

Hi, New Baby, by Andry and Kratka, goes one step further by predicting situations that may call for action on the part of the elder child. The authors suggest useful responses to the new baby, but above all, this book demonstrates to the older children that they are loved. This message that every family member is important is also communicated strongly in Sara Bonnett Stein's *That New Baby*. This is one of the "Open Family" books. As with the others in this series, there is a text for parents and one for children. The advice to parents is practical and psychologically sound. It helps families to recognize that jealousy and feelings of being misplaced are normal and should be dealt with in a loving, accepting way. The photographs, both in black and white and in color, show a black family, adding to the universality of the message. The family contains two older siblings—a boy and a girl—and the grandmother who is a permanent member of the family. Books of this sort help to prepare parents for coping with the problem of sibling rivalry in a realistic, direct fashion. Helping adults such as teachers, counselors, and librarians may want to read such books so that they can recommend procedures to parents and children. In addition, they can directly help children who are trying to deal with the situation of a new baby.

Many books of fiction also take up the problem of jealousy of the new baby. The books, aimed not only at the older siblings but also at parents, contain modeling situations for their readers to follow. One such book, *Billy and Our New Baby*, by Helene S. Arnstein, speaks directly to the parents in a guide included in the back of the book. The story describes Billy, who is perturbed because his mother is spending so much time with the new baby that he wants it returned to the hospital. Even after his mother responds to him with extra affection, Billy reverts to babyish behavior. But when his mother communicates that she understands and values him, he is helped to cope with the new child.

A number of the books on this topic emphasize the role the elder sibling can play in helping with the new baby. In Gerson's *Omoteji's Baby Brother*, Omoteji, a Nigerian boy, feels left out and useless until he decides on the perfect contribution that he can make to the festivities of his new brother's naming ceremony. In Schick's *Peggy's New Brother*, the elder sibling finds that her efforts to entertain the new baby are appreciated. Eloise Greenfield's *She Come Bringing Me That Little Baby Girl* is another book in which the elder sibling accepts the younger one because he is permitted to help in some way. *Alex and the Baby*, by Mary Dickinson, is unusual because it describes an only child who goes through the pangs of jealousy when an infant visits the house. He finds some sources of pleasure in playing with the baby, and then has the satisfaction of knowing how much his mother newly appreciates him, in comparison to the infant. A book with a similar plot is *Stevie* by John Steptoe. In this book the child resents the intrusion of a younger boy who stays with them during the week, but he misses Stevie when the family moves away.

Children who read these books, or who have the books read to them, can be asked to give suggestions for how they can help at home with their baby sisters or brothers. They can also dictate stories to their teachers or to older students or adults in the classroom or library. In these stories they can name themselves as the protagonists who have just had the experience of having a baby sibling come home to them. They can describe what they do to help with the new baby and can then illustrate their stories either with their own drawings or with photographs of themselves and their families. Their stories can be placed on the classroom or library shelves.

The best antidote to the poison of sibling rivalry is a feeling of self-worth, along with the knowledge that the family still loves and needs the person who is jealous. Myra Berry Brown's *Amy and the New Baby* confirms the family's love for Amy. Mary Jarrell's *The Knee Baby* and Ann Herbert Scott's *On Mother's Lap* also help the child to overcome a feeling of displacement. In Jarrell's book, the boy takes turns with the new baby on his mother's lap. In Scott's book, the mother makes room at the same time for everyone.

Patricia MacLachlan's *Arthur, for the Very First Time,* describes a boy's gradual development from being very self-involved to appreciating and cherishing new life, and others' feelings and ideas. Caring adults and a feisty, sensitive female friend help him in this evolution. While not primarily about the acceptance of a new sibling, this book will help a reader, especially one who has been an only child, adjust to the coming of an infant.

Sometimes, no matter how well intentioned the parents are, children still feel unwanted. In both Russell Hoban's *A Baby Sister for Frances* and Ezra Jack Keats's *Peter's Chair,* the elder siblings run away from home. But neither runs very far, and both feel much better when they realize that their parents want them back.

Norma Klein presents two sets of very understanding parents in her books *If I Had My Way* and *Confessions of an Only Child*. In the first book, Ellie reverts to infantile behavior, dreaming out her hostility by taking over the world and subjugating adults. The book is somewhat overdone but might prove helpful to children who are very angry about their lack of control over their families. Antonia, in *Confessions of an Only Child*, uses her friends and her parents to help work out her unpleasant feelings.

SIBLING RIVALRY

Authors exhibit sympathy for the elder child, but also consider the younger one if the younger sibling in the story is still a toddler. In *If It Weren't for Benjamin* by Barbara Shook Hazen, the older brother gets to lick the icing spoon, uses scissors with points, and stays up late. The parents help the young child to see that it isn't necessary to be identical to his sibling, and that he is valued for who he is. He independently comes to recognize that he'd miss Benjamin's telling him jokes, fixing his toys, and playing with him. But he also admits that there are times when he hates his brother.

Several books elaborate on this theme. In Crescent Dragonwagon's *I Hate My Brother Harry,* the little girl is permitted to express her ambivalent feelings toward her older brother. She retains both the love and hate at the end of the book. It is a little boy in Judith Viorst's *I'll Fix Anthony*, who dreams of the day he will be six years old, and big enough to get back at his older brother, who treats him badly. This sort of presentation reassures a child who has not achieved a purely loving relationship with a sibling that it is a normal condition.

Although authors demonstrate that they are very much aware of the problems for the elder children, they usually focus their happy solutions and understanding on the period when the younger sibling is an infant. A number of books reflect the problem of the rivalry between siblings once the siblings have progressed beyond babyhood. But the point of view of the younger child is the one more often championed in these books. Natalie Savage Carlson's *The Half Sisters* describes Luvvy's plight as the sister caught in the middle. Understandably attempting to be considered a fit companion for her elder sisters, Luvvy wants to be seen as mature. However, she considers her youngest sister to be a pest, and acts accordingly. The author sympathizes with Luvvy's position as a younger sibling, but disapproves of Luvvy's negligent behavior toward her youngest sister. When this baby sister dies, poor Luvvy suffers from guilt for the rest of her life.

Similarly, in Norma Klein's *Naomi in the Middle*, seven-year-old Naomi is the narrator, protagonist, and favored character. Her elder sister, Bobo, is negatively portrayed. The parents are not as kind to Bobo as they are to

Naomi. It is quite comprehensible to an empathic reader that Bobo dreads yet another addition to the household, but her feelings are not at all acknowledged by anyone in the book. Eloise Greenfield's *Sister* is a more complex book, which favors the younger girl, Doretha, over her difficult elder sister, Alberta.

●TRY THIS

Rewrite a scene from *Naomi in the Middle, The Half Sisters,* or *Sister,* from the point of view of the elder sister. Rewrite any of the "new baby" books from the point of view of the new baby. Have children do the same thing. If they cannot write, have them retell the stories orally.

Other books portraying sibling rivalry include Doris Orgel's *Bartholomew, We Love You.* While the reader's sympathy is expected to lie with the younger sister, the presentation is balanced enough so that the elder does not emerge as the victimizer. The happy ending is not that the younger one wins out, but that they learn to share and cooperate with each other. This book is useful in its depiction of the parents, who in addition to both being working people, are impartial, understanding, and capable.

In a somewhat different setting, John Branfield's *Why Me?* focuses on a younger sister whose behavior is complicated by the fact that she has diabetes. Very resentful because of this, she abuses her elder sister, her parents, and her friends. Although she is the principal character, she is not portrayed very sympathetically. Everyone tries to help her, although at times her sister is understandably angry. It does not look, even at the end of the book, as if the sibling relationship will ever be a good one, but the reader understands everyone's point of view and can accept the conclusion. Some mature readers might try to give other solutions for the family's problems or might write a different ending for this book. Ron Roy's *Where's Buddy?*, a book with a similar situation, provides readers with a more positive model of two siblings, one of whom has diabetes. Although Mark, the older brother, somewhat resents having to baby-sit for Buddy, the younger boy is shown as capable of taking care of his own physical needs under normal circumstances. Buddy is pampered by his parents, but the sibling relationship is a solid one.

Twins are often considered to be two halves of the same child. A number of books usefully present twins as experiencing the rivalry that exists between ordinary brothers and sisters. Beverly Cleary's *Mitch and Amy* and Alice Bach's *The Smartest Bear and His Brother Oliver* are two that demonstrate this approach. The bear twins have understanding, responsive parents, but Mitch and Amy's parents unwittingly foster competition between the twins. Katherine Paterson's *Jacob Have I Loved* revolves around Louise, who hates her favored twin sister. Only maturity and a sense of accomplishment in saving the life of a newborn baby help Louise to overcome her negative feelings.

Most books at least imply that the siblings will grow out of their bickering and rivalry. For some readers, this may seem an unlikely development. They will be delighted with Beryl Epstein and Dorritt Davis's *Two Sisters and Some Hornets*. In this story the sisters are elderly women in rocking chairs, recalling their childhood. As they talk about their recollections, they adopt the same argumentative patterns that they had when they were children—and the book ends with their continuing to argue over the facts. It is comforting to know that they and their relationship have survived into old age.

COOPERATION AND LOVE

Perhaps less realistic for some children, but certainly reflective of others' experiences, are the books that describe amiable, helpful, and loving relationship among siblings. If these books are not held up to readers as perfect examples to be emulated, then they can serve as confirmation of positive feelings and can, perhaps, provide alternatives to quarrelsome behavior.

In *Do You Have the Time, Lydia?* by Evaline Ness, an elder sister unwittingly hurts the feelings of her younger brother by being too preoccupied with her own adventures. She recognizes what she has done and, on her own initiative, sets it right.

There is no conflict whatsoever in some stories with siblings as the characters. In John Steptoe's *My Special Best Words*, Bweela, although she is only three years old, lovingly and competently takes care of her younger brother. They do have some verbal quarrels, but the reader recognizes this as part of the fun; the relationship remains strongly positive. The elder brother in Betsy Byars's *Go and Hush the Baby* also assumes some care-taking tasks for his young sibling and performs his job willingly and well. June Jordan contributes a strong, coping family in *New Life, New Room*. The children are realistic, lively, and inventive, while both parents are tender to each other and to the children. The brother and sister in Patricia MacLachlan's delightful *Seven Kisses in a Row* provide another excellent model for readers to appreciate and emulate. The children recognize and accept each other's idiosyncracies. All of the characters have vivid personalities and are amusing as well as captivating.

FACING RESPONSIBILITY

Siblings are often called upon to take care of each other to varying degrees, depending on the extremes of the situation. In Lucille Clifton's *Don't You Remember?* the four-year-old girl is tended by her elder brother. He must postpone going back to school so that both parents can work and his sister can be adequately supervised. The statement is made that he will resume his schooling. The arrangement does not seem to be a hardship for him, but it is a unique one.

In somewhat less supportive circumstances, Lydia, in the Cleavers', *Me Too*, tries to nurture and educate her retarded twin sister. Their father has left them because he cannot tolerate his family. In the end Lydia fails but she recognizes that her failure was inevitable, her goal unachievable. She also accepts the fact that she cannot be responsible for her sister.

Dicey, in Cynthia Voigt's *Homecoming* and the Newbery-Award-winning *Dicey's Song*, and Mary Call, in the Cleavers' *Where the Lilies Bloom*, take over the management of their families when their parents are gone. Mary Call's parents are both dead; Dicey's mother has abandoned them. Both girls hide the fact that they have no adult protection. Both are occasionally resented by their siblings for their imperious attitudes. Both are superhuman in their ability to earn a living, to respond to emergencies, and to maintain the family. These stories end happily, with adults stepping in and taking charge. But Karana, in *Island of the Blue Dolphins*, by O'Dell, never receives the benefit of someone to take care of her after she and her brother are marooned on an island. She is in this predicament because of her brother and her sense of responsibility for him. Unfortunately, despite her efforts, he dies, and she must manage her own survival alone.

In *The Bears' House*, by Marilyn Sachs, the children also do not fare well. After their father leaves them, their mother suffers a total mental collapse. The children, trying to sustain themselves, conceal their lack of parental supervision, but they fail at everything. Ultimately their situation is discovered, and the reader knows that they will be dispersed to different places. Their individual emotional problems make it impossible for them to function together.

SPECIAL PROBLEMS

In some books siblings and their relationships help to bring to the readers' attention some special situations with which they can empathize. In Paige Dixon's *May I Cross Your Golden River?* Jordan's brothers and sister play a large part in making his last year a happy one. Each of them reacts in a different but supportive way to the news that he is dying. His feelings for his family add to the poignancy of the story. Another, more common problem is explored in Barbara Corcoran's *A Trick of Light*, in which twins must begin to accept the fact that they are separate beings with individual lives to lead. In this story the boy is ready to be independent before the girl is; therein lies the conflict. It is resolved only after a series of traumas.

One of a pair of siblings suffers the most in Winthrop's *A Little Demonstration of Affection*. Jenny fears that she has incestuous feelings for her brother Charlie. Her family is a fairly happy but totally undemonstrative group. The parents never permit the children to see them touching each other or engaging in any affectionate behavior; they are equally reserved with the children. Jenny, therefore, misinteprets her response to her brother Charlie's normal show of affection. She is so moved by his hugging her, and so craves more of it, that she fears something is dreadfully wrong with her. Her father and brother at last help her to see that her needs are normal and that the family has been at fault for not exhibiting any kind of physical affection for each other. They all resolve to amend their behavior. The ending is a somewhat uneasy but plausible one.

Many other books contain examples of different sibling relationships. In order to be helped in constructing a healthy mode of behavior, children need to see that they are normal, that they are valued, and that there are many acceptable ways of relating. Adults and children will find numerous examples of the ways that sisters and brothers are presented, in a variety of books that will provide models, test situations, and questions to explore. The greater the number and variety that are at readers' immediate disposal, the more beneficial will be the impact. Sibling rivalry will not be eliminated, but readers may learn to handle it with more comfort.

DIVORCE

Love, marriage, and family have signaled emotional success in our society. Although men have not been considered total failures if they choose not to marry, their lives have been judged to be less than complete. Women, on the other hand, have been taught to anticipate marriage as a natural and proper part of existence. If a woman is not married, it is assumed that no one asked her; rarely is it considered that the single state is her choice. Only in recent years have arrangements other than marriage been socially available options. Some men and women are now recognizing that marriage is not necessarily a life goal for them. Their decision is viewed with less disapproval now in the light of changing lifestyles and society's new recognition of people's right to individuality.

Marriage itself is being viewed differently. Happy marriages are now defined by criteria other than longevity. Some marriages that have lasted a long time are acknowledged to be unsuccessful. People might choose to stay together for reasons other than constructive ones. Wives used to endure all kinds of hardships within marriage because they feared that life would be even more difficult for them if they were divorced. Husbands might stay with women that they no longer cared for because it was economically unfeasible to pay for the costs of divorce and its aftermath. Men were responsible for the total support of the family. Marriages might also continue "for the sake of the children." These pressures still exist; but more and more, people are recognizing that they must work together to keep a marriage going well, and that if their efforts fail, they must work together to make the separation a mutually successful one.

Separation and divorce are not so difficult or costly to arrange as before. What used to be an ugly, painful, drawn out procedure has, in many states, been simplified. Now the process itself is not a stumbling block when two partners decide that they will dissolve their contract. Divorce is less scandalous than it once was. Many states have instituted "no fault" divorce laws acknowledging that there has been an irretrievable breakdown of the marriage, and that no one is at fault.

Our social structure is in a state of transition, but the preponderant values continue to include the traditional expectations of lasting marriage. Ending a marriage other than by death is still considered by many observers to constitute failure. It is certainly a wrenching experience, not only to the partners but to any children involved. Both adults and children must overcome many emotional hurdles. Just as adults agonize over what they could have done to save the marriage (or bemoan having gotten themselves into it in the first place), so too the children blame themselves for the failed marriage. They imagine that if they had done their job as "good children" their parents would still be together. They also worry about whether or not their parents will continue to love and care for them, about being deserted by the remaining parent and about never again seeing their absent parent. They worry about being supplanted in their parents' affections, and they question their own self-worth.

Friends and acquaintances sometimes respond as though there has been a death in the family. They carefully avoid mentioning the child's predicament, eliminating the word "father" (or, if the child is living with the father, the word "mother") from their vocabulary when the child is within hearing distance. They apologize in nonverbal ways if their own families are intact, or they hesitate to invite the child to a family gathering for fear of unduly inflicting pangs of jealousy. Sometimes they barrage a child with questions: "What's your mother (father) doing these days?" "What's happening at your house lately?" "Is anything new?" While these probes might be kindly intended, they can confuse and hurt a child who does not really know how his or her parents are feeling or what is going on at home.

If divorce is an unusual occurrence in the community, the child's peers will sometimes avoid contact with the child, as though divorce were contagious. Even if this is not the case, it is sometimes difficult for peers to know what to say to help a child who no longer lives with both parents. In communities where divorce is less rare, children who have experienced the same situation can be very helpful in sharing feelings and offering support to each other. The sensitive adult can arrange for this kind of interaction to take place.

A large percentage of all divorced couples have children under eighteen. Agencies specializing in family help, as well as organizations such as Parents Without Partners, give advice and support. Books can be used as tools by parents, teachers, librarians, and children on a regular "Come to me whenever you need me" basis.

SUGGESTED CRITERIA

Just as with any other sort of book, the literary quality of a written work dealing with divorce can enhance or detract from its effectiveness. If it is a work of fiction, it should have more than the issue of divorce to carry its readers' interest. If the book's intent is to convey information it must do so in a noncondescending, jargon-free fashion. The topic of divorce must be kept up to date because the statistics and state laws have been changing rapidly. On the other hand, the psychological reactions of children have changed little in response to divorce. If a book communicates children's feelings and suggests some effective ways to deal with them, it is a useful book.

Books for children should handle the topic realistically. One pitfall to avoid is the "happy" ending of the parents' being reunited as a result of the child's behavior. Many children believe that it lies within their power to save their parents' marriage. This is unrealistic and can serve the child badly. Books should also try to refrain from establishing guilt for a divorce, which is almost always a complicated situation with no simple cause. In any case, blame-fixing is not useful. If a book uses it as a constituent of the plot, then the case should be presented so that the reader either senses another perspective or recognizes the futility of blaming.

The most helpful books about divorce grant children their feelings and are models for supportive behavior on the part of their peers and adults, providing options for everyone involved. Although they do not necessarily end happily, they do demonstrate that life can go on in a constructive fashion. Books on this topic should be used with children experiencing the problem, with their peers (so that empathy can be stimulated), and with parents, who often need to learn how to manage their responses.

The audience determines the use to which a book will be put. If the audience is a child whose parents have just divorced, the book will be used as therapy, comfort, and, perhaps, as a source of information and suggestions for behavior. If the audience is a group of children who have never come in contact with the situation of divorce and are now responding inappropriately to a peer who is involved in a divorce, the book may stimulate empathic and supportive behavior. Sometimes a book for children is a useful tool for reaching a parent, helping him or her deal with the child in a more constructive fashion. In reading a book to a child, a parent may also derive comfort, support, and ideas from it.

•TRY THIS

Select three books from the Bibliography at the end of this chapter. If you were to recommend these books to a reader, (1) for whom would this book be most valuable? (2) for whom would this book be of no use at all? (3) what problems are left unsolved by these books? After sharing your selections with someone else, combine your perceptions.

Books containing even the briefest mention of a divorce usually communicate very clearly the attitude of the author and/or the prevailing societal point of view. Religion, upbringing, and ethical standards contribute to the building of an attitude toward people who are involved in divorce. Accurate information contributes to a healthy perspective. The helping adult must face his or her own opinions knowledgeably before attempting to work with a child who is coping with the problem at firsthand.

•TRY THIS

Answer the following questions as accurately as you can. After you look at your answers, decide how your information and opinions will affect a child whose parents have been divorced. How will they affect children who are the peers of this child?

1. What is the most prevalent cause of divorce?
2. What is the current divorce rate? Where can you find this information?
3. What organizations help parents to cope with this problem?
4. What are the legal regulations in this state regarding divorce?
5. Which local agencies provide information on this topic?
6. What could cause you to seek a divorce from your mate?
7. How do you feel about the idea of preserving a marriage for the sake of the children?
8. What are your assumptions about the behavior of children coming from single-parent homes?

DISCUSSION OF CHILDREN'S BOOKS

BREAKING UP

Books describing the initial divorce process hold out hope for children whose parents have separated or divorced. The pattern of these books includes the child's bewilderment and unhappiness over the separation, the difficult period of adjustment when the arrangements are first being negotiated, the problem of living with one parent only and visiting the other parent periodically, and then the settling down to a satisfactory everyday existence with the single parent. The books do not pretend that the children's hoped-for happy ending—the reconciliation of the father and mother—will ever occur. They do recognize the fears and guilt feelings of the children, and they present realistic situations.

Beth Goff's *Where Is Daddy?* follows the pattern, adding the specific trauma for the very young child who is not only experiencing the loss of her father from the household but also the partial loss of the mother who now goes out of the house to work for the first time in the child's existence. In this book, the child, Janeydear, goes with her mother and her dog to live with her maternal grandmother. The child is terrified that, if she exhibits anger or bad temper, her mother will behave as her father did and not return. She considers herself the culprit in the divorce. If only she had behaved well, her father would not have left. Her well-meaning but harassed grandmother unwittingly contributes to this feeling. The child becomes fearful, quiet, and withdrawn.

At last the adults recognize how Janeydear feels, and take steps to make her more comfortable. The mother takes Janeydear to her place of business. Now Janeydear can picture her mother at work instead of worrying about where she is. Her grandmother accompanies them, becoming a partner in the process. The grandmother begins to play with Janeydear, relaxing some of her rules about permitting the dog into the house. And Janeydear's father visits her and answers her questions. The story is clearly and directly told. The characters are somewhat oversimplified, but not stereotyped. They have enough individuality so that the story can stand on its own without being used exclusively as a lesson. Commenting at the end of the book, Dr. John F. McDermott, a psychiatrist, describes the expected reactions of a young child to divorce and some of the difficulties that adults face. He recommends the use of this story as a bridge to help restore perspective to children and their parents. Young children may appreciate the opportunity to role-play this story and others like it.

Another book conveying a similar message for somewhat older children is Peggy Mann's *My Dad Lives in a Downtown Hotel.* When Joey's father leaves him and his mother and moves into a hotel, Joey is convinced that his father does not love him. Imagining that if he reforms, his father will be willing to come back home, he goes to visit his father, armed with a list of promises that he will fulfill to be a better person. Joey's mother also wants the father to come back home. The father seems rather callous about their feelings and rejects any contact with Joey's mother, even though she invites it; he even avoids mentioning her in conversation with Joey. He inconsiderately drops in on Joey and his mother at night to collect some of his belongings.

The book specifically describes the child's feelings and each of the significant occurrences at this time of his life. The father has apparently never before been much of a companion for the boy. Now that he and the mother are being divorced, he pays more attention to his son. The divorce brings all kinds of improvements in the behavior of both of his parents toward Joey. He also discovers that there are a number of children at school who are in his situation, and they decide to form a social club. It will probably serve as a support for these children. Life for the boy looks as if it will be comfortable.

The book demonstrates a realistic portrayal of a separation. The mother is not dependent, clinging, or nagging. Though obviously the injured party, she is not a martyr. She continues to work, cares about her appearance, and tries to devise special ways of attending to Joey's needs. She is an excellent model except for the fact that she keeps alive the hope that her husband will return. The husband, although inconsiderate, is not really a villain. Children could devise a "What if . . . ?" exercise, telling how Joey might respond if the father did not visit regularly or if the father remarried. When Joey's first attempt at bringing his parents back together fails, he accepts the reality of their always remaining separate.

In *A Month of Sundays*, by Rose Blue, ten-year-old Jeff keeps dreaming of his parents' getting back together. He and his mother have moved from the suburbs to the city. At first Jeff feels uncomfortable there, but eventually learns to enjoy the benefits that the city has to offer. The job that Jeff's mother takes is her first. Jeff is unhappy about it because he misses the attention she used to give him. She finally recognizes the reasons for his negative behavior, and, despite her weariness, spends time with him, and participates in plans for the block party to come. Children could suggest ways that Jeff can help at home, perhaps by writing an imaginary letter to Jeff, giving him advice.

Most books concentrate on the children's feelings. It would probably be useful if some of the books helped children to acknowledge their parents' feelings as well. Books such as those described above are useful for children who are enduring the painful beginnings of life after divorce. They help make the child aware that other people have gone through the same experience and have had the same ugly and confused feelings. They present a positive way of relating to both parents and of coping with the problems.

Unlike the three books thus far described, one book for preteens and older, *Leap Before You Look*, by Mary Stolz, specifically details the causes of the parents' marital breakdown. It foreshadows the divorce by having the father's young, pretty assistant appear at the house well before the divorce is a certainty. But since the unhappiness of the marriage is described before this, the reader understands the father's position. The mother in this book is really the cause of the unhappiness. She is a withdrawn, selfish woman who prefers her own isolation to anyone's company. Her values are totally different from her husband's. Her daughter, Jimmie, prefers her father to her mother but becomes very angry when he leaves them. She resents it even more when, after the divorce, he marries his lover.

This book, which has a complicated plot and unusual characters, requires that the reader understand the different people and not judge them. The mother is dealt with unsympathetically, but all the other characters are multidimensional and invite our compassion. Jimmie's friends are helpful in alleviating her pain. In the end, Jimmie begins to move toward a reconciliation with her father.

One of the negative aspects of too many of the books for older readers is the assumption that the mother is at fault. In these books, where the mother is blamed for the breakup of the marriage, the father is almost always a pleasant, understanding, admirable person. There is too often no indication, other than that of the mother's unpleasantness, that there is any real cause for the divorce. Mary Stolz's book describes a woman whose withdrawal from the real world is probably pathological, but no one in her family recognizes it as such. It is she who is the cause of her husband's unhappiness; it is she who is the least sympathetic character. Readers may find it an interesting exercise, in cases like this, to attempt to reconstruct the couple's courtship and marriage in order to understand how the pair came to marry in the first place.

Somewhat similarly, in Honor Arundel's *A Family Failing*, the mother carries the largest burden for the failure of the marriage. Again, it is the father whom the daughter prefers. Again, the father is a pleasant, honest, attractive person. In this story the father loses his job at the same time that the mother appears regularly on a successful television show. Both parents are journalists, but the mother is depicted as having few scruples, while the father is ethical, committed to quality and principle. He cannot accept his wife's position of being the sole wage earner in the family. Nor can he make good his intention to write a book. After manufacturing all kinds of excuses for his failure, he finally admits that he simply does not have the talent. He goes off to a rural spot in Scotland, deciding to stay there permanently rather than be subjected to the emotional hardship of Edinburgh. The mother loses her television job, but stubbornly refuses to join her husband because, she says, her pride will not let her.

No member of the family is without selfish characteristics. They impose upon the mother the entire responsibility for all the cooking and most of the cleaning in the house. The children realize that their parents have always permitted them to be independent, but they do not recognize the extent to which they have depended on their mother for their physical needs. When she becomes the only wage earner in the family, the family collapses. The son moves to a commune; the father moves to the small village in Scotland. The daughter first joins her brother, then her father. Despite the fact that it is the mother who carries the greatest responsibility for maintaining the family, they denigrate her jobs and her abilities. The implication is clear that the mother is at fault for the dissolution of the family. In the end, the daughter decides that she has no right to intervene in her parents' lives and that they must do what they decide is best. She also begins to accept them as they are without trying to change them. Mature preteens can read this book to help them come to a position of not having to fix blame for their parents' separation.

AFTERMATH OF THE DIVORCE

Books describing the lives of people some time after the divorce vary more than those dealing mainly with the period during and immediately after the breakup. In general the many problems are clearly confronted, but the prospect of a blissful solution is less assured.

Sometimes the child's nightmare comes true in these books. The parents really do not want to have anything to do with their children; they even abuse the children physically and psychologically. These books may be useful in stimulating peer empathy or in encouraging discussion about the negative feelings of a child who believes, accurately or not, that he or she is being victimized. For the child who becomes upset by these books, an adult would do well to provide supportive guidance, along with a variety of books presenting different aspects of the divorce situation.

A book in which the parents seemingly reject their child after the divorce is John Donovan's *I'll Get There. It Better Be Worth the Trip*. Davy has lived with his maternal grandmother since his parents' divorce. His father has remarried, and his mother is an alcoholic. When the grandmother dies, there is no one but his mother who is willing to take custody of him. She obviously sustains great anxiety about the idea, and the arrangement does not work out very well for Davy. His mother is overly taxed by the situation; his father and stepmother seem genuinely to care for the boy but not enough to provide a home for him. Not until the boy is independent of his family will he have any sort of security.

Growing up—or at least attaining emotional independence—seems to be the only solution for a number of characters in books dealing with the aftermath of divorce. The daughter in *A Family Failing* outgrows her need for her parents' attention. Chris, one of the secondary characters in *Leap Before You Look*, is in therapy because of her mother's lack of regard for the institution of marriage. Chris believes that even now, although her mother is still married to her second husband, she is in the process of searching for a third. Each of her aunts has been married three times. Chris is disgusted by this behavior, besides being angry with her father, who has not once visited her in all the years since his divorce from her mother. But she, too, recognizes that, when she gets a little older, she will be more able to provide for herself the emotional support that she now requires from her family.

Guy, the hero of Harry Mazer's *Guy Lenny*, though only twelve years old, also comes to the realization that he must emotionally separate from his parents in order to cope with his situation. With Guy, however, the fault is not easily assigned. Guy's mother left him and his father to marry another man, and has only sporadically written to Guy during their long separation. Her new husband is a career officer in the army, and it was not feasible for them to take Guy with them. Meanwhile, the boy has lived with his father, an easy-going blue-collar worker. Guy loves his father and feels deeply hurt by his mother's desertion. When his father becomes involved with Emily, who then helps to take care of Guy and the house, Guy angrily resents Emily's intrusion into the relationship he has with his father. Although she tries to befriend Guy, he will not permit it. He stubbornly maintains a hostile attitude toward her in hopes that his father will give her up.

Guy's parents are not villains in this book. His father becomes tired of having to cope with Guy's resentment of Emily. He is ready to marry again, and Guy is opposed to his doing so. Guy feels betrayed by his father when he learns that his father wants to marry Emily and is willing to relinquish him. Readers can discuss whether or not Guy could or should have been more responsive and pleasant to Emily. Each character's point of view is explored to some measure in this book. The book itself is not so well crafted as some of the others, but it could be a useful tool in helping children see more than a narrow view of their own situation.

Another book in which a child has an unreasonably negative response to the parent's new life is *Chloris and the Creeps*, by Kin Platt. Chloris and her younger sister Jenny live with their mother. Their father remarries after the divorce and then, when his second marriage breaks up, commits suicide. Jenny seems to have adjusted well to the situation, but Chloris has constructed a fantasy about her father. Aided and goaded by her paternal grandmother, she resents and blames her mother for what, realistically, is her father's failing. She glorifies and romanticizes this weak, self-centered, self-destructive man. (In reality he was impatient with the girls, unfaithful to his wife, and generally inconsiderate of everyone.) When the mother finally marries a man who is loving and solicitous of the children, Jenny is very happy, but Chloris cannot accept the situation, even though she is tremendously supported by her new stepfather. Her performance of a series of outlandish acts indicates that she is still enmeshed in her fantasy world. At last she is jolted back into reality when she discovers that her beloved father left money to her younger sister, but not to her.

I, Trissy, by Norma Fox Mazer, ends with the hope that Trissy will respond to all the positive efforts on her behalf by her father, her mother, and her stepfather. Trissy's behavior, like Chloris's, is inappropriate and self-centered. But the adults' concern for her is apparent throughout the story; the reader feels that she will use their help well and will grow to recognize that she is an individual in her own right, valued apart from what her mother and father do with their personal lives.

Children who are resentful of any sort of independent life their parents want to lead may find comfort and a source of perspective in these books, which describe the divorce in terms of the children's negative and inappropriate behavior. An exercise that the class can do is to write a "Dear Abby" letter from the character and to devise an answer from "Dear Abby."

MANAGING

Although most divorce settlements award custody of any children to one parent, the practice of shared or joint custody is gaining favor. This does not necessarily mean that children must stay for a specified amount of time with either parent. Nor does it require the actual physical presence of a parent. In this situation, both parents share in the responsibility of all of the decision making about their children. It is designed to guarantee that although the couple is no longer married, they still function together as parents.

There are many arrangements that families have structured in order to effect this shared responsibility: sometimes the children live in one parent's house for a specified amount of time (two or three days a week, one or two weeks, several months, and even alternate years); some couples arrange it so that the children stay in one place, and each parent shifts from one house to the other. When it is the children who do the "commuting," some parents arrange to have identical furniture, clothing, and toys in their house so that the children will feel comfortable. Often parents make sure that their own residence is in their children's school district in order to make the transition from house to house feasible.

Even if the custody is not shared or joint, many families are careful to maintain the feeling that the children have two parents; although the primary care is the responsibility of one of the parents, they want their children to be members of two-parent families, in the emotional and nurturing sense, even if not in the actual physical arrangements. Adjunct parents (any adult who functions in a parenting role) and/or the new partners of either parent also contribute to the nurturing process. The phrase "single-parent family" has replaced the outmoded "broken family" because of the recognition that any loving entity is a "whole" family. Now we need a new term broad enough to indicate that, although the parents are divorced, they continue to be involved in a concerned and loving relationship with their children.

Nevertheless, it would be foolish to pretend that there are no problems particular to the everyday management of living after a divorce settlement has been reached. And to date, it is still more likely that one parent will have the primary care of the children. If the mother is the parent with whom the child remains, the difficulties of taking on a full-time job and providing adequate care for the child are considerable. Several books recognize this fact and explore solutions. *Mushy Eggs*, by Florence Adams, describes the relationship between two young boys and their baby-sitter. There is no problem until the sitter wants to retire and return to her native Italy; then the boys are hurt and angry that she is leaving them.

Mushy Eggs is a gentle, somewhat uneventful book that contains some important unobtrusive messages. The mother is an excellent carpenter, and uses her skills to build bookcases, closets, and a boat for the boys to play in. The boys maintain a close relationship with their father, who continues to visit them on Sundays and to whose apartment they sometimes go to play. The boys have responsibilities for the maintenance of their house. They accept their situation calmly and constructively; their lives are not traumatic. They are unhappy when their beloved sitter leaves, but their mother wisely manages to take a week's vacation after the sitter's departure so that they will not feel too unhappy. Then she finds a new sitter who appears to be a warm, responsible person. Although the boys do not love her immediately, they accept her and have hope for the future.

Books of this sort are helpful not only to children who think that divorce means the end of the world for them, but also to parents who need good role models to emulate. The mother in this book is a comfortable, independent, caring person who is managing the situation well. Her job, working with computers, is a daytime job. She manages to find helpers to care for the children from breakfast through dinnertime.

In *The Night Daddy*, by Maria Gripe, the mother works at night as a nurse. When she advertises for a person to care for her child at night, a young man who is a writer is hired. At first the child rejects the idea of a person to stay with her. But she and the sitter, whom she comes to look upon as her night daddy, enjoy each other's company. The young man and she are mutually sensitive to each other's feelings and share good experiences together. The child's peers are generally unpleasant to her, but in the end they begin to respond more positively. The child considers her night daddy to be almost as good as a full-time father.

This book is not a factual or didactic book exploring solutions to the problem of the single mother. The imagery and emotional content of the man and child's relationship are the most important factors in the book. It is not a book that will appeal to every reader—some may find the mood and the happenings too vague or tenuous for their taste. But for those who are ready to appreciate the sustaining quality of the relationship and the seemingly small but actually very important adventures that these two share, the book will provide a tender and memorable experience.

Charlotte Zolotow's *A Father Like That* is also a book that deals with the situation of a single mother. The small boy's father "went away before he was born." The child dreams of a father who always takes his side, does not mind loud T.V., and who always agrees with the child's choice of clothing. The mother responds very positively to the child's dreaming. She says that she likes the father he has designed; but if he does not manage to acquire one of his own like that, she hopes that he will become that kind of father when he grows up.

The burden in almost all of the books about single parents falls upon the mother. Joan Lexau's *Emily and the Klunky Baby and the Next-Door Dog* is no exception. Emily is a young girl whose parents are divorced. Her mother, though harried and worried, tries hard to be sympathetic and responsive to her children. Emily resents her baby brother and is unhappy that her mother cannot spend as much time with her as Emily would like. Going for a walk in the park with her brother, she decides to "run away" to her father's house.

Not permitted to cross the street, however, she walks around the block and eventually returns home. The usefulness of this book lies primarily in the opportunity for the reader to empathize with both the mother and the child.

Muriel Stanek's *I Won't Go Without a Father* demonstrates helpful behavior on the part of other adults. People are kind both to Steve and to his mother. The father is gone (we do not know whether the cause is death or divorce), and Steven is jealous of all of his friends who have both parents. He is reluctant to attend an open house that his class is conducting, because he thinks he will be the only boy without a father. Eventually he does go, discovering several children there without fathers. His uncle, his grandfather, and a neighbor attend to give him and his mother support. One of Steve's problems is worrying about how things look to others. His peers and the helping adults work on this with him.

Advice can come in many forms. It can be disguised in a story or didactically administered through nonfiction. It can be directed at children or aimed specifically at parents. One nonfiction work, *The Boys and Girls Book about Divorce*, by Richard A. Gardner, is written for children. It is recommended by Parents Without Partners, an organization for adults who are single parents. The book contains an introduction for parents, guiding their behavior and describing their children's feelings.

The book is written in a direct and practical fashion. Dr. Gardner, a psychiatrist, reassures those children who feel unworthy because they believe that their parents do not love them. He tells them that, if their suspicions are true, they should not waste their time and energy looking for love where it does not exist, but should search for love in appropriate places where it can be found. He tells of the uses of anger. He gives advice on how to get along with divorced parents and with stepparents. There seem to be no problems stemming from divorce that Dr. Gardner avoids. His advice places the responsibility of healthy adjustment on the children's shoulders, but adults involved in this kind of situation would do well to read the book so that they, too, may benefit from the sound advice.

Several books now deal with the new relationships and adjustments that children must make when their divorced parents acquire other partners, and when they may also need to interact with stepsiblings. One such book, *My Other-Mother, My Other-Father*, by Harriet Langsam Sobol, brings out many points about this complicated situation.

Many sociologists and psychologists are making predictions about the future of marriage as we have known it. Almost everyone agrees that attitudes and arrangements are changing. Not many people agree on what the outcomes will be, but in the meantime, while we are in the transitional stage, the phenomenon of children and parents in the one-parent home remains. The appropriate and sensitive use of books to help deal with resultant problems can ease the pressure, helping not only the individuals most directly involved but also those outsiders who are interested and concerned.

ADOPTION AND FOSTER CARE

When children live in a household for extended periods of time they become part of the family structure. Adop.ed children are entitled by law to all of the rights of family members who are related by blood. They are permanent additions to the family. Foster children, however, lead a tenuous existence. At any moment, for any of a variety of reasons, they may be moved out and placed elsewhere. On the other hand, foster children almost always know who their birth parents and siblings are. They usually are aware of the reasons for their removal from their original homes, and they realistically expect, at some point, to be returned to their natural parents.

Adopted children rarely have much if any information about their biological parents. When a baby is born, information is recorded about the birth parents. In most states, if a baby is given up for adoption, these records are sealed. Neither the adoptive parents nor the adopted child are permitted access to them. Ostensibly intended to protect the child from the "stigma" of illegitimacy, this practice also shields the birth parents from any later recriminations on the part of the child, and assures that the child's new identity is the permanent one. Or so it was thought. Recently advocates for adopted children have succeeded in influencing the practices in some states so that adopted children may, upon reaching eighteen years of age, see their records. Some adoptees, understandably, want to know about their genetic heritage. They may not want to meet their birth parents in person, but they may need some clarification of the reasons for their being given up for adoption. They may want to learn about other members of their family of origin. Some psychologists believe that finding out about their birth parents helps adopted children feel more secure about themselves.

•TRY THIS

Imagine that you are adopted. You are happy with your parents, but you want to find out about your biological parents. What will you do?

Imagine that you relinquished your child for adoption. Why did you make this decision? What would you do if your child contacted you after eighteen years?

Write a story using either of the above scenarios.

This wish to know about their origins sometimes results in an extensive legal search, culminating in frustration, partly because records have not been kept up to date. Advocacy agencies such as Adoptees in Search have formed to help adoptees in their quest. In the best of situations, adoptees have the support of their adoptive parents in this search. It often happens that the birth parents are relieved to be located, and are eager to have information about their relinquished child. It can also be a traumatic discovery. One point of view contends that even if it is painful, in the long run it is better for all concerned to have up-to-date knowledge. Another perspective is that the pain is too great, and that the original parents have the right to their privacy and secret past. Everyone agrees that adopted children belong with their nurturing parents; no one seeks to return the adoptees to their birth parents.

Fantasies about their origins are common to all children. Even those children who are not adopted imagine from time to time that they were born to different parents, probably of royal blood. Heroes of myth and fairy tale have traditionally reflected this fantasy: Moses, Romulus and Remus, Oedipus, and many others were raised by other than their birth parents. But when the fantasy becomes reality, many adopted children need to know more about their background in order to adjust to their current lives.

•TRY THIS

Compile a list of agencies in your community or state that deal with adoption. Report on the regulations adoption agencies in your area follow with regard to the practice of updating records of birth parents, and making information available to adoptees.

Self-image is a problem for both foster children and adopted children. The foster child in one story points out that "If a kid thinks his own mother hasn't any use for him, how can he have any use for himself?" It is difficult for a child to understand that sometimes parents love their children so much that they are willing to relinquish them to the care of others, in order to guarantee their welfare. The children tend to see only the rejection, not the protection. They often see themselves as unworthy of love and respect, despite the verbal and demonstrated reassurances on the part of the adoptive parents. Books can help these children and their peers to look at the situations that force parents to relinquish their children to the care of others. They can discuss the similarities all children have, and the differences that are valuable and necessary among all children.

Most adoptions and foster child placements are arranged by agencies. Adoptions are very carefully controlled and monitored; foster care placements are not so meticulously overseen. After a trial period the adoptive family settles into a permanent relationship. When foster children remain "unadoptable" there is always the chance that the child's current placement may be abruptly terminated.

SUGGESTED CRITERIA

Language is an important factor in books on adoption. The term "birth" mother or father is preferable to "real" mother or father. The people who nurture, love, and accept a child are the ones who truly are the parents of that child.

The "happy" ending for adopted children should not be that their birth parents claim them. This may be the expected and appropriate outcome to a story about foster care, but adoptions should be seen as permanent arrangements, arrived at after serious thought on the part of both sets of parents.

The pitiful orphan is a stereotypic cardboard figure. Adopted and foster children should have qualities that make them distinct and memorable characters, aside from their condition. Similarly, adoptive parents should be depicted as real people, not saints or devils.

Wherever possible, the life of the family should be like that of any other family, except for the special emotional considerations attendant upon adoption and foster care. Traumas, catastrophes, and tragedies should occur, if at all, in the context of the plot, not as automatic consequences of adoption.

Books adhering to all of the above criteria are rare. Adopted and foster children are almost automatically viewed as pitiful, even tragic figures. While it is true that circumstances can be painful, and, indeed, sometimes tragic, readers must be able to believe in the reality of the situation and should be led to empathize with the characters, not pity them.

DISCUSSION OF CHILDREN'S BOOKS

FOSTER CHILDREN

Probably the finest example of a well-written, moving, multidimensional book on this topic is *The Great Gilly Hopkins* by Katherine Paterson. Gilly is a bright, manipulative, angry eleven-year-old who has been shifted from one foster home to another. Sometimes her behavior is the cause of her removal from a foster home. Gilly has been hurt by foster parents who she thought loved her. Now she says, "I can't go soft—not while I'm nobody's real kid—not while I'm just something to play musical chairs with ..." She maintains a dream that her mother loves her and wants to take care of her. In reality, Gilly's birth mother has no intention of ever reclaiming her.

Another foster child figures in this book. In contrast to Gilly, William Ernest is shy, fearful, and unable to express himself. He and Gilly become part of the household managed by Mame Trotter, who, despite her obesity and lack of education, emerges as a woman with limitless amounts of good sense, patience, and love. Mame is a remarkable human being. She accepts people and life as they are. She is generous and sensitive. Unfortunately Gilly learns to appreciate her qualities too late for Trotter and Gilly to make their relationship permanent.

Gilly learns some hard lessons in this story. The outcome of the book is not a fairy tale happy ending, but the reader knows that all of the characters will endure. Every person encountered in this book is interesting and three-dimensional. Miss Harris, the teacher who recognizes Gilly's intelligence and her anger, helps Gilly view school in a different way from her past disastrous encounters. Mr. Randolph, Trotter's neighbor, contributes some lessons in perseverance and love of literature. The story is fast moving and consistently engrossing, and foster children as well as their peers will gain insight from this excellent book.

Another well-written book that deals with foster children is Betsy Byars's *The Pinballs*. In this book the children who are in the care of Mrs. Mason (another understanding and loving foster mother) have many emotional problems, but are able to achieve a sense of family with each other.

The author describes each child's background so that readers can understand the characters' behavior. One of the boys has been deserted by his mother and run over by his alcoholic father; one was raised by two very old women who are now hospitalized. The girl, Carlie, has been abused by her stepfather (the third in a series) and is cynical and suspicious of everyone.

The children learn to care about each other, and help each other cope with their problems. The book is somewhat marred by its stereotypic gender role expectations (only Carlie helps with housework), but Carlie is an active girl, and Mr. Mason is a loving, gentle man, so the overall effect of the book is a positive one.

My Name Is Mike Tromsky, by Ruth Pipgras, uncovers many of the complexities involved in foster care. Although Mike is very happy living with his foster family, and his placement there is a stable one, he longs for a permanent reunion with his mother.

A book that sensitively and delicately addresses the issue of foster care is Patricia MacLachlan's *Mama One, Mama Two*. Intended for a young audience, the story describes the relationship between Maudie, whose mother is ill and cannot take care of her, and Katherine, Maudie's foster mother. Katherine is all that a foster parent should be: affectionate, patient, responsive, dependable, and steadfast, but willing to relinquish the child to her birth mother when "Mama One" is ready to resume responsibility. Maudie's anxieties and needs are acknowledged, as are the positive factors in her life.

ADOPTION

Not many books are available that meet the criteria for well-constructed and helpful literature on this topic. There are some factual books that give good advice, but there are others that either oversimplify the issues, or present the information in a dry style. Some books are written by authors who are themselves adoptees, and who have a strong point of view to convey. This could lend authenticity to a book, but some of these authors are so intent on persuading their readers that they lose their perspective, and become strident.

Books such as Carole Livingston's *Why Was I Adopted?* are designed to inform younger children about the facts and feelings of adoption. For older children, *How It Feels to Be Adopted*, by Jill Krementz, helps readers understand the range of responses to this issue. This book uses actual narrative by various adoptees.

High-quality fiction about adoption is even less plentiful. Miska Miles's *Aaron's Door* provides the reader with a model of a loving, concerned father who literally breaks down the barrier separating Aaron from the family that will provide him with a permanent loving home. In *Somebody Else's Child*, by Roberta Silman, Peter's adoptive mother helps to heal the hurt caused by unthinking remarks made by someone who didn't know Peter was adopted. *Abby*, by Jeannette Caines, directly and openly deals with the fact of adoption and how to handle it in a happy family.

More books will undoubtedly appear with this topic as part of the focus. Certainly, adoption and foster care are important dimensions of children's lives. It is to be hoped that children's book authors will respond to the need for appropriate literary fare dealing with these issues.

REFERENCES: FAMILY

BERNSTEIN, JOANNE E. *Books to Help Children Cope with Separation and Loss*. New York: Bowker, 1983. (2nd ed.)
Provides an excellent general psychological background on the issues and experience of any sort of loss in a child's world. Includes comments and annotated entries on death, divorce, desertion, serious illness, war, foster care and adoption, and other loss-related situations. Provides an extensive bibliography of children's books, each one sensitively annotated and critiqued by the author. Four hundred titles have been added to this revised edition.

BRACKEN, JEANNE, AND WIGUTOFF, SHARON. *Books for Today's Children: An Annotated Bibliography of Non-Stereotyped Picture Books*. Old Westbury, New York: Feminist Press, 1979.
Discusses and recommends over 100 books for young children containing positive values. The titles are arranged in lists of highly recommended, recommended, and recommended with some reservation. Otherwise, the books are not placed into categories, but many of them are concerned with family life.

BRACKEN, JEANNE, AND WIGUTOFF, SHARON, WITH BAKER, ILENE. *Books for Today's Young Readers: An Annotated Bibliography of Recommended Fiction for Ages 10–14*. Old Westbury, New York: Feminist Press, 1981.

Descriptions and analyses of books for older readers. Gender, peer friendships, special needs, families in transition, foster care and adoption, and views of old people are some of the categories specified. Very helpful discussion and format.

CARBINO, ROSEMARIE. *Foster Parenting: An Updated Review of the Literature*. New York: Child Welfare League of America, 1980.
This monograph cities many references in a clear, concise style.

COUNCIL ON INTERRACIAL BOOKS FOR CHILDREN. *Bulletin* (Special Issue on Parenting), Vol. 9, Nos. 4 and 5, 1978.
Several articles on child-rearing books, literature on foster care and adoption, single parenting, and critique of books on black parenting. Provides criteria, lists of resources, and book reviews.

DESPERT, J. LOUISE. *Children of Divorce*. Garden City, New York: Doubleday, 1962. Paperback.
Says that children whose parents have deep conflicts with each other and do not divorce are worse off than children whose parents actually do divorce. Calls it "emotional divorce" when parents maintain an unhappy marriage. Summarizes causes for divorce and considers rising divorce rate part of the "groping progress toward a democratic way of life" (p. 5). Recommends that parents find someone to listen to them and that they listen to and aid the children. Her advice, in general, is compatible with the other experts, including informing the child of the situation and reassuring the children that they are not to blame. Points out ways of safeguarding the children; advises parents, discusses problems and lists resources.

ELLIS, ANNE W. *The Family Story in the 1960's*. Hamden, Connecticut: Archon Books, 1970.
Analyzes family stories, mostly by British authors. Comments on the nature of family relationships throughout the world in the 1960s. Erosion of the family, emergence of lower classes as characters in books partial reflection of real social problems.

FASSLER, JOAN. *Helping Children Cope: Mastering Stress Through Books and Stories*. New York: Free Press, 1978.
Discusses the issues of separation, death, hospitalization, illness, lifestyle changes, and other potentially stress-causing situations as they are presented in books for children ages four to eight.

FELKER, EVELYN H. *Foster Parenting Young Children: Guidelines from a Foster Parent*. New York: Child Welfare League of America, 1974.
Deals with foster parents, foster children, biological children, and social agencies. Practical, realistic and comprehensive.

GALPER, MIRIAM. *Joint Custody and Co-Parenting*. Philadelphia: Running Press, 1980.
A step-by-step guide to co-parenting.

GROLLMAN, EARL E., ed. *Explaining Divorce to Children*. Boston: Beacon Press, 1972. Paperback.
Compilation of articles about divorce. Includes different experts' social and religious points of view and one chapter on explaining divorce to children.

GRUENBERG, SIDONIE MATSNER. *The Parents' Guide to Everyday Problems of Boys and Girls*. New York: Random House, 1958.
Devotes one chapter to brothers' and sisters' relationships. Gives practical, uncomplicated advice on how to respond to sibling rivalry. Helps parents to recognize subtle interactions and to be fair in dealing with quarrels. Discusses the characteristics of the eldest, middle, and youngest children. Recommends some useful procedures for managing the family.

HALEY, B. "The Fractured Family in Adolescent Literature," *English Journal*, Vol. 63, No. 2, February 1974, pp. 70–72.
An annotated bibliography of books of adolescents concerning adolescents, one of whose parents is not living at home because of death, divorce, or separation.

HYDE, MARGARET O. *Foster Care and Adoption*. New York: Franklin Watts, 1981.
Procedures for adoption and foster care are described, with commentary about the policies and politics of the process. Comparisons are made among states. Suggestions for improvement are supplied.

ILG, FRANCES, AND AMES, LOUISE BATES. *Child Behavior*. New York: Harper & Brothers, 1955.
The authors devote an entire chapter to the topic of brothers and sisters. They advise parents to accept sibling rivalry and hostility as normal. They describe the developmental aspects of sibling relationship.

KLEIN, CAROLE. *The Single Parent Experience*. New York: Walker, 1973. Paperback: Avon.
Discusses the person who is a single parent by choice. Warns potential single parents to be honest with themselves. Has a chapter on the single father. Also encourages single parents and advises them. Has chapter on homosexual parents, treating them objectively and honestly; presents their points of view and opposing ones. Chapter on adoption includes interracial adoptions. Talks about problems and pressures of child care. Informative books that considers the situation of single parenthood objectively and realistically.

MINDEY, CAROL. *The Divorced Mother*. New York: McGraw-Hill, 1969.
Contends that "successful divorce requires rational preparations." Writes as a divorcee from her own experiences as well as from research. Suggests going for psychological counseling before a divorce; asks couples to look to themselves rather than their marriage for the source of their problems. Poses questions for women to consider concerning their lives after divorce; provides several sources of information and help. Gives practical advice about financial and prosaic matters. Advises on how to prepare the children. Also discusses social life after divorce.

MUSSEN, PAUL HENRY; CONGER, JOHN JANEWAY; AND KAGAN, JEROME. *Child Development and Personality*. New York: Harper & Row, 1959.
Discusses the psychological influence of siblings on children's development. Primarily deals with traits and problems of the first-born in dealing with siblings. Hypothesizes that ordinal position is critical in determining later social interaction.

NEISSER, EDITH G. *Brothers and Sisters*. New York: Harper & Brothers, 1951.
Up-to-date despite its age, this book advises parents how best to help their children

develop positive feelings about themselves and others. The author presents useful do's and don'ts.

PUNER, HELEN W. *Helping Brothers and Sisters Get Along.* Chicago: Science Research Associates, 1952.
Helps adults recognize that selfishness, rivalry, and even hatred are normal aspects of sibling relationships. Also helps adults to feel more comfortable about not being perfect. Suggests tactics for handling family conflicts. The book is written simply and directly. It is remarkably up-to-date, despite its having been written in 1952.

QUEEN, GERTRUDE. "A Content Analysis of Children's Contemporary Fiction Books That Pertain to Broken Homes and Steprelationships." Unpublished Master's report, Palmer Graduate Library School, Long Island University, Brookville, New York, 1970.
Twenty-one books analyzed. Background information provided on topics. Useful as a suggested format for looking at books.

REGION I, ADOPTION RESOURCE CENTER. *Toward Developing Awareness of Black Culture and Issues Relating to Black Adoption: A Bibliography.* Fall, 1981.
More than forty references on African fiction, adoption, and other related topics concerning black families.

ROYCE, DAVID, AND TURNER, GLADYS. "Strengths of Black Families: A Black Community's Perspective," *Social Work*, Vol. 25, No. 25, September 1980.
Focuses on the strengths and values of black families rather than the problems. A needed viewpoint.

SALK, LEE. *What Every Child Would Like Parents to Know about Divorce.* New York: Harper & Row, 1978.
The discussion focuses on the effect of divorce on children. Dr. Salk offers advice on how to talk to children about the situation, and how to preserve security and emotional honesty in the family.

SCHLESINGER, BENJAMIN. *The One-Parent Family: Perspectives and Annotated Bibliography.* Toronto: University of Toronto Press, 1969.
Contains several essays on single parents and their situations. Valuable primarily because of its extensive list of resources.

SCHUR, GLORIA L. "A Content Analysis of Selected Fiction for Elementary School Children Depicting the Theme of Sibling Relationships and Rivalry." Unpublished Master's report, Palmer Graduate Library School, Long Island University, Brookville, New York, 1970.
Analyzes twenty-five books to see if they depict sibling relationships accurately. Finds that they do. Schur presents a very useful discussion of sibling relationships in the introduction to her analysis of the books.

SOROSKY, ARTHUR D.; BARAN, ANNETTE; AND PANNOR, REUBEN. *The Adoption Triangle.* Garden City, New York: Doubleday, 1978.
The effect of the practice of sealing original birth records on adoptees, birth parents and adoptive parents is the subtitle of this book advocating the unsealing of these records. The book contains stories of real people, and presents its case in a reasoned manner.

STEINZOR, BERNARD. *When Parents Divorce*. New York: Pantheon, 1969. Paperback: Pocket Books.
Discusses different types of marital relationships. Suggests that divorce not be a "friendly one, but a total psychologically free relationship." Talks about the advantages that divorce brings to children and makes suggestions about the separation agreement concerning the children. Believes visits should be a right, not an obligation. Makes recommendations as to how parents let their children know that they are separating. Openness in relationship is important. Suggests practical ways of carrying out the divorce agreements and gives direct advice for maintaining relationships. Advocates the working mother. In general, he sympathizes with children and parents who are divorcing.

TOMAN, WALTER. *Family Constellations*. New York: Springer, 1961.
Describes the "game" of understanding people's interactions with their families and with others as a result of their family placement. Defines the characteristics of siblings according to their place in the family (e.g., eldest brother of brothers is in charge; gets along well with males if they are not also elder brothers; is a good leader; can handle authority; is orderly, tough, would rather give than help). Toman analyzes different positions, making recommendations about the best sort of match and the most ideal arrangement for offspring. The book is fun to read, but it gives the impression of being just one step beyond astrology.

WOLF, ANNA W. M., AND STEIN, LUCILLE. *The One Parent Family* (Public Affairs Pamphlet No. 287). Public Affairs Committee and the Child Study Associations of America, 1959.
Presents problems of the single parent in the form of questions. Then considers solutions and advice. Advice is sensible and free of guilt-laying. Useful even now, many years after publication.

ZWACK, JEAN M. "The Stereotypic Family in Children's Literature," *Reading Teacher*, Vol. 26 No. 4, January 1973.
The author is concerned about the lack of alternatives to the nuclear family as presented in children's books.

SOURCES FOR MATERIALS ON THE FAMILY

ADOPTIVE PARENTS' COMMITTEE, INC. 210 Fifth Ave., New Yorks, New York 10010
(One of the oldest parent groups in existence.)
ADOPTION RESOURCE EXCHANGE OF NORTH AMERICA. 67 Irving Place, New York, New York 10003
(Information about local programs and referral services.)
ASSOCIATION OF BLACK SOCIAL WORKERS CHILD ADOPTION COUNSELING AND REFERRAL SERVICE. 271 West 125 St., New York, New York 10027
CHILD WELFARE LEAGUE OF AMERICA, INC. 67 Irving Place, New York, New York 10003
(Information and publications from federal and national organizations.)

COMMITTEE FOR SINGLE ADOPTIVE PARENTS. P.O. Box 4074, Washington, D.C. 20015

(Publishes *The Handbook for Single Adoptive Parents*.)

COMMITTEE ON ADOPTABLE CHILDREN BLACK CHILD ADVOCACY PROGRAM. 875 Avenue of the Americas, New York, New York 10001

FAMILY SERVICE ASSOCIATION OF AMERICA. 44 East 23 St., New York, New York 10010

(Counseling before or after adoption.)

NEW YORK COMMITTEE ON ADOPTABLE CHILDREN. 61 Gramercy Park North, New York, New York 10003

NORTH AMERICAN COUNCIL ON ADOPTABLE CHILDREN. 1346 Connecticut Avenue N.W., Suite 229, Washington, D.C. 20036

OPEN DOOR SOCIETY OF LONG ISLAND. c/o Ms. Shirley Damboise, 22 York Avenue, Ronkonkoma, New York 11779

Opportunity, annual newsletter on black adoption published at 2301 Glisan St., Portland, Oregon 97210

ORGANIZATION OF FOSTER FAMILIES FOR EQUALITY AND REFORM. 239 Vincent Dr., East Meadow, New York 11554

(Concerned with all aspects of foster care.)

BIBLIOGRAPHY: SIBLINGS

ALEXANDER, MARTHA. *When the New Baby Comes I'm Moving Out*. New York: Dial Press, 1979. (Ages 5–7.)
Oliver's mother is going to have a baby. Oliver feels that he is losing everything to this new baby—his high chair, crib, even his mother's lap. He decides he is going to leave home, until his mother convinces him of his importance in his new role of big brother. The book shows the anxiety and fear of a child's not knowing what his life will be like after the birth of a sibling.

AMOSS, BERTHE. *Tom in the Middle*. New York: Harper & Row, 1968. (Ages 4–8.)
A middle child, Tom, meets with frustration from both his older and his younger brother. Tom finally escapes through fantasy for some "Time Out," imagining he is hiding where neither brother can see him. He resolves his frustration, and fantasizes he and his brothers all are playing together. Realistically portrayed, it deals with the issue of being a middle child.

ANDERSON, LEONE CASTELL. *It's O.K. to Cry*. Illustrated by Richard Wahl. Chicago: Children's Press, 1979. (Ages 6–8.)
A touching story about an older brother trying to explain to his younger brother that their beloved uncle is dead. The younger boy can not remember or understand that he will not see his uncle again. The older boy finally shows him how they can keep his memory alive by remembering all their happy times together. Takes developmental stages into consideration.

ANDERSON, LONZO. *The Day the Hurricane Happened*. Illustrated by Ann Grifalconi. New York: Scribner's, 1973. (Ages 5–8.)

Graphic story of a family's bout with a hurricane on St. John in the Virgin Islands. Albie and his younger sister Eldra help prepare their house and their animals for the onslaught. Image of a coping, capable, loving black family. Written with a light dialect, not overpowering, but enough to give a sense of the speech of the people. Brother very protective of sister.

ANDRY, ANDREW C., AND KRATKA, SUZANNE C. *Hi, New Baby*. Illustrated by Thomas Di Grazia. New York: Simon and Schuster, 1970. (Ages 2–6.)
Addressing elder siblings, this well-illustrated book provides facts about new babies. It also points out situations that these siblings will have to cope with. The authors suggest activities that children can do to help themselves, their baby siblings, and the family situation in general.

ARNSTEIN, HELENE S. *Billy and Our New Baby*. Illustrated by M. Jane Smyth. New York: Behavioral Publications, 1973. (Ages 5–8.)
Billy is angry because mother and everyone else are busier with the new baby than with him. Billy decides he wants to be a baby again, crawls, cries, wants a baby bottle. At last, Billy starts enjoying helping out with the baby, still gets mad at the baby, but he loves him, too, and accepts him as part of family. A guide for parents and those who work with children included in back of book explains the situation and the emotions that the child goes through. Gives advice for adults' behavior.

ASCH, FRANK. *Elvira Everything*. Illustrated by the author. New York: Harper & Row, 1970. (Ages 7–10.)
The narrator of the story is an only child. As a gift, she receives a doll named Elvira Everything, though she really wanted a teddy bear. Elvira Everything is the nightmare-of-the-firstborn come true. The doll seems to take precedence over the child in her parents' affections. The doll is perfect. At last, the child destroys the doll, and things return to "normal." A rather bizarre solution to sibling rivalry, but if handled within the context of fantasizing, might be a fruitful discussion-starter. The illustrations by the author constitute a brilliant commentary on modern life and the contemporary family.

BACH, ALICE. *The Smartest Bear and His Brother Oliver*. Illustrated by Steven Kellogg. New York: Harper & Row, 1975. (Ages 5–8.)
Ronald wants to be different from his twin, Oliver. Ronald would rather read than feast. In order to demonstrate that they recognize their differences, the boys' parents give them each a different gift: to Ronald, a typewriter; to Oliver, a bakery truck. Although bears are the characters in this story, human siblings can identify with the situation.

BANISH, ROSLYN. *I Want to Tell You About My Baby*. Illustrated by the author. Berkeley, Calif.: Wingbow Press, 1982. (Ages 5–8.)
Narrated by a young boy, the photographs and text tell about the mother's pregnancy, the birth of the new baby boy, and the activities and feelings after the baby comes home. All of the emotions are accepted and handled in a loving way.

BERGER, TERRY. *Big Sister, Little Brother*. Illustrated by Heinz Kluetmeier. Chicago: Children's Press, 1974. (Ages 6–10.)
The conflicts felt by a boy and his older sister are shown. Color photographs enhance the book.

BLUME, JUDY. *Tales of a Fourth Grade Nothing*. Illustrated by Roy Doty. New York: Dutton, 1972. Also in paper. (Ages 9–12.)
Children find this book very amusing. Peter's younger brother, Fudge, is a monster. The child is spoiled, undisciplined, and favored by his foolish mother. Not only is Fudge permitted to run rampant, but also the parents are made to look ineffectual, though pleasant. Both parents try to control Fudge's behavior and sometimes win out, but it is too often through trickery. In the sequel, *Superfudge*, (Dutton, 1980) Fudge is entering kindergarten, and he and Peter now have a new sibling, Tootsie, to contend with. As with all of the Blume books, children enjoy the humor at the same time that they empathize with the characters.

BONSALL, CROSBY. *The Day I had to Play with My Sister*. New York: Harper & Row, 1972. (Ages 3–7.)
Elder brother tries to teach little sister to play hide-and-go-seek, but the little girl just cannot or will not follow the rules. The book takes no sides, but helps readers to understand the elder brother's point of view.

BRANFIELD, JOHN. *Why Me?* New York: Harper & Row, 1973. (Ages 12–up.)
Sarah and Jane are sisters who do not get along at all well; in fact, they seem to delight in making each other unhappy. Sarah has diabetes. The bulk of the story revolves around her adjustment to this condition. The parents seem to be unable to control their daughters' behavior. The only resolution is to wait until they grow up.

BROWN, MYRA BERRY. *Amy and the New Baby*. New York: Franklin Watts, 1965. (Ages 5–8.)
Amy has mixed feelings about her baby brother, who cries a great deal, takes much attention away from her, and stays longer than Amy expected. The parents handle the situation well, paying special attention to Amy, and letting her know that their love for her has not diminished, but at the same time also affirming that the baby is now a member of the family and will remain with them.

BULLA, CLYDE ROBERT. *Keep Running, Allen!* Illustrated by Satomi Ichikawa. New York: Crowell, 1978. (Ages 7–10.)
One perspective of life as the youngest in a family of four children. Allen races to keep pace with his older brothers and sister. One can easily empathize with his frustration as he never quite catches up. He finally attains peace when he gives up trying and stops to rest in a soft grassy field only to find his siblings joining him. They all lie on their backs and watch the cloud patterns in the sky.

BYARS, BETSY. *Go and Hush the Baby*. Illustrated by Emily A. McCully. New York: Viking, 1971. (Ages 3–8.)
The elder brother is called upon to entertain the crying baby while their mother finishes several tasks. The boy does this with imagination and good will; at last the baby falls asleep, and the brother is free to go out and play. The book conveys a warm, good feeling.

_____. *The Summer of the Swans*. Illustrated by Ted CoConis. New York: Viking, 1971. Also in paper. (Ages 10–up.)
The fourteen-year-old feels responsible for her younger, retarded brother. She also resents him and has unpleasant feelings about herself. In the end, a friend helps her to resolve her feelings.

CAINES, JEANNETTE. *Abby*. Illustrated by Steven Kellogg. New York: Harper & Row, 1973. (Ages 3–8.)
Abby is an adopted child who is loved by her parents and by her elder brother, Kevin, even though he upsets Abby sometimes. The family is black.

CARLSON, NATALIE SAVAGE. *The Half Sisters*. Illustrated by Thomas DiGrazia. New York: Harper & Row, 1970. (Ages 8–12.)
Luvvy's family is in two distinct sections. Her father has had six daughters, the three older ones by his first wife, the three younger ones from his current marriage. Luvvy is the oldest of the second set. She longs to be accepted by her older sisters and is impatient with the demands for attention made on her by her younger sister Maudie. When Maudie dies, Luvvy is distraught.

CLEARY, BEVERLY. *Mitch and Amy*. Illustrated by George Porter. New York: Morrow, 1967. Also in paper. (Ages 8–up.)
Mitch and Amy are fraternal twins who are always squabbling. Their parents unwittingly foster competition between them (Mitch does not read well; Amy cannot do multiplication). Still they enjoy being twins and manage to handle their arguments good-naturedly.

_____. *Ramona the Brave*. Illustrated by Alan Tiegreen. New York: Morrow, 1975. Also in paper. (Age 8–12.)
Ramona, six years old, is trying to be very brave despite the fact that she thinks her parents love her elder sister more than they love her, and despite the fact that she is unhappy in her first-grade class. Her parents eventually comfort her and persuade her that she is loved, and her sister helps with her empathy. A loving family. An excellent book, as are all of the books in the *Ramona* series.

CLEAVER, VERA AND BILL. *Me Too*. Philadelphia: Lippincott, 1973. (Ages 12–up.)
Lydia assumes responsibility for the teaching and care of her retarded twin sister, Lornie. She hopes to change Lornie's behavior. She must cope with their father's departure, the mother's despair, and the neighbors' disapprovl. Finally, she must accept the impossibility of her task.

_____. *Where the Lilies Bloom*. Illustrated by Jim Spanfeller. Philadelphia: Lippincott, 1969. Paperback: New American Library. (Ages 9–up.)
Mary Call's relationship with her siblings range from protective to hostile. She takes over responsibility for all of them (including her elder sister) when her father dies.

CLIFTON, LUCILLE. *Don't You Remember?* Illustrated by Evaline Ness. New York: Dutton, 1973. (Ages 3–7.)
Desire Mary Tate, black, four years old, and very lively, considers herself to have the best memory in her family. She has three older brothers, one of whom has taken a year off from school to care for her. Her parents both work, and her ambition is to grow up and work at the plant, "just like Daddy." Labor is assigned because it must get done, not because of sex roles.

_____. *Everett Anderson's Year*. Illustrated by Ann Grifalconi. New York: Holt, Rinehart, and Winston, 1974. (Ages 4–8.)
Reinforces the loving world that Everett lives in. His mother manages well, even though the father has left them. Everett misses and still loves his father. He, too, is

coping well. Only-children might particularly empathize with Everett in all of the books of this excellent series.

_____. *Good, Says Jerome*. Illustrated by Stephanie Douglas. New York: Dutton, 1973. (Ages 3–7.)
Lovely series of conversations between Jerome and his elder sister, Janice Marie. He mentions all his fears and anxieties to her, and she helps him to resolve them, always causing him to end up with a good feeling. Warm relationship between two siblings.

COLE, JOANNA, AND EDMONDSON, MADELEINE. *Twins: The Story of Multiple Births*. Illustrated by Salvatore Raciti. New York: Morrow, 1972. (Ages 10–13.)
The logistics of multiple births are explained and illustrated to show how cells and eggs divide. In this easily understood scientific explanation, fraternal and identical twins are identified. The effects of fertility drugs on multiple births are explained. Simple terms and good illustrations abound. Parents could read this to a young child.

COLMAN, HILA. *Diary of a Frantic Kid Sister*. New York: Crown, 1973. (Ages 8–11.)
Eleven-year-old Sarah is very jealous and resentful of her elder sister, Didi. The mother is too involved with her own problems to help. The father is supportive of her, but not of the mother and sisters. The book is a blow-by-blow description of a sibling relationship as seen through the eyes of the younger sister.

_____. *The Secret Life of Harold the Bird Watcher*. New York: Crowell, 1978. (Ages 8–11.)
Nine-year-old Harold prefers Nature to Athletics. In his fantasies he imagines himself a hero. He finally acquires a friend who also likes to make believe. Sympathetic portrayal of an only child of working parents.

CONTA, MARCIA MAHER, AND REARDON, MAUREEN. *Feelings between Brothers and Sisters*. Illustrated by Jules M. Rosenthal. Chicago: Raintree, 1974. (Ages 6–10.)
Color photographs illustrate the questions asked by siblings about important issues such as helping one another, fighting, jealousy of a newborn, teasing from older siblings, sharing, competition, and loneliness. The last picture displays middle-aged brothers who still argue, yet continue to work and be friendly with one another. The variety of questions within the book could be used as a means to promote discussion.

CORCORAN, BARBARA. *A Trick of Light*. Illustrated by Lydia Dabcovich. New York: Atheneum, 1973. (Ages 9–12.)
Casandra and Paige are twins. They are growing up and Paige wants to have friends of his own. Casandra is hurt, bitter, and jealous wanting Paige to herself. He is her best friend. During the course of the book, their dog, Bingo, dies, Paige saves Casandra's life, and Casandra learns to live with the idea of independence from her twin.

CROWLEY, ARTHUR. *Bonzo Beaver*. Illustrated by Annie Gusman. Boston: Houghton Mifflin, 1980. (Ages 5–8.)
About two beaver brothers who learn to enjoy each other. The story shows how a child who feels too little to do many things with the bigger and older children can

manage to overcome this limitation by means of cleverness rather than physical size or strength.

DICKINSON, MARY. *Alex and the Baby*. Illustrated by Charlotte Firmin. New York: Deutsch, 1982. (Ages 5–8.)
Alex resents an infant visitor, but eventually enjoys playing with her. Alex's mother is relieved when the baby leaves, and newly appreciates Alex.

DIXON, PAIGE. *May I Cross Your Golden River?* New York: Atheneum, 1975. Also in paper, new title, *A Time to Love, A Time to Mourn*. (Ages 12–up.)
Jordan, his brothers and sisters and mother are a close, loving family. When Jordan contracts a fatal illness, the siblings cope with this fact in different ways; but all are supportive of Jordan and each other.

DOSS, HELEN. *The Family Nobody Wanted*. New York: Scholastic, 1974. (Ages 12–up.)
An autobiographical account of a woman and her minister husband who adopt twelve children. Problems of logistics and money are resolved, along with the usual problems of brothers and sisters in a most unusual setting.

DRAGONWAGON, CRESCENT. *I Hate My Brother Harry*. Illustrated by Dick Gackenbach. New York: Harper & Row, 1983. (Ages 5–8.)
A young girl hates her older brother sometimes, and sometimes loves him. Included in the narrative are Harry's actions as support for her feelings. Parents are helpful to both children. The engaging text demonstrates the caring as well as the rivalry between the two siblings.

EPSTEIN, BERYL, AND DAVIS, DORRITT. *Two Sisters and Some Hornets*. Illustrated by Rosemary Wells. New York: Holiday House, 1972. (Ages 5–8.)
Sibling spats continue even through old age. This humorous story is about an incident recalled by two elderly sisters of their childhood, when they had an encounter with hornets. They react in old age in much the same way that they did as little children; the older sister smug and superior; the younger sister petulant.

GERSON, MARY-JOAN. *Omteji's Baby Brother*. Illustrated by Eliza Moon. New York: Walck, 1974. (Ages 4–8.)
Omoteji lives in Nigeria and is a member of the Yoruba tribe. Mother works in the market; father weaves. Omoteji feels left out when a new baby is born. There is no way he can help. Finally, he composes a song for his new brother and presents it as his gift at the naming ceremony. Everyone is very proud of him.

GLENN, MEL. "Maria Preosi," in *Class Dismissed: High School Poems*. Illustrated by Michael Bernstein. New York: Clarion Books, 1982. (Ages 10–up.)
Maria seethes because she is always compared to her sister, Tracy. She doesn't cope with this problem; she allows it to eat away at her, while she bottles up her anger. Readers might be asked to suggest scenarios for Maria so that she expresses her feelings without a destructive outcome.

GOLD, SHARLYA. *Amelia Quackenbush*. New York: Seabury Press, 1973. (Ages 8–11.)
Amelia and her older sisters cope with a free-spirit of a father, and a vague, escapist

mother. The sisters try to help Amelia with her problems and demonstrate loving support for her. Although she is sloppy and careless, her sisters, aside from gently teasing her, are tolerant and sympathetic.

GOLDMAN, SUSAN. *Cousins Are Special.* Chicago: Albert Whitman and Company, 1978. (Ages 3–7.)
Sarah is visiting her cousin Carol Sue for the first time. Carol Sue makes her feel right at home and the girls have a great time playing together. When they look at a photo album, they discover they have the same grandmother. This cousin relationship makes them feel even closer to each other.

GRAY, GENEVIEVE. *Send Wendell.* Illustrated by Symeon Shimin. New York: McGraw-Hill, 1974. (Ages 3–9.)
Wendell has six siblings. Wendell is the one who always has to run errands; he does not have anything important of his own to do. His elder siblings are always busy; his younger ones are too small. After his Uncle Robert's visit, Wendell does have things of his own to do: now Wendell has letters to write to Uncle Robert.

GREENFIELD, ELOISE. "Reggie," in *Honey, I Love.* Illustrated by Diane and Leo Dillon. New York: Crowell, 1978. (Ages 6–up.)
Reggie's younger sister is unhappy because he is more absorbed in playing basketball than in paying attention to her. The tone of the poem is regretful, but accepting, and brings up the issue of the separate interests of family members.

_____. *She Come Bringing Me That Little Baby Girl.* Illustrated by John Steptoe. Philadelphia: Lippincott, 1974. (Ages 5–8.)
Black family includes mother, father, Kevin, and baby sister. Kevin wanted a brother. He is jealous of the attention that the new baby gets. When his mother permits him to hold his new sister and to show her off to his friends, Kevin begins to feel happy again, and to plan for what he and his sister will eventually do together. The rivalry is handled lovingly on the part of the parents. Steptoe's illustrations are beautiful.

_____. *Sister.* Illustrated by Moneta Barnett. New York: Crowell, 1974. (Ages 10–17.)
Doretha is afraid that she'll be just like her older sister, Alberta. They look alike, and sometimes Doretha feels as resentful and rebellious as her sister. An unsympathetic teacher does not help when she assumes that Doretha will behave the same way that Alberta did. Doretha is helped to be herself by a school run by and for Afro-Americans. Well written, interesting book.

_____. *Talk about a Family.* Philadelphia: Lippincott, 1978. (Ages 10–up.)
Genny idolizes her older brother, and is sure that when he returns from the army he will be able to set right the problems that their parents are having. All of the siblings rely heavily on each other for emotional support, and even though the parents will, indeed, separate, the family will not be destroyed.

HAZEN, BARBARA SHOOK. *If It Weren't for Benjamin.* Illustrated by Laura Hartman. New York: Human Sciences Press, 1979. (Ages 5–8.)
Told through the perspective of the younger brother, this book provides an excellent model of how a loving family helps with the problem of sibling rivalry.

HAZEN, BARBARA SHOOK. *Why Couldn't I Be an Only Kid like You, Wigger.* Illustrated by Leigh Grant. New York: Atheneum, 1975. (Ages 5–8.)
Two boys, one from a large family and one an only child, would like to exchange places. They each think the other has a better life. They end up appreciating their own lives. A good book for discussion dealing with family size and numbers of siblings.

HILL, ELIZABETH STARR. *Evan's Corner.* New York: Holt, Rinehart, and Winston, 1967. (Ages 4–8.)
Evan, his three elder sisters, and younger brother, Adam, live with their parents in a very small apartment. Evan fixes up a place of his own to satisfy a need, but he is not totally satisfied until he recognizes Adam's needs too. A warm, sharing relationship is described here.

HIRSCH, KAREN. *My Sister.* Minneapolis: Carolrhoda Books, 1977.
Written from the view of a sibling with a retarded sister, the book covers a wide range of feelings and situations where a retarded sibling might make things difficult for a family. The child is accepting and understanding of this sister; other people are not always so accepting.

HOBAN, RUSSELL. *A Baby Sister for Frances.* Illustrated by Lillian Hoban. New York: Harper & Row, 1964. (Ages 5–8.)
Frances's new baby sister, Gloria, has disrupted the family's schedule, so Frances runs away (to under the dining room table). Parents talk about how they miss her. It is really a child's dream-come-true, to hear how sorry people are that she is gone. Very loving family.

HOGAN, PAULA Z. *Sometimes I Get So Mad.* Milwaukee: Raintree, 1980. (Ages 5–10.)
Karen, the older sister, realizes at the end of the book that her younger sister can be fun. The text also explores relationships between friends and deals with how a child can express angry feelings. It shows that conflicts do not have to ruin relationships, but rather that they can be used to make relationships stronger.

HURWITZ, JOHNSON. *Superduper Teddy.* Illustrated by Susan Jeschke. New York: Morrow, 1980. (Ages 5–7.)
Collection of short stories about a shy five-year-old boy named Teddy, his seven-year-old sister, Nora, and their parents, friends, family. Nora is more adventurous and gregarious than Teddy, which is a cause for great concern and comparison on his part. Teddy resolves his own problems. Each character in the book is made to seem important and worthwhile.

JARRELL, MARY. *The Knee Baby.* Illustrated by Symeon Shimin. New York: Farrar, Straus & Giroux, 1973. (Ages 5–8.)
The little boy wants very much to be held on someone's lap, hugged, and cuddled. His mother spends much time with the new baby. At last his mother gives him a turn on her lap and he is satisfied.

JONES, ADRIENNE. *So, Nothing Is Forever.* Illustrated by Richard Cuffari. Boston: Houghton Mifflin, 1974. (Ages 12–up.)
After Talene, Joey, and Adam's parents are killed in a car accident, the three run away to their maternal grandmother's ranch, hoping she will permit them to stay.

Their father is black; and their mother is white. Though they face bigotry, resentment, and rejection, they love each other and manage very well.

JORDAN, JUNE. *New Life, New Room.* Illustrated by Ray Cruz. New York: Crowell, 1975. (Ages 6–9.)
A new baby is expected and Rudy, age ten, Tyrone, age nine, and Linda, age six, must adjust their lives to the fact. Sensitive portrayal reflecting every family member's feelings. Their apartment has only two bedrooms. It is up to the children to decide how to live together in one room. With their parents' help, they arrive at a happy solution. This is a joyous, loving, constructive book.

KEATS, EZRA JACK. *Peter's Chair.* New York: Harper & Row, 1967. (Ages 5–8.)
Peter has a new baby sister. His parents are painting all of his old furniture pink for the baby. He feels excluded and, taking his chair, "runs away." (To just outside the house.) When he realizes that he has outgrown his chair, hears his parents' supportive words, and smells dinner, he returns to the family and resolves to tolerate his sister.

KLEIN, NORMA. *Confessions of an Only Child.* Illustrated by Richard Cuffari. New York: Pantheon, 1974. (Ages 8–12.)
Antonia's mother is pregnant. "Toe" is happy being an only child and is fearful and resentful of the intrusion of a sibling. Her friends support her negative feelings with unpleasant stories about their younger siblings. After the baby is born prematurely and dies, Toe becomes reconciled to her parents' having another. Useful modeling in this book.

KLEIN, NORMA. *If I Had My Way.* Illustrated by Ray Cruz. New York: Pantheon, 1974. (Ages 5–8.)
Ellie is about six years old when her baby brother is born. When her parents go out for the evening, she imagines how life would be if children ran the world. Her parents are very understanding and even let her suck on a bottle. After her imaginary trip, she resumes her own life, somewhat resigned to it.

KLEIN, NORMA. *Naomi in the Middle.* Illustrated by Leigh Grant. New York: Dial Press, 1974. (Ages 7–10.)
The story is narrated by Naomi, age seven. She and her elder sister Bobo, age nine, have a normal sibling relationship. When they hear of their mother's pregnancy, Naomi contemplates the problems of being the middle child, and Bobo is gloomy. The story is a vehicle for demonstrating how a loving family handles the problems of sibling relationships.

KONIGSBERG, E. L. *From the Mixed-Up Files of Mrs. Basil E. Frankweiler.* New York: Atheneum, 1967. Also in paper. (Ages 9–12.)
Claudia selects Jamie from among her siblings to be her companion when they run away from home. They learn from this experience to value each other more than they did before.

LASKER, JOE. *He's My Brother.* Chicago: Albert Whitman, 1974. (Ages 6–9.)
Jamie, a slow-learning younger brother, gets teased. Becka, the older sister, bakes brownies for him and is kind to him. His brother sometimes is impatient but then plays with him to make up for it. Jamie is good with babies and animals. The family

is very good, loving, and patient with him. Mildred and Joe Lasker write at the end that they hope "this book will enable other Jamies and their families to identify with the experiences shown and take comfort."

L'ENGLE, MADELEINE. *A Ring of Endless Light*. New York: Farrar, Straus & Giroux, 1980. (Ages 11–up.)
The fourth in the Austin family series focuses on Vicky. Her family is staying on the island where her grandfather lives. He is dying. Vicky and her brother, John, become close friends in this story. Her rivalry with her sister and her loving and protective relationship with her younger brother Bob also figure in the plot. In the story Vicky discovers that she has the gift of communicating with dolphins. The book is an investigation of love, life, and coming to terms with death.

LEXAU, JOAN. *The Trouble with Terry*. Illustrated by Irene Murray. New York: Dial Press, 1962. Paperback: Scholastic. (Ages 8–12.)
Terry and her elder brother Tommy are very good friends. Tommy is the perfect child; Terry is active. Tommy helps Terry when she is in trouble and sympathizes with her problems. Terry admires, loves, and envies her brother. They both have responsibilities because their mother is a widow and works full-time.

LITTLE, JEAN. *Home from Far*. Illustrated by Jerry Lazare. Boston: Little, Brown, 1965. (Ages 9–12.)
Jenny's relationship with her dead twin brother Michael was so close that she feels she will betray him if she permits herself to like her foster sister and brother. Her mother helps her to work it out.

LOWRY, LOIS. *A Summer to Die*. Illustrated by Jenni Oliver. Boston: Houghton Mifflin, 1977. (Ages 10–up.)
Meg envies her older sister Molly's prettiness and popularity, as well as her consistently positive outlook on life. But Molly contracts leukemia and cannot survive its onslaught. Meg learns of this condition almost at the end of Molly's life, when, at last, Meg comes to terms with her envy and accepts herself as she is.

MACLACHLAN, PATRICIA. *Arthur, for the Very First Time*. Illustrated by Lloyd Bloom. New York: Harper & Row, 1980. Also in paper. (Ages 9–12.)
Arthur, a ten-year-old boy who has always been an observer and a writer, dreads the approaching arrival of a new sibling. His parents have not been responsive or forthright with him, and he has functioned in a somewhat self-centered and narrow pattern. With the help of his great aunt and uncle. and his friend, Moira, he learns to value new life and to become much more sensitive to the feelings of others.

_____. *Seven Kisses in a Row*. Illustrated by Maria Pia Marrella. New York: Harper & Row, 1983. (Ages 7–10.)
An affectionate, humorous, and totally captivating story about Emma, an outspoken and engaging seven-year-old, her brother, Zach, who understands and loves her, and the five days they spend with their aunt and uncle while their parents are at an "eyeball convention." All of the characters learn to adjust to and accept each other's differences.

_____. *Unclaimed Treasures*. New York: Harper & Row, 1984. (Ages 9–12.)

In a story flavored with mystery and romance, Willa and Nicholas, twins, interact with many other colorful characters, survive the birth of a new sibling, and reinforce and support each other's feelings. The story progresses back and forth in time through the filter of Willa's perceptions. Beautifully told.

MALECKI, MARYANN. *Mom and Dad and I Are Having a Baby!* Illustrated by the author. Seattle: Pennypress, 1982. (Ages 5–10.)
The child narrator describes the entire procedure of home birth, with all of the family members in attendance.

MANUSHKIN, FRAN. *Bubble Bath.* Illustrated by Ronald Himler. New York: Harper & Row, 1974. (Ages 3–7.)
Two sisters play together happily, get dirty, and bathe together. They help each other and thoroughly enjoy all of their play.

MATHIS, SHARON BELL. *Teacup Full of Roses.* New York: Viking, 1972. (Ages 12–up.)
Three brothers love each other, but the eldest is the mother's favorite. Only the middle brother survives at the end of this story.

MATTMULLER, FELIX. *We Want a Little Sister.* Minneapolis: Lerner Publications, 1972. (Ages 4–8.)
This book is different from others which focus on a new baby coming, because there are already three children in the family. All of the children are allowed to visit their mother and baby sister in the hospital. The family atmosphere is positive; the comments and activities of the family center around including the other children.

MINARIK, ELSE HOLMELUND. *No Fighting, No Biting.* Illustrated by Maurice Sendak. New York: Harper & Row, 1958. (Ages 6–10.)
Cousin Joan is reading when a sister and brother, Willy and Rosa, come along and disturb her by fighting with one another. She quiets them by telling a story about a pair of alligator siblings whose fighting leads to danger. Willy and Rosa continue bickering for a few minutes, then finally subside to silent reading. The story portrays a realistic situation where an older child is bothered by younger children. In spite of fighting, love is implied between the children.

MULLIGAN, KEVIN. *Kid Brother.* New York: Lothrop, Lee and Shepard, 1982. (Ages 12–up.)
Brad's older brother, Tom, is perfect. It is difficult for Brad to be anything but Tom's shadow. After a visit with an eccentric older aunt in Albuquerque, Brad finally discovers who he is and what he wants to do, apart from his brother.

NAYLOR, PHYLLIS REYNOLDS. *All Because I'm Older.* Illustrated by Leslie Morrill. New York: Atheneum, 1981. (Ages 5–8.)
Because John is the oldest, he must keep his two younger siblings out of mischief during a trip to the supermarket. Eldest children will appreciate John's solution to his dilemma.

NESS, EVALINE. *Do You Have the Time, Lydia?* New York: Dutton, 1971. Also in paper. (Ages 5–8.)
Lydia and her brother live with their father, who is a florist. Their home is on a

tropical island. Lydia is a well-intentioned elder sister, but is so busy with so many activities that she bitterly disappoints her younger brother. She makes up for it by determining to change her ways and to complete each task that she begins.

O'DELL, SCOTT. *Island of the Blue Dolphins*. Boston: Houghton Mifflin, 1960. Also in paper. (Ages 10–up.)
Karana, a young Native American girl, is marooned on her home island because of her younger brother. After he dies, killed by wild dogs, she manages, through her courage, to survive for many years until at last she is rescued.

ORGEL, DORIS. *Bartholomew, We Love You*. Illustrated by Pat Grant Porter. New York: Knopf, 1973. (Ages 8–12.)
Kim is Emily's younger sister. Kim feels that Emily is prettier, smarter, more talented, and more favored. In the end, the two sisters learn to share somewhat more happily. The parents in this story are understanding, competent people. The mother works in a laboratory; the father is a machinery designer. The book is realistic and useful.

PATERSON, KATHERINE. *Jacob Have I Loved*. New York: Crowell, 1980. (Ages 10–up.) Also in paper.
Sarah Louise and Caroline Bradshaw are twins. Louise, the older and stronger, always feels outdone by her frailer, prettier, talented sister. Eventually, Louise becomes a nurse-midwife, delivers twins—concentrating on the weaker—and exorcises all her old hates and fears concerning her sister.

ROSEN, WINIFRED. *Henrietta, The Wild Woman of Borneo*. Illustrated by Kay Chorao. New York: Four Winds Press, 1975. (Ages 5–8.)
Henrietta is messy, clumsy, wild; her elder sister Evelyn is pretty, graceful, and neat. The girls' parents love them both, but Henrietta feels unloved. She tries to run away. Evelyn seems to support the idea but in the end, arranges it so that Henrietta returns home.

ROY, RON. *Where's Buddy?* Illustrated by Troy Howell. New York: Clarion Books, 1982. (Ages 8–11.)
Buddy is seven years old, and has diabetes. On the day that Mike, his older brother, is in charge of him, Buddy disappears. The story is a plausible one, and helps the reader understand what regimen is required, as well as conveying a message of coping with the condition. The older brother is protective of the younger, but recognizes Buddy's need for self-reliance.

SACHS, MARILYN. *The Bears' House*. Illustrated by Louis Glanzman. Garden City, New York: Doubleday, 1971. (Ages 9–12.)
Fran Ellen, her brother, and two sisters try to manage their household after their father has deserted them and their mother has suffered a nervous collapse. The relationship among the siblings is, with some exceptions, supportive, protective, and loving. The book is more complex and painfully involving than are most other stories of sibling survival.

———. *A December Tale*. Garden City, New York: Doubleday, 1976. (Ages 11–up.)
Myra and Henry Fine are foster children in the care of the rotten Mrs. Smith and her nasty family. Myra seeks help from just about everyone she knows. She wants to

escape from the Smiths and her hated brother. However, Myra is cajoled and threatened by Mrs. Smith not to expose her cruelty. Myra takes action ably when Henry is beaten so brutally that Myra fears for his life. The major message in this unrelievedly painful but well-written book is that abused children must, like Myra, take their fate into their own hands, and not permit themselves to be abused any longer. The sibling interaction is a major focus of this story.

SAMSON, JOAN. *Watching the New Baby*. Photographs by Gard Gladstone. New York: Atheneum, 1974. (Ages 8–11.)
Describes the newborn baby in terms of physical development and relationship to the world. The book is useful for siblings who ask many "why" questions about new babies. The photographs show many happy relationships between newborns and their elder siblings.

SARNOFF, JANE, AND RUFFINS, REYNOLDS. *That's Not Fair*. New York: Scribner, 1980. (Ages 5–8.)
Becky and her older brother, Bert, learn that being part of a family unit is not always easy. The story is humorous and realistic. The pictures are interesting and fun to share.

SCHICK, ELEANOR. *Peggy's New Brother*. New York: Macmillan, 1970. (Ages 5–7.)
Peggy would have preferred a dog or a cat to a baby brother. Her mother encourages her to help, but she is not very good at it. When Peggy discovers that she can make her baby brother laugh, their relationship is assured.

SCHLEIN, MIRIAM. *Billy, the Littlest One*. Illustrated by Luey Hawkinson. Chicago: Whitman, 1967. (Ages 3–6.)
Billy is the littlest one in his family. He tells how it feels to be the littlest. The child feels good about his place in the family and realizes that he will not always be so little.

SCOTT, ANN HERBERT. *On Mother's Lap*. Illustrated by Glo Coalson. New York: McGraw-Hill, 1972 (Ages 5–8.)
Michael and his family are Eskimo, but we know that only because of the illustrations. The story is very simply told. Mother arranges it so there is room for everyone and everything, making it clear that her lap can accommodate them all. This makes Michael very happy. The book recognizes rivalry and models mother's gentle, non-reproaching manner of dealing with it.

SCOTT, ANN HERBERT. *Sam*. Illustrated by Symeon Shimin. New York: McGraw-Hill, 1967. (Ages 4–8.)
Sam, the youngest of three children, is very much the baby of the family. The elder siblings are not unkind, but they do not want him touching their things. Sam's mother realizes that he needs to be permitted to do something special by himself. The rest of the family agrees and applauds when Sam is permitted to bake a raspberry tart.

SEGAL, LORE. *Tell Me a Mitzi*. Illustrated by Harriet Pincus. New York: Farrar, Straus & Giroux, 1970. (Ages 5–8.)
The three stories describe a contemporary Jewish family living in New York City. Mitzi (short for Martha) and her baby brother, Jacob, get along very well. They are

both happy, pleasant children, and their parents seem to treat them with equal caring.

SENDAK, MAURICE. *Outside over There*. Illustrated by the author. New York: Harper & Row, 1981. (Ages 5–up.)
As with many of Sendak's works, this book has a dream-like and symbolic quality. Ida, the protagonist, searches for her infant sibling who has been kidnapped by goblins (who turn out to look just like the baby). Ida's father is away on a voyage, and Ida's mother is in the arbor. Probably an excellent tool for discussion with any age group, the book is a visual delight.

SHARMAT, MARJORIE. *Goodnight, Andrew, Goodnight, Craig*. Illustrated by Mary Chalmers. New York: Harper & Row, 1969. (Ages 3–8.)
Two brothers, put to bed by their father, take a long time falling asleep. They finally fall asleep after the elder brother promises the younger one he will play with him in the morning. Loving family relationship all around.

SHARMAT, MARJORIE WEINMAN. *I'm Terrific*. Illustrated by Kay Chorao. New York: Holiday, 1977. Also in paper. (Ages 5–8.)
In this delightful story, Jason Everett bear is an only child, and enjoys his mother's total attention and approval. But there comes a time when Jason must decide to stop being a "mother's bear" and start being his own person.

SHYER, MARLENE FANTA. *Welcome Home, Jellybean*. New York: Scribner, 1978. (Ages 8–12.)
Twelve-year-old Neil's life changes completely when his parents bring his thirteen-year-old sister Geraldine home to stay after she has spent nearly all her life in an institution for the retarded. Neil endures fights at school, Geraldine's disruptive behavior, and the father's departure from the household. Neil develops compassion for his sister, and the acknowledgement of and joy in her small accomplishments. The story ends on a hopeful note.

STEIN, SARA BONNETT. *That New Baby*. Illustrated by Dick Frank. New York: Walker, 1974. (Ages 3–8.)
This is one in the series of "Open Family Books for Parents and Children Together." It contains a text for parents which points out that most elder children are jealous of younger ones to some extent. Through beautiful photographs (this time of a black family) and an excellent text, the message comes through that every family member is valued. The advice given to parents is practical, direct, and psychologically sound.

STEPTOE, JOHN. *Birthday*. New York: Holt, Rinehart, and Winston, 1972. (Ages 5–8.)
It is Javaka's birthday. He is the firstborn of a community of black people. The community is represented as the ideal way of life. Everyone is part of the extended, loving family.

––––––. *My Special Best Words*. New York: Viking, 1974. (Ages 5–8.)
Bweela, three years old, lives with her one-year-old brother Javaka and her father. Bweela is very good with Javaka. She helps him with his toilet training, nose blowing, and speech. They quarrel with each other, Javaka telling Bweela to

TAKEABREAK, and Bweela retorting YOUADUMMY. Both children are bright and happy.

_____. *Stevie*. New York: Harper & Row, 1969. Also in paper. (Ages 7–10.)
Robert experiences the pangs of sibling rivalry over Stevie, a young boy who stays at Robert's house. In the end, Robert misses Stevie when he leaves.

TALBOT, CHARLENE JOY. *A Home with Aunt Florry*. New York: Atheneum, 1974. (Ages 9–12.)
Jason and Wendy, Twelve-year-old orphaned twins, come to stay with their eccentric Aunt Florry in New York. Their relationship with each other is ideal. They never argue, are kind to each other, share happily, and are also very self-sufficient. Some of the messages in this book include a plea for tolerance of different lifestyles and for children's taking responsibility for themselves.

TAYLOR, MILDRED D. *Song of the Trees*. Illustrated by Jerry Pinkney. New York: Dial Press, 1975. (Ages 9–12.)
The first book in an excellent trilogy (the other two are *Roll of Thunder, Hear My Cry*, which won the Newbery Award, and *Let the Circle Be Unbroken*) about a memorable family. The sibling bond is strong within the context of the entire family setting in this recounting of the events of the family's managing in the South during the Depression.

TAYLOR, SYDNEY. *All-of-a-Kind Family Downtown*. Illustrated by Beth and Joe Krush. Chicago: Follett, 1972. Also in paper. (Ages 8–12.)
Fourth in a series containing *All-of-a-Kind Family, More-All-of-a-Kind Family*, and *All-of-a-Kind Family Uptown*. The stories describe a Jewish family containing five sisters and one brother growing up in New York in the early twentieth century. The sisters do everything together and always think of one another's feelings. The family is pious, just, loving, and cooperative. Although the children occasionally do naughty things, they always confess and set it right. The stories are very well written and convey a flavor of the era.

TERRIS, SUSAN. *Amanda the Panda and the Redhead*. Illustrated by Emily McCully. Garden City, New York: Doubleday, 1975. (Ages 3–8.)
Amanda is ignored because her parents are too busy with her brother. But they are essentially loving and responsive people and by evening, all is well.

_____. *The Drowning Boy*. Garden City, New York: Doubleday, 1972. (Ages 12–up.)
Jason is twelve years old and hates his life. His elder sister and his father are perfectionists. His mother is caring for her hopelessly senile mother. She has quit her job and does nothing but tend to grandma and grow tomatoes. Jason has been attending school for disturbed boys. When he spends the summer caring for a young autistic child, his success with the boy helps him. He also recognizes that he has to change. Issues in this book include old age, family relationships, care of autistic children, fear, and coping with difficulties.

THOMAS, IANTHE. *Walk Home Tired, Billy Jenkins*. Illustrated by Thomas DiGrazia. New York: Harper & Row, 1974. (Ages 5–8.)

It is time to go home from the playground, and Billy Jenkins is very tired. His sister, Nina, lovingly and imaginatively makes the trip home a magic ride for the two of them. Illustrations of the people and the city are beautifully and gently done.

VAN LEEUWEN, JEAN. *Amanda Pig and Her Big Brother Oliver*. Illustrated by Ann Schweninger. New York, Dial Press, 1982. (Ages 5–8.)
Amanda adores her older brother and wants to do everything he does. Their father is very nurturing, and Oliver is amazingly understanding. Eventually, Amanda listens to her mother and becomes involved in a block-building project all by herself.

VIGNA, JUDITH. *Daddy's New Baby*. Illustrated by the author. Chicago: Whitman, 1982. (Ages 5–8.)
A little girl is jealous of her baby stepsister. She comes to accept the baby after making her smile. Not a new idea, but the context of stepsiblings provides a mirror for children in this situation.

VIORST, JUDITH. "Some Things Don't Make Any Sense At All," in *If I Were in Charge of the World and Other Worries*. New York: Atheneum, 1982. (Ages 5–10.)
The young child in the poem wants to know why his mom just had another baby, especially since she's told him that he's terrific. Wonderfully humorous, and hits the mark of sibling jealousy.

_____. *I'll Fix Anthony*. Illustrated by Arnold Lobel. New York: Harper & Row, 1969. (Ages 5–8.)
A charmingly written and illustrated book, depicting sibling rivalry. Anthony, the elder boy, is thoroughly nasty and mean to his younger sibling. The younger boy, dreaming of the day when he will become six years old,. imagines all the ways that he will take his revenge. Excellent for demonstrating that younger brothers have feelings.

VOIGT, CYNTHIA. *Homecoming*. New York: Atheneum, 1981. (Ages 10–up.)
Dicey, an admirable heroine, leads her younger siblings to the home of a distant relative after they have been abandoned by their emotionally disturbed mother. Dicey finally manages to transfer her brood to her estranged grandmother's house, despite the fact that the old woman seems to want no part of them. The interaction between Dicey and her siblings comprises most of the story. The sequel, *Dicey's Song*, (1982) continues the story. It won the Newbery Award.

WATSON, CLYDE. *Tom Fox and the Apple Pie*. Illustrated by Wendy Watson. New York: Crowell, 1972. (Ages 5–8.)
Tom is the youngest in a very large family. Though greedy and lazy, he is the pet of the family. In this story, leaving his virtuous brothers and sisters to their work, he runs off to the fair. He does buy a balloon for his favorite sister but eats an entire apple pie without sharing a bit of it. He is mildly punished by his mother, but goes to bed happily unrepentant. Any youngest child would enjoy this story. Elder siblings would also probably appreciate the pattern it presents.

WEISS, NICKI. *Chuckie*. Illustrated by the author. New York: Greenwillow Books, 1982. (Ages 5–8.)
Baby Chuckie has all of the attention, and Lucy resents him until the day that Chuckie says his first word, and it's "Lucy."

WILLIAMS, BARBARA. *Jeremy Isn't Hungry*. Illustrated by Martha Alexander. New York: Dutton, 1978. (Ages 4–7.)
Jeremy and Davey's mother is trying to get ready for a school program. She asks Davey to feed little Jeremy, but Jeremy decides to play with the food instead of eat it. Davey discovers that it isn't easy to take care of his little brother, even for a short while, and begins to appreciate his mother's task.

WINTHROP, ELIZABETH. *A Little Demonstration of Affection*. New York: Harper & Row, 1975. (Ages 12–up.)
Jenny, the youngest in a family of three, adores her eldest brother, John. She and John have had a close and happy relationship. Charlie, the middle child, has been left out. This summer John finds other friends and Jenny and Charlie become inseparable. Jenny fears that her feelings for Charlie are unnatural and evil, but they at last recognize that they need affection and love and that they are normal.

WRIGHT, BETTY REN. *I Like Being Alone*. Milwaukee: Raintree, 1981. (Ages 7–10.)
With the support of her Aunt Rose and her parents, Brenda constructs a tree house so that she can get away from her siblings and have some time alone. Brenda enjoys the company of others, but she values her own privacy. She does not reject her numerous siblings, but she is permitted to have the opportunity to be her own person.

ZOLOTOW, CHARLOTTE. *Big Sister and Little Sister*. New York: Harper & Row, 1976. (Ages 5–8.)
No one likes to always be the one who is "taken care of." By showing that sometimes big sisters need help too, perhaps both big and little sisters can see a way to a happier relationship.

BIBLIOGRAPHY: DIVORCE

ADAMS, FLORENCE. *Mushy Eggs*. Illustrated by Marilyn Hirsch. New York: Putnam 1973. (Ages 3–8.)
David and Sam live with their mother, a computer operator, and their wonderful baby-sitter, Fanny, in New York, while their father lives in New Jersey. The boys learn that Fanny is going away and are very sad, hoping that some day they will love their new baby-sitter as much as they loved Fanny. Here is a story of a family managing after a divorce. The mother functions well, and the children are cooperative and understanding.

ADLER, CAROLE S. *The Silver Coach*. New York: Coward, McCann and Geoghegan, 1979. (Ages 9–12.)
Twelve-year-old Chris and her six-year-old sister, Jackie, spend the summer with their paternal grandmother. Their parents are divorced, and this summer marks their acceptance of the situation.

ANDERSON, PENNY S. *A Pretty Good Team*. Chicago: Children's Press, 1979. (Ages 6–8.)
Jeff senses something is wrong between his parents. Things aren't the same as they

used to be. The happiness is gone. Then Mother tells Jeff she and father are going to get a divorce. She does not break the news very gently, rather she blurts it out to Jeff and later apologizes. The book is realistic in the sense that Mother's reason for being so blunt is that she is so busy with her own problems. Discussion section at the end of the book is very useful.

ARUNDEL, HONOR. *A Family Failing*. Nashville: Nelson, 1972. Also in paper. (Ages 11–up.)
Joanna's parents both work, but when her father loses his job and her mother becomes a TV personality, their family life becomes difficult and the parents separate. Joanna's father moves out and makes a new life for himself. Joanna realizes that she must view her parents independently from herself. She must accept the fact that they are individuals, not just her parents.

AVI. *Sometimes I Think I Hear My Name*. New York: Pantheon, 1982. Also in paper. (Ages 11–up.)
Conrad's aunt and uncle try to protect him from finding out that he lives with them because his divorced parents really don't want him. He decides to confront his parents rather than go on a planned vacation to England. When both his parents demonstrate that they are incapable of giving him love and security, he returns to his aunt and uncle, finally accepting his situation and himself. Part of the plot involves Conrad's relationship with a lonely, angry and rejected young girl whose upper class parents are emotionally abusive.

BATES, BETTY. *Bugs in Your Ears*. New York: Holiday, 1977. (Ages 10–up.)
Carrie, a 13-year-old girl, finds her life completely changed when her mother marries Dominic Ginetti, a man with three children. The adjustments of the two families are humorous and lifelike. Carrie's acceptance of her new father is made more difficult because she has a fantasized memory of her own father, even though he was a drinker and her mother divorced him when Carrie was a year old. No one listens to Carrie. Even the judge grants the adoption without listening to Carrie's feelings about an official adoption into the Ginetti family. Carrie's gradual acceptance of and by her new family illustrates realistically the problems and adjustments that have to be made by all blended families.

BAWDEN, NINA. *The Runaway Summer*. Philadelphia: Lippincott, 1969. (Ages 9–12.)
Mary's parents are getting divorced. They do not really care about her, so they send her to live with her grandfather and aunt. Mary meets friends, is happy, and decides to live there permanently. She realizes that for her, her parents' divorce was not a calamity.

BERGER, TERRY. *A Friend Can Help*. Photographs by Heinz Kluetmeier. Milwaukee: Advanced Learning Concepts; Chicago: Children's Press, 1974. (Ages 7–10.)
A simple book, but very helpful and reassuring. The photographs clearly reflect the characters' emotions. The main character's parents are divorced. The divorce is evidently a useful arrangement for everyone concerned. Susan, a friend, helps considerably with her understanding and companionship.

_____. *How Does It Feel When Your Parents Get Divorced?* Photographs by Miriam Shapiro. New York: Julian Messner, 1977. (Ages 8–12.)

Sensitive photographs by Miriam Shapiro help illustrate a child's feelings about divorce. Although not in story form, the book is easy to read and excellent for children eight years old and up. It states and explores real feelings.

BLUE, ROSE. *A Month of Sundays.* Illustrated by Ted Lewin. New York: Franklin Watts, 1972. (Ages 8–10.)
When Jeff's parents divorce, Jeff moves to New York with his mother. With the help of Matthew and his adopted mother, Mrs. Walters, Jeff begins to enjoy city life and gets used to his new situation. A useful book for children who feel that divorce and a change of lifestyle signal the end of their world.

BLUME, JUDY. *It's Not the End of the World.* New York: Bradbury Press, 1972. Also in paper. (Ages 10–12.)
Karen's parents go through a divorce, and Karen and her sister and brother react normally. They try to get their parents back together; they worry about whether or not their parents love them. A friend whose parents are also divorced introduces Gardner's book, *The Boys and Girls Book about Divorce*, to Karen. It helps them both.

BROOKS, JEROME. *Uncle Mike's Boy.* New York: Harper & Row, 1973. (Ages 10–up.)
Pudge's parents are divorced. His father's brother, Uncle Mike, takes care of Pudge, helping him to accept his younger sister's death, his mother remarriage, and his father's mental breakdown. The plot is complicated but exposes the problems many children must face when their parents divorce.

CAIN, BARBARA, AND BENEDEK, ELISSA. *What Would You Do? A Child's Book about Divorce.* Indianapolis: Saturday Evening Post, 1976. (Ages 6–8.)
Deals with questions a child may have about divorce and concomitant problems: moving, new school, new friends. The use of color in the illustrations effectively depicts the feelings the participants are experiencing (anger, jealousy, loneliness, etc.).

CAINES, JEANNETTE. *Daddy.* New York: Harper & Row, 1977. (Ages 6–8.)
Warm, sensitive book about a child whose father comes to get her each Saturday. It describes the anxiety of the transition and the pleasures of the time spent with Daddy and Paula in their apartment. The characters are black.

CHARLIP, REMY, AND MOORE, LILLIAN. *Hooray for Me!* Illustrated by Vera B. Williams. New York: Parents Magazine Press, 1975. (Ages 5–8.)
Many kinds of families are illustrated here, including blended families and extended families.

CLEARY, BEVERLY. *Dear Mr. Henshaw.* Illustrated by Paul O. Zelinsky. New York: Morrow, 1983. (Ages 8–11.)
Ten-year-old Leigh Botts writes regularly to his favorite author, Mr. Henshaw. He takes the author's advice and begins a diary. Through his letters we learn about Leigh's feelings about his parents' divorce, his difficulties at school, and his wishes and dreams. All of this is told humorously and sensitively. A winner of a book.

CLIFTON, LUCILLE. *Everett Anderson's Year.* Illustrated by Ann Grifalconi. New York: Holt, Rinehart and Winston, 1974. (Ages 4–8.)

Reinforces the loving world that Everett lives in. His mother manages well, even though the father has left them. Everett misses and still loves his father. He, too, is coping well.

CLYMER, ELEANOR. *Luke Was There*. Illustrated by Diane de Groat. New York: Holt, Rinehart and Winston, 1973. (Ages 8–12.) (Wel-Met Award.)
Julius's mother has been married and divorced twice. He and his half-brother, Danny, are sent to an institution when their mother becomes ill. Luke, a sensitive counselor, proves to be a positive force in the boys' life.

COLMAN, HILA. *After the Wedding*. New York: Morrow, 1975. (Ages 10–up.)
An 18-year-old finds that marriage, even to someone you love, is not easy. As her relationship with Peter weakens, Kate realizes she will have to face reality and life alone. A modern realistic novel which discusses the question of exactly what the responsibilities are of a husband and wife to each other.

DANZIGER, PAULA. *The Divcorce Express*. New York: Delacorte Press, 1982. (Ages 10–up.)
Phoebe's parents have been divorced for a year. Her parents share joint custody, but she lives with her father most of the time because he is an artist and works at home, and her mother's interior decoration profession takes her outside the home. The story deals with Phoebe's adjustment to her parents' new lifestyles and partners. While this book is amusing, and contains significant concerns for children of divorce, it needs to be discussed in the light of the somewhat romanticized happy ending, and the plot that is based heavily on coincidence.

DONOVAN, JOHN. *I'll Get There. It Better Be Worth the Trip*. New York: Harper & Row, 1969. Also in paper. (Ages 12–up.)
After his parents' divorce, Davy lives with his grandmother until she dies, whereupon he goes to stay with his alcoholic mother, thinks about moving in with his remarried father, and worries about a homosexual encounter with his best friend. The involved feelings of the parents, the competition for the boy's loyalty, the difficulty of sorting out what is right, are all presented in this book.

DRESCHER, JOAN. *Your Family, My Family*. Illustrated by the author. New York: Walker, 1980. (Ages 4–7.)
A pleasant non-fictional description of different kinds of families. This little book can help children recognize that all sorts of families exist in today's society, and that there is a chance for happiness in any of them.

EICHLER, MARGARET. *Martin's Father*. Illustrated by Beverly Maginnis. Chapel Hill, North Carolina: Lollipop Power, 1971. (Ages 3–7.)
Martin and his father live together. The story describes the commonplace daily activities that the two engage in together. A gentle, matter-of-fact presentation.

GARDNER, RICHARD A. *The Boys and Girls Book about Divorce*. Illustrated by Alfred Lowenheim. New York: Science House, 1970. Also in paper. (Ages 12–up.)
Written by a child psychiatrist, this book discusses a child's feelings about divorce, uses of anger and love, reactions toward working mothers and stepparents, and provides many practical suggestions for adjustment to the new situation. The author

confronts all of the problems realistically. He does not mince words. His advice is reasonable and helpful.

GLASS, STUART M. *A Divorce Dictionary, A Book for You and Your Children.* Boston: Little, Brown, 1980. (Ages 10–up.)
Defines and explains the vocabulary associated with divorce. It shows how each term applies in actual circumstances through anecdotes and case histories. Clear and concise.

GLENN, MEL. "Jason Talmadge," in *Class Dismissed: High School Poems.* Photographs by Michael Bernstein. New York: Clarion Books, 1982. (Ages 11–up.)
Jason feels unwanted by both his natural father and his stepfather. He thinks, bitterly, that his parents want to exclude him from their lives.

_____. "Richie Miller," in *Class Dismissed: High School Poems.* Photographs by Michael Bernstein. New York: Clarion Books, 1982. (Ages 11–up.)
The bickering in Richie's house is constant. His parents threaten each other with divorce, but never follow through. The home atmosphere is tense and ugly.

GOFF, BETH. *Where Is Daddy? The Story of a Divorce.* Illustrated by Susan Perl. Boston: Beacon Press, 1969. (Ages 4–7.)
A little girl who cannot understand her parents' divorce blames herself, and she is afraid that her mother won't come back whenever she goes off to work. Gradually her mother and grandmother help her to accept the new situation and not to blame herself for the divorce. Parents will also find this book informative and useful.

GREENE, CONSTANCE C. *A Girl Called Al.* Illustrated by Byron Barton. New York: Viking, 1969. Also in paper. (Ages 11–up.)
Alexandra's mother and father are divorced. She puts on a show of not caring, but is unhappy. The elderly janitor befriends her; after his death, her mother begins to pay more attention to her as a person. Her father sends her money but no love; she keeps looking for substitutes for him. A useful book for purposes of empathy.

GREENFIELD, ELOISE. *Talk about a Family.* Illustrated by James Calvin. Philadelphia: Lippincott, 1978.
Genny hopes that her brother, Carry, will save their parents' marriage when he returns from a thirteen-month army stint. A realistic view of a marital break-up.

GRIPE, MARIA. *The Night Daddy.* Illustrated by Harold Gripe. New York: Delacorte Press, 1971. Also in paper. (Ages 8–up.)
The story of the friendship between a girl and a writer who is hired to stay with her at night while her mother works as a nurse. The setting is Sweden, but the story provides a feasible solution for some families here.

HAZEN, BARBARA SHOOK. *Two Homes to Live In: A Child's-Eye View of Divorce.* Illustrated by Peggy Luks. New York: Human Sciences Press, 1978. (Ages 4–8.)
Niki comes to accept the fact that her parents have divorced each other, but that no one has divorced her. She also accepts the fact that many children's parents are divorced, and it's okay to have pajamas in two places.

HELLBERG, HANS-ERIC. *Grandpa's Maria.* Illustrated by Joan Sandin. Translated from the Swedish by Patricia Crampton. New York: Morrow, 1974. (Ages 7–10.)

Seven-year-old Maria considers her grandfather to be her daddy. Her parents are divorced. When she meets her father for the first time, their relationship is somewhat strained because his second wife disapproves of his seeing Maria. Maria adores her grandfather, who understands Maria and enjoys her company. Maria's mother goes to a mental hospital; she has obviously not weathered the divorce as well as her husband has. In the end it appears that all will be well for everyone. The author invites his readers to write to him and promises to engage in a correspondence.

HELMERING, DORIS WILD. *I Have Two Families.* Nashville: Abington, 1981. (Ages 5–8.)

Patty and Michael experience normal anxieties when their parents divorce. They live with their father, but regularly visit their mother and her new partner. Both parents love and care about them. Their adjustment seems complete.

HOLLAND, ISABELLE. *The Man Without a Face.* Philadelphia: Lippincott, 1972. Also in paper. (Ages 12–up.)

Charles is emotionally drained by his mother's multiple divorces and his elder sister's cruelty to him. He becomes attached to his tutor, fears he is sexually attracted to him, learns later that the tutor is a homosexual, and ultimately comes to recognize his own feelings as that of admiration and gratefulness. The tutor does not take advantage of the boy's love even though he loves the boy.

IRWIN, HADLEY. *Bring to a Boil and Separate.* New York: Atheneum, 1980. (Ages 11–up.)

For a while Kate, age thirteen, avoids talking about her parents' separation, but eventually deals with it. There is respect for everyone in this story. Neither parent is the villain.

KINDRED, WENDY. *Lucky Wilma.* New York: Dial Press, 1973. (Ages 4–8.)

Wilma and her father, Charlie, spend every Saturday together. They visit museums and parks and play lovingly and happily together. At the end of each Saturday, Wilma's father returns to his own house, and Wilma goes home to her mother. The book demonstrates that children need not be miserable because of parents' divorcing.

KLEIN, NORMA. *Breaking Up.* New York: Avon, 1980. Also in paper. (Ages 12–up.)

Allie, a 15-year old girl, torn between her divorcing parents, deals with her over-protective father, her gay mother, and her stepmother, who misjudges her age and taste.

_____. *It's Not What You Expect.* New York: Pantheon, 1973. Also in paper. (Ages 4–8.)

Carla and Oliver Simon's father leaves home for the summer. There is no apparent reason for his going except that he is undergoing a personal crisis. The marriage has evidently been a strong one, and at the end of the summer, he returns. There is a hint that he has had an affair, but there is no question that his wife wants him back and accepts him without recrimination.

_____. *Taking Sides.* New York: Pantheon, 1974. Also in paper. (Ages 9–up.)

After her parents' remarriage and second divorce, Nell and her brother live with their father in New York. The book consists of Nell's observations and reflections as her life changes and progresses. This book is one of the few in which there is the recognition that the father may be better at nurturing children than the mother is. Unfortunately, circumstances occur that force the children to wind up with their mother. Both parents are different from the stereotype.

LESHAN, EDA. *What's Going to Happen to Me?* New York: Four Winds Press, 1978. (All ages.)
A guide for children whose parents separate or divorce. It addresses divorce honestly, looks at feelings of all kinds, and makes suggestions for coping, along with a "further reading" section. LeShan acknowledges that divorce is a painful and frightening experience for children. She underlines the importance of being aware of the feelings children are having.

LEXAU, JOAN. *Emily and the Klunky Baby and the Next-Door Dog.* Illustrated by Martha Alexander. New York: Dial Press, 1972. (Ages 5–8.)
A little girl resents her little brother and is upset that her divorced mother cannot pay more attention to her, so she attempts to run away to her father's house. Her mother expects much from her, and the pressure is more than the child can tolerate. But the mother recognizes the problem and sets aside her own work to attend to her children. The message here is for parents.

_____. *Me Day.* Illustrated by Robert Weaver. New York: Dial Press, 1971. (Ages 7–10.)
Rafer has an unhappy birthday until his divorced father comes to spend the whole day with him as a surprise. The reader gets the feeling that the father does not really care about his family, and that this day will be only a temporary oasis in Rafer's otherwise barren life.

MANN, PEGGY. *My Dad Lives in a Downtown Hotel.* Illustrated by Richard Cuffari. Garden City, New York: Doubleday, 1973. Also in paper. (Ages 8–12.)
Joey blames himself for his parents' divorce. But after spending time with his father, talking more with his mother, and finding a friend who also has no father living at home, Joey accepts the situation more happily. There are some very moving sections of this book; for example, Joey lists his faults and promises to reform if only his father will come home. Joey's mother is the defeated person in this story.

MAYLE, PETER. *Divorce Can Happen to the Nicest People.* New York: Macmillan, 1979. (Ages 7–10.)
A handbook written especially for young children. Gives reassurance, sympathy, and advice on how to cope with a separation or a divorce. Written in simple, honest language and is fair to both parents.

MAZER, HARRY. *Guy Lenny.* New York: Delacorte Press, 1971. Also in paper. (Ages 9–12.)
Twelve-year-old Guy feels betrayed by his father, who wants to marry again. Guy eventually must live with his mother, who has come back to get him after having deserted him about seven years before. This story presents realistic dilemmas for families involved in divorce.

MAZER, NORMA FOX. *I, Trissy*. New York: Delacorte Press, 1971. Also in paper. (Ages 9–12.)
The story of an imaginative girl who blames her mother for her parents' divorce. Eventually, she begins to be able to see herself and each of her parents in a realistic, individual light. Trissy behaves in a very self-centered manner throughout the entire book. She, not her parents, is the cause of problems in the aftermath of the divorce. Her parents' understanding provides a base for her to build a more mature and responsible way of behaving.

MERRIAM, EVE. "Two People," in *A Word or Two with You*. Illustrated by John Nez. New York: Atheneum, 1981. (All ages.)
Although the parents in this poem disagree about almost everything, the poet realizes that they love one another anyway.

MOORE, EMILY. *Something to Count On*. New York: Dutton, 1980. (Ages 9–12.)
Lorraine and Jason's parents separate. The children blame themselves. Lorraine, a bright, talented, but disruptive fifth grader, narrates this story about separation, family life, friendship, and the difference a good teacher can make. Most of all the book helps us to understand the feelings and responses of a seemingly unmanageable child.

NEWFIELD, MARCIA. *A Book for Jodan*. Illustrated by Diane de Groat. New York: Atheneum, 1975. (Ages 6–10.)
Jodan is heartsick at her parents' divorce. Though they both reassure her that they love her, she is very unhappy. She and her mother move to California; her father remains in Massachusetts. At the end of a holiday visit, her father gives her a special book that he has made, just for her. It recalls their happy times together and serves as a secure reminder of her father's love. A story that demonstrates the effort going into a constructive relationship.

NEUFIELD, JOHN. *Sunday Father*. New York: Signet, 1977. (Ages 12–up.)
A 13-year-old is frustrated and angry over her parents' divorce. Her main aim is to get her mother and father back together again. She refuses to relate to her new stepmother even when confronted with the fact of her father's remarriage. At the end she accepts the fact that her parents will not remarry.

NORRIS, GUNILLA. *Lillian*. New York: Atheneum, 1968. (Ages 8–12.)
Lillian's parents divorce, and she is afraid her mother will stop loving her now that she is so busy with her job. With her mother's help, Lillian grows more self-reliant, self-confident, and less fearful. Readers will find their own anxieties mirrored in this book.

OKIMOTO, JEAN DAVIES. *My Mother Is Not Married to My Father*. New York: Putnam, 1980. (Ages 7–10.)
Eleven-year-old Cynthia and her six-year-old sister make an excellent adjustment to their parents' divorce and their mother's subsequent dating.

OPPENHEIMER, JOAN L. *Gardine vs. Hanover*. New York: Crowell, 1982. (Ages 12–up.)
The focal point of this book is the relationship between step-siblings, and the effect on each of the children of joining two families.

PARIS, LENA. *Mom Is Single*. Illustrated by Mark Christianson. Chicago: Children's Press, 1980. (Ages 8–12.)
A child describes the changes in his life since his parents' divorce. He shows some of his feelings of anger, fear, and resentment. The photographs emphasize that this is a realistic situation. The book ends on an accepting note.

PARK, BARBARA. *Don't Make Me Smile*. New York: Knopf, 1981. (Ages 9–12.)
Charles is devastated when his parents decide to divorce. He compares divorce to helplessly watching a car smash your bicycle. "It's all smashed to pieces, and it will never be the same. It's too late,- That's divorce." A psychiatrist helps Charlie say what's on his mind without yelling. His perceptions are humorously stated, and hit the mark.

PECK, RICHARD. *Father Figure*. New York: Signet, 1978. Paperback. (Ages 12–up.)
When Jim and Byron's mother kills herself, their grandmother decides it's time they see their father, who left them many years before. The boys come to terms with their father, after going through the pain of mourning, and the additional challenge of accepting themselves and their father for who they all are.

PERL, LILA. *The Telltale Summer of Tina C*. New York: Seabury Press, 1975. (Ages 10–up.)
Tina's mother has wearied of upper class life and is now living a somewhat Bohemian existence with her new husband. Tina comes to terms with her mother and begins to establish better communications with her father.

PERRY, PATRICIA, AND LYNCH, MARIETTA. *Mommy and Daddy Are Divorced*. New York: Dial Press, 1978. (Ages 5–8.)
Ned, a pre-schooler, tells in the first person about the things he and his younger brother Joey do with Daddy on Saturdays. Ned expresses unhappiness when his father leaves at the end of the day. Mother offers a matter-of-fact explanation of why they divorced. This book concentrates mostly on the children's relationship to the father on his visit day. Illustrated with excellent photographs.

PEVSNER, STELLA. *A Smart Kid like You*. New York: Seabury Press, 1975. (Ages 11–up.)
Nina's parents are divorced. She discovers, when she enters junior high, that her math teacher is her father's new wife. She and her friends harass the teacher, until good sense prevails. Nina's father helps her to adjust to the new situation.

PLATT, KIN. *Chloris and the Creeps*. Philadelphia: Chilton, 1973. (Also in paper.) (Ages 12–up.)
Chloris cannot accept her parents' divorce, her father's subsequent suicide, or her mother's dating and eventual remarriage. She is hateful and destructive to her mother and her mother's new husband. She imagines her father to have been a super-human person. Through therapy and patience Chloris' mother, sister, and stepfather nurture her to a point where the reader has hopes that she will change her attitude and behavior.

PURSELL, MARGARET SANFORD. *A Look at Divorce*. Photographs by Marcia S. Forrai. Ontario: Lerner Publications, 1977. (Ages 6–10.)
Photos and text combine to present a matter-of-fact look at divorce. Addresses

changes in parents' feelings and family patterns. Reassuring comments for young readers predict better family relationships eventually.

RICHARDS, A., AND WILLIS. I. *How to Get It Together When Your Parents Are Coming Apart*. New York: McKay, 1976. (Ages 11–up.)
This guide is an attempt to help adolescents cope with their parents' marital problems, divorce, and the aftermath. Young people were interviewed and their stories make up most of the book. Separate sections address various issues: marital problems, the divorce process, adjustment after the divorce, and a guide to getting help: various sources, addresses, helpful information.

ROFES, ERIC, ed. *The Kids' Book of Divorce*. Lexington, Massachusetts: Lewis Publishing Co., 1981. Also in paper. (Ages 8–up.)
Twenty students of Cambridge's Fayerweather Street School, aged 11–14 years, discuss various aspects of divorce, including custody arrangements, parents' friends, how they were first told about their parents' divorce, and the consequences of the divorce from their perspectives. This book's impact is in the faithful reproduction of children's words as they respond to divorce and describe how they feel.

SACHS, MARILYN. *The Bear's House*. Illustrated by Louis Glanzman. Garden City, New York: Doubleday, 1971. (Ages 9–12.)
When Fran Ellen's father deserts her family, her mother totally collapses. The elder brother assumes direction of the family, but it does not work. Eventually a teacher, recognizing the extremity of the situation, takes steps to salvage their lives. But the book itself is painful to read. Fran Ellen lives in two worlds and is in danger of retreating forever into her fantasies. Everyone's plight is emotionally wrenching in this story. Perhaps its usefulness lies in assuring unhappy readers that there are people in much worse straits than they.

SCHUCHMAN, JOAN. *Two Places to Sleep*. Illustrated by Jim LaMarche. Minneapolis, Minnesota: Carolrhoda Books, 1979. (Ages 5–10.)
A seven-year-old boy lives with his father after his parents are divorced. He visits his mother on weekends and has trouble accepting the situation. He is just beginning to adjust to his new lifestyle and needs reassurance that he is still loved. This book might be especially helpful for a child living with a single male parent.

SEVERANCE, JANE. *When Megan Went Away*. Illustrated by Tea Schook. Chapel Hill, North Carolina: Lollipop Power, 1979. (Ages 7–12.)
Shannon and her mother are unhappy because Megan, her mother's lover, has moved out of their house. The feelings a child experiences when one of the nurturing adults in the house has left are well stated here. The difference in this book is that it involves a lesbian relationship.

SHARMAT, MARJORIE. *Sometimes Mama and Papa Fight*. Illustrated by Kay Chorao. New York: Harper & Row, 1980. (Ages 4–8.)
Kevin and his sister get very upset when his parents fight. They learn that some fighting can be a natural part of family life, without necessarily leading to divorce.

SINBERG, JANET. *Divorce Is a Grown Up Problem*. Illustrated by Nancy Gray. New York: Avon, 1978. Paperback. (Ages 3–8.)
Written to help young children better understand their reactions to the divorce of

their parents. Feelings such as fear, anger, sadness, alienation, and confusion are acknowledged. The book ends on the reassuring note that both parents still love the child. The author includes a brief preface for the parents and some helpful advice for coping with the situation. There is also an annotated bibliography of other relevant books.

SITEA, LINDA. "*Zachary's Divorce*" in *Free to Be You and Me*. New York: McGraw-Hill, 1974. Also in paper. (Ages 5–8.)
The aftermath of divorce is described through the eyes of Zachary, a young boy. He feels as if he has been divorced, although his mother assures him that it is his parents who divorced each other. Zachary's mother is supportive, understanding, and coping. Zachary's friend Amy lives with her father because her parents are divorced. Zachary decides that there are two kinds of divorce: the "mommy" kind and the "daddy" kind. He feels very much out of control and dominated by the grown-up world. But time will pass, and he will recover from his bad feelings. A very useful little story.

SLOTE, ALFRED. *Love and Tennis*. New York: Macmillan, 1979. (Ages 11–up.)
Fifteen-year-old Buddy is an excellent tennis player who gets a chance to train at a famous coach's school. Meanwhile, he falls in love, and must come to grips with his parents' divorce, his mother's remarriage, his father's girlfriend, the loss of his first love, and his own life goals.

SMITH, DORIS BUCHANAN. *The First Hard Times*. New York: Viking, 1983. (Ages 10–up.)
Ancil resents her new stepfather and is pained by all of her family's acceptance of him. Her friend, Lloyd, helps her to cope.

_____. *Kick a Stone Home*. New York: Crowell, 1974. (Ages 10–up.)
Sara Jane, the adolescent protagonist, has difficulty coping with boy-girl relationships, her parents' divorce, and her own feelings. She at last comes to terms with herself and feels a sense of great accomplishment.

SOBOL, HARRIET LANGSAM. *My Other-Mother, My Other-Father*. Illustrated by Patricia Agre. New York: Macmillan, 1979. (Ages 10–up.)
Andrea tells how she feels about being a stepchild and about the advantages and disadvantages of having two sets of parents. Her relationships seem to work out fine, making this a very positive book. The photographs show good interaction among all parties involved.

SPILKE, FRANCINE SUSAN. *The Family That Changed: A Child's Book about Divorce*. Illustrated by Tom O'Sullivan. New York: Crown, 1979. (Ages 5–8.)
Aimed at the very young child, the book helps parents to inform their preschoolers about divorce. Very much an introduction to impending divorce, the book anticipates anxieties and fears.

STANEK, MURIEL. *I Won't Go Without a Father*. Illustrated by Eleanor Mill. Chicago: Whitman, 1972. (Ages 6–9.)
Steve is angry and jealous of anyone who has a father; but, with the support of his

uncle and grandfather, he learns to become less defensive and more accepting of his family situation.

STOLZ, MARY. *Leap Before You Look*. New York: Harper & Row, 1975. Also in paper. (Ages 12–up.)
Jimmie adores her father and resents his remarriage. Living with her mother, brother, grandmother, and aided by her friend Chris, who is bothered by several divorces in her family, Jimmie gradually adjusts and reconciles herself with her father.

SUROWIECKI, SANDRA LUCAS. *Joshua's Day*. Chapel Hill, North Carolina: Lollipop Power, 1972. (Ages 3–6.)
Joshua, who lives with his mother, goes to a day-care center while she works. She is coping well without a husband, and Joshua seems fine.

VIGNA, JUDITH. *Daddy's New Baby*. Illustrated by the author. Chicago: Whitman, 1982. (Ages 5–7.)
A little girl is jealous of her baby stepsister. She rescues the baby from an accident, and makes her smile. Not a new idea, but useful for the special adjustment of new stepsiblings.

WHITE, ANN S. *Divorce*. Illustrated by Ginger Giles. New York: Franklin Watts, 1979. (Ages 8–up.)
A frank book on the mechanics and terminology of divorce. It deals with feelings, the law, and court.

ZOLOTOW, CHARLOTTE. *A Father like That*. illustrated by Ben Shecter, New York: Harper & Row, 1971.
The story is of a young boy's fantasy of what the ideal father for him would be. He depicts a husband who cares for his wife and contributes to the care of his child. The mother is sensitive to the child's needs and encourages him to be that type of person if he does not happen to have a father like that while growing up.

BIBLIOGRAPHY: ADOPTION AND FOSTER CARE

ADLER, C. S. *The Cat That Was Left Behind*. New York: Ticknor and Fields, 1981. (Ages 11–up.)
Thirteen-year-old Chad has recently become a foster child to the Sorenic family. Because of Chad's past experiences in foster homes, he has little trust for this new foster family. During the course of the story he befriends as stray cat. At the same time the Sorenics, especially his stepsister Polly, work very hard at building Chad's trust within the family. By the story's end Chad has accepted the family, who are then making plans to adopt him.

AMES, MILDRED. *Without Hats, Who Can Tell the Good Guys?* New York: Dutton, 1976. (Ages 10–12.)
Anthony Lang, Jr., an 11-year-old, has been sent to live with the Diamonds, until, he says, his father can come back for him. He is not happy with this family at first.

He likes no one. Eventually he learns to really care about Hildy, his sister, Mr. and Mrs. Diamond, and even senile Mrs. Puckett. When his dream of someday living with his father is shattered, Tony's love for his foster family supports him through that difficult and maturing period of his life. A realistic insight into the life of foster child who gradually learns to accept and love his new family.

BATES, BETTY. *Bugs in Your Ears*. New York: Holiday, 1977. (Ages 10–up.)
Carrie, a 13-year-old girl, finds her life completely changed when her mother marries Dominic Ginetti, a man with three children. The adjustments of the two families are humorous and life-like. Carrie's acceptance of her new father is made more difficult because she has a fantasized memory of her own father, even though he was a drinker and her mother divorced him when Carrie was a year old. No one listens to Carrie. Even the judge grants the adoption without listening to Carrie's feelings about an official adoption into the Ginetti family. Carrie's gradual acceptance of and by her new family illustrates realistically the problems and adjustments that have to be made by all blended families.

BLUE, ROSE. *A Quiet Place*. Illustrated by Tom Feelings. New York: Franklin Watts, 1969. (Ages 9–12.)
Nine-year-old Matthew is a black foster child who spends his spare time in his "quiet place" at the library. He has been to a variety of foster homes and only his current one has been like a real home to him. When the library is closed for two years, Matt feels threatened again with loss and despair. He experiences the fear of being abandoned by his foster parents. It is only through their loving reassurance that he overcomes his fear. Matthew's life is a good one now. His mother and father are loving, understanding people. His big sister has been in trouble, but now she has a fine boyfriend who helps her to stay on the right track. He also has a baby brother. All are foster children. All benefit from the warmth of the home. The whole family is black. Parents have had other adopted children and have been successful at it.

_____. *Seven Years from Home*. Illustrated by Barbara Ericksen. Milwaukee: Raintree, 1976. (Ages 9–12.)
Mark is adopted. His younger brother, Peter, is their parents' child by birth. Suddenly, at eleven years of age, Mark is anxious about his position in the family and desperately wants to find his birth parents. Their sons are important to them and they want to be evenhanded in their treatment of both. Issues of adoption and sibling rivalry are addressed graphically in this book, but the ending is a little too pat for believability. Nevertheless, the book invites serious discussion and could be useful for initiating some talk about adopted children's feelings.

BRENNER, BARBARA. *A Year in the Life of Rosie Bernard*. New York: Harper & Row, 1971. Also in paper. (Ages 8–12.)
Rosie's mother has died, and her father, despite his promise to keep Rosie with him, must, because of the pressures of the Depression, take an acting job that keeps him on the road. He therefore brings Rosie to her maternal grandparents' house in Brooklyn. Rosie, a spunky, bright, sensitive, and engaging girl, spends the year with this family and grows to love and appreciate them. Many issues are found in this well-crafted book: reaction to death, foster care, old age (the grandfather and grandmother emerge as strong characters) and certainly a heroine who defies stereotyping.

BUCK, PEARL. *Matthew, Mark, Luke and John*. Illustrated by Mamoru Fuhai. New York: John Day Company, 1966. (Ages 10–up.)
This book shows the hardships that so many children of American fathers and Korean mothers have had to endure. They are outcasts—literally left to care for themselves or die. One child learns to survive and becomes the father figure to three other children like himself. When they stumble onto a Christmas party at an army base, Matthew finds a friend who wants to adopt him. Matthew worries about his "charges," Mark, Luke and John. Eventually homes are found for the other boys. The adoption is not as important in the book as the social issue about children of mixed parentage.

BUNIN, CATHERINE AND SHERRY. *Is That Your Sister?* New York: Pantheon, 1976. (Ages 6–12.)
A six-year-old child explains all about adoption. Since she is of a different race from her parents, she has become an "expert" on explanations. A warm, true story with photographs of her family.

BUTTERWORTH, WILLIAM. *LeRoy and the Old Man*. New York: Four Winds Press, 1980. Also in paper. (Ages 12–up.)
LeRoy goes to stay with his grandfather, whom he is meeting for the first time in his life. LeRoy's father has deserted him and his mother. The grandfather is unforgiving of his son, but takes in his grandson and teaches him his value system. The old man is strong, capable, and well respected by the community. LeRoy eventually will make a permanent home here.

BYARS, BETSY. *The Pinballs*. New York: Harper & Row, 1977. (Ages 9–12.)
Three foster children, or "pinballs" as Carlie labels them, are sent to stay with the Masons. Each of the three has a problem that must be confronted, discussed and accepted. Carlie, the ringleader, helps both Thomas J. and Harvey while at the same time she grows and matures into a sincere, loving sister to both boys. A well-written, sensitively handled story.

CAINES, JEANNETTE. *Abby*. Illustrated by Steven Kellogg. New York: Harper & Row, 1973. (Ages 5–8.)
Abby is an adopted child who is loved by her parents and by her elder brother, Kevin, even though he upsets Abby sometimes.

COLMAN, HILA. *Tell Me No Lies*. New York: Crown, 1978. (Ages 10–12.)
Angela finds her birth father, learns the truth about her birth, and comes to terms with her parents and with her prospective adoptive father.

DUPRAU, JEANNE. *Adoption: The Facts, Feelings, and Issues of a Doubled Heritage*. Julian Messner, 1981. (Ages 12–up.)
Explores changes in adoption laws and policies over the years. Describes present-day adoption process. Examines the conflicts and feelings of the child, adoptive parents, and birth mothers. Detailed, objective, sensitive, readable, extensive.

GREENFIELD, ELOISE. *Grandmama's Joy*. Illustrated by Carole Byard. New York: William Collins Publishers, 1980. (Ages 6–8.)
Rhondy has lived with her grandmother since she was a baby. Grandma calls Rhondy her "Joy" and always says everything will be all right as long as she has her

Joy. But when Grandma finds out they have to move not even Rhondy can make her happy until she reminds Grandma that they still have each other.

HOLLAND, ISABELLE. *Alan and the Animal Kingdom*. New York: Dell, 1977. (Ages 9–12.)
Alan has been shipped from one relative to another since his parents died. His love for animals seems greater than his love or belief in people. Alan eventually learns you have to rely on people and puts his trust in his "new" family.

HUNT, IRENE. *Up a Road Slowly*. Chicago: Follett, 1966. (Ages 9–12.) (Newbery Medal.)
Seven-year-old Julie and her nine-year-old brother Chris are sent to live with their Aunt Cordelia when their mother dies. Their father can't cope with the situation. Both have a hard time adjusting to these changes. The story describes their growth and acceptance of their aunt and their situation. Excellent characterization with realistic interaction and dialogue.

JONES, ADRIENNE. *So, Nothing Is Forever*. Boston: Houghton Mifflin, 1974. (Ages 12–up.)
Three children from an interracial marriage, fifteen-year-old Talene, thirteen-year-old Joey, and two-year-old Adam, decide to stay with their maternal grandmother Anna Hallet when their parents are killed in a car crash. They refuse to be separated and put into different foster homes. They are unsure of their grandmother's welcome since she never contacted their mother (her daughter) after the marriage. The gradual acceptance by the grandmother of her grandchildren and vice-versa brings the reader clearly into the world of the homeless, frightened, fiercely proud, and lovable Bardon children.

KREMENTZ, JILL. *How It Feels to Be Adopted*. New York: Knopf, 1982. (Ages 11–up.)
Using actual testimony from a variety of adopted children and teenagers, the author helps readers explore feelings and experiences of families involved in adoption. Different races are represented as well as many family situations. The author's photographs underline the authenticity of the book.

LAPSLEY, SUSAN. *I Am Adopted*. New York: Bradbury Press, 1974. (Ages 5–8.)
A simple picture book about two adopted children, Charles and Sophie, narrated from a child's point of view. Charles describes their everyday activities and the family's love, warmth, and caring shine through.

LEVITIN, SONIA. *Journey to America*. Illustrated by Charles Robinson. New York: Atheneum, 1970. (Ages 9–12.)
Lisa's family decides to escape the Nazis by emigrating to America. Their decision is a difficult one, complicated by the fact that the father must go first. The children and their mother stay for a while in Switzerland, where two of them are subjected to terrible treatment in a foster care facility. Finally, they are reunited in America.

LIVINGSTON, CAROLE. *Why Was I Adopted?* Illustrated by Arthur Robins. Secaucus, New Jersey: Lyle Stuart, 1978. (Ages 4–10.)
A thorough and humorous presentation of the whys and hows of adoption. Keeps the "specialness" of being adopted in proper perspective with individual abilities

and everyday acceptable behavior and the necessity of parental discipline. Included are common questions asked by adoptees with down-to-earth answers.

LOBEL, ARNOLD. *Uncle Elephant*. Illustrated by the author. New York: Harper & Row, 1981. Paperback: Scholastic. (Ages 4–8.)
Uncle Elephant adopts his unknown nephew when his parents are lost at sea. The two develop a tender, loving relationship while they are together and the book illustrates the sense of loss each feels when their time together is over.

MACLACHLAN, PATRICIA. *Arthur, for the Very First Time*. Illustrated by Lloyd Bloom. New York: Harper & Row, 1980. Also in paper. (Ages 9–12.)
With the help of his great aunt and uncle, and his friend, Moira, Arthur learns to value new life and to become much more sensitive to the feelings of others. Moira is a child whose parents have deserted her. She lives with her grandfather, and is not certain until the end of the book that he really loves her. A social worker who comes to check on her understands the relationship, and approves of Moira's placement in her grandfather's house. A tender, well-written story.

_____. *Mama One, Mama Two*. New York: Harper & Row, 1982. (Ages 5–11.)
Maudie is living with a foster family until her birth mother is well enough to care for her. Mama Two often relates to Maudie the story of how she became a foster child. There is warmth and understanding in the story line as well as in the colorful illustrations. Maudie is tenderly accepted as part of her new family. She is given love and reassurance. It is clear that Mama Two will be able to relinquish Maudie to Mama One's care when the time comes, but will also remain available.

MILES, MISKA. *Aaron's Door*. Boston: Little, Brown, 1977. (Ages 9–11.)
Aaron, a newly adopted boy, trusts no one and is afraid of loneliness and rejection. He closes himself off by hiding behind his bedroom door. When *Aaron's Door* is finally broken down, the wall against the world crumbles. He begins to trust.

MYERS, WALTER DEAN. *Won't Know till I Get There*. New York: Viking, 1982. (Ages 11–up.)
Earl Goins has gone from one foster home to another; his mother won't have him, but she refuses to permit him to be permanently adopted. He finally arrives at the comfortable home of the Perrys, where he causes many problems, but where he also finds understanding. Earl is certainly not what his foster brother Stephen expected, but Stephen learns a lesson in acceptance as the story progresses. There are also some excellent scenes in an old age home where the two boys work for a summer.

PARKER, RICHARD. *Paul and Etta*. Nashville: Thomas Nelson, 1972. (Ages 9–12.)
Young Paul Aintree is being considered for adoption by the Milford family. This family consists of Mr. & Mrs. Milford and their spoiled little girl, Etta. The story basically revolves around the rivalry and battles between Paul and Etta, who both possess strong personalities and wills. A good character study into realistic sibling rivalry. The thoughts and feelings of Paul are expressed through realistic dialogue and situations.

PATERSON, KATHERINE. *The Great Gilly Hopkins*. New York: Crowell, 1978. (Ages 9–up.)

Gilly is a very intelligent, though angry and unhappy, girl. She seems to get pleasure from making people dislike her. In reality, she craves love and security. The story tells of Gilly's dream of being reunited with her birth mother; her placement with Trotter, the obese, wise, and loving foster mother; and William Ernest, the painfully insecure little boy who is also Trotter's foster child. This is a masterfully written story, in which all of the characters are vivid individuals, helping readers to understand better the problems of foster care.

PIEPGRAS, RUTH. *My Name Is Mike Trumsky*. Illustrated by Peg Roth Haag. Chicago: Child's World, 1979. (Ages 7–10.)
Mike lives with his foster family, the Westons. Although he is comfortable living there and has a good relationship with all of them, he really wants to see and be with his mother. The dialogue between Mike and his friends and Mike and his foster family gives a clear depiction of foster care. In the end there is the possibility of a permanent reunion between Mike and his mother at some time in the future.

POWLEDGE, FRED. *So You're Adopted: A Book about the Experience of Being Adopted*. New York: Scribner, 1982. (Ages 12–up.)
Informal in tone, but very informational, the book offers advice and explores the issues of adoption. Excellent resource list included.

PURSELL, MARGARET SANFORD. *A Look at Adoption*. Minneapolis: Lerner Publications, 1978. (Ages 5–8.)
Useful Information about the topic geared to young children's level without being condescending.

SACHS, MARILYN. *A December Tale*. New York: Doubleday, 1976. (Ages 9–11.)
A very painful tale of ten-year-old Myra Fine, who must learn to cope with an ineffectual and rejecting father, a very difficult younger brother, a world that refuses to help her, and an inappropriate foster care placement. As an escape, she spends time in conversation with her imaginary friend, St. Joan of Arc. When she finally defends her younger brother Henry from their abusive foster mother, she relinquishes her fantasies and finds the strength for some real solutions. Children may find this story too difficult to handle without adult support.

SILMAN, ROBERTA. *Somebody Else's Child*. Illustrated by Chris Conover. New York: Frederick Warne & Company, 1976. (Ages 8–10.)
Peter, an adopted ten-year-old in a loving family, has a new friend, Puddin' Paint, a bus driver. When Puddin' Paint mentions that he never had his own children, and wouldn't want "somebody else's child," he upsets Peter and his feelings of belonging. Peter's mother is very supportive and together they decide that people outside an adoptive family haven't had the experience to understand their special feelings. In an adventure searching for the bus driver's lost dogs (almost like his children), they learn a lot about love.

STEIN, SARA BONNET. *The Adopted One*. Photographs by Erika Stone. New York: Walker, 1979. (Ages 3–8.)
One of the *Open Family* series. Four-year-old Joshua is adopted. Joshua questions his mommy about his birth mother. He wants to discover some things about his beginning. The accompanying text for adults provides clear explanations as to why

children may ask certain questions. It models helpful ways of responding to these questions.

YOLEN, JANE. *Children of the Wolf*. New York: Viking, 1984. (Ages 12–up.)
Set in a Christian orphanage in India in the 1920's and based on several accounts of the wolf girls of Midnapore, India, the story, above all, leads the reader through the coming of age of its protoganist, Mohandas, a nurturing, sensitive boy. At the same time it provides a picture of what an institution for orphans was like. The story of the wolf girls is a fascinating, though sad one.

YOUNG, MIRIAM. *Miss Suzy's Birthday*. New York: Parents' Magazine Press, 1974. (Ages 5–8.)
A surprise birthday party for a mother squirrel is given by her four adopted squirrels. A tender and reassuring story for members of an adoptive family.

•THREE•

SEX

SEX EDUCATION HAS NOT YET BECOME a comfortable topic in either schools or libraries. Almost everyone agrees that there should be some instruction on this topic for young children, but when it comes to specifically determining who, what, where, when, and how, opinions vary widely. Some parents object to having the topic even mentioned at school, while others wish that the schools would handle the issue totally. Most parents want to have a say in the manner of the instruction. Often libraries, recognizing the controversial nature of the information, either maintain shelves "by permission only" or simply do not purchase the controversial literature.

At present, children receive their sex instruction in a variety of ways. They sometimes learn about the process in a totally satisfactory manner from their parents who are knowledgeable and comfortable in their beliefs and attitudes. They are sometimes helped in their search for answers by sympathetic and informed teachers, counselors, or friends. They can also acquire needed information from objective librarians who know what the resources are and how to handle them. But most of the time children receive their information, both accurate and inaccurate, from their peers. They also seem to be adept at acquiring pornographic material aimed at titillation rather than education. Much of their informal education comes from movies and television, and much comes from the fiction that they read, which is not consciously trying to instruct in matters sexual but which succeeds in imparting many lessons.

Few communities can arrive at consensus in determining the approach, set of values, and even quantity of information that they are willing to have their children exposed to. The dilemma, then, remains. How can an interested, positive, supportive adult communicate the necessary information to inquisitive young people? What information is necessary? Where can the materials be found? What steps can be taken to help young people feel comfortable about the topic and informed enough to behave responsibly? What values are valid for contemporary times? Before attempting to answer these questions, it would be useful for adults to examine their own attitudes and values.

•TRY THIS

Answer the following questions as honestly as you can. Do not share the answers with anyone unless you want to.

What was the primary source of most of your information about sex? Your parents? Teachers? Books? Peers? Experience? Other?

How much time elapsed between your learning about puberty and the onset of your puberty?

How well prepared did you consider yourself to handle the new situations and physical conditions imposed by puberty?

How did you feel about your body when you were a teenager?

How do you feel about your body now?

What is your opinion about premarital or extramarital sex for yourself? For an eventual (or current) spouse? For your children (if you have any or will have any)? For other people?

How linked do you think sex and love should be? For men? For women?

How "special" do you consider sexual intercourse to be in a relationship between two people?

What is your opinion of homosexuality?

What is your definition of pornography?

What, if any, are your personal rules about sex?

What are your opinions about masturbation?

What, if any, taboos do you hold for yourself?

How do you react to dirty jokes? To X-rated films?

How generalized or universal would you like your attitudes to be?

How do you feel about people who disagree with you?

Who do you feel should be responsible for educating children about sex?

When do you believe sex education should begin?

Attitudes play an important role in determining the quality of education, no matter what the content. In trying to teach children what we want them to know about sex, our attitudes and theirs come very strongly into play—but our feelings are colored by our knowledge and experience. Some of us are afraid that our students or children know more about sex then we do; we even suspect that some of them have a very active acquaintance with information that we are ignorant of.

Furthermore, we wonder where direct information about sexuality and sex practices should begin and where it should end. Some people believe that instruction ends with marriage. Some think that it should stop when a person has experienced intercourse. (After all, they reason what more would anyone need to know?)

At a conference of publishers, educators, counselors, and representatives from various religious organizations, consensus was reached about several courses of action to follow. It was agreed that any material aiming to instruct about sex should stress the broad range of sexual behavior and responses in human relationships, not only those pieces of behavior labeled sex acts. Thus, sexuality rather than sex should be emphasized. Current research in physiological responses, family relations, education and psychology should be taken into consideration in any program of instruction. An overemphasis on physiology and too much duplication of known facts should be avoided. The conference participants agreed that this kind of education should be perceived as a developmental program based on acknowledged human sexual conditions and needs from birth to old age. (See *Publishers Weekly* article in References.)

Mary S. Calderone, for many years the director of the Sex Information and Education Council (SIECUS), advises that we affirm the presence of sexuality in all human beings as a developing and continuing force from birth to death. She quotes Wallace Fulton, one of the founders of SIECUS, as stating that the intent of this organization is "to establish sexuality as a health entity, and to dignify it by openness of approach." (*Sex Education and the Schools,* page 3.) Most educators agree that this healthy and positive attitude toward sex is necessary in any program of sex education.

The content of sex education is important. For adolescents in particular, whose formal sex instruction is too often linked with units on drugs, crime, and other abuses, instruction on sex should be integrated into the regular curriculum. For all children, this integration is important. Adults generally manage to read and learn more about sex in the context of their normal living; they do not separate this learning into a compartment. Books that present sex in the light of normal and positive human interaction generally are regarded as the most positive influences.

Even after it is accepted that sexuality and learning about sex are appropriate to all ages, the specific question of direct, formal instruction remains. How can the questions of a very young child who cannot yet read be handled? How much information is appropriate for a nine-year-old? How can positive values and behaviors be presented in a manner acceptable to a twelve-year-old? How can we, as adults, insure that we are up to date in our information? How can we test that our values and our personal behavior are constructive?

•TRY THIS

Do this activity with a group of classmates or colleagues. Without signing your name, list three questions that you still have regarding sex or sexuality. Your questions may pertain to physiological facts about your own body or that of someone of the opposite sex. Your questions may be about sensations, process, or myths. They may reflect a desire to clarify or to be initially informed.

Place your questions in a box. Draw out the questions one at a time. Who, in the group, has some answers? What sources can you find, in addition to peers, that can provide answers? Answer or attempt to answer every question in this box. How comfortable is the group with this procedure?

Once a procedure is established for the continued education of adults, it is easier to address the education of children. The presentation of information about sex varies according to the developmental level of the student. Infants and very young children receive most of their ideas from experiencing the way that people interact in front of them and with them. Children who are accustomed to seeing their parents in affectionate embraces will probably feel differently about their own sexuality from children whose families are undemonstrative. Children receive many messages from the way adults respond to their games of "Doctor." Adult reactions to children's masturbating also teach lessons. The pattern of how adults answer children's questions in general will guide children to what specific questions that they can risk asking about sex. Adult conversations overheard by children also form a powerful part of the informal educational system. Comments about the behavior of married couples, reactions to films and television, and responses to the way that other adults dress and behave are components of sex instruction.

Most educators, counselors, and psychologists, as well as religious advisers, agree that it is important for adults to help children feel comfortable with their sexuality, curiosity, and behavior. A guilty or furtive feeling because of sexual activity is not helpful. The experts also advise that adults take into consideration the child's physical, intellectual, and emotional development in determining the extent of the information to be given in response to specific questions. You may have heard about young John who asks his mother, "Mommy, where did I come from?" Mother then launches into an elaborate and detailed description from the progress of the egg to possible positions for intercourse. After a long lecture, during which time the child listens attentively, the mother asks John what else he wants to know. "Well," says he, "Timothy comes from Baltimore, and I still don't know where I come from."

On the other hand, when children do ask us pointed and specific questions, we should try not to evade them or give them incomplete answers. When they ask how the sperm and egg got together, they really do want to know about intercourse.

Reproduction education is not all there is to sex education. The facts of reproduction are, of course, an important element, but human beings engage in sexual activity for reasons in addition to the desire to have children. Not all sexual activity includes intercourse. Children want to know about their bodies, how they are constructed, and why. They want to know about the opposite sex. They want to be reassured that they are normal. And they need to grow to accept themselves, their bodies, and their functions with ease and self-liking. An era of Freudian education, which has taught that sex is at the root of all negative behavior, has done some damage. Many adults need to reexamine their own feelings about sex; they must refrain from imposing their mis-education on children.

Of primary importance in any program of education is the interaction between learners and teachers. Good sex education programs benefit from discussions among peer groups and adult leaders, parents, counselors, teachers, and any other interested adults. Multi-aged sessions among students are not recommended because of the readiness of some children to acquire greater detail than others, and because it is generally acknowledged that the younger children are usually satisfied with briefer answers than the older ones. William A. Block, a doctor specializing in sex education, identifies three developmental levels of sexuality: the dormant stage, the awakenened period, and the active stage. He assigns age levels to these stages, but, as with any developmental concept, the ages will vary according to the group and the individual. He suggests that the first stage lasts until age nine, the second until age fourteen, and the third to age nineteen. He does not mention adults because his primary interest is in providing a public school program of sex education for its students. Block (see References) advises adults to take the stage of the child into consideration whenever questions need answering. He asserts that in the dormant stage, children are very inquisitive but have not become intensely concerned about sex. The time of greatest preoccupation is during the awareness period, when sexual curiosity and exploration are high. He believes that this is, perhaps, the most critical time for education.

Most adults draw upon books and other materials to help them in their explanations. Many children actively seek out books and other references to help guide them in their quest for information. There are many books now available that have, as their primary intent, the proper sexual instruction of young children. There is an equally great number of books that instruct without, perhaps, intending to do so. The first category of books is usually in the realm of nonfiction; the second, of course, lies within fiction and fantasy. But all nonfiction is not necessarily successful in teaching the lessons that it purports to communicate. Values and attitudes lie close to the surface, influencing the factual information. Adults and children should be aware of these hidden messages and should respond to them knowingly.

In recent years numerous books have been directed toward a very young audience of preschool and primary school children. Authors and publishers have recognized that children become interested in matters sexual before their teen-age years. Some of the books are consciously written for the parent to serve as interpreter to the young child. The books represent a wide range of attitudes, values, and information and can be used as valuable tools for education.

Many books have been written specifically for sex education. Most are nonfiction and obviously didactic. The illustrations vary from an approach that is carefully objective with clinical diagrams unattached to human bodies, through romanticized, sweet paintings of affectionate parents and amiable babies, to explicit cartoons or photographs depicting sex play and intercourse. The words are equally as varied, including dry, detailed scientific descriptions, sentimental descriptions and euphemisms substituting for anatomical labels, and slyly humorous observations phrased in vernacular terminology.

One of the aims of this chapter is to acquaint concerned adults with the variety, intent, styles, and general usefulness of such books; it is hoped that the adults may thus acquire the resources to help young readers locate the appropriate tools of instruction. Perhaps greater adult familiarity and comfort with the materials will help to remove the restrictions that are often unnecessarily imposed.

SUGGESTED CRITERIA

Whether or not the intent is didactic, books communicating information about sex should take into consideration the reader's developmental level. An appropriate amount of information should be transmitted. Whatever information is included should be accurate, with carefully selected terminology. Some books consciously use vernacular terms because their intent is to eliminate some of the mystery and high-handedness that some adults communicate, while others use the vernacular to demonstrate to their readers that they, the authors, are on the young people's level. Some authors, fearing that clinical terms will confuse the child, use euphemistic language in order to romanticize or idealize sex. Often the euphemisms are confusing. Accurate dictionary terms are preferred to either the vernacular or the euphemistic.

In all books the approach should maintain dignity. Distortions in the guise of humor should be avoided. A balanced presentation, neither dour nor caricatured, is preferable.

Values should be communicated clearly with the author's acknowledgement of the intent. But books should indicate that there are many attitudes and sets of values toward sex and should not impart feelings of guilt if the readers disagree with the message of the book. No book can be acceptable to all people; no book should attempt to make all readers conform to its point of view. Moralizing about behavior is usually not so useful in books as indicating consequences of various behaviors. Care should be taken to avoid perpetuating myths, since values based on mythology have little chance of lasting.

Books should acknowledge and value sexuality in all human beings; sexual activity should not be relegated to young adults. Enjoyment should be presented as well as problems. Sex should be part of healthy living rather than a problem, but when problems are presented, they should be realistic. The solutions should be feasible rather than contrived or romanticized. The "happy ending" should not always be marriage.

Sex education should be more than reproduction education. If the intent is to communicate only the facts of birth, then there should at least be an indication to the reader that there is more to be learned. Care should be taken to include a discussion of the role and function of both sexes; for example, fathers should not be left out of the birth process. In books giving sexual information, both sexes should be invited to learn; boys are inquisitive about girls, and girls about boys. In books addressed to either sex, facts about both sexes should appear.

Stereotypes about the interest, arousability, capability, and behavior of males and females should be avoided. Expectations that marriage is the aim of every woman and that all couples will want to have children should also be handled as opinion rather than rule. Care should be taken to label opinion as such; far too many books present their view of morality as the only proper way. Illustrations should take into account the injunction against stereotypes; multiethnic characters should people these books.

Prurient or demeaning humor should be avoided. Books with titillation as the intent are in danger of imparting negative and uncomfortable lessons rather than constructive ones. The aim of sex education materials should be to make each reader comfortable and informed about his or her sexuality and the processes of sex.

DISCUSSION OF CHILDREN'S BOOKS

BOOKS FOR YOUNG CHILDREN

Most books on this topic for young children describe the birth process. They rarely take into consideration the other aspects of sexuality in a child's life. John Steptoe's *My Special Best Words* is one of the exceptions. In this book, three-year-old Bweela lives with her one-year-old brother and their father. Bweela tries to toilet-train her brother and the two children romp together in the bathroom. They are comfortable with their bodies. The illustrations help to convey the sense of joy and comfort with themselves and each other. As usual, Steptoe is educational at the same time that he is disturbing the complacency of some of the reading public.

The illustrations in Sara Bonnett Stein's *Making Babies* are the most important feature of the book. They are beautiful and informative photographs, showing the universality of sexual curiosity, and reactions to pregnancy and birth. The text, directed toward parents of very young children, is useful, and the suggestions for activities that parents and children can do together to help the communication process are very helpful. The text for the children is not as good. The assumption is conveyed that all normal boys and girls want to grow up to be parents. There is also the statement that dogs mating are "loving each other." But, despite these minor flaws, the book's intention to help the education process of children as young as three years of age is carried out reasonably well.

Another book designed for very young children, Andry and Schepp's *How Babies Are Made*, is also very useful. Although flowers and animals are discussed in addition to human beings, this information does not become confusing. The context is always in terms of the child's wanting to know. The illustrations are pleasant and attractive combinations of paper sculpture; they do not caricature or demean. The text, which is clear and nonmoralizing, uses terminology that is not complex, but is accurate.

Deliberately and successfully avoiding sexist implications is *Did the Sun Shine Before You Were Born?* by Sol and Judith Gordon. The illustrations picture children engaged in different kinds of activities that are not stereotypically gender-linked. Love and affection are illustrated. Options for different lifestyles are presented as normal and viable, with choices presented in many forms. Different heritages are pictured. The entire book presents a balanced, positive, healthy view of life and sex.

Sometimes otherwise excellent books miss the opportunity to educate readers to a balanced sex role perspective. Some of them contribute accuracy and useful details, but imply that the main role of the father is to stand and wait. Perhaps readers should write to the publishers suggesting that these books be revised in light of contemporary needs. Parents would do well to guide their children in the reading of books so that questions will be encouraged and answers provided.

One book useful for the prompting of questions is supposedly designed for seven- to ten-year-olds. But *The Birth of Sunset's Kittens*, by Carla Stevens, could easily be absorbed and enjoyed by younger children, especially if interested adults are present to provide direction. The photographs help to satisfy curiosity in a socially acceptable way. The vocabulary is informative and nonthreatening. Uterus, amnion, placenta, and umbilical cord are described; but for some inexplicable reason, the vagina is described as "a special opening" without ever being called a vagina. Nevertheless, the book is clear and informational enough to be useful with a wide variety of children.

BOOKS FOR OLDER CHILDREN

Nonfiction

Most of the books for children eight years of age and older recognize that the children will be interested in detail and description of the sex act as well as of the process of birth. Most of these books also take into consideration the questions of approaching puberty. The methods of presentation vary widely in the factual books. Depending on the particular intent and point of view of the authors, the books range from objective, almost clinical presentations to intensely personal ones.

Be wary of books whose authors are intolerant of people who disagree with them or who try to convey guilt feelings to those adults who hold different values. Be ready to comment on books with ridiculing humor. Even more important, watch out for material in which too much information is conveyed through words or pictures that will be threatening to young children. When the emphasis is on mature bodies and advanced sex play, the implications may make the young intended audience overly anxious. Some books imply that intercourse always ends in mutual orgasm or that it is always for the purpose of reproduction. Simplistic explanations invite many questions. That is fine; questions should be encouraged. But if a book is misleading, children must learn how to find the questions that will provide them with useful answers.

Wardell Pomeroy's books *Boys and Sex* and *Girls and Sex*, are direct and frank. He addresses readers twelve years of age and older. He treats topics that concern them now, not years later. He speaks about masturbation, sex play, homosexuality, petting, dating, and other questions, including intercourse. He expresses his opinion, but labels them as such and indicates his rationale.

Eric Johnson's book *Love and Sex in Plain Language* is exactly what the title promises. Dealing with personal and social values and with the pleasure of sex as well as some of the problems, it stresses personal responsibility on the part of each individual. The book is aimed at readers as young as ten years of age. It speaks frankly but in a calm and reassuring tone.

Fiction

As has been stated many times, works of fiction, particularly if they are well crafted, can convey lessons more effectively than can many books calculated to teach. The lessons may be unintentional on the part of the author, but they are learned, nevertheless, by impressionable readers. In recent years, fiction has included such previously taboo topics as premarital sex, sex play, homosexuality, and even incest.

A hint of incest occurs in Elizabeth Winthrop's *A Little Demonstration of Affection*. But it turns out that what Jennie fears as an abnormal incestuous desire is, in reality, a simple craving for some physical familial affection.

Jennie's family is singularly undemonstrative. A hug from her brother is enough to make Jennie react so strongly as to imagine all sorts of peculiarities about herself. Jennie is finally helped by her father to understand that her feelings are normal.

Both *I'll Get There. It Better Be Worth the Trip*, by John Donovan, and *The Man without a Face*, by Isabelle Holland, deal briefly with homosexuality. In each case, the hero, a young teen-ager, fears that he has homosexual tendencies. In each case, an older male reassures the hero that love for another male is normal and need not develop into a homosexual relationship. Most books of fiction and nonfiction maintain the attitude that homosexuality is to be avoided at almost all cost, and that homosexuals are "sick" people. The two above-mentioned books handle the situation in a fairly reasonable manner, but the societal fear comes through clearly.

Also dealing with this topic, but in a much more comprehensive and direct manner, is Nancy Garden's *Annie on My Mind*. The story is powerful in its character portrayal and intensity. In this novel, Liza and Annie are lovers, although neither was aware of her own orientation before they met. The development of their relationship is the topic of the story. Also figuring in the plot are two female teachers who are lifelong lovers, and who are punished by the school committee for their sexual preference. The issue is dealt with sensitively, providing a sympathetic view of homosexuality.

Menstruation is a favorite topic in novels written for readers ten years of age and up. Some books deal with the emotional issues and problems created by peers who are entering adolescence. It becomes a competition to see who will begin menstruating first in Judy Blume's *Are You There, God? It's Me, Margaret*. There is so much pressure placed on these girls to grow up that one girl lies about having her period in order to be "one-up" on her friends. Self-image hangs desperately on size of breasts and condition of puberty in this story. Readers should probably be guided through this book by sympathetic adults. Perhaps a box could be set up into which readers of this and any other book could place their questions. Several small-group sessions might be organized to answer the questions. It would be useful if the teacher reads the questions first and comes prepared with some sources of answers.

Judy Blume presents the problems of boys and their entry into puberty in *Then Again, Maybe I Won't*. Tony has nocturnal emissions and uses binoculars to view a female neighbor in the nude. The information may not suffice for inquisitive readers. A question box may help in dealing with this book, but more likely some informal discussion groups in which young people compare their own experiences and feelings would be more helpful.

Norma Klein presents "unconventional" attitudes in two of her books, *Mom, the Wolf Man and Me* and *It's Not What You Expect*. Klein is always direct; she does not deal in subtlety. In *Mom, the Wolf Man and Me*, the young heroine's mother has never been married and Brett does not want her to be. Brett, whose image of marriage is negative, fears that she and her mother will change and become stereotypes if her mother marries. She indicates that she is comfortable with sexual information, having learned all about it at school. She and her mother have a frank, open relationship in which her mother answers all her questions honestly.

In *It's Not What You Expect*, sex is again handled casually. One of the characters becomes pregnant and undergoes an abortion as a logical matter of course. Everyone knows about it and accepts it comfortably. The mother mentions that times have changed since she had *her* abortion, before she was married to the children's father and when she was dating another man. The father's extramarital episode is tolerated. This book can raise some questions about expected modes of behavior and different lifestyles. For fun, students can place the setting of this book in Victorian times to see how that would influence the behavior of the characters. Or students can take each character separately, saying how they would behave in contemporary times if they were in the character's place.

Honor Arundel also discusses controversial sexual behavior in her novels—but she presents the consequences. She also describes the motivations and situations leading up to the problems that arise. In *The Longest Weekend* Eileen is an unwed mother. Her mother is understanding to the point of taking over the care and love of the infant. The author attempts to remain nonjudgmental, but in the end Eileen marries Joel, the father of the child. A number of issues arise here for fruitful discussion. The students can discuss "Who was right?" They can decide what they would have done in Joel's or Eileen's place. They can discuss the book with their parents and ask what their parents would have done in the circumstances that the book describes.

Any discussion of sex is more valuable if parents and children can talk together. Situations can be arranged for peers to have discussions under the guidance or direction of a knowledgeable adult. But, in the long run, parents and children should understand and respect each other's points of view and come to terms with their value systems. Books can help. They can be vehicles for understanding and exploration, but they cannot take the place of close, supportive family interaction. Librarians, teachers, parents, and counselors can accumulate materials that present different approaches and convey an assortment of attitudes in order to have resources on which to base their discussions. No matter what emerges as the selected set of values, it cannot help but be more constructive if it has been influenced by accurate information and by an increased awareness and appreciation of human sexuality.

REFERENCES: SEX

BLOCK, WILLIAM A. *What Your Child Really Wants to know about Sex and Why.* Englewood Cliffs, New Jersey: Prentice-Hall, 1972.
A straightforward presentation, stressing the importance of recognizing children's

sexuality. Freudian orientation. Generally practical advice. Divides children's development of sexuality into three stages: the dormant period, age five to nine; the awakened period, age ten to fourteen; and the active period, age fifteen to nineteen. Recommends patterns of answers to questions about sex depending on the stage of the child. Also suggests some useful activities for the classroom.

BREASTED, MARY. "Nothing but the Facts—of Life," *New York Times Book Review*, 23 September 1973, p. 8.
Prefers good fiction to manuals for learning about sex. Reviews three children's books.

BREWER, JOAN SCHERER. "A Guide to Sex Education Books: Dick Active, Jane Passive," *Bulletin of the Council on Interracial Books for Children*, Vol. 6, Nos. 3 and 4, 1975.
An excellent analysis of the general attitude that books convey about sex. Brewer criticizes the maintenance of the expectation of a passive role for females. She points out the negative way that homosexuality is discussed and comments that bisexuality is rarely discussed. Brewer reviews fifteen sex education books; her comments are incisive and informative.

CAMPBELL, PATRICIA J. *Sex Education Books for Young Adults, 1892–1979*. New York: Bowker, 1979.
Provides a history and analysis of fiction and non-fiction. Each chapter covers a decade. The last chapter contains an annotated guide and selection criteria for these books aimed at an audience of readers twelve years old and up.

CHILD STUDY ASSOCIATION OF AMERICA. *What to Tell Your Child about Sex*, revised ed. New York: Pocket Books, 1974. Paperback.
Discusses sexual development in children up to age seventeen. Excellent explanations presented in nonjudgmental fashion. Useful annotated bibliography. Provides list of questions and answers. An excellent resource.

COUNCIL ON INTERRACIAL BOOKS FOR CHILDREN. *Bulletin* (Special Issue on Homophobia), Vol. 14, Nos. 3 and 4, 1983.
The entire double issue deals with how homosexuality is and should be handled in materials for the child audience.

DEL SOLAR, CHARLOTTE. *Parents' Answer Book*. New York: Grosset and Dunlap, 1969.
Poses questions and supplies answers. Presents myths and helps substitute reality. The questions have been asked by children; the answers indicated often provide choices, depending on the sitation. A useful book.

FEINGOLD, MAXINE. "A Content Analysis of Materials for the Early Sex Education of Children," Unpublished Master's report, Palmer Graduate Library School, Long Island University, Brookville, New York, 1969.
Cites many authorities on developmental aspects of sex. Describes the attributes of sexual development for three stages: three- to four-year-olds, five- to eight-year-olds, and nine- to twelve-year-olds. Recommends that concerned adults make themselves knowledgeable about the stages in order to help select useful materials for helping children understand sex.

FRANK, JOSETTE. "Sexuality in Books for Children," in *Issues in Children's Book Selection*. New York: Bowker, 1973.
Questions what is the appropriate age level for fiction treating sex explicitly. Lists criteria for acceptable books as integrity of purpose, authenticity, moral and social validity, and resolutions offered. Praises several books and suggests that parents, teachers, and librarians recommend acceptable books to young readers.

GRANNIS, CHANDLER B. "Publishers Can Play a Key Role in Sex Education," *Publishers Weekly*, Vol. 203, No. 11, 12 March 1973, pp. 30–31.
A report of a conference combining religious leaders, SIECUS representatives, and publishers' representatives to set guidelines for publishing information about sex. Consensus was that sexuality should be stressed rather than sex. Sexuality includes "love, intimacy, fidelity, family life" and the way that people regard themselves physically.

HILU, VIRGINIA, ed. *Sex Education and the Schools*. New York: Harper & Row, 1957.
Despite the age of this book, it is timely and useful now. The contributors, Mary Calderone, Alan Guttmacher, Millicent McIntosh, and Richard Unsworth, engage in conversation with one another, offering their recommendations for healthy conveying of information and attitude about sex.

JENKINS, C. A., AND MORRIS, JULIE L. "Recommended Books on Gay/Lesbian Themes," in *Bulletin of the Council on Interracial Books for Children*, Vol. 14, Nos. 3 and 4, 1983, pp. 16–19.
More than twenty-five books, mostly for readers over twelve years of age, are described and recommended.

MERCER, JOAN BODGER. "Innocence Is a Cop-Out," *Wilson Library Bulletin*, Vol. 46, No. 2, October 1971, pp. 144–146.
Pleads for recognition that children are reading books at a young age and understanding them, even when topics such as sex and drugs are included. Asks adults not to pretend innocence.

MINNESOTA COUNCIL ON FAMILY RELATIONS. *Family Life Literature and Films: An Annotated Bibliography*, 1972.
Massive annotated bibliography containing references for adults and children on all aspects of sex education as well as other topics relating to family life.

NEUFELD, JOHN. "The Thought, Not Necessarily the Deed: Sex in Some of Today's Juvenile Novels," *Wilson Library Bulletin*, Vol. 46, No. 2, October 1971, pp. 147–152.
Asks authors to write about the whole child, including acknowledgement of sexuality. Praises honesty in books for young people.

POWERS, G. PAT, AND BASKIN, WADE. *Sex Education: Issues and Directions*. New York: Philosophical Library, 1969.
A book of readings including many different points of view. Representatives of many institutions, attitudes, and professions have contributed offerings. Useful sources are listed. Many options are presented.

STANEK, LOU WILLETT. "The Maturation of the Junior Novel: From Gestation to the Pill," in *Issues in Children's Book Selection*. New York: Bowker, 1973.

Presents the difficulties in writing about the adolescent's sexual drive. Analyzes the formula upon which most junior novels are based and criticizes most contemporary books for following the standard formula.

USLANDER, ARLENE S. "Everything You've Always Wanted to Know about Sex Education," *Learning*, Vol. 3, No. 2, October 1974, pp. 34–41.
Useful advice and discussion about how to respond to children's questions in the classroom.

WERSBA, BARBARA. "Sexuality in Books for Children," in *Issues in Children's Book Selection*. New York: Bowker, 1973.
Wants to see more recognition of enjoyment of sexuality in children's books from picture books to novels for young adults. Accuses books of presenting "the Old Morality disguised as the New Sex."

WHITE, EULA T., AND FRIEDMAN, ROBERTA. "Sex Is Not a Four-Letter Word," *Wilson Library Bulletin*, Vol. 46, No. 2, October 1971, pp. 153–162.
The authors discuss sex education programs in schools and recommend a long list of useful references directed at the teenager. A very useful article.

WHITLOCK, KATHERINE, AND DILAPI, ELENA M. "Friendly Fire: Homophobia in Sex Education Literature," in *Bulletin of the Council on Interracial Books for Children*, Vol. 14, Nos. 3 and 4, 1983, pp. 20–23.
Provides guidelines for evaluating sex education materials for treatment of homosexuality.

WOLKSTEIN, DIANE. "Old and New Sexual Messages in Fairy Tales," *Wilson Library Bulletin*, Vol. 46, No. 2, October 1971, pp. 163–166.
Interprets a number of fairy tales as exploring sexuality and responding to sexual needs. Recommends that new tales show sexuality and sensuality as important factors of life.

BIBLIOGRAPHY: SEX

ANDRY, ANDREW C., AND SCHEPP, STEVEN. *How Babies Are Made*. Illustrated by Blake Hampton. New York: Time-Life Books, 1968. (Ages 3–10.)
This book with colorful pictures starts with flowers and animals and then discusses human reproduction. The pictures are a combination of cartoon and collage. They are not at all demeaning or tending to caricature. The text contains accurate information, gently and objectively conveyed. A widely useful book.

ARUNDEL, HONOR. *The Longest Weekend*. New York: Thomas Nelson, 1969. (Ages 12–up.)
Eileen, a young, unwed mother, struggles with her parents' wishes and her own feelings and desires. The author is not judgmental, but the happy ending is that Eileen and Joel (the father of the child) marry. Interesting complications and realistic dialogue make this a good book for discussion.

BENDICK, JEANNE. *What Made You You?* New York: McGraw-Hill, 1971. (Ages 5–8.)

A straightforward book for small children dealing with birth, conception, and growth.

BLUME, JUDY. *Are You There, God? It's Me, Margaret.* New York: Bradbury Press, 1970. Also in paper. (Ages 10–up.)
Margaret is twelve. She and her friends are preoccupied with their physical maturation. They wish that they had large breasts; they talk constantly about menstruation and boys. The story hits home with many pre-adolescent girls.

_____. *Then Again, Maybe I Won't.* New York: Bradbury Press, 1973. Also in paper. (Ages 10–up.)
Tony is a young adolescent learning how to deal responsibly with his new sexual feelings. Blume is explicit about young people's fears and curiosity. In this book she presents the phenomena of nocturnal emissions and uncontrollable erections. She manages to do this in a very humorous context.

BRENNER, BARBARA. *Bodies.* Illustrated by George Ancona. New York: Dutton, 1973. (Ages 8–10.)
A happy combination of didacticism and fun. Sexuality is described as normal. Photographs depict children clothed and unclothed without embarrassment or condescension.

BURGESS-KAHN, JANE. *Straight Talk about Love and Sex for Teenagers.* Boston: Beacon Press, 1979. (12–up.)
Among the topics discussed in this book are dating, falling in love, petting, premarital sex, pregnancy, homosexuality, VD, living together, abortion, marriage, and the family. A generally informative book which includes a selected bibliography and an index.

CALDERONE, MARY S., AND JOHNSON, ERIC W. *The Family Book about Sexuality.* Illustrated by Vivian Cohen. New York: Harper & Row, 1981.
Lengthy, exhaustive treatment of the factual, emotional, and attitudinal aspects of sex. Appropriate for adolescents of both sexes. Emphasis on normalcy of curiosity and feelings. Non-judgmental; matter-of-fact, explicitly illustrated. Considers responsibility as well as function. Very well done.

CLIFTON, LUCILLE. *The Times They Used to Be.* Illustrated by Susan Jeschler, New York: Holt, Rinehart and Winston, 1974. (Ages 10–up.)
Tassie, thirteen years old, knows nothing about sex. When she begins menstruating, she thinks that it is "sin" breaking out of her body. Her friend, Sylvia (the narrator of the story), is also ignorant. Finally, Sylvia's mother explains about menstruation to both of them. The clearest point is that ignorance leads to fear and misinterpretation.

COLE, JOANNA. *My Puppy Is Born.* Photographs by Jerome Wexler. New York: Morrow, 1973. (Ages 5–up.)
A factual book about the birth of puppies. The photographs are in black and white, but they are excellent. The photographs show the actual birth of a puppy, the sac being broken by its mother, and the new puppies nursing.

COLE, JOANNA, AND EDMONDSON, MADELEINE. *Twins: The Story of Multiple Births.* Illustrated by Salvatore Raciti. New York: Morrow, 1972. (Ages 10–12.)

The logistics of multiple births are explained and illustrated to show how cells and eggs divide. In this easily understood scientific explanation, fraternal and identical twins are identified. The effects of fertility drugs on multiple births are explained. Simple terms and good illustrations abound. Could be read to a young child.

DAY, BETH, AND LILEY, MARGARET. *The Secret World of the Baby*. Photographs by Hennert Nilsson, Suzanne Szasz et al. New York: Random House. 1968. (Ages 10–up.)
A well-illustrated account of the physiological and psychological development of a child from conception to several years after birth.

DESCHWEINITZ, KARL. *Growing Up*, 4th ed. New York: Macmillan, 1965. (Ages 7–11.)
A detailed and informative book on how babies are born. Uses animals as examples, and relates these directly to humans. Photographs and drawings are used as illustrations. The terminology is accurate and not overpowering. Gives the message that reproduction is the reason for sexual intercourse and states that people marry those whom they wish to be the parent of their children. These value judgments might lead to a discussion or debate.

DONOVAN, JOHN. *I'll Get There. It Better Be Worth the Trip*. New York: Harper & Row, 1969. Also in paper. (Ages 12–up.)
Davy, among his other problems, fears that he has homosexual tendencies when he and his friend engage in some affectionate play. His father helps him to deal with his fears.

DRAGONWAGON, CRESCENT. *Wind Rose*. Illustrated by Ronald Himler. New York: Harper & Row, 1976. (Ages 5–9.)
A poetic, joyful celebration of the fruits of a loving relationship between a man and a woman. The mother explains to Wind Rose all of the details of her conception and birth that are suitable for her level of understanding.

GARDEN, NANCY. *Annie on My Mind*. New York: Farrar, Straus & Giroux, 1982. (Ages 12–up.)
Liza and Annie are lovers. They have moved into this relationship gradually and reluctantly, but it is a solid one. The story includes two female teachers who have been lovers for many years, and who are punished because of Liza and Annie's using their house as a rendezvous. The book dispels many stereotypes about lesbians, and offers a sensitive portrayal of the characters and the choices they make. A powerful work.

GIRARD, LINDA WALVOORD. *You Were Born on Your Very First Birthday*. Illustrated by Christina Kieffer. Chicago: Whitman, 1983. (Ages 5–8.)
Father and mother love each other, show affection and joy in the birth of their child. Contains a description of the process from embryo to birth.

GORDON, SOL. *Girls Are Girls and Boys Are Boys*. Illustrated by Frank C. Smith. New York: John Day, 1975. (Ages 5–8.)
This excellent book reflects the author's awareness of a multiethnic audience. It focuses on an acknowledgment of the needs and emotions of both girls and boys. The language is clear, communicating information and constructive values directly.

GORDON, SOL AND JUDITH. *Did the Sun Shine Before You Were Born?* Illustrated by Vivien Cohen. New York: Third Press–Joseph Okpaku, 1974. (Ages 5–8.)
Realistic Illustrations. Excellent explanations. Clear, accurate terminology. Many incidental learnings are included. There is a boy with a doll, a female doctor, loving sexual relations (rather than clinical), multiethnic representation, option not to get married and/or have children, picturing of different kinds of families (including one-parent families), sexual organs depicted without exaggeration, distortion, or romanticizing. A balanced view, in general.

HALL, LYNN. *Sticks and Stones.* Chicago: Follett, 1972. (Ages 12–up.)
Seventeen-year-old Tom Naylor's life is almost ruined by gossip that he is a homosexual. The boy is forced to re-evaluate his friendship with another boy, and his own sense of right and wrong when he comes to an almost tragic decision about his life.

HANCKEL, FRANCES, AND CUNNINGHAM, JOHN. *A Way of Love, A Way of Life: A Young Person's Introduction to What It Means to Be Gay.* Photographs by Alix Olson; Illustrations by Larry Stein. New York: Lothrop, Lee and Shepard Books, 1979. (Ages 12–up.)
Attempts to present the view that gender identity and erotic preference are established very early in life and should be accepted as they are. Portraits are included of representative gays living fulfilled, productive lives. The authors see the primary audience as young people who are gay or uncertain of their sexual orientation; it is informative for others as well. This forthright look at sexual preferences defines terms, explains male and female physical and sexual development, and various kinds of sexual relationships. It is frank, explains terms used in slang as well as formal usage. The authors include extensive references and an index. This book is for the sophisticated reader with a basic knowledge of physical and emotional sexuality.

HETTLINGER, RICHARD F. *Growing Up with Sex.* New York: Seabury Press, 1970. Also in paper. (Ages 12–up.)
An informative and comprehensive book dealing with all aspects of sex.

HODGES, BRUCE E. *How Babies Are Born—The Story of Birth for Children.* Illustrated by Richard Cuffari. New York: Simon and Schuster, 1967. Also in paper. (Ages 7–up.)
Terry's mother is going to have a baby, so Terry's father, a doctor, takes the opportunity to explain the process of birth and conception through many comparisons between animals and humans.

HOLLAND, ISABELLE. *The Man without a Face.* Philadelphia: Lippincott, 1972. (Ages 12–up.)
Charles is emotionally drained by his mother's multiple divorces and his elder sister's cruelty to him. He becomes attached to his tutor, fears he is sexually attracted to him, learns later that the tutor is a homosexual, and ultimately comes to recognize his own feelings as that of admiration and gratefulness. The tutor does not take advantage of the boy's love even though he loves the boy.

JOHNSON, ERIC W. *Love and Sex in Plain Language*, revised ed. Illustrated by Russ Hoover. Philadelphia: Lippincott, 1973. Also in paper. (Ages 10–up.)

A discussion of personal and social values surrounding love, sex, birth, and sex-related problems. Talks plainly of erection, pleasurable sex relations, and the fact that humans engage in sexual activities for reasons other than reproduction. Stresses personal responsibility. A very informative, balanced presentation.

JOHNSON, ERIC W., AND JOHNSON, CORINNE B. *Love and Sex and Growing-Up*. Philadelphia: Lippincott, 1970. (Ages 10–12.)
A less complex, less specific volume than *Love and Sex in Plain Language*, this presentation is intended to prepare prepubescent readers for the greater mass of information to follow. It focuses on clarification of the reproduction process, and on a tolerance for different social attitudes.

KLEIN, NORMA. *It's Not What You Expect*. New York: Pantheon, 1973. Paperback: Avon. (Ages 12–up.)
Sex is handled casualy and in line with the "new" morality in this book. Abortion is the logical solution to unplanned pregnancy and is accepted without trauma by the characters; further, it is not punished. Premarital sexual intercourse is the expected mode. All the characters are comfortable in their heterosexual relationships. The father is permitted to have a summer affair and is welcomed home without recrimination. The mother was more experienced sexually before marriage than the father was. This is a book that can generate much discussion.

_____. *Mom, the Wolf Man and Me.* New York: Pantheon, 1972. Also in paper. (Ages 10–up.)
More an indication of alternative lifestyles than informative about sex, the story tells of Brett and her mother, who, up to now, has never been married. Brett doesn't mind it when her mother's male friend sleeps over, but she does object to her mother's plan to get married. Brett's mother has always been frank with Brett, and Brett has received sex education at school, and is informed about many matters, including contraception.

LANGONE, JOHN. *Like Love Lust*. Boston: Little, Brown, 1980. (Ages 12–up.)
Not a "guide" or "how to" book on sex but one which emphasizes "caring, sharing, communication." The author explores emotions, values, raises questions about human relationships including sex, pornography, homosexuality, and prostitution.

LEVENSON, SAM. *A Time for Innocence*. Illustrated by Whitney Darrow, Jr. New York: Simon and Schuster, 1969. (Ages 8–12.)
"A kid's eye view of the Facts of Life" is the subtitle of this very humorous book filled with the misinformation children have about sex.

LIPKE, JEAN. *Birth*. Illustrated by Robert Fontaine. Minneapolis: Lerner Publications, 1972. (Ages 5–up.)
A factual account of birth, delivery, and the baby after birth. The book explains the stages of labor.

MAY, JULIAN. *How We Are Born*. Illustrated by Michael Hampshire. Chicago: Follett, 1969. (Ages 8–12.)
An illustrated book about how we are born, with love being the key incentive for enjoying sex and bearing children.

MAY, JULIAN. *Living Things and Their Young*. Illustrated by Don Merghan. Chicago: Follett, 1969. (Ages 8–12.)
This book describes the differences and similarities between animal and human births.

_____. *Man and Woman*. Illustrated by Tak Murakin. Chicago: Follett, 1969. (Ages 8–12.)
A book dealing simply and expressively with intercourse, love, birth, and the process of becoming an adult.

McCOY, KATHY, AND WIBBELSMAN, CHARLES. *The Teenage Body Book*. New York: Pocket Books, 1978. (Ages 12–up.)
Topics include male and female body development, appearance, birth control, medical needs of young adults, pregnancy, parenthood, venereal disease. The format is sample questions, followed by answers and elaboration on the topic. Clear illustrations accompany the text. A lengthy appendix gives state by state guide to adolescent health and birth control clinics, as well as further reading.

MILLER, JANE. *Birth of a Foal*. New York: Scholastic, 1977. (Ages 5–8.)
A factual story with pictures about the birth and care of a new foal—a Welsh Mountain Pony. Not only does the story convey the physical, but also the emotional needs of the new foal and the mother.

POMEROY, WARDELL B. *Boys and Sex,* revised ed. New York: Delacorte Press, 1981. Also in paper. (Ages 12–up.)
Speaks directly and clearly about sex play, masturbation, homosexuality, intercourse, and other questions that boys and girls ask. Girls would also benefit from reading it.

POMEROY, WARDELL B. *Girls and Sex*, revised ed. New York: Delacorte Press, 1981. Also in paper. (Ages 12–up.)
Boys would also benefit from reading this. Stresses positive self-concept. Expresses strong opinions on topics such as the positive value of petting and the negative consequences of dating married men.

PURSELL, MARGARET STANFORD. *A Look at Birth*. Illustrated by Maria S. Forrai. Minneapolis: Learner's Publications, 1978. (Ages 6–10.)
Begins with a picture of a couple embracing and explains that together a man and woman are able to create a child. The story describes the stages of pregnancy through delivery. Home birth is mentioned, although the photographs of the delivery take place in a hospital. The father and other siblings are active participants.

READING, J. P. *Bouquets for Brimbal*. New York: Harper & Row, 1980. (Ages 12–up.)
Macy and Annie are best friends. Although Macy does not know it, Annie is a lesbian. Both girls become involved in sexual relationships during the summer that they are working at a summer stock theater. At first, Macy cannot tolerate her friend's involvement with a woman, but in the end the two young women resume a stronger, more mature friendship.

RUDOLPH, MARGUERITA. *Look At Me*. Illustrated by Carla Kuskin. New York: McGraw-Hill, 1967. (Ages 4–6.)

An explanation, in poetry, of a child's body parts and physical features. Designed to give children understanding of, and pride in their bodies.

RUSHNELL, ELAINE EVANS. *My Mom's Having a Baby*. New York: Grosset & Dunlap, 1978. (Ages 5–12.)
Based on the Emmy Award winning "ABC Afterschool Specials" program, contains drawings and photographs from the teleplay. The story is about a boy whose parents are about to have another baby. When the boy has his physical checkup, the doctor makes arrangements to show him and his friends a cartoon film about reproduction. Some myths about reproduction are discussed as well as the facts.

SCOPPETTONE, SANDRA. *Happy Endings Are All Alike*. New York: Harper & Row, 1979. (Ages 12–up.)
Jaret and Peggy love each other. They are required to decide how they will resolve the societal pressures placed on them because of their lesbian relationship. Male chauvinism and rape are included in the drama.

_____. *Trying Hard to Hear You*. New York: Harper & Row, 1981. Also in paper. (Ages 12–up.)
Jeff and Phil become involved in a homosexual relationship. The story unravels the events of a summer and the revelation of this relationship to their peers. The subject and events are handled realistically in the book, and the conclusion does not dispel the boys' choice of sexuality, or make any value judgments.

SEVERANCE, JANE. *When Megan Went Away*. Illustrated by Tea Schook. Chapel Hill, North Carolina: Lollipop Power, 1979. (Ages 7–12.)
Shannon and her mother are unhappy because Megan, her mother's lover, has moved out of their house. The feelings a child experiences when one of the nurturing adults in the house has left are well stated here. The difference in this book is that it involves a lesbian relationship.

SHEFFIELD, MARGARET. *Where Do Babies Come From?* Illustrated by Sheila Bewley. New York: Knopf, 1973. (Ages 7–10.)
The illustrations in this book are a major asset. They are paintings of real-looking people—frank but not titillating. They contain no distortions and are not idealized; their realism is not frightening. The text is a reasonable companion to the pictures. It is direct and utilizes accurate terminology. The information is not so complex as to be confusing but contains enough detail to be useful with children across a wide age span.

SHOWERS, PAUL AND KAY SPERRY. *Before You Were a Baby*. Illustrated by Ingrid Fetz. New York: Crowell, 1968. (Ages 8–10.)
The story begins with cells under the microscope and ends when the baby comes. It is very accurately and sensitively told. Could be read to a young child.

SIMON, NISSA. *Don't Worry, You're Normal: A Teenager's Guide to Self-Health*. New York: Crowell, 1982. (Ages 11–up.)
Direct, clearly conveyed information, using accurate terminology, and avoiding all condescension, this helpful book talks about the details of sexual development,

sexuality, sexual behavior, and other issues of concern to adolescents. The contraception section lacks only a discussion of the cervical cap. Otherwise, the material seems comprehensive and specific.

STEICHEN, EDWARD. *The Family of Man*. New York: Museum of Modern Art, 1955. (All ages.)
A collection of photographs of people from sixty-eight nations—their struggles and their love, likenesses and differences. Included in context of the cycle of life are pictures of lovers, marriage ceremonies, pregnant women and babies being born, held and nursed. The book leads the reader through a beautiful collection of pictures and some relevant poetry.

STEIN, SARA BONNETT. *Making Babies*. Photographs by Doris Pinney. New York: Walker, 1974. (Ages 5-8.)
Another in the Open Family Series. It is a discussion of the importance of an open atmosphere for growing up, understanding sex, love, birth, and families. The photographs and the text respond to a very beginning level of inquiry. The value system is somewhat imposed in this book; dogs are described as "loving" each other when they are mating and it is presumed that all boys and girls want to be parents. For those who want these values conveyed, this is an excellent book.

STEPTOE, JOHN. *My Special Best Words*. New York: Viking, 1974. (Ages 5-8.)
Bweela, three years old, lives with her one-year-old brother Javaka and her father. Javaka is not yet toilet-trained, so Bweela teaches him. The book is full of "special" words, including the family's personal bathroom language. The illustrations are explicit: Javaka has a penis. A frank, educational, and endearing book.

STEVENS, CARLA. *The Birth of Sunset's Kittens*. Photographs by Leonard Stevens. New York: Young Scott Books, 1969. (Ages 7-10.)
A clear and sensitive book picturing and discussing the birth of four kittens. The transition to information about humans is well made.

WINTHROP, ELIZABETH. *A Little Demonstration of Affection*. New York: Harper & Row, 1975. (Ages 12-up.)
Jenny fears that she has incestuous feelings toward her brother, Charles. Her family is undemonstrative, never showing affection outwardly. Jenny is so moved by her brother's hugging her that she fears she is abnormal. Eventually her father helps her to work out her feelings.

YOLEN, JANE. *The Gift of Sarah Barker*. New York: Viking 1981. (Ages 11-up.)
Two young Shaker teenagers fall in love. The characters are well-drawn as is the dilemma which faces Abel and Sarah: how to reconcile their feelings of love for each other with the edicts of their religious community which, among other things, strictly enforces separation of the sexes. Sexuality and love are treated gently and with honesty and respect.

ZAPLEEN, SIMONE. *Mommy, Where Do Babies Come From?* Illustrated by Tina Cacciola. New York: Platt and Munk, 1974. (Ages 5–8.)
Two children learn about many different kinds of birth on their search to discover where babies come from.

ZINDEL, PAUL. *My Darling, My Hamburger*. New York: Harper & Row, 1969. Also in paper. (Ages 12–up.)
A novel dealing with abortion, premarital sex, and interpersonal relationships.

FOUR

GENDER ROLES

WHAT WAS BEGUN MORE THAN ONE HUNDRED YEARS AGO as women's battle for the vote has broadened today into a quest for equality of opportunity and respect for both men and women. People of all classes have become conscious of the feminist movement and of the issues involved in it. Men, too, have added their voices and energy, recognizing that liberation from stereotypic and self-destructive roles is essential for everyone, not only for women.

Although media such as television, radio, motion pictures, magazines, newspapers, comic strips, adult books, and children's books continue to produce a number of traditionally stereotyped programs, situations, and characters, they also reflect the growing awareness of the transition in gender role definitions and behaviors. The trend is a positive one, signifying the concerns of an increasingly independent and enlightened public.

Many research studies by psychologists, teachers, and professionals in affiliated areas have confirmed the abuses of the stereotypes of gender roles. One significant study by Broverman et al. (see References) concludes that clinical psychologists have regularly defined anything but conventional gender role behavior as abnormal. This definition extends to characteristics beyond behavior and indicates that male characteristics are valued far above female. The authors of the article contend that "abstract notions of health will tend to be more influenced by the greater social value of masculine stereotypic characteristics than by the lesser valued feminine stereotypic characteristics" (p. 1). The study goes on to demonstrate that the concept of the healthy adult and the healthy male are congruent, while the concept of the healthy female differs from that of the healthy adult. Aggression, independence, objectivity, leadership, sense of adventure, ambition, self-confidence, and logic are among those valued male characteristics that are considered unhealthy for women to exhibit.

•TRY THIS

Recognizing that each of us is at a different level from everyone else in our attitudes toward masculine and feminine characteristics and roles, complete the following chart to inform yourself more completely about your own position. Be honest with yourself; no one else need see this. The purpose of this self-test is to help you recognize and articulate your own attitudes so that you can examine the areas that are likely to influence you in your work with children. If you are uncomfortable with some of your responses, use this information to determine what your next step will be.

Attribute	Admirable in Men/Women/Both/Neither				Usually found in Men/Women/Both/Neither			
Intelligence								
Health								
Compassion								
Physical strength								
Good grooming								
Ambition								
Assertiveness								
Acquiescence								
Loquacity								
Sexual appeal								
Flirtatiousness								
Obedience								
Tenacity								
Silence								
Good manners								
Strong emotions								
Self-control								
Quick temper								

The assigned female characteristics of being talkative, tactful, gentle, religious, neat, vain, quiet, and dependent on others for security are considered to be signs of emotional problems in males and in the generalized category of "adult" when evidenced to any great extent. The authors of the study suggest that clinicians examine their own biases in order to serve their clients well. They conclude: "The cause of mental health may be better served if both men and women are encouraged toward maximum realization of individual potential rather than to an adjustment to existing restrictive sex roles" (p. 7).

The psychologists have not caused the problem. They are reflecting the attitudes that society has consistently held about men and women who deviate from the expected norm. We are moving slowly from this position, but any change is still a battle that we must wage with care. The gains that have been made are that women have moved more into men's positions. That is, women wear clothes styled like men's, take jobs that have traditionally been reserved for men, and adopt some "male" behaviors, such as greater independence, admission of ambition, and carefully controlled assertiveness. The women's movement has educated the general public considerably.

Nevertheless, a great gap still remains between the new attitudes and behaviors that demonstrate them. Men who take on women's tasks tend to be looked at askance. Men who are gentle, passive, self-effacing, religious, and emotional open themselves to criticism. Though few people question the desire of women to climb to the level of male esteem, they wonder why any man would consent to give up his superior position. Their doubts are understandable. Men, men's tasks, male characteristics, and male behaviors generally remain those valued over corresponding female categories. Certain men are apprehensive about their ability to remain independent and secure without the measuring rod of the "inferior" women beneath them. To some minds, there are, in addition, questions about the effect equal job opportunity will have on the economy; about the future of the family with so many mothers working, and about the rising divorce rate, which is attributed by some people to the newfound independence and opportunities for women.

Once people become aware of their preconceptions and fears, they can then begin to deal with today's realities. We are a society in transition—in which women and men can govern their own behavior, maintain the traditional mode, move dramatically beyond it, or adopt some middle ground. It is important that everyone have a sense of the options available to them so that they may choose consciously and productively.

People's roles are linked with their personality characteristics. Just as male traits are valued above female, so, too, male roles are the more favored ones. Housekeeping, child nurturing, nursing, serving as a flight attendant, and other jobs traditionally assigned to women are regarded as inferior to positions conventionally reserved for men. A doctor is more valued than a nurse, a pilot more than a flight attendant, an athlete more than a cheerleader. Until recently, young girls did not aspire to positions of authority. Female lawyers, police, physicians, judges, and pilots are still considered to be the exception and, indeed, the "strange ones" in some areas.

An anecdote circulating among many women's groups concerns the attitudes of these females toward themselves: the riddle was told at a party of a man and his son who were involved in a tragic automobile accident. The father was killed and the son was rushed to the hospital for emergency surgery. Just before performing the operation the surgeon looked down at the child and exclaimed, "My God, that's my son!" The question is, how could that be? None of the people at the party could come up with the right answer. They guessed that the surgeon was mistaken, that it was a long-lost son, or that the dead man was the boy's stepfather. Although the people at the party were all physicians and surgeons, both male and female, not one of them guessed that the surgeon was the boy's mother! Similarly, when children in school are queried as to their occupational aspirations, most girls continue to select those jobs that are designated as conventionally open to females, while most boys select those assigned to conventional adult males, despite the fact that their parents might be employed in unstereotypic positions.

There are, of course, those occupations that are considered to be lower status jobs, which, nevertheless, are reserved for men. Ditchdigging (at least here in the United States), heavy janitorial work, professional gardening, street cleaning, and garbage collecting, even dishwashing, are considered to be in the male domain when they are performed for payment. Some of these jobs are slowly being opened to females, in approximately the same proportions and with the same public reaction of shock as in the more highly prestigious areas. We see female toll collectors, road workers, truck and bus drivers, and gasoline station attendants. On the other hand, we are also beginning to notice more male nursery-school teachers, telephone operators, flight attendants and nurses. The number of males taking hitherto female assignments is not as great as the movement in the other direction, but it is discernible.

•TRY THIS

Draw up a list of occupations that you believe are primarily the responsibility of men. Draw up a similar list of occupations for women. Rank them by prestige, salary level, and interest. Present the list, without the gender designation, to an elementary school class. Have the students mark which jobs they feel are available to them. Compare the sex of the students with your designated list; discuss the results with the students.

One of the dangers of any movement is that it will go too far and become too extreme in its direction. Most advocates of women's rights are careful to say that women should feel comfortable if they have decided not to join the paid labor force. If women choose to remain full-time housekeepers and mothers, that choice should be supported. But information and encouragement about all available career and leisure-time options should be communicated to everyone. Similarly, males and females should feel free to behave as they choose without other people's constraints being forced upon them, as long as they are within legal and ethical boundaries. Society, however, has exerted such a strong influence on gender role behavior that sometimes it is difficult to say whether a certain role is a person's true inclination or whether that person has simply been socialized into thinking that it is. Today's educators, counselors, and leaders in general have the responsibility of presenting models and providing materials that expand people's options.

Language has been used as an effective tool for both imprisonment in, and release from, gender role constraints. A "spinster" is generally an object of pity and derision; a "bachelor" is to be envied. Professors and administrators are referred to as "he"; teachers are "she." The universal pronoun, until recently, has been "he." "Man" has stood for person, and we have no pronouns in the singular form that represent both males and females. Some attempts have been made to create new pronouns, but it is this author's opinion that the pronoun "they" will soon come to be both singular and plural, representing the generic form. In fact, in 1974, the NCTE, in its *Guidelines for Non-Sexist Language in NCTE Publications*, indicated that "they" and "their" could be used as singular generic pronouns.

The use of "person," rather than "man," is fairly widespread if somewhat awkward. Fireperson, mailperson, chairperson, and others will probably be replaced with short forms of the terms or with different names entirely—firefighter, letter carrier or postal worker, and chair, or head, are preferable terms.

Books for children have reflected societal attitudes in limiting choices and maintaining discrimination. Most traditional books show females dressed in skirts or dresses even when they are engaged in activities inappropriate for this sort of costume. Illustrations also have conventionally placed females in passive observer roles, while males have been pictured as active. Studies have demonstrated time and time again that illustrations confirm the subordinate, less valued role for the female, while stressing the active, adventuresome, admirable role for the male. (See annotated References for specific examples.) Often a happy ending for a story occurs when a "tomboy" reforms and becomes a "proper" young lady. When a female is permitted to retain her active qualities, it is usually made clear to the reader that she is the notable exception and that all the other girls in the story are "normal"; that is, interested in dolls and clothing, passive, obedient, graceful, and conventionally pretty.

Publishers of children's reading texts sometimes consciously maintain this situation because they try to appeal to boys' interests. Their contention has been that, since most of the children who are in need of remedial reading are boys, boys should have stories that will especially appeal to them. They have not been as concerned with girls because they have subscribed to the belief that girls will read anything but that boys stay away from stories that have girls as the main characters. This phenomenon has held true to a certain degree. Some boys have been taught to be embarrassed if they enjoy fairy tales and stories with emotional relationships. But although girls may read a greater variety of books, boys enjoy books that have active female characters. Pippi Longstocking, Charlotte and Fern in E. B. White's *Charlotte's Web*, Mary and Laura in the Laura Ingalls Wilder series, and Alice in Carroll's *Alice in Wonderland* attract boys and girls who enjoy reading well-constructed stories. All readers relate to heroes, male and female, who are well balanced in their action and inventiveness.

Publishers have now recognized that sexist bias harms everyone, girls and boys, women and men. Many publishers of children's texts issue guidelines to authors and artists to assist them in writing nonsexist, nonracist books. Some of these are listed in References at the end of this chapter. Readers may wish to adapt and adopt those that seem most pertinent.

SUGGESTED CRITERIA

While not every book can adhere to all of the criteria, a library or classroom collection should contain enough of an array so that all of the criteria are, at least, encountered by the children at one time or another. Good literature usually presents no problem in this regard.

Wherever possible, characters should be individuals, consistent with their own personalities and the context of their situations. Males and females can be portrayed negatively, provided they appear in an individualized setting rather than in a stereotypic fashion, and if the negative characteristics are not generalized to include all people of that character's gender.

The same kind of sensitivity should be displayed toward genders as a group as for any heritage; that is, the same attention should be paid to avoiding common stereotypes of occupation, reaction, or behavior.

Occupations should, within the context of literary consistency, be gender-free. Women and men should be pictured doing similar tasks and with roughly the same distribution of responsibility and prestige. In at least some books parents should function both as parents and in their other occupations. Both fathers and mothers should be shown as responsible for care of the house, children, and decisions about their lives.

Attributes such as mechanical competence should not be restricted by sex. Achievements should be judged equally, not through a filter of gender role differences. A woman should not be complimented for throwing a ball well "for a girl." Nor should a man be praised for taking care of a house "as competently as a woman could."

Cooperation between males and females should be part of the action of some books. Competition should not be the sole mode of relating.

Clothing should be functional and differentiated. Males and females should be dressed in clothing appropriate to their activities, economic situation, and historical setting, and consistent with their personalities, rather than wearing a gender-stereotyped "uniform."

Females need not always be weaker, shorter, or more delicate than males. A normal range of differences is preferable. Illustrations showing real people in real situations convey a message well. Imaginative and impressionistic illustrations can also be very important in affirming or combating stereotypes.

Both males and females should be independent when appropriate, and dependent upon each other when that is in context. Males and females should each be logical or emotional, depending on the situation. Above all, both males and females should be treated with dignity and respect for their individual characteristics.

Language that indicates bias should be avoided. The McGraw-Hill Book Company provides thorough recommendations regarding the use of language. The suggestions include a number of situations in which care should be exercised in the use of language and provide excellent examples of appropriate terms. Following are excerpts from the guidelines.

MCGRAW-HILL GUIDELINES FOR EQUAL TREATMENT OF THE SEXES

In references to humanity at large, language should operate to include women and girls. Terms that tend to exclude females should be avoided whenever possible.

The word *man* has long been used not only to denote a person of male gender, but also generically for humanity at large. To many people today, however, the word *man* has become so closely associated with the first meaning (a male human being) that they consider it no longer broad enough to be applied to any person or to human beings as a whole. In deference to this position, alternative expressions should be used in place of *man* (or derivative constructions used generically to signify humanity at large) whenever such substitutions can be made without producing an awkward or artificial construction. In cases where *man*-words must be used, special efforts should be made to ensure that pictures and other devices make explicit that such references include women.

Here are some possible substitutions for *man*-words:

no	*yes*
mankind	humanity, human beings, human race, people
man's achievements	human achievements, people's achievements
If a man drove 50 miles at 60 mph …	If a person (or driver) drove 50 miles at 60 mph …

no	*yes*
the best man for the job	the best person (or candidate) for the job
man-made	artificial, synthetic, manufactured, constructed, of human origin
grow to manhood	grow to adulthood, grow to manhood or womanhood, mature

The English language lacks a generic singular pronoun signifying *he* or *she*, and therefore it has been customary and grammatically sanctioned to use masculine pronouns in expressions such as "one . . . *her*," "anyone . . . *he*," and "each child opens *his* book." Nevertheless, avoid when possible the pronouns *he*, *him*, and *his* in reference to the hypothetical person or humanity in general.

Various alternatives may be considered:

1. Reword to eliminate unnecessary gender pronouns.
2. Recast into the plural.
3. Replace the masculine pronouns with *one, you, he or she, her or his*, as appropriate. (Use *he or she* and its variations sparingly to avoid clumsy prose.)
4. Alternate male and female expressions and examples.
5. To avoid severe problems of repetition or inept wording, it may sometimes be best to use the generic *he*, but to add in the preface and as often as necessary in the text, emphatic statements to the effect that the masculine pronouns are being used for succinctness and are intended to refer to both females and males.
6. Some authors alternate *he* and *she* in successive chapters, and use both as the generic pronoun.

These guidelines can only suggest a few solutions to difficult problems of rewording. The proper solution in any given passage must depend on the context and on the author's intention. For example, it would be wrong to pluralize in contexts stressing a one-to-one relationship, as between teacher and child. In such cases, the expression *he or she* or either *he* or *she* as appropriate will be acceptable.

Occupational terms ending in *man* should be replaced whenever possible by terms that can include members of either sex unless they refer to a particular person who is in fact male. . . .

Different pronouns should not be linked with certain work or occupations on the assumption that the worker is always (or usually) female or male. Instead, either pluralize or use *he or she* and *she or he*. . . .

Males should not always be first in order of mention. Instead, alternate the order, sometimes using: *women and men, gentlemen and ladies, she or he, her or his*. . . .

Language that assumes all readers are male should be avoided. . . .

The language used to designate and describe females and males should treat the sexes equally. Parallel language should be used for women and men. For example, in speaking of people attending college, "co-eds" should not be used. "Students" serves equally well for males and females. Note that *lady* and *gentleman, wife* and *husband*, and *mother* and *father* are role words. *Ladies* should be used for women only when men are being referred to as *gentlemen*. Similarly, women should be called *wives* and *mothers* only when men are referred to as *husbands* and *fathers*. Like a male shopper, a woman in a grocery store should be called a *customer*, not a *housewife*.

Women should be identified by their own names (e.g., Indira Gandhi). They should not be referred to in terms of their roles as wife, mother, sister, or daughter unless it is in these roles that they are significant in context. Nor should they be identified in terms of their marital relationships (Mrs. Ghandi) unless this brief form is stylistically more convenient (than, say, Prime Minister Gandhi) or is paired up with similar references to men.

A woman should be referred to by name in the same way that a man is. Both should be called by their fully names, by first or last name only, or by title.

Unnecessary reference to or emphasis on a woman's marital status should be avoided. Whether married or not, a woman may be referred to by the name by which she chooses to be known, whether her name is her original name or her married name.

Whenever possible a term should be used that includes both sexes. Unnecessary references to gender should be avoided.

Terms for women should maintain the same dignity accorded to terms for men.

no	*yes*
the fair sex, the weaker sex	*women*
the distaff side	*the female side* or *line*
the girls or *the ladies* (when adult females are meant)	*the women*
girl, as in: I'll have my *girl* check that.	I'll have my *secretary* (or my *assistant*) check that. (Or use the person's name.)
lady used as a modifier, as in *lady* lawyer	*lawyer* (A woman may be identified simply through the choice of pronouns: *The lawyer made her summation to the jury.* Try to avoid gender modifiers altogether. When you *must* modify, use *woman* or *female,* as in: *a course on women writers,* or *the airline's first female pilot.*)
the little woman, the better half, the ball and chain	*wife*
female-gender word forms, such as *authoress, poetess, Jewess*	*author, poet, Jew*

no	yes
female-gender or diminutive word forms, such as *suffragette, usherette, aviatrix*	*suffragist, usher, aviator* (or *pilot*)
libber (a put-down)	*feminist, liberationist*
sweet young thing	*young woman; girl*
co-ed (as a noun)	*student*

(*Note:* Logically, *co-ed* should refer to any student at a co-educational college or university. Since it does not, it is a sexist term.)

housewife	*homemaker* for a person who works at home, or rephrase with a more precise or more inclusive term.
career girl or *career woman*	name the woman's profession: *attorney Ellen Smith; Maria Sanchez, a journalist* or editor or business executive or doctor or lawyer or agent
cleaning woman, cleaning lady, or *maid*	*housekeeper, house* or *office cleaner*
The sound of drilling disturbed the housewives in the neighborhood.	The sound of drilling disturbed everyone within earshot (or everyone in the neighborhood).
Housewives are feeling the pinch of higher prices.	Consumers (customers or shoppers) are feeling the pinch of higher prices.

Women should be treated as part of the rule, not as the exception. Generic terms, such as doctor and nurse, should be assumed to include both men and women, and modified titles such as "woman doctor" or "male nurse" should be avoided. Work should never be stereotyped as "woman's work" or as "a man-sized job." Writers should avoid showing a "gee-whiz" attitude toward women who perform competently. ("Though a woman, she ran the business as well as any man" or "Though a woman she ran the business efficiently.")

Women should be spoken of as participants in the action, not as possessions of the men. Terms such as *pioneer, farmer* and *settler* should not be used as though they applied only to adult males.

Clearly, the use of language plays an important part in communicating equal valuing of the sexes. Most publishers are keenly aware of the need for authors to consider their words carefully. Those people who fear that the feminist movement is too extreme quarrel with the suggestions for language reform and care. They dislike the term *Ms.* and prefer to maintain the traditional use of the male universal pronouns. They argue that people should understand that *he* is meant to include both males and females. But most proponents of the language guidelines as exemplified by McGraw-Hill argue persuasively that, although the intent to represent all people may indeed be there, until our society includes equal treatment of the sexes as a regular practice, females will be excluded not only in word but also in deed.

•TRY THIS

Examine an article in today's newspaper or in any current magazine, and/or three children's books of your choice. Using *only* the language criteria, place a piece of masking tape over each word that does not meet the nonsexist standard (for example, if *congressman* is used as the universal term to include male and female senators and representatives, place a piece of tape over that word).

Write an appropriate nonsexist word on the masking tape to replace the offender. Try this with children, too.

One must recognize that a story existing only as a didactic device is not a lasting or even very effective story. The talent of an author to present a gripping plot, a vivid character, or a moving description supersedes the appropriate use of pronouns. Unfortunately, a number of books are currently being produced with little to commend them other than their good intentions. There are enough examples of both good writing and good intent to draw upon. Therefore, in this chapter, as in the others, only those books recommended for young readers will be listed.

Women's groups and publishers have compiled many bibliographies to help us provide children with entertaining, enlightening materials that, at best, challenge the traditional constraints of gender role behavior and that, at least, are moving toward a nonsexist stance. Every day new books, articles, and other information are published with this intent. Teachers, counselors, parents, and librarians have undertaken the responsibility of guiding young people to a better sense of the options that a nonsexist society makes available to them. The young audiences are seen as the most accepting of the new trend and the most likely to influence the course of future events.

It is for this reason that children's literature should help in recognition of different points of view about mores in our society. Books should be a reflection of our lives, our past, and our future trends. They should present a diversity of life patterns and a range of opinions. And, as a matter of fact, they do. Although many books retain conventional patterns and attitudes, there are a number of recent books that encourage young readers to accept more contemporary ideas of gender role responsibility.

DISCUSSION OF CHILDREN'S BOOKS

FOLK AND FAIRY TALES

It is logical to expect that, since folk and fairy tales rely so strongly on patterns and tradition, all of these stories would reflect a heavily gender role stereotyped format. Most of them do. The typical hero is strong, brave, and active, highly extroverted, nonintellectual, and willing to take great physical risks. It is usually the male who initiates action and controls the situation. Conversely, the heroine is weak, demure, passive, in need of rescuing, somewhat pensive (although never scholarly), and, above all, obedient. She seldom is in control of her own destiny. Her greatest reward is to become the bride of her prince-rescuer and to serve him happily ever after. Sometimes there are females in these tales who are not constrained by the burden of being the heroine. Servants, witches, fairy godmothers, and wicked stepsisters can be powerful, intelligent, average in looks, or even ugly, strong, and disobedient.

Most of our folk and fairy tales come from and mirror early nineteenth century values and ideas. We read them as the result of the setting down of these tales drawn from the oral tradition by the Grimm brothers and Andrew Lang. But other collections are available to children that reflect the oral traditon without being held hostage by the early nineteenth century European perspective. One such volume is currently out of print, but worth hunting for in libraries, and perhaps requesting reprinting: Rosemary Minard compiled *Womenfolk and Fairy Tales* because of her desire to provide for children a literary diet well balanced with fantasy, while at the same time offering an image of the female appropriate for contemporary times. She provides a variety of African, Irish, Scandinavian, Japanese, Chinese, and other stories. They range from "East of the Sun and West of the Moon" and Walter de la Mare's "Mollie Whuppie," which have heroines who perform daring and clever deeds and who marry the prince, to "The Stolen Bairn and the Sidh," which has as its heroine a mother who rescues her child from the fairies, and "The Chinese Red Riding Hoods," who trick the wicked wolf. The collection is an entertaining and excellent one. The stories conform to the traditional patterns of folk tales, with three the magic number and the youngest child usually the one who accomplishes the daring deeds. The fantasy and imagination are stimulating to the reader. And the heroines are admirable. The males are not denigrated; they are, however, not as dominant in the stories as the females are. This is a useful and balancing book.

Some writers feel so strongly about the heretofore unbalanced treatment of women in fairy tales that they have gone to the other extreme and made the men victims. Jay Williams, in the admittedly humorous and charmingly illustrated book *The Practical Princess*, has Princess Bedelia performing all kinds of clever acts. After brilliantly outwitting a snobbish and vicious dragon, she rescues the sleeping prince. Unfortunately, all of the males in the book are simpletons; further, they permit themselves to be ordered about and humiliated by her. A later fairy tale, *Petronella*, is far more equitable in its treatment of males and females, although the prince is the clown character in the story. In fact, the hero is the sorcerer. Stereotypes of the perfect prince, the princess, and the villain are overturned, and the story remains an engaging one.

Some writers deliberately invent fairy tales designed to influence the attitudes of contemporary children. Harriet Herman's *The Forest Princess* has this intention. Her princess, a magical creature who grows up alone in the forest, learns to take care of herself in many ways, such as constructing her own furniture and relating to wild animals. One day the prince of a nearby kingdom is tossed by a storm onto the beach nearby. He and the princess spend some time together. After a while they both go to the prince's kingdom, where everything is different from the forest. The princess is made to conform to the expectations of the kingdom, which are very restrictive for females, but needless to say, she makes a great impact upon the entire kingdom. The story is not so heavy-handed as others with the same didactic intent, and the writing is good. The book is a worthwhile addition to a fairy tale library.

Richard A. Gardner has also created several tales with a didactic intent. Dr. Gardner's *Fairy Tales for Today's Children* are written in a light, smooth fashion. "Hans and Greta" describes both children as equally intelligent and courageous. They return home after vanquishing the witch, knowing that they cannot change their stepmother, but agreeing to use their own natural qualities to try to get along with her when she is in good moods and to try to avoid her when she is in bad moods. "The Ugly Duck" does not turn into a swan but learns to cope with his different appearance. "Cinderelma" never meets a fairy godmother, but goes to the ball because of her own initiative. After agreeing to marry the prince, she stays with him at his castle and they mutually decide that they are not suited for each other. She eventually starts her own business and marries a man who shares her interests. The fantasy in Dr. Gardner's stories is not so rich as that in traditional fairy tales, but the lessons are explicit. They are taught humorously, but their point is clear. The messages are worthwhile, and perhaps counteract the myths of romantic, unreflective love at first sight, and happily-ever-after weddings.

Jane Yolen, an author who has written many contemporary fairy tales with a flavor of the traditional, makes no attempt to teach lessons. Her aim is to stretch the imagination and to communicate a sense of universality. Her language is poetic, her plots, complex. She usually manages, within the context of the fairy tale, to create characters who are active, intense, thoughtful, and complete, whether they are males or females.

The collection *The Girl Who Cried Flowers and Other Tales* contains women with special characteristics as central figures. In "Silent Bianca" the heroine's words emerge frozen from her mouth; she cannot be heard until her words thaw. As she is noted for her wisdom, her words are valued; people must, thus, take the time to listen. The prince asks her to marry him because of her beauty, her powerful intellect, and her silence. She acquiesces gracefully to his proposal, and the reader has the sense that a shared rule will follow.

A second tale is contrary to tradition in that the need to satisfy others is what destroys Olivia, the girl whose tears turn into flowers. Olivia is exploited by all of the people in her community, who care only about the free source of flowers that she provides them. When, after her marriage, she is forbidden by her husband ever again to weep, her former friends desert her. Her inappropriate virtue, total obedience to others, causes her to die. The third heroine, the most active of the three, has as her chief characteristic an insatiable curiosity about the future. After she accepts the task of becoming the Weaver of Tomorrow, her curiosity is sated, but she has chosen a lonely life. The allusions to the Devil make the reader suspect that she has been influenced by evil; nevertheless, she takes control of her fate. Her ending is not conventional.

These women are unique in their qualities, as are the woman in Yolen's other stories. In *The Emperor and the Kite*, Djeow Seow uses ingenuity and courage to rescue her father, the Emperor. In *The Girl Who Loved the Wind*, Danina manages to escape from the sheltered, safe world that her father has designed for her. In *The Magic Three of Solatia*, Sianna becomes the wise and just ruler of her country. She also demonstrates bravery, inventiveness, intelligence, compassion, and the ability to be a wonderful mother. She is a dutiful but independent daughter. Her qualities are extraordinary, and she is a believable and admirable woman. Among her teachings are that it is acceptable and useful for people, even men, to cry; that tenderness should not be reserved to female behavior; and that every act has its consequence that must be considered before the action is undertaken. She is truly a model to be emulated. But even with all of the lessons to be learned, the stories retain their entertaining quality. The morals do not intrude upon the reader's enjoyment of the magic of the tales.

Any collection of fairy or folk tales has lessons to teach and morals to impart. Young readers should be helped to recognize what they may be absorbing. They should become aware of the messages being communicated. One activity that students can use with any fairy tale is to note who initiates the action. Is it a male or a female? What would happen in any of these tales if the initiator's sex were changed? Another activity could be to list those qualities considered admirable in females and those considered admirable in males in specific stories, and to discuss how this matches with contemporary times. Another possible approach might be to reconstruct the society that constitutes the setting of the tale in order to see what changes the readers would render in the society to make the tale more acceptable.

CLASSICS

Classics are stories that have withstood the test of time and remain popular over a long period of years. Most people also ascribe to classics a certain literary quality and a sense of universal appeal. This second characteristic is not true of all acknowledged classics. *Little Women*, for example, is generally considered to be a "girls' book." Some stories, such as *Charlotte's Web*, are thought of as modern classics because it looks as if their popularity will endure for a long time. Most classics are products and reflections of their time but manage to supersede the temporal; they indicate to the reader a sense of timelessness, at least in values that they impart to the reader.

Frances Hodgson Burnett's *The Secret Garden* contains a number of interesting characters. The heroine is bold, assertive, capable of initiating her own behavior, and independent. The boys in the story are equally unusual for their time. One of them is, at first, weak, spoiled, and dependent. Another is kind, gentle, and wise beyond his years, with a capacity for loving and nurturing that is admired by everyone else in the book. Both boys and girls enjoy reading this book despite the fact that its main character is a girl.

Little Women, by Louisa May Alcott, also contains several unusual characters, Marmee and Jo in particular. Jo is one of literature's exemplars of the active young woman. Most of the values transmitted by this book are concerned with people's relationships to each other as respected individuals. There is also much emphasis on the responsibility of each human being to care about and for every other person. But boys do not usually like to be seen reading this book; its title and its reputation classify it "for girls only." Perhaps at some time in the future this will no longer be the case, and boys will be permitted to enjoy it without fear of embarrassment.

Other classics with females as the major characters include *Caddie Woodlawn,* by C. R. Brink, and *The Courage of Sarah Noble,* by Alice Dalgliesh. The heroines are daughters in pioneer families. Boys seem willing to read both of these books, perhaps because of their historical topics, perhaps because of their active male characters, perhaps because of their literary quality and compelling story line. These books, and those in *The Little House* series by Wilder, although they contain female figures who are somewhat different from the conventional, also consistently reaffirm the traditional position of male superiority, strength, and wisdom.

Classics should be used to compare modern times with those of the book's setting. Often the books will contain assertions that are no longer valid, but were perhaps appropriate for the time. A useful study could involve students' selecting classics and commenting on what, in their opinion, made each book a classic. Then they could produce some suggested changes to make these classics contemporary in social terms. Debates could be held on whether or not to amend the classics. Students could examine all of the work of selected authors, such as Alcott, Burnett, and Sorenson, for evidence of consistent attitudes toward males and females. Students could construct bulletin boards of the "Best Balanced Characters," being certain to leave space for opposing opinions and comments, as well as additions to the list. The main purpose of all of these activities is to give students the experience of comparing contemporary expectations with historical treatment of males and females in high quality books.

NONFICTION

Factual books aimed at providing appropriate gender role models can sometimes send messages different from what they intend:

One message to examine is the implication that females must strive to be more competent in their jobs than men, or they will not be respected. Some books ostensibly telling the reading audience that both males and females can aspire to the same careers in fact indicate that competiton between the sexes is the expected norm. Much more beneficial is Eve Merriam's book for young children, *Boys and Girls, Girls and Boys*, which emphasizes mutual respect and cooperation as well as equality. Another very useful book is Harlow Rockwell's *My Doctor*, which describes what goes on during a visit to the doctor's office for a checkup. The primary intent of the books is to remove a child's fear of visiting the doctor by a clear and specific picture of what the young patient can expect. The doctor in this book is a woman, and one of the parents in the waiting room is a male. Here is a book that unobtrusively provides a model and a nod of approval for these roles.

Some of the most convincing and positive books encouraging readers to build an acceptance of new roles for both males and females are those that describe real people already doing real things that defy the stereotype. These books are particularly effective when they are illustrated with photographs. Some examples of such books are the entire *What Can She Be?* series, which includes descriptions of an architect, a lawyer, a newscaster, and others. All are women; all are successful; all have full, balanced lives. The series, by Gloria and Esther Goldreich, is well written and well photographed. It includes all sorts of social circumstances, heritages, problems, and issues. Designed for a wide age range, it can be used even beyond the upper age limit of ten years suggested by the publishers.

HISTORY AND BIOGRAPHY

There are many excellent histories of the women's movement: Dale Carlson's *Girls Are Equal Too,* Elaine Landau's *Women, Women, Feminism in America,* Janet Harris's *A Single Standard,* and Ruth Warren's *A Pictorial History of Women in America* are a few. For those readers, mostly older children, who enjoy reading this category of book, these histories (or, as they are coming to be known, "herstories") are valuable, fascinating, and illuminating. Students' research would benefit from the use of these books in addition to standard historical texts and encyclopedias.

Famous women ought to be included as part of the regular social studies curriculum rather than in a separate category. Significant authors, artists, and scientists deserve to be studied as representatives of their professions, regardless of their sex. Students can update their textbooks by doing research on women previously not included. Student-authored additions can be appended to the texts, updating and improving their study.

Biographies should become part of the accepted compilation of texts used in studying history, to help make it come alive. It is easy to be discouraged when a visit to any library or bookstore produces evidence that biographies of males far outnumber biographies of females, out of all proportion to their representation in history and society. But it is heartening to see on the shelves the increasing number of books about women who have made important contributions to the world. Most of the recent biographies deal with women who have been concerned with the feminist cause. But others, such as biographies of poets and queens, have also appeared.

In reading a biography it is essential that the student recognize the biographer's bias. Because of the difficulty in determining what is truth and what is romanticized when one reads about an admired character, it is useful to try to acquire more than one book about any given person. In reading of Sarah Emma Edmundson, who disguised herself as a male for several years during the Civil War and served as a soldier and as a spy, one can uncover numerous disputes about what really happened and what she was really like. There is even a difference of opinion about her name. Reading one biography of "Emma Edmonds" invites the assumption that the heroine not only hated being a woman but also that she had no regard for any women. The reader might also be puzzled by the lack of insight provided into Emma's character, thoughts, and motivations. The authors of the biography refer to Emma as "he" during the time that she masquerades as Frank Thompson. Few details of her life in the army are provided. The reader is expected to be satisfied with vague explanations of separate pup tents and cursory physical examinations.

But the book *Girl Soldier and Spy: Sarah Emma Edmundson*, by Mary Hoehling, develops Sarah's character and permits the reader to share her feelings. Of course, the character's emotions are no more than informed speculation on the part of the author, but the account of the research that she did for the book is impressive. She went beyond written records to seek out family members and people who knew of Sarah, both in her male and female identities. During the course of the book, Hoehling never lets the reader forget that the main character is a woman. Sarah retains the qualities of an attractive young woman even when she is pretending to be a man. True, she wants to prove to her father that she can be as good as a boy, but the reader does not feel she is resentful of her womanhood. In one book she seems to be a strange creature, out of place in this world, always wishing to be a man. In *Girl Soldier and Spy* there are excellent reasons for her actions, and she is in control of her situation. She is a pitiful figure in one book, an admirable one in the other.

An interesting project for students would be to research this and other little known characters to compose their own version of the character's life. Reading differing books such as the two described above could lead students to debate the authors' believability. Since most notable people have had several biographies written about them, it would not be difficult to find such information. Another activity for a group of students could be to assemble as many different versions of a subject's life as they could find. Each group member would read one or more of the accounts, and compare notes. Criteria could be designed for judging the accuracy of a book. In those cases of general agreement about the details of a person's life, they could decide which of the biographies was the most appealing, most useful, or best written.

Harriet Tubman is one woman about whom a number of books have been written, all of which are in accord about the details of her remarkable life. The points of view are generally consistent—that Harriet was a brave, successful, unusual woman. The methods of presentation, however, vary from straightforward telling of the story to acquainting the reader with the horrors of slavery. Jacob Lawrence's *Harriet and the Promised Land* relies on the power of illustrations to convey the difficulty of Harriet's task and the strength that she needed to endure. Lawrence's book is a controversial one because some critics believe that the illustrations are too harsh for children. Some critics even believe that the illustrations are demeaning of black people, although the artist is himself black. Readers should be made aware of the controversy so that they will be encouraged to judge for themselves how they feel about the pictures. It is also a good idea to encourage students to recognize that they must read factual work as well as fiction with a critical mind.

Other black women who helped the cause of black people and who were courageous and strong have had biographies written about them. Sojourner Truth, Juliette Derricotte, Maggie Mitchell Walker, Ida Wells Barnett, Septima Poinsette Clarke, Charlotte Forten, Shirley Chisholm, and others can be found on the biography shelves. Most of the authors are respectful of their topic and knowledgeable about their heroines. Polly Longsworth, for example, has written a well constructed fictionalized autobiography of Charlette Forten. The book makes the point that the abolitionist and women's liberation movements are compatible and similar.

Amelia Earhart, Florence Nightingale, Eleanor Roosevelt, Emily Dickinson, Edna St. Vincent Millay, Chris Evert Lloyd, Maria Tallchief, Elizabeth Blackwell, and numerous others in every field of endeavor can be found described in books. Most of these women defied social convention and family pressure in order to accomplish what they did. Most of them endured ridicule and abuse, but persevered. *Nellie Bly, Reporter*, by Nina Brown Baker, describes the challenging and socially effective reporting done by this woman. The book also bemoans the fact that Nellie Bly is probably better remembered for her stunt of going around the world alone in fewer than eighty days than she is for her work in cleaning up "insane asylums," prisons, and other abusive institutions. Nellie Bly had a life in which fame, prosperity, poverty, and adversity were all ingredients. Whatever she achieved was on her own initiative and only after struggling against opposition.

Margaret Sanger, Pioneer of Birth Control, by Lader and Meltzer, also describes a woman who had to overcome tremendous barriers. Sanger was a determined woman. She was roundly criticized for her controversial views about marriage and for her ideas of appropriate behavior for women, but her work far outlasted her notoriety and countinues to have far-reaching consequences for the world in general. This biography, like many of the others, makes no pretense that its subject is uncontroversial or flawless. It demonstrates that personal contentment is not necessary for public good. It also describes people who dare to be different because of principle, not whim.

Linda Peavy and Ursula Smith have written *Women Who Changed Things*, a provocative book containing succinct but sensitive biographies of nine women, each of whose life, in different ways, made a difference to society. The authors selected women who had previously been neglected by historians and biographers; readers of this volume will come to empathize with and know them, and will want to learn more about them. Young readers can interview men and women they know, who may even now be making a significant contribution, who may be changing things. A series of these interviews, written for publication, might be appropriate for the school newspaper, or even for a text, compiled by the students, for use in their history classes.

GIRLS AS MAIN CHARACTERS

Many works of fiction have, as their main characters, girls who dare to be different. Sometimes, as with the young women in O'Dell's *Island of the Blue Dolphins* and George's *Julie of the Wolves*, this difference spells survival. In both books the young women, alone in the wilderness, must cope with their environment in order to remain alive. In both cases the heroines face their situations with courage and intelligence. Julie must also cope with problems of personal and societal nature throughout the book. Her spiritual survival becomes an issue. For Karana, the physical is the challenge. Readers who wonder if the books would be as effective if the main characters were male may change the gender of the characters to see if this affects the story. A poll can be conducted to see how many male readers would prefer that these main characters be male.

Other tales of survival with female protagonists should also be read with this question in mind. Howard's *The Ostrich Chase* is the story of a young woman who refuses to be bound by the traditions of her tribe. Her elderly grandmother, aiding her in her rebellion, almost loses her life in the process. Khuana, however, manages to surmount the problems and to retain her womanly qualities as well. Maude, the heroine of *The Maude Reed Tale*, by Norah Lofts, overcomes social pressure that is as strong as any physical barrier. She manages to change her mother's expectations of her and to do what she wants with her life, despite the fact that she lives in the Middle Ages, a time when the social system was cast in stone.

But these women are rarities. They are the striking examples set against the more conforming females. Even books such as *Queenie Peavy,* by Burch, make it clear that the strong-willed, intelligent, self-managing, disobedient heroines are anomalies beyond the norm. How comfortable are young girls with using these females as models? How admirable and believable do young males find them to be? Some heroines are extremely lonely and somewhat unhappy young women, despite their bravado. They, like Fitzhugh's *Harriet the Spy*, crave friends and want others to like and accept them. The adventures that they have and the ideas they act upon are humorous and clever. But what child would want to be in their situation? These supergirls do not lead enviable lives although their exploits are fun to read about.

A more constructive female model is to be found in the character of Beth Lambert in Bette Greene's *Philip Hall Likes Me: I Reckon Maybe*. Although competition between males and females is a primary issue in the book, Beth emerges as an admirable character to be emulated and respected by the reader. Beth, who is very bright, can do everything extremely well. At first, she permits her liking for Philip Hall to inhibit her; she doesn't want to show him up. But her good sense wins out when she realizes that she has a responsibility to herself to do her very best.

The main character of Vera and Bill Cleaver's *Ellen Grae* is another bright, sensitive, and appealing character. In each of the three books in which she appears, she maintains integrity and strength. Rosie Bernard is also a feisty, bright, and interesting female. She engages the reader in her adventures in *A Year in the Life of Rosie Bernard*, by Barbara Brenner.

These heroines are good to have; we need more of them. We should also learn to expect to find as many competent females as males in stories. Our expectations are sure to influence authors. If students are made aware of this necessity, they can begin to write letters to favorite authors, suggesting that more females be used as equals and compatriots of males. Authors enjoy reading fan mail and may respond to their readers' suggestions.

WOMEN IN CHILDREN'S BOOKS

Rarely the main characters in children's books, women usually appear incidentally as mothers, teachers, or adult foils for the plot.

Ellen MacGregor's *Miss Pickerell* series does have a humorous woman as its protagonist. She is a very intelligent, if eccentric, person who has fabulous adventures. She is much brighter than most of the males in the books. Her eccentricities are harmless and her appearance is unthreatening. She is an exceptional person. But like Mary Poppins, who also has her faults, it is good to encounter a remarkable female character.

Mary Poppins and Miss Pickerell are unmarried and childless. Mothers are seldom protagonists. Sometimes, though, they are unforgettable characters; not only is the mother in *A Wrinkle in Time*, by Madeleine L'Engle, beautiful and brilliant, but the fact that she is a scientist, working in a laboratory, is also useful in a contemporary book. Working mothers generally have to put up with much criticism in fiction; their children are often seen to suffer from their lack of time and interest. Kerr's *Dinky Hocker Shoots Smack* and several other books contain children who resent their mother's involvement outside the house. These mothers do not seem to be able to handle the situation well. The daughters are interesting and active characters, and they manage to communicate their feelings in sometimes dramatic ways, redeeming the books from sexist accusations. Children might benefit from discussing what they would do if their mothers behaved as these mothers do. The mothers in *The Terrible Thing That Happened at Our House*, by Marge Blaine, *Mushy Eggs*, by Florence Adams, and *Mom, the Wolf Man and Me*, by Norma Klein, manage to maintain their jobs and a nurturing role with their children.

Contrary to reality, not many fictional mothers have paid jobs. The role of the mother in most children's books is still that of the housekeeper and cook. Differing from this, and providing another view of males as well, is *The Night Daddy*, by Maria Gripe. In this story, the mother copes well with her job and her parental responsibilities by working at night and hiring a young man to baby-sit while she is gone. Not much is made of the mother's work in most of the books that do mention mothers and their jobs. But two charming and useful books, Eve Merriam's *Mommies at Work* and Joe Lasker's *Mothers Can Do Anything*, picture mothers in all sorts of roles in addition to their mothering ones. Again, the Goldreich series—particularly those that picture the women at home with their families as well as outside the home at work— are worthwhile books to have and to refer to.

A book that centers on the problem of a mother's losing her job is *My Mother Lost Her Job Today*, by Judy Delton. The mother and her little girl discuss the situation, comfort each other, and plan for the future. Acknowledging that many children live in homes where both parents work outside the house, Kathleen Kyte has written a book of advice for these children called, *In Charge: A Complete Handbook for Kids with Working Parents*.

Activities in which children are asked to describe the work that their mothers and fathers do and then to try to find matching characters in books may reveal that parents' jobs are rarely described. The students may then write job descriptions for parents in the stories that exclude them. An activity related to books of fiction could have children describe the characteristics of "ideal" parents. They could then locate books that contain parents matching these descriptions and books that conflict with, or differ from the descriptions. They then can be encouraged to aim for a rethinking and expanding of their descriptions and of those qualities that they consider to be beneficial. They can search for fictional working mothers who are members of different ethnic heritages, and compare their treatment in the stories.

Students can list positive qualities for boys and for girls, again matching characters in literature. They can compare their lists with each other, with the books, and even categorize the descriptions according to age levels.

Older women, particularly grandmothers, are emerging as sometimes interesting and unique individuals. Udry's *Mary Jo's Grandmother* presents a woman who is independent and capable, while the grandmother in Klein's *Naomi in the Middle* is a tennis-playing, somewhat brusque individual who unashamedly confesses to an antipathy toward infants.

MEN IN CHILDREN'S BOOKS

The feminist movement contends that its quest is not only for a change in the status of women, but also for men. *Human* liberation is the goal. It is, therefore, useful to consider the treatment of males in children's books. Young readers as well as concerned adults can apply to males the same criteria suggested for females, as males have been victimized by stereotypic expectations almost as severely as females. Readers may observe how young male characters are treated and expected to act. They may reflect on the literary role of the father and should watch for the imposition of a competitive system in which males are required to win. When stories are free of these restrictions they should be recommended to friends. Publishers and authors are receptive to letters written by readers of their books and take into consideration those readers' comments and suggestions.

All of Patricia MacLachlan's books avoid stereotypes and tell wonderfully crafted, humorous, engaging stories. In *The Sick Day*, Emily's father stays home with her when she is sick (her mother is at work) and lovingly and tenderly responds to her needs. Other fathers, such as Ramona Quimby's in all of the *Ramona* books by Beverly Cleary, and Bweela and Javaka's father in *My Special Best Words* and *Daddy Is a Monster ... Sometimes*, by John Steptoe, are models of nurturing adult males, not because they are perfect fathers, but because they exhibit characteristics that counteract the stereotype.

Readers should note the books that deviate from the imposed artificial requirements that males must be interested only in sports, must never cry, must have only male friends, and must always be strong and brave. Peter, the protagonist in *A Special Gift,* by Marcia L. Simon, loves to dance, but is intimidated by his peers, and reluctant to let them know of his talent. Finally, he comes to accept and value his special interests. Dance is also an option for males in Rachel Isadora's two books, *Max* and *My Ballet Class*.

A work of nonfiction, *Oh Boy! Babies!*, by Alison Herzig and Jane Mali, describes, through dialogue and photographs, an elective course on child care. This course is offered to fifth and sixth graders in an all male school. Real babies are brought into the classroom and the boys learn to bathe, diaper, feed, and nurture the infants.

For older children, Jess, in *Bridge to Terabithia*, by Katherine Paterson, is sensitive and artistic. Furthermore, his best friend is female. Ramon, in *Shadow Like a Leopard*, by Myron Levoy, rejects the "macho" facade his father and peers try to impose on him, and Alan, in *Alan and Naomi*, also by

Levoy, patiently and tenderly befriends Naomi in an attempt to help her regain her equilibrium after she has been traumatized by her father's brutal murder.

Slowly but surely, books and the media are reflecting society's direction. Active critical reading and responding will help speed the process.

REFERENCES: GENDER ROLES

AHLUM, CAROL, AND FRALLEY, JACQUELINE M. *Feminist Resources for Schools and Colleges: A Guide to Curricular Materials.* Old Westbury, New York: Feminist Press, 1973.
An excellent and complete compilation of resources. The Clearinghouse on Women's Studies directed this project. The annotated bibliography includes lists of books and articles on sexism in education, materials for the elementary school teacher. The children's books listed are not annotated, but all other entries are.

ALLYN AND BACON, INC. *Sensitivity Guidelines for Artists.* Specific in terms of avoidance of stereotype. Very useful for purposes of analysis.

BENEFIC PRESS. *Checklist for Female-Male Roles in Books.* Brief, but fair to both sexes.

BERNSTEIN, JOANNE. "The Changing Roles of Females in Books for Young Children," *The Reading Teacher*, Vol. 27, No. 6, March 1974, pp. 545–549.
Deplores the relatively small quantity of books in which females are the main characters and are viewed positively. Suggests that boys would benefit in many ways from reading such books. Describes several books in which girls are active, valued characters.

BRACKEN, JEANNE, AND WIGUTOFF, SHARON. *Books for Today's Children: An Annotated Bibliography of Non-Stereotyped Picture Books.* Old Westbury, New York: Feminist Press, 1979.
Discusses and recommends over 100 books for young children containing positive values. The titles are arranged in lists of books that are highly recommended, recommended, and recommended with some reservation. Otherwise, the books are not placed into categories.

BRACKEN, JEANNE, AND WIGUTOFF, SHARON, WITH BAKER, ILENE. *Books for Today's Young Readers: An Annotated Bibliography of Recommended Fiction for Ages 10–14.* Old Westbury, New York: Feminist Press, 1981.
Descriptions and analyses of books for older readers. Gender, ethnicity, acculturation and racism, peer friendships, special needs, families in transition, foster care and adoption, and views of old people are some of the categories specified. Very helpful discussion and format.

BROOKLINE PUBLIC SCHOOLS. "Report of the Sex-Role Stereotyping Commission, 1974." (Robert I. Sperber, Superintendent of Schools, Brookline, Massachusetts 02146.)
Provides guidelines for evaluating written materials. Also serves as a model for what school systems can do to combat sexism in the schools.

BROVERMAN, INGE K.; BROERMAN, DONALD M.; CLARKSON, FRANK E.; ROSENKRANTZ, PAUL S.; AND VOGEL, SUSAN R. "Sex-Role Stereotypes and Clinical Judgments of Mental Health," *Journal of Consulting and Clinical Psychology*, Vol. 34, No. 1, February 1970, pp. 1–7.
Important and revealing report of a study conducted with clinical psychologists, demonstrating that male characteristics are viewed as positive for adults, and female characteristics are not. Further, the study concludes that unstereotypic sex-role behavior is viewed as abnormal.

COHEN, MARTHA. *Stop Sex Role Stereotypes in Elementary Education: A Handbook for Parents and Teachers*. Hartford: Connecticut Public Interest Research Group, 1974.
The pamphlet contains discussions of sex-role stereotyping, and suggestions for helping children recognize and deal with it. An excellent set of criteria is offered for examining texts and trade books. Descriptions of materials, strategies, and workshops useful for educating people to combat sex-role stereotyping are presented. Fairly extensive annotated bibliography of children's books, films, and materials for teachers and parents is included. The list of addresses of key publishers and organizations adds a bonus to this invaluable pamphlet.

COOPER, SUSAN. "Womenfolk and Fairy Tales," *New York Times Book Review*, 13, April 1975, p. 6.
Cooper reviews Rosemary Minard's book *Woomenfolk and Fairy Tales* unfavorably. She disagrees with the author's premise that girls and boys need admirable heroines. She considers this to be "an adult neurosis foisted upon children." She believes that readers identify with all characters, male and female, and that "an anthology based on a feminist approach is fettered by self-consciousness."

COUNCIL ON INTERRACIAL BOOKS FOR CHILDREN. *Bulletin* (Special Issue on Romance Series for Young Readers), Vol. 12, Nos. 4 and 5, 1981.
Articles analyzing and criticizing the sexist implications of many of the romance novels so popular with young readers. Listing of books on male-female friendships (such as *Bridge to Terabithia*, and *Growin'*) as an antidote to the romances.

———. *Guidelines for Selecting Biasfree Textbooks and Storybooks*, 1980.
A set of articles compiled into a useful manual for teaching children about bias of all sorts in the books they read.

———. *Winning "Justice for All."* Sponsored by the Women's Educational Equity Act Program, U.S. Department of Health, Education and Welfare, 1980.
A social studies and language arts curriculum to help children overcome stereotypes, particularly those of gender role.

DEGROOT, ROSEANN M. "A Comparison of the Parental Image Found in Selected Children's Books of the Nineteen-Thirties with Those of the Nineteen-Sixties," Unpublished Master's report, Palmer Graduate Library School, Long Island University, Brookvile, New York, 1970.
This paper describes the changing role of the father as well as that of the mother.

Talks of the problem of the absentee parent and surrogate parents. Lists characteristics and checks whether either or both parents exhibit them.

FEMINISTS ON CHILDREN'S LITERATURE. "A Feminist Look at Children's Books," *School Library Journal*, Vol. 18, No. 5, January 1971, pp. 19–24.
Reprinted in Fritz J. Luecke, ed., *Children's Books, Views and Values* ed. Middletown, Connecticut: Xerox Educational Publications, 1973.
Finds an extreme imbalance in language and in number of female characters compared to male. Divides books into categories: "sexist," "cop-outs," "positive images," and "especially for girls." Particularly focuses on Newbery Award winners, but includes others as well. Hopes eventually to omit the last category entirely.

FEMINISTS ON CHILDREN'S MEDIA. *Little Miss Muffet Fights Back: Recommended Non-Sexist Books about Girls for Young Readers*, 1971.
This annotated listing was one of the first of its kind. It presents brief but descriptive annotations of children's books judged to be nonsexist. The criteria for judging are not listed. Some of the books are not as adequately described as others, but this is a good basic beginning for readers interested in accumulating books with a positive image of females.

GERSONI-STAVN, DIANE. "Feminist Criticism: An Overview," *School Library Journal*, Vol. 20, No. 5, January 1974, p. 22.
Reviews the negative stereotyping of girls in children's books. Cautions critics to engage in humanistic criticism that supports both males and females. Also pleads for maintenance of aesthetic standards. Gives excellent advice to readers and critics. A very thoughtful, constructive article.

_____. "Reducing the 'Miss Muffet' Syndrome: An Annotated Bibliography," *School Libary Journal*, Vol. 18, No. 5, January 1972, pp. 32–35.
Reviews the progress that books have made in depicting females. Although many more females now appear in books, much still needs to happen in describing "everyday" females. There is also a notable lack of excellence in biographies for younger and middle-grade children. Approximately forty books for younger intermediate and older children are described positively in their treatment of female characters.

_____. *Sexism and Youth*. New York and London: Xerox, 1974.
Chapter after chapter, this book examines the socialization of females in society. It talks about omission of females from history, stereotyping in picture books, television, etc. This book also reviews books for children and gives examples of imprinting sex typecasting on children. A very worthwhile resource book.

GINN AND COMPANY. *Treatment of Minority Groups and Women*, 1975.
Provides criteria for art and design as well as content. Includes extensive list of extremely useful concerns and criteria. Contains suggestions for settings as well as different sorts of people.

GREENLEAF, PHYLLIS TAUBE. *Liberating Young Children from Sex Roles*. Somerville, Massachusetts: New England Free Press, 1972.

A discussion of teachers' experiences with preschool children in trying to liberate them from sex-role stereotypes. Practical suggestions and a realistic look at the problems involved in changing stereotypic attitudes and behavior make this a very useful pamphlet.

HAGAN, ELIZABETH, AND THE CENTRAL NEW JERSEY CHAPTER OF NATIONAL ORGANIZATION FOR WOMEN. "Sex Role Stereotyping in Elementary School Readers." Princeton: Women on Words and Images, 1970.
Concludes that elementary school texts are not taking seriously the expectations and potential of girl students. Fifteen reading series were examined, from primer to sixth-grade level. The observations provide a useful framework for others who would like to replicate the study.

HEIDE, WILMA SCOTT. "On Women, Men, Children, and Librarians," *School Library Journal*, Vol. 20, No. 5, January 1974, pp. 17–21.
Defines sexism and sexist behavior. Urges librarians to actively include feminist literature, displays, and programs in libraries.

HEINS, ETHEL. "The Fifties Revisited," *The Horn Book*, December 1982.
A commentary on the romance novels for young people, and their failure to provide a literate and mature perception of relationships.

HOUGHTON MIFFLIN COMPANY. *Avoiding Stereotypes.*
Presents a position statement on minorities and women. Also has compiled annotated bibliographies of its publications dealing with these populations.

HOWE, FLORENCE. "Educating Women: No More Sugar and Spice," *Saturday Review*, 16 October 1971, pp. 76–77.
Criticizes the extensive sex-role stereotyping in children's trade books and texts, both fiction and nonfiction. Hopes for far-reaching reform in curriculum as well as evidence of greater sensitivity in texts and literature.

INTERRACIAL BOOKS FOR CHILDREN. "10 Quick Ways to Analyze Books for Racism and Sexism," *Bulletin*, Vol. 5, No. 3, 1974, p. 1.
Criteria to use when examining children's books. Incisive and useful.

JONES, BARTLETT C. "A New Cache of Liberated Children's Literature—In Some Old Standbys," *Wilson Library Bulletin*, Vol. 49, No. 1, September 1974, pp. 52–56.
Criticizes feminist complaints and research in children's literature. Locates many classics in which he claims females have a very positive image. Suggests extensive research be done to see if literature does have an effect on self-image and identity. Concludes that the situation is not at all desperate for female image in children's books.

KNODEL, BEA. "Still Far from Equal: Young Women in Literature for Adolescents." Paper presented at the Annual Meeting of the National Council of Teachers of English, April 1982. (Eric Document Reproduction Service No. ED 217 425.)
Criticizes the treatment of females in most books. Pleads for more books with admirable young heroines in them.

KOLBENSCHLAG, MADONNA. *Kiss Sleeping Beauty Good-bye*. New York: Doubleday, 1979. Also in paper.

Basing her comments on the problems and personalities of Sleeping Beauty, Cinderella, Snow White, Goldilocks, Beauty, and some of the Princesses who inhabit the fairy tales, the author examines their characteristics and interactions and relates them to today's society.

KRAM, JUDITH. "How to Combat Sexism in Textbooks," *Bulletin of the Council on Interracial Books for Children*, Vol. 6, No. 1, 1975, pp. 3–8.
Suggests activities and strategies for changing the texts used in a public school system. Letter-writing campaigns and other procedures are recommended. Specific helpful resources are listed.

LANES, SELMA. "On Feminism and Children's Books," *School Library Journal*, Vol. 20, No. 5, January 1974, p. 23.
Urges differentiation between art and propaganda. Criticizes books that display male or female characteristics rather than universal human behavior. But Lanes agrees with the cause of feminism and welcomes healthy propaganda. She cautions against an unbalanced preoccupation with propagandistic literature in a total reading diet.

LEWIS, SUSAN. "Exploding the Fairy Princess Myth," *Scholastic Teacher*, Vol. 99, No. 3, November 1971, pp. 6–12.
Criticizes texts, books, counselors, and educators for accepting the fairy princess stereotype. Offers "A Chauvinistic Index for Educators" (p. 11). Also provides a list of resources for women's studies.

LIEBERMAN, MARCIA. "Some Day My Prince Will Come: Female Acculturation through the Fairy Tale," *College English*, Vol. 34, No. 3, December 1972, pp. 383–395.
Analyzes the Lang versions of fairy tales and demonstrates the negative effects of these on women. Beauty and passivity are presented as the most important female qualities in these tales; marriage is a female's greatest reward. The author argues powerfully that fairy tales inculcate stereotypic sex-role behaviors into child readers.

LOEB, ROBERT H., JR. *Breaking the Sex-Role Barrier*. New York: Franklin Watts, 1977.
Selected research discusses high school students' stereotypic views of sex roles. Survey format encourages readers to evaluate their own belief system before reading current research, which supports most differences between the sexes as cultural rather than biological.

LUCKENBILL, W. BERNARD. "Fathers in Adolescent Books," *School Library Journal*, Vol. 20, No. 6, February 1974, pp. 26–30.
Fifty books for adolescents are examined. Most fathers and mothers are narrowly stereotyped. But author warns against overly contrived, didactic presentations.

LURIE, ALISON. "Fairy Tale Liberation," *New York Review of Books*, Vol. 15, No. 11, December 1970, pp. 42–44.
The author argues that folk and fairy tales help prepare children for women's liberation, since so many of the characters are women and so many women are strong. She then goes on to suggest collections of tales.

MCGRAW-HILL BOOK COMPANY. *Guidelines for Equal Treatment of the Sexes in McGraw-Hill Book Company Publications.*
The guidelines are concerned with eliminating stereotypes for both males and females in McGraw-Hill publications. Vocabulary is directly dealt with; examples of positive and negative language are given. The guidelines are very specific and very helpful.

MOBERG, VERNE. *A Child's Right to Equal Reading.* Washington, D.C.: National Education Association, 1972.
Specific instructions on how to conduct community workshops to recognize and combat sexism in children's books.

MORAN, BARBARA K. "Women's Rights Address Book," *Woman's Day*, October 1972, p. 25.
A very valuable list of more than sixty national groups and agencies, with a concise description of what each agency offers.

NADESAN, ARDELL. "Mother Goose: Sexist?" *Elementary English*, Vol. 41, No. 3, March 1974, pp. 375–378.
Invites readers to draw their own conclusions from the quotes and excerpts included in the article. Most of the findings support the conclusion that males are better treated than females are.

NILSEN, AILEEN PACE. "Women in Children's Literature," *College English*, Vol. 32, No. 8, May 1971, pp. 918–926.
Critiques Caldecott Award winners from 1951 to 1970. Suggests several causes of unfairness toward females in children's books. Recommends that good books be written with interesting, strong females so that both boys and girls will want to read them.

OLIVER, LINDA. "Women in Aprons: The Female Stereotype in Children's Readers," *Elementary School Journal*, Vol. 74, No. 5, February 1974, pp. 253–259.
After pointing out the stereotypes in children's readers, Oliver recommends guidelines for the treatment of women. She then goes on to criticize several stories, specifically providing a framework for other readers to do the same.

POGREBIN, LETTY COTTIN. "Down with Sexist Upbringing," *Ms.* Preview Issue, Spring 1972.
This article, which includes the annotated bibliography "A Basic Library for Liberated Children," tells in a personal, powerful style of the negative effects of sexism in children's books and TV shows. The author criticizes books from nursery rhymes to texts. She provides her own list of approved books for the reader.

_____. "Girls' Liberation," *New York Times Book Review,* Section 7, Part 3, 6 May 1973, pp. 44.
A witty and challenging article pointing out the sexism in science books, calendars, and psychologically oriented books, such as Joan Fassler's works. Pogrebin raises provocative questions for readers to consider. (Fassler has since revised her books to reflect societal changes.)

_____. *Growing up Free/Raising Your Child in the 80s.* New York: McGraw-Hill, 1980.

Guidelines for role-free family life. Advice on every aspect of relationships. Deals with sexism and the culture of childhood. This is a comprehensive book that attempts to address a very large topic.

PRIDA, DOLORES, AND RIBNER, SUSAN. "Feminists Look at 100 Books: The Portrayal of Women in Children's Books on Puerto Rican Themes," *Bulletin of the Council on Interracial Books for Children*, Vol. 4, Nos. 1 and 2, Spring 1972.
Commentary, analysis, and annotated bibliography of children's books containing Spanish-speaking female characters. The same damaging stereotypes adhere to Puerto Rican female characters as to their Anglo counterparts, perhaps with greater intensity.

RUPLEY, WILLIAM H.; GARCIA, JESUS; AND LONGNION, BONNIE. "Sex Role Portrayal in Reading Materials: Implications for the 1980s," *The Reading Teacher*, Vol. 34, No. 7, April 1981, pp. 786–791.
Citing some discrepancies in the research, the authors nevertheless conclude that it is important for teachers to examine the reading materials they use in their classrooms for evidence of gender-role bias. They note some advances in basal readers in this regard, but report that supplementary materials retain their sexist imbalance.

SCOTT, FORESMAN AND COMPANY. *Guidelines for Improving the Image of Women in Textbooks.*
Provides examples of negative presentations and positive sample ways to correct them. Pertains primarily to textbooks, but could be useful as well for trade books.

SCOTT, KATHRYN P. "Effects of Non-Sexist Reading Materials on Children's Preferences, Sex-Role Attitudes, and Comprehension." Paper presented at the Annual Meeting of the National Reading Conference, 1978. (Eric Document Reproduction Service No. EP 169 496.)
Summarizes research indicating that students' interest in reading material may be enhanced by using more interesting stories about females; children's comprehension is increased, and their attitudes toward role behavior is more flexible. The plea is made for more research into the impact of materials with nontraditional male role models.

SHARGEL, SUSAN, AND KANE, IRENE. *We Can Change It*. San Francisco: Change for Children, 1974.
Annotated bibliography of ninety-three nonsexist, nonracist children's books. Includes some ideas for using these books in the classroom. Also lists publishers' and alternative publishers' addresses.

SNEE, BETH. "Sexism and Ten Techniques to Combat It through Children's Books," 1979. (Eric Document Reproduction Service No. ED 188 168.)
Summarizes the studies to date on sexism in children's books. Includes ideas for activities to use in classrooms to lessen sexism.

STACEY, JUDITH; BEREAUD, SUSAN; AND DANIELS, JOAN; eds. *And Jill Came Tumbling After: Sexism in American Education*. New York: Dell, 1974.
An informative anthology of articles on sexism in education from nursery school through college.

STEWIG, JOHN, AND HIGGS, MARGARET. "Girls Grow Up to Be Mommies: A Study of Sexism in Children's Literature," *Library Journal*, Vol. 98, No. 2, 15 January 1973, pp. 236–241.
Criticizes some carelessly mounted research and praises some that is excellent. Confirms the conclusions that women "play a subordinate, home-related role" in picture books.

TIBBETTS, SYLVIA-LEE. "Sex Differences in Children's Reading Preferences," *The Reading Teacher*, Vol. 28, No. 3, December 1974, pp. 279–281.
Examines the acknowledged assumption that girls will read anything, but boys will read only these books pertaining to boys and their interests. Concludes that this bias is societally imposed rather than an inherent sex characteristic. Females and things female are considered inferior and therefore are rejected. Thus a societal change is in order, rather than publishers' conforming to current malpractice.

WEITZMAN, LENORE J.; EIFLER, DEBORAH; HOKADA, ELIZABETH; AND ROSS, CATHERINE. "Sex Role Socialization in Picture Books for Pre-School Children," *American Journal of Sociology*, Vol. 77, No. 6, May 1972, pp. 1125–1150.
The Caldecott Award winners in particular are examined in light of their influence on acceptance of sex-role stereotyping. Other award winners and popular books for children are also analyzed. Illuminating article, evidencing careful research.

WOMEN ON WORDS AND IMAGES. *Dick and Jane as Victims: Sex Stereotyping in Children's Readers*. Princeton: National Organization for Women, 1972.
One hundred thirty-four readers from fourteen different publishers were analyzed. This well-written, well-researched, well-documented study presents a powerful case for change in textbooks. The same recommendations can be carried over to all books for children. An extremely useful reference.

YODER, JANICE MILLER. "Cracking the Glass Slipper through Adolescent Literature." Paper presented at the Conference on English Education, March 1978. (Eric Document Reproduction Service No. ED 155 704.
Cites some research that looks closely at the content of young adult novels and analyzes several novels for adolescents in the light of their treatment of sexuality and gender role. Concludes that the more recent novels offer adolescents more options than they once had.

SOURCES FOR MATERIALS ON GENDER ROLES

BETHANY PRESS. 2320 Pine Blvd., P.O. Box 179, St. Louis, Missouri 63166
CONNECTICUT PUBLIC INTEREST RESEARCH GROUP. P.O. Box 1571, Hartford, Connecticut 06101
FEMINIST PRESS. SUNY College at Old Westbury, P.O. Box 334, Old Westbury, New York 11568
KNOW INC. P.O. Box 86031, Pittsburgh, Pennsylvania 15221
LOLLIPOP POWER, INC. P.O. Box 1171, Chapel Hill, North Carolina 27514
NATIONAL FOUNDATION FOR THE IMPROVEMENT OF EDUCATION: RESOURCE

CENTER ON SEX ROLES IN EDUCATION. 1201 16th St., N.W., Rm. 628, Washington, D.C. 20036

NATIONAL ORGANIZATION FOR WOMEN (local branches in each state). Central Office: 425 13th St., N.W., Suite 1048, Washington, D.C. 20004

NEW SEED PRESS. 1665 Euclid Ave., Berkeley, California 94709

ORGANIZATION FOR EQUAL EDUCATION OF THE SEXES. 744 Carroll St., Brooklyn, New York 11215. (Publication: *TABS: Aids for Ending Sexism in Schools.*)

PEER (Project on Equal Education Rights). (*Cracking the Glass Slipper: PEER'S Guide to Ending Sex Bias in Your Schools.* Washington, D.C.: NOW Legal Defense and Education Fund, 1979. 1029 Vermont Ave., N.W., Suite 800, Washington, D.C. 20005. A packet of information addressed to educators to help them change their schools to be more equitable.)

WOMEN ON WORDS AND IMAGES. 30 Valley Rd., Princeton, New Jersey 08540

BIBLIOGRAPHY: GENDER ROLES

ADAMS, FLORENCE. *Mushy Eggs.* Illustrated by Marilyn Hirsch. New York: Putnam, 1973. (Ages 5–10.)
The women in this story are admirable and have several dimensions. The housekeeper-baby-sitter has her own friends and family, and the boys' mother copes well with her computer job and the boys. They all seem none the worse for wear.

ADLER, C. S. *The Magic of the Glits.* Illustrated by Ati Forberg. New York: Macmillan, 1979. (Ages 9–12.)
Jeremy feels that his summer is ruined because he has to wear a cast on his leg, and he also is in charge of a seven-year-old girl whose mother has recently died, and whose stepfather can't take care of her. Jeremy displays his creativity by inventing imaginary creatures to entertain Lynette, and discovers that he enjoys this pastime, and grows fond of the little girl. She turns out not to be a helpless orphan, but someone who takes charge of her own life.

_____. *The Once in a While Hero.* New York: Coward, McCann and Geoghegan, 1982. (Ages 9–12.)
Patrick has five sisters and enjoys the company of girls as much as he does that of boys. He also enjoys activities outside of sports. When a bully keeps badgering him, he worries that he won't be able to handle it, but eventually, all turns out well, and he acknowledges that he likes himself as he is. The conventional fight with the bully occurs, but with a twist that makes the reader believe with Pat that it isn't necessary to be a hero all the time.

ADOFF, ARNOLD. *I Am the Running Girl.* Illustrated by Ronald Himler. New York: Harper & Row, 1979. (Ages 7–11.)
Book-length poem about a young woman who loves to run. Other women are shown joyously celebrating their abilities.

ALCOTT, LOUISA MAY. *Little Women.* Boston: Little, Brown, 1868. Also in paper. (All ages.)

Portraits of four sisters in a loving family, each with an individual personality and a different vision of her future life. A classic. Jo is one of the sources of the literary image of the active female.

ALDA, ARLENE. *Sonya's Mommy Works.* Illustrated by the author. New York: Julian Messner, 1982. (Ages 5–8.)
Sonya has responsibilities, develops self-confidence, and spends quality time with each parent. She worries, gets reassured, and has an understanding grandmother. A realistic and specific picture of a family with two parents who work outside the home.

ANCONA, GEORGE. *And What Do You Do?* Photographs by the author. New York: Dutton, 1976. (Ages 8–12.)
About the careers of twenty-one people, the book contains excellent photographs. The introduction states that although a woman or a man is shown doing a job, each job can be done by either.

ANDRE, EVELYN M. *Things We Like to Do.* New York: Abingdon Press, 1968. (Ages 5–8.)
A large picture book depicting children of both sexes in various activities that are fun to do: play with friends, bake a cake, play with dolls.

ARMSTRONG, LOUISE. *How to Turn War into Peace.* Illustrated by Bill Basso. New York: Harcourt Brace Jovanovich, 1979. (Ages 5–8.)
A child's guide to resolving conflict and much more. The message is not hidden in comfortable fantasy and painless, polite complaint. Direct language and real children demonstrate how to resolve conflicts. A girl is given equal rights to anger, intelligence, pride, and the ability to resolve a problem by seeing reason.

ASBJORNSEN, P. C. *The Squire's Bride.* Illustrated by Marcia Sewall. New York: Atheneum, 1975. (Ages 7–10.)
Retelling of an old Norwegian tale in which a young woman outwits the old Squire who wants to force her to marry him.

BABBITT, NATALIE. *Phoebe's Revolt.* New York: Farrar, Straus & Giroux, 1968. (Ages 7–10.)
Set in the Victorian era. A girl decides she does not want to wear ruffles and frills and likes her father's clothes instead. Finding that her father's clothes are not right, either, she finally finds a comfortable compromise.

BAKER, NINA BROWN. *Nellie Bly, Reporter.* Illustrated by W. Blickinstoff. New York: Henry Holt, 1956. (Ages 8–12.)
An interesting biography of a determined and intelligent woman. Contains telling commentary about early twentieth-century America.

BAVER, CAROLINE FELLER. *My Mom Travels a Lot.* Illustrated by Nancy Winslow Parker. New York: Frederick Warne, 1981. (Ages 5–8.)
The young narrator's mother has a job that requires a lot of travel. There are advantages and disadvantages as far as the little girl is concerned: she likes going to the airport, but she doesn't like getting only her father's good night kiss, or the fact that her mother must sometimes miss an important event, like a school play.

BERENSTAIN, STAN AND JAN. *He Bear, She Bear*. New York: Random House, 1977. (Ages 4–6.)
A delightful story for children with excellent illustrations by the authors. Many occupations are illustrated and discussed; all are appropriate for either a male or female.

BLAINE, MARGE. *The Terrible Thing That Happened at Our House*. Illustrated by John C. Wallner. New York: Parents' Magazine Press, 1975. (Ages 5–10.)
When a young girl's mother resumes her career, the child feels as if her world has fallen apart. She is intolerant of the new arrangements that the family makes. Resenting her parents' new roles, she wants her old, comfortable life back again. After a confrontation, the family together decide on a course of action satisfactory to all. The solution is a good one.

BLAIR, R. V. N. *Mary's Monster*. New York: Coward, McCann and Geoghegan, 1975. (Ages 7–10.)
A charming and well-documented biography of Mary Anning, who began to collect "curiosities" as a child. The large dinosaur bones she discovered in Cornwall, England, made her famous. She was instrumental in the development of geology as a science. The author emphasizes her curiosity and her single-minded pursuit of her unconventional interests.

BLASSINGAME, WYATT. *Combat Nurses of World War II*. Illustrated by Gil Walker. New York: Random House, 1967. (Ages 9–up.)
A historical recounting of the teamwork among those who were involved in the battles of World War II. Free of sentimentality and of the exploitation found in some depictions of war-related events.

_____. *Eleanor Roosevelt*. New York: Putnam, 1967. (Ages 7–10.)
Despite its simple language, it captures the subject's sensitivity and her determination to work for human rights.

BOEGEHOLD, BETTY. *Pippa Mouse*. Illustrated by Cyndy Szekeres. New York: Dell, 1973. Also in paper. (Ages 5–8.)
The entire *Pippa Mouse* series delights young children at the same time that it offers them a lively, bright model for their consideration. Pippa is spunky and cheerful; the stories are fun.

BONSALL, CROSBY. *And I Mean It, Stanley*. New York: Harper & Row, 1974. (Ages 5–8.)
The friendship between a giant dog named Stanley, and an active, imaginative little girl who builds contraptions in a junk yard.

BRENNER, BARBARA. *A Year in the Life of Rosie Bernard*. New York: Harper & Row, 1971. Also in paper. (Ages 8–12.)
Rosie's mother has died, and her father, despite his promise to keep Rosie with him, must, because of the pressures of the Depression, take an acting job that keeps him on the road. He therefore brings Rosie to her maternal grandparents' house in Brooklyn. Rosie, a spunky, bright, sensitive, and engaging girl, spends the year with this family, and grows to love and appreciate them. Many issues are found in this

well-crafted book: reaction to death, foster care, old age (the grandfather and grandmother emerge as strong characters) and certainly a heroine who defies stereotyping.

BRINK, CAROL RYRIE. *Caddie Woodlawn*. Illustrated by Trina Schart Hyman. New York: Macmillan, 1935. Also in paper. (Ages 9–12.)
A frontier story of the lively childhood adventures of Caddie and her brothers in the 1860s. Caddie's adventurous and active qualities are admired.

BROEKEL, RAY. *A New True Police Book*. Chicago: Children's Press, 1981. (Ages 6–8.)
Discusses some of the jobs that a police officer does. States at the beginning of the book that both men and women can join the police force. The photographs show both men and women working at their jobs.

BROWNMILLER, SUSAN. *Shirley Chisholm*. Garden City, New York: Doubleday, 1970. Also in paper. (Ages 9–12.)
A biography of Shirley Chisholm, the first black woman to become a U.S. representative. The book provides an insight into the business of American politics.

BUCKMASTER, HENRIETTA. *Women Who Shaped History*. New York: Macmillan, 1966. Also in paper. (Ages 10–up.)
An excellent compilation of short biographies of six women who were important contributors to our country's development. Well written, well balanced, and well selected.

BURCH, ROBERT. *Queenie Peavy*. Illustrated by Jerry Lazare. New York: Viking, 1966. (Ages 9–12.)
Queenie is a strong, intelligent, capable thirteen-year-old. Her self-motivation and determination help her to overcome her father's negative influence and the teasing that she endures because he is in the penitentiary. She does things that only boys are usually thought of as doing and is frequently in trouble. In the end, the support of many adults and her own intelligence win.

BURNETT, FRANCES HODGSON. *The Secret Garden*. Philadelphia: Lippincott, 1911. Also in paper. (Ages 9–12.)
A sensitive, assertive girl comes to live in a new place, discovers a secret garden, new friends, and how to care about others.

BURT, OLIVE. *Black Women of Valor*. Illustrated by Paul Frame. New York: Julian Messner, 1974. (Ages 9–12.)
Tells the stories of four black women who demonstrated their courage and ability: Juliette Derricotte, Maggie Mitchell Walker, Ida Wells Barnett, Septima Poinsette Clark. The book also contains a long list of other black women of valor.

_____. *Sacajawea*. New York: Franklin Watts, 1978. (Ages 9–12.)
Researches the life of the young Native American woman who guided the Lewis and Clark expedition into the Northwest Territory in the early part of the nineteenth century. The text examines a variety of historical records and hypothesizes about her life after the expedition. The tone is more scholarly than most biographies written for this age group.

BYARS, BETSY. *The Midnight Fox.* Illustrated by Ann Grifalconi. New York: Viking, 1968. Also in paper. (Ages 10–up.)
Tommy's parents are going on a long-planned-for trip to Europe, and he reluctantly goes to spend the time that they are gone on a farm. He doen't like sports. He hated camp, does not like animals, and would rather spend his time with his best friend or constructing models. When he gets to the farm he does like it because he discovers a fox and goes frequently to observe the fox. In the end he is able to save the lives of the fox and her baby. The story is gentle, and beautifully written. The reader is pleased that Tommy is not required to change in order to be happy. He remains his own self, and is content.

CAINES, JEANETTE. *Just Us Women.* Illustrated by Pat Cummings. New York: Harper & Row, 1982. (Ages 5–9.)
Aunt Martha and the young narrator of the story are about to embark on a wonderful trip where the two of them will do just exactly as they please, and will have a marvelous time. A joyful account of the relationship between a niece and her aunt, and their sense of independence.

_____. *Window Wishing.* Illustrated by Kevin Brooks. New York: Harper & Row, 1980. (Ages 5–8.)
Grandma Meg is not old, but she is a grandmother, and it is important for children to encounter a variety of women who are grandmothers. Grandma Meg is a wonderful character. She wears sneakers all the time, and leads a very active life. When the two children visit her she takes them fishing, and "window wishing" (her name for looking in the windows of shops and wishing for what they can one day have). Unconventional in many ways, Grandma Meg demonstrates her love and provides her grandchildren with memories they will cherish. As with all of the author's books, the characters are black.

CARLSON, DALE. *Girls Are Equal Too: The Women's Movement for Teenagers.* New York: Atheneum, 1973. (Ages 11–up.)
Raises strong issues and presents clear arguments reflecting the feminist position. Good sections on women's rights and job inequality and on the history of women's rights.

CLEARY, BEVERLY. *Ramona the Brave.* New York: Scholastic, 1975. Paperback. (Ages 8–12.)
Continues the story of Beezus and Ramona. Their mother has begun to work and the girls find themselves facing the problems of "latchkey" children everywhere. Ramona's relationship with her father is shown in some detail. *Ramona and Her Mother* and *Ramona and Her Father* further explore the issues of the working mother and unfulfilled father. Everyone supports the idea of the father's finding a satisfying way of making a living.

_____. *Ramona the Pest.* New York: Morrow, 1968. (Ages 8–11.)
Everyone calls curious, lively Ramona a "pest," but she has a different image of herself during her first few months of kindergarten. Overturns the image of the typical little girl.

CLEAVER, VERA AND BILL. *Ellen Grae.* Illustrated by Ellen Raskin. Philadelphia: Lippincott, 1967. (Ages 9–12.)
Ellen Grae is imaginative beyond belief, and is, in fact, not usually believed by the other characters in the book. A nonconformist in many ways, often to the dismay of her parents and other adults, she is, however, sensitive and appealing.

_____. *Hazel Rye:* Philadelphia: Lippincott, 1983. (Ages 9–12.)
When we first meet Hazel she is content to remain ignorant, unlettered, and unambitious. She is her father's darling, and his sole companion. She is dirty, quick-tempered, and self-indulgent. By the time we reluctantly leave her, she has begun to quest for knowledge and a wider circle of friends and interests. What is more, she now knows the extent to which her father has been involved in keeping her isolated and restricted. We wonder how Hazel will manage to overcome his destructive intervention in her life. The book's characters are all well-drawn and special. Felder, a young boy who assists in Hazel's awakening, is a gentle, extraordinarily intelligent, talented person, reminiscent of Dickon in *The Secret Garden*, except that Felder is a voracious reader. He is particularly gifted in making things grow and in understanding human beings.

_____. *Lady Ellen Grae.* Illustrated by Ellen Raskin. Philadelphia: Lippincott, 1968. (Ages 9–12.)
Another very well-written story by the Cleavers. Ellen Grae is the imaginative, sensitive, loving, bright heroine, who manages, despite her eccentricities, to endear herself to everyone. In this book, her parents decide that she should learn "ladylike" ways. The parody on stereotypic feminine characteristics is somewhat broad, but the demonstration that individual differences are far more acceptable than mindless conformity helps the reader to overlook the flaws.

_____. *Me Too.* Philadelphia: Lippincott, 1973. (Ages 12–up.)
Lydia tries to teach her retarded twin, Lorna. Devoting an entire summer to her sister's education, she endures the hostility of neighbors and the desertion of a friend. She is clever, energetic, introspective, nasty at times, and a clear individual. She is free of sex-role stereotypes. She finally accepts the fact that her sister will remain retarded and that there is little that she can do for her.

_____. *Where the Lilies Bloom.* Illustrated by Jim Spanfeller. Philadelphia: Lippincott, 1969. Also in paper. (Ages 9–up.)
Set in Appalachia. A fourteen-year-old girl cares for her family after the sickness and death of their father, whom they bury and pretend is still alive. Her strength is impressive but is insufficient without the help of her siblings and outside circumstances.

CLIFTON, LUCILLE. *Don't You Remember?* Illustrated by Evaline Ness. New York: Dutton, 1973. (Ages 5–8.)
Desire Mary Tate, black, four years old, and very lively, considers herself to have the best memory in her family. She has three older brothers, one of whom has taken a year off from school to care for her. Her parents both work, and her ambition is to grow up and work at the plant, "Just like Daddy." Division of labor because it must get done, not because of sex role.

_____. *Good, Says Jerome*. New York: Dutton, 1973. (Ages 5–8.)
Jerome, frightened by many things, asks his sister for reassurance. She usually has good comforting answers for him and helps him deal with many aspects of life. Jerome is not punished or derided for his feelings.

COERR, E. *Jane Goodall*. New York: Putnam, 1976.
This famous ethologist (investigator of animal behavior in the natural habitat), even as a tiny girl, was curious about nature. Because she could not afford to pay for a university education, some researchers considered her unqualified to study animal behavior. The author describes her pioneering work on chimpanzee behavior and her efforts to protect wildlife—activities which continue today.

COHEN, MIRIAM. *The New Teacher*. New York: Macmillan, 1972. Also in paper. (Ages 5–8.)
A group of boys and girls at a racially mixed city school get a new teacher and decide that they like her. The activities of the children are not determined by sex. The book provides a good model for nonsexist activities.

COLMAN, HILA. *Diary of a Frantic Kid Sister*. New York: Crown, 1973. (Ages 9–12.)
Written in a narrative/diary form, this is the sensitive story of an eleven-year-old girl's relationships with her mother and her elder sister, all of whom are having difficulty determining their roles.

COONEY, BARBARA. *Miss Rumphius*. Illustrated by the author. New York: Viking, 1982. (Ages 5–9.)
Alice's grandfather is an artist. He impresses upon her that she must do something to make the world more beautiful. Alice lives a very active and adventure-filled life. When she becomes old, she plants lupus seeds in many places, and in so doing, beautifies her world. As a very, very old woman, she passes on her legacy to her niece, who also promises to make the world more beautiful.

DALGLIESH, ALICE. *The Courage of Sarah Noble*. Illustrated by Leonard Weisgard. New York: Scribner, 1954. (Ages 7–10.)
A girl travels into the wilderness in 1707 with her father. She lives with neighboring Indians while her father returns for the rest of the family. She exhibits patience and adaptability. A classic.

DELTON, JUDY. *My Mother Lost Her Job Today*. Illustrated by Irene Trivas. Chicago: Whitman, 1980. (Ages 5–8.)
A young girl is frightened because her mother comes home angry and hurt, having just lost her job. The two females share their concerns and give each other loving support. They determine that everything will eventually be resolved, and may even turn out better than before.

DE PAUW, LINDA GRANT. *Seafaring Women*. Boston: Houghton Mifflin, 1982. (Ages 10–up.)
Women have been pirates, warriors, traders, whalers and sailors, as this interesting book reports. Though most seafaring people are male, there is an interesting history containing accounts of the females who went to sea, some of them because they were a part of the captain's family.

EICHLER, MARGARET. *Martin's Father*. Chapel Hill, North Carolina: Lollipop Power, 1971. (Ages 5–8.)
Martin and his father go through a typical day together. There is no mother, and the two males perform what is conventionally considered to be women's work.

ENGEBRECHT, P. A. *Under the Haystack*. New York: Thomas Nelson, 1973. (Ages 11–up.)
When deserted by her mother and stepfather, Sandy, a thirteen-year-old girl courageously manages to take care of her sisters and the farm where they live. She must work hard, defend herself, and cope with heavy responsibility.

FABER, DORIS. *Lucretia Mott: Foe to Slavery*. Champaign, Illinois: Garrard, 1971. (Ages 8–12.)
The biography of a Quaker woman who spent her life fighting for suffrage and educational rights for women and blacks.

FITZHUGH, LOUISE. *Harriet the Spy*. New York: Harper & Row, 1964. Also in paper. (Ages 9–12.)
An amusing, brash portrayal of a sometimes stubborn eleven-year-old girl who wants to be a spy and writes down all her observations of family and community life in her secret notebook. Harriet is clever and inventive, but not very sensitive to other people's feelings. The other children in the book are also not stereotyped.

FLORIAN, DOUGLAS. *People Working*. Illustrated by the author. New York: Crowell, 1983. (Ages 3–6.)
In a colorful and ebullient book, people of all ages and backgrounds are shown busily at work. Males and females work together and at separate tasks, at home, under the ground, on land and water, in cities and in the country, and this book shows them all. Fun.

GARDNER, RICHARD A. *Dr. Gardner's Fairy Tales for Today's Children*. Illustrated by A. Lowenheim. Englewood Cliffs, New Jersey: Prentice-Hall, 1974. (Ages 8–up.)
Four fairy tales loosely adapted from classical versions. The characters behave in rational, constructive fashion rather than adhering to traditional patterns. The stories are fun.

GAUCH, PATRICIA LEE. *This Time, Tempe Wick?* Illustrated by Margot Tomes. New York: Coward, McCann & Geoghegan, 1974. (Ages 7–10.)
Temperance Wick, a bold, unselfish girl, defies rebellious American soldiers in order to protect her mother, house, and horse during the Revolutionary War.

GEORGE, JEAN CRAIGHEAD. *Julie of the Wolves*. Illustrated by John Schoenherr. New York: Harper & Row, 1972. (Ages 12–up.)
An Eskimo girl runs away from an unhappy situation. Living in the frozen wilderness, she courageously makes friends with the wolves and learns their ways. She must face problems not only of individual survival but also of the changing ways of her people.

GERAS, ADELE. *Apricots at Midnight and Other Stories from a Patchwork Quilt*. Illustrated by Doreen Caldwell. New York: Atheneum, 1982. (Ages 9–up.)

Aunt Pinny is a storyteller. She is also an older woman who has never married, but who, nevertheless, has lived a rich and passionate life because of her understanding of others' needs, her imagination, and her zest for living. Gloriously well written and engrossing.

_____. *Voyage*. New York: Atheneum, 1983. (Ages 10–up.)
Mina takes charge of her brother and mother on their long journey to America. She also manages to buoy up the spirits of most of the passengers in steerage. She is an exuberant, self-assured, artistic girl whose energy enlivens the voyage. Another passenger on the ship, Clara Zussmann, an old woman, is an elderly version of Mina. Her provision of small luxuries in the midst of deprivation adds quality to the voyage that enriches all of the passengers. Geras's prose is elegant and moving. Each vignette is a piece of the tapestry woven by the author.

GLENN, MEL. "Eric Theodore," in *Class Dismissed: High School Poems*. Illustrated by Michael Bernstein. New York: Clarion Books, 1982. (Ages 11–up.)
Eric judges his manliness by how many girls he has dated. The girls seem to him to all be the same, and he feels empty.

GOLDREICH, GLORIA AND ESTHER. *What Can She Be? A Lawyer*. Photographs by Robert Ipcar. New York: Lothrop, Lee & Shepard, 1973. (Ages 7–12.)
Part of the series devoted to describing women in professions formerly considered to be for men only. This book describes how Ellen Green manages to be a lawyer, wife, and mother. Ms. Green has a varied clientele and is shown to be an able attorney, as well as a competent, happy, well-adjusted woman. An excellent, well-conceived book.

_____. *What Can She Be? A Newscaster*. Photographs by Robert Ipcar. New York: Lothrop, Lee & Shepard, 1973. (Ages 7–12.)
A straightforward book about a woman who works as a TV and radio newscaster and also has a good family life. Other books in this unfailingly excellent series contain descriptions of a musician, architect, veterinarian, film producer, farmer, geologist, police officer and computer scientist. Different heritages are represented, and all of the women are portrayed as having lives outside their work as well as being competent at their tasks.

GOODSELL, J. *Eleanor Roosevelt*. New York: Crowell, 1970. (Ages 7–10.)
This biography explains how shy and self-conscious Eleanor learns to assert herself. After her husband's polio attack, she shoulders a wider role in promoting his career and the progressive policies they both espoused. The text stresses her compassion for the suffering of others and her sense of justice—qualities which made her one of the best loved women of our time.

GOODYEAR, CARMEN. *The Sheep Book*. Chapel Hill, North Carolina: Lollipop Power, 1972. (Ages 5–8.)
Describes the cycle of raising sheep for their wool, which then becomes yarn and eventually a garment. The illustrations by the author are appropriate to the text. The farmer is a woman. The message of the text is didactic without being dull.

GRANT, ANNE. *Danbury's Burning*. Illustrated by Pat Howell. New York: McKay, 1976. (Ages 5–8.)

During Revolutionary times, Sybil Ludington rode through towns rousing them, and warning that the British were coming. This sixteen-year-old Connecticut counterpart of Paul Revere should become better known to students of history.

GREENE, BETTE. *Morning Is a Long Time Coming*. New York: Dial Press, 1978. (Ages 11–up.)
In this sequel to *Summer of My German Soldier*, eighteen-year-old Patty goes off on her own to Europe. She does not find the new family she so desperately seeks, but she does find a new love, and some insights into herself and her family.

———. *Philip Hall Likes Me: I Reckon Maybe*. Illustrated by Charles Lilly. New York: Dial Press, 1974. (Ages 9–12.)
Beth Lambert is black, eleven years old, and extraordinarily bright and competent. She is a lively, ambitious, successful young woman, who wants to be a veterinarian, and the reader knows that she will succeed. Some of the action in the book revolves around the issue of Beth's competition with her friend Philip. Their relationship is further explored in the sequel, *Get on Out of Here, Philip Hall* (1981).

———. *Them That Glitter and Them That Don't*. New York: Knopf, 1983. (Ages 11–up.)
Carol Ann Delaney bears the burden of care for her entire family. She is very talented musically, and must choose, in the end, between conforming to her parents' and friends' expectations, and following her own dream. Because she is a gypsy, she is the victim of prejudice. The story is a rich one, going well beyond issues of stereotyping, poverty, and family problems.

GREENFIELD, ELOISE. "Harriet Tubman," in *Honey I Love*. Illustrated by Diane and Leo Dillon. New York: Crowell, 1978. (Ages 6–up.)
Using vernacular language, the poet describes a child's perception of Harriet Tubman's courageous exploits. All of the poems in this collection are personal, evocative, and well crafted.

GREENFIELD, HOWARD. *Gertrude Stein, a Biography*. New York: Crown, 1973. (Ages 12–up.)
A frank and clearly written biography of the controversial woman. Her personal life is described and explained, as well as her public accomplishments.

GRIMES, NIKKI. *Growin'*. Illustrated by Charles Lilly. New York: Dial Press, 1978. (Ages 9–12.)
Pump Jackson's father is dead, and she doesn't get along very well with her mother, who doesn't seem to understand her passion for writing poetry. Pump makes friends with Jim, the class bully, who, it turns out, is a talented artist. Finally Pump realizes that she may have misjudged her mother, who, indeed, at one time also wrote poetry.

GRIPE, MARIA. *The Night Daddy*. Illustrated by Harold Gripe. New York: Delacorte Press, 1971. (Ages 9–12.)
An unusual story about the relationship between a young girl and her adult male baby-sitter who stays nights while her mother works. The story takes place in Sweden.

HAMILTON, VIRGINIA. *Sweet Whispers, Brother Rush*. New York: Philomel Books, 1981. (Ages 12–up.)
A masterful story about a black family, past and present, and a young girl's coming of age. Tree, fourteen years old, is very protective of her seventeen-year-old brother Dabney (Dab). Dab is "slow" and "different." Brother Rush, a handsome ghost, appears to Tree and tells about the family's past, including the emotional neglect of Dab by their mother. Dab has a rare illness and eventually dies. When Tree recovers from her mourning, she begins to accept her own womanhood.

HANLON, EMILY. *The Swing*. New York: Bradbury Press, 1979. (Ages 9–12.)
The two main characters, Emily, a hearing-disabled eleven-year-old, and Danny, a thirteen-year-old having a difficult time mourning his father's death, lock horns with each other in this well-written story dealing strongly with how to be an individual in a society that demands conformity.

HARRIS, JANET. *A Single Standard*. New York: McGraw-Hill, 1971. (Ages 10–up.)
Although this book contains a historical approach to the feminist movement, it stresses the sociological and psychological implications more than the history. The book relates to every aspect of women's lives.

HART, CAROLE. *Delilah*. New York: Harper & Row, 1973. Delilah is an active, happy girl who enjoys drums and playing basketball. She helps her father fix dinner on "his night" to cook. Acceptance of other-than-usual roles and interests for women and men are portrayed here. Delilah has good relationships with both parents. Told from the perspective of the child. Delilah emerges as a well-balanced person.

HASKINS, JAMES. *Fighting Shirley Chisholm*. New York: Dial Press, 1975. (Ages 12–up.)
The dynamic black representative is described here in excellent detail. Haskins's book is very frank and inclusive.

HENRIOD, LORRAINE. *Marie Curie*. Illustrated by Fermin Rocher. New York: Putnam, 1970. (Ages 7–10.)
A "beginning to read" biography dispelling the myth that radium was discovered accidentally. In simple but clear language it points out the care and study that Marie Curie devoted to her profession.

HERMAN, HARRIET. *The Forest Princess*. Illustrated by Carde Petersen Duinell. Berkeley Calif.: Over the Rainbow Press, 1974. Paperback. (Ages 5–10.)
A modern-day fairy tale in which a princess wakes a sleeping prince with a kiss and then enchants him with her independence and self-assurance.

HERZIG, ALISON AND MALI, JANE. *Oh Boy! Babies!* Illustrated by Kathrine Thomas. Boston: Little, Brown, 1980. (Ages 10–up.)
An all-male school offers an elective on baby care to fifth and sixth graders with real babies! This is a delightful book full of photographs and quotes that show the boys learning to hold, bathe, diaper, feed and love babies.

HEYN, LEAH. *Challenge to Become a Doctor: The Story of Elizabeth Blackwell*. Old Westbury, New York: Feminist Press, 1971. (Ages 9–12.)
The biography of the struggle of a determined woman to become a doctor despite the

discrimination evident in the all-male profession. Blackwell, in fact, became the first woman physician.

HEYWARD, DUBOSE, AND ZARSSONI, MARJORY. *The Country Bunny and the Little Gold Shoes*. Boston: Houghton Mifflin, 1939. Also in paper. (Ages 5–8.)
A story about a rabbit who is a mother and a strong, proud Easter Bunny at the same time. While she is out delivering Easter eggs, her little bunnies, boys and girls alike, are taking care of the house. Note the early copyright date.

HOCHMAN, SANDRA. *The Magic Convention*. Illustrated by Ben Shecter. Garden City, New York: Doubleday, 1971. (Ages 8–up.)
A girl goes to a professional magician's convention, sees an exciting performance by a woman magician, and decides more than ever that she wants to be a magician.

HOCHSCHILD, ARLIE RUSSELL. *Colleen the Question Girl*. Illustrated by Gail Ashby. Old Westbury, New York: Feminist Press, 1964. Paperback. (Ages 5–10.)
Colleen is an intelligent young girl who questions everyone about serious and confusing topics—race, discrimination, wealth, and status.

HOEHLING, MARY. *Girl Soldier and Spy: Sarah Emma Edmundson*. New York: Julian Messner, 1959. (Ages 10–up.)
A well-written account of this unusual woman. The author always refers to her heroine as a woman, and it is as a woman that Sarah accomplishes her adventures. Her qualities are womanly, even when she is pretending to be a man. The author values women and presents the story so that readers may do so as well.

HOLMAN, FELICE. *Victoria's Castle*. Illustrated by Lillian Hoban. New York: Norton, 1966. (Ages 5–8.)
Victoria is an only child with a wild imagination with which she builds a castle and a fantasy world filled with unusual animals.

HOPKINS, LEE BENNETT. *Girls Can Too!* Illustrated by Emily McCully. New York: Franklin Watts, 1972. (Ages 5–8.)
A book of positive poems about the different things girls can do, think, and feel.

_____. *I Loved Rose Ann*. New York: Four Winds Press, 1976. (Ages 7–10.)
Harry tells his story about why he is so angry at Rose Ann, whom he used to love. The book's value lies not only in the humor of the story, but especially in the fact that the second part of the book tells the same story, only this time from Rose Ann's perspective. In Rose Ann's account we gain much information about stereotyping and its consequences, but not in a didactic or heavy-handed manner. Excellent book.

HOWARD, MOSES L. *The Ostrich Chase*. Illustrated by Barbara Seuling. New York: Holt, Rinehart and Winston, 1974. (Ages 10–12.)
Khuana, a young woman of the Bushman tribe, violates tradition by learning to hunt and to build fires. Because of these skills, she is able to save her grandmother's life and to conquer the desert. She nevertheless remains interested in womanly things as well. She is an admirable character.

HUNT, IRENE. *Up a Road Slowly*. Chicago: Follett, 1966. Also in paper. (Ages 12–up.)

Julie goes to live with a strict aunt when her mother dies. Julie learns to admire her aunt enough to want to stay with her instead of returning to live with her remarried father.

HUNTER, KRISTIN. *The Soul Brothers and Sister Lou*. New York: Scribner, 1968. Also in paper. (Ages 12–up.)
Detailed portrayal of a group of black teen-agers, both boys and girls, growing up in Harlem. Lou is bright, active, and ambitious.

ISADORA, RACHEL. *Max*. Illustrated by the author. New York: Macmillan, 1976. (Ages 5–8.)
Max accompanies his sister to her dance class and recognizes the advantages of such a class. He joins in, and enjoys it as much as he does his sports.

_____. *My Ballet Class*. New York: Greenwillow Books, 1980. (Ages 6–8.)
A very simple story of a girl attending her ballet class. The teacher is a man and boys also attend the class. Rachel's father calls for her after class, carrying a younger child.

_____. *No, Agatha!* Illustrated by the author. New York: Greenwillow, 1980. (Ages 5–8.)
Agatha accompanies her parents on a ship to England. The adults try to make her conform to what "nice" little girls do, but Agatha is lively and irrepressible.

JACOBS, WILLIAM JAY. *Mother, Aunt Susan, & Me: The First Fight for Women's Rights*. New York: Coward, McCann & Geoghegan, 1979. (Ages 9–12.)
In an interesting format, the reader is introduced to Sojourner Truth, Susan B. Anthony, and Elizabeth Cady Stanton, the mother of the teenaged narrator of the story.

JEWELL, NANCY. *Try and Catch Me*. Illustrated by Leonard Weisgard. New York: Harper & Row, 1972. (Ages 4–8.)
An active girl is self-sufficient and energetic. As she goes about her play, a boy teases her and seems to disapprove of what she is doing. But in the end, he approaches her and invites her to join him in a swim. Both the boy and the girl are described in positive ways.

JORDAN, JUNE. *Fannie Lou Hamer*. Illustrated by Albert Williams. New York: Crowell, 1972. (Ages 5–8.)
A well-told biography of a brave black woman who fought for the rights of black people and who began a cooperative in Mississippi.

KAUFMAN, JOE. *Busy People*. New York: Golden Press, 1973. (Ages 5–7.)
A book about community life and careers that includes women and men, blacks and whites, in nonstereotyped roles.

KELLER, GAIL FAITHFULL. *Janes Addams*. Illustrated by Frank Aloise. New York: Crowell, 1971. (Ages 7–9.)
A clear description of the work and personality of Jane Addams. Simply, but in useful detail, her life is well narrated.

KINGMAN, LEE. *Georgina and the Dragon*. Illustrated by Leonard Shortall. Boston: Houghton Mifflin, 1972. (Ages 7–10.)
Georgina Gooch is determined to live up to her suffragist great-grandmother's tradition. She crusades for equal rights and manages to raise the level of consciousness of her whole neighborhood. She is fun—her energy and intelligence are outstanding.

KLEIN, NORMA. *Girls Can Be Anything*. Illustrated by Roy Doty. New York: Dutton, 1973. (Ages 5–8.)
Marina's friend Adam tells her she has to be the nurse or the stewardess when they play. But Marina's parents inform her that she can be anything, even a doctor, pilot, or U.S. President. Marina reports this to Adam, and they change the way they play their games.

_____. *Mom, the Wolf Man and Me*. New York: Pantheon, 1972. Also in paper. (Ages 10–up.)
Brett and her mother are females who do not conform to a stereotype. Brett's mother has never been married and is very frank about her sex life. She is a competent working woman, and she and Brett share an open and affectionate relationship.

_____. *Naomi in the Middle*. Illustrated by Leigh Grant. New York: Dial Press, 1974. (Ages 7–10.)
Most of the characters in this book are female; all are individuals. They are pictured wearing comfortable clothes and doing activities of all sorts. The grandmother is an interesting character in her own right. She is not very fond of infants, preferring "more complicated" older children. The shop teacher is female. And so is Alice, Bobo's pet rat.

_____. *A Train for Jane*. Illustrated by Miriam Schottland. Old Westbury, New York: Feminist Press, 1974. (Ages 5–8.)
A verse-story telling how, despite all efforts of persuasion by her parents, Jane insists on a train for a Christmas present. It is fine for other girls to want "girls toys" but she loves her train.

KONIGSBURG, E. L. *From the Mixed-up Files of Mrs. Basil E. Frankweiler*. New York: Atheneum, 1967. Also in paper. (Ages 8–12.)
Claudia and Jamie run away from home and hide in the Metropolitan Museum of Art, where they get involved in a mystery centered around a work of art formerly owned by Mrs. Basil E. Frankweiler. Both Claudia and Mrs. Frankweiler are strong females with individual personalities.

KRAUS, ROBERT. *Another Mouse to Feed*. Illustrated by Jose Aruego and Ariane Dewey. New York: Windmill/Wanderer Books, 1980.
When Mr. and Mrs. Mouse become exhausted from overwork, caring for their thirty-one children, the little mice decide to take over. Everyone enjoys the results.

KRAUSS, RUTH. *I'll Be You and You Be Me*. Illustrated by Maurice Sendak. Lenox, Massachusetts: Bookstore Press, 1973. Also in paper. (Ages 8–up.)
Warm ideas, in poetry form, about friendship between boys and girls.

KYTE, KATHLEEN. *In Charge: A Complete Handbook for Kids with Working Parents.* New York: Knopf, 1983. Also in paper. (Ages 10–up.)
Sensible ideas and advice for young people whose parent(s) work outside the house.

LADER, LAWRENCE, AND MELTZER, MILTON. *Margaret Sanger, Pioneer of Birth Control.* New York: Crowell, 1969. Also in paper. (Ages 12–up.)
A biography of Margaret Sanger, who fought to make birth control a right for all women, especially the poor. She was strong enough to maintain her own individuality.

LANDAU, ELAINE. *Women, Women, Feminism in America.* New York: Iulian Messner, 1970. (Ages 12–up.)
Presenting a case for equality of the sexes, the author describes many instances of discrimination as the basis for her argument. She also tells of countries, such as Israel and Sweden, where great advances in the cause of equality have been made. A well-written, persuasive book.

LARRICK, NANCY. AND MERRIAM, EVE, eds. *Male and Female Under 18.* New York: Avon, 1973. Paperback. (Ages 8–up.)
Comments and poems contributed by girls and boys, aged eight to eighteen, reflecting how they feel about their sex roles. The responses range from strong support of tradition to militant anger.

LASKER, JOE. *Mothers Can Do Anything.* Chicago: Whitman, 1972. (Ages 3–8.)
This book demonstrates the variety of jobs that mothers can hold, including scientist, artist, and lion tamer. The illustrations are fun, and the message is an important one.

LASKY, KATHRYN. *My Island Grandma.* New York: Fredrick Warne, 1979. (Ages 7–10.)
Abbey's grandma is a rugged and resourceful woman. She teaches Abbey much about her surroundings. Grandma carries wood, pumps water, takes down and puts up shutters. She also has a very gentle side and takes the time to look at and enjoy nature.

LAWRENCE, JACOB. *Harriet and the Promised Land.* New York: Simon and Schuster, 1968. (Ages 5–8.)
In verse and colorful pictures, this book describes the courageous black woman, Harriet Tubman, who escaped from slavery and helped many others to escape also. Her life was difficult and unconventional, as she persevered in her heroic actions despite grave danger.

L'ENGLE, MADELEINE. *A Wrinkle in Time.* New York: Farrar, Straus, 1962. Also in paper. (Ages 12–up.)
Meg is the heroine of this adventure about two children who travel into space with three wise, magical creatures to find their scientist-father. Their mother, too, is brilliant and a scientist. The other two books in the series, *A Swiftly Tilting Planet* and *A Door in the Wind* continue the same unstereotyped characterizations.

L'ENGLE, MADELEINE. *The Young Unicorns.* New York: Farrar, Straus, 1968. (Ages 12–up.)

A mystery set in New York with a blind musician, Emily, and a scientific whiz, Sue, as heroines of the story. All of the other books in the Austin family series contain strong and unstereotypic female characters. The males are also free of gender-role impositions.

LEVINSON, IRENE. *Peter Learns to Crochet*. Illustrated by Ketra Sutherland. Berkeley: New Seed Press, 1973. Paperback. (Ages 5–8.)
Peter wants to learn to crochet but has trouble finding someone to teach him, until he asks his teacher, Mr. Alvarado.

LEVITIN, SONIA. *Rita, the Weekend Rat*. Illustrated by Leonard Shortall. New York: Atheneum, 1971. (Ages 8–12.)
Cynthia is a second grader who hates being a girl. She has a rat named Rita, whom she cares for on weekends. She begins to reconcile herself to being a girl, by the end of the book, and does not stop being active or taking care of Rita and her baby rats.

_____. *Alan and Naomi*. New York: Harper & Row, 1977. Also in paper. (Ages 10–up.)
A beautifully written, tragic yet heroic story of the attempts of a young boy, Alan, to help his friend, Naomi, recover from the horror of the Holocaust. Alan is a sensitive, thoughtful male, as is his father in this book that explores many issues.

LEVOY, MYRON. *Shadow Like a Leopard*. New York: Harper & Row, 1981. (Ages 11–up.)
In order to prove his worth to a street gang, fourteen-year-old Ramon Santiago robs an old man, Arnold Glasser, at knife-point. Glasser is an artist; Ramon is a poet. The two characters form a surprising alliance, and help each other to find a way out of their problems. Both are unforgettable characters: feisty, intelligent, talented, and unwilling to conform to what others want to force them to be.

LEWIS, MARJORIE. *Ernie and the Mile-Long Muffler*. Illustrated by Margot Apple. New York: Coward, McCann & Geoghegan, 1982. (Ages 6–9).
Ernie learned to knit from his Uncle Simon, a sailor, when Ernie was at home with the chicken pox, and was bored. Uncle Ernie is a great character, and a wonderful model for male adults. Ernie decides to knit a mile-long muffler as a project. He doesn't quite make it, but along the way he learns some lessons about arithmetic, friendship, and perseverance. An excellent book.

LOFTS, NORAH. *The Maude Reed Tale*. Illustrated by Anne and Janet Grahame Johnstone. Nashville: Thomas Nelson, 1972. Also in paper. (Ages 10–up.)
The setting is the Middle Ages. Maude, about twelve years old, has a twin brother, who runs away from home to be a minstrel. Maude wants to be a wool merchant. The conflicts of personal and societal values, besides the cleverness of the heroine, make the book a vital one. The writing is of excellent quality.

LONGSWORTH, POLLY. *Emily Dickinson: Her Letter to the World*. New York: Crowell, 1965. (Ages 10–up.)
A nicely constructed biography of Emily Dickinson. Her reclusive behavior is accepted as a logical result of her way of life, rather than being presented as a mystery.

LONGSWORTH, POLLY. *I, Charlotte Forten, Black and Free*. New York, Crowell, 1970. (Ages 10–12.)
Charlotte Forten serves as the narrator of this fictionalized autobiography. Her life is eventful and rich. She meets and works against slavery with many famous people. The book describes other abolitionists, such as the Grimké sisters and William Lloyd Garrison, and tells the stories of such notable blacks as Frederick Douglass, James Forten, and William Wells Brown, among others. The fight for women's rights is seen as parallel to and compatible with abolition.

LYSTAD, MARY. *Jennifer Takes Over P.S. 94*. Illustrated by Ray Cruz. New York: Putnam, 1972. (Ages 3–8.)
Jennifer imagines how she would run the school, while sitting on the "punish bench" for kicking a girl who hit her first.

MACGREGOR, ELLEN. *Miss Pickerell Goes to Mars*. Illustrated by Paul Galdone. New York: McGraw-Hill, 1951. Also in paper. (Ages 9–12.)
Miss Pickerell is an old woman who travels from one exciting adventure to another, all over the universe. She is much brighter than most of the males, and accomplishes more than most people. There is a long series of Miss Pickerell books.

MACLACHLAN, PATRICIA. *Arthur, for the Very First Time*. Illustrated by Lloyd Bloom. New York: Harper & Row, 1980. Also in paper. (Ages 9–12.)
Arthur, a ten-year-old boy who has always been an observer and a writer, dreads the approaching arrival of a new sibling. His parents have not been responsive or forthright with him, and he has functioned in a somewhat self-centered and narrow pattern. With the help of his great aunt and uncle, and his friend, Moira, he learns to value new life and to become much more sensitive to the feelings of others. Moira is a child whose parents have deserted her. She lives with her grandfather, and is not certain until the end of the book that he really loves her. A social worker who comes to check on her understands the relationship, and approves of Moira's placement in her grandfather's house. A tender, well-written story.

_____. *Cassie Binegar*. New York: Harper & Row, 1982. (Ages 9–12.)
No character in any of this author's books is stereotypic. In this story of changes, interactions, and, above all, love, Cassie, the young protagonist, learns to accept herself and her world. The story is remarkable for its evocation of strong feelings, lightened by an overlay of wit. The grandmother, despite her age, is a passionate lover of life and people, and understands Cassie's feelings. She is an admirable model, as are all of the male characters, who are permitted poetic and gentle thoughts, dreams and actions, without any loss of strength or dignity.

_____. *The Sick Day*. Illustrated by William Pène Du Bois. New York: Pantheon, 1979. (Ages 5–8.)
Emily and her father spend some loving time together while Emily is sick with a bad cold, and her mother is at work. Emily's father is tender, nurturing, and fun.

MANN, PEGGY. *Amelia Earhart, First Lady of Flight*. Illustrated by Kiyo Komoda. New York: Coward, McCann, 1970. (Ages 10–12.)
A biography of the first woman to become a well-known aviator. Earhart is one of the women most written about.

MARZOLLO, JEAN. *Close Your Eyes*. Illustrated by Susan Jeffers. New York: Dial Press, 1978. (Ages 5–8.)
Sensitive story about a father's and child's nighttime fantasies, "Close your eyes and you can play with woolly lambs on a lazy day." Father is playful, caring and gentle. His androgynous personality is portrayed in a warm storyline and beautiful illustrations.

MATHIS, SHARON BELL. *Listen for the Fig Tree*. New York: Viking, 1974. Also in paper. (Ages 12–up.)
Sixteen-year-old Muffin Johnson is blind. She is extraordinarily competent. She manages all of the details of housekeeping, sews and shops, and has excellent relationships with people. Her mother is weak, and almost destroyed over the death of the father. Muffin takes care of her. The male characters in this story are not stereotyped. Muffin is a super woman. The only chink in her armor surfaces when someone attempts to rape her. Her feelings about her black heritage are a strong part of the book. Muffin's blindness adds a dimension to the book, as does the strong support of the black community.

_____. *Sidewalk Story*. Illustrated by Leo Carty. New York: Viking, 1971. Also in paper. (Ages 9–12.)
Lilly Etta Allen is the nine-year-old protagonist. By her refusal to accept an unfair situation, she manages to help her friend Tanya deal with eviction. Lilly Etta enlists the aid of the newspapers and also acts on her own to protect her friend's possessions.

MAURY, INEZ. *My Mother the Mail Carrier*. New York: Feminist Press, 1976. (Ages 7–12.)
Written in Spanish and English, the story shows how a single-parent is an effective mother, mail carrier, and a person all at the same time. The son, Lupita, loves his mother very much and is very proud of her.

MAY, J. *Billie Jean King: Tennis Champion*. Mankato, Minnesota: Crestwood House, 1974.
This biography of Billie Jean King is written in simple language with many photographs of the subject. Emphasis is given to her childhood interest in sports, her introduction to tennis, and to her non-traditional role in competitive tennis.

MCGOVERN, ANN. *Half a Kingdom*. Illustrated by Nola Langner. New York: Frederick Warne, 1977. (Ages 7–10.)
Signy, a poor peasant girl, rescues Prince Lini from the evil trolls. When they marry, they decide to rule jointly and make the kingdom a more democratic place.

MCKINLEY, ROBIN. *The Blue Sword*. New York: Greenwillow Books, 1982. (Ages 11–up.)
Harry Crewe, an unusually tall, strong and intelligent young woman, is the protagonist of this fantasy-adventure set in the Homelander Empire and the Kingdom of Damar. Women warriors, ethnic conflict and magic are but a few of the ingredients in a very well-written story.

MELTZER, MILTON. *Tongue of Flame: The Life of Lydia Marie Child*. New York: Crowell, 1965. Also in paper. (Ages 12–up.)

A well-written account of the life and times of Lydia Maria Child, who fought for such causes as abolition, women's rights, and rights of Native Americans. This book is one of the excellent series of biographies entitled "Women of America."

MERRIAM, EVE. *Boys and Girls, Girls and Boys*. Illustrated by Harriet Sherman. New York: Holt, Rinehart & Winston, 1972. Also in paper. (Ages 3–8.)
An unpretentious book showing children, boys and girls alike, of various ethnic heritages, exploring, being active and enjoying life.

_____. *Mommies at Work*. New York: Knopf, 1961. Also in paper. (Ages 5–8.)
Shows what women can do outside the house—a very broad and varied range, all compatible with being a mother.

MERRILL, SUSAN. *Washday*. New York: Seabury Press, 1978. (Ages 5–8.)
A little girl describes the fun her family shares on washday. Everyone joins in to help. Even Papa. Cooperation is the rule as Papa makes cocoa while Mama builds a fire. In all of the illustrations Papa is shown helping with the children or helping with the housework. This book could be used as a tool to discuss the importance of a family working together and sharing responsibilities.

MINARD, ROSEMARY, ed. *Womenfolk and Fairy Tales*. Illustrated by Suzanna Klein. Boston: Houghton Mifflin, 1975. (Ages 7–10.)
Females are the major characters in all of the stories in this book. In general, they exhibit such qualities as intelligence, courage, and integrity. The introduction is a valuable addition to the tales themselves.

MITCHELL, JOYCE SLAYTON, ed. *Free to Choose: Decision-making for Young Men*. New York: McGraw-Hill, 1974. Also in paper. (Ages 12–up.)
Good advice to young men from a number of authors, ministers, psychologists, and other professionals interested in helping young people grow up in a liberated society.

NATHAN, DOROTHY. *Women of Courage*. Illustrated by Carolyn Cather. New York: Random House, 1964. (Ages 10–up.)
Biographies of five brave women: Susan B. Anthony, women's rights crusader, Jane Addams, social reformer who worked for the poor, Mary McLeod Bethune, educator of black children, Amelia Earhart, daring aviator, and Margaret Mead, anthropologist searching for the "secrets of human nature."

NEILSON, WINTHROP AND FRANCIS. *Seven Women: Great Painters*. Philadelphia: Chilton, 1969. (Ages 12–up.)
Serious critique of seven famous painters, from Angelica Kauffmann to Georgia O'Keeffe.

NESS, EVALINE, compiler and illustrator. *Amelia Mixed the Mustard and Other Poems*. New York: Scribner, 1975. (All ages.)
A collection of poems dedicated to all females. Each one of the poems has a heroine at its center. The mood is light; the poems are well selected.

NESS, EVALINE. *Do You Have the Time, Lydia?* New York: Dutton, 1971. (Ages 5–8.)
Lydia and her brother live with their father, who is a florist. Lydia is a little dynamo.

NOBLE, IRIS. *Emmeline and Her Daughters: The Pankhurst Suffragettes*. New York: Julian Messner, 1974. (Ages 12–up.)

Detailed story of the British Pankhurst family. The mother and three daughters were ardent and active fighters for women's rights.

NOLAN, MADEENA SPRAY. *My Daddy Don't Go to Work*. Illustrated by Jim LaMarche. Minneapolis: Carolrhoda Books, 1978. (Ages 5–8.)
The father in this story stays home and does the cooking and cleaning because he cannot find another job. His wife goes outside the home to work. He is anxious, and thinks of looking for employment in another geographic area. The entire family agrees that it is very important for the family to stay together, so the father continues to stay at home. The family is black.

NORTON, MARY. *The Borrowers*. New York: Harcourt Brace Jovanovich, 1953. Also in paper. (Ages 8–up.)
The first of a series of books about little people called Borrowers who live under the floors and in the walls of human's houses. In this book, Arietty, an adventurous female, is taken out by her father to learn how to borrow—something usually done only by males.

O'DELL, SCOTT. *Island of the Blue Dolphins*. Boston: Houghton Mifflin, 1960. Also in paper. (Ages 10–up.)
Karana, a young Native American girl, is alone on her home island after her people have left and her brother has been killed by wild dogs. She manages her own survival courageously for many years until, at last, she is rescued.

_____. *Sing Down the Moon*. Boston: Houghton Mifflin, 1970. Also in paper. (Ages 7–up.)
A courageous young Navajo woman experiences all sorts of dangers: she is kidnapped by Spaniards, endures the Long Walk to Fort Sumner, and manages to return, with her husband and child, to their original home. The story focuses on the character of the young woman rather than on the hardships of the Navajos.

OPPENHEIM, SHULAMITH. *The Selchie's Seed*. New York: Bradbury Press, 1975. Also in paper. (Ages 9–up.)
Marian's heritage is the seal folk, who sometimes are able to shed their sea-skins and live on land as human. She is drawn to the sea, and, at her coming-of-age, no one and nothing can prevent her return. Beautifully written, the story is a haunting one.

ORTIZ, VICTORIA. *Sojourner Truth, A Self-Made Woman*. Philadelphia: Lippincott, 1974. (Ages 12–up.)
In reading the story of this remarkable black woman, much history is learned. The link between the feminist and abolitionist movement is described. Sojourner Truth, a pioneer for black civil rights, vigorously fought for her people until her death.

PARLIN, JOHN. *Amelia Earhart*. Illustrated by Anthony D'Adamo. New York: Dell, 1962. Paperback (Ages 8–10.)
A pioneer in aviation, Amelia Earhart ventured because she felt that "Women must try to do things men have tried. When they fail, their failure must be but a challenge to others."

PATERSON, KATHERINE. *Bridge to Terabithia*. New York: Crowell, 1977. (Ages 9–12.)

A beautifully written story about the friendship of a boy, Jess, and a girl, Leslie, neither of whom is a conventional character. Leslie runs as swiftly as Jess, and is bold, and willing to take chances. Jess is sensitive and artistic. When Leslie dies, suddenly and unexpectedly, Jess goes through each of the stages of mourning, from denial to guilt, anger, and grief. In the end he decides to give to others of the "magic" Leslie taught him in their imaginative play, and he begins with his little sister.

PATTERSON, L. *Coretta Scott King*. Champaign, Illinous: Garrard, 1977.
This biography of Ms. King describes her life as a lively talented child in an energetic family. She goes North to college and to pursue a musical career, defying the constraints placed on blacks in our society prior to the Civil Rights Movement. The author emphasizes Ms. King's role in her husband's career and as a spokesperson on her own for human rights.

PEAVY, LINDA, AND SMITH, URSULA. *Women Who Changed Things*. New York: Scribner, 1983. (Ages 12–up.)
Well-written accounts of nine women who are not very well known, but who, by their talent, determination, and intelligence were able to make a difference in the world. Included are a mountain climber, a medical inspector, a psychologist, a social worker, a journalist, an educator, an astronomer, and a woman who founded an organization of craftspeople that provided jobs for many other women. None of these women were world-famous in their time, but each of them has an interesting story, and provides an excellent model for young readers.

PERL, LILA. *That Crazy April*. New York: Seabury Press, 1974. (Ages 9–12.)
Eleven-year-old Cress's mother is very much involved in the women's movement. Her father cheerfully participates in the maintenance of the house, and supports his wife's interests. Cress resents her mother's activities. In the end she realizes that she will develop her own interests and personality and will learn to survive on her own terms. The book raises interesting questions.

PFEFFER, SUSAN BETH. *The Beauty Queen*. Garden City, New York: Doubleday, 1974. (Ages 12–up.)
A girl is coerced by her mother to enter the local beauty contest. She wins the titles of Miss Great Lakes and Miss Harrison County. After much thought, she realizes that being a beauty queen has no real meaning for her; she rejects her titles and the values they represent.

PHELPS, ETHEL JOHNSON. *The Maid of the North: Feminist Folk Tales from around the World*. Illustrated by Lloyd Bloom. New York: Holt, Rinehart and Winston, 1981. (Ages 11–up.)
A collection of tales from the oral tradition of many countries. Approximately seventeen different heritages are represented. The heroines are resourceful, intelligent, active, courageous and self-confident. The author has provided an introduction describing the sources for the tales.

PHELPS, ETHEL JOHNSTON. *Tatterhood and Other Tales*. Illustrated by Pamela B. Ford. New York: Feminist Press, 1978. (Ages 8–12.)
A collection of traditional tales from Norway, England, China, and other countries.

Each tale portrays a witty and resourceful woman who actively sets about to determine her own fate.

PLOTZ, HELEN, ed. *Saturday's Children: Poems of Work.* New York: Greenwillow, 1982. (Ages 11–up.)
One of the sections of this excellent book contains poems exclusively about women at work.

POWELL, MEREDITH, AND YOKUBINAS, GAIL. *What to Be?* Chicago: Children's Press, 1972. (Ages 5–8.)
A little girl tries to decide what to be when she grows up. Her choices are varied. She considers everything from a lumberjack or an astronaut to a dancer or a beautician. The book offers good choices for girls, or even for boys. It shows the many professions in which women can be involved.

REAVIN, SAM. *Hurray for Captain Jane!* Illustrated by Emily Arnold McCully. New York: Parents' Magazine Press, 1971. (Ages 5–8.)
Jane goes on a fantasy ocean voyage while she is taking a bath. The captain of the ship, she saves the ship from crashing into an iceberg. When she awakens from her fantasy, she plans to pilot a plane for her next adventure.

REIT, SEYMOUR, AND GOLDMAN, LOUIS. *A Week in Hagar's World: Israel.* London: Macmillan, 1969. (Ages 5–8.)
A week in the life of a little Jewish girl who lives in a kibbutz in Israel, illustrated beautifully by photographs. The nonsexist aspects of kibbutz life are displayed.

RICH, GIBSON. *Firegirl.* Illustrated by Charlotte Purrington Farley. Old Westbury, New York: Feminist Press, 1972. (Ages 6–10.)
A girl has ambition to become a fire fighter and learns all about what it takes to realize this goal.

ROCKWELL, HARLOW. *My Doctor.* New York: Macmillan, 1973. (Ages 5–8.)
Description of a regular medical checkup, and the doctor is a woman. The description is matter-of-fact; the message is not intrusive.

RODGERS, MARY. *Freaky Friday.* New York: Harper & Row, 1972. Also in paper. (Ages 10–up.)
A girl magically becomes her mother for a day and sees herself from a new perspective.

SACHS, MARILYN. *Call Me Ruth.* Garden City, New York: Doubleday, 1982. (Ages 9–up.)
Ruth and her mother emigrate from Russia to New York City. Ruth's father had worked for nine years to save enough money to send for them. Ruth loves America from the moment she arrives; her mother hates it. They are poor; their apartment has no toilet or bath; the father is ill, and soon dies. Afterward, the mother becomes active in the Labor Movement, causing enormous embarrassment to Ruth. Ruth is a very bright, academically talented child; she works hard at school, loves to read, and is considered a model child. The author presents several points of view clearly and sympathetically. She also conveys an accurate historical view of early twentieth century labor and immigrant issues.

_____. *Peter and Veronica*. Illustrated by Louis Glanzman. Garden City, New York: Doubleday, 1969. Also in paper. (Ages 8–12.)
Peter and Veronica are good friends despite their differences of sex, religion, and social acceptablility and despite pressures exerted by parents and peers. They finally realize that even good friendship can sometimes be very painful. Veronica is strong, pugnacious, and awkward. She begins to change in physical appearance but does not want that to affect her relationship with people.

SAWYER, RUTH. *Roller Skates*. Illustrated by V. Angelo. New York: Viking, 1936. Also in paper. (Ages 9–12.)
Lucinda is the lively, bouncy heroine of this story. The episodes take place in very upper-class old New York. Lucinda is unusual for her time but beautifully in tune with today.

SCOTT, ANN HERBERT. *Sam*. Illustrated by Symeon Shimin. New York: McGraw-Hill, 1967. (Ages 5–8.)
Sam wants to play, but his mother, father, sister, and brother all send him away—they are too busy. When Sam begins to cry, they all realize the cause of his unhappiness. Mother finds a task for him: she helps him learn how to bake a raspberry tart. Beautiful illustrations. Loving, aware family. Child permitted to cry, not criticized.

SEED, SUZANNE. *Saturday's Child—36 Women Talk about Their Jobs*. Chicago: J. Philip O'Hara, 1973. Also in paper. (Ages 11–up.)
Thirty-six women who have had successful careers in architecture, theatre, law, carpentry, science, and so on, talk about their training, how they chose their jobs, and how their jobs affect their families.

SHULEVITZ, URI. *Rain Rain Rivers*. New York: Farrar, Straus & Giroux, 1969. (Ages 5–8.)
The author-illustrator poetically describes the positive effects of rain. The central character is an active and responsible girl. A boy could also have been this central character. The fact that it is a girl creates a positive basis for young readers' sex-role redefinition.

SIEGEL, BEATRICE. *An Eye on the World*. New York: Frederick Warne, 1980. (Ages 11–up.)
Margaret Bourke-White, the subject of this biography, was a respected, talented, and courageous photographer. She was noted for her dedication to her work, and for the stories she told through her camera. She was a fighter for political, social, and economic equality.

SIMON, MARCIA L. *A Special Gift*. New York: Harcourt Brace Jovanovich, 1978. (Ages 9–12.)
Peter loves to dance and play basketball. He has been keeping his ballet a secret, however, and when he wins a role in The Nutcracker, he must come to grips with his "double life." Some adults and children in the story react negatively to his ballet; some think it is "weird." Peter realizes that dancing is what he wants to do and his confidence convinces others of its value. Sympathetically written, the book makes the case that one should do what one is best at, no matter what the gender.

SMUCKER, BARBARA. *Runaway to Freedom*. New York: Harper & Row, 1977. (Ages 9–up.)
More than an adventure story, this account of the escape of two young women from slavery tells of friendship and courage. Twelve-year-old Julilly protects and supports her friend, Liza, who is severely disabled because of her former master's beatings.

SORENSEN, VIRGINIA. *Plain Girl*. Illustrated by C. Geer. New York: Harcourt, Brace, 1956. Also in paper. (Ages 9-12.)
Esther is a member of an Amish family. The story revolves around the conflict between the teachings of her group and the rest of the world. Esther is a strong heroine because she struggles to think for herself and to make decisions about how she will behave.

SPEARE, ELIZABETH GEORGE. *The Witch of Blackbird Pond*. Boston: Houghton Mifflin, 1958. Also in paper. (Age 12.)
Kit Tyler, orphaned as a young teen-ager, decides to leave her native island of Barbados to live with her maternal aunt, Puritan uncle, and two female cousins. She has been educated and encouraged to lead an active life. The role of the female in Colonial days, as well as the impact of politics and religion, is dramatically described in this book. The women in it are individuals, as are all the characters.

SUKOWIECKI, SANDRA LUCAS. *Joshua's Day*. Illustrated by Patricia Reilly Vevitrall. Chapel Hill, North Carolina: Lollipop Power, 1972. (Ages 5–8.)
Contemporary story of a single working mother and her son's experience in a city day-care center.

TAVES, ISABELLA. *Not Bad for a Girl*. New York: M. Evans, 1972. (Ages 9–12.)
A little girl prefers to play baseball rather than dolls. Though the coaches object, her father takes her side.

TERRIS, SUSAN. *Amanda the Panda and the Redhead*. Illustrated by Emily McCully. Garden City, New York: Doubleday, 1975. (Ages 3–8.)
The family functions in an equitable, unself-conscious manner. Father and mother both cook, clean, and nurture children. Clothing of mother, teacher, and children is comfortable.

THANE, ELSWYTH. *Dolley Madison: Her Life and Times*. New York: Macmillan, 1970. (Ages 12–up.)
An interesting description, not only of Dolley Madison, but also of the times she lived in and of several of the famous people she knew. Many details of life during the early development of America are described. Although not a complete account of the era, it should interest serious students sufficiently to lead them to further reading.

THAYER, JANE. *Quiet on Account of Dinosaur*. New York: Morrow, 1965. (Ages 5–8.)
A girl loves studying dinosaurs and grows up to be a scientist, museum director, and dinosaur expert.

THOMAS, MARLO; STEINEM, GLORIA; AND POGREBIN, LETTY COTTIN. *Free to be You and Me*. New York: McGraw-Hill, 1974. Also in paper. (Ages 6–up.)
Collection of stories, poems, and songs dealing with people's potential to become whatever they want to become.

TOBIAS, T. *Marian Anderson*. New York: Crowell, 1972. (Ages 7–10.)
This biography of Marian Anderson is written in very simple language with many illustrations and large print. The text details the magnificent singer's childhood interest in music and the encouragement she received from her family as well as the obstacles she faced as a black woman in her professional career.

TURKLE, BRINTON. *Rachel and Obadiah*. New York: Dutton, 1978. (Ages 5–8.)
Rachel and Obadiah are brother and sister. They live on Nantucket in the 1700s and are Quakers. Both want to earn a coin for running through town with the news of a ship sighting. Rachel wins because Obadiah wanders off. Rachel has a good self-image; she knows she is her brother's equal, even in those pre-liberation times.

UDRY, JANICE MAY. *Mary Jo's Grandmother*. Illustrated by Eleanor Mill. Chicago: Whitman, 1970. (Ages 5–8.)
One snowy Christmas, Mary Jo visits her old but independent grandmother, who lives alone in the country. When her grandmother has an accident, Mary Jo gets help. Both Mary Jo and her grandmother are capable females.

VAN WOERKOM, DOROTHY. *The Queen Who Couldn't Bake Gingerbread*. Illustrated by Paul Galdone. New York: Knopf, 1975. (Ages 5–8.)
An adaptation of a German folk tale about a king in search of the perfect wife—one who bakes gingerbread, darns socks, and cures his loneliness. She must be beautiful, too. The Princesses he interviews cannot bake gingerbread, but can bake other things that are beautiful. The Queen he picks is wise and has a mind of her own. In the end the king bakes the gingerbread himself.

VESTLY, ANNE-CATH. *Hello Aurora*. Illustrated by Leonard Kessler. Translated by Eileen Amos; adapted by Jane Fairfax. New York: Crowell, 1974. (Ages 7–10.)
A very didactic but charming story about a Norwegian family. Mother is a lawyer. Father, who is studying for his doctorate, stays home with Aurora, the young daughter, and Socrates, the baby. The father is not tremendously adept, but he and Aurora manage fairly well. The neighbors disapprove of the arrangement, and Aurora is uncomfortable; the reader is totally drawn into the situation.

VIORST, JUDITH. "And Then the Prince Knelt Down and Tried to Put the Glass Slipper on Cinderella's Foot," in *If I Were in Charge of the World and Other Worries*. Illustrated by Lynne Cherry. New York: Atheneum, 1981. (Ages 7–10.)
In this poem Cinderella has second thoughts about marrying a prince she hardly knows.

VOIGT, CYNTHIA. *Dicey's Song*. New York: Atheneum, 1982. (Ages 9–up.)
Dicey has protected and tended her younger siblings throughout a difficult year; their mother has been hospitalized for mental illness, and they are now living with their maternal grandmother, a very strong, and seemingly eccentric woman. The relationship between Dicey and her grandmother constitutes the major portion of this sensitive and intricate book. This is the sequel to *Homecoming*, in which Dicey and her siblings are abandoned by their mother and must make their way without parental help. Dicey's strength carries them through.

WABER, BERNARD. *Ira Sleeps Over*. Boston: Houghton Mifflin, 1972. Also in paper. (Ages 5–8.)

Ira does not bring his teddy bear when he goes to sleep at his friend's house. He finds out when he gets there that his friend has a teddy bear, too. Nicely supportive of children and their feelings.

_____. *Nobody's Perfect.* Boston: Houghton Mifflin, 1971. (Ages 5–8.)
A series of small humorous incidents involving friendship between girls and boys.

WANDRO, MARK, R. N., AND BLANK, JOANIE. *My Daddy Is a Nurse.* Illustrated by Irene Trivas. Reading, Mass. Addison-Wesley, 1981. (Ages 4–8.)
With accompanying remarks by a helpful adult, this book can help change some preconceptions about gender-role careers. For those children who are not burdened by these stereotypes, the book can be a useful reinforcement. It tells of ten fathers who work as nurses, weavers, flight attendants, dental hygienists, librarians, and other jobs generally associated with women workers.

WARREN, RUTH. *A Pictorial History of Women in America.* New York: Crown, 1975. (Ages 10–up.)
A useful overview of the role of women in America's development. The book focuses on the women rather than the historical context. Many women are included. The text is interesting and well written.

WEINER, SANDRA. *I Want to Be a Fisherman.* New York: Macmillan, 1977. (Ages 7–10.)
Christine is the central character in this true story about a family earning its living by fishing. The photographs taken by the author accent the sensitivity and authenticity of the work.

WERTH, KURT, AND WATTS, MABEL. *Molly and the Giant.* New York: Parents Magazine Press, 1973. (Ages 5–8.)
Molly outwits a giant and is brave and clever enough to get herself and her sisters married to three princes in this modern tale. Perhaps some day there will be a different happy ending.

WHITE, E. B. *Charlotte's Web.* Illustrated by Garth Williams. New York: Harper & Row, 1952. Also in paper. (Ages 7–12.)
Charlotte, a clever and witty spider, saves the life of her "true friend" Wilbur, the pig, in this story of a deep friendship.

WILDER, LAURA INGALLS. *Little House in the Big Woods* and *Little House on the Prairie.* Illustrated by Helen Sewell. New York: Harper & Row, 1932 and 1935. Also in paper. (Ages 7–11.)
The first two books in a series about a little girl growing up with her family and leading an interesting frontier life. The characters, who actually lived, are accurately portrayed. They display courage and strength.

WILLIAMS, JAY. *Petronella.* Illustrated by Friso Menstra. New York: Parents Magazine Press, 1973. Also in paper. (Ages 5–8.)
Petronella, the youngest of three children, sets off to seek her fortune and rescue a prince. She finds a prince, but it turns out he is really just a parasite dependent on the enchanter at whose house he is staying. Petronella ends up marrying the wise, kind enchanter rather than the nitwit prince.

_____. *The Practical Princess*. Illustrated by Friso Menstra. New York: Parents' Magazine Press, 1973. Also in paper. (Ages 5–9.)
A turnabout fairy tale. Princess Bedelia is intelligent, brave, and active. She kills a dragon and rescues a prince from a wicked sorcerer. Unfortunately, she is the only positive character in the book; all of the others are males, and they are dolts. The book is amusing, but it is derisive humor. Children can discuss the problem of having a strong female but weak males in a story.

WOOD, JAMES PLAYSTED. *Emily Elizabeth Dickinson*. Nashville: Thomas Nelson, 1972. (Ages 11–up.)
A personalized biography of the poet, emphasizing the mystery of Emily's choosing to remain, for the last years of her life, inside her house. The description of Amherst during the nineteenth century adds flavor to the book.

WRIGHT, BETTY REN. *I Like Being Alone*. Milwaukee: Raintree, 1981. (Ages 7–10.)
With the support of her Aunt Rose and her parents, Brenda constructs a tree house so that she can get away from her six siblings and have some time alone. Brenda enjoys the company of others, but she values her own privacy. She does not reject her numerous siblings, but she is permitted to have the opportunity to be her own person.

YOLEN, JANE. *Dragon's Blood*. New York: Delacorte Press, 1982. (Ages 12–up.)
Both the young male and female protagonists in this fantasy novel strive for and gain their independence by means of their wits, talent, and perseverance. Both are nurturing, sensitive people, willing to take risks to accomplish their goals. The story is rich in detail and adventure, and weaves a tapestry of setting, plot, and character. The sequel, *Heart's Blood*, is the second of the Pit Dragon trilogy.

_____. *The Emperor and the Kite*. Illustrated by Ed Young. Cleveland: World, 1967. (Ages 5–8.)
Loyal Djeow Seow rescues her father, the Emperor, who has been captured by evil men and locked in a high tower. Written in a poetic style, it is a story of a girl's love, courage, and ingenuity.

_____. *The Girl Who Cried Flowers and Other Tales*. Illustrated by D. Palladini. New York: Crowell, 1974. (Ages 9–12.)
Three of these five tales have female protagonists. They are far from conventional: one contains a wise and frostily silent queen; one has a woman who takes upon herself the burden of designing the world's fate; one is destroyed by her desire to please.

_____. *The Girl Who Loved the Wind*. Illustrated by Ed Young. New York: Crowell, 1972. (Ages 5–8.)
Danina is kept from the outside world by her father, who wants to protect her from all sad things. But despite the garden wall, Danina hears the wind's voice and eventually accepts the wind's challenge to discover the world for herself.

_____. *The Magic Three of Solatia*. Illustrated by Julia Noonan. New York: Crowell, 1974. (Ages 10–up.)
Sianna is a wise and strong and active heroine. The reader sees her grow from

childhood into womanhood, retaining all of these qualities. These imaginative stories sustain a poetic and folkloric quality that is very satisfying.

_____. *Pirates in Petticoats*. Illustrated by Leonard Vosburgh. New York: David McKay, 1963. (Ages 10–up.)
An engagingly written series of descriptions of female pirates. Interesting from a historical view.

ZOLOTOW, CHARLOTTE. *The Summer Night*. Illustrated by Ben Shecter. New York: Harper & Row, 1974. (Ages 5–8.)
When a little girl cannot sleep, her father tries all kinds of remedies for her sleeplessness and finally accompanies her on a walk. The father is tender and understanding.

_____. *William's Doll*. Illustrated by William Pène duBois. New York: Harper & Row, 1972. (Ages 3–8.)
William likes to do "male" activities, such as sports and playing with trains, but he also wants a doll. His father, brother, and friends (male) are perturbed by this. Grandmother comes to his rescue by getting him a doll and explaining that he can practice for the time when he becomes a father himself. This book will serve as the basis for much discussion.

•FIVE•

HERITAGE

A TEACHER IN A SUBURB OF A LARGE CITY ordered a new set of books for the class library. She deliberately selected books containing a variety of characters representing different heritages, and set the books in random order on a table. She then noted, somewhat to her surprise, because she had not planned this as an experiment, that the children gravitated to the books that described their own individual heritage. Their reaction is not unique. Given the opportunity, most of us choose, at least sometimes, to read about ourselves, or some extensions of ourselves. That is not to say that fantasy and strange experiences are not important to include in our reading fare; it must be noted that fantasy reinforces, validates, and helps us to see our emotions (females usually identify with the princess as males usually do with the prince).

If any segment of our society is excluded from literature, the implication is clear that the group is not valued by society. Until ten or fifteen years ago it was rare in books to find representatives of any group other than white Protestants. Color, religion, and national origin constitute an important portion of a person's heritage. Culture, of course, is also a piece of our heritage; it is often included as part of the environment in which we live, and in the particular ways in which our group practices its rituals. Further, our own individual family lines must be included in our personal heritage. Witness the popularity and effect of the television series, "Roots," on the behavior of our nation. Our interest in our own personal roots is an extension of our need for validating our entire heritage.

Some people, however, are either so certain that their own heritage is superior to others, or so insecure in their own identities that they act in a racist fashion and demean others. Their behavior toward people is based on religion, color of skin, or national origin rather than individual characteristics. Racist practices include ostracism; economic, social, and political deprivation; social slight; educational and job discrimination; denial of human dignity; and even murder. Racists create, believe, and then use stereotypic descriptions to excuse their actions. They also use stereotypes to foster and maintain divisions among people. Racists are generally frightened, insecure individuals who feel threatened by those who are different from themselves.

Most of us try to respect other cultures and tolerate unconventional customs and lifestyles. We want to be just and caring. We never intentionally judge people on the basis of their ethnic characteristics. We try to be open-minded about appearances and behaviors, and hope that we suffer from few, if any, damaging preconceptions about genetic inferiority or superiority. Valuing individuals, we recognize that all people, no matter what their group membership may be, are unique. Although we recognize the difficulty in speaking out, we try to act to eliminate unjust practices wherever they occur, no matter how uncomfortable the situation and despite peer pressure to remain aloof or silent.

But we all know that human beings are not perfect. We mean well, but we are products of our society. And our society, in common with all modern societies, fosters racism. We carry within ourselves the influence of our parents', grandparents', teachers', and communities' experiences as well as our own. We retain the teachings of the books we have read, the lectures we have heard, the films we have seen. We cannot claim total objectivity about anything, nor can we acquire all of the necessary information we need about any given group.

It is not the intention of this author to impart guilt or a sense of hopelessness to the reader. Rather, recognizing that we share a common condition and affliction, we can set about remedying it to the best of our ability. If we learn to diagnose the extent of the problem within ourselves we may determine what next steps we may take to help ourselves grow. Assisting each other at the same time that we are helping ourselves, we can also aid children at an early age to change the negative attitudes that have afflicted our society in the past.

Racism is a harmful and corrosive problem for the perpetrator as well as for the victim. It is our hope that this section will provide a format for working with the issues of any group with a common heritage as they are presented in children's books.

Especially for those of us who are involved with children, our responsibility must be actively maintained. What criteria do we consider when we build a library? How do we handle racist attitudes in books? How aware are we of the connotations and innuendos in the books our children read? How do we manage the classics? What of the popular fantasies and novels and even works of so-called nonfiction that are rife with racist ideas? How do we manage to keep progressing with our own sense of openness and world-mindedness, and at the same time influence children who are, perhaps, not at the same level of awareness that we are? How can we recognize our acts of omission?

The focus here is on books. Each of the abovementioned questions should also be applied to all other media, and, indeed, to our social behavior. It is important to remember that there are many minorities in the United States who need to see themselves in the literature. The presentation of people of other countries, of people who speak a language other than English, of poor people, leaves much to be desired. The eventual client is the child. If, in our analyses and comments we can help children to value themselves and each other, then we will have succeeded in our primary objective.

Our task is first to cultivate self-awareness and then to recognize how other people react to certain language, how they feel about themselves and their world, how their modes of response compare with ours, and what their backgrounds and values are. Cultural differences may be difficult for some people to tolerate, but they are an aspect of society that is to be valued rather than feared.

The more people are encouraged to value their own diversity the more they should be able to value others'. Respect and admiration should lead to a sense of comfort and joy that eventually invites the cooperation that is an ultimate aim in human relations. We must each keep taking the next steps that will lead us through these stages, continuing to examine our own reactions in order to guarantee our steady progress. And even after comfort and collegiality are reached, we must continue to learn more and more about each other.

No person can be said to have reached a state of total awareness. Some of us may still be at the point where culturally different people are either invisible, "strange," or frightening. The fact that books in the past excluded any but all-white characters has exacerbated this problem. Other children have not been able to find themselves in books. They have not been able to identify with heroes or heroines, or even with ordinary children who simply "belong." Nancy Larrick brought this appalling gap to the attention of the children's book publishers and the public in her important and influential article in the *Saturday Review* of September 11, 1965 (see References). In the past several years more and more culturally diverse books have been published. One of our first steps, then, in working toward nonracist and antiracist classrooms is to stock them with books that include a variety of people, cultures, points of view, lifestyles, and situations.

Knowledge about one's own heritage, characteristics, and the problems imposed by society are essential for learning and growth. Tolerance of onself and one's people is important as a next step. Acceptance and valuing must follow in order for true self-pride to grow. Finally, the ability to make one's own decisions comfortably will result in a sense of independence and collegiality. The steps must be repeated with each new situation, and must be practiced consistently.

Sometimes our own good intentions cause us to be less effective than we would wish. We want our students, our peers and community to progress to our level of awareness and behavior. We try to force people to move more quickly than they are able. We must work hard to remember that people are where they are, not where they should be. It is not the "shoulds" we can successfully attend to; it is the reality of the present situation. We can help people to take next steps; it is not feasible to force them to take leaps. Meanwhile, we can continue to advance in our attitudes and behaviors.

•TRY THIS

Select three books for young children that you believe demonstrate a good level of awareness and valuing. List the qualities that support your judgment. Find one way each of the books could have done an even better job. Do the same with three books for older children. Compare your observations with a peer.

SUGGESTED CRITERIA

How can we assess books' usefulness in helping readers to become more aware and more valuing of other cultures and differences? What criteria can we establish that will help us not only to locate racist inferences, but also to recognize positive gains? Many individuals and groups have provided us with lists of criteria. Eventually it is the reader who must compile one personally. One invaluable aid, not only to constructing criteria but also to fostering greater awareness of the situation is the *Bulletin* published by the Council on Interracial Books for Children. This organization focuses on trying to eliminate racism, sexism, and other antihuman factors from children's books. It exerts a powerful influence on publishers, educators, authors, and readers. The publication contains articles analyzing how books deal with issues. It also lists helpful resources and provides critiques of current books. The reader is helped to look at books from different perspectives, and is given ideas for how to proceed with other such books. Some critics feel that the council is a censoring agency because of its strong statements about books it finds objectionable. The council's intent is not to censor but to educate. Sometimes it uses harsh criticism to make its points, but readers are always free to make up their own minds, and the council's arguments are always thought-provoking.

Care should be taken to find books written from an authentic cultural perspective. As Rudine Sims points out, "There is a difference between being talked *to* and being talked *about*." (See References.) Members of a particular group should be able to see themselves mirrored in literature with as many facets of their heritage as possible presented and developed. This can occur only if the shelves of a classroom, home, or library contain many books about many heritages.

In any population people, despite their common heritage, differ in lifestyle, economic condition, personality, interests, and abilities. The literature should reflect this. Characters should occupy positions of authority or status apart from their heritage. Standards, aspirations, relationships, and viewpoints should result from the story line and character development rather than from preconceptions about specific groups. Children who are white and middle class should not necessarily set the norms; those in power should have their position because of ability, not color, religion, class, or sex; victims should not always be members of one particular group.

When stories take place in cities or in geographic areas where there is a range of heritages represented, the characters in the stories should reflect this variety. Omission of this multicultural population should be commented on, and readers should be invited to discuss the reasons for the omission., When characters of different heritages are represented, they should be three-dimensional, and beyond the stereotype.

The language of any book is an important factor in its quality as well as its impact. The cadences and vocabulary of a particular regional or ethnic group are important features of that group. Literature should reflect the linguistic richness of a culture. Dialect should not be used as a differentiating mechanism with negative intent. Language should avoid insulting or demeaning implications. Talented authors convey through their characters' language the music of authentic speech. They also name their characters authentically, not according to the impressions of people outside the culture.

Books, even when they are works of fiction, should report history accurately. Because historic portrayal depends on the perspective and background of the author, several books about the same event or famous person should be available to young readers. It is important for authors to include authentic detail and setting. The best of the books, no matter what the age of the intended audience or the genre of the literature, contain nuances reflecting the flavor of the heritage, a quality very difficult to achieve, and rare in authors whose primary experience is outside that of the group depicted in the book.

Books reflect their authors' credentials. Most good authors write from their own experience. They illuminate and extend their perceptions through research and imagination, and, above all, their talent as story tellers and their sensitivity to people enhance their writing.

In addition to the writing, illustrations figure importantly in the impact of books. In some books, only the illustrations give readers clues to the ethnic heritage of the characters. Good illustrations avoid stereotypes, tokenism, quaintness, and demeaning implications. They are accurate and respectful of their subject.

•TRY THIS

Select three books for young children (preschool to age eight) and three books for older children (eight to twelve). Use the Bibliography at the end of this chapter as a source, if you wish. Analyze the books for evidence of a nonracist approach. For example, try to find specific evidence of nonstereotypic illustrations. In examining the story line try to find examples of situations where minority members have constructive power. List the books you have found, and the positive characteristics you have discovered.

It is important to be able to recognize the positive as well as the negative aspects of any book. It is also necessary to filter one's observation through such qualities as literary excellence, the effectiveness of the story, the side effects of the message, and the universality of the human experiences described in the book. The mood of the story, the author's ability to cause the reader to empathize with the characters—in short, the overall impact of the book—must always be considered. The more knowledgeable the readers are, the more able they will be to determine whether or not the author has presented historical, anthropological, and emotional truth.

What steps can we expect authors to take in order to provide the reading public with fewer racist books? First, they must examine their own racial biases and fantasies before presenting them in print. Those authors who already possess advanced skills of communication must take special care. Their words are read by many children and adults. Their ideas are received, internalized, and acted upon. Their impact is enormous. We frequently admonish ourselves and our students not to believe all that we read, but we willingly suspend disbelief when a writer is powerful, and particularly when we are confronted, not with facts, but with fantasy. Then the messages seep into our systems without our having weighed or even recognized the information.

Authors, then, must take care to present characters in a varied and unstereotypic fashion. They should try to examine their own work with a diagnostic eye, looking for positive images for a variety of people, and trying to weed out negative inaccuracies or artificial characters that would foster racist attitudes and responses in their readers.

We, on our part, can communicate to publishers and authors both our positive and negative criticisms. We can examine our own perceptions, compare them with others' and ask for validation, and be alerted when we find ourselves so immersed in a book that we are not actively questioning the author's intent and methodology. We must learn to recognize positive factors, and to keep our minds open for negative implications. Once we have reached the point of easily detecting overt negative racial attitudes we can look for subtle indications, and act to overturn them.

Books are currently published with a variety of audiences in mind. Some books reflect an attempt to educate "the outsider," and are at the earliest level of fostering awareness. Some seek to inform the reader about long-neglected and little-known history. A fairly large body of books deals with constructing and reinforcing a sense of pride and positive self-image for children, while, at the same time, helping the uninformed reader to develop awareness and appreciation of others' qualities and contributions. Differences are cherished rather than discouraged in the best of these books.

Folktales and informational books about countries of origin are increasing in number. These folk and fairy tales are particularly valuable for offsetting the prevailing sense of the folktales' coming only from Europe.

•TRY THIS

Find and compare folktales from different countries that are "Cinderella" stories.

Find folktales that have the following elements:

1. A simpleton who wins out over his or her smarter siblings
2. A beast who is transformed into a prince or princess
3. A hero who is a trickster
4. A series of three tasks required for the hero(ine) to win a prize
5. A child abandoned at birth, who grows up to become the ruler of a country

Discuss the implications of your findings.

Poetry anthologies have become somewhat more inclusive and contemporary in their selections. In fiction for the older child more varied protagonists are appearing. Moreover, there is a greater sense of this country's multiethnic construct. Although many gains have been made, more are needed. We have noted the exceptions, not the rule. And we must continue to criticize and analyze even the new, well-intentioned books to secure the progress they and we have made.

One of the chief criticisms of books in the past was that in stories for young children it appeared that only middle class Christian white people existed in this world. All families, all neighborhoods, all people seemed to be white, middle class, and suburban. This situation could not continue in a society where people were interested in moving away from racism. Nonwhite, non–middle class children were made to feel as if they were invisible. They were told, by omission, that they did not exist, or, if they did, that they were not considered important enough to mention. They were unvalued. Fortunately, more and more excellent authors and illustrators are acknowledging the world's diversity.

This chapter looks primarily at works of fiction. Nonfiction is important for children to read, but the scope of nonfiction about different heritages is too large to be confined to one chapter. Indeed, the fiction is so extensive as to permit only a sampling to be reviewed here. But this author hopes that a format and frame will be provided for the reader to continue as an individual to critically examine the literature, and to make judgments of a constructive nature. Criteria specific to any given heritage will be discussed in the context of that heritage later on in this chapter.

Native Americans, a group different from people of other heritage because they did not come here as immigrants or captives, will be discussed first. This was their land, wrested from them by white invaders. Then Afro-American characters in children's books will be examined, as a model for investigating and critiquing the literature. After these two major groups are presented, a general discussion will follow of the treatment of other heritages in children's books.

NATIVE AMERICAN HERITAGE

The Native American, or American Indian, was our first victimized ethnic group. Although many of the first white settlers sought religious freedom and had, themselves, been oppressed for their beliefs, they were intolerant of others. Fearful and contemptuous of the people who already inhabited the country, they viewed these natives, for the most part, as less than human. Their religion was considered to be pagan and, therefore, no religion at all. Their manner of dress was an affront to the standards of the Europeans. Because of this superior feeling on the part of the colonists, their disregard for the rights of the American Indians was not considered to be persecution. By converting the "heathens" to the true and proper religion of Christianity, they felt that they were repaying helpfulness on the part of Native Americans with the greatest kindness of all—initiation into white culture.

No recognition was paid to the lifestyles, beliefs, and temperaments of the native tribes. It was assumed that any response to the whites other than gratitude would be inappropriate. So convinced were the new settlers of their righteousness that the chronicles they wrote of their times reflected their attitude—that the Indians were barbaric, naive, and in need of enlightenment. This point of view unfortunately has permeated our history books and, until now, few people have questioned its validity.

Our history books and works of fiction have stressed the image of the intrepid pioneer, fighting valiantly against all odds to make something of the land. As Americans we have been proud of a heritage of tenacity and valor. We have not been encouraged to think about the people whose lands we usurped, and we have not been correctly informed about their customs and characteristics. It has been to our advantage to glorify our white predecessors, at the same time demeaning the Native Americans. As Americans we like to believe that justice and righteousness have always been on our side. We view ourselves as moral people who would not hurt others unless we had to.

But this has not been the case with American Indians. We began, systematically, to persecute them as soon as we landed on this continent. We have not yet stopped. Up to the past ten years, very few books even hinted at the true account of our treatment of these peoples. Our storybooks have either villainized or romanticized them; our histories have distorted information. It is, therefore, necessary that we acquaint ourselves with some of the facts.

Several books that could constitute a beginning for building background information about the history, culture, and present-day situation of Native Americans are Stan Steiner's *The New Indians*, Robert Burnette's *The Tortured Americans*, and Virgil Vogel's *The Indian in American History*. Each book discusses how the United States has treated the Indians; each suggests ways to change the miserable conditions in which they still exist; and each helps the reader to build a clearer perspective and understanding of the relationship between history and the present.

Vine Deloria's *Custer Died for Your Sins* should be required reading for anyone interested in understanding how complex and difficult are the realities confronting the Native American. Deloria is an Oglala Sioux from the Standing Rock Reservation. He is an acknowledged, although by no means uncontroversial, leader of the movement for tribal self-determination. He criticizes other Native Americans, churches, practices of the United States government, Republicans and Democrats, and anthropologists. But his book, exceptionally well written, is laced with a wry humor that helps the reader to accept the importance of what he says without resenting it. His points of discussion enlighten the reader and raise many questions. His detailing of history sheds an enormous amount of light on fuzzy areas obscured by traditional texts. The bulk of his book helps the reader look at today's Indians; it suggests new approaches to aid them to achieve appropriate status in their own land.

Other books for young adults and older readers attempt to change white Americans' views concerning the building of the American West. In a well-researched book, *Bury My Heart at Wounded Knee*, Dee Brown describes the history of Native American–white relations from a point of view that is sympathetic to the Indian people. The recounting of treachery and atrocities, particularly on the part of white soldiers, is difficult to read without revulsion. His descriptions of the battles and the events leading up to them provide important information for modern Americans. This book, in combination with Deloria's, can constitute background for enlightened reading of current fiction concerning the American Indian. Of course, the more informed one becomes, and the more sources one consults, the more able one is to interpret and evaluate any work.

HISTORICAL OVERVIEW

A short chronology of United States relations with Native Americans may help the reader to assume a perspective when reading works of historical fiction or when teaching young children.

When Columbus reached the shores of the West Indies, mistakenly thinking that he had reached India, he called the natives of the land "Indians." Since most of the tribes had no specific names to call themselves, other than "the people," this misnomer remained. After the colonists had settled in, and more and more kept coming, the once helpful and friendly tribes began to recognize that they were being pushed out of their homes, and that there was no recourse from the whites' incursion.

Some tribes participated in the wars between the whites. Although not absolutely confirmed, conjecture is that the practice of taking the scalps from one's victims was introduced to the American Indians either by the Spaniards in the seventeenth or the English in the eighteenth century (some time before the French and Indian War). It is, however, verified that the Puritans and other settlers paid bounties to mercenaries for Native American scalps. At first the whole head of a victim was required as proof of the kill, but eventually the scalp alone was accepted. Only Indian scalps were redeemable for the bounty.

Before the American Revolution, Indian lands were somewhat protected by the English Crown. Even after the colonists won the war, it was considered unlawful to take land without either purchasing it or making some attempt at treaties. The new American government attempted to maintain peaceful relations with the Native Americans. But although the Northwest Territory Ordinance and the Articles of Confederation insured the rights of the American Indians to their own government and their property, the Congress was, by 1800, beginning to demand Indian loyalty to the government of the United States. Indian affairs were administered by the United States government through the Secretary of War. The Indians, though still technically considered to be separate foreign nations existing on American soil, came more and more under American domination.

In 1804 the infamous removal of the Cherokee from their lands was made "legal" under the provisions of the Louisiana Purchase. The Cherokee nation, which had conformed in every way to white demands and expectations, was nevertheless forced to relinquish all lands and possessions. Soon after, other tribes were ordered removed to the West. President Andrew Jackson's attitude and behavior toward the Native Americans was totally oppressive and without regard for their legal or human rights. When the Chief Justice of the Supreme Court, John Marshall, declared the occupation of Indian land to be illegal, Jackson refused to enforce the ruling and, in effect, told Marshall to enforce it himself, if he could. Meanwhile Congress kept appropriating funds to "civilize and educate the heathen natives." Presidents after Jackson were no less cruel when it came to destruction of Native Americans. The demand that they change their ancient ways was pressed on all tribes.

In 1824 the Bureau of Indian Affairs was established to handle the problems "caused" by the Native Americans. The bureau was contained in the War Department until 1849, when it was transferred to the Department of the Interior. For the rest of the nineteenth century, the United States conducted a systematic and ruthless campaign of genocide against all Native American tribes. Under the most cruel conditions, Indian nations were removed forcibly from their lands. Their possessions were confiscated, and they were forced to endure killing marches across many miles to substandard land. Torn from their well-established patterns of life, they were forced to try farming a land that was almost totally barren. Some of them were set down in swamp lands, where many of them succumbed to fever. Most of the tribes were decimated on their "long marches." The remaining people found it almost impossible to survive the hostile conditions of the new lands to which they were sent. They were removed time and time again, whenever the whites discovered that their land contained lead or gold deposits or anything remotely useful. Those people who did not die of disease or starvation were subject to constant military harassment.

In 1887 the Allotment Act was passed, permitting the United States to divide all Indian lands into small allotments and to make all acreage that remained after the Indians had received their "share" available to white settlers. At this point there were only about 250,000 Native Americans remaining in the United States, where before there were more than a million. Most of them were contained in the land reserved for them alone (reservations) but subject to United States law. The Bureau of Indian Affairs was, and still is, responsible for administering the funds assigned to Native Americans and for protecting their rights. The BIA has been prey to graft, pressures of politicians, and mismanagement by unqualified staff. But there have been people in the bureau who have truly held the interests of the American Indians to be their responsibility and who have tried to accomplish gains in Native Americans' economic, political, and educational welfare.

In the twentieth century, the policy of the United States government has become somewhat more responsive to Native American needs. Laws have been enacted granting citizenship, permitting tribes to incorporate, and granting compensation for land lost. But schools, which in general have been established and run by the government, have discouraged the practice of native religion, ancient tribal customs, and speaking of the native tongue, and have attempted to thrust upon the tribes an acceptance of the English language, Christianity, and white ways.

Termination, a government policy exercised for a period of time in recent decades, has endangered many tribes. This practice of purchasing reservation land, in effect dispersing the tribes, requires them to seek new places and new ways of life. Generally, the Native Americans so dispersed were unsuccessful in establishing a viable economic and cultural position for themselves; indeed, some of the slums of Chicago and other midwestern cities are testimony to the destructive impact of the termination policy. Outspoken native leaders have denounced this policy and have influenced change. The BIA and the government now recognize that tribal self-determination rather than assimilation will probably be more effective in helping Native Americans to be contributing citizens of the United States. It is to be hoped that termination will not recur as established United States policy.

An era of change has begun. Native Americans are again practicing once forbidden religious rites and speaking their ancient languages. At last a knowledge of—and respect for—the customs and beliefs of tribal ancestors is being communicated in schools and communities. No longer is the white way the preferred way. Young Indians are being encouraged to write about their heritage, and there are many tribal newspapers and publications across the country. Indian associations whose membership is composed largely if not exclusively of Native Americans are gaining in influence. American Indian voices are being heard in Congress, in the news media, and in books. Native Americans are relying on their own abilities and leadership as tribes more and more control their own affairs. No longer will the Indians remain silent—no longer can we depict them as a vanishing race. We must heed their voices; we must end the oppressive and abusive practices that have continued.

•TRY THIS

Find histories of American Indians in encyclopedias and history texts. Compile traditional descriptions of the removal to "Indian territory." Then, do the same with any of the books written after 1965 from an Indian perspective. Analyze the differences in factual presentation. Do the same with the Battle of Little Big Horn and with the massacre at Wounded Knee.

What kind of information are our children receiving? Every child has had several units of work about the Indian. Not every classroom makes use of a variety of materials beyond the conventional text, so as to convey an accurate notion of the history, diversity, and plight of these people. Rey Mickinock, author and member of the Ojibway nation, points out that even talented illustrators include inaccuracies in their pictures. They dress characters in inappropriate and incorrect costumes and mix tribal characteristics. Mickinock goes on to describe many other errors, oversights, and misconceptions conveyed to the young reading public by authors and illustrators ignorant of such details. Mary Gloyne Byler, in her informative *Introduction to American Indian Authors for Young Readers: A Selected Bibliography*, published by the Association on American Indian Affairs, further describes and then corrects some of the mistakes made in books for young children. After having examined hundreds of books, Byler comes to this conclusion: "Only American Indians can tell non-Indians what it is to be Indian. There is no longer any need for non-Indian writers to 'interpret' American Indians for the American public."

•TRY THIS

Find a book by a Native American describing life on a reservation. (Any of Virginia Driving Hawk Sneve's books would be useful here.) Contrast the information and attitudes transmitted with a book about the same topic by a non-Indian. (Coatsworth's *The Cave* or Barnouw's *Dream of the Blue Heron* can be consulted.) Contrast two books in the same way on the topics of schooling, history, and folklore. Comment on your findings compared with Mary Gloyne Byler's conclusions.

The literary treatment of Native Americans has been distorted both in an idealized as well as negative manner. The Indian has been viewed either as a noble savage or as a marauder. It is seldom apparent that the Native American was threatened by the settlers and that tribes were aware that if they did not fight for their land they would lose it. Those American Indians who are portrayed in the stories as having positive qualities usually are praised for adapting to white ways, or helping white people. One book talks of famous Indian heroines such as Milly Hadjo Francis, who saved a white soldier at the expense of her own father's life. Many of these women betrayed their own people in order to help whites. Almost all of them were successful by white standards, married white men, and lived in white society.

Assimilation, once the government's aim, is not the goal of the "new Indian," although it does occur as one of the "happy" endings in some fictionalized history for children. It is a demonstration of ignorance when authors speak in global terms of and for Indians. Any investigation of the customs, lifestyles, and values of Native Americans demonstrates the necessity for specifying the tribe and the location. Native Americans vary as greatly as do whites. Their commonalities are also great; but in order to do justice to them, books must demonstrate a recognition of the differences.

•TRY THIS

Select a group of tribes, such as those belonging to the Cherokee or Sioux nations. Find as many works of fiction and nonfiction as you can that specifically describe the group you selected. Write a summary of their major characteristics, roles of the men and women, government, means of livelihood, and history of how they came to be where they are. Compare your findings with students who have investigated other tribal confederations or groups.

SUGGESTED CRITERIA

One of the signals of respect for Native Americans is the care that the author takes in detail. If the characters in a book are American Indians, with no indication of their tribe or special origin, the book is usually less than effective. Therefore, look for the name of the tribe and the setting of the story when selecting books on this topic. The adequate research that most authors attempt to do in order to validate their stories is particularly important in the case of books about the Native American. Not only should the details be accurate but also the values conveyed in the text should reflect as closely as possible the attitudes of the real life counterparts of the characters. If the author is not a Native American, then perhaps consultants could be located to authenticate the text.

Not all American Indians agree about any given question. For example, the label "Indian" is not an accurate one, but it is less objectionable to some groups than to others. Any label is likely to be inadequate. Recognizing this, an author who uses tribal names or demonstrates a sensitivity to the preference on the part of some people to be called Native Americans would be satisfying part of the criterion of treating the subject with respect.

Probably the most important criterion is respect. Others include refraining from comparing tribal ways unfavorably with those of whites. Any indication that manner of dress, family relationships, or religious beliefs are "quaint" or "weird" is a negative factor to be avoided.

Authors should not use such adjectives as "strange" or "savage" when describing differences. People *are* different from one another, and our differences are to be encouraged and valued. The differences should be apparent in their actual description, not in their labeling. An overly sentimental description is just as detrimental to understanding and appreciation as one that is critical. Overly idealized descriptions violate the criterion of accuracy. For example, much is made in many books of the American Indian's belief that no one can own land; but it would be false to assume that tribes had no sense of territory. Land is an important consideration for the contemporary Indian. One of the ways that Indian nations have been able to strengthen themselves in recent times has been through the acquisition of land. It is essential for authors and readers to recognize that although the ideas Native Americans have about personal property and administration of the law are somewhat different from those of most white societies, their sense of protocol and behavior is clear and consistent.

In considering the contemporary Native American, authors should avoid patronizing statements. Respect and recognition of the tribal point of view is essential even through a white perspective, and assimilation should not be the goal or the happy ending. Scrupulous research is necessary. Here again, consultation with members of the tribe would be of great value.

History should be presented in perspective. In too many books, when the Indians are victorious, the battle is called a massacre. When the whites win, it is a "victorious battle," usually "heroically" fought. Stereotypes should be avoided both for the Native American and the white settler.

In books of folklore, the complexity of the symbols and the messages of the tales should be conveyed accurately. Some collections miss the whole point of the stories. Some of them—as with any attempt to set down in writing what has been part of the oral literature—are obscure and badly told. Here, too, the reader should search for the author's credentials, since an understanding of the background and specific meaning of the tale is necessary for its proper telling and a knowledgeable author would demonstrate this understanding.

Illustrations are very influential and particularly critical in the case of books on Native Americans. Physical features, dress, and environment should be depicted correctly. It is a hopeful sign that Native American illustrators as well as writers have been recognized in recent years and have been employed by publishers who care about presenting the Indian people's perspective.

DISCUSSION OF CHILDREN'S BOOKS

FOLKLORE

For a long time, folklorists have been interested in the Indian Pourquoi, or explanatory tales. Recognizing the different origins of the various tales, they have appropriately labeled them according to the group from which they came. One such work is *Skunny Wundy: Seneca Indian Tales*, by Arthur C. Parker, himself a Seneca Indian. The Seneca belong to the Iroquois Nation, and these animal tales convey the special qualities attributed to them by the Iroquois. Other collections describe Zuni ways, Papago and Pima myths, Paiute, Algonquin, Hopi, Kiowa, and many other individual tribal customs and beliefs. Jamake Highwater, a Blackfoot Indian, has written a number of books based on Cherokee folklore. All of them are beautifully written, and well worth acquiring. In *Cherokee Animal Tales*, George Scheer adds notes informing the reader about contemporary life, as well as some recent history.

The complexity of the tales is such that it is sometimes difficult to convey the intended meaning. Alex Whitney's *Stiff Ears: Animal Folktales of the North American Indians* tries to teach a lesson with each of the stories. In contrast are Betty Baker's stories in the collection *At the Center of the World* and Margaret Hodges's *The Fire Bringer: A Paiute Indian Legend*. Contemporary tribal education is emphasizing the continuation of the old tales.

Undoubtedly more members of the Indian nations will set down the tales as they have heard them so that their special qualities will be communicated in print.

HISTORY

Alice Dalgliesh wrote the now classic *Courage of Sarah Noble* in 1954. Although no real issues are raised in the story and the tone is somewhat that of implied white superiority, the fact that the father leaves the little girl in the care of an American Indian family (no tribal name is given) and the girl is lovingly cared for is useful to counteract the otherwise negative image of Indians. The setting is Connecticut, but the two families seem to be the only ones around; thus the opportunity is missed for a description of communal life. It would have been interesting to have seen what east coast Indians were like and how their friendly relations with the whites affected them. Nevertheless, the story of Sarah and her family is a positive one to use in contrast with the very negative others.

Another more recent story of the same genre is *Little Yellow Fur*, by Wilma Pitchford Hays. Again, it is told from the perspective of the white settlers, but it conveys a sympathetic attitude based on the recollections of the author's own childhood and has that sort of authenticity. Certainly it is valid to have some stories from this perspective, as long as there are others to balance it from the Indian point of view.

History for the older child has been written with a more empathic attempt in terms of the Native American. Betty Baker's *Killer-of-Death* describes how the Apache (a word meaning "enemy") came to accept that name. The ways of the tribe are included in what appears to be accurate detail. The hero of the story is well described, and the reader's sympathy is with him throughout the story; he understandably becomes the enemy of all whites as a result of the perfidy of the white community. The book describes the white practice of scalping Native Americans, even women and children. It also indicates some of the rivalries among tribes. Treating customs without condescension, this book maintains the reader's respect as well as attention. Although it is fictionalized history, it has the ring of truth and adds to the reader's store of information and attitude.

Sing Down the Moon, by Scott O'Dell, is another story that helps illuminate history. The main character in this tale is a young Navajo woman who exhibits remarkable determination and tenacity. She has many adventures, not the least of which is the Long Walk that she and her people must endure when they are removed from their beloved Canyon de Chelly. Although she proves to be emotionally stronger than her husband, he is a fit partner for her; together they leave the unsuitable land designated for them by the whites and return to their own home. Navajo readers have noted inaccuracies in descriptions of hair (Navajo do not wear braids, only buns and headbands) and other details.

The unutterable hardships that the Navajo suffered are not fully described. But the story is a moving one. The author's intention is to convey the fortitude of the Navajo people through the example of the young woman and her husband. The reader finishes the book with respect for these individuals and with some questions about United States policy regarding the Navajo. *White Shell Horse*, by Jane and Paul Annixter, also tells of the successful return of the Navajo to their original homes in Arizona. The hero is a young man named Agapito who retains his faith in the old ways and in his visions. The story conveys the message that the Navajo learned to use strategies other than warfare in order to cope with their white enemies; it ends with the hope that faith and talk will help the Navajo to maintain their own ways and to succeed in their own terms. The story is well written and respectful.

More factual accounts of the sequence leading to the defeat in warfare of the Indian nations can be found in Dee Brown's *Wounded Knee: An Indian History of the American West*, adapted for young readers by Amy Ehrlich. This clearly written book is powerful in terms of counteracting what the history texts would have had us believe in years past. Alex Bealer's *Only the Names Remain: The Cherokees and the Trail of Tears* is another informative and illuminating factual book, telling of the Cherokee Nation and its accomplishments as well as the criminal acts perpetrated against it. Peter Collier's *When Shall They Rest? The Cherokees' Long Struggle with America* continues the story to the present day, helping the reader to understand some contemporary problems. Children can examine conventional history texts and insert extra pages adding the new information that they receive from books with a Native American perspective.

CUSTOMS

Some books of nonfiction link history and contemporary life by describing various tribes as they once lived. Ann Nolan Clark's *Circle of Seasons* is one of these. The author, who has written many books for use in the education of young Native Americans, tells in this book about the Pueblo Indians. She describes their religious customs, using as a theme the different seasons of the year, and presents the reader with many details of Pueblo life, dress, and belief.

S. Carl Hirsch's *Famous American Indians of the Plains* uses excellent paintings by well-known artists to illustrate the ways of the Plains Indians. The reader is invited to respect and admire the accomplishments of the Plains Indians while at the same time learning about their customs and situation. There are many such books that children can use as references and instruction on the differences in lifestyles among the diverse tribes of North America. (Other titles are included in the Bibliography at the end of this chapter.) It is necessary to seek out those books that treat the topic accurately and in a noncondescending fashion.

CONTEMPORARY LIFE

Among the books giving factual descriptions of contemporary Native Americans, Alfred Tamarin's *We Have Not Vanished* is useful in describing the several tribes of Native Americans living in the eastern part of the United States. They inhabit almost all of the states from Maine to Florida. The book describes the history of each of the tribes, its customs, and its present-day political structure. *Circle of Life: The Miccosukee Indian Way*, by Nancy Henderson and Jane Dewey, a book with a similar intent, provides a close look at the modern Miccosukee Indians. It offers an optimistic outlook, tracing the history of the tribe to the present, when the tribe has control over governmental funds and projects. This management over their own education and economy is one of the most hopeful signs of progress for the Native Americans. It will, perhaps, serve as a model for government treatment of other tribes.

Some Native Americans left the reservation either voluntarily or because their tribes were victims of the termination policy that the United States effected in the 1950s. Books like Carol Ann Bales's *Kevin Cloud: Chippewa Boy in the City* describe in detail the sordid existence that some Native Americans are subjected to in urban slums. The similarity to black slums is evident, but there are important differences. Although the mood is one of despair, the attempt to remember old stories and customs and the loving behavior of the extended family toward one another gives the reader some cause for hope. The photographs by the author are excellent in their stark detail.

The Key, by Florence Parry Heide, contains a story called "Wild Bird," which describes the life of a young Native American and his grandfather living in the slum section of the city. The grandfather tries to keep the boy's vision alive with his tales of the old days and old ways. The boy enjoys listening to his grandfather, but the old man and the reader both know that the boy's life is doomed by the squalor and oppression of the life that they lead. This is indeed a depressing story, but it is well written and helps the reader to recognize the problems of urban Indians.

Another depressing but well-constructed and truthful book is Hal Borland's *When the Legends Die*. Only mature readers could handle this book, which contains a great deal of personal violence. It is the story of a Ute, Tom Black Bull, who is orphaned as a very young child and who grows up to be an angry and troubled young man. After venting his hatred on horses and people, he returns in the end to his birthplace, determined to learn more about himself and his people.

Several recent books have been written by white authors, but treat contemporary Native Americans in a sympathetic fashion. In *Dakota Sons*, by Audree Distad, Tad, a white boy, comes to respect, and wants to learn more about Indian ways because of his friend Ronnie, who is a Dakota Sioux. The story provides a vehicle for understanding between the two races and, as such, is useful.

Six Days from Sunday by Betty Biesterveld, who has lived among the Navajo, presents their lifestyle lovingly. Willie Little Horse, who must go away to school, is very anxious about the prospect, though his family believes that it will be a good experience for him. He really does not want to leave his family or his well-known and loved existence. The book is optimistic about the possibility of taking advantage of new knowledge while retaining what is good about the old ways.

Students may arrange to establish a pen-pal correspondence with children attending a reservation school. They will learn much to counteract the inaccuracies of many of the books.

School is described as a somewhat mixed situation in *Ride the Crooked Wind*, by Dale Fife, and *Dream of the Blue Heron*, by Victor Barnouw. Both books indicate that it is difficult for the young students to adjust to school, particularly since white ways are thrust upon them and the attempt is made to destroy old ways. But in each book the rebellious young men recognize the value of acquiring new information and skills in order to maintain what is good of the old ways, emphasizing the necessity for self-pride and a valuing of one's heritage.

Some of the most useful and encouraging books about the contemporary Native American have been written by Virginia Driving Hawk Sneve, a Sioux Indian. Three of her books for young readers, *Jimmy Yellow Hawk, High Elk's Treasure,* and *When Thunders Spoke* (all illustrated beautifully by Oren Lyons), not only authentically reflect the life of the Plains Indians but also indicate a hope for the future that is based on their actions today. Besides conveying a sense of the history of the people, the books also describe the beliefs held by some of the tribes and the problems of the conflicting new ways. All include families that are happy to be together; all tell interesting stories in a competent fashion.

Partly because it is difficult to secure many of the books written by Native Americans, and partly because of the conviction that many different points of view should be aired and considered, this author differs from Mary Gloyne Byler's conclusion in her *Introduction to American Indian Authors for Young Readers: A Selected Bibliography* that only books by Native Americans should be presented to young readers on the topic of Native Americans. The teacher, librarian, parent, and child are urged to read all materials with care and sensitivity, and to accept very little without verifying authenticity. Questions and research stemming from this reading can be effective in counteracting the generations of misinformation and distortions and in building a new and healthy respect for the first Americans.

AFRO-AMERICAN HERITAGE

Like people of other heritages living here in the United States, Afro-Americans participate in and belong to the general American culture as well as to their own distinct groups. Art, music, literature, traditions, language and history form the basis of a particular perspective within the larger framework of cultural ingredients shared with the rest of the American population. Thus, jazz and spirituals are certainly a valued part of American culture, but they are specifically owned by Afro-Americans. European folklore has been translated into English and widely distributed to American children. It has become part of all Americans' background, but the specific heritage of any group goes beyond what has been adopted by the population as a whole.

Books by, about, and for Afro-Americans have increased in number over the past decade. They vary widely in their intent, style, topic, and authenticity. However, the preponderance of literature for children continues to exclude the Afro-American heritage. It is important for teachers, librarians, and parents to find books of quality that contain this heritage and to present them not only to black readers, but to all children.

•TRY THIS

Locate several books that, upon examination, include no black characters. Imagine that the characters are black. How does this change the story? How difficult was this to do? Now locate several picture books that have only white characters in them. Design new illustrations so that some or all of the characters are black. How does this change the story? How does this change the effect of the book? Invite children to perform these same exercises.

DISCUSSION OF CHILDREN'S BOOKS

SELF-IMAGE

Many nonfiction books have been created with the express purpose of helping the black reader to affirm a positive self-image, and to cause the white reader to adapt, amend, or dispel any negative preconceptions about blacks. Although this chapter emphasizes works of fiction, a description of at least a few of these very effective books should be useful. Rudine Sims has described and critiqued a number of books containing Afro-American characters and themes, providing educators with a methodology for reading these books in her important work, *Shadow and Substance: The Afro-American Experience in Contemporary Children's Fiction*. She discusses realistic fiction with a social conscience, the melting pot, and works written from black or white perspectives. Her focus is on images of today's children rather than those from the past. Her intent is to help adults select appropriate literature for children.

Some children's books are very direct in their message. Ann McGovern's *Black Is Beautiful* is a compilation of lovely photographs and simple text. The text is didactic in intent and approach, but it is effective next to the photographs. Other books talk about emotions, trying to help readers to accept themselves and their feelings no matter what their color. These books are intended to convey universal responses. *Don't Worry, Dear* by Joan Fassler, deals with thumb-sucking, stuttering, and the need for a "security blanket." The illustrator has chosen to represent these feelings common to all children by picturing a black family. Both parents are very supportive and understanding of the child's needs. The problems get resolved as the child grows older. Readers identify with the circumstances.

Whenever possible, more heritages should be included in a book that purports to speak to all children.

FOLK TALES

The realm of oral literature is a rich and wide one. Unfortunately, our libraries and our classrooms have acquired an unbalanced collection of literature drawn from the folk. There have been many reasons for this, not the least of which has been the assumption that most Americans draw their heritage from Europe. Too often there has been no indication of the existence of any source other than the European for the folk tales, although many of them began in countries far removed from their European settings. Children of all races have been deprived of the imaginative, colorful, and rich heritage derived from Asia, Africa, and North and South America. They have remained ignorant of the interrelationships throughout all of folk literature, and the effect societies and cultures have had upon each other. They have missed the important implications of the universality of many of the themes folk tales and myths share, no matter what the country of origin.

Fortunately, we are gaining more insight into our previous errors. Libraries and classrooms are beginning to be stocked with more of a variety. Children are beginning to ask about their own and others' backgrounds, and to value diversity in a way that was not possible before. There are many collections of African folk tales in print. Not all of them are well written; appallingly few are even adequately illustrated. Perhaps a constructive activity might be to search out photographs and magazine illustrations that are attractive and realistic, substituting them for the unsatisfying illustrations already contained in some books.

Folk tales appeal to readers of all ages. Some stories are too difficult for very young readers to handle by themselves. Some, because of their sexual content, are meant for adults only. Folk tales compiled for children are almost always effective and enjoyable when read aloud. Teachers would do well to read these tales regularly to their classes as a steady diet. The tales augment the curriculum in almost any subject area. Discussions about the differences and similarities among the different countries and peoples would provide material for many research projects, lessons, and other classroom activities. Such tales are also an informative device for learning about customs and climates of other lands.

Readers should take care to verify authors' expertise. Some of the collections are taken from other literary sources, and are several steps removed from authenticity. Others are told patronizingly by white "friends" of Africa. Still others are authentic but are not very interestingly told. There are quite a few, however, that are written with competence and flavor.

Joyce Cooper Arkhurst's *The Adventures of Spider: West African Folk Tales* introduces Spider, that mischievous, magical, amusing, amazing character. The author maintains a respectful attitude toward the stories and the customs described in them. The style of the writing is clear and smooth in these tales, which abound in cleverness and good humor. Spider's adventures are detailed in mythlike stories as well as in less complex folk stories. Most anthologies of African tales contain at least several episodes about Spider.

Harold Courlander, who has traveled extensively in Africa, and who is a folklorist, has compiled several volumes of folk tales. One of them, in association with George Herzog, is called *The Cow-Tail Switch and Other West African Stories*. This one and another, in which Courlander was assisted by Albert Kofi Prempeh, called *Hat-Shaking Dance and Other Tales from the Gold Coast*, afford the reader an excellent, entertaining, and informative view of these tales. The notes included at the end of each of these books tell where each story comes from, and describe more of the customs of the people. The illustrations in books of folk tales are rarely as good as the text. But in Terry Berger's *Black Fairy Tales*, the illustrations are fitting companions to the colorful and intricate stories. Elton Fax's illustrations outshine the written word in Verna Aardema's *Tales from the Story Hat*. But the stories are well worth reading. Some of them help the reader to recognize the origin of many of the Uncle Remus tales. The notes add interest to the stories. The glossary serves also to aid the reader's appreciation of the tales. All of these stories were adapted from other literary sources. Three of them came from Henry M. Stanley's *My Dark Companions and Their Strange Stories*. The stories are generally well told by the author.

Most books containing African myths and stories will prove to be worth the reading. They are almost unfailingly complex, but clear. Their messages are gentle, but pointed. Their action is rarely violent, but seldom placid. The annotated Bibliography at the end of this chapter will list more collections that the reader can enjoy. These tales will almost inevitably communicate a sense of history and culture difficult to acquire in any other way.

HISTORY

Not enough black history has been written into textbooks. But more and more publishers are moving to fill that void. Many books have been written in fictionalized form, presenting a true history of black people in the United States. Ann McGovern and Jacob Lawrence have each produced a book about Harriet Tubman. The two are very different from each other. Lawrence's illustrations are stark and dramatic in *Harriet and the Promised Land*. The book won the Brooklyn Art Book for Children Citation, and was selected by *The New York Times* as one of the best illustrated children's books of the year. The artist is black. The text is by Robert Kraus, but it is the illustrations that carry the book. McGovern's *Runaway Slave* tells the story of Harriet Tubman in a smooth narrative, sympathetically conveying the details of her incredible life. Moses, as she was called, never got caught, and never lost a passenger from her Underground Railroad ventures.

Stories of the Underground Railroad have been told by several authors. F. N. Monjo wrote an "I Can Read History" book called *The Drinking Gourd*, which is based on historical fact. It tells the story of one of the stations on the Underground Railroad, run by a minister. In this story the minister's son, Tommy, who is always in trouble, discovers and then helps a black family attain freedom. The book is written in an unpatronizing style. The young white boy is responsible for saving the lives of the black runaway slaves, but at no time do the fugitives lose their dignity or sense of self-possession. They are not passive; they are ready to fight to the death rather than lose their freedom. At the end of the story there is a thoughtful discussion between the boy and his father about what it means to be breaking a bad law. Black history is often presented from a white perspective. In some cases, such as the Underground Railroad, it is just as much a part of white history as it is black. *Brady*, by Jean Fritz, is the story of a young white boy whose father, a minister, is a conductor on the Underground Railroad, but no one in the family knows about it. Brady grows in the story from an immature child who cannot keep his mouth shut about anything, and who does not have an opinion about slavery, to a young man who has courage and the ability to keep silent when he should. He carries a runaway slave to the next station on the Underground Railroad and becomes his father's partner.

The struggle for abolition of slavery, and the deep feelings that split the country, are part of this story. It is written so that readers will understand how the white community was split over the issue of slavery. Brady's mother, a Southerner, disapproves of her husband's views, but dutifully stands by him, even when half of his congregation becomes angry enough to absent themselves from his services. The book succeeds in communicating the conflict and growth in the boy. It dramatizes the courage of white people who recognized and fought the evil of slavery.

Florence Freedman's *Two Tickets to Freedom* also demonstrates the willingness of whites to take risks to help fight slavery. But it focuses much more on the lives of Ellen and William Craft, who ingeniously managed to escape their bondage. They overcome enormous odds, manage to get to England, where they raise a family, and then return to the United States after the Civil War, where they establish the Woodville Cooperative Farm School for rural black children. This book is more factual than *Brady*. It is equally dramatic, and emphasizes the black rather than the white experience. The Crafts' story is one of the three love stories in Julius Lester's *This Strange New Feeling*. As with all of Lester's books, the writing is powerful, and well researched.

A very important book that helps readers acquire perspective is Lester's *Long Journey Home: Stories from Black History*. This book dramatically demonstrates the role black people took in maintaining the Underground Railroad. Few students know that it was not only whites who maintained stations for fugitive slaves; many of the conductors as well as those who received runaways in their homes were former slaves themselves. Black people were often the source of their own freedom; many did not have to rely upon the kindness and generosity of sympathetic whites. The book tells very well by means of firsthand accounts some of the horrors of slavery without oversentimentalizing the stories.

Two other books, both also written by black authors, and both very readable and useful are Lucille Clifton's *The Black BC's* (*sic*) and Deloris L. Holt's *The ABC's of Black History*. Clifton's book can be read at two levels: each letter has a simple verse helping the young reader to fill in some of the concepts of black pride and history that the longer, more complex text then expands upon. Each letter takes up a full page, but that page is filled with factual and attitudinal information. Holt's ABC presents a person from black history for each of the letters of the alphabet. The people Holt has selected range from contemporary figures such as Duke Ellington, Martin Luther King, Malcolm X, and Benjamin Quarles, to figures from the past, such as Deborah Sampson Gannett, Pedro Alonso Nino, Harriet Tubman, and others. Both of these books would be valuable additions to any library.

Contemporary history is also depicted in books for children. June Jordan's *Dry Victories* compares the time of Reconstruction and the Civil Rights era. The book is a conversation between two young black men, discussing, in black speech, their perception of the history of the black American. The book's many valuable illustrations include photographs, articles from newspapers, and reproductions of posters. The illustrations help the text to convey to the reader the author's message of no real victory for black Americans. In her afterword the author says that she is angry. "... and you should be too. Then we can do something about this after-mess of aftermath, following on so much tragedy." The book ends with the comment that the Poor People's March on Washington accomplished nothing, and that blacks are still in need of proper housing, social conditions, and economic and political power.

Many new books for older readers contain black characters and make allusions to the problems of minorities in the United States. Readers from the ages of eight to twelve are considered to be much more sophisticated and mature now in their reading preferences than they were before. Racial violence and abuses are realistically portrayed. For the older child, however, the plot and characters are emphasized. The literary quality of a long and complicated text makes a tremendous difference in books for these older readers. Whereas, in a picture book, the illustrations can help to carry the message and make an impact, for the older child the words convey the bulk of the effect. Therefore, teachers, parents, and librarians must seek out books that not only have high literary quality, but also help to move toward a constructive society.

Children are always learning and growing. They need to be helped to deal with the information they encounter in the books they read. Their favorites are sometimes harmful to them in racial awareness. Even books that are acknowledged to be aesthetically fine can be marred by authors' lack of self-perception. The benevolence of the white and the contrasting dependence of the minority member can be a message in well-meaning but ultimately harmful books, particularly those classics written in a less informed era by white authors.

While it is true that having lived an experience adds authenticity to the recounting of it, in this author's opinion, it is useful, but not totally necessary for success. If an artist has insight, empathy, accurate information, and talent, then the resulting work can be effective in achieving its stated goals. If any of the four ingredients is lacking, then the product will be less powerful in its positive achievement.

William Armstrong explains in an author's note at the beginning of *Sounder* that his first teacher, a black man who taught in a "... one-room Negro school," told him the story that he then retells in this book. The plot is of a poor black Southern family who sharecrop on a white man's land. They are very poor and hungry. The father is a strong, vigorous man. The mother is a passive person who believes it is God's will that the black man was "born to lose." There are other children in the family, and there is a hound called Sounder. The dog is the only character in the book who has a name. The others are called "the boy," "the mother," or "the father." None of the white characters is named either. The father is caught after stealing a ham. He is dragged off, unresisting, to jail. The dog tries to interfere, is shot, crippled, and deformed as a result. The father is kept imprisoned for a number of years, during which time his son keeps searching for him to no avail. The son eventually meets a teacher (it is not clear whether he is black or white) and begins to satisfy his craving for learning. When the father does return, he, like the dog, is crippled and deformed. Both the man and the dog are feeble relics of their former selves. At the end of the story, the father and the dog both die. The son continues his education. The author leaves the reader with the impression that the ghosts of the man and dog remain youthful and strong, and that the hope of the boy and his people will be fulfilled through quiet acceptance of one's lot, and through education.

Critics of this book reprove the author for not naming any of the characters except the dog. They claim that the lack of names dehumanizes the people. They decry the seeming valuing of the animal over the humans. In this author's opinion, Armstrong means to use the dog as the symbol for the man. The dog's powerful voice is stilled by the ugliness of oppression. It becomes full-bodied again after the man has regained his freedom. The dog and the man are symbolically linked in the book. When the man dies, so does the dog. Here, too, the critics resent the analogy. They point out that the man is made to go off by himself to a private place to die, in the same way that the mother has explained that animals do. The injuries to both dog and man are almost identical. Perhaps Armstrong means to tell the reader that this is the way some human beings are treated by some others.

For white readers, the book presents a clear and strong indictment of an oppressive system. It arouses a deep sense of sympathy with and anger at the treatment of the blacks. It invites questions about a country's so-called democratic system that permits these abuses to occur. But it might also cause a white reader to think, "Why didn't anyone fight back? Why didn't the family seek legal help? Why did the man steal the ham? Why didn't they attempt to hide the ham and evidence, once he did steal it? Why was the mother so defeatist, and so discouraging of her son's ambition?" And these questions might possibly lead the reader to feel just a little smug or superior, without ever investigating the truth of the implications.

The black reader might also have some questions about the story. The analogy using the dog and other animals may be useful as a literary device, but it can also be demeaning to a black person. The total defeatism of the mother, and the passive behavior, even in seeking out his father, and then an education, on the part of the son might be somewhat perplexing to the reader. Nowhere in the book is it explained why the father must remain imprisoned for so long. He is supposedly let off early (after so many years?) because of his severe injuries (caused by a mine explosion). There is no mention made beforehand of the length of his sentence, only that he went to "hard labor." Is it not difficult to believe that the stealing of a ham, most of which was returned, would call down such a punishment? Why did the author choose to treat his character so very harshly?

For those readers who have never been deeply moved by the plight of the black victim, this book could constitute an important experience of growth. For those who already understand and decry white oppression, it might possibly be an reminder of white abuse. But it might also help to affirm some negative images in the minds of those readers who believe that black people are essentially incapable of asserting their own rights. There is no one correct interpretation or criticism of this book. The reader and interested adults must decide for themselves what the message is. They must also decide for themselves how to proceed. But it would be helpful to be aware of the author's special background in order to fully process the various reactions to the book.

Julius Lester's *To Be a Slave* also graphically portrays the horrors wrought upon blacks. He helps the reader to see slaves as individuals. Many of them, despite all odds, maintained their selfhood, and managed to overcome their specific hardships. He gives us their own words, and helps us to understand more deeply what they signify by adding his own comments. After offering the reader descriptions of some of the ways some slaves managed to enjoy themselves, Lester adds, "... whatever pleasure the slave was able to provide for himself was a remarkable testimony to the ability to retain humanity under the most inhuman conditions." Lester does not leave it to the inexperienced reader to draw conclusions. He helps every reader to acquire a deeper perception.

It is an author's responsibility, in this transitional time in history, to make a work that includes minorities in it a part of the movement toward a better society. Good work is read and accepted by so many people that it lies in the author's power to make an impact, the results of which will be felt by future generations. It is also the parent's, librarian's, and the teacher's responsibility to bring to the young reader's attention those ideas, attitudes, and facts that will help to construct a new and healthy community for everyone.

OTHER AMERICAN HERITAGES

There are more examples in literature of the two heritages already included in this chapter (the Native American and the Afro-American) than there are of all of the other heritages combined. It is very important for librarians, teachers, parents, and children to try to find books of quality containing characters representing the diversity of populations that now live in the United States. In order to approach books with a critical understanding and the ability to sort out inaccuracies, distortions, stereotypes, derogatory language, romanticization, and omissions, it is necessary for readers first to acquaint themselves with the history, culture, and current status of these groups.

Books should be read with an awareness of the author's perspective, the authenticity of the text, the accuracy of the illustrations, and in comparison with other books on the same topic. The criteria mentioned in the first two sections of this chapter pertain to literature about any heritage, and should be applied to every book. Every collection of children's books should reflect the diversity within groups as well as between them. The authors of these books should either be members of the specific heritage or knowledgeable "outsiders." Books should be supplemented with current newspaper and magazine articles, and, wherever possible, with conversations with people whose heritage is that of the group being studied.

HISPANIC AMERICANS

Hispanic Americans differ from each other as much as they, as a group, differ from other groups. The blending of Spanish, Native American, and African parentage constitutes their rich heritage. They live in South America, Central America, Mexico, and the Caribbean as well as in various sections of the continental United States. They share a common language, although the differences in vocabulary, intonation, and pronunciation are at least as marked as the differences among English-speaking people. They have a common history, with variations depending on the degree and kind of interaction between the conquering Spaniards and the indigenous populations. Hispanics are generally Catholic, but a significant number embrace other religious beliefs.

In personality, appearance, political opinions, social class, economic status, lifestyle, and education, Hispanics are varied in the same way that the general American population is.

Hispanics were the first Europeans to establish settlements on the North American continent. The Caribbean was the first region colonized by Spain at the end of the fifteenth century (as a result of Columbus's voyages). Spain rapidly and extensively moved into the "New World" from then on, and occupied much of the Caribbean, as well as the east coast of continental North America. Because no women came with the Spanish explorers and colonists, and because the Spaniards initiated an extensive import of slave labor, children born of the Spanish conquests had Native American ("Indian") and African as well as Spanish heritage. This section will describe a few books dealing with Puerto Ricans and Mexican-Americans. There are few if any books that successfully contain stories with Cuban or other Latin American characters. It is hoped that writers and publishers will remedy this deficit in the near future, particularly since the Hispanic population is the fastest-growing and largest minority in the United States.

Puerto Ricans

Puerto Ricans are citizens of the United States, whether they reside in Puerto Rico, in other lands, or in any of the states on the continent. They are not foreigners. The most prevalent reason for Puerto Ricans to migrate from their land is the search for work. Contrary to the myth that Puerto Ricans "are lazy and come here to be on welfare," they generally come motivated by the desire to better their family situation through steady employment. If they wanted to be on welfare, they could stay in Puerto Rico where the weather is mild, the natural beauty is lush and colorful, everyone speaks their language, and where they have an extended family with whom to visit and share troubles and triumphs.

What is more, contrary to the erroneous impression given by the bulk of the literature, Puerto Ricans belong to different economic classes, and live both in urban areas and rural areas in Puerto Rico and elsewhere. On the mainland the majority live in New York or other large cities, but it is important for young readers to see a balanced and accurate picture of people in order to prevent them from forming prejudicial impressions. Milton Meltzer's book *The Hispanic Americans* provides an excellent resource for learning about not only Puerto Ricans, but also other Hispanic Americans. He includes anecdotes about individuals and families, comments about the importance of bilingual education, and describes the effects of institutional racism in relationship to this population. The photographs contribute to the already rich details of the book.

In one of its 1983 issues, the *Bulletin* of the Council on Interracial Books for Children (Volume 14, Numbers 1 and 2) devotes most of its pages to a discussion of Puerto Ricans in children's literature and history texts, and the articles, particularly those by Sonia Nieto, are very informative. Dr. Nieto describes several books of fiction and nonfiction with Puerto Rican themes. She analyzes them for their accuracy and quality. She bemoans the fact that so few excellent books exist that contain Puerto Rican characters seen in a clear light.

Most of the books that are available are aimed at an audience of readers aged ten and up. Nicholasa Mohr, a Puerto Rican author, has written a number of books about life in the *barrio* of New York City. Her characters are vivid and three-dimensional. The stories are not gentle or fantasy, and occasionally there is some stereotype labeling that jars the reader, but on the whole, they are engrossing, informative, and worthwhile. Myron Levoy's *Shadow like a Leopard*, is another realistic book set in Spanish Harlem. This book, too, is for older readers, contains excellent plot and characterization, and is compelling reading. Ramon, the protagonist, does not permit the facts of his mother's hospitalization, his father's imprisonment, and a gang of hoodlums' threats to defeat him. His talents, intelligence, street wisdom, and capacity for loving help him to overcome any barriers.

The wealth of folklore that belongs to Puerto Rico is not easily available in English-language books. One anthology edited by Kal Wagenheim includes stories, some of them based on folk tales, by Belavel, Marques, Soto, Diaz Alfaro, Gonzalez, and Diaz Valcarcel. This book, *Short Stories from Puerto Rico*, is published in English by the Institute of Puerto Rican Culture, and is a worthy purchase for any classroom or library. For younger children, *Juan Bobo and the Pig* is a folk tale retold in English by Bernice Chardiet. Many more such books are needed.

Scholastic Book Clubs publish a number of books in both Spanish and English for young children. Their quality is generally excellent, and the message, that the Spanish language should be valued in Anglo schools and libraries, is an important one. *Mi Mama, la Cartera (My Mother the Mail Carrier)*, by Inez Maury, published by the Feminist Press, is an example of a book printed in both Spanish and English that provides an excellent image of a Hispanic family, a strong woman, and a charming presentation.

Mexican Americans

A remarkable book, *Growing Older*, by George Ancona, describes, among others, an active, vibrant Mexican American woman who is old and zestful. Jacqueline Bernard chronicles the lives of three Mexican Americans who figured in the history of the American Southwest in *Voices from the Southwest: Antonio Jose Martinez, Elfego Baca, Reies Lopez Tijerina*. Another factual book helping young readers to value the contributions of Mexican Americans is Patricia de Garza's book, *Chicanos: The Story of Mexican-Americans,* and Rudy Acuña, a Mexican American writer, has contributed two valuable histories, one for young readers (*The Story of the Mexican Americans: The Men and the Land*) and one for older students (*A Mexican American Chronicle*). Paula Paul conveys respect for traditional Mexican culture in *You Can Hear a Magpie Smile.* Leo Politi retells some Mexican legends in *Three Stalks of Corn,* one of the few examples of these tales in books for English-speaking children.

It is important to find books that value the culture, heritage, and language of Hispanics (as it is with any heritage). Take care to find books that do not demean the language with false dialect or condescending phrases. Writers of quality tune their ears to the cadence and patterns of the language and communicate their respect through their portrayal.

ASIAN AMERICANS

As with other groups, Asian Americans differ from each other as well as from other populations. Although they share a racial construct, they vary as much as do Caucasians and blacks. Books that lump all Asians in one pot err greatly. Unfortunately, the literature is very sparse in its portrayal of any Asian Americans.

Milton Meltzer's *The Chinese Americans* points out the distortions, prejudices, and racist practices perpetrated against Chinese Americans. He also details their contributions and progress. Lawrence Yep has written a number of stories that depict Chinese American characters in realistic and non-stereotypical settings and situations. *Dragonwings* contributes information about the same historical attitudes toward Chinese Americans that Meltzer's book does, but the facts are set into a stirring tale. Yep's *Sea Glass* explores the conflict between old and new ways, and between self-valuing and external pressures. Again, the Chinese American community emerges clearly.

Chinese folk and fairy tales are better represented in children's books than some of the other Asian populations. *Yeh-Shen: A Cinderella Story from*

China, retold by Ai-Ling Louie, beautifully introduces this forerunner of the European versions of *Cinderella*. Diane Wolkstein respectfully retells the story of *White Wave*, the moon goddess. In both books the illustrations heighten the impact of the story.

Yoshiko Uchida has written a number of books containing Japanese American characters, telling of their tragedies and victories, their strengths and foibles. *Journey Home* and *A Jar of Dreams* describe Japanese American families enduring prejudice and difficult economic times, but surmounting their difficulties by means of their reservoirs of tradition and strength. Uchida's writing is swift-moving and enjoyable.

For younger children, Taro Yashima's books *Crow Boy* and *Umbrella* provide delightful images and information about Japanese characters. Children ages seven and up can appreciate *Isamu Noguchi: The Life of a Sculptor*, by Tobi Tobias. Simply told, the book makes readers aware of the ugly practice of interning Japanese Americans in concentration camps. The same topic is explored in Jeanne Wakatsuki Houston and James Houston's more mature *Farewell to Manzanar*.

Vietnamese Americans are rarely found in American children's books. *First Snow*, by Helen Coutant, is one of the exceptions. Basically a book explaining how the old grandmother views death, the story manages to portray the tender relationship between Lien and her grandmother. A book that contains much specific information about Vietnamese heritage is *The Land I Lost: Adventures of a Boy in Vietnam*, by Huynh Quang Nhuong. It tells a gripping story, interspersed with humor, by means of a series of anecdotes. In one of them, the author's grandmother manages to rout a bully through her knowledge of martial arts. Through these recollections, the reader gains an acquaintance with the land and people of Vietnam.

The paucity of books with Asian American characters indicates that there is much to be done in the area of multicultural awareness on the part of publishers and writers of children's literature. It is to be hoped that more writers will attempt to portray their own roots through children's literature.

JEWISH AMERICANS

Differing from the above accounts, the literature containing Jewish characters has grown rapidly and prolifically in the past decade. In addition to a substantial body of literature on the Holocaust (see the chapter on war), the awarding of the Nobel Prize for literature to Isaac Bashevis Singer for his writings in Yiddish is a reflection of the wealth of books including the folklore and flavor of the Jewish population.

Singer's *The Power of Light: Eight Stories for Hannukah* is but one of the many exquisitely told collections of tales of miracles, realities, and, above all, people, that the author has written from his store of Jewish oral tradition as well as from his own imagination. *Yussel's Prayer: A Yom Kippur Story*, is retold by Barbara Cohen in a loving folkloric style. Jewish literature is rich in folklore, and the literature for children reflects this legacy.

Since there is so much to choose from, readers may be particularly selective. They can look for respectful rather than ridiculing humor, avoidance of the extremities of physical stereotyping, careful rendition of language, and presentation of varying characteristics of women (not all of them are smothering, overprotective, or aggressive housekeepers) and men (not all of them are weak, impractical, philosophical dunderheads).

In addition to folk tales, books portray Jewish life in otherwise nonethnic stories by the mention of religious or cultural customs. Joan Fassler's *My Grandpa Died Today* is one example: it is mentioned that the mirrors in the house are covered during the time of mourning. In Rose Blue's *Grandma Didn't Wave Back*, Debbie's grandmother has "tchachkes," a Yiddish word for bric-a-brac, little mementos that are meaningful to her.

Other books specifically use the setting of a Jewish home to flavor the plot and create their characters. All of the *Hannah* books by Mindy Skolsky portray Hannah and her grandmother in the context of Jewish food and celebrations. The classic *All of a Kind Family* series by Sydney Taylor contributes a perspective on Jewish family life at the turn of the century in New York's Lower East Side.

Some books explore some of the specifically religious aspects of Jewish heritage. *How Yossi Beat the Evil Urge*, by Miriam Chaikin, an author of many books with Jewish themes, centers on a Chasidic community and its practices. Judy Blume's popular *Are You There God? It's Me, Margaret*, and the wonderfully absorbing *A Year in the Life of Rosie Bernard*, by Barbara Brenner, both contain young female characters who reflect on their Judaism and have questions and conflict over their religious identity.

Children can use the stories they read to compare religious practices, find other books about different religions, do research on contemporary religious groups, discuss what the difference is between religion and culture, and examine the causes and practices of religious bigotry.

The Bibliography contains books on other populations, not categorized according to specific population, first of all because there are not enough numbers in each category to separate them, and secondly because, as with special needs, the issue is a global one, with the necessity of paying special attention to certain details. With the constant updating of new publications, and increasing public awareness of the roots of racism, caring adults will be able to provide children with the basis for healthful and constructive attitudes toward themselves and others.

REFERENCES: HERITAGE

ABEL, MIDGE B. "American Indian Life as Portrayed in Children's Literature," *Elementary English*, Vol. 50, No. 2, February 1973, pp. 202–208.

Gives historical overview of the variety of children's books concerning Native Americans. Criticizes the poor quality of most illustrations.

ALEXANDER, RAE. "What Is a Racist?" *Bulletin of the Council on Interracial Books for Children*, Vol. 1, No. 1, Autumn 1970.
Cites research that demonstrates damaging effect of literature on black children. Recommends the exclusion of any book that may give pain to even one black child. Critiques a number of books.

ARNEZ, NNEKA NANCY. "An Annotated Bibliography of Selected Non-Racist Books for Black Children," *Negro Educational Review*, Vol. 32, Nos. 3–4, July–October 1981.
Reports on a study finding that books by black authors are more likely to describe black characters in vivid and genuine fashion than white authors. Recommends that black parents purchase and encourage the reading of these books by black authors. Supplies an annotated list of seventeen expecially fine books for black children.

ASIAN AMERICAN CHILDREN'S BOOK PROJECT. *"How Children's Books Distort the Asian American Image,"* Bridge, Vol. 4, No. 3, July 1976, pp. 5–7.
Including criteria for analyzing books on Asian Americans, this article points out stereotypes, myths, and misrepresentations.

BAKER, AUGUSTA. "The Changing Image of the Black in Children's Literature," *Horn Book Magazine*, February 1975, pp. 79–88.
Traces the history of the black in children's literature. Provides questions to be used as criteria for judging quality of these books. Supports the search for black authors. Supports the positive direction of contemporary books. Hopes for a sense of universality on the part of the reading public.

BANFIELD, BERYL. "Beyond 'Roots': Readings on the Slavery and Reconstruction Periods," *Bulletin of the Council on Interracial Books for Children,* Vol. 8, No. 2, 1977, pp. 9–11.
Discusses the necessity for reading materials about this historical period that provide an Afro-American perspective, are historically accurate, and are readable and readily available. Lists and describes teacher resources and students' materials.

BAXTER, KATHRINE. "Combating the Influence of Black Stereotypes in Children's Books," *Reading Teacher*, Vol. 27, No. 6, March 1974, pp. 540–544.
Excellent article analyzing both subtle and blatant stereotyping in children's books. Criteria presented for judging books. Recommendations made for helping children recognize racist implications.

BECK, KATY AND ARMIN. "All They Do Is Run Away," *Civil Rights Digest*, August 1972.
Discusses impact of racial insults upon children. Recommends inservice programs so that teachers can learn how to handle this problem.

BERNSTEIN, JOANNE E. "Minorities in Fiction for Young Children," *Integrated Education*, Vol. 11, No. 3, May–June 1973, pp. 34–37.
Ninety-eight stories with school settings analyzed to see how roles of minority group members are portrayed. Is optimistic about current trend toward multiethnic portrayals. Bibliography (not annotated).

BINGHAM, JANE. "The Pictorial Treatment of Afro-Americans in Books for Young Children 1930–1968," *Elementary English*, Vol. 48, No. 7, November 1971, pp. 880–886.
Investigated illustrations in forty-one recommended books, which had black characters in them. Criteria are offered for judging the impact of the illustrations. Recommendations are made, based on the findings of the study.

BIRTHA, JESSIE. "Portrayal of the Black in Children's Literature," *Philadelphia Library Association Bulletin*, Vol. 24, July 1969, pp. 187–197.
Suggests guidelines for examining books, with specific evaluative criteria. Offers her own list of notable books portraying black people. Author is a black librarian.

BRACKEN, JEANNE, AND WIGUTOFF, SHARON. *Books for Today's Children: An Annotated Bibliography of Non-Stereotyped Picture Books*. Old Westbury, New York: Feminist Press, 1979.
Discusses and recommends over 100 books for young children containing positive values. The titles are arranged in lists of books that are highly recommended, recommended, and recommended with some reservation. Otherwise, the books are not placed into categories.

BRACKEN, JEANNE, AND WIGUTOFF, SHARON, WITH ILENE BAKER. *Books for Today's Young Readers: An Annotated Bibliography of Recommended Fiction for Ages 10–14*. Old Westbury, New York: Feminist Press, 1981.
Descriptions and analyses of books for older readers. Gender, ethnicity, acculturation and racism, peer friendships, special needs, families in transition, foster care and adoption, and views of old people are some of the categories specified. Very helpful discussion and format.

BRITTON, JEAN E. *Selected Books about the Afro-American for Very Young Children, K–2*. Boston: Commonwealth of Massachusetts, Department of Education, Division of Curriculum and Instruction, Bureau of Curriculum Innovation. (182 Tremont St., Boston, Massachusetts 02111.)
This bibliography was compiled with the assistance of the Massachusetts Commission against discrimination. It includes guidelines for evaluating books and an indication of the books that children in the town of Roxbury particularly enjoyed.

BRODERICK, DOROTHY M. *Image of the Black in Children's Fiction*. New York: Bowker, 1973.
Excellent historical and background information for learning about and understanding the negative treatment of blacks in children's books. The author includes quotes from books written for children that are demeaning to blacks. She demonstrates the pervasive negative attitudes and behaviors specifically and powerfully.

BROWN, DEE. *Bury My Heart at Wounded Knee*. New York: Holt, Rinehart and Winston, 1971.
History of U.S. relations with the Native Americans written from a point of view sympathetic to the American Indian people. Shocking details of atrocities, lies, and betrayals.

BRYAN, ASHLEY. "On Poetry and Black American Poets," *Horn Book Magazine*, Vol. 55, No. 1, February 1979, pp. 42–49.
Bryan quotes several black poets to illustrate his point that in describing the multi-faceted black experience in this nation black poets speak not only to black Americans, but to all humanity. Poetry crosses the barriers of age, sex, and race, allowing the dreams, joys and pains of one person, one people to be felt by all people.

BURNETTE, ROBERT. *The Tortured Americans*. Englewood Cliffs, New Jersey: Prentice-Hall, 1971.
Describes present-day political and economic situation of the Rosebud Sioux. Recommends an investigation of the entire field of Indian affairs. Also recommends the establishment of a Federal Indian Commission instead of the BIA and the passage of a new act to grant American Indians control over themselves. Burnette is a Sioux who has for a long time been involved in the battle of independence for American Indians.

BYLER, MARY GLOYNE, ED. *American Indian Authors for Young Readers: A Selected Bibliography*. New York: Association on American Indian Affairs, 1973.
In her introduction to the annotated bibliography, Byler explains why she decided to include only work written by Native Americans. Unfortunately, many of the items in her bibliography are difficult to secure, except directly from the publisher. It is to be hoped that libraries, schools, and bookstores across the country will take the trouble to purchase these books.

CANE, SUZANNE S.; CHATFIELD, CAROL A.; HOLMES, MARGARET C.; AND PETERSON, CHRISTINE C., eds. *Selected Media about the American Indian for Young Children*. Boston: Commonwealth of Massachusetts, Department of Education, Division of Curriculum and Instruction, Bureau of Curriculum Innovation, 1970.
Excellent and useful pamphlet listing books for children and adults, museums in Massachusetts, other sources of information, and publishers' addresses. The editors examined hundreds of items and found most to be of poor quality. The annotations indicate both positive and negative features of each entry.

CARLSON, RUTH KEARNEY. *Emerging Humanity: Multi-Ethnic Literature for Children and Adolescents*. Illustrated by Louise Noack Gray and Ernest Jaco. Dubuque, Iowa: William C. Brown, 1972.
Excellent reference containing discussions, bibliographies, and practical suggestions for activities relating to minority groups. The two chapters specifically relating to blacks are informative and extensive.

CITRON, ABRAHAM F. "Rightness of Whiteness." Detroit: Office of Urban Education, 1971. (College of Education, Wayne State University, Detroit, Mich. 48202.)
Discusses the impact of language, environment, and books on white and black children. Cites research; provides useful bibliography.

CLAPP, OUIDA H. "Language Arts—The Invisible Child," *Instructor*, Vol. 80, No. 6, February 1971, pp. 63–65.
Pleads for inclusion of books containing black characters, particularly in order to help the black child.

CORNELIUS, PAUL. "Interracial Children's Books: Problems and Progress," *Library Quarterly*, Vol. 41, No. 2, April 1971, pp. 106–127.
Reviews criticism and research leading to the awareness of the dearth of representation for minority groups in children's books. Presents a history of books dealing with black characters. Describes a number of books, organizations, and movements designed to change the system. Presents current issues about children's books containing black characters. Critiques several books. Useful overview.

COUNCIL ON INTERRACIAL BOOKS FOR CHILDREN. *Bulletin*, Vol. 14, Nos. 1 and 2, 1983. (Special issue on Puerto Ricans in Children's Literature and History Texts: A Ten-Year Update.)
Contains articles by such people as Sonia Nieto, Sharon Wigutoff, Iris Santos-Rivera, Juan Hernandez-Cruz, and Analda Colon-Munoz critiquing books and text containing material on Puerto Rico and Puerto Ricans. Includes criteria and analyses.

_____. *Guidelines for Selecting Biasfree Textbooks and Storybooks.* New York: Council on Interracial Books for Children, 1980.
A set of articles compiled into a useful manual for teaching children about bias of all sorts in the books they read.

_____. *Winning "Justice for All."* New York: Council on Interracial Books for Children, 1980. (Sponsored by the Women's Educational Equity Act Program, U.S. Dept of Health, Education and Welfare.)
A social studies and language arts curriculum to help children overcome stereotypes, particularly those of gender role.

_____. *Bulletin,* Vol. 7, No. 5, 1976. (Special issue on Language and Racism and Sexism.)
A discussion on how language can be used to further stereotypes and negative attitudes toward females and nonwhite people.

_____. *Bulletin,* Vol. 11, Nos. 3 and 4, 1980. (Special Issue on Children, Race and Racism.)
Several articles on how to help children develop positive race awareness.

COX, JUANITA, AND WALLIS, BETH S. "Books for a Cajun Child-Lagniappe or a Little Something Extra for Multicultural Teaching," *Reading Teacher*, Vol. 36, No. 3, December 1982, pp. 263–266.
This annotated bibliography of children's books dealing with Cajun themes is a valuable resource not only for teachers in the French-speaking Acadian community, but also for any teachers who care that their children be exposed to as many cultures as possible.

DAVIS, MAVIS WORMLEY. "Black Images in Children's Literature: Revised Editions Needed," *School Library Journal*, Vol. 18, No. 5, January 1972, pp. 37–39.
Criticizes language and character portrayal demeaning blacks in many children's books. Praises others for their positive treatment. Recommends revision of the negative books.

DELORIA, VINE, JR. *Custer Died for Your Sins*. New York: Macmillan, 1969.
Controversial, personal, and impressive. Deloria is former Executive Director of the National Congress of American Indians. He is a Standing Rock Sioux. His opinions and interpretations of current and past events compel the reader to raise many questions.

DENBY, ROBERT V. "Literature by and about Negroes for the Elementary Level," *Elementary English*, Vol. 46, No. 7, November 1969, pp. 909–913.
A listing of ERIC documents including rationale, background readings for teachers, and bibliographies on blacks in children's literature. The documents listed are through 1968, including some which are no longer in print but are still available on microfiche.

DOUGLASS, JOSEPH H. "Mental Health Aspects of the Effects of Discrimination upon Children," *Young Children*, May 1967, pp. 298–304.
Discusses effects of discrimination on children, and, by extension, on society.

DUSOLD, LENORE. "A Study of the Portrayal of the American Indian in Selected Children's Fiction." Unpublished Master's report, Palmer Graduate Library School, Long Island University, Brookville, New York, 1970.
Examines a number of children's books, analyzing them for prejudice toward the Native American. Establishes criteria such as rejecting assimilation as a goal, combatting stereotypes, and valuing of the culture. Applauds the current goals of self-determination through tribal power and nationalism. Bibliography and discussion of the books is included.

EDELMAN, MARIAN WRIGHT. *Portrait of Inequality: Black and White Children in America*. Washington, D.C.: Children's Defense Fund, 1980.
Statistics and discussion that document the disparity between all societal benefits to black and white families. The book urges enlightened advocacy and provides many suggestions for action.

FISHER, LAURA, "All Chiefs, No Indians: What Children's Books Say about American Indians," *Elementary English,* Vol. 51, No. 2 February 1974, pp. 185–189.
An excellent analysis of the cliches, stereotypes, and distortions presented in children's books that deal with Native Americans. Fisher recommends a number of books that she judges to be better than most in fostering healthy attitudes in the reader.

FOUNDATION FOR CHANGE. "Black Women Are Proud," January 1973.
One of a series of pamphlets presenting historical information about minorities. The aim is to help minority children build and reinforce a postive self-image.

FRASER, JAMES. "Black Publishing for Black Children," *School Library Journal*, Vol. 20, No. 3, November 1973, pp. 19–24.
Traces the history of black publishing; that is, enterprises "owned and operated by black people producing literature by black writers with the needs and interests of black people in mind." Gives an overview of companies and their publications. Supplies a list of publishers and their addresses.

GAST, DAVID K. "The Dawning of the Age of Aquarius for Multiethnic Children's Literature," *Elementary English*, Vol. 47, No. 5, May 1970, pp. 661–665.
A very influential article, listing different approaches to beware of in children's books dealing with the black experiences.

GILLILAND, HAP. "The New View of Native Americans in Children's Books," *Reading Teacher*, Vol. 35, No. 8, 1982, pp. 912–916.
Reviews the past record of published books for children about Native American, and finds that there are a number of current books that are interesting, true-to-life and respectful of Native American ways. Supplies a list of these books, and describes them.

GLANCY, BARBARA J. "Annotated Bibliography of Integrated and Black Books for Children," in *Black Image: Education Copes with Color*, ed. Grambs and Carr. Dubuque, Iowa: William C. Brown, 1972.
Classifies books in age groupings. Includes books with black characters with content related to racial problems, and also with content not related to racial problems in separate lists.

_____. "Why Good Interracial Books Are Hard to Find," in *Black Image: Education Copes With Color,* ed. Grambs and Carr. Dubuque, Iowa: William C. Brown, 1972.
Discusses the roles of publishers, reviewers, sales, library and teacher selection tools in seeing to it that interracial books become available to children.

GRAHAM, LORENZ. "An Author Speaks," *Elementary English*, Vol. 50, No. 2, February 1973, pp. 185–188.
Graham, a black author, tells about his life and his decision to become a writer.

GRANSTROM, JANE, AND SILVEY, ANITA. "A Call for Help: Exploring the Black Experience in Children's Books," *Horn Book Magazine*, Vol. 48, No. 4, August 1972, pp. 345–404.
Reproduces a panel discussion among concerned educators and librarians concerning the black experience as negatively portrayed in children's books.

GRIESE, ARNOLD A. "Ann Nolan Clark—Building Bridges of Cultural Under-standing," *Elementary English*, Vol. 49, No. 5, May 1972, pp. 648–658.
A description of Ann Nolan Clark and her work. Pays particular attention to her literary style and to her contribution to young Native Americans self-image.

GRIFFIN, LOUISE. *Multi-Ethnic Books for Young Children: An Annotated Bibliography for Parents and Teachers.* Washington, D.C.: National Association for the Education of Young Children, 1970.
Lists books available up to 1970 for minority, non-middle-class children. Many cultures listed. Adult books suggested for parents and teachers. Annotations are very useful.

HALL, SUSAN J. "Tarzan Lives! A Study of the New Children's Books about Africa," *Bulletin of the Council on Interracial Books for Children*, Vol. 9, No. 1, 1978, pp. 3–7.
The author finds that factual errors, patronizing vocabulary, and racism abound in children's books about Africa.

HAMILTON, VIRGINIA. "Ah, Sweet Rememory," *Horn Book Magazine*, Vol. 57, No. 6, December 1981, pp. 633–640.

The award-winning author discusses the way her heritage has informed her fiction. All of her books are influenced by the journey of black people through America, "the dream of freedom tantalizingly out of reach."

HENRY, JEANETTE, ed. *Index to Literature on the American Indian*. San Francisco: Indian Historian Press, 1973 (regularly updated).

Lists an enormous quantity of periodicals, texts, and books published about the American Indian. Produced by Indians under the direction of the American Indian Historical Society. Has a section on Juvenile literature, and a special supplementary index to the young people's periodical, *The Weewish Tree*. None of the entries is annotated, unfortunately, but the vast amount of material listed is invaluable.

HIRCHFELDER, ARLENE, ed. *American Indian and Eskimo Authors: A Comprehensive Bibliography*. New York: Association on American Indian Affairs, 1974.

Introduction by Mary Gloyne Byler points out the gains made because of changes in non-American Indian attitudes. Bibliography is annotated helpfully and is extensive. Children's books are not included in this list, although some of the entries also appear in *American Indian Authors for Young Readers*.

JENKINS, ESTHER C. "Multi-Ethnic Literature: Promises and Problems," *Elementary English*, Vol. 50, No. 5, May 1973, pp. 693–699.

Describes goals of a multiethnic literature program and recommends ways of setting one up.

KEATING, CHARLOTTE MATTHEWS. *Building Bridges of Understanding between Cultures*. Tucson: Palo Verde Publishing Company, 1971.

Several chapters of this book pertain to books concerning black Americans. One chapter is devoted to black Americans, one to selections with multiethnic representation, one to Africa, and one to the Caribbean. The annotations are extensive, interesting, and very personalized. The author may not be critical or sensitive enough to the negative implications of some of the books that she recommends; but her intentions are honest, and the book is, in general, a valuable one.

KERCKFOFF, RICHARD, AND TRELLA, SHERRY CRANE. "Teaching Race Relations in the Nursery School," *Young Children*, April 1972, p. 240.

Describes how reading certain books to young children helped them to develop constructive racial attitudes.

KLEIN, BARRY T., ed. *Reference Encyclopedia of the American Indian*, 3rd ed., Vol. 1. New York: Todd Publications, 1978.

A very thorough listing of government agencies, museums, libraries, associations, courses, government publications, magazines and periodicals, and other resources on the Indians of North America. Several thousand entries are included in the extensive bibliography. An invaluable resource.

LANES, SELMA G. "Black is Bountiful," in *Down the Rabbit Hole*. New York: Atheneum, 1971.

Discusses several books, including classics, in terms of their treatment of black characters and their effect on the reader. Also reviews the criticisms of some books. Presents interesting points of view for the reader to consider.

LARRICK, NANCY. "The All-White World of Children's Books," *Saturday Review,* 11 September 1965, pp. 63–85.
Presents a powerful argument against stereotypes in children's books. Helps the reader to recognize subtle negative implications in books. Expresses hope that publishers will take heed.

LATIMER, BETTYE I. "Children's Books and Racism," *Black Scholar*, May–June 1973, pp. 21–27.
This article, excerpted from *Starting Out Right*, includes the listing of the most common flaws in books about blacks.

_____, ed. *Starting Out Right: Choosing Books about Black People for Young Children* Madison, Wisconsin: Department of Public Instruction, 1972.
Presents sixteen criteria for judging books involving blacks. Several chapters discuss the issues involved in books for children. The authors annotate more than two hundred books according to their established criteria. They are in alphabetical order by title. The authors suggest several ways of effecting change. A very useful publication.

LESTER, JULIUS. "The Kinds of Books We Give Children: Whose Nonsense?" *Publishers Weekly,* Vol. 197, No. 8, 23 February 1970, p. 86.
Recommends that we begin to acquaint our children, through books, to the real world.

LESTER, JULIUS, AND WOODS, GEORGE. "Black and White: An Exchange," *New York Times Book Review*, 24 May 1970, pp. 1, 34–38.
Correspondence between Julius Lester and George Woods concerning their opinions on the way books affect black and nonblack readers. Both points of view are well stated and represent two perspectives.

MACCANN, DONNARAE. "Overdue," *Wilson Library Bulletin*, Vol. 46, No. 9, May 1971, pp. 880–881.
Recommends a careful analysis of the images in children's books.

MACCANN, DONNARAE, AND WOODARD, GLORIA, EDS. *The Black American in Books for Children: Readings in Racism*. Metuchen, New Jersey: Scarecrow Press, 1972.
A series of informative articles, all dealing with issues of minorities in children's books.

MAEHR, JANE. *The Middle East: An Annotated Bibliography of Literature for Children*, 1977. (Available from ERIC Clearinghouse on Early Childhood Education, University of Illinois, 805 West Pennsylcania Ave., Urbana, Illinois 61801. Catalog No. 161.)
Books containing characters and information about Iran, Iraq, Israel, Jordan, Kuwait, Lebanon, Saudi Arabia, Syria, Turkey and the United Arab Republic

(Egypt) are described here. The other countries are excluded only because no books in English could be found to represent them.

MATHIS, SHARON BELL. "True/False Messages for the Black Child," *Black Books Bulletin*, Vol. 2, Nos. 3 and 4, Winter 1974, pp. 12–19.
Criticizes a number of books demeaning blacks by their use of stereotyes and "poison-words." Illuminating article.

MAY, JILL P. "To Think Anew: Native American Literature and Children's Attitudes," *Reading Teacher*, Vol. 36, No. 8, April 1983, pp. 790–794.
Discusses in detail a course of study used with gifted fifth and sixth graders, using literature to help dispel negative impressions of Native Americans, and to motivate the students to learn more about this heritage.

MICKINOCK, REY. "The Plight of the Native American," in *Issues in Children's Book Selection*. Reprinted from September 1971 *School Library Journal*. New York: Bowker, 1973.
The author, a member of the Ojibway Nation, discusses the inaccuracies and misconceptions printed in many children's books. He recommends several books for their accuracy and usefulness. He also clears up a number of false images some books have presented.

MYERS, WALTER. "The Black Experience in Children's Books: One Step Forward, Two Steps Back," *Bulletin of the Council on Interracial Books for Children*, Vol. 10, No. 6, 1979, pp. 14–15.
A revealing article about attitudes of some of the public to books with black characters, and to the issue of criticizing racism in books. Myers points out "Good literature for my children is literature that includes them and the way they live.

NABOKOV, PETER, ed. *Native American Testimony: An Anthology of Indian and White Relations, First Encounter to Dispossession*. New York: Crowell, 1978.
Documentation of Native Americans' voices, telling of their impressions of and encounters with whites. Illustrated with photographs and maps, the book helps dispel preconceptions and distortions by providing the reader with authentic first-person accounts from a Native American perspective.

NATIONAL CONFERENCE OF CHRISTIANS AND JEWS. *Books for Brotherhood*.
The books in this annual listing are selected "on the basis of their contribution to the search for community in a pluralistic society . . ." The children's and young people's list includes books about different minorities. Notations are helpful.

NEWMAN, JEFFRY. "Indian Association Attacks Lies in Children's Literature," *Bulletin of the Council on Interracial Books for Children*. Vol. 2, No. 3, Summer 1969.
Decries the lack of accuracy about Native Americans, especially in children's books. Presents list of criteria for evaluating books on Native Americans.

PARKS, CAROLE A. "Good-bye Black Sambo," *Ebony*, November 1972, pp. 60–70.
Describes a number of black children's book authors and their writing. Applauds the rise in numbers of these authors and the emergence of black publishing companies.

ROLLINS, CHARLEMAE. "The Role of the Book in Combating Prejudice," *Wilson Library Bulletin*, Vol. 42, No. 2, October 1967, p. 176.
Useful history of treatment of black characters in children's books. Analysis of some books included.

_____. ed. *We Build Together*. Urbana, Illinois: National Council of Teachers of English, 1967.
Although this bibliography was reprinted in 1974, it was not revised. Somewhat out-of-date, it is still useful. It contains a discussion of the history and scope of books containing black characters, as well as an extensive categorized annotated bibliography.

ROLLOCK, BARBARA, ed. *The Black Experience in Children's Books*, New York: New York Public Library, 1979. (Office of Branch Libraries, New York Public Library, 8 E. 40th St., New York, New York 10016.)
The most complete listing of books relating to black people. Everything that has a black character in it is included. Annotations are very informative. The list, originally compiled by Augusta Baker, is regularly updated.

SCHAFSTALL, MARILYN, AND FRANCOIS, LILLIAN. *Native Americans in Selected Children's Media*. Toledo, Ohio: Toledo-Lucas County Public Library, 1978.
Almost 400 titles of books portraying an accurate view of Native Americans.

SCHMIDT, NANCY J. "Books by African Authors for Non-African Children," *Africana Library Journal*, Vol. 2, No. 4, Winter 1971, p. 11.
Interesting reviews of several books on Africa.

SCHON, ELIZABETH. *A Hispanic Heritage: A Guide to Juvenile Books about Hispanic People and Culture*. Metuchen, New Jersey: Scarecrow Press, 1980.
Annotated bibliography containing themes and characters from all of the Spanish-speaking countries of the world. Gives critical analyses of how successful the authors have been in relating authentic descriptions and accurate details.

SEALE, DORIS. "Bibliographies about Native Americans: A Mixed Blessing," *Bulletin of the Council on Interracial Books for Children*, Vol. 12, No. 3, 1981, pp. 11–15
A critical examination of eight bibliographies of books containing references to Native Americans. Reminds the educator and librarian of criteria for selection.

SHARGEL, SUSAN, AND KANE, IRENE. *We Can Change It*. San Francisco: Change for Children, 1974.
An excellent, though brief, annotated bibliography of nonsexist, nonracist books. Also suggests several ways of dealing with books so that children will learn to combat racist and sexist attitudes and practices.

SHEPARD, RAY ANTHONY. "Adventures in Blackland with Keats and Steptoe," *Bulletin of the Council on Interracial Books for Children*, Vol. 3, No. 4, Autumn 1971.
Makes distinction between black and white illustrators. "Steptoe shows love for his people ... [and] celebrates the ethnic differences of Blacks." Compares Ezra Jack Keats and John Steptoe: "For the Black reader, ... the difference is simple. In Keats there is someone who looks like me, and in Steptoe there is someone who knows what is going on."

SIMS, RUDINE. *Shadow and Substance: Afro-American Experience in Contemporary Children's Fiction*. Urbana, Illinois: National Council of Teachers of English, 1982. A clear and persuasive consideration of 150 books of contemporary realistic fiction about Afro-Americans, classifying them into four categories: social context, melting pot, reflections of Afro-American experience, and work by the image-makers. The author's critiques and comments are incisive and informative. The monograph is very useful; it would be even more so with an index. It is arranged so that the books are listed at the end of the chapter in which they are discussed, and the monograph itself is concise enough (110 pages) so that items are not too difficult to find.

STEINER, STAN. *The New Indians*. New York: Harper & Row, 1968. A report of the contemporary progress of American Indian protest. Steiner is a supporter of Vine Deloria, Jr. He speaks as an advocate of the "new Indians." The book is informative and provocative.

STENSLAND, ANNA LEE. *Literature by and about the American Indian: An Annotated Bibliography for Junior and Senior High Students*. Urbana, Illinois: National Council of Teachers of English, 1979. Study Guide is provided, serving as a useful format for working with other books. Short biographies of Native American authors add to the book's value. This update of the 1973 list contains many more reviews of children's books, totaling almost 800, and including fiction and nonfiction.

THOMPSON, JUDITH, AND WOODARD, GLORIA. "Black Perspectives in Books for Children," *Wilson Library Bulletin*, Vol. 44, No. 4, December 1969, pp. 416–424. Comments on the need for writers to include a black perspective based on black experience. Criticizes books which place black characters in subsidiary roles. Lists acceptable books for young children and older children.

TWAY, EILEEN, ed. *Reading Ladders for Human Relations*, 6th ed. Washington, D.C.: American Council on Education and the National Council of Teachers of English, 1982. Contains discussion of necessity for positive self-image. Reviews many books considered to be helpful in this area. Also includes multiethnic literature.

VASQUEZ, SUE ANN. *Educational Materials by and about the American Indian*. Concord, California: Indian Education Project, 1977. Almost 1,000 listings, not all of them easily accessible, some with annotations. Includes books, records and films. Native American authors are identified. Criteria for selection are provided.

VOGEL, VIRGIL J. *The Indian in American History*, Chicago: Integrated Education Association, 1968. (ERIC Document No. 033 783.) Obliteration, defamation, disembodiment, and disparagement are the four ways the author discloses have been used to malign the Native American. Bibliography includes useful sources of information.

WAGONER, SHIRLEY A. "Mexican-Americans in Children's Literature since 1970," *Reading Teacher*, Vol. 36, No. 3, December 1982, pp. 274–279. Analyzes the trends in literature about the Mexican American, and concludes that there is much improvement needed. Includes an annotated list of books that are, in general, recommended, and includes specific comments on their quality of presentation.

WALTON, JEANNE. "The American Negro in Children's Literature," *Eliot-Pearson School*, February 1964. (Alumnae Office, Eliot-Pearson School, Tufts University, Medford, Massachussetts 02155.)
Criticizes certain books for having defects when describing blacks. Provides annotated bibliography.

WOLFE, ANN G. *About 100 Books . . . a Gateway to Better Intergroup Understanding*. New York: American Jewish Committee, Institute of Human Relations, 1972.
Includes books published between 1969 and 1972. Several hundred books examined; one hundred chosen. Several minorities represented. Annotations are brief but useful.

WUNDERLICH, ELAINE. "Black Americans in Children's Books," *Reading Teacher*, Vol. 28, No. 3, December 1974, pp. 282–285.
Recalls Nancy Larrick's 1965 study on black characters in children's books. Finds that the situation has improved in the past ten years, but cautions responsibility on teachers' part to accent books that have high literary quality and that provide positive identity base for black children. List of references is useful.

YOUNG, JACQUELINE LEE. "Criteria in Selection of Black Literature for Children," *Freedomways*, Vol. 13, No. 2, 1973, pp. 107–116.
Discusses self-image and its psychological importance. Includes a short story to exemplify necessary black-oriented themes.

YEP, LAWRENCE. "The Ethnic Writer as Alien," *Bulletin of the Council on Interracial Books for Children*, Vol. 10, No. 5, 1979, pp. 10–11.
The author reflects on the influence his heritage has had on his writing.

SOURCES FOR MATERIALS ON HERITAGE

The Directory of Ethnic Publishers and Resource Organizations, 2d ed., compiled by Marjorie K. Jeramo (American Library Association, 1979).

AFRO-AMERICANS

AFRO-AM PUBLISHING COMPANY, INC. 910 S. Michigan Ave., Rm. 556, Chicago, Illinois 60605
AMURU PRESS, INC. 161 Madison Ave., New York, New York 10016
ASSOCIATION FOR THE STUDY OF AFRO-AMERICAN LIFE AND HISTORY, INC. 1401 14th St., N.W., Washington, D.C. 20005
BLACK ANTI-DEFAMATION COALITION. 1765 N. Highland, Box 246, Los Angeles, California 90028
BROADSIDE PRESS PUBLICATIONS. 74 Glendale Ave., Highland Park, Michigan 48203

COUNCIL ON INTERRACIAL BOOKS FOR CHILDREN. 1841 Broadway, Rm. 500, New York, New York 10023

COMBINED BLACK PUBLISHERS. 7848 S. Ellis Ave., Chicago, Illinois 60619

DRUM AND SPEAR PRESS. 1902 Belmont Rd., N.W., Washington, D.C. 20009

FITZGERALD PUBLISHING COMPANY. P.O. Box 264, St. Albans, New York 11412

INSTITUTE OF POSITIVE EDUCATION. 7524 S. Cottage Grove, Chicago, Illinois 60619

JOHNSON PUBLISHING COMPANY. Book Division, 820 S. Michigan Ave., Chicago, Illinois 60605

NAACP. 186 Remsen St., Brooklyn, New York 11201

NEW DAY PRESS. c/o Karamu House, 2355 E. 89 St., Cleveland, Ohio 44106

JULIAN RICHARDSON ASSOCIATES. 540 McAllister St., San Francisco, California 94102

THIRD PRESS: JOSEPH OKPAKU COMMUNICATIONS. 444 Central Park West, New York 10025

U.S. COMMITTEE FOR UNICEF. 331 East 38th St., New York, New York 10016.

ASIAN AMERICANS

BRIDGE: ASIAN AMERICAN PERSPECTIVES (a quarterly). 32 E. Broadway, New York, New York 10002

CHINESE CULTURAL CENTER. 159 Lexington Ave., New York, New York 10016

INDOCHINESE CURRICULUM CENTER. 601 E. 12th St., Kansas City, Missouri 64106

INDOCHINESE EDUCATION SERVICE CENTER. 500 S. Dwyer Ave., Arlington Heights, Illinois 60005

INDOCHINESE MATERIALS CENTER. U.S. Dept. of Education, 324 E. 11th St., Kansas City, Missouri 64106

JAPANESE AMERICAN CURRICULUM PROJECT. P.O. Box 367, 414 E. Third Ave., Ave., San Mateo, California 94401

SOUTHEAST ASIA RESOURCE CENTER. P.O. Box 4000D, Berkeley, California 94704

HISPANIC AMERICANS

NATIONAL PUERTO RICAN COALITION. 701 N. Fairfax St., Suite 310, Alexandria, Virginia 22314

JEWISH AMERICANS

ANTI-DEFAMATION LEAGUE, B'NAI B'RITH. 823 United Nations Plaza, New York, New York 10017

NATIVE AMERICANS

AMERICAN INDIAN HISTORICAL SOCIETY. 1451 Masonic Ave., San Francisco, California 94117

(Publishes *The Weewish Tree*, a magazine for young people featuring stories, poetry, and articles by Native Americans.)

INDIAN AFFAIRS. 432 Park Ave. South, New York, New York 10016

INDIAN EDUCATION PROJECT. Mount Diablo Unified School District, 1135 Lacey Lane, Concord, California 94520

INDIAN HISTORICAL PRESS. 1451 Masonic Ave., San Francisco, California 94117

MONTANA COUNCIL FOR INDIAN EDUCATION. 517 Rimrock Road, Billings, Montana 59102

NATIONAL CONGRESS OF AMERICAN INDIANS. 202 E St., N.E., Washington, D.C. 20002 (Publishes a monthly newsletter, *The Sentinel.*)

BIBLIOGRAPHY: NATIVE AMERICANS

ALLEN, TERRY. *The Whispering Wind: Poetry by Young American Indians*. Garden City, New York: Doubleday, 1972. (Ages 10–up.)
Fourteen Native American poets' works. Poets are described in introductory remarks before each section of poetry. Not all the poetry is directly about the experience of being a Native American, but much of it is. The quality is excellent.

ANNIXTER, JANE AND PAUL. *White Shell Horse*. New York: Holiday, 1971. (Ages 12–up.)
Agapito maintains his faith and inherits his uncle's powers of foreseeing. He embodies the Navajo virtues and values and, in the end, returns with his people to their homeland. They manage to use weapons other than warfare to cope with the whites.

BAKER, BETTY. *At the Center of the World*. Illustrated by Murray Tinkelman. New York: Macmillan, 1973. (Ages 8–11.)
These tales, based on Papago and Pima myths, are retold by the author. The illustrations are very well done. All are old creation myths.

_____. *Killer-of-Death*. Illustrated by John Kaufmann. New York: Harper & Row, 1963. (Ages 12–up.)
Story of how the Apache (meaning "enemy") came to accept that as their name. Details of tribal customs included here. Killer-of-Death is the hero. His tribe is all but wiped out by the whites' treachery. As a result of this, his feud with a fellow brave is eradicated, and he becomes a fierce enemy of all whites. In the end he recognizes the need to acquire knowledge to continue to exist in a white man's world. One of the few books to describe the whites' practice of scalping Native Americans, even the children.

BAKER, OLAF. *Where the Buffaloes Begin*. Illustrated by Stephen Gammell. New York: Murray, 1981. (Ages 5–8.)
The drawings vividly recreate the sense of power and beauty of the buffalo, as well as the sense of respect the Native Americans had for these great beasts. The story is told as seen through the eyes of Little Wolf, a young boy.

BALES, CAROL ANN. *Kevin Cloud: Chippewa Boy in the City*. Illustrated with photographs. Chicago: Reilly and Lee, 1972. (Ages 7–10.)

Although the mood of the story is not a positive one, the family is loving, and old stories and customs are remembered. The plight of the Cherokee in the city is used as an example of white oppression of this group.

BARNOUW, VICTOR. *Dream of the Blue Heron*. Illustrated by Lynd Ward. New York: Delacorte Press, 1966. Also in paperback. (Ages 9–12.)
Wabus is a Chippewa boy who is caught in a struggle between his grandfather, who wants to continue with the old ways, and his father, who admires and wants to practice white ways. In the end, Wabus decides to be a lawyer and to speak for his people. Well-written, but somewhat double-edged story.

BARON, VIRGINIA OLSEN, ed. *Here I Am*. Illustrated by Emily Arnold McCully. New York: Dutton, 1969. (Ages 6–up.)
A number of poems by Native Americans are included in this anthology of poems written by young people in some of America's minority groups. Poems are of uneven quality, but are all very expressive.

BAYLOR, BYRD. *God on Every Mountaintop*. Illustrated by Carol Brown. New York: Scribner, 1981. (Ages 9–12.)
Sacred myths of the Southwest Native Americans, well told and illustrated. Sources are included for further study.

BEALER, ALEX W. *Only the Names Remain: The Cherokees and the Trail of Tears*. Illustrated by William Sauts Bock. Boston: Little, Brown, 1972. (Ages 9–12.)
Author, though not a Native American, has been interested and involved in Native American affairs since his boyhood. This book tells of the history of the Cherokee nation since the white man came to America. It tells of their strength and their tragedy. Clearly demonstrates the illegal and immoral behavior of the whites as individuals and as institutions.

BELTING, NATALIE. *Our Fathers Had Powerful Songs*. Illustrated by Laszlo Kubinyi. New York: Dutton, 1974. (Ages 8–12.)
The author has created lyrical poems based on the song lore of a variety of western Native American tribes. The poems deal with death, creation, and animal traditions. Somewhat romantically illustrated but a well-constructed book.

BIERHORST, JOHN, ed. *The Fire Plume: Legends of the American Indians*. Illustrated Aland E. Cober. New York: Dial Press, 1969. (Ages 9–12.)
Tales from the Algonquin tribes. Well told, dramatic, useful.

BIERHORST, JOHN, adaptor. *Songs of the Chippewa*. Illustrated by Joe Servello. New York: Farrar, Straus & Giroux, 1974. (All ages.)
A beautiful book. Well researched and carefully presented.

BIESTERVELD, BETTY. *Six Days from Sunday*. Illustrated by George Armstrong. Chicago: Rand McNally, 1973. (Ages 12–up.)
The author, who has lived among the Navajo, writes of them respectfully and with affection. Willie Little Horse is anxious about going to school. He really does not want to leave home. The family is understanding of his feelings but determined that he will go. Much is discussed about the value of the old ways compared to new ways.

BLUENOSE, PHILIP, AND CARPENTER, WALTER S. *Knots on a Counting Rope.* Illustrated by Joe Smith. New York: Holt, Rinehart and Winston, 1964. (Ages 7–10.)
The grandfather tells his young grandson the story of his name and about the counting rope as an allegory of life. He keeps tying knots on the rope as he goes through life. When there is no more room for knots, life is over and death will come. Lovely illustrations.

BORLAND, HAL. *When the Legends Die.* Philadelphia: Lippincott, 1963. Also in paper. (Ages 12–up.)
For older readers—a hard, ugly look at the life of one Ute Indian. Tom Black Bull was orphaned young and grew up tough. At the end of the story, he determines to learn more about himself and his people.

BROWN, DEE. *Tepee Tales of the American Indian.* Illustrated by Louis Mofsie. New York: Holt, Rinehart and Winston, 1979. (Ages 8–up.)
A fine collection of Native American folk tales and myths thoroughly researched by a respected author. The illustrator is a Native American who grew up in New York. More than two dozen American Indian tribes are represented in this collection. Brown divides the stories into several categories, providing a short, but adequate introduction at the beginning of each section. This is a fine addition for school libraries, especially since there are so many units on the Native American.

_____. *Wounded Knee: An Indian History of the American West,* adapted for young readers by Amy Ehrlich from Brown's *Bury My Hear at Wounded Knee.* New York: Holt, Rinehart and Winston, 1974. (Ages 11–up.)
An accounting of the many broken promises of the United States government to Native Americans. Angering and shameful behavior on the part of the whites.

CARLSON, VADA, AND WITHERSPOON, GARY. *Black Mountain Boy: A Story of the Boyhood of John Honie.* Illustrated by Andrew Tsinajinnie. Chinle, Arizona: Navajo Curriculum Center, 1968. (Ages 10–up.)
Told in the first person by John Honie, a Navajo medicine man. Navajo values come through clearly in his account of his boyhood. Excellent for positive self-image.

CLARK, ANN NOLAN. *Circle of Seasons.* Illustrated by W. T. Mars. New York: Farrar, Straus & Giroux, 1970. (Ages 8–11.)
The author has been a teacher in schools for Native Americans for many years and has written many books about them. This book tells of the Pueblo Indians and their celebrations of different seasonal ceremonies, including Christian ones.

CLIFFORD, ETH. *The Year of the Three-Legged Deer.* Boston: Houghton Mifflin, 1971. Also in paper. (Ages 10–up.)
1819–1820 is the year described in this book, which is set in Indianapolis. The story is about Jesse Benton, white trader, his Lenni-Lenape Indian wife, and their two children. During this year many events take place, including the trials and convictions of three white men who murdered some Delaware Indians; the death of Chilili, the young daughter; and the removal of the Delaware Nation beyond the Mississippi River. Jesse's wife and son leave him to go with the Lenni-Lenape. This is a sad, thought-provoking book.

COATSWORTH, ELIZABETH. *The Cave*. Illustrated by Allan Houser. New York: Viking, 1958. (Ages 7–10.)
Beautiful and authentic story of a Navajo boy and his special understanding of the task of a shepherd.

COLLIER, PETER. *When Shall They Rest? The Cherokees' Long Struggle with America*. New York: Holt, Rinehart and Winston, 1973. Also in paper. (Ages 12–up.)
A factual telling of the history of the Cherokees, up to today. The author acquaints the reader not only with the shameful past history of U.S. treatment of the Cherokees, but also with the problems foisted upon the Cherokees today.

CURRY, JANE LOUISE. *Down from the Lonely Mountain*. Illustrated by Enrico Arno. New York: Harcourt, Brace & World, 1965. (Ages 9–12.)
California Indian tales. Excellent for reading aloud.

DALGLIESH, ALICE. *The Courage of Sarah Noble*. Illustrated by Leonard Weisgard. New York: Scribner, 1954. (Ages 7–10.)
A girl travels into the wilderness in 1707 with her father. She lives with Indians while her father returns for the rest of the family. She exhibits patience and adaptability.

DEPAOLA, TOMIE. *The Legend of the Bluebonnet*. Illustrated by the author. New York: Putnam, 1983. (Ages 5–8.)
Based on Comanche Indian lore, this is the story of an orphaned girl who sacrifices what she loves best to save her tribe. The decision is the girl's alone; it is an active and heroic act that she performs. The Indian tribe is named and the illustrations are authentically Comanche.

DISTAD, AUDREE. *Dakota Sons*. Illustrated by Tony Chen. New York: Harper & Row, 1972. (Ages 8–11.)
Tad, a white boy, makes friends with Ronnie, a Dakota Sioux. Despite the prejudice of some of the townspeople and some of the other young people, their friendship flourishes.

FIFE, DALE. *Ride the Crooked Wind*. Illustrated by Richard Cuffari. New York: Coward, McCann & Geoghegan, 1973. (Ages 10–up.)
Po has lived with his grandmother since the death of his parents. When his grandmother is hospitalized with tuberculosis, he is sent to the Indian Boarding School. He believes in the traditional ways of the Paiute, and has learned them well. The story tells how he begins to bend somewhat because of his competent, successful uncle. This book, valuing the traditions, suggests ways that Native Americans can retain their pride in the old ways and utilize the new.

FRITZ, JEAN. *The Good Giants and the Bad Pukwudgies*. Illustrated by Tomie dePaola. New York: Putnam, 1982. (Ages 5–8.)
Adapted from a collection of tales of the Wampanoag Indians of New England, the story is a somewhat modernized amalgam of several tales, telling of the creation of the islands off Cape Cod. Fun and well-written, the book would whet young readers' appetites for more authentic tales of these Native Americans.

GOBLE, PAUL. *The Gift of the Sacred Dog*. New York: Bradbury Press, 1980. (Ages 7–10.)
The story tells of the coming of the horse (the sacred dog) because of the bravery of a young boy who seeks to help his people. Beautifully and respectfully told.

_____. adaptor. *Star Boy*. Adapted and Illustrated by Paul Goble. New York: Bradbury Press, 1983. (Ages 7–10.)
Based on Blackfoot tipi designs, the illustrations accompany a Blackfoot tale explaining why the people annually build a Sun Dance lodge, round as the earth and sky.

GRIDLEY, MARION E. *Indian Tribes of America*. Illustrated by Lone Wolf. Northbrook, Illinois: Hubbard Press, 1973. (Ages 11–up.)
A useful reference to help differentiate among the different tribes and to appreciate their special qualities. The author conveys a sense of the contributions that each tribe has and of the heritage behind each tribe.

HAYS, WILMA PITCHFORD. *Little Yellow Fur*. Illustrated by Richard Cuffari. New York: Coward, McCann & Geoghegan, 1973. (Ages 7–10.)
Based on the author's own childhood experiences, the story tells of a little blonde girl who lives with her pioneer family on what was once Sioux land.

HEIDE, FLORENCE PARRY. *The Key*. Illustrated by Ati Forberg. New York: Atheneum, 1972. (Ages 11–up.)
The first story in this collection, "Wild Bird," is about a young Native American who lives with his grandfather in a small room in the city. The grandfather tries to instill in the boy a knowledge and valuing of his heritage.

HENDERSON, NANCY, AND DEWEY, JANE. *Circle of Life: The Miccosukee Indian Way*. Photographs by David Pickens. New York: Julian Messner, 1974. (Ages 8–10.)
A close look at modern Miccosukee life. The book also describes the past history and customs of the tribe. The tribe now has control over government funds and programs. This means that now the Miccosukee people can control their own education and culture. They can teach and practice their own ways. They can also manage their own economic affairs. The book is respectfully written, and holds out hope of survival and dignity for Native Americans.

HIGHWATER, JAMAKE. *Many Smokes, Many Moons: A Chronology of American Indian History through Indian Art*. Philadelphia: Lippincott, 1978. (Ages 12–up.)
Beginning with a creation story, the text continues with informative narrative of the history, mostly of the Native Peoples of North America. Illustrations by, and photographs of artifacts of, Native Americans illuminate and extend the reader's enjoyment.

_____. *Moonsong Lullaby*. Photographs by Marcia Keegan. New York: Lothrop, Lee and Shepard, 1981. (All ages.)
Beautiful photographs of the activities of a Cherokee camp, its activities and natural environment. The lullaby affirms the positive quality of life.

HILLERMAN, TONY. *The Boy Who Made Dragonfly.* Illustrated by Laszlo Kubinyi. New York: Harper & Row, 1972. (Ages 10–up.)
A folk tale, originated somewhere around the fifteenth century. It tells of the Zuni ancient ways. The virtues extolled here are charity, obedience, and reverence, as well as loyalty to one's people. A well-told tale.

HIRSCH, S. CARL. *Famous American Indians of the Plains.* Illustrated by Lorence Bjorklund. Chicago: Rand McNally, 1973. (Ages 12–up.)
The book is lavishly illustrated with paintings by famous artists, as well as the drawings by Bjorklund. Tells with respect of the accomplishments, customs, and circumstances of the Plains Indians.

HODGES, MARGARET. *The Fire Bringer: A Paiute Indian Legend.* Illustrated by Peter Parnell. Boston: Little, Brown, 1972. (Ages 7–up.)
Beautifully told and illustrated story of how the coyote and a Paiute boy brought fire to people.

HUNGRY WOLF, BEVERLY. *The Ways of My Grandmother.* New York: Morrow, 1980. (Ages 12–up.)
Collected in the manner of all good oral historians, the book contains stories, accounts of daily life, myths and legends, and informative passages on history and customs of the author's People. A member of the Blackfoot Nation, she writes movingly and informatively of their traditional way of life.

JONES, HETTIE. *Coyote Tales.* Illustrated by Louis Mofsie. New York: Holt, Rinehart and Winston, 1974. (Ages 8–12.)
Coyote is a recurrent character in Native American tales, which are similar in many ways to the African tales of Spider. Illustrations (by a Native American illustrator) are excellent.

JONES, HETTIE, ed. *The Trees Stand Shining: Poetry of the North American Indian.* Illustrated by Robert Andrew Parker. New York: Dial Press, 1971. (Ages 6–up.)
Chants, songs, and poems of Native Americans across the country. Beautifully illustrated.

KATZ, JANE B., ed. *This Song Remembers: Self Portraits of Native Americans in the Arts.* Boston: Houghton Mifflin, 1980. (Ages 12–up.)
A very well-researched and designed book of written and artistic representations of Native Americans, as they view themselves. A good representation of cultures and work are included.

KEEGAN, MARCIA. *The Taos Indians and Their Sacred Blue Lake.* New York: Julian Messner, 1972. (Ages 8–11.)
Photos and captions (written by Taos Indians) are interesting and excellent. Story is somewhat nonexistent but states that the Taos Indians, in 1971, had the Blue Lake region returned to them by the United States government. The photos and captions carry the book.

KIRK, RUTH. *David, Young Chief of the Quileutes: An American Indian Today.* New York: Harcourt, Brace & World, 1967. (Ages 8–10.)
Describes contemporary lives of Quileute Indians in the state of Washington. David

Hudson, eleven years old, is designated as their chief. The book is illustrated with photographs by the author. The text is of a surface nature but interesting.

LEWIS, RICHARD, ed. *Out of the Earth I Sing*. New York: Norton, 1968. (All ages.)
Illustrations are powerful and remarkable photographs of original art work by the people who are represented by the poetry. Many Native American songs, chants, and poems are included.

McCONKEY, LOIS. *Sea and Cedar: How the Northwest Coast Indians Lived*. Illustrated by Douglas Tait. Seattle: Madrona Press, 1973. (Ages 10–up.)
Tells of the traditional customs of the Northwest Coast Indian group. Customs described respectfully. White man's interference told of at the end. Excellent illustrations.

McDERMOTT, GERALD. *Arrow to the Sun*. New York: Viking, 1974. (Ages 5–8.)
Adaptation of a Pueblo Indian tale. Very stylized illustrations. The story is similar to other hero tales in which the father is a deity and the son must prove himself to be worthy.

McLUHAN, T. C. *Touch the Earth*. New York: Promontory Press, 1971. (Ages 10–up.)
A collection of writings and saying of Native Americans, accompanied by wonderful photographs. This is a powerful book, obviously the result of considerable research. "In this book, the Indians speak for themselves of the quality of their life." Very well done.

MARRIOTT, ALICE, AND RACHLIN, CAROL K. *American Indian Mythology*. New York: Crowell, 1968. Paperback: Apollo. (All ages.)
Contains many myths from various tribes. Retold by authors who heard them from Native American storytellers. Authors are anthropologists; collection is excellent. Introduction is long, aimed at adult readers, and somewhat condescending.

MARTIN, FRAN. *Raven-Who-Sets-Things-Right: Indian Tales of the Northwest Coast*. Illustrated by Dorothy McEntee. New York: Harper & Row, 1975. (Ages 10–up.)
A retelling of stories originally transmitted by native storytellers of the Pacific Northwest coastal Indians.

MATSON, EMERSON N. *Longhouse Legends*. Illustrated by Lorence Bjorklund. Camden, New Jersey: Thomas Nelson, 1968. (Ages 10–up.)
Well-told, interesting tales of the Pacific Northwest Indians.

MELTZER, MILTON. *Hunted like a Wolf: The Story of the Seminole War*. New York: Farrar, Straus & Giroux, 1972. Also in paper. (Ages 12–up.)
Interesting and informative account of the Seminoles of Florida, their relationship with black people, and their resistance to white encroachment in their land. Here again the treachery of the United States government is made clear.

MILES, MISKA. *Annie and the Old One*. Illustrated by Peter Parnell. Boston: Little, Brown, 1971. (Ages 6–8.)
A Navajo girl tries to prevent her grandmother's death. In the end she accepts death as a necessary part of life. The customs of the Navajo are described in the process of

the story; the illustrations are beautifully done, and the text is respectful of Navajo ways.

NATIONAL GEOGRAPHIC SOCIETY. *The World of the American Indian*. Washington, D.C.: National Geographic Society, 1974. (Ages 8–up.)
This large format book is thoroughly researched and gives an historical, cultural and societal picture. It is an excellent reference book, complete with maps. The text draws on Native American as well as non-Indian authors.

O'DELL, SCOTT. *Island of the Blue Dolphins*. Boston: Houghton Mifflin, 1960. Paperback: Dell. (Ages 12–up.)
This story, a modern classic of courage and survival, is based on a true story. Karana is abandoned on an island after all her people have left and her brother has been killed. She manages to survive for many years and is rescued, at last, by missionaries.

_____. *Sing Down the Moon*. Boston: Houghton Mifflin, 1970. Also in paper. (Ages 10–up.)
Describes the Long Walk of the Navajo. The main character, a young Navajo woman, is remarkable in her courage and strength. The story focuses on the character of the young woman rather than on the hardships of the Navajos. Some customs are described in this very well-written book.

PARKER, ARTHUR C. *Skunny Wundy: Seneca Indian Tales*. New edition of 1926 version. Illustrated by George Armstrong. Chicago: Whitman, 1970. (Ages 8–up.)
Author, a Seneca Indian, was an anthropologist and museum director. The stories are somewhat reminiscent of the Anansi tales of Africa. Skunny Wundy is a magical, clever character. (Mighty hunters are called Skunny Wundy; good storytellers are called Skunny Wundy.) These are animal tales, well told, and convey the special qualities that the Iroquois believed the animals had.

PERRINE, MARY. *Salt Boy*. Illustrated by Leonard Weisgard. Boston: Houghton Mifflin, 1968. Also in paper. (Ages 4–9.)
Salt Boy is a young Navajo boy who wants his father to teach him how to rope a horse. His father promises to do so when Salt Boy becomes more responsible about caring for his mother's sheep. Salt Boy rescues a lamb and earns his roping lesson. The Navajo valuing of sheep is clearly conveyed here.

PORTER, C. FAYNE. *The Day They Hanged the Sioux and Other Stories from Our Indian Heritage*. Philadelphia: Chilton, 1964. Also in paper. (Ages 12–up.)
Nine stories of outstanding Native Americans. An appendix includes some selected folklore told to the author by contemporary young Native Americans. The entire book gives a perspective of history different from the usual white-oriented text.

RAMA OJIBWAY ELDERS: SAM SNAKE, ELIJAH YELLOWHEAD, ALDER YORK, DAVID SIMCOE, AND ANNIE KING. *The Adventures of Nanabush: Olibway Indian Stories*. Set down by Emmerson and David Coatsworth. Illustrated by Frances Kagige. New York: Atheneum, 1980. (Ages 9–12.)
Vividly told stories of Nanabush in his many manifestations. The illustrations are a fitting accompaniment.

RASKIN, JOSEPH AND EDITH. *Indian Tales.* Illustrated by Helen Siegl. New York: Random House, 1969. (Ages 8–10.)
Very well-told stories. Illustrations add to appeal of text. Respectful recounting, mostly of animal tales.

RICHTER, CONRAD. *The Light in the Forest.* New York: Knopf, 1953. Also in paper. (Ages 12–up.)
For older readers. The story of True Son who is captured and raised by Tuscarawas. He is forced to return to his white family but cannot exist there. Nor can he become part of the Native American tribe again. In the end, he is alone and without a future.

RUSHMORE, HELEN, AND HUNT, WOLF ROBE. *The Dancing Horses of Acoma and Other Acoma Indian Stories.* Illustrated by Wolf Robe Hunt. Cleveland: World, 1963. (Ages 12–up.)
Stories recounted to author by her illustrator, Wolf Robe Hunt. Most of them are well told and clear, even though there are many complicated details. Some of the tales include the magic characters Spider Woman and Spider Boy. Author is respectful of the old traditions. Illustrations are excellent.

SANDOZ, MARI. *These Were the Sioux.* Illustrated by Amos Bad Heart Bull and Kills Two. New York: Hastings House, 1961. Also in paper. (Ages 10–up.)
A factual but personal description of the customs and beliefs of the Sioux.

SCHEER, GEORGE F. *Cherokee Animal Tales.* Illustrated by Robert Frankenberg. New York: Holiday, 1968. (Ages 8–10.)
These well-told tales include mythic explanations of natural phenomena. Of particular value is the history of the Cherokee, which the author provides in a respectful style.

SLEATOR, WILLIAM. *The Angry Moon.* Illustrated by Blair Lent. Boston: Little, Brown, 1970. (Ages 5–8.)
A retelling of a Tlingit Indian story. Tlingit motifs form the inspiration for the exciting illustrations. In this story the moon is the villain, capturing a young girl. Lupan, her friend, rescues her with the aid of the magical Old Grandmother.

SNEVE, VIRGINIA DRIVING HAWK. *High Elk's Treasure.* Illustrated by Oren Lyons. New York: Holiday, 1972. (Ages 9–up.)
Fictionalized history. Dramatic account of contemporary Lakota Sioux family and their adventures. Some history comes out in the telling of the story, which conveys a sense of pride in being Native Americans but also indicates some of the problems.

_____. *Jimmy Yellow Hawk.* Illustrated by Oren Lyons. New York: Holiday, 1972. (Ages 12–up.)
Adventures of a young modern Sioux Indian who lives on a reservation in South Dakota. Conveys a sense of the mixture of old ways and new.

_____. *When Thunders Spoke.* Illustrated by Oren Lyons. New York: Holiday, 1974. (Ages 12–up.)
Norman Two Bull, who lives with his parents in the Dakota reservation, changes his ideas in this story about the old ways and new ways. There is conflict in the family

concerning how to live in modern times as a Native American. In the end, the reader feels that Norman, still respecting the old ways, will try to use whatever new ways are appropriate for his success. Excellent illustrations; well-written text.

SPEARE, ELIZABETH GEORGE. *The Sign of the Beaver*. Boston: Houghton Mifflin, 1983. (Ages 10–up.)
Authentically depicted story of colonial life. Matt and his Native American neighbors form a mutually respectful relationship.

SYME, RONALD. *Geronimo, the Fighting Apache*. Illustrated by Ben F. Stahl. New York: Morrow, 1975. (Ages 8–12.)
This biography, sympathetic to Geronimo and the Apache, is drawn from many documents. Quotes from Geronimo and others alive at the time convey a sense of authenticity.

TAMARIN, ALFRED. *We Have Not Vanished*. Chicago: Follett, 1974. (Ages 12–up.)
Informative, useful book describing the Native Americans still living on the East Coast of the United States from Maine to Florida. The history, political structure, and customs are briefly described.

TUNIS, EDWARD. *Indians*. Revised ed. New York: Crowell, 1979. (Ages 10–up.)
Informative drawings and text describe the lives of Native Americans before any white people came to their shores.

WHITNEY, ALEX. *Stiff Ears: Animal Folktales of the North American Indians*. New York: Walck, 1974. (Ages 7–10.)
Brief folktales from the Hopi, Chippewa, Iroquois, Chinook, Pawnee, and Cherokee people. Each tale teaches a lesson. The author provides readers with a short explanatory introduction to each story.

WOLF, BERNARD. *Tinker and the Medicine Men*. New York: Random House, 1973. (Ages 9–12.)
Tinker is six years old. The book pictures his way of life as a part of the Navajo Nation. His father is a medicine man, using both traditional and peyote practices. In addition to describing the family relationship and Navajo conditions, the author leads the reader through a peyote ceremony. The photographs aid greatly in the telling. The author is respectful and admiring of the Navajo way of life in Monument Valley.

WONDRISKA, WILLIAM. *The Stop*. New York: Holt, Rinehart and Winston, 1972. (Ages 6–9.)
A little boy stays in Monument Valley with an injured colt, while his brother goes to get his father and uncles. The illustrations are paintings of the valley at different times of day and night. People and their stories are insignificant next to the magnificence of this valley, which is part of the Navajo reservation.

YELLOW ROBE, ROSEBUD. *An Album of the American Indian*. New York: Franklin Watts, 1969. (Ages 9–11.)
Illustrated with paintings, drawings, and photos. Authentic detail. Native American culture, history, and viewpoints.

YELLOW ROBE, ROSEBUD. *Tonweya and the Eagles, and Other Lakota Indian Tales.* Illustrated by Jerry Pinkney. New York: Dial Press, 1979. (Ages 9–12.)
Recounted from the oral tradition, these animal tales convey the flavor of Lakota life.

BIBLIOGRAPHY: AFRO-AMERICANS

AARDEMA, VERNA. *Tales from the Story Hat.* Illustrated by Elton Fax. New York: Coward, McCann, 1960. (Ages 8–10.)
All but one of these stories are based on folk tales. The book shows that the Uncle Remus stories are taken from Africa. One of them has a wily rabbit as the hero; three are from Henry M. Stanley's *My Dark Companions and Their Strange Stories.* Notes about the stories and a glossary contain useful information. Stories are well told and illustrations are excellent.

ABDUL, RAOUL. *The Magic of Black Poetry.* Illustrated by Dane Burr. New York: Dodd, Mead, 1971. (Ages 12–up.)
Collection of poetry written by black people all over the world, some of them anonymous, across a great span of years. Many are by notable living poets. Also contains a section describing the poets.

ADOFF, ARNOLD. *Black Is Brown Is Tan.* Illustrated by Emily Arnold McCully. New York: Harper & Row, 1972. (Ages 3–8.)
Interracial family. Author Adoff (who is white) is married to Virginia Hamilton (who is black). Positive feelings of warmth, energy and togetherness are conveyed. Family members each have good feelings about themselves.

_____. ed. *Black Out Loud.* Illustrated by Alvin Hollingsworth. New York: Macmillan, 1969. (Ages 9–up.)
Anthology of modern poems by black Americans. Consistently high quality.

_____. ed. *I Am the Darker Brother.* Illustrated by Benny Andrews. New York: Macmillan. 1968. (Ages 12–up.)
Poems about the black experience by many black poets.

_____. *Malcolm X.* Illustrated by John Wilson. New York: Crowell, 1970. (Ages 7–10.)
Tells simply, and in a factual manner, the details of Malcolm X's life. Very specific in its recording of what Malcolm believed and what happened to him. The heroic quality of his life emerges clearly.

_____. *My Black Me: A Beginning Book of Black Poetry.* New York: Dutton, 1971. (Ages 8–up.)
Excellent accumulation of poetry by many black poets. Poems deal largely with black identity: families, history, pride. Brief description of poets included.

ALEXANDER, MARTHA. *The Story Grandmother Told.* New York: Dial Press, 1969. (Ages 5–8.)
Lisa asks her grandmother to tell her a particular story. In describing which story she

wants, she tells the whole thing herself; then her obliging grandmother retells it for her. Warm, loving relationship. Illustrations nicely done. Neighborhood is pictured as integrated.

ALEXANDER, RAE PACE, AND LESTER, JULIUS, eds. *Young and Black in America.* New York: Random House. 1970. (Ages 11–up.)
Excellent collection of self-descriptive essays about eight black people whose contributions have been outstanding. Introductory notes by Julius Lester accompanying each account aid the reader.

ANDERSON, LONZO. *The Day the Hurricane Happened.* Illustrated by Ann Grifalconi. New York: Scribner, 1973. (Ages 5–8.)
Graphic story of a family's bout with a hurricane on St. John in the Virgin Islands. Albie and his younger sister Eldra help prepare their house and their animals for the onslaught. The father, who is constable, must warn the rest of the island. Image of coping, capable, loving black family. Written with a light dialect, not overpowering, but enough to give a sense of the speech of the people.

ARKHURST, JOYCE COOPER. *The Adventures of Spider: West African Folk Tales.* Illustrated by Jerry Pinkney. Boston: Little, Brown, 1964. Paperback: Scholastic. (Ages 7–11.)
Stories from Liberia and Ghana. Spider is a clever, mischievous character who usually outwits his foes, but sometimes he catches himself. The stories explain natural phenomena. In the telling, details of African foods, the work that the people do, and some of the customs are described. Most of the stories are good-humored; no one gets badly hurt.

ARMSTRONG, WILLIAM. *Sounder.* Illustrated by James Barkley. New York: Harper & Row, 1969. Paperback: Scholastic. (Ages 11–up.)
Black Southern family, very poor. Father is jailed for many years because he steals a ham. Dog, Sounder, is crippled and deformed as a consequence of his trying to save the father. Father also comes home crippled and deformed. Man and dog die at the same time. Son begins an education, and the hope for a better life. Very movingly written story, criticized by some because of its depiction of the black as a passive accepter of the white man's injustice. Provides much food for discussion.

ARMSTRONG, WILLIAM. *Sour Land.* New York: Harper & Row, 1971. (Ages 12–up.)
Sequel to *Sounder.* Intelligent, sensitive black teacher, Moses Waters, lives his life avoiding conflict and violence. One white family loves and tries to protect him, but to no avail; he is senselessly murdered at the end of the book. The tragic consequence of racism are made clear.

BAMBARA, TONI CADE. *Tales and Stories for Black Folks.* Garden City, New York: Doubleday, 1971. (All ages.)
Collection of stories about the lives of black people, told from a black perspective.

BARON, VIRGINIA OLSEN, ed. *Here I Am!* Illustrated by Emily Arnold McCully. New York: Dutton. 1969. (Ages 6–up.)
An anthology of poetry written by children from various heritages. The verse, collected from all over the United States, contains an excellent range of mood and message.

BERGER, TERRY. *Black Fairy Tales*. Illustrated by David Omar White. New York: Atheneum. Also in paper. (Ages 8–12.)
Excellent illustrations. All are tales from South Africa. Complex, fascinating stories. The style of the telling is such that readers will be captured by the intricacy of the plots, and will also acquire information about Swazi, Shangani, and 'Msuto ways.

BIRD, PAULINE. *"Harlem 1960 & 1968,"* in Nancy Larrick, ed., *I Heard a Scream in the Street*. New York: Dell, 1970. (Ages 10–up.)
The difference in self-pride in the black population is illustrated in this two-part comparison between 1960, when "The whiter you are the better you are," and 1968, the beginning of the realization that "Black is beautiful."

BLUE, ROSE. *Black, Black, Beautiful Black*. Illustrated by Emmett Wigglesworth. New York: Franklin Watts, 1969. (Ages 5–8.)
Danita is excited about going to the zoo. Text recounts all the beautiful and shiny and attractive black objects and animals that she sees. Then she sees her own reflection—black and beautiful. Nicely done for self-image.

BONTEMPS, ARNA, ed. *American Negro Poetry*. New York: Hill and Wang, 1963. (Ages 10–up.)
Diverse selection of poetry across a span of many years. Biographical descriptions of the poets are included.

BRYAN, ASHLEY. *Walk Together Children, Black American Spirituals*. New York: Atheneum, 1974. (Ages 6–up.)
Beautiful woodcuts by the author, who selected the spirituals. The music is included with the words. Twenty-four songs are presented in this valuable book.

BURROUGHS, MARGARET TAYLOR. *Jasper the Drummin' Boy*. Illustrated by Ted Lewin. New York: Young Readers Press, 1970. (Ages 8–12.)
Jasper, a black boy, loves the drums. His mother has him take piano lessons but cannot take the love of drummin' away from him. To help raise money for the Community Civic Fund, Jasper and his friends perform on homemade instruments (wash tubs, cake pans, etc.) Their families are disgraced by this until the famous Stomp King hears them and is impressed. Jasper is finally appreciated—drumming and all. A fun story.

BURT, OLIVE. *Black Women of Valor*. Illustrated by Paul Frame. New York: Julian Messner, 1974. (Ages 9–11.)
Tells the stories of four black women who demonstrated their courage and ability: Juliette Derricotte, Maggie Mitchell Walker, Ida Wells Barnett, and Septima Poinsette Clark. The book also contains a long list of other black women of valor. Valuable addition to information about black history.

———. *Negroes in the Early West*. Illustrated by Lorence F. Bjorklund. New York: Julian Messner, 1979. (Ages 9–11.)
Except for some outdated terminology, this book presents a fascinating account of the role that black people played in the development of the West. Many of the names in this book will be familiar to the readers. Well-told descriptions of the lives of these interesting people.

BUTTERWORTH, WILLIAM. *LeRoy and the Old Man*. New York: Four Winds Press, 1980. Also in paper. (Ages 12–up.)
LeRoy goes to stay with his grandfather, whom he is meeting for the first time in his life. LeRoy's father has deserted him and his mother; the grandfather is unforgiving of his son, but takes in his grandson and teaches him his value system. The old man is strong, capable, and well repected by the community. LeRoy eventually will make a permanent home here.

CAINES, JEANNETTE. *Window Wishing*. Illustrated by Kevin Brooks. New York: Harper & Row, 1980. (Ages 5–8.)
Grandma Meg is not old, but she is a grandmother, and it is important for children to encounter a variety of women who are grandmothers. Grandma Meg is a wonderful character. She wears sneakers all the time, and leads a very active life. When the two children visit her she takes them fishing, and "window wishing" (her name for looking in the windows of shops and wishing for what they can one day have). Unconventional in many ways, Grandma Meg demonstrates her love and provides her grandchildren with memories they will cherish. As with all of the author's books, the characters are black.

CHILDRESS, ALICE. *A Hero Ain't Nothing but a Sandwich*. New York: Coward, McCann and Geoghegan, 1973. (Ages 10–14.)
A novel that pulls no punches and offers no easy solutions probes the problems of Benjie—a thirteen-year-old Harlem boy well on his way to becoming a heroin addict. The book tells the story from Benjie's point of view, with comments from his mother, stepfather, and pusher friends.

CLIFTON, LUCILLE. *All Us Come Cross the Water*. Illustrated by John Steptoe. New York: Holt, Rinehart and Winston, 1973. (Ages 5–9.)
Ujamaa tries to trace his heritage; he wants to know his country of origin. His family helps, but his friend says it does not matter. "All us crossed the water."

_____. *The Black BC's*. Illustrated by Don Miller. New York: Dutton, 1970. (Ages 3–9.)
An ABC book that presents a concept for each letter and then explains it further. There is a short verse for the letter, and then a clarification in addition to it on the same page. It is an excellent vehicle for enhancing self-image.

_____. *The Boy Who Didn't Believe in Spring*. Illustrated by Brinton Turkle. New York: Dutton, 1973. (Ages 3–7.)
Contemporary version of an old theme. King Shavazz and his friend Tony, both young boys, go on a search for spring. The language is contemporary and vernacular. The illustrations are accurate in detail, and the mood is positive. The city setting is realistically but not negatively portrayed. Pictures are of a completely integrated neighborhood, with individual ethnic characteristics illustrated.

_____. *Don't You Remember?* Illustrated by Evaline Ness. New York: Dutton, 1973. (Ages 3–7.)
Desire Mary Tate, black, four years old, and very lively, considers herself to have the best memory in her family. Her family promises her all kinds of pleasant experiences "next time." She fears that they have forgotten, but on her birthday, they all remember. Loving, coping.

CLIFTON, LUCILLE. *Everett Anderson's Year*. Illustrated by Ann Grifalconi. New York: Holt, Rinehart, and Winston, 1974. (Ages 4–8.)
Reinforces the loving world that Everett lives in. His mother manages well, even though the father has left them. Everett misses and still loves his father. He, too, is coping well.

———. *Good, Says Jerome*. Illustrated by Stephanie Douglas. New York: Dutton, 1973. (Ages 3–7.)
Loving series of conversations between Jerome and his elder sister, Janice Marie. He mentions all his fears and anxieties to her, and she helps him to resolve them, always causing him to end up with a good feeling. Warm relationships between these two siblings.

———. *My Friend Jacob*. Illustrated by Thomas Di Grazia. New York: Dutton, 1980. (Ages 6–10.)
This story describes the relationship between an eight-year-old black child, Sam, and his fourteen-year-old white, mentally disabled (probably with Down's syndrome) friend, Jacob. The children teach and learn from one another. They demonstrate a loving and understanding friendship. The families live in the same neighborhood and participate in activities together.

———. *Some of the Days of Everett Anderson*. Illustrated by Evaline Ness. New York: Holt, Rinehart and Winston, 1970. (Ages 3–8.)
The entire series about Everett Anderson is worth reading. In this one the energetic boy of six goes through the week in a lively manner. The charm and personality of the boy emerge through each of the short poems. The illustrations reflect the same sense of warmth and energy.

COLMAN, HILA. *End of the Game*. Photographs by Milton Charles. New York: World, 1971 (Ages 8–12.)
Donny is a nine-year-old black child who gets invited to spend three weeks with a well-to-do white family. Timmy, their son, is Donny's age. Timmy's mother treats Donny very differently from white children. She bends over backwards to be kind and never reprimands or punishes him. In the end Donny's mother berates him for behaving like a white man's fool and upbraids Timmy's mother for her racism. A useful, mind-opening book.

COURLANDER, HAROLD, AND HERZOG, GEORGE. *The Cow-Tail Switch and Other West African Stories*. Illustrated by Madye Lee Chastain. New York: Holt, Rinehart and Winston, 1962. (Ages 9–12.)
Notes at the back of the book tell where each tale comes from and what its significance is. Courlander has traveled extensively in Africa and is a well-known and respected folklorist.

COURLANDER, HAROLD, AND ALBERT KOFI, *Hat-Shaking Dance and Other Tales from the Gold Coast*. Illustrated by Enrico Arno. New York: Harcourt, Brace & World, 1957. (Ages 8–12.)
Stories, from the Ashanti, are very well told. Most are about Anansi. The notes at the end tell more about the background.

DAVIS, OSSIE. *Langston*. New York: Delacorte, 1982. (Ages 12–up.)
A different approach to biography (this is a play within a biography), this description of Langston Hughes also includes some of his writing.

DEASY, MICHAEL. *City ABC's*. Photographs by Robert Perron. New York: Walker, 1974. (Ages 5–8.)
Good photos of a variety of places in a city help change the negative image that cities have. Mixture of people pictured. No special connotations for any particular group of people. Constructive actions pictured.

DETREVINO, ELIZABETH BORTON. *I, Juan de Pareja*. New York: Farrar, Straus & Giroux, 1965. (Ages 12–up.)
Juan is a slave who spends most of his life serving the great painter Velasquez. He secretly and illegally becomes a competent painter on his own. When he confesses to the king, his master frees him.

DOOB, LEONARD W., ed. *A Crocodile Has Me by the Leg—African Poems*. Illustrated by Solomon Irein Wangboje. New York: Walker, 1967. (Ages 9–up.)
Authentically researched and presented, these poems deal with love, family, nature and cultural events. Woodcuts enrich and flavor this collection of poems about African life. Illustrator is Nigerian.

FASSLER, JOAN. *Don't Worry, Dear*. Illustrated by Stewart Kranz. New York: Behavioral Publications, 1971. (Ages 3–8.)
Jenny is a small child who wets her bed, stutters occasionally, and sucks her thumb. Her mother is very understanding. The story takes the reader to point at which Jenny outgrows all these habits—a very comforting conclusion. Jenny's father is also supportive. The illustrations show that the family is black. Useful for a book to have a black family represent the universal and understanding family.

FEELINGS, MURIEL. *Jambo Means Hello*. Illustrated by Tom Feelings. New York: Dial Press, 1974. (Ages 5–10.)
Beautiful illustrations accompany the simple text. Each of the twenty-four letters has a word and its definition, and then a more complete explanation of the customs associated with the word. For example, after the definition of *arusi* (a wedding), the author explains how weddings are celebrated.

_____. *Zamani Goes to Market*. Illustrated by Tom Feelings. New York: Seabury Press, 1970. (Ages 6–9.)
Zamani is the real name of the author's son. The book, inspired by the Feelings' visit with a West Kenyan family, tells of Zamani's being at last old enough to accompany his father and brothers to market. The flavor of the place and the group are communicated as well as the universal emotions of love and family caring.

FEELINGS, TOM. *Black Pilgrimage*. New York: Lothrop, Lee and Shepard, 1972. (Ages 12–up.)
Autobiography of one of our most gifted black artists. Traces his struggle as a young aspiring black artist in a white-dominated system, and his decision to leave America. Recounts his feelings about Ghana and his subsequent removal to South America. Illustrations in this book are beautiful. Text is clearly written and conveys very well a sense of self-respect and pride in being black.

FIFE, DALE. *Adam's ABC's*. Illustrated by Don Robertson. New York: Coward, McCann and Geoghegan, 1971. (Ages 6–10.)
The book is calculated to improve and support black children's positive self-image. The ABC's are introduced through a simple narrative describing Adam's pleasant day. He lives in the city with both of his parents, an elder sister, and a baby brother. His family is comfortable and loving. Stereotypes are avoided. Useful, realistic illustrations and actions are characteristics of this book.

FOLSOM, FRANKLIN. *The Life and Legend of George McJunkin: Black Cowboy*. Nashville: Thomas Nelson, 1973. (Ages 10–up.)
McJunkin was a competent cowboy, as well as a naturalist, meterorologist, and rancher. He undertook many responsibilities and discharged them well. Interesting account of his life, drawn from research.

FOX, PAULA. *The Slave Dancer*. Illustrated by Eros Keith. Scarsdale, New York: Bradbury Press, 1973. (Ages 11–up.)
Jessie, a thirteen-year old boy, is kidnapped from New Orleans and forced to serve on a slave ship. He has to play the fife so that the slaves will exercise. When the ship encounters trouble, all but Jessie and Ras, a young slave, are killed. Ras is helped to freedom by an old Black man, who runs a station on the underground railroad. Ugly, harrowing descriptions of the conditions of the slave ship and the cruelty of the crew. Very well written, but raises an interesting debate about black versus white perspective in the telling of a tale.

FREEDMAN, FLORENCE. *Two Tickets to Freedom*. New York: Simon and Schuster, 1971. (Ages 9–12.)
Ellen and William Craft, the hero and heroine of this book, escape from slavery by using their wits. They have many adventures and meet many interesting people before they escape to England. After the Civil War, they return to the U.S., where they found a school for poor rural black children.

FRITZ, JEAN. *Brady*, Illustrated by Lynd Ward. New York: Coward McCann, 1960. (Ages 9–12.)
Brady finally learns how to keep a secret when he discovers that his father is a conductor on the Underground Railroad.

GIOVANNI, NIKKI. "The Funeral of Martin Luther King Jr.," in Arnold Adoff, ed., *Black Out Loud*. Illustrated by Alvin Hollingsworth. New York: Macmillan, 1970. (All ages.)
Martin Luther King's gravestone proclaims, "Free at Last." Giovanni, a well-known black poet, mourns his passing with this poem. Particularly useful for discussion is the expressed idea that "death is a slave's freedom."

———. *Spin a Soft Black Song: Poems for Children*. Illustrated by Charles Bible. New York: Hill and Wang, 1971. (Ages 7–11.)
A book of poems reflecting black experiences and feelings.

GLASSER, BARBARA, AND BLUSTEIN, ELLEN. *Bongo Bradley*. Illustrated by Bonnie Johnson. New York: Hawthorn, 1973. (Ages 7–11.)
Bradley Clark's father is a jazz musician; his mother is a nurse. Bradley goes to

North Carolina for the summer to visit his father's family. There he learns about his father's roots, about music, and about more of his people.

GORDY, BERRY, SR. *Movin' Up*. New York: Harper & Row, 1979. (Ages 12–up.)
Told in an informal, anecdotal sytle, this autobiography of the founder of Motown Records was completed shortly before his death at the age of ninety. Alex Haley's introduction to the book points out that it was written from a series of taped sessions during which "Pop" Gordy reminisced about his life. The flavor of the man's personality and energy comes through clearly.

GRAHAM, LORENZ. *Hungry Catch the Foolish Boy*. Illustrated by James Brown, Jr. New York: Crowell, 1973. (Ages 7–10.)
The Prodigal Son retold in Liberian English. Beautiful rhythm to the words. Dramatically simple illustrations. Graham, a minister's son, was born in New Orleans. He has retold other Bible stories in this style: *David He No Fear*, and *Every Man Heart Lay Down*. All are excellent.

_____. *John Brown: A Cry for Freedom*. Illustrated with photographs. New York: Crowell, 1980. (Ages 11–up.)
A biography of this controversial figure, which makes a case for his having deep religious convictions about freeing slaves, rather than the view that some historians have promoted of his being a wild, insane monster. This account does not, however, portray him as a saint.

_____. *Whose Town?* New York: Crowell, 1969.
David Williams, eighteen years old, is an intelligent, quiet, young black man, who wants to go to medical school after college. A series of tragic events deprives his father of a job, gets David into trouble with the police, and makes everyone wonder whether they can ever be safe and comfortable again. In the end, David does graduate from high school, with a scholarship to college, but there is not total hope that the future will be bright. Discussions in the book about Black Power—and what course of action to take—are useful. This is a sequel to *North Town* and *South Town*, which also tell about David Williams and the struggles that his family endure.

GRAY, GENEVIEVE. *A Kite for Bennie*. Illustrated by Floyd Sowell. New York: McGraw-Hill, 1972. (Ages 5–8.)
Bennie lives with his mother, sister, and two brothers in a poor neighborhood; they are on welfare. Bennie sees, is fascinated by, and desirous of, a kite. Many kind people (including his brother's parole officer) contribute to his building a kite. Mutually helpful and loving family. The quality of togetherness comes through strongly.

_____. *Send Wendell*. Illustrated by Symeon Shimin. New York: McGraw-Hill, 1974. (Ages 3–9.)
Wendell is the one in his family always sent on errands—his older siblings are too busy; his younger ones are too small. But he goes happily. His Uncle Robert, a successful California farmer, comes to visit. He invites Wendell to come to help on the farm when he gets big enough. After that, Wendell also has something to do

when his mother needs an errand run; he writes to Uncle Robert. Good, happy family story. Uncle Robert is a great character—big, wealthy, happy, and loving.

GREENE, BETTE. *Philip Hall Likes Me, I Reckon Maybe.* Illustrated by Charles Lilly. New York: Dial Press, 1974. (Ages 8–11.)
Flavorful story about a black community in rural Arkansas. Beth Lambert is the eleven-year-old protagonist; Philip is the boy whom she loves. Her adventures are fun. The community is social and active. The parents are proud of their children and want the best for them. The sequel, *Get on Home, Philip Hall*, continues the story.

GREENFIELD, ELOISE. *Honey, I Love.* Illustrated by Diane and Leo Dillon. New York: Crowell, 1978. (Ages 6–up.)
Inspired by everyday experiences, these sixteen poems are soft and gentle slices in the life of a young black child. Black vernacular is used naturally and resonantly. The Dillons' illustrations are both magical and affirming.
_____. *Mary McLeod Bethune.* New York: Crowell, 1978. (Ages 7–10.)
Explains in very simple language how a little girl with a burning desire to read grew up to start many schools for blacks in the South at the turn of the century. The author also describes Ms. Bethune's efforts to preserve the heritage of black Americans.

_____. *She Come Bringing Me That Little Baby Girl.* Illustrated by John Steptoe. Philadelphia: Lippincott, 1974. (Ages 5–8.)
Black family includes mother, father, Kevin, and baby sister. Kevin wanted a brother. He is jealous of the attention that the new baby gets from all the relatives and neighbors, as well as from his parents. When his mother permits him to hold his new sister and to show her off to his friends, Kevin begins to feel happy again and to plan for what they will eventually be able to do together. Steptoe's illustrations are beautiful.
_____. *Sister.* Illustrated by Moneta Barnett. New York: Crowell, 1974. (Ages 10–up.)
Author is black. Doretha and her sister Alberta live with their mother. Father dies of a heart attack and is sorely missed by everyone. Alberta drops out of school and rebels against convention. Doretha is sensitive and perceptive but has problems in school. She is afraid that she will be like her sister. Finally a school, run by Afro-Americans, affords her some hope.

GREENFIELD, ELOISE, AND LITTLE, LESSIE JONES. *Childtimes: A Three-Generation Memoir.* Illustrated by Jerry Pinkney and photographs from the authors' family albums. New York: Crowell, 1979. (Ages 10–up.)
A poetic set of memoirs of three strong black women, their times, and their families. The book makes the people and the eras come alive.

GUIRMA, FREDERIC. *Tales of Mogho, African Stories from Upper Volta.* New York: Macmillan, 1971. (Ages 8–10.)
Creation myth and other tales passed along by storytellers. Interlaced with words of the Mossi people in the More language. The words are set down here in print for the first time. A glossary is provided for the reader. Like other African tales, these are complex and rich in detail.

GUY, ROSA. *The Friends.* New York: Holt, Rinehart and Winston, 1973. (Ages 12–up.)
The Cathy family, from the West Indies, live in Harlem. The girls, Phyllisia and

Ruby, are victimized at school. Mother dies of breast cancer; father is stern and harsh in his bereavement. Edith, a friend of Phyl's, is looked down upon by both Phyl and her father, but she proves to be Phyl's truest friend. At end, everyone has grown in some way, and looks as if the family will make it. Very sad, very powerful story.

HALEY, GAIL E. *A Story, a Story*. New York: Atheneum, 1970. (Ages 5–8.)
Beautifully told, beautifully illustrated story of how many African folk tales come to be called Spider tales. Tells how Anansi, by his wits, caused Nyame, the sky god, to share all his stories with Anansi.

HAMILTON, VIRGINIA. *The House of Dies Drear*. Illustrated by Eros Keith. New York: Macmillan, 1968. (Ages 10–up.)
Mystery story. Black family purchases very large, historic old house in Ohio. Father is a college professor. House was a station on the Underground Railroad. Descendant of one of the slaves who hid there was bequeathed a fabulous underground cavern full of treasures. The cavern is under the house. Good adventure story, with message of black pride contained in it.

_____. *M. C. Higgins, the Great*. New York: Macmillan, 1974. (Ages 12–up.)
Interesting and complex story of a black family living in the mountains of Ohio. M. C. is the unusual hero of the story. The plot involves family love and pride and process of growing up.

_____. *Paul Robeson, The Life and Times of a Free Black Man*. New York: Harper & Row, 1974. (Ages 12–up.)
Well-written account of this talented and controversial man. Hamilton, who very much sympathizes with and admires Robeson, hopes that his country will raise him to the position of esteem she feels that he deserves.

_____. *The Planet of Junior Brown*. New York: Macmillan, 1971. (Ages 12–up.)
Junior Brown is a very fat (almost three hundred pounds), very disturbed young man. He has one friend who is also a friend to many young black boys who live in abandoned houses all over the city. Junior finally joins them.

_____. *Sweet Whispers, Brother Rush*. New York: Philomel Books, 1981. (Ages 12–up.)
A masterful story about a black family, past and present, and a young girl's coming of age. Tree, fourteen years old, is very protective of her seventeen-year-old brother Dabney (Dab). Dab is "slow" and "different." Brother Rush, a handsome ghost, appears to Tree and tells about the family's past, including the emotional neglect of Dab by their mother. Dab has a rare illness and eventually dies. When Tree recovers from her mourning, she begins to accept her own womanhood.

_____. *Time-Ago Lost: More Tales of Jahdu*. Illustrated by Ray Prather. New York: Macmillan, 1973. (Ages 7–10.)
Mama Luka, the storyteller, is sad because her building will be torn down; she will have to relocate. Lee Edward is worried that she will move away too far for him to visit, but his father reassures him that it will take a very long time for the building to be torn down. Meanwhile, Mama Luka tells him more about that great character Jahdu.

HAMILTON, VIRGINIA. *The Time-Ago Tales of Jahdu.* Illustrated by Nonny Hogragian. New York: Macmillan, 1973. (Ages 7–10.)
Lee Edward is a young black child whose baby-sitter, Mama Luka, tells him stories of Jahdu, magical young boy. Jahdu is similar to Anansi in some ways. The stories and this book are aimed at helping black children to develop and to maintain a sense of self-pride and positive ambition. The people live "in a fine good place called Harlem." The stories are told in a very stylized but interesting fashion, and the character of the storyteller is well captured.

———. *Zeely.* Illustrated by Symeon Shimin. New York: Macmillan, 1967. (Ages 10–12.)
Elizabeth and John Perry go for a vacation to their uncle's farm. They are black. While they are there, they meet a strikingly beautiful black girl named Zeely. Six-and-a-half feet tall, she is undoubtedly a descendant of the Watusi. Zeely helps Elizabeth to be herself and to be proud of it. It is a growing summer for both Elizabeth and her brother.

HAYDEN, ROBERT. *Eight Black American Inventors.* Reading, Massachussetts: Addison-Wesley, 1972. (Ages 9–12.)
An excellent resource book for any school library. The book shows the importance of black inventors in our lives.

HEIDISH, MARCY. *A Woman Called Moses.* Boston: Houghton Mifflin, 1976. (Ages 12–up.)
A well-written biography of Harriet Tubman that goes beyond the simplified versions written especially for younger readers. This account is told through the voice of Harriet, herself, as she looks back over her long years of life. Encountered in the book are such famous figures as John Brown, Frederick Douglass, William Lloyd Garrison, and others, so that readers gain a sense of history beyond Harriet's contributions.

HILL, ELIZABETH STARR. *Evan's Corner.* Illustrated by Nancy Grossman. New York: Holt, Rinehart and Winston, 1967. (Ages 5–8.)
Evan lives in two rooms with his parents, three sisters, and two brothers. They share a kitchen with neighbors down the hall. They are black; both parents work. When Evan wants a place of his own, his mother says that everyone can have a corner. Evan furnishes his corner, then helps his little brother to do the same. Although the family is very poor, the mood is not depressed. All the members love, appreciate, and respect each other. They enjoy their lives, and everyone does what he or she can. They do not sit back and complain; they are active and constructive.

HOEXTER, CORINNE. *Black Crusader, Frederick Douglass.* Chicago: Rand McNally, 1970. (Ages 10–up.)
Conveys well a sense of the man and his times. Other figures are also described in the book, making it a valuable contribution to the learning of black history. Douglass emerges as a brilliant, courageous, far-seeing man. The author respects her subject and handles it well.

HOLT, DELORIS. *The ABC's of Black History.* Illustrated by Samuel Bhang, Jr. Pasadena: Ritchie Ward Press, 1953. (Ages 9–12.)
Written by a black teacher. Each letter offers the name of a black person who

achieved much and who contributed to the struggle for freedom. Contemporary as well as long-dead heroes and heroines are presented. This book contains an impressive array of people about whom more should be known and taught.

HOPKINS, LEE BENNETT, ed. *Don't You Turn Back*. Illustrated by Ann Grifalconi. New York: Knopf, 1969. (Ages 11–up.)
The title comes from a line in the poem called "Mother to Son." It stresses the positive determination of the black people to keep on going. The poems in this collection reflect this courage, despite the fact that "life for me ain't been no crystal stair."

_____. ed. *On Our Way: Poems of Pride and Love*. Photographs by David Parks. New York: Knopf. 1974. (Ages 8–up.)
Twenty-two poems by black poets, singing of the special black experience. A beautiful collection, visually as well as poetically.

_____. *This Street's for Me*. Illustrated by Ann Grifalconi. New York: Crown, 1970. (Ages 7–9.)
City poems conveying a sense of the moods and activities of the city. Nicely integrated illustration. Poems are general: there are no special references to any minority groups or customs. Useful for dispelling negative stereotypes about the city.

HORVATH, BETTY. *Hooray for Jasper*. Illustrated by Fermin Rocker. New York: Franklin Watts, 1966. (Ages 10–up.)
Black family in the suburbs. Warm relationship between Jasper and his grandfather. Jasper wants to be bigger. He follows his grandfather's advice, does a good deed, and feels bigger. Pleasant story.

HOWARD, VANESSA. *A Screaming Whisper*. Photographs by J. Ponderhughes. New York: Holt, Rinehart and Winston, 1972. (Ages 12–up.)
Vanessa Howard is a young black poet who was born in 1955. She began writing when she was twelve. Her poem "For My Children" could be used as a guide to writers. In it, she says, "My children are unique, my children have names."

_____. "Monument in Black," in June Jordan and Terri Bush, eds. *The Voice of the Children*. New York: Holt, Rinehart and Winston, 1970. (Ages 9–12.) The poet suggests using Black Americans to honor on coins and with statues. She alludes to the many black soldiers who died in Vietnam for our country and have not been recognized.

HUNTER, KRISTIN. *The Soul Brothers and Sister Lou*. New York: Scribner, 1968. (Ages 12–up.)
Louretta has seven brothers and sisters and mother at home, plus her sister's baby. Father has left home; sister was never married. Lou sings well and achieves success singing with a group. She tries to act so that she will accomplish her goals.

ISADORA, RACHEL. *Ben's Trumpet*. New York: Greenwillow Books, 1979. (Ages 6–10.)
Ben loves music, particularly trumpet music. He pretends he has a horn, and plays wonderful music in his imagination. A friendly professional trumpet player helps turn his fantasies into reality.

JOHNSON, ALICIA LOY. "A Black Poetry Day," in Arnold Adoff, ed., *Black Out Loud—An Anthology of Modern Poems by Black Americans*. Illustrated by Alvin Hollingsworth. New York: Macmillan, 1970. (Ages 6–12.)
The poet wants a day to celebrate black poets, and ultimately, all areas of achievement by blacks.

JONES, ADRIENNE. *So, Nothing Is Forever*. Illustrated by Richard Cuffari. Boston: Houghton Mifflin, 1974. (Ages 12–up.)
The children in this interracial family are left to take care of themselves after their parents are killed in a car accident. Their uncle will take responsibility for them in a year, but they must first survive that year.

JORDAN, JUNE. *Dry Victories*. New York: Holt, Rinehart and Winston, 1972. (Ages 12–up.)
Black perspective, in black dialect, of Reconstruction and the Civil Rights Era. Directed at both black and white readers. Excellent illustrations and photographs. Jordan points out that at the end of each of these periods of alleged victory for blacks, they were defeated politically, economically and socially.

_____. *Kimako's Story*. Illustrated by Kay Burford. Boston: Houghton Mifflin, 1981. (Ages 4–9.)
Kimako Anderson is almost eight years old, and she is already a rugged and engaging individual. Through her account of her activities we are admitted into her world and see the city through her eyes. A delightful book.

_____. *New Life: New Room*. Illustrated by Ray Cruz. New York: Crowell, 1975. (Ages 6–9.)
A beautiful, warm story about a coping black family. The parents wisely permit the children to work out their own solution to the problem of space in their small apartment.

_____. *Who Look at Me*. New York: Crowell, 1969. (Ages 9–up.)
Poem accompanied by reproductions of twenty-seven paintings. Very effective.

KEATS, EZRA JACK. *Hi Cat*. New York: Collier, 1970. (Ages 5–8.)
Archie and Peter perform on the city street, but Willie, the dog, and a cat spoil their theater. A fun story, in which the pictures are even more important than usual in a Keats book.

_____. *A Letter to Amy*. New York: Harper & Row, 1968. (Ages 5–8.)
Peter writes a letter to Amy inviting her to his party. Through a misunderstanding, Amy is hurt by Peter. But she shows up at his party and all is well.

_____. *Peter's Chair*. New York: Harper & Row, 1967. (Ages 5–8.)
Peter has a new baby sister, and his parents are painting all his old furniture pink for the baby. He feels excluded and taking his chair, "runs away." He actually remains close by. When he realizes that he has outgrown his chair and when he hears his parent's supportive words and smells dinner, he returns to the family, resolving to tolerate his sister.

_____. *The Snowy Day*. New York: Viking, 1962. (Ages 3-6.)

Peter has a lovely, joyful time in the snow. This is the reader's first introduction to Peter and his family.

_____. *Whistle for Willie*. New York: Viking, 1964. (Ages 4–6.)
City setting, pleasant and sunny. Peter is an inventive, charming child. He tries to learn to whistle so that he can call his dog, Willie. He finally succeeds, and everyone is very proud of him.

KIRN, ANN. *Beeswax Catches a Thief*. New York: Norton, 1968. (Ages 4–8.)
Adaptation of a Congo folk tale. A version of the Tar Baby story, only here it is the tortoise who is coated with beeswax and the jackal who gets caught. Nicely told and illustrated by the author.

LARRICK, NANCY, ed. *On City Streets: An Anthology of Poetry*. Illustrated by David Sagarin. Philadelphia: M. Evans, 1968. (Ages 10–up.)
Poems by prominent poets mirror both the excitement and the bleaker aspects of city living. Photographs reflect varying facets of the city.

LAWRENCE, JACOB. *Harriet and the Promised Land*. Verses by Robert Kraus. New York: Simon and Schuster, 1968. (Ages 6–10.)
Jacob Lawrence is a black artist. His paintings form the book, accompanied by Kraus's verses. The combination conveys very powerfully the sense of Harriet Tubman's heroism. The paintings are stark. The book won the Brooklyn Art Book for Children award and was selected by *The New York Times* as one of the best-illustrated children's books of the year.

LESTER, JULIUS. *Black Folktales*. Illustrated by Tom Feelings. New York: Grove Press, 1969. (Ages 10–up.)
Powerful retelling of tales from Africa, the South, and from black sections of cities. In many cases, the white man is the enemy. The illustrations are excellent. The book adds to each reader's store of perceptions and events.

_____. *The Knee-High Man and Other Tales*. Illustrated by Ralph Pinto. New York: Dial Press, 1972. (Ages 3–8.)
Retelling of tales from slavery times. All contain trickery and competition, with one creature outwitting another. Very well told stories, each of which could be allegorical.

_____. *Long Journey Home: Stories from Black History*. New York: Dial Press, 1972. Also in paper. (Ages 12–up.)
Fascinating and very well told accounts of people who did not so much make a giant mark in the history books, but were individuals who should be known. Book demonstrates that many black people were the source of their own freedom, not having to rely on the kindness and generosity of Whites. A very important book.

_____. *This Strange New Feeling*. New York: Dial Press, 1982. (Ages 11–up.)
Three love stories that transcend the people in them, and become testimony to the power of the human spirit and the resolve for freedom. Beautifully written, based on fact, the stories bring the characters very close to the reader.

_____. *To Be a Slave*. Illustrated by Tom Feelings. New York: Dial Press, 1968. (Ages 12–up.)

Accounts in slaves' own words of what it means to be a slave. Proceeds from the transportation of slaves from Africa to the time after Emancipation. Lester's comments guide the reader to a deeper understanding of the time and the people. The bibliography adds to the potential sources of information. A very powerful, well-constructed, important book.

LEWIS, RICHARD, ed. *Out of the Earth I Sing.* New York: Norton, 1968. (All ages.) Well-selected collection of poems. The illustrations, powerful and remarkable, are photographs of original art work of the people who are represented by the poetry. The sources of the poetry are mostly other written works; the sources of the art are mostly museums.

LEXUA, JOAN M. *Benjie on His Own.* Illustrated by Don Bolognese. New York: Dial Press, 1970. (Ages 4–8.) One day Benjie's grandmother fails to pick him up from school. He manages, despite a number of problems, to find his way home through the hostile city streets. He discovers that his grandmother is ill. The ghetto then turns into a supportive place, and people help him in his time of need.

LITTLE, LESSIE JONES, AND GREENFIELD, ELOISE. *I Can Do It Myself.* Illustrated by Carole Byard. New York: Crowell, 1978. (Ages 5–8.) Donny is ready to take a step toward self-reliance: he plans to go on his own to the flower shop to purchase a birthday gift for his mother. He has made careful plans for this day, and must overcome such obstacles as getting past a vicious dog, and persuading his brother that he can, indeed, do it by himself. A loving book.

LONGSWORTH, POLLY. *I, Charlotte Forten, Black and Free.* New York: Crowell, 1970. (Ages 10–12.) Fictionalized autobiography. Charlotte Forten's life is rich and eventful. She is active all her life in the fight for equal rights for black people. The book describes other abolitionists, such as William Lloyd Garrison, and tells the stories of such notable blacks as Frederick Douglass, James Forten, and William Wells Brown, among others.

McGOVERN, ANN. *Black Is Beautiful.* Illustrated by Hope Warmfeld. New York: Four Winds Press, 1969. (Ages 5–8.) Excellent photographs demonstrating the beauty of blackness. The text is poetic. Different kinds of people are pictured. This book is a good one to reinforce positive self-image or to change a once negative perspective.

———. *Runaway Slave.* Illustrated by R. M. Powers. New York: Four Winds Press, 1965. Also in paper. (Ages 7–10.) Well-told story of the remarkable woman Harriet Tubman, or Moses, as she was known. The simple facts of her life are incredible. Her courage and strength were legend. She never got caught, and she never lost a passenger on her Underground Railroad.

MATHIS, SHARON BELL. *Listen for the Fig Tree.* New York: Viking, 1974. Also in paper. (Ages 12–up.) Kwanza, an African celebration, figures strongly in this complex and interesting story. Muffin Johnson, the heroine, is sixteen years old and blind. The black community is very important to Muffin and is very supportive of her. The sense of community and black identity is stressed in the book.

_____. *Sidewalk Story*. Illustrated by Leo Carty. New York: Viking, 1971. (Ages 9–11.)
Lilly Etta Allen is the nine-year-old protagonist. She manages to help her friend, Tanya, overcome the effects of being evicted. She calls the newspapers, contacts a sympathetic reporter, and saves the day.

_____. *Teacup Full of Roses*. New York: Viking, 1972. (Ages 12–up.)
Two of the brothers in this black family are destroyed, partly because of the mother's favoritism. Very moving.

MELTZER, MILTON. *All Times, All Peoples: A World History of Slavery*. Illustrated by Leonard Everett Fisher. New York: Harper & Row, 1980. (Ages 8–12.)
Tracing the history of slavery from ancient times to the present, the author tells readers that there are currently ten million slaves in various places in the world (counting those political prisoners who are forced to labor against their will). He ends with a plea for action on the part of the free world.

MENDOZA, GEORGE. *And I Must Hurry for the Sea Is Coming In*. Illustrated by DeWayne Dalrymple. Englewood Cliffs, New Jersey: Prentice-Hall, 1971. (Ages 8–up.)
Young black child is pictured as the captain of a large, beautiful sailboat. He handles the ship masterfully and withstands all obstacles. The reader knows that this child will persevere and overcome even though the reader sees, at the end of the book, that the child is really sailing a toy boat in the water of a fire hydrant in the city. The rest of the book is his fantasy. Beautifully done.

MESSER, RONALD K. *Shumway*. Nashville: Thomas Nelson, 1975. (Ages 11–up.)
The South in the 1950's was an ugly place to be. The story describes an uneasy friendship between a white boy named Shumway and a black boy named Lyle. Shumway is ignorant and naive, but spunky. The incidents in the story indicate the extent of the poor whites' hatred against blacks.

MONJO, F. N. *The Drinking Gourd*. Illustrated by Fred Brenner. New York: Harper & Row, 1970. (Ages 5–8.)
Tommy Fuller, a white child, is always in trouble and always being punished by his parents; but he redeems himself by helping a family of fugitive slaves escape through the Underground Railroad. Although Tommy saves the black family by using his wits to escape detection, the family is not demeaned or depicted as weak. Each family member is named, and Jeff, the father, helps to educate Tommy. The family is dignified, courageous, and determined to win their freedom.

MUSGROVE, MARGARET. *Ashanti to Zulu, African Traditions*. Illustrated by Leo and Diane Dillon. New York: Dial Press, 1976. (Ages 7–10.)
A unique alphabet book which describes the traditions of many African tribes. The book uses many native words and describes aspects of the life of the various tribes. Beautiful illustrations.

MYERS, WALTER DEAN. *Fast Sam, Cool Clyde and Stuff.* New York: Viking, 1975. (Ages 12–up.)
Reminiscences of the adolescent years of a young black boy in New York City. His group of friends is close-knit and constructive. They are unusually naive despite their rough surroundings. The language is that of the city. The plot is thin, but there is much here that destroys the negative stereotype of the young Black in the city.

ORTIZ, VICTORIA. *Sojourner Truth, A Self-Made Woman.* Philadelphia: Lippincott, 1974. (Ages 12–up.)
In reading the story of this remarkable black woman, much history is learned. The link between the feminist and abolitionist movement is described. Sojourner Truth, a pioneer for the cause of black civil rights, vigorously fought for her people until her death.

PETRIE, PHIL W. "It Happened in Montgomery," Raoul Abdul, compiler, in *The Magic of Black Poetry.* Illustrated by Dane Burr. New York: Dodd, Mead, 1972. (Ages 10–up.)
Dedicated to Rosa Parks, the black woman who refused to give up her seat on a bus, this poem celebrates her determination and bravery in undertaking such a courageous act. The poet describes how "A weary woman turned the page of History."

SCHRAFF, A. E. *Black Courage.* Illustrated by Len Ebert. Philadelphia: Macrae Smith, 1969. (Ages 9–up.)
Twenty-one black heroes of the American West are described here. Not all of the stories have happy endings, but all of the heroes have made contributions; thus readers may take pride in their undertakings.

SHEPARD, RAY ANTHONY. *Conjure Tales by Charles W. Chestnutt.* Illustrated by John Ross and Clare Romano. New York: Dutton, 1973. (Ages 9–up.)
Retelling of the 1899 *The Conjure Woman.* Tales of slaves and their attempt to relieve their plight through the use of magic. Sometimes it worked; sometimes it did not. Tales are well told.

SMUCKER, BARBARA. *Runaway to Freedom.* New York: Harper & Row, 1977. (Ages 9–up.)
More than an adventure story, this account of the escape of two young women from slavery tells of friendship and courage. Twelve-year-old Julilly protects and supports her friend, Liza, who is severely disabled because of her former master's beatings.

STEPTOE, JOHN. *Birthday.* New York: Holt, Rinehart and Winston, 1972. (Ages 4–8.)
Idealized black community. All the people in it are loving, joyful, and productive. All have African names. Javaka is the firstborn of the community, and it is his birthday, so there is a celebration. Pictures and text combined give the reader a strong, positive sense of the community and each person in it.

———. *Stevie.* New York: Harper & Row, 1969. Also in paper. (Ages 4–8.)
Robert's mother takes care of Stevie while his mother works. Robert resents Stevie's demanding, babyish ways. But when, after some time, Stevie and his parents move away, Robert remembers the good things about Stevie and misses him. Both families

are close and caring. The illustrations are strong and appropriate. The text is written in black dialect that conveys the thoughts of the character very well.

_____. *Train Ride.* New York: Harper & Row, 1971. Also in paper. (Ages 6–10.)
Written in Black English, the story is that of a group of black children who decide to take a train ride uptown from Brooklyn, where they live, to Times Square. They do so, have a marvelous time, and return home late, knowing that they will be everely punished. Their worried parents do punish them, but the reader knows that this intrepid band will repeat their experience. The children like themselves and each other. The illustrations are of a realistic but supportive city.

_____. *Uptown.* New York: Harper & Row, 1970. Also in paper. (Ages 5–8.)
The entire book is a conversation between Dennis and John about what they will be when they grow up. They discuss junkies, black pride, clothing, the army, karate, and hippies. They come to no conclusions but agree that they will continue to be alert and to enjoy life. All of John Steptoe's books depict black characters.

TAYLOR, MILDRED D. *Let the Circle Be Unbroken.* New York: Dial Press, 1981. (Ages 8–12.)
Happily, this third book in the series about the Logan family is every bit as powerful as the first two. The story is compelling, the characters vivid, the history passionate. Sibling relations and family interaction emerge as important elements in the plot.

_____. *Roll of Thunder, Hear My Cry.* New York: Dial, 1976. Also in paper. (Ages 8–12.)
Moving story of a black family in the South during the 1930's. Many sub-plots form the book, but the basic theme is the injustice of white society contrasted with the strength and moral fortitude of the black family.

_____. *Song of the Trees.* Illustrated by Jerry Pinkney. New York: Dial Press, 1975. (Ages 8–12.)
The first book in the trilogy. The setting is rural Mississippi during the Depression. The story is about a black family and their battle to protect their trees from a white lumberman. A sense of pride and togetherness impresses the reader.

THOMAS, IANTHE. *Lordy, Aunt Hattie.* Illustrated by Thomas di Grazia. New York: Harper & Row, (Ages 4–8.)
A loving tone poem of growing up in the Deep South. The child, Jeppa Lee, and her Aunt Hattie engage in a conversation that demonstrates their warmth, affection, and positive sense of self.

_____. *My Street's a Cool Morning Street.* Illustrated by Emily A. McCully. New York: Harper & Row, 1976. (Ages 5–8.)
Charming illustrations of the bristling and busy life of a city street in the early morning. A black child walks down "his" street and reacts to it on his way to school. Full of joy and delight in his city-world.

_____. *Walk Home Tired, Billy Jenkins.* Illustrated by Thomas di Grazia. New York: Harper & Row, 1974. (Ages 5-8.)
It is time to go home from the playground, and Billy Jenkins is very tired. His sister,

Nina, lovingly and imaginatively makes the trip home a magic ride for the two of them. Illustrations of the people and the city are beautifully and gently done.

THUM, MARCELLA. *Exploring Black America: A History and Guide*. New York: Atheneum, 1975. (Ages 10–up.)
Combines an informative and comprehensive historical account of black people in the United States with a guide to places of historical and cultural significance for black people. An invaluable, well-constructed resource.

WALKER, ALICE. *Langston Hughes, American Poet*. Illustrated by Don Miller. New York: Crowell, 1974. (Ages 7–9.)
One of a series of biographies including a number of black Americans. The author, who knew Hughes personally, tells simply and sympathetically of his youth. She indicates the problems that Hughes had because of his father's negative attitudes. Not much is said of his adult years, but the poet is introduced to young readers, who may then be motivated to read more about and by Langston Hughes.

WEINER, SANDRA. *It's Wings That Make Birds Fly*. New York: Pantheon Books, 1968. (Ages 6–9.)
Otis is a sensitive young man. He and his friends have a difficult time of it in New York. They are good boys but are destroyed by their environment. The author notes that Otis was killed by an automobile while he was playing in the street. All the text is from tape recordings made of the boys' conversation.

YARBROUGH, CAMILLE. *Cornrows*. Illustrated by Carole Byard. New York: Coward, McCann and Geoghegan, 1979. (Ages 5–9.)
As Mama and Great-Grammaw braid the children's hair into cornrows, they tell of the meaning of the designs of the cornrows, and they present some of the tradition and richness of Afro-American history.

YOUNG, BERNICE ELIZABETH. *Harlem, The Story of a Changing Community*. New York: Julian Messner, 1972. (Ages 8–10.)
The history of Harlem from early Dutch times to the present. Gives a good sense of its transition. Author is a black writer.

BIBLIOGRAPHY: ASIAN AMERICANS

BUNTING, EVE. *The Happy Funeral*. Illustrated by Vo-Dinh Mai. New York: Harper & Row, 1982. (Ages 5–9.)
After Laura's grandfather dies she is included in all of the ceremonies celebrating his life, and marking his death. She understands that her grandfather was ready for death after a long, full life, but she is unhappy to lose him. Chinese rituals are respectfully described and illustrated.

COUTANT, HELEN. *First Snow*. Illustrated by Vo-Dinh Mai. New York: Knopf, 1974. (Ages 5–8.)
Lien and her family moved from Vietnam to New England. It is winter, and Lien's grandmother is dying. Lien asks her grandmother to explain what dying means. She understands when her grandmother directs her to experience the snow. Recognizing the cyclical nature of life, she is content.

DAVIS, DANIEL S. *Behind Barbed Wire*. New York: Dutton, 1982. (Ages 12–up.)
Fully researched and detailed account of the internment of Japanese-Americans during World War II.

FOLEY, BERNICE WILLIAMS. *A Walk among the Clouds*. Illustrated by Mina Gow McLean. Chicago: Children's Press, 1980. (Ages 6–8.)
A folk tale from China which teaches that kindness to others is often repaid. The tale uses beliefs of the people to explain forces of nature. Colorful illustrations.

FRITZ, JEAN. *Homesick: My Own Story*. Illustrated by Margot Tomes. New York: Putnam, 1982. (Ages 10–up.)
Told from the perspective of the author as a ten-year-old girl, the story contains all sorts of sensory images and memories, laced with the details of China in the years 1925 to 1927. The author is an accomplished writer who makes all of the incidents ring true.

HOUSTON, JEANNE WAKATSUKI, AND JAMES HOUSTON. *Farewell to Manzanar*. Boston: Houghton Mifflin, 1973. Also in paper. (Ages 12–up.)
Written from the perspective of Jeanne Wakatsuki as a seven-year-old girl growing up in one of the largest of the internment camps for Japanese-Americans during the Second World War. The story details the author's impressions and reactions to this dehumanizing experience.

HOU-TIEN, CHENG. *The Chinese New Year*. Scissor cuts by the author. New York: Holt, Rinehart and Winston, 1976. (Ages 6–12.)
This book describes the many days of celebration that go on to signify the end of winter and the coming of spring. The Little New Year, the five days of The Chinese New Year, and the Lantern Festival or Feast of the First Full Moon, are described. The scissor cuts are excellent.

HUYNH QUANG NHUONG. *The Land I Lost: Adventures of a Boy in Vietnam*. Illustrated by Vo-Dinh Mai. New York: Harper & Row, 1982. (Ages 9–12.)
Only on the last two pages of this book does war enter into the story, and then it is the war between the French and the Vietnamese, who are led by Ho Chi Minh. The author tells of his family and friends, and the life they led before the war. Customs, beliefs, and adventures are described in the context of a dearly loved community and lifestyle.

LOUIE, AI-LING, adaptor. *Yeh-Shen: A Cinderella Story from China*. Illustrated by Ed Young. New York: Philomel Books, 1982. (Ages 8–up.)
First appearing in a book from the T'ang dynasty (A.D. 618–907), this story predates the earliest European version of Cinderella by about one thousand years, leading scholars to believe that this was one of the many folk and fairy tales adopted and adapted from Asia by European retellers.

MELTZER, MILTON. *The Chinese Americans*. Illustrated with photographs. New York: Crowell, 1980. (Ages 10–up.)
With his customary sensitivity and expertise, the author describes the history, trials, and accomplishments of the Chinese people in America. A very readable and informative book.

SADLER, CATHERINE EDWARDS, adaptor. *Treasure Mountain: Folktales from Southern China.* Illustrated by Cheng Mun Yun. New York: Atheneum, 1982. (Ages 9–12.)
Tales of the Chuang, Han, T'ung and Yao tribes, taken from the oral tradition.

SAKURI, RHODA. *Speak for Yourself.* Illustrated by Guy Buffet. Boston: Houghton Mifflin, 1977. (Ages 7–10.)
Joy must go to classes after her regular school day is over, in order to learn about her heritage. At first she is resentful of this, but at last she begins to appreciate her culture.

SAY, ALLEN. *The Bicycle Man.* Illustrated by the author. Oakland, California: Parnassus Press, 1982. (Ages 5–9.)
The author recalls an incident from when he was growing up during the American occupation of Japan. The story is a gentle one, telling of the friendly visit and demonstration of bicycle-riding prowess of two American soldiers. The details of the Japanese Sport Day are beautifully presented in words and pictures.

TOBIAS, TOBI. *Isamu Noguchi: The Life of a Sculptor.* Illustrated with photographs. New York: Crowell, 1974. (Ages 7–11.)
Too few books portray notable Japanese Americans. This account of the talented sculptor tells of his development, not only as a sculptor, but also as a person who confronts his situation as the son of a Japanese father and a white American mother.

UCHIDA, YOSHIKO. *A Jar of Dreams.* New York: Atheneum, 1981. (Ages 9–12.)
Rinko and her family struggle economically during the Depression years, which are the backdrop for this story about learning to value one's heritage. All of the author's books portray a close-knit, caring Japanese-American family.

_____. *Journey Home.* New York: Atheneum, 1979. (Ages 9–12.)
This book is the sequel to *Journey to Topaz,* and tells of the extreme hardships the family encounters upon returning home from the internment camp.

_____. *Journey to Topaz.* Illustrated by Donald Carrick. New York: Scribner, 1971. (Ages 9–12.)
Yuki and her family are torn from their comfortable Berkeley home and placed in the internment camp for Japanese-Americans in Utah. The family endures terrible deprivation with a surprising amount of tolerance for their oppressors.

WOLKSTEIN, DIANE. *White Wave: A Chinese Tale.* Illustrated by Ed Young. New York: Crowell, 1979. (Ages 7–up.)
The moon goddess visits and befriends a poor young man, and he is appropriately grateful. The beautiful illustrations and the well-told tale combine to make a fine book.

YASHIMA, TARO. *Crow Boy.* Illustrated by the author. New York: Viking, 1955. Also in paper. (Ages 5–8.)
Chibi's schoolmates tease him because he is shy and different from them. A new teacher encourages him to express his talents and all of his peers appreciate him at last. Illustrations enhance the text.

_____. *Umbrella.* Illustrated by the author. New York: Viking, 1958. Also in paper. (Ages 5–8.)
As with the other work of this author, the story is sensitively and beautifully told, and the illustrations delight the eye.

YEP, LAWRENCE. *Child of the Owl.* New York: Harper & Row, 1977. (Ages 12–up.)
Casey must stay with her grandmother in Chinatown after having lived a very assimilated and transient existence with her gambler-father. In the story, Casey at last values her heritage.

YEP, LAWRENCE. *Dragon of the Lost Sea.* New York: Harper & Row, 1982. (Ages 11–up.)
Based upon an old Chinese myth, the story follows a shape-changing dragon and her companion, Thorn, a human boy, in their adventures to combat evil.

_____. *Dragonwings.* New York: Harper & Row, 1975. (Ages 12–up.)
Telling the story of one family's emigration from China to America, the author creates special characters who somehow translate into universal reflections of many people.

_____. *Sea Glass.* New York: Harper & Row, 1979. (Ages 12–up.)
Craig Chin can't fit into any of the worlds he has been forced to live in. His peers, family, and community look at him with displeasure. Except for Uncle Quail, who takes him into yet another world.

BIBLIOGRAPHY: HISPANIC AMERICANS

ACUNA, RUDY. *A Mexican American Chronicle.* New York: American Books, 1971. (Ages 12–up.)
Provides a different view of the Spanish "conquerors" and presents an extensive study of Indian civilizations in Mexico. The book proceeds to modern times and takes a militant perspective in discussing contemporary problems facing Mexican Americans.

ACUNA, RUDY. *The Story of Mexican-Americans: The Men and the Land.* New York: American Books, 1969. (Ages 6–9.)
Gives young readers an excellent introduction to the history of Mexican Americans in the Southwest. Includes a thorough look at Indian heritage as well as Spanish.

ANCONA, GEORGE. *Growing Older.* Photographs by the author. New York: Dutton, 1978. (Ages 10–up.)
An excellent book of biographies, including those of two Mexican Americans, illustrating the beauty and energy of the lives of people who have now grown old.

BARRY, ROBERT. *Ramon and the Pirate Gull.* Illustrated by the author. New York: McGraw-Hill, 1971. (Ages 5–8.)
Ramon, a young boy who lives in Ponce, Puerto Rico, sights a rare gull, captures it, and returns it to the Marine Research Station in San Juan.

BELPRE, PURA. *Once in Puerto Rico.* Illustrated by Christine Price. New York: Frederick Warne, 1973. (Ages 8–11.)
Puerto Rican tales and legends including historical and animal tales. Told in an interesting style.

_____. *Santiago.* Illustrated by Symeon Shimin. New York: Frederick Warne, 1969. (Ages 6–9.)
Santiago's mother and teacher respond sensitively to him when they realize how much he misses his native Puerto Rico.

BERNARD, JACQUELINE. *Voices from the Southwest: Antonio Jose Martinez, Elfego Baca, Reies Lopez Tijerina.* New York: Scholastic Books, 1972 (Ages 10–up.)
Chronicles the lives of three Mexican Americans who figured in the history of the American Southwest. Antonio Jose Martinez, Elfego Baca, and Reies Lopez Tijerina are the men who are described here.

BOUCHARD, LOIS KALB. *The Boy Who Wouldn't Talk.* Illustrated by Ann Grifalconi. Garden City, New York: Doubleday, 1969. (Ages 7–10.)
Carlos decides to stop talking because he is primarily Spanish-speaking and is uncomfortable with English. Carlos helps a blind boy who, in turn, helps Carlos to put things into a different perspective.

BUCKLEY, PETER. *I Am from Puerto Rico.* Illustrated with photographs. New York: Simon and Schuster, 1971. (Ages 10–up.)
The photographs are the most valuable part of this book because they graphically demonstrate the diversity of the Puerto Rican population.

CHARDIET, BERNICE. *Juan Bobo and the Pig.* Illustrated by Hope Meryman. New York: Walker, 1973. (Ages 5–9.)
A classic folk tale of the simpleton, found in many cultures, and retold here in a flavorful style.

COLORADO, ANTONIO J. *The First Book of Puerto Rico.* New York: Franklin Watts, 1972. (Ages 12–up.)
Although this edition is out of date, the photographs and information about the history, economics, and people of Puerto Rico are useful.

DE GARZA, PATRICIA. *Chicanos: The Story of Mexican-Americans.* Illustrated with photographs. New York: Julian Messner, 1973. (Ages 9–12.)
The history of Mexican Americans up to the present, as told through the accounts of individuals.

EVERTON, MACDUFF. *El Circo Magico Modelo/Finding the Magic Circus.* Illustrated by the author. Minneapolis: Carolrhoda Books. (Ages 5–9.)
The book's colorful illustrations are done in the style of the Huichol Indians' yarn paintings. The story is based on a real-life trip that the author and his son took to Mexico to visit friends and to revisit the Yucatan Circus where the author was once a performer. Spanish words are translated with a pronunciation guide at the back of the book. A very worthwhile addition to any library.

KOUZEL, DAISY. *The Cuckoo's Reward/El Premio del Cuco.* Illustrated by Earl Thollander. New York: Doubleday, 1977. (Ages 5–8.)

Told in both English and Spanish, the story is an adaptation of a Mayan legend explaining why the cuckoo lays her eggs in other birds' nests.

LASANTA, MIRIAM. "My Soul Speaks Spanish," in *The Voice of the Children*. New York: Holt, Rinehart and Winston, 1970. (Ages 8–12.)
This Puerto Rican poet is proud to be what she is. She does not want to be labeled.

LEVOY, MYRON. *Shadow like a Leopard*. New York: Harper & Row, 1981. (Ages 11–up.)
In order to prove his worth to a street gang, fourteen-year-old Ramon Santiago robs an old man, Arnold Glasser, at knife-point. Glasser is an artist; Ramon is a poet. The two characters form a surprising alliance and help each other to find a way out of their problems. Both are unforgettable characters: feisty, intelligent, talented, and unwilling to conform to what others want to force them to be.

MANN, PEGGY. *Luis Muñoz Marín: The Man Who Remade Puerto Rico*. New York: Coward, McCann and Geoghegan, 1976. (Ages 12–up.)
The story of Muñoz Marín's political struggles and achievements in improving the economy of Puerto Rico. Take care that this is not the only book to use as an indicator of the political and economic perspective of Puerto Ricans.

MARTEL, CRUZ. *Yagua Days*. Illustrated by Jerry Pinkney. New York: Dial Press, 1976. (Ages 5–9.)
Adan's parents take him for a visit to his relatives in Puerto Rico where he has a wonderful time with his extended family, and appreciates the beauty of the land, and the diversity and caring of the people.

MAURY, INEZ. *My Mother, the Mail Carrier/Mi Mama, la Cartera*. New York: Feminist Press, 1976. (Ages 4–7.)
Written in Spanish and English, the story centers on how a single parent can be an effective mother, mail carrier, and individual, all at the same time. The little boy loves his mother very much, and is very proud of her.

MELTZER, MILTON. *The Hispanic Americans*. New York: Crowell, 1982. (Ages 11–up.)
An excellent examination of three Hispanic peoples: Puerto Rican, Mexican and Cuban. The focus is on both their background and their current position in the United States. Photographs and personalized anecdotes make this a readable and informative book.

MOHR, NICHOLASA. *Felita*. Illustrated by Ray Cruz. New York: Dial Press, 1979. (Ages 8–12.)
Because of the bigotry eight-year-old Felita and her family encounter when they move away from the barrio, they decide that the new neighborhood is not better than their old one, and they move back to where they know they will have a supportive community. Felita's grandmother helps her to respect her Puerto Rican heritage.

NEWLON, CLARK. *Famous Puerto Ricans*. New York: Dodd, Mead, 1975. (Ages 12–up).
Carmen Maymi, Roberto Clemente, Luis Pales Matos, Herman Badillo, Concha

Melendez, and La Familia Figueroa are among the accomplished people described here. Readers should be encouraged to do further research and compile their own lists of notable Hispanics.

PAUL, PAULA G. *You Can Hear a Magpie Smile*. New York: Elsevier/Nelson, 1980. (Ages 9–12.)
A new doctor learns to value the ancient ways of healing in a remote Mexican village. The child, Lupe, will grow up to be respectful of both old and new ways.

PERL, LILA. *Piñatas and Paper Flowers: Holidays of the Americas in English and Spanish*. Illustrated by Victoria de Larrea. Spanish version by Alma Flor Ada. New York: Clarion, 1983. (Ages 7–10.)
Although the tone is a little condescending, and assumes that the reader is totally ignorant ("Christmas in January? How is that possible?" introduces the section on Three Kings' Day), there is interesting information in this book. Aimed more toward the non-Hispanic reader, it is a useful compendium of holiday customs.

_____. *Puerto Rico: Island between Two Worlds*. New York: Morrow, 1979. (Ages 12–up.)
A great amount of information is packed into this book about every aspect of Puerto Rico. It is clear that the author feels that it is a place worth learning about and visiting. Her presentation can be used as the basis for further research and debate.

POLITI, LEO. *Three Stalks of Corn*. New York: Scribner, 1976. (Ages 8–11.)
Corn legends form the background for the grandmother and her cooking of delicious Mexican food.

ROSARIO, IDALIA. *Idalia's Project ABC: An Urban Alphabet Book in English and Spanish*. New York: Holt, Rinehart and Winston, 1981. (Ages 4–7.)
Not like the usual alphabet book, this one is substantive in its depiction of positive urban life as well as some of the problems encountered in the city. An excellent book for any classroom.

SANDOVAL, RUBEN. *Games Games Games*. Photographs by David Strick. New York: Doubleday, 1977. (Ages 5–teen.)
A delightfully illustrated description of traditional games played by children of Mexico, and in the contemporary barrios in California.

SINGER, JULIA. *We All Come from Puerto Rico*. New York: Atheneum, 1977. (Ages 9–up.)
Although this book romanticizes Puerto Rico and makes it seem that there are no problems there, and although it focuses mainly on the light-skinned and the middle class, it is valuable because it demonstrates that Puerto Rico is a land of many different people. There is no stereotypic version of a Puerto Rican person.

WAGENHEIM, KAL, ed. *Short Stories from Puerto Rico*. San Juan, Puerto Rico: Institute of Puerto Rican Culture. Available also from Schocken, 1978. (Ages 12–up.)
This beautiful collection of stories contains several that are derived from the oral tradition, some that are concerned with contemporary times, and some that reflect historical themes. A very valuable book.

WHITE, FLORENCE M. *Cesar Chavez: Man of Courage*. Illustrated by Victor Mays. Champaign, Illinois: Garrard, 1973. (Ages 9–12.)
An admiring account of the labor leader's courage and vision.

BIBLIOGRAPHY: JEWISH AMERICANS

For books containing the topic of the Holocaust, see the bibliography at the end of the chapter on war. Holocaust entries are specially noted there.

ADLER, DAVID A. *The House on the Roof*. New York: Bonim Books, 1976. (Ages 5–7.)
The children's grandfather secretly brings in materials to their apartment house so that he can surprise them by building a Sukkah (little house) for Succoth (the harvest festival).

ARRICK, FRAN. *Chernowitz*. New York: Bradbury Press, 1981. Also in paper. (Ages 11–up.)
Bobby has never been very popular, but now he is the victim of a viciously anti-Semitic bully, who manages to align all of Bobby's former friends against him. Bobby does not confide in his parents until the situation reaches dangerous proportions. While the book is flawed in some of its developments, it does provide some insights and questions about the issue of gang psychology. The bully is a boy who is regularly beaten severely by his father. Realistically, Bobby recognizes at the end that no matter what he does, the bully will not become reasonable or appreciative of Jews.

BAER, EDITH. *A Frost in the Night: A Girlhood on the Eve of the Third Reich*. New York: Pantheon, 1980. (Ages 11–up.)
The book ends with the appointment of Adolf Hitler as Chancellor of Germany. Not a Holocaust story, the action takes place in Germany when the horror was in its infancy. Eva is a young Jewish girl whose life has been ideal until this time. It is her story that is told here.

BERNSTEIN, JOANNE E. *Dmitry, a Young Soviet Immigrant*. Illustrated by Michael J. Bernstein. New York: Clarion Books, 1981.
The photographs and text combine to present a clear picture of Dmitry and his family, who have recently emigrated from the Soviet Union. The family must struggle with their identities as Jews (they didn't go to Israel because they "didn't feel Jewish enough") with their difficult financial situation, their isolation from family and friends, the new language, customs, and expectations. The book ends on an encouraging note; the family will do well.

BLAINE, MARGE. *Dvora's Journey*. Illustrated by Gabriel Lisowski. New York: Holt, Rinehart and Winston, 1979. (Ages 8–11.)
For Jews in Russia at the turn of the century, life was not only difficult, it was dangerous. Twelve-year-old Dvora and her family risk the hardships of escape across the border in order to reach a ship, and passage to America.

BLUE, ROSE. *Grandma Didn't Wave Back*. Illustrated by Ted Lewin. New York: Franklin Watts, 1972. (Ages 7–10.)

It is difficult for Debbie, who loves her dearly, to understand why her grandmother must go to live in a nursing home. In the end all agree that this placement is the best solution. The book incidentally includes some Yiddish words and flavor.

BLUME, JUDY. *Are You There, God? It's Me, Margaret*. New York: Bradbury Press, 1970. Also in paper. (Ages 10–up.)
Margaret talks regularly to God about all of her problems. She spends some time and energy trying to sort out how she feels about religion. Her paternal grandmother wants her to be Jewish. Her maternal grandparents want her to be Christian. Her parents practice no religion and are distressed by her interest in going to religious services. Margaret finally comes to the conclusion that she will have to take more time and thought in order to decide what religion she will select.

BRENNER, BARBARA. *A Year in the Life of Rosie Bernard*. New York: Harper & Row, 1971. Also in paper. (Ages 8–12.)
Rosie's father is Jewish. Her mother was Christian. When Rosie is staying with her maternal grandparents she decides that she will investigate the Jewish religion. Eventually she postpones any decision about what religion she will choose to be.

CHAIKIN, MIRIAM. *How Yossi Beat the Evil Urge*. Illustrated by Petra Mathers. New York: Harper & Row, 1983. (Ages 8–10.)
A warmly told story of a young boy, growing up in an Orthodox, Chasidic family and community, who seems to be unable to concentrate on his studies. Although his teachers seem unsympathetic, his friends, his family, and his special talent see him through.

———. *I Should Worry, I Should Care*. Illustrated by Richard Egielski. New York: Harper & Row, 1979. (Ages 7–10.)
The flavor of life in Brooklyn in the 1930s as part of a working-class Jewish family comes through strongly in each of the books about Molly (there are three). In each of the stories, Jewish foods, customs, and language figure as part of the setting. Molly is a somewhat self-centered but sensitive young girl who cares about others and their feelings, but sometimes forgets to show it. She is a very human protagonist, and the family is a loving one.

CHAPMAN, CAROL. *The Tale of Meshka the Kvetch*. Illustrated by Arnold Lobel. New York: Dutton, 1980. (Ages 5–9.)
Written in folk tale style, this amusing story is enhanced by the illustrations. The old woman learns an important lesson about the value of focusing on the positive rather than always complaining.

COHEN, BARBARA. *Yussel's Prayer: A Yom Kippur Story*. Illustrated by Michael J. Deraney. New York: Lothrop, Lee and Shepard Books, 1981. (Ages 5–9.)
Yussel, a poor cowherd, teaches the entire congregation a lesson about the sincerity of prayer when only he can reach the ear of God. A loving tale, told in the style of a folktale.

COLMAN, HILA *Ellie's Inheritance*. New York: Morrow, 1979. (Ages 9–12.)
The sequel to *Rachel's Legacy*, the story of Ellie's mother. Set in the 1930s, the book shows how a young Jewish woman and her father redefine their lives after Rachel's

death and after all of their money is lost in the Stock Market crash. Ellie begins a career and learns to deal with people who are anti-Semitic. Fascism on the rise is also a topic in this story.

EISENBERG, PHYLLIS ROSE. *A Mitzvah Is Something Special*. Illustrated by Susan Jeschke. New York: Harper & Row, 1978. (Ages 5–9.)
Lisa's two grandmothers are very different from each other, at least in their behavior. But they both love Lisa, and they both enjoy it enormously when Lisa does a mitzvah (good deed) and invites them both over for an evening.

FASSLER, JOAN. *My Grandpa Died Today*. Illustrated by Stewart Kranz. New York: Behavorial Publications, 1971. (Ages 3–8.)
A boy's grandfather dies, and he feels sad and empty until after the funeral, when his parents encourage him to go outside and play. At first he feels guilty about resuming his normal activities, but then he realizes that this is what his grandfather would have wanted for him. Jewish mourning customs are alluded to in this book and might provide a context for the discussion of other cultures' rituals.

FAST, HOWARD. *The Jews: Story of a People*. New York: Dial Press, 1968. Also in paper. (Ages 12–up.)
A wonderfully readable, comprehensive study of Jewish history, including photographs and maps. The author raises many questions about the survival of the Jews, persecution, and population patterns. He also supplies some possible answers. The book concludes with the creation of the Jewish State in Israel, and leaves the reader with more questions to try to answer.

GIRION, BARBARA. *A Tangle of Roots*. New York: Scribner, 1979. Also in paper. (Ages 11–up.)
Beth's mother dies suddenly of a cerebral hemorrhage. The story details all of Beth's reactions, the Jewish ritual of the funeral and mourning, and the way that the family tries to readjust their lives afterward. Beth's relationships with her friends and family change after her mother's death. All of the responses are believable and the pace of the book is appropriate to the topic. Many details of Jewish family life are unobtrusively included. Beth's disbelief when she is told of her mother's death, her grief and reassessment of her own life, her fear of desertion, and her gradual recovery are well developed in the book.

FITZGERALD, JOHN D. *The Great Brain*. Illustrated by Mercer Mayer. New York: Dell, 1967. Paperback. (Ages 8–12.)
The image of the Jew in this book is not handled well. But the book is so well written and so popular that it might be a good idea to bring the issue up for discussion with young readers. Abie Glasman appears in two chapters of this book. He is an elderly Jewish itinerant peddler who has been persuaded by the townspeople to stop his traveling and open a variety store in Adenville, Utah. He literally starves to death because he is too proud to ask for help, and because the townspeople assume that because he is a Jew, he is wealthy. In their guilt, they give him a Christian burial to salve their consciences. Many discussions can arise from this act alone.

GOFFSTEIN, M. B. *Family Scrapbook*. Illustrated by the author. New York: Farrar, Straus & Giroux, 1978. (Ages 8–11.)

Seven tales of a Jewish family and their everyday adventures are sensitively, amusingly, and lovingly told.

GOLDREICH, GLORIA, ed. *A Treasury of Jewish Literature from Biblical Times to Today*. New York: Holt, Rinehart and Winston, 1982. (Ages 12–up.)
Selections of writings from the time of the Torah to the present. An excellent sampling is included, representing a vast and varied heritage.

HERMAN, CHARLOTTE. *The Difference of Ari Stein*. New York: Harper & Row, 1976. (Ages 8–12.)
Ari's family is orthodox. Ari's friends in this new neighborhood in Brooklyn try to lead him astray, but in the end, family and tradition win out. Jewish customs well portrayed.

HEYMAN, ANNA. *Exit from Home*. New York: Crown, 1977. (Ages 12–up.)
A Russian Jewish boy from a pious family moves away from his religion and becomes active in the Revolution of 1905. He escapes to America. The book is one of the few that points out the conflict between secular and religious Jews.

HURWITZ, JOHANNA. *Once I Was a Plum Tree*. New York: Morrow, 1980. (Ages 8–12.)
Gerry Flam's family's name used to be Pflamenbaum, or "Plumtree". They have become assimilated, and even somewhat alienated from their Jewish background. Gerry finally finds the opportunity to learn about her heritage from a family who are escapees from the Holocaust.

_____. *The Rabbi's Girls*. Illustrated by Pamela Johnson. New York: Morrow, 1982. (Ages 8–12.)
Carrie's father is a rabbi, and the family has moved from one congregation to the next for the past eleven years. Rabbi Levin is an idealist, and is often not practical or selfish enough to suit the influential members of his congregation. This story takes place in 1923, in Ohio. The family endures anti-semitism, illness, and, finally, the death of the father, but the tone of the story is one of hope and determination, and the strength of the characters emerges as the overriding element.

ISADORA, RACHEL. *Jesse and Abe*. Illustrated by the author. New York: Greenwillow Books, 1981. (Ages 4–8.)
Jesse enjoys visiting his grandfather, Abe, at work. Abe works backstage at a Broadway theater. Jesse learns how much his grandfather is valued one night when Abe is late for work. Jesse also becomes aware of how much he loves Abe.

ISH-KISHOR, SULAMITH. *A Boy of Old Prague*. Illustrated by Ben Shahn. New York: Pantheon, 1963. Also in paper. (Ages 10–up.)
Set in Old Prague, in the sixteenth century, the story is narrated by Tomas, a young serf who is sent to be the servant of a Jew, as a punishment for stealing food. All of the superstitions and prejudices of the time are described in the story, and Tomas finds himself constantly astonished by the truth. The ending is tragic: the ghetto is burned, and many Jews are tortured and murdered. But Tomas's life is changed as a result of his new understanding, and the reader is taught some ugly history lessons.

LASKY, KATHRYN. *The Night Journey*. Illustrated by Trina Schart Hyman. New York: Frederick Warne, 1981. (Ages 11–up.)

Rachel's great-grandmother tells her stories about life long ago in czarist Russia, and how Jews were treated in those times. The book is full of flavorful language and customs of Jewish families. The old great-grandmother is greatly valued in the family, but particularly so by Rachel.

MELTZER, MILTON. *Remember the Days: A Short History of the Jewish American.* Illustrated by Harvey Dinnerstein. Garden City, New York: Doubleday, 1974. Also in paper. (Ages 10–up.)
A well-written and informative account of Jews in America from 1654 to contemporary times. Facts such as the origin of the term "anti-Semitism" and explanations of the sources of stereotyping behavior help to illuminate the history, not only of the Jewish American, but also of our country in general.

SACHS, MARILYN. *Call Me Ruth.* Garden City, New York: Doubleday, 1982. (Ages 9–up.)
Ruth and her mother emigrate from Russia to New York City. Ruth's father had worked for nine years to save enough money to send for them. Ruth loves America from the moment she arrives; her mother hates it. They are poor; their apartment has no toilet or bath; the father is ill, and soon dies. Afterward, the mother becomes active in the labor movement, causing enormous embarrassment to Ruth. Ruth is a very bright, academically talented child; she works hard at school, loves to read, and is considered a model child. The author presents several points of view clearly and sympathetically. She also conveys an accurate historical view of early twentieth century labor and immigrant issues.

SEVELA, EPHRAIM. *Why There is No Heaven on Earth.* New York: Harper & Row, 1982. (Ages 11–up.)
The young narrator tells of his growing up in a small city in Russia, around the time of the World War II. He tells of the anti-Semitism, the politics, the way of life of the poor people, and of a friend of his named Berele Mats. He idolizes his friend, and says that because Berele died young there can be no heaven on earth. The style of the prose is that of an old folk tale, rich in sensory images, and flavored with the sounds of the people's accents and sayings.

SINGER, ISAAC BASHEVIS. *The Power of Light: Eight Stories for Hannukah.* Illustrated by Irene Lieblich. New York: Farrar, Straus & Giroux, 1980. (Ages 8–up.)
Each of the stories tells of a miracle. Imbedded in the tales is much about Jewish tradition. Masterfully written, the stories provide ethical as well as dramatic content. The Nobel Prize-winning author has several collections of tales for children, all dealing with Jewish themes.

SKOLSKY, MINDY WARSHAW. *Hannah and the Best Father on Route 9W.* Illustrated by Karen Ann Weinhaus. New York: Harper & Row, 1982. (Ages 8–11.)
The fourth in the series of Hannah books (*The Whistling Teakettle, Carnival and Kopek*, and *Hannah Is a Palindrome* are the other three) continues the story of Hannah, a young Jewish girl growing up in the 1930s in rural New York. Her family and friends participate in the gentle and engaging adventures attendant upon owning a diner on Route 9W, and growing up with Jewish customs and traditions. The other three books focus on the relationship between Hannah and her grandmother. Everyone appreciates Hannah, who is a bright, loving child.

SNYDER, CAROL. *Ike and Mama and the Once-in-a-Lifetime Movie.* Illustrated by Charles Robinson. New York: Coward, McCann & Geoghegan, 1981. (Ages 7–10.) Jewish speech and customs flavor this series of books (this is the third one) about Ike and his mother, living in the Bronx in the era of the First World War. In this episode Ike and his friends manage to appear in a D. W. Griffith film.

SOBOL, HARRIET LANGSTON. *Grandpa: A Young Man Grown Old.* Illustrated by Patricia Agre. New York: Coward, McCann & Geoghegan, 1980. (Ages 10–up.) The life of Morris Kaye, a Jewish immigrant—a modest, dignified "young man grown old"—described in words and actual family photographs from two vantage points: Morris's, as he looks back on seventy-eight years, and that of his seventeen-year-old granddaughter Karen, who loves and respects him for what he has accomplished and for the part he has played in her own growing up.

SUSSMAN, SUSAN. *There's No Such Thing as a Chanukah Bush, Sandy Goldstein.* Illustrated by Charles Robinson. Niles, Illinois: Whitman, 1983. (Ages 6–10.) Although Robin goes to a public school, the preparation for and celebration of Christmas occupies a substantial amount of class time. Robin, who is Jewish, is very uncomfortable and somewhat envious of all of the trappings of Christmas. Her friend, Heather, who attends Catholic School, wants to know why Robin can't have a tree, and call it a Chanukah Bush, as Sandy Goldstein (whom we never meet) does. Robin's family help her to work through the problem, assuring her that though they will not have a tree, she can wholeheartedly celebrate with her friends on their holidays, as they can with her.

TAYLOR, SYDNEY. *All-of-a-Kind Family Downtown.* Illustrated by Beth and Joe Krush. Chicago: Follett, 1972. Also in paper. (Ages 8–12.) Fourth in a series containing *All-of-a-Kind Family, More-All-of-a-Kind Family*, and *All-of-a-Kind Family Uptown*. The stories describe a Jewish family containing five sisters and one brother growing up in New York in the early twentieth century. The sisters do everything together and always think of one another's feelings. The family is pious, just, loving, and cooperative. Although the children occasionally do naughty things, they always confess and set it right. The stories are very well written and convey a flavor of the era.

BIBLIOGRAPHY: OTHER HERITAGES

The paucity of books on heritages other than the ones already listed is an obvious problem. Listed here are only a few books that specifically deal with different heritages. While there are others, there is an insufficient amount to use as a significant body of material for classroom use. It is to be hoped that authors and publishers will take note of this situation and remedy it.

LEVOY, MYRON. *The Witch of Fourth Street and Other Stories.* Illustrated by Gabriel Lisowski. New York: Harper & Row, 1972. (Ages 6–10.) Eight stories about people living in the Lower East Side of Manhattan in the early 1900s. All of the families are immigrants from different countries of the world; all have in common their dream of a better life for themselves and their children. With flavorful words and pictures, the stories engage children at the same time that they instruct them about the feelings and customs of each group.

PELLOWSKI, ANNE. *First Farm in the Valley: Anna's Story.* Illustrated by Wendy Watson. New York: Philomel Books, 1982. (Ages 10–up.)
The fourth in a series of stories about a community of Polish-Americans who settled in Latsch Valley, Wisconsin, in the late nineteenth and early twentieth century. The stories focus particularly on one family, modeled from the author's own, and follow the family through four generations. Although this book is the fourth in the series, chronologically, it takes place first. Each of the stories describes Polish customs and heritage in a loving, detailed, and respectful manner.

SANDIN, JOAN. *The Long Way to a New Land.* New York: Harper & Row, 1981. (Ages 5–8.)
The detailed illustrations by the author add to the information children can receive from this story about the emigration of a Swedish family to America in the last half of the nineteenth century.

SPIER, PETER. *People.* New York: Doubleday 1980. (All ages.)
A beautifully illustrated book dealing with all aspects of people's appearance. The author provides us with a wonderful profusion of different types of eyes, noses, colors, hair. The overall effect is to value diversity.

STEICHEN, EDWARD. *The Family of Man.* Prologue by Carl Sandburg. New York: Museum of Modern Art, 1955. (All Ages.)
This book brings home the point that we all are, in fact, part of the human family. Through verse and pictures, the author illustrates the common experiences all people share: birth, happiness, grief, having a mother, having a father, the right to vote, the joys of children, the aloneness people experience—and many more. Could be very useful in a classroom for discussion.

SIX

SPECIAL NEEDS

THE YEAR 1981 WAS DESIGNATED BY THE UNITED NATIONS as "The International Year of Disabled Persons." During this year public awareness and sensitivity were aroused. Projects were funded to help make buildings and streets accessible to people in wheelchairs; devices aiding people who are hearing- or sight-impaired were added to public institutions such as libraries and schools. Laws had already been passed in several states providing for special education for exceptional children. In 1975, with implementation scheduled for September 1978, Public Law 94-142 was enacted by the Congress of the United States. Aimed at correcting some of the problems that children with special needs had encountered in the public schools, The Education for All Handicapped Children Act requires that disabled children be placed in an educational environment that will be least restrictive. That is, children who until now had been deprived of appropriate placement must be incorporated into the regular classroom wherever possible (mainstreamed), and provided with an educational plan most suitable for them. Parents are invited to participate in the decision-making process; no educational plan is implemented until parents have approved it.

This law also prohibits the detrimental labeling of children with special needs. Language is an important factor in any movement. Describing people by their characteristics and behavior is preferable to viewing them as creatures of their disability, with no other distinguishing attributes. "Cripple," "retard," and other terms depriving disabled people of their individuality should not be used. Developmental disabilities or impaired mobility should be described as such, without implying that these conditions constitute the whole person.

This chapter deals with children's literature containing characters who have special needs. The category includes not only children who are physically disabled but also those with emotional problems; those who are substance abusers; children who have, themselves, been abused; gifted children; and characters who feel, act, or look different from most of their peers. Almost any child might fit into one of these categories. Each child in the world has special needs, and has the right to receive respect, sensitivity, and appropriate humane behavior from others.

Many of us are somewhat uncomfortable when we are with people who are considerably or noticeably different from ourselves. We are used to a certain range of abilities, and a fairly narrow set of standards of appearance. We often label groups and ourselves by appearance and behavior. People tend to dress and behave alike within the confines of their own group, thus creating their own "uniforms." They form a contrast to other groups, and often deliberately set themselves apart. When we do this on purpose, we understand that we are inviting positive reactions from some people, and negative ones from others. But when we have no control over these factors, then we are likely to suffer from other people's responses.

"Normal" children, too, are victims of certain myths that prevail about disabled people. They are often afraid to talk to or even stand near people with disabilities because they are afraid that the disability is contagious. Even adults become anxious about their own physical well-being when they are faced with someone else's condition. Just as the death of a person reminds us of our own mortality, a disability reminds us of our own vulnerability. Sometimes this reminder makes us empathic; sometimes it causes us to be fearful.

When we do not know people as friends, we are sometimes tempted to classify them by their obvious attributes ("the blond;" "the fat one"). We would do well to help ourselves and our students move away from these limiting and dehumanizing categorizations toward a response to the whole, complex individual. We should also acknowledge that all people have the ability to give as well as receive, and can participate in activities that involve the whole community.

Although we, as helping adults, would prefer to think of ourselves as open-minded and unbiased, we do ourselves and others a disservice if we do not confront our own feelings and prejudgments. How can we change our negative attitudes if we are unwilling to admit that they exist?

•TRY THIS

Place an X in the appropriate column. Think about the implications of your answers. Determine which of your attitudes or behaviors you will want to change in the future. Assess which ones you will want to affirm and strengthen.

Attitudes/Beliefs	True	False	Don't Know
1. I pity disabled people.			
2. I have friends who are disabled.			
3. Disabled people should be integral members of the work force.			

4. People who use wheelchairs cannot engage in sexual intercourse.			
5. Most communications disabilities are paired with mental retardation.			
6. Disabled people are usually sweet and kind.			
7. Disabled people develop "super" powers in areas other than their disability			
8. Disabled people must rely upon and be cared for by "normal" people.			
9. Handicapping barriers are imposed on disabled people by our society.			
10. I am comfortable talking to disabled people about their disabilities.			

When we are able to confront our fears, ignorance, superstitions, and lack of ease, and build on our knowledge, comfort, and positive experiences, we can help children to approach and cope with their feelings toward people with disabilities. Movies, television, newspapers, and books often reinforce stereotypes and inaccuracies, simply because the writers have not taken the trouble to research their topic extensively enough. Many resources are available, free of charge, to the public. A list of some helpful agencies and organizations is included at the end of this chapter.

•TRY THIS

Answer the following questions. Add others that will help test your knowledge. Find out how you can expand your current information.

How much help do disabled people need? How do I offer help? How do people with special needs feel about being with people who are different from themselves? How do people with special needs feel about talking about their particular condition? How regularly should "typical" children come into contact with children with special needs? How do I show my interest and curiosity to people about their special need? What is the best learning environment for a child with special needs? How can I determine this? What aspects of a child's life are affected by his or her special need? Which ones have nothing to do with the special need? What agencies offer information about particular special needs? What laws has my state passed that affect disabled people? What percentage of the population of my state is disabled? . . . my community? . . . the country?

STEREOTYPES

Social psychologists tell us that stereotypes of disabled people are maintained because groups that are unlike the cultural majority are isolated, have few opportunities to develop intimate relations with nondisabled people, and are treated in ways that correspond to their stereotypes. What is more, they are rewarded for living up to others' image of them, and punished in subtle ways for breaking out of the mold. They are expected to be helpless, sweet-natured (or constantly complaining), nonsexual, passive, and uninterested in anything but their own condition.

Because specific mental, emotional, or physical impairments are not generally characteristic of the protagonists in children's books, disabled people seem illegitimate in ordinary society. Or because of their absence from the books they may feel invisible.

Another problem occurs when a disabled person is depicted as an evil villain. In many folk and fairy tales people with physical deformities, people who are smaller or larger than the expected standard size, and people who do not conform to the current societal norms of beauty are used as devices to frighten and menace the child protagonists. Witness too how many stories have characters with a patch on one eye, or wearing a wooden leg as a signal that the person is wicked.

Often, when a person in a children's book is disabled, we know that the character is bound to die soon, and be assured a seat with the angels. They are "too good to live." The romanticized stereotype is so strong that we are sometimes surprised when we encounter a disabled person who has normal emotions and behaves in the same way as a nondisabled person.

We have moved away from using a disabled person as a comic foil, but many books portray disabled people as the butt of the other characters' bad humor. This unfortunate and ugly behavior does occur in real life. When it occurs in a book, adults should intervene with young readers and invite them to think about the effect of this demeaning behavior both on the bully and on the disabled person.

Sometimes a disability is portrayed as being something that with positive thinking, prayer, and hard work the disabled person can not only overcome, but also can make disappear. This has the effect of making it seem as if disabled people are the cause of their own disabilities, and presents an unrealistic fantasy that cures can be effected just from wishing them to be so, and from "good" behavior. This does disabled people an incredible injustice; the implication is that if they worked hard enough their disabilities would disappear.

Disabled people, like Native Americans and blacks, are very often expendable in the story. Sometimes in the process of saving the life of a protagonist, and sometimes just in the course of the plot, they die, which is a convenient way of getting rid of them and gives the impression that their very presence is a problem that can only be solved by their disappearance.

People with special needs may be described as "loners." They are portrayed as not having normal friendships, sexual involvement, or social interactions. They do not seem to have normal feelings or desires. Sometimes society behaves in a way that excludes disabled people from social circles, not because they cannot function well in these circles but because nondisabled people have negative attitudes and translate these attitudes into restrictive behavior.

Disabled people, no matter how old they are, are often looked upon and treated as children. Their capabilities, maturity, and sexuality are ignored in favor of a protective, patronizing attitude. They are sheltered from bad news, hard work, and other realities of everyday existence.

Disabled people are sometimes depicted as being superhuman. In this respect an analogy may be drawn to the treatment of females. Sometimes, in books as well as life, in order to gain acceptance, women must display heroic qualities: they must be the first of their sex to have accomplished something (the first woman doctor, judge, astronaut). So too it is with disabled people. They must save someone's life, be superheroic or supercompetent. They are not permitted to have ordinary flaws, to be average, nonspectacular people. And that, again, is an injustice.

One way for children to judge the fairness of a book is to have them look at these stereotypes and then to use them as a filter in the books that they read. They should notice if in a wide range of population there is no mention of any person with disabilities. Perhaps they can design some characters for inclusion in these books, or they can judge how the book would differ if any of the existing characters were described as having disabilities.

•TRY THIS

Look for books in which there are characters who are disabled.

1. List the characters and their disabilities. How many of them die during the course of the story? Describe their personalities; compare them to their nondisabled peers. Note the language used to describe the disabled characters.
2. Discuss how the story would be affected if the disability were removed.
3. Equip other characters with the disability; how would the action change?

Gifted people, not usually included in the category of disability, do have special needs, and are victims of stereotypic classification. The mad scientist; spoiled, conceited "brain"; weak, unathletic boy; unpopular, unattractive girl; emotionally disturbed outcast—all are commonly held preconceptions that can be found in real life as well as literature.

SUGGESTED CRITERIA

People with special needs are individuals. They have complex personalities, and are capable of many activities. They are as talented in as many areas as any other people are, and are as untalented in equally as many areas as their nonspecial peers. They can be angry, pleasant, nasty, loving, and irritable in the same proportions as anyone else, and literature should portray them in this balanced way.

Readers should look for books in which disabled people are respected, not pitied. Although they should not necessarily perform heroic acts, and should certainly not be superhuman, the characters should be depicted as capable of helping themselves and others. They should be shown as coping with their disability, rather than being rewarded with a miraculous cure because of their positive thoughts and/or good behavior. If a book is to deal with a disability, its effect is diminished if the "problem" simply goes away. What is the disabled person's view of him or herself? If it is negative, what has caused this? What changes occur in the course of the story to help modify this attitude?

Special attention should be paid to the language used to describe disabled people. It should be specifically descriptive of a behavior or condition. A person should be described as having epilepsy rather than as "the epileptic." If it is known that someone has Down's syndrome, that specific term is preferable to the more general, "mentally retarded." The word "disability" is preferred to "handicap." Joan Tollison comments in her "Open Letter" (see References), "It might be possible to draw a parallel between 'handicapped' and 'Negro,' between 'disabled' and 'Black,' and between 'cripple' and 'nigger.'" Barbara Baskin and Karen Harris state (in *Notes from a Different Drummer*) that "... a *disability* is a reality, for example, the loss of vision. The restrictions and opportunities imposed by society determine whether or not the disability becomes a *handicap*."

Accuracy is particularly important when an author is describing the behavior of a disabled character. Generalities or invented characteristics mislead readers, and cause them either to have unrealistic expectations or to misunderstand the consequences of a specific disability. Similarly, the setting should also be described accurately. Institutions are rarely romantic, ideal havens, or, conversely, torture chambers. With the current emphasis on placement in regular schools and halfway houses, most people with disabilities are now likely to have a setting that is outside an institution. If "special" classes or schools are described in a book, it should be made clear that this is the least restrictive environment for the disabled person.

Any book of quality avoids the pairing of physical attributes with personality traits or intellectual ability. A person who is physically attractive need not be emptyheaded ("beautiful but dumb"); a person with a spinal deformity need not be wicked. Using a physical characteristic as a literary signal diminishes the impact of the writing.

Disabled people are generally capable of loving relationships. They belong to families, and can maintain close friendships. Their desires and sexuality do not differ from those of the general population, and books should reflect this fact.

Books should also take care that violence or tragedy is not a by-product of disability. If either occurs as a realistic result of an action of the plot, it should not be linked only with a disabled person. (Too often, disabled people are depicted either as victims or perpetrators of violence.)

It is important to notice the attitudes of the nondisabled characters toward the disabled. How does the author indicate what the desired behavior should be? If the attitude of a favored character toward disabilities is disrespectful and negative, how is the reader informed of this? If these attitudes change for the better, how realistic is this change? Facts embedded skillfully into a work of fiction accomplish much more than moralizing. For example, if, without special attention called to it, a disabled person is shown as effective at his or her job, then young readers are more likely to assume that disabled people can be expected to be competent at their work. (Studies have demonstrated that disabled employees perform well at their jobs, are highly motivated, and have a lower absentee rate and incur fewer disabling job-related injuries than the rest of the population. They also have been proven to do work that is equal in quantity and quality to that of their nondisabled peers.)

When disabled people are characters in books (and they should appear in at least the same proportion as they exist in real life), they should be as fully dimensional as the other characters, with the same flaws, strengths, problems, feelings, and responses. They should also be varied in their race, economic background, social class, religion, age, and lifestyle as well as being represented in different genres such as poetry, fiction, folktales, nonfiction, adventure tales, and fantasy in the array of books available to young readers.

Disabled people should appear as minor characters as well as protagonists. Not freaks, they should be incorporated into the action as individuals able to perform a wide variety of tasks and able to handle their own lives.

Gifted individuals should also be described in a balanced, nonstereotypic manner. A talent should be part of a character's overall makeup, not something unnatural, superimposed, and having an existence of its own. Giftedness should be valued, not ridiculed; gifted characters should not necessarily be nasty, conceited, or isolated, unless the plot and interaction with the other characters logically calls for these qualities.

Interaction with people with special needs is the best way to counteract negative preconceptions. Becoming conscious of the stereotypes or lack of them in books that they read will also contribute to children's better relationships with all people in their daily lives.

DISCUSSION OF CHILDREN'S BOOKS

LEARNING PROBLEMS

Learning disabilities should not be confused with mental retardation. These disabilities sometimes carry the same symptoms as brain damage, but no hard evidence can be found to support this diagnosis. Learning disability is not generally considered to be a medical problem. Children who, for any of many reasons, although mentally competent, cannot succeed in schoolwork are often diagnosed to have a learning disability. They may have visual or auditory perception problems, and they may have difficulty with muscular coordination. When the difficulty is particularly in the area of reading, the condition is often called dyslexia (specific language disorder). It is always a controversial diagnosis. Some experts believe that most "learning disabilities" are, in fact, the results of poor or improper teaching methods. Whatever the cause, the treatment is usually the same: the children engage in activities involving their muscles and sense of touch. They are encouraged to find physical ways of getting meaning from written symbols. Good teachers also try to find materials and topics that interest these children so that they will be drawn into the reading process through their own volition rather than by external pressure.

In *Kelly's Creek*, by Doris Buchanan Smith, the young boy must practice meaningless perceptual exercises, and does not benefit from them. He hates to do them. He would much rather play in the creek that runs near his house, where he has a friend who values him, and where he can do things he enjoys. He displays special knowledge about pond life, and demonstrates that he is mentally competent, even if he cannot read.

Several important lessons may be learned from this book. Although motor skills are usually an important factor in helping children overcome learning disabilities, the most important ingredient in their (or anyone's) learning process is motivation and the pairing of educational materials with the interests of the child. Small successes build on each other and self-esteem follows, and contributes to the overall success of the program. Kelly's school experience is limiting rather than enhancing his abilities because the focus is on mechanical exercises rather than on getting personal meaning from learning. Joe Lasker's book about a boy whose family understands and helps him deal with his learning disabilities brings up other factors, such as peer acceptance and the valuing of a person's positive qualities. The book, *He's My Brother*, is lovingly narrated by Jamie's older brother.

Not many books include characters who exhibit learning disabilities. Some of the books containing this topic demean the children who are having learning difficulties; some distort the behaviors; some treat the issue as a mysterious malady that cannot be overcome. It is important for readers of these books to verify the accuracy of the details, and discuss some alternative treatment of the characters.

Rose Blue's *Me and Einstein*, helps children to recognize that dyslexia has little, if anything, to do with a person's potential for success, or with innate ability. It is pointed out in the book that famous people such as Winston Churchill, Thomas Edison, Woodrow Wilson, and Albert Einstein probably had this condition. The book deals with the dilemma of a bright, motivated boy for whom reading is an ordeal. He wants help, but doesn't know how to ask for it because he doesn't know what's wrong. He expends a great deal of energy trying to hide his condition, and because he is so bright, he manages to do this until he reaches the fourth grade. Then, in response to his teacher's thinking that he is simply not trying hard enough, he begins to get into trouble. Eventually he receives help, and enrolls in a special program for children with learning disabilities. For some people this is an unsatisfactory solution; they would prefer that the problem be handled within the context of the regular classroom, but it must also be recognized that not all teachers are capable of devoting the extra time and energy needed for children with special needs. In those cases, it might be preferable to provide some special help until the regular classroom can be a nurturing place.

NEUROLOGICAL DISABILITIES

Another condition that is too often confused with mental retardation is cerebral palsy. Although this impairment affects muscular control, it does not hamper thought. A frustrating concomitant is the lack of control over the muscles that work the speech organs, making it difficult for people with cerebral palsy to be understood.

Let the Balloon Go, by Ivan Southall, clearly and accurately describes the condition from the perspective of John, a twelve-year-old Australian boy who attempts to demonstrate to his overprotective mother and the rest of the world that despite his disorder he is capable of doing many things for himself. For younger children, *About Handicaps,* by Sara Bonnett Stein, helps to validate "normal" children's feelings about themselves and children with disabilities. Joe, Matthew's playmate, is pictured as a child with cerebral palsy. Matthew learns how to respond to Joe and to deal with his own fears when his father recognizes that Matthew is having difficulties, and lovingly and sensitively helps him handle them. The book's excellent photographs enhance the text. As with other "Open Family" books, a separate, simultaneous text is provided for adults' use.

INTELLECTUAL DISABILITIES

The language of disability is nowhere more complicated than in the realm of the intellect. Conventionally called retardation, intellectual impairment can result from congenital conditions such as Down's syndrome, brain tissue anomalies, chromosomal disorder, or prenatally acquired infections. Disorders of growth, poor nutrition, tumors, and certain degenerative diseases may also cause this condition, which is demonstrated by subnormal intellectual functioning.

Until the advent of laws providing for the mainstreaming of children with special needs into the regular classroom wherever possible, children with intellectual disabilities were shut off from any contact with other youngsters. They were labeled either "trainable," which meant that they had very low IQ scores (usually, under 55, but always depending on the capacity of the program to handle a certain number of students) and were not expected to learn how to do very much more than the minimal tasks of self-care, or "educable," which meant that they had scored somewhere between 55 and 80 (depending on the program's requirements) and could be taught to do minimal academic and functional tasks. This labeling usually had the detrimental effect of holding back these students from achieving what they could. The assumption was made that their limitations were of such magnitude that they could never take care of themselves, or function in "normal" society. Now the focus is on what they *can* do and many books are available to help other children understand and respond constructively to them.

One gem of a book that deals with this topic is Lucille Clifton's *My Friend Jacob*, which tells of the friendship between Sam, an eight-year-old black child, and Jacob, a seventeen-year-old white retarded young man. Jacob and Sam share a mutually rewarding friendship, and help both their mothers to understand the quality of their relationship. No labeling is present in the text; the illustrations are specific and sensitively drawn. This book helps set aside stereotypes and builds understanding.

Another excellent book is Harriet Sobol's *My Brother Steven Is Retarded*. The story is told from the perspective of Beth, Steven's eleven-year-old sister. Her negative feelings are presented without imparting a sense of guilt to the reader. The photographs permit us to enter into the family, and greatly enhance the text. For younger children, a similar book is Lucia Smith's *A Special Kind of Sister*, which again permits a nondisabled sibling to express her negative as well as positive emotions, and does not assign blame or negative attributes to the disabled child.

A sibling also narrates the story of *Welcome Home, Jellybean*, by Marlene Shyer. Neil is younger than his sister Geraldine (Jellybean), who has lived in an institutional setting since she was an infant because her parents felt that they couldn't deal with her intellectual disability. When the mother finally cannot cope any longer with her guilt, and insists on bringing Geraldine home, life changes considerably for the entire family. Neil feels embarrassment, anger, pride, love, and a variety of ambivalent emotions; Neil's father eventually moves out of the house. In the end it looks as though Geraldine, Neil, and their mother will make a good life for themselves. The strengths of this story lie in the vivid descriptions of Geraldine's behavior, and in Neil's growing understanding for her needs and his ability to nurture.

Readers and helping adults may benefit from discussing the dilemma faced by many families when their child's condition mandates an institutional setting. Sometimes home care is not feasible, and the family should be helped not to feel guilty when their decision is made for everyone's benefit.

PHYSICAL DISABILITIES

MOBILITY IMPAIRMENT

The range of disabilities resulting in impairment of mobility is a wide one. Conditions such as cerebral palsy, spastic diplegia, spina bifida, polio, scoliosis, and juvenile rheumatoid arthritis may involve only moderate impeding of walking, while these same conditions and others may require people to use a wheelchair, crutches, braces, prosthetic devices, or a cane to aid them in moving around.

Accessibility is a major problem for people whose mobility is impaired. Curbs, narrow door openings, stairs, gravel paths, slopes that are too steep, faulty illumination, doors that are difficult to open, inconvenient placement of facilities such as telephones, toilets, drinking fountains, light switches, handles, and knobs can cause them to become formidable obstacles.

Attitudinal barriers are sometimes more difficult to overcome than the physical ones. One book that helps dispel fears and false notions is *Don't Feel Sorry for Paul* by Bernard Wolf. Paul wears prosthetic devices that help him to be able to ride horseback and engage in ordinary everyday activities. The graphic photographs help satisfy a nondisabled child's need to look closely at a prosthetic device without being rude. Another book that does this is the already mentioned *About Handicaps* by Sara Bonnett Stein. A man who has a prosthesis for a hand shows how it works to Matthew (and to the young reader, who might be inquisitive about its form and operation). Another work of nonfiction, *What Do You Do When Your Wheelchair Gets a Flat Tire? Questions and Answers about Disabilities*, edited by Douglas Biklen and Michele Sokoloff, contains questions asked by children and answered by disabled children. It includes not only the factual responses, but also the emotional reactions of these children. The photographs portray a wide range of disabilities and a variety of children from different backgrounds.

The classic *Door in the Wall*, a Newbery Award winner by Marguerite de Angeli, is set in the Middle ages, in the wake of the bubonic plague. In it,

Robin, the young protagonist, has been left with withered and weak legs as a result of an unnamed illness. In one part of the story he is called "Cruikshanks" by his peers, and the monks tell him that it is not a derogatory term, but simply a description that identifies him. Children might be invited to discuss the effects of name-calling and the consequences of labeling a person by how he looks rather than honoring his given name. They may also trace the historic development of attitudes through the ages toward disabled people. Positive qualities in the book include Robin's acceptance of his disability, and his determination to function in the world as a contributing, competent, active individual. Students might want to debate whether Robin's heroism causes him to be accepted (this would signal an unconstructive perspective on the part of the author) or whether he has already been accepted for himself before his heroic act. Some people think that his disability is an advantage in this adventure, making it less likely that the enemy would suspect Robin. Others disagree, and say that this is another case where a disabled person must be heroic in order to gain respect and recognition. Whatever the outcome of the debate, there is sure to be some new learning on the part of the students. Most people agree that the story is very well written, and invites the reader's empathy and admiration rather than pity.

Another work of fiction also brings the reader into a sense of identification with the main character, and focuses on the story more than on the disability. *Deenie*, by Judy Blume, describes the reactions of its protagonist to the news that she has scoliosis. She is a typical adolescent, and she behaves in normal fashion. Her mother is too much the "pushy" cardboard shrew, but the story is amusing as well as informative, and helps the reader to acquire an understanding of what it is like to be threatened by a lack of mobility, and to have to make some difficult choices about treatment. It also explores the changes in Deenie's perceptions of other disabled people.

For younger readers, many books, among them Eloise Greenfield's *Darlene*, show that a wheelchair need not be a deterrent to enjoyment of life. *The Balancing Girl*, by Bernice Rabe, describes a classroom in which a little girl who uses a wheelchair demonstrates her abilities and engages in all sorts of activities, despite her motor disability. Other books with identical themes are listed in the Bibliography.

It is important for children to read books in which the disabled characters learn to help themselves rather than depend totally on others. Another example of this sort of book is *Run, Don't Walk,* by Harriet Savitz. In this story two teen-agers help to educate and persuade their community to cease its discrimination. Savitz is also the author of *Wheelchair Champions*, which tells of real people who have gained prowess in various sports. This book lists organizations and publications dealing especially with sports for people who use wheelchairs.

What If You Couldn't ...? by Janet Kamien is directed at nondisabled children in an attempt to help them empathize with and understand people who are disabled. In conjunction with some materials from the Children's Museum of Boston, the activities in this book can spark many others. Simulations such as wearing a sling on one or both arms, using crutches or a wheelchair, and attempting to accomplish tasks such as cleaning a room, playing a game, or moving from one place to another across some barrier stimulate discussion and additional activities.

HEARING DISABILITY

People who have a hearing impairment are not only those who simply live in a silent world. Hearing disorders can involve the distortion or muffling of sounds as well. Sometimes a hearing aid can totally control the disability; sometimes it serves as a partial correction; at other times it is not recommended, because it would do no good at all. Frequently a child with a hearing problem goes undiagnosed for a long time because of the mistaken impression that the child is "slow" or a behavior problem. Teachers and parents must be alert to the signs of a hearing disorder: frequent colds and infections, runny or inflamed ears, distorted speech, rubbing or pulling on the ears, use of gesture rather than speech, frequent requests for repetition of statements by others, talking too loudly, and/or seeming inattention may be behaviors that a child who has a hearing disability may exhibit. If a hearing disorder is suspected, the child should be examined immediately by a specialist.

Just because a person has a hearing impairment does not mean that the ability to enjoy conversations, music, and the other pleasures applicable to speech and sound are lost. Deaf people can often dance, play musical instruments, and sing.

One controversy in the education of people with hearing disabilities involves the issue of whether or not to use sign language. Some experts believe that only oral communication permits deaf people to function in the hearing world. They argue that if sign language is taught, people will grow to rely solely on that means of communication, and will never be fluent talkers. Other people argue that a combination of lip-reading, speech, and signing provides "total" communication for hearing-impaired people, and constitutes the ideal program of instruction. A powerful drama, *Children of a Lesser God*, by Mark Medoff, explores this controversy, and presents the issues as comparable to those of any activist group trying to win recognition from society. Incidentally, many of the performers in this play are themselves hearing-impaired.

Most of the books about this disability are nonfiction. Some of them, like *Handtalk: An ABC of Finger Spelling and Sign Language*, by Remy Charlip, Mary Beth Miller, and George Ancona, teach how to communicate without oral speech. This book is delightfully illustrated, and manages to convey a sense of joy in the process. Others, like *Claire and Emma*, by Diana Peter, and

I Have a Sister, My Sister Is Deaf, by Jeanne Peterson, discuss the everyday life of a deaf child, while conveying specific information about hearing disorders and how to manage them.

In some works of fiction, a deaf character is made to be mysterious, afflicted by God, or abnormal in ways beyond what can realistically be expected of a hearing-disabled person. Sometimes the deaf character is a nonperson, a foil for the other characters. In contrast, Emily Hanlon's *The Swing*, contains Beth, an eleven-year-old girl who has been deaf since birth, who demonstrates courage, insight, and a sense of her own talents and limitations. She is treated naturally by the other characters, and is portrayed well by the author. Margaret, the fourteen-year-old protagonist in Barbara Corcoran's *A Dance to Still Music*, has many problems, and suffers from a sense of isolation. She runs away to escape from what she believes to be an uncaring mother and the unwelcome prospect of "banishment" to a school for deaf children. At the end of the book she has been helped by a wonderful woman (who is almost too good to be true) to acknowledge and resolve her problems. Incidental factual information about hearing disabilities is well integrated into this novel.

SPEECH IMPAIRMENT

Communication is a very important part of human interaction. The usual mode of interacting with others is through speech. People with a hearing impairment often find it difficult to be understood, because they cannot themselves hear the speech sounds that they are manufacturing. If someone has been deaf from birth it is much more difficult. A person like Helen Keller is enormously admired for surmounting the difficulties attendant upon having multiple disabilities, particularly those affecting her ability to communicate.

Children's books that convey this sense of overcoming the problem while still retaining the disability are important for both disabled and nondisabled readers. Not everyone can be a genius, or become famous. Most people, however, can, with understanding and help from others, manage to make their thoughts and feelings known to others.

Speech problems can be as massive as total muteness; they also include more common concerns, such as stuttering, lisping, and other minor speech disorders. Most children's books covering this topic are about characters who are mute. In some of the books, such as E. B. White's *Trumpet of the Swan,* the disability is the primary focus of the plot. In this story Louis, a swan, uses a trumpet as a substitute for his voice, and makes his way in the world very successfully. In Jane Yolen's *Dragon's Blood*, the dragon is deliberately bred to be mute because the lack of a raucous cry is a great advantage to a fighting beast. But this dragon can communicate in a very special way with a limited number of people: she can transmit her feelings and thoughts through her mind.

Frank Jupo's book *Atu, the Silent One* tells of a young hunter, an African Bushman, who is mute. He communicates by his paintings both to his peers and to future generations. Although he cannot tell his people's stories orally, his talent as an artist accomplishes something that speech cannot. Another mute person, the uncle in Meindert DeJong's *Journey from Peppermint Street*, speaks eloquently through gesture and writing, and is a strong, sensitive, and admirable character.

Aaron, the twelve-year-old boy in *The Half-a-Moon Inn*, by Paul Fleischman, achieves self-responsibility through a harrowing adventure. Aaron is mute, and the story transports readers into the world of this boy who cannot speak, but whose thoughts and behavior communicate graphically to his audience.

Books about speech problems other than muteness are difficult to find. Although some books contain characters who have difficulty with speech, or who stutter, the disabilities are either not described accurately, or there is the implication that the problem is all a figment of the character's imagination. The "defects" disappear as soon as other events make the plot take an upward turn. In some of the stories, the character's speech returns or is improved after he or she has performed some remarkable task, saved someone's life, or developed an amazing talent. As is the case in too many of these areas of disability, many more books are needed that show knowledge and sensitively portray a disabled character integrated into a well-constructed plot.

VISUAL DISABILITY

Although some people have no vision at all, and neither see nor sense light, most visually impaired people have at least some vision. Some people can see only distorted images; others can see only at a certain distance. There are many aids for people with sight dysfunction: corrective lenses help a large percentage; surgery is performed successfully on most cataracts, glaucoma, detached retinas, and to provide cornea transplants. The development of the Braille alphabet and "talking books" have been a boon to people who want to enjoy the pleasures of reading. The training of guide dogs has also liberated a number of visually-disabled people from dependence on others.

Vision is an important factor in school success, and teachers and parents should be alert to the signals of visual problems. They should watch for signs of eyestrain or fatigue, such as squinting or frowning, redness or watery eyes, frequent headaches, or rubbing of the eyes. Also significant are the practices of holding reading material very close to the face, or very far away, and copying incorrectly from a chalkboard or another piece of paper. Other signs of trouble are double or blurred vision, frequent eye infections, and awkward movement (bumping into things, tripping, spilling when pouring liquids). Sometimes children are not aware that they are not seeing as clearly as they should; sometimes they are aware of the fact, and want to hide it. This situation can sometimes be detected because the child seems fearful or irritable, has problems making friends, and doesn't seem to want to engage in any new activities.

Many authors have included blind characters as major elements in their stories. There are books for young, middle grade, and older children, both fiction and nonfiction. One story that can be appreciated by children of all ages is Jane Yolen's *The Seeing Stick*. In this moving story, told in poetic language rich in sensory images, an old man journeys to the palace of the emperor to teach the princess, Hwei Ming, to "see" in a way different from the usual. By means of the carvings on his stick, the old man helps Hwei Ming to use her sense of touch to visualize the details of the stories he tells her. Eventually she learns this technique so well that she teaches it to the blind children of her kingdom. It is only at the end of the story that we are informed that the old man, too, is blind. The beautiful illustrations complement the text.

Children are probably familiar with the classic *Little House* series by Laura Ingalls Wilder because of the television program based on it. Several books describe the trauma of and then the coping with Mary's blindness. She emerges as a strong person, not only dealing with her own disability, but also, like Hwei Ming, helping others like herself.

Another sensitively written story about a competent blind person is Patricia MacLachlan's *Through Grandpa's Eyes*. John and his grandfather enjoy each other's company, and John acquires new dimensions of perception because of his talented grandfather.

Yet another superbly competent blind person is met in Sharon Bell Mathis's powerful novel for older children, *Listen for the Fig Tree*. Muffin, the sixteen-year-old protagonist has become blind over a period of years. She has prepared for this condition with the aid of her father, another very strong character. After the father is killed, Muffin's mother falls apart, and it is up to Muffin to maintain their household. She is helped by the emotional support of a close-knit black community. The descriptions of Muffin's ability to cope with everyday routines are flawlessly handled by the author. The other characters also ring true in this sometimes painful but always inspiring book. As with all of Mathis's books, the characters are black, and the story is lovingly and respectfully told.

In addition to the many books with blind characters in them, there are a number of books that deal with the not so total condition of limited sight. Jean Little's *From Anna* describes the evolution of Anna's self-perception from loser to competent achiever because her problem is handled appropriately. Some of the books that talk about limited sight and corrective glasses demean or ridicule the wearer of glasses. Adults should discuss these books with children and ask them to suggest different dialogue and behavior for the characters. They may want to invent their own stories about visual problems. An alert adult can sense many anxieties by actively listening to the stories children invent.

SPECIAL CATEGORIES

Although the next categories are not a usual part of the Disabilities Rights Movement, people who look different, are chronically ill, are victims of child abuse, substance abusers or associated with substance abusers, and the gifted and talented population have substantial special needs, and require particular understanding and attention on the part of helping adults. They therefore are included in this chapter.

SPECIFIC HEALTH PROBLEMS

Diabetes, epilepsy, leukemia, and other physical conditions that sometimes can be controlled by medicine, but that always have an effect on a person's life, can be found in a number of books. The same criteria apply to the use of these books as to the others involving physical disabilities. The important thing to remember in these books is that the characters should have a life outside their illness. They should be permitted to exhibit their own distinctive personalities, and should be part of a story that contains more than the symptoms and treatments of their physical conditions. In books where the characters have diabetes, epilepsy, or other treatable conditions, it is unfortunate when the situation is kept a guilty secret, as if it were something to be ashamed of. An open discussion could dispel some of the myths surrounding these health problems. Books such as *Epilepsy*, by Dr. Alvin and Virginia B. Silverstein, clarify and define what epilepsy is, and what it isn't. Another helpful book, *You Can't Catch Diabetes from a Friend*, by Lynne Kipnis and Susan Adler, accomplishes the same task for diabetes.

Another plot element that needs to be discussed deals with characters who have a particular illness but forget or refuse to take their medicine. They know what to do and how to do it, but they neglect to do so, and someone else in the story has to rescue them. This is the case in Ron Roy's *Where's Buddy?*, but the story is redeemed because Buddy proves to be responsible and more capable of caring for himself than his overprotective parents had thought.

Some illnesses, such as leukemia, are less controllable by the individual who suffers from them, and necessitate hospitalization and extensive medical treatment. These are discussed in the chapter on death because of their serious life-threatening implications. However, they are listed as well in the annotated Bibliography at the end of this chapter.

CHILD ABUSE

Sexual, physical, and emotional abuse are the topics of several books for preadolescent and older children. This painful, delicate issue is more prevalent in real life than has been previously suspected. Sometimes the reading of one of these books can help a young person recognize that he or she is a victim of abuse, and alerts him or her to seek help. In Louise Moeri's *The Girl Who Lived on the Ferris Wheel*, Til, the young protagonist, is not quite sure until she is almost killed by her mother that she is being abused. She keeps on wondering if, perhaps, her mother is simply punishing her the way other children's parents do. She has a conversation with a friend about this question, and begins to suspect that her mother is not a normal parent. She does, in the end, determine that she will never again be victimized or forced into a situation that is too painful for her to bear.

Victims of child abuse almost always feel that, in some unknown way, they must be to blame. They fear that the abuse is in their imagination, that their punishment is deserved. They are ashamed of their bruises, and try to hide the fact of their abuse from others. They often protect the abuser, who, in many cases, is a parent. Harvey, one of the foster children in *The Pinballs*, by Betsy Byars, lies about the fact that his father, in a drunken stupor and rage, has run him down with a car, breaking both his legs. Til does not tell about her mother's abuses, for fear that something worse will happen if she does. Hildy, the abused teen-ager in the poem "Hildy Ross," by Mel Glenn, does not want to "turn in" her father, even though he beats her.

Sometimes the parent is a substance abuser who only hurts the child when under the influence of alcohol or drugs. Often, though, the parent is emotionally disturbed, and is not aware of the ramifications of his or her abusive act. Will, the severely battered boy in Michelle Magorian's *Good Night, Mr. Tom*, is confused about his mother's irrational behavior, and disoriented when he is brought into the loving, healthful environment of the countryside far away from London. When he returns to his mother and almost dies as a result of her insane brutality, he sees, too late, what the situation is. He must be rescued by outsiders. Occasionally the parents are portrayed as well-intentioned people who cannot cope with the realities and expectations of ordinary existence. Almost always, the abuser has, himself or herself, been a victim of abuse.

It is difficult for a book to free itself of the violence and hysteria surrounding this topic. Most of the books listed in the Bibliography about this issue have some flaws, but are of sufficient quality to warrant inclusion. One rare book that is not primarily about abuse, but that is exquisitely written, and deals with many issues as it tells a compelling story, hints of what appears to be abusive behavior on the part of the mother. Virginia Hamilton's *Sweet Whispers, Brother Rush* manages to convey to the reader a sense of the mother's confusion and despair that lead her to confine her child to his bed, and to leave him, eventually, to the ministrations of his younger sister. Vy, the mother, is not a stereotypic child abuser. She is neither disturbed nor a substance abuser. She is a rich character whose behavior is complex. The reader does not hate her, but feels for her. Dabney, her son, has a congenital illness that impairs his intellect and claims his life at an early age. He, like the others, is a unique character. If this book is read with a concern for child abuse, it may help to make readers beware of easy answers and pat expectations. Social and psychological agencies are currently focusing on helping abusive parents, rather than condemning them.

Children can benefit from several works of nonfiction that offer information and advice about this difficult topic. *Private Zone*, by Frances Dayee, is addressed to children and adults, and includes behaviors to watch for that are indicators that children might be victims of abuse. Advice on how to recognize sexual abuse and what to do if assaulted is given to children. The book is aimed at an audience of children under nine years of age. *Child Abuse*, another factual book, for older readers, by Edward F. Dolan Jr., gives five suggestions for what to do if there is abuse at home.

An agency that sends free pamphlets about this topic is Children's Village, U.S.A. Located in California, it has a toll-free number that people can call for information and advice.

SUBSTANCE ABUSE

Although a number of books for adolescents deal with the issue of substance abuse in its own right, apart from child abuse, the topic is often either handled in a very heavy-handed, nonliterary fashion, or mentioned as a factor in a character's behavior pattern but not fully explored. Sensationalism is difficult to avoid in a disability whose effects are more devastating on the people near the substance abuser (in terms of emotional and, sometimes, physical damage) than to the "victim." Unfortunately, substance abuse and child abuse often go hand in hand. Even if there is no overt bodily hurt, the emotional pain that the family of a substance abuser endures is equivalent to, and often deeper than, physical bruises.

Laughter in the Background, by N. B. Dorman, graphically details the moment-to-moment experience of living with an alcoholic parent. Marcie tries to compensate herself for her mother's alcoholism by gorging herself on food. She is obese, unhappy, friendless and trapped until she takes matters into her own hands and requests to be removed from her house. The book leaves us with not much hope for her mother, but support groups and the help of loving and competent foster parents bring Marcie to a point where we know she will continue to progress to stability and success.

In the books where there is a daughter of an alcoholic mother, there is a pattern of the daughter's taking responsibility for what is traditionally regarded as the mother's role. The father in these stories is generally irresponsible, weak, and ready to blame anyone but himself for the difficult situation. All of the books described in this section have these ingredients.

Laurie, the sixteen-year-old daughter in Jane Claypool Miner's *Why Did You Leave Me?*, is one such character. The emphasis in this story is on her reaction to her alcoholic mother's return after two years away. Part of the time has been spent in a special treatment center. Laurie finds it difficult to relinquish her caretaking position, and feels anger, jealousy, and resentment, as well as self-pity. She behaves in a self-defeating fashion throughout most of the book. In the end she is helped to move from her negative stance by a nineteen-year-old woman who is a recovered alcoholic. Her mother regularly attends Alcoholics Anonymous, and it looks as if she will be successful in overcoming her drinking problem.

The role of AA, Alanon, and Alateen in helping alcoholics and their families is mentioned in most of the books on alcohol abuse. *Francesca, Baby*, by Joan Oppenheimer, is almost totally an advertisement for these organizations, but the story is an engrossing one, and the product is worth advertising. Francesca, the protagonist, could be Laurie's twin. She too is sixteen years old, and has the primary responsibility for her younger sister's welfare as well as for the running of the house. Her joining Alateen makes a major difference in everyone's behavior, leading to optimism in the end about the prospect of her mother's eventual recovery.

There are many books that contain a young protagonist who has "fallen into evil ways," and has become addicted to drugs or alcohol. Most of these stories are "formula" books: they portray shallow characters whose parents do not understand them, whose friends are wild and only out for a good time, and who succumb to the temptations of drugs, alcohol, and crime, but who are rescued by a person who loves them. Adolescents might enjoy these stories as escapist adventure tales, but they are not likely to gain insight or information from them. Readers should try to find books where the characters are more than vehicles for a message, and where the information is accurate and clearly conveyed. Substance abuse is a serious societal problem, and young people should be able to acquire helpful advice through the medium of literature as well as through responsible agencies and adult helpers.

EMOTIONAL DYSFUNCTION

Emotional problems afflict all of us at one time or another. Literature would be dull, indeed, if the characters in stories always behaved in rational, dispassionate, logical ways. The occasional outburst or slump is part of normal functioning, and it would be an enormous disservice to children if we labeled such behavior aberrant or demanded professional treatment for it. Books that contain characters who are emotionally unstable should try to communicate the message to their readers that it is not likely that they will fall victim to these problems, and that the problems are usually caused by some unusual or intense factor in the characters' lives.

It is conceivable that a person who has to cope with any of the disabilities mentioned in this chapter will experience serious emotional dysfunction, sometimes as a direct but temporary result of a specific incident, sometimes as a more general and permanent reaction to the difficulties of life. Some authors try to convey the thoughts of the person who is emotionally distaught, but more often the character is seen through the eyes of a narrator.

Those literary characters who are seriously disturbed, if well crafted by the author, remain with the reader for a long time, and help the reader to empathize with people whose responses are out of the normal range of expectation. Fran Ellen, in Marilyn Sachs's *The Bears' House*, tries to cope with a harsh world by escaping into the fantasy of the safe and compact toy bears' house her teacher has brought into the classroom. Junior Brown, in Virginia Hamilton's *The Planet of Junior Brown*, leaves the pain of this world for a safer planet. Naomi, the girl who has seen her father beaten to death by Nazis, runs back into silence when she is confronted by the bloody fist fight that Alan engages in with an anti-Semitic bully in Myron Levoy's masterful novel *Alan and Naomi*. All of these stories are powerful tales of human suffering and interaction. All of them deal with intimate relationships and the quest for acceptance and security. All of them are literary works of quality rather than clinical examinations of mental illness.

Specific symptoms of emotional dysfunction are described in some books: Florence Parry Heide's protagonist in *Growing Anyway Up* performs elaborate rituals to make her private world a safe one; Alexandra's journal in Patricia Windsor's *The Summer Before* details her feelings and observations. In some of the stories it is the mother of the protagonist who is experiencing emotional problems so severe that they cause her to be unable to function. Fran Ellen's mother has lapsed into an almost catatonic state because of the desertion of her husband. It is the mother's condition that causes the trauma for the children. They try desperately to maintain their household, take care of the baby, and stay together, but in the end, they are taken charge of by a social worker who will try to place them in appropriate homes. It is this resolution that prompts Fran Ellen to escape into the bears' house.

Their mother's mental collapse causes Dicey and her siblings to search for a safe haven in Cynthia Voigt's *Homecoming*. The sequel, *Dicey's Song*, won the Newbery Award; both books are equally moving and well crafted. Other books with emotionally disabled mothers are listed in the Bibliography. There are some fathers who are emotionally disturbed, but for some reason the books in which they appear are not of as high a quality as those where the mothers are disabled.

Some books depict characters who have temporary, or not quite as severe, emotional problems. Trissy, in Norma Fox Mazer's book, *I, Trissy*, loses her sense of proportion and behaves in a destructive fashion, but is brought back to balance by the end of the book. Chloris, in *Chloris and the Creeps*, by Kin Platt, seems to be relinquishing her obsessive false image of her father, and the reader hopes that her behavior will change for the better by the time the story has ended.

It is important to find books in which, if any of the characters behaves in such a way as to warrant a diagnosis of emotional dysfunction, the behavior be accurately described and not lightly "cured." Children should be invited to discuss what is within the realm of normalcy, and what behaviors invite professional attention.

APPEARANCE

Many books contain characters who feel that they look so different from the rest of their peers as to cause them serious concern. Some of these books contain an element of humor; most of them end with the problem resolved either by the character's peers accepting and valuing the differences, or by a change in the character's appearance. It is important to stock a number of such books in the classroom or library so that children may use them for bibliotherapy. It is always comforting to find a literary character who manages to survive looking different. Those children who feel they are too tall might enjoy Robin McKinley's *The Blue Sword*, in which the main character, Harry, is a very tall young woman who looks considerably different from her peers, and who turns out to have great gifts, and to be valued for her appearance by the people of a land she did not know existed. At the other end of the continuum, very short children might empathize with the feelings of the dwarfed characters in M. E. Kerr's *Little Little*. In any case, a discussion of the valuing of differences, and respect for others' feelings, will serve well in the matter of physical appearance.

Eating disorders often result in such a difference in the character's appearance so as to cause negative reactions from their peers. Obese children tend to be derided; children with anorexia nervosa, despite the fact that they are emaciated, often think of themselves as "too fat." In the case of anorexia nervosa, if the problem is not solved, the person will die. In *Second Star to the Right*, by Deborah Hautzig, Leslie, typical of all anorexics, reacts to her need to be successful, loved, and secure by almost starving herself to death. Often, the same sort of pressure drives a person to compulsive overeating. *The Pig-Out Blues*, by Jan Greenberg, describes the negative relationship between a mother and her daughter, ostensibly because of the daughter's weight, and the ultimate loss of weight by the daughter because she has found acceptance by other people. This is a recurring theme in the plethora of books that deal with obese children. The causes of eating disorders are usually environmental rather than physiological.

There is a controversy about obesity: some people feel that fat people should be accepted as they are, and not badgered to lose weight, or be made to feel ugly and unpopular. They argue that they should be permitted to remain fat, and should be considered attractive. They resent a "happy ending" of a diet that works, with a thin person emerging from the discarded flesh of the former fat one.

In all eating disorders self-image is the key. Children might want to share their experiences with each other, and give their opinions of the importance of weight as a factor in appearance. They might want to discuss Judy Blume's book *Blubber* as an example of children's cruelty to each other, and, perhaps, make some suggestions about how to handle this situation.

GIFTEDNESS

Although intellectual, artistic, creative, or leadership talent are not disabilities, people who are gifted do have special needs, and are looked upon by the rest of society in sometimes destructive ways. Most heroes and heroines in fantasies and fairy tales are gifted in one way or another, but it is more difficult to find children in stories about everyday life who are gifted, and whose talents are respected, and not instruments for inviting punitive behavior.

The *Encyclopedia Brown* series by Donald Sobol is excellent for showing a child who is valued for his cleverness. Ramona, the creative little girl in Beverly Cleary's series of books, is another example of the bright child who is in no way scorned or feared. On the other hand, Madeleine L'Engle's *Time* trilogy contains a number of wonderfully gifted characters, including Charles Wallace, a young boy whose extraordinary intelligence is perceived by some of the general public as "weird" and "retarded." L'Engle's series of books on the Austin family portray unusually gifted people who are admirable, loving, and balanced.

Books also contain descriptions of characters who are gifted in ways other than the intellect. Taro Yashima's *Crow Boy* has outstanding powers of observation and mimicry; Nancy Garrett has extrasensory perception in Lois Duncan's *A Gift of Magic*. Marcia Simon's young male protagonist in *A Special Gift* is a talented dancer; a mute boy in Glen Rounds's *Blind Outlaw* is remarkably gifted in working with animals.

In looking for books that provide a sensible and positive perspective on giftedness, attributes that seem reasonable in the context of the story, avoidance of derogatory stereotypes (thick glasses, fragile health, unpopularity with peers, arrogant self-interest, emotional imbalance) should be sought. A great variety of books, characters, heritages, and talents should be represented.

CAVEATS

With any issue it may be tempting for a helping adult to reach for a book that seems to have the topic of concern as its major focus, without examining how well the author has crafted the book as a whole. It is very important to remember that a book is a special device: its words can weave a spell that transports the reader into another world, another century, another reality. Authors are human beings with human failings. They cannot be held responsible for readers' failure to use their own good judgment and critical ability when they read. It is the concerned adult's responsibility to help young readers to exercise their skills of discrimination during the act of reading.

REFERENCES: SPECIAL NEEDS

ANDERSON, HOYT. "Don't Stare, I'll Tell You Later!" *The Exceptional Parent*, December 1980.
Discusses how to explain a person's disability to children. Lists helpful suggestions for parents in order to promote empathy and understanding on the part of children who are not disabled. The author was born with cerebral palsy.

ANGUS, JEAN RICH. *Watch My Words: An Open Letter to Parents of Young Deaf Children*. Forward Movement Publications, 1974. (Paperback.)
The mother of two hearing-impaired children supplies practical suggestions as she tells their story from kindergarten through college.

AYRAULT, EVELYN WEST. *Growing Up Handicapped: A Guide to Helping the Exceptional Child*. New York: Seabury Press, 1977.
The author, born with cerebral palsy, is a clinical psychologist who focuses on working with disabled people and their families. She contributes much information and many helpful suggestions to parents and other adults who are interested in working with disabled children. Her advice is practical; she is aware of the pitfalls of overprotection and ignorance.

BANFIELD, BERYL, AND THE CIBC STAFF. "Teaching About Handicapism," *Bulletin of the Council on Interracial Books for Children*, Vol. 8, Nos. 6 and 7, 1977. pp. 22–25.
Classroom activities and exercises for uncovering stereotypes in books and media, and for teaching about the disability rights movement.

BARBE, W. B., AND RENZULLI, JOSEPH, eds. *Psychology and Education of the Gifted*. New York: Irving Publishers, 1975.
Probably the most comprehensive volume available on this topic, the book is important reading for all adults who work with this population.

BASKIN, BARBARA H., AND HARRIS, KAREN H. *Books for the Gifted Child*. New York: Bowker, 1980.
Discusses academically talented children's reading needs and provides a list of intellectually demanding books for use with gifted readers.

_____. *Notes from a Different Drummer: A Guide to Juvenile Fiction Portraying the Handicapped*. New York: Bowker, 1977.
A comprehensive annotated bibliography with helpful comments and information about the inclusion of disabled characters in children's books. The bibliography includes books that are not recommended as well as those that are, and the authors explain their criteria and their judgments. An invaluable aid for librarians and teachers. Juvenile fiction written between 1940 and 1975 is analyzed in this edition.

_____., eds. *The Special Child in the Library*. Chicago: American Library Association, 1976.
Compendium of articles including bibliographies on how to provide library services to children with special needs. Gifted are also included in this collection, which provides theoretical discussions, clinical reports, and practical suggestions for practicing bibliotherapy.

BENNIE, E. H., AND SCLARE, A. E. "The Battered Child Syndrome," *American Journal of Psychiatry,* Vol. 125, No. 7, 1969.
A clinical review of the psychological aspects of treating children who have been abused. Parental attitudes, early recognition, and the possibilities of predicting child abuse are discussed.

BIKLEN, DOUGLAS, AND BOGDAN, ROBERT. "The Language of Handicapism and the Disability Rights Movement, *Family Involvement,* September–October 1976.
Discusses the problem of demeaning and prejudicial language and treatment when the general public deals with disabled people. Very informative.

BOURNE, RICHARD, AND NEWBERGER, ELI H. *Critical Perspectives on Child Abuse.* Lexington, Massachusetts: D. C. Heath, 1979.
Thirteen essays presenting an analytic approach to practice and policy as well as theory of child abuse. Each essay views the issue from a different perspective. Excellent introduction and overview.

BRETON, MARGARET. "Resocialization of Abusive Parents," *Social Work,* March 1981, pp. 119–122.
Recommends procedures for working with parents who abuse their children, and holds out hope that they can be helped to become nurturing parents. Discusses the problem of inadequacy of resources to deal with this problem.

BUCKLEY, LILLIAN A. "Gifted and Talented Characters in Children's Fiction," *New England Journal of Reading,* Vol. 16, No. 1, 1981.
A list of twenty-five novels that contain gifted characters. Annotations are brief, but useful.

CAMPLING, JO D. *Images of Ourselves: Women with Disabilities Talking.* Boston: Routledge and Kegan, 1981.
Women from a broad spectrum of backgrounds, ages, and disabilities write about their feelings, problems and perceptions.

CHANNING, L. *What Everyone Should Know about Child Abuse.* Bete Company, 1980.
Part of a packet of materials distributed by various agencies, this simple booklet counteracts myths, and contributes much information about child abuse. It also provides some suggestions about how to react to abuse, and how to help abused children.

CORMAN, CHERYL. "Bibliotherapy—Insight for the Learning-Handicapped," *Language Arts,* Vol. 52, No. 7, October 1975, pp. 935–937.
Additional resources of annotated bibliographies are provided, to complement the author's plea for the use of classroom guidance through books.

COUNCIL ON INTERRACIAL BOOKS FOR CHILDREN. *Bulletin,* Vol. 8, Nos. 6 and 7, 1977.
Special issue on "Handicapism in Children's Books." Contains many articles and reviews of books pertaining to attitudes toward disabled people as evidenced in children's books.

_____. *Bulletin,* Vol. 11, Nos. 1 and 2, 1980. (Special issue on "American Sign Language/Hearing Impairment in Children's Materials.")

Articles focus on how deaf people are portrayed in children's books, and include self-perceptions by hearing-impaired authors.

COUNCIL ON INTERRACIAL BOOKS FOR CHILDREN. *Bulletin*, Vol. 13, Nos. 4 and 5, 1982. Special issue on "Handicapism in Children's Books: A Five Year Update."
Exactly as the title indicates, this issue updates the previous examination of materials, and provides thoroughly annotated entries of recommended materials as well as criticisms of items not judged to be free of negative stereotypes and attitudes.

_____. *Guidelines for Selecting Biasfree Textbooks and Storybooks.* New York: Council on Interracial Books for Children, 1980.
A set of articles compiled into a useful manual for teaching children about bias of all sorts in the books they read.

CRISCUOLO, NICHOLAS P. "Open Discovery Spots for Gifted Readers," *Gifted Child Quarterly,* Vol. 18, No. 2, Summer 1974, pp. 72–73.
Describes mini-interest centers teachers can set up in elementary school classrooms to challenge gifted readers.

CUSHENBERY, DONALD C., AND HOWELL, HELEN, *Reading and the Gifted Child: A Guide for Teachers.* Springfield, Illinois: Thomas, 1974.
Designed to dispel the idea that gifted children are best left to their own devices, presents many ideas and resources to use for this population.

DAVOREN, E. "Foster Placement of Abused Children," *Children Today,* Vol. 4, No. 2, 1975, p. 41.
Briefly deals with the issue of placement from the points of view of foster parents, abusive parents, and children.

DOBO, PAMELA J. "Using Literature to Change Attitudes toward the Handicapped," *Reading Teacher,* Vol. 36, No. 4, December 1982, pp. 290–292.
Advocates the use of children's literature to find out what information, attitudes and feelings children have about disabled people. Lists sources for finding books on this topic. Urges both cognitive and affective consideration.

DOLAN, EDWARD F., JR., *Child Abuse.* New York: Franklin Watts, 1980.
Extensive amount of information, including suggestions for older children on what to do if they are subject to abuse at home.

FRASIER, MARY M., AND McCANNON, CAROLYN. "Using Bibliotherapy with Gifted Children," *Gifted Child Quarterly,* Vol. 25, Spring 1981, pp. 81–85.
Annotated list of books that contain gifted children who solve their particular problems. Useful for discussion as well as models.

GALLAGHER, JAMES J. *Teaching the Gifted Child,* 2d. ed. Boston: Allyn and Bacon, 1975.
The most comprehensive text available on this topic. Discusses identification, characteristics, content modifications, training of personnel, gifted under-achievers and special problem areas. A "must" for anyone interested in working with this population.

GEISER, ROBERT L. *Hidden Victims: The Sexual Abuse of Children.* Boston: Beacon Press, 1979.

A detailed, factual presentation of all of the aspects of this difficult issue, including pornography, molestation, incest, and rape. Description of the array of people who perform these acts of sexual abuse. Proposes recommendations for programs that will help prevent, and possibly correct this situation.

GLIEDMAN, JOHN, AND ROTH, WILLIAM (for the Carnegie Council on Children). *The Unexpected Minority: Handicapped Children in America.* New York: Harcourt Brace Jovanovich, 1980.
Provides a well-researched view of disabled people as an oppressed minority group in the United States. Argues powerfully for removal of legal restrictions as well as societal, psychological, and economic barriers. Criticizes the medical model of viewing disabled people.

GENSLEY, JULIANA T. "Let's Teach the Gifted to Read," *Gifted Child Quarterly,* Vol. 19, No. 1, Spring 1975, pp. 21–22.
Presents a process that involves research, interpretation, analysis, synthesis and evaluation. All are necessary components in any reading program, but particularly in one for the gifted.

HANDELMAN, GLADYS. "Child Abuse! The Nuclear Family Explodes," *Columbia,* February 1983, pp. 31–36.
A sympathetic discussion of how parents who abuse their children need help to learn how to rehabilitate themselves and their children.

HAYNES, JOHN. "No Child Is an Island: Three Books That Focus on Handicapped Children," *Children's Literature in Education, Vol. 15,* 1974, pp. 3–18.
A detailed literary and critical analysis of three children's books containing disabled characters. The author provides a model for such analysis, and demonstrates a sensitivity to the problems of disabled people. The terminology is British, and somewhat different from the terms in accepted use in the United States, but the concepts are congruent.

HERBRUCK, CHRISTINE COMSTOCK. *Breaking the Cycle of Child Abuse.* Minneapolis: Winston Press, 1979.
Case histories of parents who abused their children. Five types of abuse are identified and contrasted with neglect. Feelings are discussed sympathetically. The book essentially describes the work of Parents Anonymous, a support group for these parents.

HOPKINS, CAROL J. "Developing Positive Attitudes toward the Handicapped through Children's Books," *Elementary School Journal,* Vol. 81, No. 1, September 1980, pp. 34–37.
Identifies materials for use in regular elementary school classrooms to create awarencess of the abilities of disabled children. Lists a number of children's books. Focus is on the positive, critical evaluation of the books is omitted.

JACOBS, LEO M. *A Deaf Adult Speaks Out.* Washington, D.C.: Gallaudet College Press, 1974.
Deaf himself, the author's parents, wife and one child are also deaf. Jacobs is teacher of the deaf as well as an author who includes in this book a discussion of communication, the deaf community, aspects of deafness, educational methods, and strategies for help.

JOURNAL OF CHILDREN AND YOUTH, Spring 1980. Special issue on "Educating our Gifted and Talented Children."
Many of articles relating the education of gifted students.

KEMPE, C. HENRY AND RUTH. *Child Abuse.* Cambridge, Massachusetts: Harvard University Press, 1978.
Part of the Harvard University Press series on Child Development, this report describes the Kempes' work with parents who have been identified as potential child abusers.

LASS, BONNIE, AND BROMFIELD, MARCIA. "Books about Children with Special Needs: An Annotated Bibliography," *Reading Teacher,* Vol. 34, No. 5, February 1981, pp. 530–533.
Criteria for selection of books are clearly stated, with a rationale provided. Books are discussed and recommended.

LITTON, FREDDIE W.; BANBURY, MARY M.; AND HARRIS, KAREN. "Materials for Educating Nonhandicapped Students about Their Handicapped Peers," *Teaching Exceptional Children,* Fall 1980.
Materials described include mainstreaming resource materials and children's books.

LUKAWEVICH, ANN. "Three Dozen Useful Information Sources on Reading for the Gifted," *Reading Teacher,* Vol. 36, No. 6, February 1983, pp. 542–548.
A useful annotated bibliography of resources for use in the classroom with gifted children. Included are articles and books on various aspects of the teaching of reading.

MARTIN, H. P. ed. *The Abused Child: A Multi-Disciplinary Approach to Developmental Issues:* Cambridge, Massachusetts: Ballinger, 1976.
Focusing on child abuse as a syndrome, this collection of articles describes the characteristics of abused children, how their environment figures into their problems, and how they handle the situation. Includes specific programs and proposals for treatment, criticizes some current treatments.

NORTHCOTT, WINIFRED H. ed. *The Hearing Impaired Child in a Regular Classroom: Preschool, Elementary, and Secondary Years.* Alexander Graham Bell Association, 1973.
All personnel and clients are represented in this collection of articles concerned with integrating hearing-disabled children into regular classroom settings.

POWERS, HELEN. *Signs of Silence: Bernard Bragg and the National Theatre of the Deaf.* New York: Dodd, Mead, 1972.
This important institution has done much to make the general public more conscious of the capabilities of deaf people, and more appreciative of the beauty of signing.

REGION I ADOPTION RESOURCE CENTER. *Adoption of Children with Special Needs: A Bibliography.* January 1982.
More than forty annotated references relevant to adopting children with special needs.

RENZULLI, JOSEPH S. *The Enrichment Triad.* Connecticut: Creative Press, 1977.
An important model of curriculum construction for gifted students. Renzulli is one of the major proponents of education for the gifted.

SANFORD, L. T. *The Silent Children: A Parent's Guide to the Prevention of Child Sexual Abuse.* Garden City, New York: Doubleday, 1980.
Teaches parents of children seven years of age and older how to warn their children about sexual abuse. Deals with family atmosphere; gives an overview of child molestation and incest. Provides exercises for parents' use with children.

SCHWARTZ, ALBERT V. "Books Mirror Society: A Study of Children's Materials," *Bulletin of the Council on Interracial Books for Children,* Vol. 11, Nos. 1 and 2, 1980, pp. 19–24.
An extensive evaluation of books dealing with deafness and or deaf characters. Criteria are established and used as a filter for the evaluation. Most books are found wanting, but a number are recommended.

_____. "Disability in Children's Books: Is Visibility Enough?" *Bulletin of the Council on Interracial Books for Children,* Vol. 8, Nos. 6 and 7, 1977, pp. 10–15.

SMITH, DEBRA MOREY, AND STACKHOUSE, SHEILA. *Mental Retardation: An Issue in Literature for Children.* Arlington, Texas: Association for Retarded citizens of the United States, 1981. Pamphlet.
Comprehensive, sensitively annotated bibliography of childrens's books dealing with mental retardation.

STANOVICH, KEITH E. AND PAULA. "Speaking for Themselves: A Bibliography of Writings of Mentally Handicapped Individuals," *Mental Retardation,* Vol. 17, No. 2, April 1979, pp. 83–86.
Annotated listing of articles and books, all written by people with some condition of mental disability.

TOLLIFSON, JOAN. "An Open Letter ...," *Bulletin of the Council on Interracial Books for Children,* Vol. 8, Nos. 6 and 7, 1977, p. 19.
Straightforward and persuasive comments on society's perceptions of disabled people, with some suggestions for how to correct them.

TWAY, EILEEN. "The Gifted Child in Literature," *Language Arts,* Vol. 57, No. 1, January 1980, pp. 14–20.
Excellent overview of how the gifted child is portrayed in children's books. Analyses of books are thorough and informative.

WATSON, EMILY STRAUSS. "Handicapism in Children's Books: A Five Year Update," *Bulletin, of the Council on Interracial Books for Children,* Vol. 13, Nos. 4 and 5, 1982, pp. 3–5.
Summarizes a number of books containing disabled characters, and recommends a number, although many other books fail to meet the criteria for balanced portrayal of disabilities.

WEST, NANCY, ed. "Educating Exceptional Children," an *Annual Edition,* Dushkin Publishing Group, 1982.
One of a series of excellent *Annual Editions,* each a compendium of informative articles on a particular topic. This volume contains forty-eight articles on mainstreaming, strategies for helping non-disabled children understand their disabled peers, educating visually, auditorily, physically, emotionally, learning, and behaviorally disabled, as well as gifted children.

WRIGHT, DAVID. *Deafness,* Briarcliff Manor, New York: Stein and Day, 1975. Paperback.
Inspiring autobiography of this British poet who became deaf at the age of seven. Explores many aspects of his world, examines the history of education of the deaf, discusses causes and treatment of deafness.

YURA, MICHAEL T., AND ZUCKERMAN, LAWRENCE. *Raising the Exceptional Child: Meeting the Everyday Challenges of the Handicapped or Retarded Child.* New York: Hawthorn Books, 1979.
Basing their advice on the work of Rudolph Dreikurs and Alfred Adler, the authors, both professionals in the area of family guidance, detail a number of situations and behaviors that can cause problems in families where there are disabled children. They offer practical, specific solutions for the families to employ.

ZAMES, FRIEDA. "The Disability Rights Movement Five Years Later," *Bulletin of the Council on Interracial Books for Children,* Vol. 13, Nos. 4 and 5, 1982, pp. 18–21. Update on the legal, political, and social status of the disability civil rights movement. Discusses what has been accomplished, and what still needs to be done.

SOURCES FOR MATERIALS ON SPECIAL NEEDS

AL-ANON FAMILY GROUP HEADQUARTERS. P.O. Box 182, Madison Square Station, New York, New York 10010

ALEXANDER GRAHAM BELL ASSOCIATION FOR THE DEAF. 3417 Volta Place, N.W., Washington, D.C. 20007

AMERICAN ASSOCIATION FOR GIFTED CHILDREN. 15 Gramercy Park, New York, New York 10003

AMERICAN CANCER SOCIETY, INC. 777 Third Ave., New York, New York 10017

AMERICAN CIVIL LIBERTIES UNION. 22 East 40 St., New York, New York 10016
(The ACLU has published a series of books on disability rights, the mental patient, teachers, and developmentally delayed individuals.)

AMERICAN COALITION OF CITIZENS WITH DISABILITES. 1346 Connecticut Avenue, N.W., Washington, D.C. 20036

AMERICAN DIABETES ASSOCIATION. 18 East 48th St., New York, New York 10017

THE ASSOCIATION FOR THE GIFTED, COUNCIL FOR EXCEPTIONAL CHILDREN. 1920 Association Drive, Reston, Virginia 20091

ASSOCIATION FOR RETARDED CITIZENS. National headquarters, 2709 Avenue E East, P.O. Box 6109, Arlington, Texas 76011

CANCER INFORMATION SERVICE OF THE NATIONAL CANCER INSTITUTE. Toll-free telephone 800-638-6694

CANDLELIGHTERS FOUNDATION, NATIONAL CANCER INSTITUTE. Building 3, Room 10A 18, Bethesda, Maryland 20205

CENTER FOR INDEPENDENCE OF THE DISABLED OF NEW YORK CITY. 853 Room 10A 18, Bethesda, Maryland 20205

CENTER FOR INDEPENDENT LIVING. 2539 Telegraph Ave., Berkeley, California 94704 (A nonprofit organization run for and primarily by disabled people)

CHILD WELFARE LEAGUE OF AMERICA. 67 Irving Place, New York, New York 10003

CHILDREN'S DEFENSE FUND. 1520 New Hampshire Ave., N.W., Washington, D.C. 20036. Toll-free telephone 800-424-9602

CHILDREN'S DIVISION OF AMERICAN HUMANE ASSOCIATION. 5351 South Roslyn St., Englewood, Colorado 80110

CHILDREN'S VILLAGE U.S.A. National Headquarters, 6463 Independence Ave., Woodland Hills, California 91267
(Distributes materials on child abuse.)

CLEARINGHOUSE ON CHILD ABUSE AND NEGLECT INFORMATION.Herner and Co., 1700 North Moore St., Arlington, Virginia 22209

CONNECTICUT ASSOCIATION FOR THE GIFTED. Peter H. Cobb, President, 259 Naubuc Ave., East Hartford, Connecticut 06118

DEAFNESS. John Tracy Clinic, 806 W. Adams Blvd., Los Angeles, California 90007

DIRECTORY OF ORGANIZATIONS INTERESTED IN THE HANDICAPPED. Committee for the Handicapped, People to People Program, Suite 610, LaSalle Bldg., Connecticut Ave. and L St., N.W., Washington, D.C. 20036

DISABILITY RIGHTS AND EDUCATION DEFENSE FUND (DREDF). 2032 San Pablo, Berkeley, California 94702

DISABLED IN ACTION NATIONAL. Emily Strauss Watson, National Coordinator, c/o Disabled in Action of Metropolitan New York, P.O. Box 1273, New York, New York 10009

DOWN'S SYNDROME CONGRESS. 1640 West Roosevelt Rd., Room 156-E, Chicago, Illinois 60608

EPILEPSY FOUNDATION OF AMERICA. 1727 L St., N.W., Washington, D.C. 20036

EQUAL PAY. Women's Action Alliance, 370 Lexington Ave., New York, New York 10017
(Subscriptions are $10 for individuals, $20 for institutions. Vol. 11, No. 1–2, Winter-Spring 1981 is an entire issue on mainstreaming.)

THE EXCEPTIONAL PARENT. 296 Boylston St., Third Floor, Boston, Massachusetts 02116

FEDERATION OF CHILDREN WITH SPECIAL NEEDS. 120 Boylston St., Room 338, Boston, Massachusetts 02116

FIDELCO GUIDE DOG FOUNDATION. P.O. Box 142, Bloomfield, Connecticut 06002

GALLAUDET COLLEGE. 7th St. and Florida Ave., N.E., Washington, D.C. 20002

THE GIFTED CHILD QUARTERLY. 1426 Southwind, Westlake Village, California 91361

GUIDE DOG FOUNDATION FOR THE BLIND. 371 Jericho Turnpike, Smithtown, New York 11787

GUIDE DOGS FOR THE BLIND. P.O. Box 1200, San Rafael, California 94902

GUIDING EYES FOR THE BLIND. Granite Springs Rd., Yorktown Heights, New York 10598

INTERNATIONAL ASSOCIATION OF PARENTS OF THE DEAF. 814 Thayer Ave., Silver Spring, Maryland 20910

INTERNATIONAL GUIDING EYES. 5528 Cahuenga Blvd., North Hollywood, California 91601

JOURNAL FOR THE EDUCATION OF THE GIFTED. School of Education, Ruffner Hall, Room 103, University of Virginia, Charlottesville, Virginia 22903

C. HENRY KEMPE NATIONAL CENTER FOR PREVENTION AND TREATMENT OF CHILD ABUSE AND NEGLECT. 1205 Oneida St., Denver, Colorado 80220

THE KIDS ON THE BLOCK, INC. 1712 Eye St., N.W., Suite 1005, Washington, D.C. 20006

LEADER DOGS FOR THE BLIND. 1039 Rochester Rd., Rochester, Michigan 48063

LIBRARY FOR DEAF ACTION. Box 50045, F Station, Washington, D.C. 20004

MAINSTREAM, INC. 1200 15th St., N.W., Washington, D.C. 20005

MASSACHUSETTS ASSOCIATION FOR CHILDREN WITH LEARNING DISABILITIES. 1296 Worcester Rd., Framingham, Massachusetts 01701
(The association published The Specific Learning Disabilities Gazette.)

MUSCULAR DYSTROPHY ASSOCIATION OF AMERICA. 1790 Broaday, New York, New York 10017

NATIONAL ASSOCIATION FOR GIFTED. 8080 Spring Valley Dr., Cincinnati Ohio 43236

NATIONAL ASSOCIATION FOR RETARDED CHILDREN. 2709 Ave. E. East, Arlington, Texas

NATIONAL ASSOCIATION OF THE DEAF. 814 Thayer Ave., Silver Spring, Maryland 20910

NATIONAL ASSOCIATION OF RETARDED CHILDREN. 420 Lexington Ave., New York, New York 10017

NATIONAL CENTER FOR LAW AND THE DEAF. Gallaudet College, 7th St. and Florida Ave., N.E., Washington, D.C. 20002

NATIONAL CENTER FOR PREVENTION AND TREATMENT OF CHILD ABUSE AND NEGLECT. 125 Oneida St., Denver, Colorado 80220

NATIONAL CENTER ON CHILD ABUSE AND NEGLECT. Information Clearing House, P.O. Box 1182, Washington, D.C. 20013

NATIONAL CLEARINGHOUSE FOR ALCOHOL INFORMATION. P.O. Box 2345, Rockville, Maryland 20852

NATIONAL COMMITTEE FOR PREVENTION OF CHILD ABUSE. 332 S. Michigan Ave., Suite 1250, Chicago, Illinois 60604

NATIONAL CYSTIC FIBROSIS RESEARCH FOUNDATION. 202 E. 44th St., New York, New York 10017

NATIONAL DOWN'S SYNDROME SOCIETY. 146 East 57th St., New York, New York 10022

NATIONAL EASTER SEAL FOR CRIPPLED CHILDREN AND ADULTS. 2023 W. Ogden Ave., Chicago, Illinois 60612

NATIONAL FOUNDATION—MARCH OF DIMES. P.O. Box 2000, White Plains, New York 10602

NATIONAL INFORMATION CENTER FOR THE HANDICAPPED. Box 1492, Washington, D.C. 20013
(Publishes the periodical *Closer Look* free of charge. Also distributes free information packets. A project of the Office of Education, HEW, Bureau of Education for the Handicapped.)

NATIONAL INSTITUTE OF NEUROLOGICAL DISEASES AND STROKE. National Institutes of Health, Information Office, Bethesda, Maryland 20014

NATIONAL MULTIPLE SCLEROSIS SOCIETY. 257 Park Ave. South, New York, New York 10010

NATIONAL SOCIETY FOR PREVENTION OF BLINDNESS. 79 Madison Ave., New York, New York 10016

NATIONAL/STATE LEADERSHIP TRAINING INSTITUTE—GIFTED/TALENTED. Ventura County Superintendent of Schools, 535 East Main St., Ventura, California 93009

NEW ENGLAND RESOURCE CENTER FOR CHILDREN AND FAMILIES. Judge Baker Guidance Center, 295 Longwood Ave., Boston, Massachusetts 02115

OFFICE OF GIFTED & TALENTED. 6th and D St., S.W., Washington, D.C. 20202

PACER CENTER, INC. 4704 Chicago Ave. South, Minneapolis, Minnesotta 55401

(Parent Advocacy Coalition for Educational Rights provides up-to-date information on PL94-142 and other educational laws. They publish a newsletter, *Pacesetter*.)

COUNCIL ON EXCEPTIONAL CHILDREN. 1920 Association Dr., Reston, Virginia 22091

PARENTS ANONYMOUS. 22330 Hawthorne Blvd., Torrance, California 90505

PILOT DOGS. 625 West Town St., Columbus, Ohio 43215

PUBLIC AFFAIRS PAMPHLETS. 381 Park Ave. South, New York, New York 10016 (Send for their list of publications. All pamphlets are $.50 each.)

ROEPER REVIEW: A JOURNAL ON GIFTED CHILD EDUCATION. Roeper City and Country School, Bloomfield Hills, Michigan 48013.

THE SEEING EYE. P.O. Box 375, Morristown, New Jersey 07960.

SILENT NEWS. The Silent News, Inc., 343 Forest Ave., Paramus, New Jersey 07652 (Monthly newspaper for the deaf. $8 per year.)

SPECIAL OLYMPICS, INC. 1701 K St., N.W., Suite 203, Washington, D.C. 20006

TEACHING GIFTED CHILDREN. Croft—NEI, 24 Rope Ferry Rd., Waterford, Connecticut 06386

UNITED CEREBRAL PALSY ASSOCIATION, INC. 66 E. 34th St., New York, New York 10016

U.S. DEPARTMENT OF HEALTH AND HUMAN SERVICES. President's Committee on Mental Retardation, Office of Human Development Services, Washington, D.C. 20201

U.S. DEPARTMENT OF HEALTH AND HUMAN SERVICES. Public Health Service: Alcohol, Drug Abuse and Mental Health Administration, 5600 Fishers Lane, Rockville, Maryland 20857

BIBLIOGRAPHY: SPECIAL NEEDS

The items in this bibliography are listed in alphabetical order by author, not sorted according to specific special needs. Each subtopic is listed in the index, so that separate lists may be constructed. Many of the books contain mention of more than one special need. Readers may benefit from applying the criteria mentioned in the chapter to any of the books dealing with special needs. Bracketed descriptions are included in the entries to indicate what conditions of special needs are dealt with in each book.

ADAMS, BARBARA. *Like It Is: Facts and Feelings about Handicaps from Kids Who Know.* Illustrated by James Stanfield. New York: Walker, 1979. (Ages 8–12.) Photographs and directly worded text describe individual children, each with a particular disability such as hearing, speech, visual, and orthopedic handicaps, and retardation, learning disabilities, and behavior disorders. The text generally is presented from the perspective of a disabled person speaking to the nondisabled public.

ALLAN, MABEL ESTHER. *View beyond My Father*. New York: Dodd, Mead, 1978. (Ages 12–up.) [vision]
A blind girl growing up in Britain in the 1930s fights her parents' stifling overprotectiveness to gain a measure of independence.

ANDERS, REBECCA. *A Look at Alcoholism*. Minneapolis: Lerner Publications, 1978. (Ages 7–11.) [substance abuse]
A very "sobering" textbook on alcoholism in language that young children can understand.

_____. *A Look at Mental Retardation*. Photographs by Maria Forrai. Foreword by Muriel Humphrey. Minneapolis: Lerner Publications, 1976. (Ages 7–11.) [intellectual disability]
Text and photographs describe problems faced by people who are mentally disabled.

ARRICK, FRAN. *Chernowitz*. New York: Bradbury Press, 1981. Also in paper. (Ages 11–up.) [child abuse]
Bobby has never been very popular, but now he is the victim of a viciously anti-semitic bully, who manages to align all of Bobby's former friends against him. Bobby does not confide in his parents until the situation reaches dangerous proportions. While the book is flawed in some of its developments, it does provide some insights and questions about the issue of gang psychology. The bully is a boy who is regularly beaten severely by his father. Realistically, Bobby recognizes at the end that no matter what he does, the bully will not become reasonable or appreciative of Jews.

ARTHUR, CATHERINE. *My Sister's Silent World*. Chicago: Children's Press, 1979. (Ages 6–9.) [hearing]
The story about Heather, who is deaf, is told by her older sister and enhanced by color photographs. A small child would benefit from the text and pictures and gain some understanding of what it must be like to be a deaf child. The sister covers such areas as deafness not being contagious and the use of hearing aids, lip reading, and sign language. Heather goes to a special school and likes to do many of the same things that other children like to do.

AUSTRIAN, GEOFFREY. *The Truth about Drugs*. Garden City, New York: Doubleday, 1971. (Ages 12–up.) [substance abuse]
A description of drug usage, effects, history, and the reasons people take them, documented with case histories. A useful glossary of terms is included. An unbiased view.

AVI. *Sometimes I Think I Hear My Name*. New York: Pantheon, 1982. Also in paper. (Ages 11–up.) [child abuse]
Conrad's aunt and uncle try to protect him from finding out that he lives with them because his divorced parents really don't want him. He decides to confront his parents rather than go on a planned vacation to England. When both his parents demonstrate that they are incapable of giving him love and security, he returns to his aunt and uncle, finally accepting his situation and himself. Part of the plot involves

Conrad's relationship with a lonely, angry and rejected young girl whose upper class parents are emotionally abusive.

BALDWIN, ANNE. *A Little Time*. New York: Viking Press, 1978. (Ages 8–12.) [intellectual disability]
Sarah, the middle child of five children, narrates the story. One of her younger brothers, Matt, has Down's Syndrome. When their mother becomes ill, the family must make a decision about how to best help Matt. Children might want to discuss how the father might have helped more with Matt. The story is a satisfying one.

BIKLEN, DOUGLAS, AND BARNES, ELLEN. *You Don't Have to Hear to Cook Pancakes: A Workbook in Understanding People*. Syracuse, New York: Human Policy Press, 1978. (Ages 8–12.) [general]
A workbook of exercises to help sensitize children to the issues and feelings of handicapped/disabled people.

BIKLEN, DOUGLAS, AND SOKOLOFF, MICHELLE. *What Do You Do When Your Wheelchair Gets a Flat Tire? Questions and Answers about Disabilities*. Syracuse, New York: Human Policy Press, 1978. (Ages 7–11.) [general]
Children with various disabilities tell what it's like to be disabled. They answer questions about their particular disabilities, how they get around, their likes and dislikes, how they want others to treat them.

BLUE, ROSE. *Me and Einstein*. New York: Human Press, 1979. (Ages 8–12.) [learning disability]
Bobby has dyslexia, a reading problem which some famous people also have had. Among them are Thomas Edison, Winston Churchill, Woodrow Wilson, and Albert Einstein. The story makes it clear that Bobby is a bright, competent boy, and that the appropriate educational program will help him.

BLUME, JUDY. *Blubber*. New York: Bradbury, 1974. Also in paper. (Ages 8–up.) [appearance]
Linda is slightly overweight, but not really obese. She has become the object of ridicule for Wendy, a bully and class ringleader. The other children in the class go along with Wendy's cruelty because they are afraid that if they don't, they will also become her victims. Adults will want to discuss the behavior of the children in this story, as well as the outcome.

_____. *Deenie*. New York: Dell, 1977. Paperback (Ages 9–12.) [scoliosis]
Thirteen-year-old Deenie has always avoided contact with disabled people. When Deenie finds that she has scoliosis and must wear a confining brace for four years, she has a rough time adjusting to the situation, but her view of disabled people changes.

BODE, JANET. *Rape: Preventing It; Coping with the Legal, Medical, and Emotional Aftermath*. New York: Franklin Watts, 1979. (Ages 12–up.) [sexual abuse]
Using case histories and extensive interview material, this book discusses rape as a "social problem." The author looks at the legal, medical, and emotional aftermath of rape and includes specific practical information on preventive and protective measures. Very informative and eye-opening.

BOURKE, LINDA. *Handmade ABC: A Manual Alphabet*. Illustrated by the author. Reading, Massachusetts: Addison-Wesley, 1981. Also in paper. (All ages.) [hearing] Using bold black-and-white line drawings, Bourke shows the correct fingerspelling for each letter of the alphabet. Each page is bordered by something beginning with that letter ("vine" for "v") and the fingers are holding or wearing something else ("handcuff" for "h").

BRANFIELD, JOHN. *Why Me?* New York: Harper & Row. 1973. (Ages 12–up.) [diabetes] Sarah and Jane are sisters who do not get along at all well; in fact, they seem to delight in making each other unhappy. Sarah has diabetes. The bulk of the story revolves around her adjustment to this condition. The parents seem to be unable to control their daughter's behavior. The only resolution is to wait until they grow up.

BRIGHTMAN, ALAN J. *Like Me*. Boston: Little, Brown, 1976. (Ages 5–8.) [intellectual disability] Narrated by a child who has Down's syndrome, this photo story invites sympathetic understanding on the part of nondisabled children.

BROTHER AND SISTER GROUP, AND GROUP WORK RECREATION PROGRAM, ASSOCIATION FOR THE HELP OF RETARDED CHILDREN. *It's Tough . . . To Live with Your Retarded Brother or Sister*. (Ages 7–12.) [intellectual disability] In question and answer form, the pamphlet gives information for the school-age sibling of a retarded person. (Address for free copy: Academic Therapy, 1539 Fourth St., San Rafael, California 94901.)

BUTLER, BEVERLY. *Light a Single Candle*. New York: Dodd, Mead, 1964. (Ages 12–up.) [vision] In learning to accept her newly sightless condition and continue to lead a full, rich life, fourteen-year-old Cathy Wheeler encounters not only obstacles such as doors and curbs, but also those of people's prejudices and fears. Through her own determination and hard work and the help of her very supportive family and friends, Cathy manages to get through her initial depression as well as a semester at a dismal school for the blind. The author, who is blind, vividly describes how Cathy learns to have confidence in herself, get around well with her guide dog, Trudy, make many friends, and achieve in her classes at the public high school.

BYARS, BETSY. *The Pinballs*. New York: Harper & Row, 1977. (Ages 9–12.) [child abuse] Three foster children, or "pinballs" as Carlie labels them, are sent to stay with the Masons. Each of the three has a problem that must be confronted, discussed, and accepted. Harvey, one of the children, has been run over by his drunken father, and Carlie has been sexually abused. A well-written, sensitively handled story.

_____. *The Summer of the Swans*. Illustrated by Ted CoConis. New York: Viking, 1971. Also in paper. (Ages 10–up.) [intellectual disability] Fourteen-year-old Sara feels responsible for Charlie, her younger, retarded brother. She also resents him and has unpleasant feelings about herself. Charlie's thoughts and feelings are described in a sensitive way. In the end, a friend helps her to resolve her feelings.

CARPENTER, RUE. "Stout," in *Rainbow in the Sky*, ed. by Louis Untermeyer. New York: Harcourt, Brace & World, 1973. (Ages 8–up.) [appearance]
This is a short poem about the trials of an overweight boy, particularly noting what the boy feels when he must sit quietly, yet "feels quite wild."

CHARLIP, REMY; MILLER, MARY BETH; AND ANCONA, GEORGE. *Handtalk: An ABC of Finger Spelling and Sign Language*. Illustrated with photographs by George Ancona. New York: Four Winds Press, 1980. Reprint of edition published by Parents Magazine Press, 1974. (All ages.) [hearing]
All ages will enjoy learning about the ways people can talk without using their voices: finger spelling (making words letter by letter with the fingers) and signing (using the hands to convey a picture for a word or idea). Full-color pictures show children how it's done. A striking, accessible introduction to signing.

CHILDREN'S VILLAGE U.S.A. *Child Abuse and You*. A guidebook by the Children's Village U.S.A. [child abuse]
Systematically describes what child abuse is, how to detect it, report it, who inflicts abuse, what one can do about it, what a community can do, and how to become part of the National Campaign for the Prevention of Child Abuse.

CHILDRESS, ALICE. *A Hero Ain't Nothing but a Sandwich*. New York: Coward, McCann and Geoghegan, 1973. Also in paper. (Ages 12–up.) [substance abuse]
A novel that pulls no punches and offers no easy solutions probes the problems of Benjie, a 13-year-old Harlem boy well on his way to becoming a heroin addict. The book tells the story from Benjie's point of view, with comments from his mother, stepfather, and pusher friends. The book is often funny, but overall shows a very depressing view of life. Excellent discussion on drug dangers.

CLARK, LEONARD. "Charles," in *A Flock of Words*, collected by David Mackay. Illustrated by Margery Gill. New York: Harcourt, Brace & World, 1970. [vision]
Although his parents despair because of his blindness, Charles uses other senses and becomes a marvelous pianist.

CLEARY, BEVERLY. The *Ramona* series. Illustrated by Alan Tiegreen and Louis Darling. New York: Morrow, 1975–1983. Also in paper. (Ages 8–12.) [gifted]
Ramona, the younger sister of Beezus, is creative, imaginative, and a nonconformist. Beezus is bright, obedient, and academically successful. Both children feel that they are lacking in some way because they measure themselves according to their sibling's abilities. All of the books support the idea of being oneself. Each of the books in this delightful series tells an excellent story while, at the same time, portraying two very intelligent characters.

CLEAVER, VERA AND BILL. *Me Too*. Philadelphia: Lippincott, 1973. (Ages 12–up.) [intellectual disability]
Lydia tries to teach her retarded twin, Lorna. Devoting an entire summer to her sister's education, she endures the hostility of neighbors and the desertion of a friend. She is clever, energetic, introspective, nasty at times, and a clear individual. She is free of sex-role stereotypes. She finally accepts the fact that her sister will remain retarded and that there is little that she can do for her.

CLIFTON, LUCILLE. *My Friend Jacob*. Illustrated by Thomas DeGrazia. New York: Dutton 1980. (Ages 6–10.) [intellectual disability]
This story describes the relationship between an eight-year-old black child, Sam, and his fourteen-year-old white, intellectually disabled (probably with Down's syndrome) friend, Jacob. The children teach and learn from one another. They demonstrate a loving and understanding friendship. The families live in the same neighborhood and participate in activities together.

COHEN, MIRIAM. *See You Tomorrow, Charles*. Illustrated by Lillian Hoban. New York: Greenwillow Books, 1983. (Ages 5–8.) [vision]
Charles joins the first grade. He and the other children learn a great deal about each other, and come to respect each other's abilities. This same multi-ethnic classroom, with its interacting children, appears in other Cohen/Hoban books.

CORCORAN, BARBARA. *Axe Time, Sword Time*. New York: Atheneum, 1976. (Ages 12–up.) [learning]
Elinor, coming of age in the 1940s, struggles hard against her reading disability. Her story shows what such a problem meant at a time when little was known about the diagnosis and treatment of learning disabilities.

_____. *A Dance to Still Music*. New York: Atheneum, 1974. (Ages 10–up.) [hearing]
Margaret feels it's the end of her world when she becomes deaf as a teenager. Her mother is worse than no help. She runs away, and is befriended by Julie, an amazingly patient, noble character. Finally Margaret is willing to enter a program especially for deaf people. She is at last beginning to accept herself.

CURTIS, PATRICIA. *Cindy, a Hearing Ear Dog*. Photographs by David Cupp. New York: Dutton, 1981. (Ages 7–up.) [hearing]
Not a work of literature, but a factual account of the training of a dog to be an interpreter of sounds for hearing-impaired people. The book would be even more informative if it included information about which hearing-impaired people benefit most from the services of these dogs. The photographs are appealing.

_____. *Greff, the Story of a Guide Dog*. Illustrated by Mary Bloom. New York: Lodestar Books (Dutton), 1982. (Ages 9–up.) [vision]
Illustrated with descriptive and appealing black and white photographs, this book details the training of a guide dog.

DAVIDSON, MARGARET. *Louis Braille, the Boy Who Invented Books for the Blind*. New York: Hastings House, 1971. (Ages 9–12.) [vision]
Blinded at the age of three in his father's harness shop, Louis Braille is helped by the village priest to go to the Royal Institute of Blind Youth in Paris. At fifteen, he perfects the raised-dot alphabet which enables blind people to read with their hands. His brief, courageous life is devoted to helping others with his disability.

DAVIDSON, MICKI. *Helen Keller*. New York: Hastings House, 1971. (Ages 7–10.) [gifted, vision, hearing]
A biography focusing on the childhood of this remarkable of woman who overcame the handicaps of being blind and deaf, and became a model for the world of a superheroic, super-capable person.

DAVIDSON, MICKI. *Helen Keller's Teacher*. New York: Four Winds Press, 1965. (Ages 9–12.) [gifted, vision]
The story of Annie Sullivan—poor, orphaned, and nearly blind herself, whose discoveries at the Perkins Institute enabled her to teach deaf-blind Helen Keller. Annie's grim childhood and Helen's amazing accomplishments are realistically described in this true story of extraordinary determination.

DAYEE, FRANCES S. *Private Zone*. Illustrated by Marina Megale Horosko. Edmonds, Washington: Charles Franklin Press, 1982. (Ages 3–9.) [sexual abuse]
A tasteful, nonoffensive presentation of what a young child needs to know to prevent and/or report sexual assault. Included is information by experts for adult use, as well as symptoms in children's behavior that indicate they may have been sexually assaulted. Advice on what to do if a child is sexually assaulted, and a listing of additional books on the subject are added.

DE ANGELI, MARGUERITE. *The Door in the Wall*. Illustrated by the author. New York: Doubleday, 1950. Also in paper. (Ages 9–12.) [mobility]
Set in medieval times, when the bubonic plague was rampant. Robin, the ten-year-old protagonist, learns to live with a disability that has impaired the use of his legs. Aided by monks, he learns to read, write, whittle, and get around using crutches.

DEJONG, MEINDERT. *Journey from Peppermint Street*. New York: Harper & Row, 1968. (Ages 8–11.) [speech, hearing]
Uncle Siebren is mute. His nephew is afraid of him at first but soon recognizes his gentleness and strength. Uncle Siebren communicates wonderfully with his hands, as well as in writing.

DORMAN, N. B. *Laughter in the Background*. New York: Elsevier/Nelson, 1980. (Ages 11–up.) [substance abuse, eating disorder]
Marcie's mother is an alcoholic. Marcie is obese and slovenly. She seems helpless to do anything about her situation until she is almost raped by one of her mother's boyfriends. Then she takes charge of her own life and demands to be taken out of her mother's custody. Marcie emerges as a strong young woman who will overcome her problems.

DUE, LINNA A. *High and Outside*. Harper and Row, 1980. Also in paper. (Ages 12–up.) [substance abuse]
Niki is a seventeen-year-old star athlete and honor student who from both her parents' and teachers' point of view has everything a teenager could want or need. This is a modern family in which mother and father are "Joyce" and "Carl" and Niki partakes in her parents' daily ritual of cocktails. From the first few pages the reader is aware that Niki is a lonely and desperate girl who drinks more than a cocktail with dinner. Niki tries to commit suicide but decides "If I liked my wrist enough not to cut it anymore, maybe I could learn to like the rest of me." The story ends with Niki accepting the help of Al-Anon. She will overcome her problem.

DUNCAN, LOIS. *A Gift of Magic*. Little, Brown, 1971. (Ages 10–up.) [gifted]
Nancy Garrett has extrasensory perception. Her gift causes her anxiety and grief at first, but she learns to control and value herself.

FANSHAWE, ELIZABETH. *Rachel.* Illustrated by Michael Charlton. Scarsdale, New York: Bradbury Press, 1975. (Ages 5–8.) [mobility]
Rachel is a little girl in a wheelchair who goes to a regular school and does many of the same things that nondisabled children do. The emphasis is on what Rachel *can* do, not what she cannot do. The theme of accepting people with differences is an important one and is well presented. The illustrations wonderfully complement the text.

FASSLER, JOAN. *Howie Helps Himself.* Illustrated by Joe Lasker. Chicago: Whitman, 1975. (Ages 5–8.) [mobility]
Howie, a child in a wheelchair, relies on others to wheel him around. The book recounts various aspects of his home and school life, but is colored by Howie's frustrations, due to his being unable to control his own wheelchair. Throughout the book, Howie tries and strains to make his wheels move, until, one day, he turns himself around as his Dad comes to pick him up from school, and slowly with great effort, he wheels himself over to his Dad.

_____. *One Little Girl.* New York: Human Sciences Press, 1969. (Ages 5–up.) [learning]
Laurie has a learning problem. She is slow at some things and quicker at others. When attitudes change on Laurie's part and the adults around her, everyone becomes happier.

FITZHUGH, LOUISE. *Harriet the Spy.* New York: Harper & Row, 1964. (Ages 10–up.) [gifted]
Eleven-year-old Harriet wants to be a writer and in order to get a head start on her career, spends part of every day on her spy route "observing" and noting in her singular, caustic, comic way, everything of interest to her.

FLEISCHMAN, PAUL. *The Half-a-Moon Inn.* Illustrated by Kathy Jacobi. New York: Harper & Row, 1980. (Ages 10–up.) [speech]
Aaron is mute. On his twelfth birthday, his mother helps him to accept his need for independence. He endures extreme hardships, but eventually overcomes them. The muteness is not just a device, and Aaron is not just a mute; he is a full character, as are all of the others in this excellent book.

FORRAI, MARIA S., AND PURSELL, MARGARET S. *A Look at Physical Handicaps.* Illustrated by the authors. Minneapolis: Lerner Publications, 1976. (Ages 5–8.) [mobility]
Excellent black-and-white photographs and a simple text convey the message. Physical handicaps are defined and explained in terms of causes. Several types of handicaps and special ways of adjusting to them are shown.

FRIIS-BAASTAD, BABBIS. *Don't Take Teddy.* New York: Scribner, 1967. (Ages 10–12.) [intellectual disability]
Mikkel is determined not to let anyone put his retarded brother, Teddy, in an institution. The Norwegian boys are very close and Mikkel accepts much responsibility for caring for Teddy. He even leads him through the mountains to his uncle's cabin to keep Teddy from being sent away. Eventually, Mikkel's parents enter Teddy

into a special day school near their home. The ending is an ideal one, but not unrealistic.

GALE, NORMAN. "Bobby's First Poem," in *Pick Me Up*, ed. William Cole. New York: Macmillan, 1972. (All ages.) [sexual abuse]
Because children don't always recognize tickling as an early potential form of sexual abuse, this poem, read aloud, may be useful in introducing this awareness.

GARFIELD, JAMES B. *Follow My Leader*. New York: Viking, 1957. Also in paper. (Ages 9–12.) [vision]
When a firecracker explodes, Jimmy loses his sight; with a guide dog, he learns to do things he had thought impossible.

GARRIGUE, SHEILA. *Between Friends*. Scarsdale, New York: Bradbury Press, 1978. (Ages 10–up.) [intellectual disability]
Ten-year-old Jill has just moved to New England. Jill makes friends with a retarded girl, Dede, who lives on her street, because she is lonely and all of the other neighbors who are her age are away on summer holidays. Jill likes Dede and becomes interested in how much mentally retarded children can do (although at first she is very uncomfortable with them). When Dede moves to a warmer climate, Jill realizes she will miss Dede even though her friendship with Dede has been an assortment of mixed emotions.

GEORGE, JEAN CRAIGHEAD. *Julie of the Wolves*. Illustrated by John Schoenherr. New York: Harper & Row, 1972. (Ages 12–up.) [gifted]
An Eskimo girl runs away from an unhappy situation. Living in the frozen wilderness, she courageously makes friends with the wolves and learns their ways of survival. She must face problems not only of individual survival but also of the changing ways of her people.

GILLHAM, BILL. *My Brother Barry*. London: Andre Deutsch, 1981. (Ages 8–11.) [speech]
Nine-year-old James has a mentally disabled brother who can't talk. James loves Barry and usually doesn't mind watching out for him, but sometimes feels that the responsibility gets to be a bit too great. His caretaking behavior sometimes gets in the way of his making friends and having time for himself. James is terrified that something terrible has happened when Barry is lost for over twenty-four hours. Fortunately James and his friend Tommy are able to assist the police with information that helps them to find Barry unharmed.

GLENN, MEL. *Class Dismissed: High School Poems*. Illustrated by Michael Bernstein. New York: Clarion Books, 1982. (Ages 12 and up.) [general]
A sensitive and powerful set of poems, each told from the point of view of an individual high school student. Although written by an adult, the poems clearly portray the special feelings and problems of the young people. The photos are worthy of special mention.

———. "Ernest Mott," in *Class Dismissed! High School Poems*. Photographs by Michael Bernstein. New York: Clarion Books, 1982. (Ages 12–up.) [emotional dysfunction]

Ernest has managed to control his feelings after several years of therapy and drugs, but he is afraid to be mainstreamed "back to people who still have fear in their faces."

_____. "Hildy Ross," in *Class Dismissed! High School Poems*. Photographs by Michael Bernstein. New York: Clarion Books, 1982. (Ages 12–up.) [child abuse]
Hildy is an abused teenager who has ambivalent feelings about her father. Even though he beats her, she "can't see turning him in."

_____. "Nancy Soto," in *Class Dismissed! High School Poems*. Photographs by Michael Bernstein. New York: Clarion Books, 1982. (Ages 12–up.) [emotional dysfunction]
Nancy suffers from an excruciating shyness. Her inability to speak out loud in the classroom is a major source of pain and embarrassment for her.

_____. "Rhonda Winfey," in *Class Dismissed! High School Poems*. Photographs by Michael Bernstein. New York: Clarion Books, 1982. (Ages 12–up.) [substance abuse]
Rhonda is under constant stress: for good grades, college entrance, first place. She depends on valium to see her through the "jungle" that is high school.

GREENBERG, JAN. *The Pig-Out Blues*. New York: Farrar, Straus & Giroux, 1982. (Ages 10–up.) [appearance, eating disorder]
Jody overeats and is very self-centered. Friends and another family help her to start becoming aware of other people's problems and feelings.

GREENFIELD, ELOISE. *Darlene*. New York: Methuen, 1980. (Ages 5–8.) [mobility]
This slim picture book effectively shows that there is much a wheelchair-bound girl can enjoy.

GROLLMAN, SHARON. *More Time to Grow*. Boston: Beacon Press, 1977. (Ages 7–10.) [intellectual disability]
Carla's feelings toward her retarded brother Arthur are responded to with an explanation about what it means to be mentally retarded. Questions and activities and a guide for parents and teachers are also included in the book, as is an annotated listing of recommended organizations, books, pamphlets and films.

HAMILTON, VIRGINIA. *The Planet of Junior Brown*. New York: Macmillan, 1971. Also in paper. (Ages 12–up.) (Newbery Honor Book and National Book Award Finalist.) [emotional dysfunction, appearance]
Junior Brown is a very fat (almost three hundred pounds), very unhappy young man. Buddy, his friend, has created a community of homeless children by finding abandoned buildings for them to live in. Junior, who, incidentally, is a talented musician, finally moves out of his destructive home setting into the constellation that Buddy directs. As with all of Hamilton's books, the writing is exceptional and the characters are black.

_____. *Sweet Whispers, Brother Rush*. New York: Philomel Books, 1981. (Ages 12–up.) [illness, intellectual disability, neglect]
A masterful story about a black family, past and present, and a young girl's coming of age. Tree, fourteen years old, is very protective of her seventeen-year-old brother

Dabney (Dab). Dab is "slow" and "different." Brother Rush, a handsome ghost, appears to Tree and tells about the family's past, including the emotional neglect of Dab by their mother. Dab has a rare illness and eventually dies. When Tree recovers from her mourning, she begins to accept her own womanhood.

HANLON, EMILY. *The Swing.* New York: Bradbury Press, 1979 (Ages 9–12.) [hearing disability]
The two main characters, Emily, a hearing-disabled eleven-year-old, and Danny, a thirteen-year-old having a difficult time mourning his father's death, lock horns with each other in this well-written story dealing strongly with how to be an individual in a society that demands conformity. The information about hearing loss and its effects is accurately woven into the story.

HAUTZIG, DEBORAH. *Second Star to the Right.* New York: Greenwillow Books, 1981. (Ages 12–up.) [appearance]
Leslie is bright, athletic, and very eager to please, especially her mother, who is a holocaust survivor. In her zeal to lose weight (and, clearly, hating herself, and any notion that she will mature into womanhood) she almost starves herself to death. At first rejecting the fact that she has anorexia nervosa, she ultimately begins her slow climb back to normalcy.

HEIDE, FLORENCE PARRY. *Growing Anyway Up.* Philadelphia: Lippincott, 1976. (Ages 10–up.) [emotional dysfunction]
Florence has an elaborate system for protecting herself from further emotional harm. Her Aunt Nina, a wholesome, loving woman, helps her to establish a more realistic perspective.

HERMES, PATRICIA. *What If They Knew?* New York: Dell Yearling, 1980. (Ages 9–12.) [epilepsy]
Beginning fifth grade in a new school comes as a terrible blow to Jeremy, who suddenly becomes concerned about keeping her epilepsy secret. By the end of the school year, after an epileptic episode, her friends and family persuade her of their good intentions, and she becomes more self-sufficient. Although the book is somewhat flawed (layer upon layer of secrets unrealistically intrude on the plot), the points made in the book are pertinent to the topic.

HICKS, CLIFFORD B. *Alvin's Secret Code.* New York: Scholastic, 1963. (Ages 9–12.) [gifted]
Alvin Fernald, his friend Shoie, and his sister, the Pest, are off again—on another hilarious adventure—this time as Secret Agents, hot on the trail of spies.

HILDICK, E. W. *The Case of the Invisible Dog.* Illustrated by Lisl Weil. New York: Macmillan, 1977. (Ages 8–12.) [gifted]
All of the McCurtle mysteries involve a group of bright youngsters who use their imaginations and their intelligence to solve mysteries.

HIRSCH, KAREN. *My Sister.* Illustrated by Nancy Inderieden. Minneapolis: Carolrhoda Books, 1977. (Ages 5–8.) [intellectual disability]
Written from the perspective of a sibling with a retarded sister, the book covers a wide range of feelings and situations where a retarded sibling might make things difficult for a family. The child's behavior is accepting and understanding of this

sister; other people's is not always so accepting. Positive and negative attitudes and emotions are presented in a supportive manner. The story ends with the brother knowing that no matter how much he wishes, his sister will never be normal, but he accepts her as she is.

HOLLAND, ISABELLE. *Dinah and the Green Fat Kingdom.* Philadelphia: Lippincott, 1978 Also in paper. (Ages 11–up.) [appearance, cerebral palsy]
Dinah is twelve years old, and has been overweight for several years. Her family, especially her mother, has launched an intensive campaign to make her lose weight. She is helped to accept herself, and also to lose weight by a nun who is a nutritionist at a school for children with special needs. Her puppy, her father, and Sebastian, a boy who has cerebral palsy, and who is very good with animals, and very intelligent, also contribute to her changed self-image.

HOLMES, BURNHAM. *The First Seeing Eye Dogs.* New York: Contemporary Perspectives, 1978. (Ages 8–10.) [vision]
From its beginning in World War I in Germany to The Seeing Eye, a school for blind people and guide dogs, the story of guide dogs is told. The history of the school is covered as well as the resistance guide dogs have faced in many places, public and private. The story is told mostly through the experience of Morris Frank and his guide dog, Buddy.

HULL, ELEANOR. *Alice with Golden Hair.* New York: Atheneum, 1981. (Ages 10–up.) [intellectual disability]
Alice is retarded and lives in an institution. She obtains a resident job in a nursing home for old people, and handles her new responsibilities well.

HUNT, IRENE. *The Lottery Rose.* New York: Scribner, 1976. (Ages 10–up.) [intellectual disability]
Georgie is an abused child. His mother and her boyfriend have mistreated him for all of his seven years. He eventually goes to a Catholic school where he is treated better than he ever was before. He slowly begins to heal emotionally, and eventually establishes a loving and permanent relationship with a woman whose life has been full of tragedies. Although the book contains some cliches (a mentally retarded boy dies), the language and power of the book are extraordinary. Be prepared to cry; this is a very touching story.

HUNT, NIGEL. *The World of Nigel Hunt.* New York: Garrett, 1967. (Ages 12–up.) [intellectual disability]
The diary of Nigel Hunt, a British child with Down's syndrome. His physician's and his father's comments preface his diary.

HYDE, MARGARET O. *Cry Softly! The Story of Child Abuse.* Philadelphia: Westminster Press, 1980. (Ages 10–up.) [child abuse]
Helps children and concerned adults to understand that child abuse is present in families at all socioeconomic levels. Provides a list of organizations that help abusive parents as well as their children.

HYDE, MARGARET O. *Know about Alcohol.* Illustrated by Bill Morrison. New York: McGraw-Hill, 1978, (Ages 9–up.) [substance abuse]
Simple description of alcohol, its use and abuse. Information about AA, plus resources for further information.

HYDE, MARGARET O. *Mind Drugs.* New York: McGraw-Hill, 1972. (Ages 12–up.) [substance abuse]
A candid, factual approach to usage of drugs from several fields, e.g., medicine, psychiatry, social psychology, and public health. Abuse, addiction, and preventive measures are discussed.

IRWIN, ANN. *One Bite at a Time.* New York: Franklin Watts, 1973. (Ages 12–up) [appearance]
A very fat girl in ninth grade is miserable and plans to run away. When her music teacher and a boy classmate display interest and kindness, she resolves to stay in school and try to overcome her eating and social problems.

JOHNSTON, NORMA. *Of Time and Seasons.* New York: Atheneum, 1975. (Ages 11–up.) [gifted]
Bridget is a member of a very gifted faimly. She is the only one without talent. She eventually discovers that she also has a special talent, an ability to help her family through a crisis.

JUPO, FRANK. *Atu, the Silent One.* Illustrated by the author. New York: Holiday, 1967. (Ages 5–8.) [speech, gifted]
Atu is a young African Bushman, living before the era of recorded history. He is mute, but he is able, through his talent as an artist, to leave a beautiful and graphic record of his people's activities and customs.

KAMIEN, JANET. *What If You Couldn't. . . ? A Book about Special Needs.* New York: Scribner, 1979. (Ages 6–12.) [general]
Janet Kamien's format is creative and interesting. She approaches six exceptionalities from the "What if you couldn't?" perspective and this would certainly appeal to children. A good adjunct to the Boston Children's Museum activities to help non-disabled children experience, to a limited extent, how it feels to be disabled.

KATZ, BERNARD AND JONATHAN. *Black Woman.* New York: Pantheon, 1973, (Ages 10–up.) [gifted]
Lucy Terry Prince (1730–1821), an eighteenth-century slave, seeks education and legal redress for her family through the courts.

KENT, DEBORAH. *Belonging.* New York: Dial Press, 1978. (Ages 12–up.) [vision]
Meg is blind. She is also self-sufficient, and attempting to find out how she can be her own person, without conforming to the preconceptions of peers as well as adults. The author conveys very well how Meg feels and functions. Excellent sensitivity to the physical perceptions of visually disabled people is imbedded into a good story.

KERR. M. E. *Dinky Hocker Shoots Smack.* New York: Harper & Row, 1972. Also in paper. (Ages 12–up.)
Concerns several adolescents not accepted by the adult community. Centers on Dinky, an overweight girl who is neglected by her community-oriented parents.

KILLEA, MARIE. *Karen.* Englewood Cliffs, New Jersey: Prentice-Hall, 1952. (Ages 11–up.) [cerebral palsy]
A true story about a child who has cerebral palsy and her parents' attempts to help her live a good life.

KIPNIS, LYNN, AND ADLER, SUSAN. *You Can't Catch Diabetes from a Friend.* Illustrated by Richard Benkof. Gainesville, Floria: Triad, 1979. (Ages 7–11.) [diabetes]
Using a series of photographs and simple, but specific text, the book follows the experiences of several children who have diabetes through their daily routines. The children are of different ages and backgrounds, but they all handle their condition competently.

KONIGSBERG, E. L. *From the Mixed-Up Files of Mrs. Basil E. Frankweiler.* New York: Atheneum, 1967. (Ages 8–10.) [gifted]
Adventure, suspense, and humor abound when twelve-year-old Claudia and her younger brother elude the security guards and live for a week in New York's Metropolitan Museum of Art.

LANGONE, JOHN. *Goodbye to Bedlam: Understanding Mental Illness and Retardation.* Boston: Little, Brown, 1974. (Ages 12–up.) [emotional dysfunction, intellectual disability]
Clear, objective description of "mental illness" and "retardation." Historical anecdotes enrich the text.

LARSEN, HANNE. *Don't Forget Tom.* New York: Crowell, 1978. (Ages 5–7.) [intellectual disability]
About a mentally disabled boy named Tom. Using photographs of Tom and his family and the simple language of the text, the book informs young readers about mental retardation. Some of Tom's difficulties are mentioned in a very tactful manner, such as the fact that he isn't toilet trained and that he sometimes get angry and sad about some things he can't do. The approach used in presenting these issues is realistic and appropriate. The original version was written in Danish.

LASKER, JOE. *He's My Brother.* Chicago: Whitman, 1974. (Ages 6–9.) [learning disability]
Jamie, a slow-learning younger brother gets teased. Becka, the older sister, bakes brownies for him and is kind to him. His brother sometimes is impatient but then plays with him to make up for it. Jamie is good with babies and animals. The family is very loving and patient with him. Mildred and Joe Lasker write at the end that they hope "this book will enable other Jamies and their families to identify with the experience shown and take comfort."

LASKER, JOE. *Nick Joins In.* Chicago: Whitman, 1980. (Ages 6–9.) [mobility]
When Nick, who uses a wheelchair, goes to public school for the first time, he is worried about getting around and being accepted. The teachers encourage questions from the other children, and Nick's parents patiently answer his own questions. Stresses many of the things which Nick can do as well as or better than the other children. Pictures are excellent, showing a racially integrated class and teaching staff, and a female construction worker. Nick seems to be the only disabled child in the school.

LE GUIN, URSULA K. *Very Far Away from Anywhere Else.* New York: Atheneum, 1976. (Ages 11–up.) [gifted]
Owen, a talented 17-year-old, has identity problems and finds facing home, school,

and daily life very difficult. Through his relationship with Natalie, a creative and talented musician, he begins to find himself and learns to deal with life.

L'ENGLE, MADELEINE. *A Ring of Endless Light*. New York: Farrar, Straus & Giroux, 1980. (Ages 11–up.) [gifted]
This fourth book in the Austin family series focuses on Vicky. Her family is staying on the island where her grandfather lives. He is dying. Vicky and her brother John become close friends in this story. Vicky also discovers that she has the gift of communicating with dolphins. The book is an investigation of love, life, and coming to terms with death.

L'ENGLE, MADELEINE. *A Wrinkle in Time*. New York: Farrar, Straus, 1962. Also in paper. (Ages 10–up.) [gifted]
A scientist has vanished. Now an eerie midnight visitor leads three children in search of him—through a "wrinkle in time." Other books in the *Time* trilogy are: *A Wind in the Door* and *A Swiftly Tilting Planet*. Two of the children in the family are unusually gifted: Charles Wallace's intellect and depth of understanding, and Meg's math ability are outstanding. The rest of the family is also very talented. (The author's series about the Austin family also contains gifted families.)

LEVINE, EDNA S. *Lisa and Her Soundless World*. New York: Human Sciences Press, 1974. (Ages 6–8.) [hearing]
The book begins with a discussion of our senses and how we use them. It then introduces Lisa, an eight-year-old girl who is deaf. Hearing aids, instruction in lip-reading, sign language, and finger spelling help her to communicate.

LEVOY, MYRON. *Alan and Naomi*. New York: Harper & Row, 1977. Also in paper. (Ages 10–up.) [emotional dysfunction]
A beautifully written, tragic yet heroic story of the attempts of a young boy, Alan, to help his friend, Naomi, recover from the horror of the Holocaust. Naomi gradually becomes able to relate to other children and go to school, until a violent incident sends her back into emotional crisis.

LIPSYTE, ROBERT. *One Fat Summer*. New York: Harper and Row, 1977. (Ages 11–up.) [appearance]
Robert Marks is extraordinarily obese. He is ashamed of his body, but keeps on gorging himself with food. His friend Joan has a huge crooked nose. Over the course of a summer Joan has her nose fixed, and Bob loses weight. The process of changing is much more painful and difficult for Bob than for Joan.

LITTLE, JEAN. *From Anna*. Illustrated by Joan Sandin. New York: Harper & Row, 1972. (Ages 9–12.) [vision]
Anna's vision problem is discovered after she and her family emigrate to Canada from Nazi Germany. Because of her previously unexplained disability, Anna had been awkward and clumsy in her movements, and had therefore been rejected by others. She becomes very competent after she has the opportunity to cope with her visual impairment.

LIVINGSTON, MYRA COHN. "Being Fat," in *The Moon and a Star and Other Poems*. Illustrated by Judith Spahn. New York: Harcourt, Brace & World, 1965. (Ages 9–12.) [appearance]

This poem shows an interesting perspective on obesity. Some fat people feel that their stomachs are all that people can think about, or even talk to.

LONG, JUDY. *Volunteer Spring.* New York: Dodd, Mead, 1976. (Ages 11–up.) [intellectual disability]
Although Jill, an eighth grader, volunteers to work at a nearby mental institution, she is unprepared for the range of mental and physical disabilities she encounters there. The staff of the hospital are caring, able professionals, and Jill overcomes her antipathy and decides to continue at her task.

MACDONALD, CYNTHIA. "Accomplishments," in *Don't Forget to Fly,* collected by Paul Janeczko. New York: Bradbury Press, 1981. (Ages 12–up.) [child abuse]
The desperate attempts of a child to please an uncaring, unresponsive mother prove fruitless, even in the last shocking stanza of this poem.

MACK, NANCY. *Tracy.* Illustrated by Heinz Kluetmeier. Milwaukee: Raintree, 1976. (Ages 5–8.) [cerebral palsy, mobility, intellectual disability]
The book follows Tracy, who has cerebral palsy, through a day in school and at home. She rides a bike, works at a desk, slides on the playground slide and turns a jump rope. The excellent photographs include pictures of Tracy receiving therapy and using her wheelchair.

MACLACHIAN, PATRICIA. *Through Grandpa's Eyes.* Illustrated by Deborah Ray. New York: Harper & Row, 1979. (Ages 6–9.) [vision]
John spends time with his blind grandfather and learns to appreciate nature while discovering how to use all of his senses. The author's prose creates an atmosphere of caring which is augmented by Ray's soft drawings. Both grandparents are seen as productive, creative people. The grandmother sculpts, the grandfather plays the cello. Males are seen performing domestic tasks. The grandparents love each other and enjoy their lives.

MAGORIAN, MICHELLE. *Good Night, Mr. Tom.* New York: Harper & Row, 1981. (Ages 12–up.) [child abuse]
Willie Beech is at first disoriented when he is sent to the country with other evacuated city children. Willie has been abused by his mother to the point where he has no conception of what a normal relationship is. He meets with understanding and affection, and finally is rescued from near death by Mr. Tom, his elderly benefactor.

MANN, JOHN S., M. D. *The Good Drug and the Bad Drug.* Illustrated by Lynn Siveat. New York: M. Evans, 1970. (Ages 8–12.) [substance abuse]
A primer in anatomy and the effects of drugs on our bodies. An unbiased approach with the emphasis on basic biology, the book is nicely illustrated.

MATHIS, SHARON BELL. *Listen for the Fig Tree.* New York: Viking, 1974. Also in paper. (Ages 12–up.) [vision, substance abuse, gifted]
Sixteen-year-old Muffin Johnson is blind. She is an extraordinarily competent and gifted young woman. She manages all of the details of housekeeping, sews and shops, and has excellent relationships with people. Her mother is almost destroyed over the death of the father and is frequently in an alcoholic stupor. Muffin takes care of her with remarkable facility. Her feelings about her black heritage are a strong part of the book.

MAZER, NORMA FOX. *I. Trissy.* New York: Delacorte Press, 1971. Also in paper. (Ages 9–12.) [gifted, emotional dysfunction]
The story of an imaginative girl who blames her mother for her parents' divorce. Eventually, she begins to be able to see herself and each of her parents in a realistic, individual light. Trissy behaves in a very self-centered manner throughout the entire book. She, not her parents, is the cause of problems in the aftermath of the divorce. Her parents' understanding provides a base for her to build a more mature and responsible way of behaving.

McKILLOP, PATRICIA A. *The Riddle Master of Hed.* New York: Atheneum, 1976. (Ages 10–up.) [gifted]
Morgon is a prince of Hed. He tries to be a simple prince but is drawn into riddles and mysterious adventures which he must use his head to solve.

McKINLEY, ROBIN. *The Blue Sword.* New York: Greenwillow books, 1982. (Ages 11-up.)
Harry Crewe, an unusually tall, strong, and intelligent young woman, is the protagonist of this fantasy-adventure set in the Homelander Empire and the Kingdom of Damar.

McLEAN, SUSAN. *Pennies for the Piper.* New York: Farrar, Straus & Giroux, 1981. (Ages 10–up)
Ten-year-old Victoria and her mother have tried to plan adequately for what they know is inevitable: the mother's approaching death from heart disease. Also in the story is a young boy whose mother has neglected, abused, and finally rejected him. The book provides readers with a remarkable view of the human spirit.

MEINKE, PETER. "This Is a Poem to My Son Peter," in *Don't Forget to Fly,* collected by Paul Janeczko. New York: Bradbury Press, 1981. (Ages 10–up.) [child abuse]
An interesting perspective is presented in this poem about a father apologizing to his son for beating him. The anguish of the father is evident in his admission that the child was the victim of his father's need to inflict pain.

MELTON, DAVID. *A Boy Called Hopeless by M. J.* New York: Scholastic, 1977. (Ages 10–up.) [neurological]
A story of Jeremiah, a brain-damaged boy, and his family as told by his sister. It tells of the "patterning" program used for some brain-damaged children. it includes some of the positive results for Jeremiah.

MINER, JANE CLAYPOOL. *Why Did You Leave Me?* New York: Scholastic, 1980. Paperback. (Ages 12–up.) [substance abuse]
Laurie, the sixteen-year-old daughter of an alcoholic mother, remembers and resents her mother's behavior during her drunken binges. The mother has spent some time in a special treatment center for alcoholics. Laurie finds it difficult to relinquish her caretaking position and feels anger, jealousy, and resentment, as well as self-pity. In the end she moves from her negative stance, with the help of a nineteen-year-old woman who is a recovered alcoholic. Her mother regularly attends Alcoholics Anonymous, and it looks as if she will be successful in overcoming her drinking problem.

MITCHELL, JOYCE SLAYTON. *See Me More Clearly: Career and Life Planning for Teens with Physical Disabilities.* New York: Harcourt Brace Jovanovich, 1980. (Ages 12–up.) [general]
Specific disabilities are described and discussed, with the objective of helping people who have these disabilities learn survival skills and become self-supporting. Topics such as sexuality are also included.

MOERI, LOUISE. *The Girl Who Lived on the Ferris Wheel.* New York: Dutton, 1979. (Ages 10–up.) [child abuse]
Til's father visits with her every Saturday and takes her to an amusement park, where they ride the ferris wheel. Til is afraid to tell him that she hates the ride to the extent that it gives her nightmares. She is also afraid to tell anyone that her mother physically abuses her. When Til realizes that her mother is insane, and that she, Til, is in danger of her life, she finally gets help.

O'BRIEN, ROBERT C. *Mrs. Frisby and the Rats of NIMH.* New York: Atheneum, 1971. Also in paper. (Ages 8–10.) [gifted]
The doctors at NIMH have created a race of super intelligent rats who can read the labels on medicine bottles and the instructions on how to open their cages. The dilemma and responsibilities of intelligence are explored.

O'DELL, SCOTT. *Island of the Blue Dolphins.* Boston: Houghton Mifflin, 1960. Also in paper. (Ages 10–up.) [gifted]
Karana, a young Native American girl, is alone on her home island after her tribe has left and her brother has been killed by wild dogs. She manages her own survival courageously for many years until, at last, she is rescued by missionaries.

OMINSKY, ELAINE. *Jon O: A Special Boy.* Englewood Cliffs, New Jersey: Prentice-Hall, 1977, (Ages 5–8.) [intellectual disability]
The photographs provide a graphic presentation of the manifestations of Down's syndrome. The text describes the family interactions and feelings.

O'NEILL, MARY. "The Milk Man's Little Boy," in *People I'd Like to Keep.* Illustrated by Paul Galdone. New York: Doubleday, 1964. (Ages 6–12.) [hearing]
The poet, using the voice of a young child, is delighted on milk-bill day. He accompanies his father, the milkman, who speaks on his fingers "with lightning speed and dazzling grace" as the son translates for the customers. A very positive, joyous poem.

O'NEILL, MARY. "Mimi's Fingers," in *Fingers Are Always Bringing Me News.* Illustrated by Don Bolognese. New York: Doubleday, 1969. (Ages 6–9.) [visual]
Mimi is a well-adjusted blind girl who can experience the world with her sensitive fingers. Still, in the last line of the poem, Mimi acknowledges her inability to see as she asks the reader to "...tell me about blue?"

OPPENHEIMER, JOAN. *Francesca, Baby.* New York: Scholastic, 1976. Paperback (Ages 12–up.) [substance abuse]
Francesca's mother is an alcoholic. Francesca and her sister protect their mother from outsiders, and cut themselves off from any social contact because they are ashamed. Finally they get help from Alanon and force their mother to help herself.

PATERSON, KATHERINE. *The Great Gilly Hopkins*. New York: Crowell, 1978. (Ages 9–up.) [gifted]
Gilly is a very intelligent, though angry and unhappy, girl. She seems to get pleasure from making people dislike her. In reality, she craves love and security. A masterfully written story, in which all of the characters are vivid individuals: Mr. Randolph, the self-sufficient, book-loving blind neighbor; Trotter, the obese, wise, loving foster mother; William Ernest, the painfully insecure little boy.

PETER, DIANA. *Claire and Emma*. Illustrated by Jeremy Finlay. New York: John Day, 1977. (Ages 6–9.) [hearing]
Claire and Emma are sisters who were born deaf. The book, illustrated with color photographs, graphically and specifically explains many of the details of their condition, including the use of hearing aids, the difficulty of communication, and the procedures for helping the sisters function in a hearing world.

PETERSON, JEANNE WHITEHOUSE. *I Have a Sister, My Sister Is Deaf*. Illustrated by Deborah Ray. New York: Harper & Row, 1977. (Ages 5–8.) [hearing]
Told from the perspective of the sister of a deaf child. The narrator describes how other people react to her sister and how she feels about her sister's condition.

PHIPSON, JOAN. *A Tide Flowing*. New York: Atheneum, 1981. (Ages 11–up.) [mobility]
Mark's problems with his family are seemingly insurmountable until his friend Connie, who is disabled, helps him.

PLATT, KIN. *The Boy Who Could Make Himself Disappear*. Philadelphia: Chilton, 1968. Also in paper. (Ages 12–up.) [child abuse, speech, emotional dysfunction]
Roger is a child who is abused, unloved, and unwanted by his sadistic, selfish parents, who are divorced. Although he becomes totally out of touch with reality in the end, he at last has a friend who cares for him and who holds out hope that he can make a new life for himself. As with many Platt books, the writing is excellent, and the situation is very painful. Readers should be warned of this, and the book should be used with care.

PLATT, KIN. *Chloris and the Creeps*. Philadelphia: Chilton, 1973. Also in paper. (Ages 12–up.) [emotional dysfunction]
Chloris cannot accept her parents' divorce or her father's subsequent suicide. She is hateful and destructive to her mother, her mother's new husband, and their home because she thinks of her father as a kind of superman. Through therapy, sensitive response, and patience, Chloris's mother, sister and stepfather nurture her. A sudden awakening to her father's real nature seems also to help.

RABE, BERNICE. *The Balancing Girl*. Illustrated by Lillian Hoban. New York: Dutton, 1981. (Ages 5–8.) [mobility]
Margaret is talented at balancing things: blocks, books on her head, dominoes, and herself on braces, with crutches. She also can get around pretty well in her wheelchair. The story revolves around Tommy's jealously of Margaret's ability and the attention she gets because of it. A gentle portrayal of an engaging heroine and an episode in first grade.

RILEY, JOCELYN. *Only My Mouth Is Smiling.* New York: Morrow, 1982. (Ages 11–up.) [emotional dysfunction]
Thirteen-year-old Merle lives with her unstable mother and antagonistic grandmother. When her mother flees with her family to a lake in Wisconsin, Merle begins to build a life for herself despite warnings that her mother will soon have another bout with severe mental illness. The reality of children dealing with a mentally ill parent is depicted here as well as the uncertainty of future custody of the children. The grandmother is a complex, but stable influence.

ROBINSON, VERONICA. *David in Silence.* Philadelphia: Lippincott, 1966. (Ages 12–up.)
A working-class industrial town in England provides the setting for this sensitive and positive novel about David, a deaf teen-aged boy trying to settle in a new town with a hearing group of friends. Deafness is neither downplayed nor given the upper hand. The reader is made aware of all the tools David has at his disposal. Lip-reading, special schooling, and sign language are all integral but not overpowering parts of his life. Robinson has done her research well, but keeps technicality to a minimum. Essentially a warm and upbeat book about a special group of young people who learn with and through one another.

ROSENBERG, MAXINE B. *My Friend Leslie.* Photographs by George Ancona. New York: Lothrop, Lee & Shepard, 1983. (Ages 5–8.) [general]
Leslie has multiple handicaps. This photographic essay depicts her fellow kindergartners as helpful, mutually respectful, and enjoying each other's company.

ROUNDS, GLEN. *Blind Outlaw.* New York: Holiday, 1981. (Ages 7–up.) [speech, vision]
A mute boy, talented in working with animals, tames a wild blind horse. The step-by-step progress of the horse, led by the patient boy, results in an evocatively beautiful story.

ROY, RON. *Where's Buddy?* Illustrated by Troy Howell. New York: Clarion Books, 1982. (Ages 8–11.) [diabetes]
Buddy is seven years old, and has diabetes. On the day that Mike, his older brother, is in charge of him, Buddy disappears. Mike finds him trapped in a cave, and although Buddy has not taken his medicine, it is clear to the reader that he knows what regimen is required, and can cope with his condition.

SACHS, MARILYN. *The Bears' House.* Illustrated by Louis Glanzman. Garden City, New York: Doubleday, 1971. (Ages 9–12.) [emotional dysfunction]
Fran Ellen, her brother, and her three sisters try to manage their household after their father has deserted them and their mother has suffered a nervous collapse. Fran Ellen finds refuge in the fantasy of a toy bears' house her teacher has brought into the classroom. At the end of the book the reader is not certain that Fran Ellen will emerge into the real world again.

SACHS, MARILYN. *Call Me Ruth.* Garden City, New York: Doubleday, 1982. (Ages 9–up.) [gifted]
Ruth and her mother emigrate from Russia to New York City. Ruth's father had worked for nine years to save enough money to send for them. Ruth loves America

from the moment she arrives; her mother hates it. They are poor; their apartment has no toilet or bath; the father is ill, and soon dies. Afterward, the mother becomes active in the Labor Movement, causing enormous embarrassment to Ruth. Ruth is a very bright, academically talented child. She works hard at school, loves to read, and is considered a model child. The author presents several points of view clearly and sympathetically. She also conveys an accurate historical view of early twentieth century labor and immigrant issues.

SACHS, MARILYN. *A December Tale*. Garden City, New York: Doubleday, 1976. (Ages 11–up.) [child abuse].
Myra and Henry Fine have been placed in the home of an abusive woman and her ineffectual family. Myra feels that she hates her brother Henry. She thinks that if Henry weren't around, her father would permit her to come home. When Henry is beaten so brutally that Myra fears for his life, she realizes that she loves him and she finally takes hold of their situation. The major message in this unrelievedly painful but well-written book is that abused children must, like Myra, take their fate into their own hands, and not permit themselves to be abused any longer.

SACHS, MARILYN. *Dorrie's Book*. Illustrated by Anne Sachs. Garden City, New York: Doubleday, 1975. (Ages 9–12.) [gifted]
Dorrie is very bright, but self-centered, and, until her siblings are born, is a pampered only child. Her giftedness is mentioned throughout the book. Reactions of adults to gifted children are depicted somewhat realistically. Her educational program is alluded to, but not specifically described. Her teacher is, fortunately, very flexible and responsive. This book is well written, and very funny in parts.

SAVITZ, HARRIET MAY. *Run, Don't Walk*. New York: Franklin Watts, 1979. (Ages 12–up.) [mobility]
Two disabled teenagers fight for their rights when their high school imposes barriers, both physical and emotional. They are strong and independent people, and they also display the vulnerabilities of all teenagers.

SAVITZ, HARRIET MAY. *Wheelchair Champions: A History of Wheelchair Sports*. Illustrated with photographs. New York: Crowell, 1978. (Ages 9–12.) [mobility]
A factual account of the athletes and events that comprise wheelchair competition.

SEIXAS, JUDITH S. *Alcohol: What It Is, What It Does*. New York: Greenwillow Books, 1977. (Ages 6–9.) [substance abuse]
An informative, simple book for younger children.

SEIXAS, JUDITH S. *Living with a Parent Who Drinks Too Much*. New York: Greenwillow Books, 1979. (Ages 9–up.) [substance abuse]
Describes alcoholism and the behavior of alcoholics in clear, direct terms. Suggests what children can do to help themselves. Demonstrates understanding of the specific problems of children whose parents are alcoholics.

SHAPIRO, PATRICIA GOTTLIEB. *Caring for the Mentally Ill*. New York: Franklin Watts, 1982. (Ages 11–up.) [emotional dysfunction]
A brief overview of what emotional dysfunction is, how it is treated, what resources are available, and the legal rights of the "mentally ill."

SHARBURNE, ZOA. *Why Have the Birds Stopped Singing?* New York: Morrow, 1974. (Ages 9–12.) [epilepsy]
Katie has an epileptic seizure in the house of her great-great-great-grandmother who also had epilepsy when it was not understood. Katie in present time leads a normal life with medication.

SHARMAT, MARJORIE. *Nate the Great.* New York: Coward, McCann and Geoghegan, 1972. (Ages 6–8.) [gifted]
Another child detective who is bright and capable, and fun.

SHARP, CONSTANCE. "I Show the Daffodils to the Retarded Kids," in *Don't Forget to Fly,* collected by Paul Janeczko. New York: Bradbury Press, 1981. (Ages 10–up.) [intellectual disability]
The reaction of several intellectually disabled children to a daffodil provides a glimpse into the various ways in which these children can learn. Children are named, are presented as real, feeling, joyous people.

SHYER, MARLENE FANTA. *Welcome Home, Jellybean.* New York: Scribner, 1978. (Ages 8–12.) [intellectual disability]
Twelve-year-old Neil's life changes completely when his parents brings his thirteen-year-old sister Geraldine home to stay after she has spent nearly all her life in an institution for the retarded. Neil endures fights at school, Geraldine's disruptive behavior, and his father's departure from home. Neil develops compassion for his sister, and the acknowledgement of and joy in her small accomplishments. The story ends on a hopeful note.

SILVERSTEIN, DR. ALVIN AND VIRGINIA B. *Alcoholism.* Philadelphia: Lippincott, 1975. (Ages 11–up.) [substance abuse]
Comprehensive description of alcoholism—its history, physiological effects, manifestations, treatment and implications.

SILVERSTEIN, DR. ALVIN AND VIRGINIA B. *Epilepsy.* Philadelphia: Lippincott, 1975. (Ages 11–up.) [epilepsy]
Dispels myths and defines and describes the condition. Helps to clarify what it is, and what it isn't.

SILVERSTEIN, DR. ALVIN AND VIRGINIA B. *Runaway Sugar.* Illustrated by Harriet Barton. Philadelphia: Lippincott, 1981. (Ages 7–10.) [diabetes]
A factual, specific account of what diabetes is, how it affects people, and what can be done for it.

SIMON, MARCIA L. *A Special Gift.* New York: Harcourt Brace Jovanovich, 1978. (Ages 10–13.) [gifted]
Marcia Simon has written a deeply probing novel about a young boy's coming to terms with himself—his determined but unsteady shaping of values and friendships, and his acceptance of his love for dancing as a special gift rather than a problem.

SIMON, SEYMOUR. *Einstein Anderson, Science Sleuth, Shocks His Friends.* New York: Viking, 1980. Also in paper. (Ages 9–12.) [gifted]
Like the *Encyclopedia Brown* series, these stories revolve around a bright young boy,

who, using logic and facts, solves mysteries. All of Anderson's solutions are based on scientific information.

SLEPIAN, JOAN. *The Alfred Summer*. New York: Macmillan, 1980. Also in paper. (Ages 11–up.) [intellectual disability]
Lester, who has cerebral palsy, narrates this story about friendship. Alfred is retarded and epileptic. Myron is overweight. Claire completes the group. The four decide to build a boat. On an excursion to get oarlocks for the boat, Alfred and Lester experience the joy of being out on their own. When Alfred has a seizure, Lester finds strength and coordination he didn't know he possessed to help Alfred. No condescension is evident in this unusual story.

SLOTE, ALFRED. *Hang Tough, Paul Mather*. Philadelphia: Lippincott, 1973. Also in paper. (Ages 9–12.) [leukemia]
Paul is twelve years old and has leukemia. The descriptions of his reactions to medication are graphic, but the book essentially conveys a hopeful message. The boy's devotion to baseball carries him through some of the bad times with his illness.

SMITH, DORIS BUCHANAN. *Kelly's Creek*. Illustrated by Alan Tiegreen. New York: Crowell, 1975. (Ages 7–12.) [learning]
Kelly has a learning disability. At home and in school he feels like a failure. His only true friend is Philip, a college biology student doing an ecological study of the creek behind Kelly's house. On the creek Kelly feels intelligent and whole. His parents, worried about his lack of progress in school, forbid him to go to the creek until he improves his schoolwork. Finally, with Philip's help, his interest and knowledge of water life are recognized and valued.

SMITH, GENE. *The Hayburners*. New York: Delacorte Press, 1974. (Ages 10–up.) [intellectual disability]
Joey is a mentally retarded adult who does odd jobs. He nurtures a calf so that it becomes a prize winner, and, in the process, leads young Will and his family to value him. Readers might speculate about how the family would feel about Joey if the calf did not win a prize.

SMITH, LUCIA. *A Special Kind of Sister*. New York: Holt, Rinehart and Winston, 1977. (Ages 5–8.) [intellectual disability]
Written from the perspective of the older sister of Andy, who is mentally retarded, the story describes the negative aspects of the family's life. Children might attempt to write the story from Andy's point of view.

SOBOL, DONALD J. *Encyclopedia Brown Carries On*. Illustrated by Ib Ohlsson. New York: Four Winds Press, 1980. Also in paper. (Ages 8–11.) [gifted]
All of the books in this series depict a young boy who is very bright and who is valued by his parents and peers for his intelligence. The stories permit the reader to try to solve the mysteries along with Encyclopedia Brown, thus challenging their problem-solving skills.

SOBOL, HARRIET LANGSAN. *My Brother Steven Is Retarded*. Photographs by Patricia Agre. New York: Macmillan, 1977. (Ages 8–11.) [intellectual disability]
A beautiful, sensitive book told from the perspective of the eleven-year-old sister of

a retarded boy. The photographs bring the reality of the family situation close to the reader.

SOUTHALL, IVAN. *Let the Balloon Go*. Illustrated by Ian Ribbons. New York: St. Martin's 1969 (Ages 9–12.) [cerebral palsy]
John is a twelve-year-old Australian boy. He has cerebral palsy and has been overprotected by his mother. The plot involves John's slow and painful bid for more independence, and incidentally includes much factual material about cerebral palsy.

STARBIRD, KAYE. "Eat-It-All-Elaine," in *Poem Stew*, selected by William Cole. Illustrated by Karen Ann Weinhaus. Philadelphia: Lippicott, 1981. (Ages 7–10.) [appearance]
Because her camp-mates call her "Eat-It-All Elaine," Elaine continually pleases them with the oddities she eats. This is a good example of children living up to expectations of others.

STEIN, SARA BONNETT. *About Handicaps*. New York: Walker, 1974. (Ages 6–9.) [general]
Good photographs, explanatory material for adults, and a text for children tell the story of Matthew and his friend Joe, who has cerebral palsy. Matthew's fears are explored and questions are answered with understanding. The book's photographs graphically demonstrate the workings of an artificial arm and hand.

STOLZ, MARY. *The Edge of Next Year*. New York: Harper & Row, 1974. (Ages 12–up.) [substance abuse]
A moving story of the devastating effects of a mother's death on her family. The husband becomes an alcoholic, and the two boys must try to fend for themselves. In the end there is hope that the father will recover.

SULLIVAN, MARY BETH, AND BOURKE, LINDA, WITH SUSAN REGAN. *A Show of Hands: Say It in Sign Language*. Illustrated by Linda Bourke. Reading, Massachusetts: Addison-Wesley, 1980. (Ages 6–10.)
Conveys a positive attitude about sign language and its use. Depicts a wide variety of people with hearing impairment, some of them famous.

TER HAAR, JAAP. *The World of Ben Lighthart*. New York: Dell, 1977. Paperback. (Ages 11–up.) [vision]
As the result of an accident, Ben Lighthart, who was about to enter high school, loses sight in both eyes. In the hospital, and later at home, Ben begins the long journey through anger, fear, and darkness to find a new life.

VOIGT, CYNTHIA. *Dicey's Song*. New York: Atheneum, 1982. (Ages 9–up.) [emotional dysfunction]
Dicey has protected and tended her younger siblings throughout a difficult year; their mother has been hospitalized for mental illness, and they are now living with their maternal grandmother, a very strong and seemingly eccentric woman. The relationship between Dicey and her grandmother constitutes the major portion of this sensitive and intricate book. This is the sequel to *Homecoming*, in which Dicey and her siblings are abandoned by their mother and must make their way without parental help. Dicey's strength carries them through.

WAHL, JAN. *Jamie's Tiger*. New York: Harcourt Brace Jovanovich. 1978. (Ages 4–7.) [hearing]
A little boy becomes deaf from German measles. Includes information about lip reading and sign language. A textbook about deafness for the very young, both hearing and hearing-impaired.

WHITE, E. B. *The Trumpet of the Swan*. New York: Harper & Row, 1970. (Ages 9–up.) [speech]
Sam, a young boy, is one with nature. He one day observes a swan and her mate with their cygnets. Louis, one of them, is born without a voice. Louis' determination enables him to provide for himself in life.

WHITE, PAUL. *Janet at School*. New York: Crowell, 1978. (Ages 5–8.) [mobility]
A five-year-old child with spina bifida finds her own ways of doing things that others do. A straightforward, caring account of her daily life.

WILLIAMS, JAY, AND ABRASHKIN, RAYMOND. *Danny Dunn and the Homework Machine*. New York: McGraw, 1958. (Ages 8–10.) [gifted]
Adventures of Danny, a bright young man, and his friends, with a miniature automatic computer.

WINDSOR, PATRICIA. *The Summer Before*. New York: Harper & Row, 1973. Also in paper. (Ages 12–up.) [emotional dysfunction]
The accidental death of her boy friend causes Alexandra to have an emotional breakdown. The shock is so severe that the potential for her recovery seems slight.

WINTHROP, ELIZABETH. *Knock, Knock, Who's There?* New York: Holiday, 1978. (Ages 11–up.) [substance abuse]
After Sam and Michael's father dies of pernicious anemia, they become aware of the fact that their mother is an alcoholic. They also learn that their parents' marriage was less than happy. The boys force their mother to face her alcoholism. Details are graphic; there is no miraculous cure, but the family has hope that the mother will recover. While the book has many gaps in its: we don't know how about the father; some of the other characters are shadowy; we're not sure what happens to the mother when she goes home to "dry out"; the details of the alcoholism and the boys' reaction to it are useful for a discussion of substance abuse.

WOLF, BERNARD. *Anna's Silent World*. Philadelphia: Lippincott, 1977. (Ages 8–10.) [hearing]
Though born deaf, Anna is able to function well, thanks to firm family support, special training, and sound-amplifying technology.

WOLF, BERNARD. *Connie's New Eyes*. Philadelphia: Lippincott, 1976. (Ages 10–12.) [vision]
Connie, a young blind woman, and Blythe, the seeing eye dog who helps her carry on her life, manage very well together.

WOLF, BERNARD. *Don't Feel Sorry for Paul*. Philadelphia: Lippincott, 1974. (Ages 8–up.) [mobility]
Paul Jockimo has malformed hands and feet and wears prostheses on his right arm and both legs. He is a determined seven-year-old who has worked very hard learning

to use these prostheses. He can run, write, play ball, and do many other activities that nonhandicapped children can do. He has even won ribbons competing in horse shows. His supportive family and many doctors, therapists, and technicians have assisted him. Paul's hard work and the achievement of his goals could be good examples to children who read this book. Bernard Wolf's black-and-white full-page photographs demonstrate the work of the prostheses. Readers of all ages may find these pictures fascinating and informative.

WRIGHTON, PATRICIA. *A Racecourse for Andy*. New York: Harcourt Brace Jovanovich, 1968. (Ages 9–up.) [intellectual disability]
Set in Australia, this beautifully written story tells of Andy, a mentally retarded young man, and his circle of friends. Andy's friends include him in their games. When he is tricked by a tramp into paying three dollars to buy a racetrack, his friends become concerned. All is righted in the end, with no one the loser, and Andy's dignity intact.

YASHIMA, TARO. *Crow Boy*. New York: Viking, 1955. (Ages 3–5.) [gifted]
A picture book story of Chibi (Tiny Boy), who has the ability to observe and record minute details, and thus wins the admiration of his peers.

YOLEN, JANE. *The Boy Who Had Wings*. New York: Crowell, 1974. (Ages 5–8.) [gifted]
Aetos, a Greek boy, is born with wings. He is rejected by his family and forbidden to use his wings until, one day, he must use them to save his father's life. He then loses them forever. An allegory of how people view the gifted. Sparks much discussion and debate.

YOLEN, JANE. *Dragon's Blood*. New York: Delacorte Press, 1982. (Ages 12–up.) [speech, gifted]
Both the young male and female protagonists in this fantasy novel strive for and gain their independence by means of their wits, talent, and perseverance. Both are nurturing, sensitive people, willing to take risks to accomplish their goals. Rich in detail and adventure, the story weaves a tapestry of setting, plot, and character. A mute dragon serves as the instrument of the boy's success; her muteness functions as an advantage in battles. The sequel, *Heart's Blood*, is the second of the *Pit Dragon* trilogy.

YOLEN, JANE. *The Seeing Stick*. New York: Crowell, 1977. (Ages 5–8.) [vision]
The emperor's daughter learns to "see" by touching a seeing stick. The wise old man who brings her the stick is also blind. The young princess and the old man work together to help other blind people. Beautifully told and illustrated, this book is a treasure.

SEVEN

OLD AGE

OUR SOCIETY IS NO LONGER DOMINATED BY THE YOUNG. We may still worship at the altar of perpetual youth, but the nation's median age is constantly rising, and we can no longer ignore that substantial part of our population that is over sixty-five years of age. Different cultures have responded to the phenomenon of aging in a variety of ways. Some, particularly in Asia, venerate their old people. They respect the long years of experience and knowledge that accrue with age. They assign to old people almost magical qualities of wisdom and ability. Some nomadic groups, for their own survival, expect their aged members to disappear gracefully from the society once they become burdensome because they can no longer fend for themselves. Between these two extremes lies a great range of treatment of the elderly, some prescribed and ritualized, some purely idiosyncratic. Our society provides no consistent behaviors. We are confused about what to do. The stereotypes we have constructed about old people often inhibit us from treating them in humane and rational ways. On the one hand we pay lip service to how much we respect old people's wisdom. On the other, we force them into retirement homes, or isolate them in communities restricted only to old people. We sometimes behave as if we are pretending that they don't exist. With the decline of the extended family their isolation has become even more marked.

Fortunately, the aged population is not waiting for the rest of us to rescue them. Through such organizations as the Gray Panthers and the American Association of Retired Persons, and such activities as elder hostels, they have been taking charge of their own advocacy, and have helped educate the rest of the population to their abilities and needs. Problems have been imposed upon them, not through their own failings, but as a function of unresponsive social and governmental services. Pressure to withdraw from the work force, insufficient social security benefits, hoodlums who prey on old people, inadequate and expensive medical care, and a society that tends to ostracize the elderly present barriers that are difficult to overcome.

•TRY THIS

Answer these questions to the best of your ability.

1. How should old people live: with their families? Where alone? in planned communities?
2. How many people over age sixty-five are in my community? my state? the country?
3. What should the regulations be about retirement age? What are they in my place of work? in my state?
4. What are the most usual sources of income for old people?
5. What stereotypes do I subscribe to about old people? How can I change these perceptions?

A society that excludes its elderly people deprives itself of firsthand encounters with the wealth of past experience these people afford us, not only of world and local history, but also of cultural and family roots. Children need the multigenerational perspective old people can provide. They also need models for treating people with dignity and respect, no matter what their age. Books can aid in the development of a mutually rewarding interaction with old people. There are many descriptions of the aged in children's books, and fortunately, a number of them are accurate and constructive ones.

SUGGESTED CRITERIA

Although old age is the last developmental stage of life, aging and death should not automatically be linked with each other in books for children. The emphasis should be on life and its activities and interactions. Death is a separate matter, and should be confronted as such. It is, however, reasonable to expect old people to think and talk about death, and to acknowledge some sort of preparation for dealing with it.

Senility, when included as part of a plot, should be factually accurate. Children need to know about this problem, but the library should be balanced with books that describe capable, intellectually competent old people as well. Senility is less prevalent in the aged population than is commonly imagined, and the myth that all old people become senile should be counteracted. With proper nutrition and exercise, and barring neurological diseases, senility is not a necessary concomitant of aging.

Another myth that needs to be dispelled is that all old people primarily function in relationship to their families. Some people never marry, and continue to be active participants in society; some people live far from their families or choose not to spend most of their time with their relatives. Books should reflect the variety of relationships possible. Old people should appear in roles additional to that of grandparents. Children should recognize that there is as great a range of elderly people as there is in the rest of the population. Children should be helped to see that they may find many opportunities to interact with old people who are not in their immediate family, and who have identities separate from their family ties.

Old people have as many varied personalities and responses as young people. Individuality does not disappear with age. It should not be assumed that just because people are over sixty-five they have lost their distinctive character traits. More stories are now available that picture old people as unique individuals. This includes their social interaction. The sexuality of old people should be acknowledged. They are not necessarily intentionally without sex partners, and their faculties can remain active as long as they live. They should be shown as capable of establishing new relationships and also as enjoying their continuing marriage to long-time partners.

Children should not always be the rescuers of old people, and elderly people should not always be victims. The image of the helpless, dependent old person should not dominate the literature. It is demeaning and condescending to present the child-hero as the more intelligent, assertive, perceptive character. Friendships between children and old people can exist, and should be depicted realistically, with each partner contributing to the relationship.

All characters should be treated with dignity. The qualities of an old person should not be ridiculed, or made to seem quaint because of the association with old age. Old people should not be required to be seers, saints, or sages. Their reason for existence should not be simply to serve others. They are entitled to the same foibles and flaws as the rest of the population. Just as young people are not always beautiful, old people are not invariably physically unattractive. Old people should not automatically be assigned the characteristics of being crotchety, forgetful, wicked, or feeble. Many old people retain an energy level that equals and even surpasses a young person's.

Characters over sixty-five should, at times, be pictured as active, and engaged in vital projects. The stereotype of the passive, sedentary senior citizen should not be the predominant image. In those books where the old age, nursing, or retirement home figures in the plot, it should not be presented as the expected place of residence for an old person. In reality, only about five percent of the aged population lives in these institutions. Most of them live in their own homes, or share housing with each other or their families. When this sort of placement is deemed necessary, it should be described realistically and in appropriate perspective.

Since old people belong to a range of cultures, classes and communities, this diversity should be depicted in the books that make up the classroom or library collection. Children must learn to refrain from pigeon-holing our elderly population in any way.

DISCUSSION OF CHILDREN'S BOOKS

A number of books have recently been published for children under eight years of age describing the problems as well as the positive characteristics of the aged. Ironically, this seems to be a more difficult topic to handle than death is. Old people vary in life as much as young ones do, and this diversity must be recognized in the stories. In *Annie and the Old One* by Miska Miles, the reader should not be tempted to assume that all old Navajo grandmothers are wise, gentle, and prepared to die gracefully. The book is positive and helpful to children who anticipate the death of a grandparent. Annie tries to do all that she can to prevent her grandmother's demise, but the old woman explains to her that there is no possible way to avoid death. The old woman is a wise and attractive person. She understands Annie's feelings, and tries to help her cope with them. She does not seek death, but faces it with equanimity.

Nana Upstairs and Nana Downstairs, by Tomie de Paola, describes a succession of very long-lived grandmothers. The book graphically tells about an old person so helpless that she must be tied into a chair to keep from falling off. The description is neither painful nor romanticized. The ninety-four-year-old great-grandmother remains a part of the family and is cherished, particularly by Tommy, the four-year-old boy. He wants to be tied into a chair, too, and keeps his great-grandmother company every Sunday. After she dies, and a long time later, Tommy's grandmother shifts to the upstairs, taking her place in the cycle of the family's old people. In this book it is clear that the family expects its old people to remain with them. They are valued.

A grandmother far from the stereotype is portrayed in Jeanette Caines's *Window Wishing.* Grandma Mag doesn't like to cook, but when the children come to spend their vacation with her, she makes them wonderful lemonade, teaches them how to fish, and takes them "window wishing" (her name for window-shopping). They picnic in the cemetery, and Grandma Meg models a healthful attitude for the children. As with all of Ms. Caines's writing, the characters are black. They are individuals, and their universality contributes to the value of this excellent book.

Another grandmother who has a spicy personality is the one in the *Hannah* series by Mindy Skolsky. In *Carnival and Kopeck*, Hannah and her grandmother have a dreadful argument, which makes them both distraught. In the end their deep affection for each other wins out over their mutually stubborn dispositions.

Arnold Lobel's *Uncle Elephant* is not a grandparent. He is a caretaker and rescuer of the young boy when the parents are lost at sea. Uncle Elephant is the epitome of an active, energetic individual. Sally Wittman has also created a lively, vital old character in the person of *The Wonderful Mrs. Trumbly*. She is an older person who is still attractive, newly married, and has her own interests, as well as befriending the young protagonist of the book.

In order to provide the opportunity for young readers to be exposed to different models of aging, teachers and parents should attempt to provide as great a variety of portraits of the aged as possible. Children can bring in photographs of grandparents, elderly relatives, and neighbors. They can cut out pictures of old people from magazines and newspapers. They can make a bulletin board or scrapbooks entitled "What Old People Look Like" or "What Old People Do" or, simply, "Old People".

For older students, Myron Levoy's *A Shadow like a Leopard* describes a friendship between fourteen-year-old Ramon Santiago and seventy-six-year-old Arnold Glasser. The two help each other in a mutually appreciative and often stormy relationship. Arnold Glasser is nobody's grandfather. He is independent and prickly, and sometimes despondent, as is his young friend, Ramon. By the end of the book, the problems for both of them seem well on their way to being resolved.

Old Arthur, by Liesel Moak Skorpen, presents another picture of old age. This gentle, nicely understated story points out that, even though someone is of little use in one place, it is still possible to be valued in another. Old Arthur is a dog who is not useful on the farm anymore. He is slow, sleepy, and foregetful. He escapes being put to death by the farmer simply because he falls asleep and drops out of sight on the way to being killed. Picked up by the dog catcher, he is brought to the pound. At last a little boy comes who does not want a frisky puppy. Although everyone tries to talk him out of it, he wants a dog with Old Arthur's qualities. He likes the way that the dog looks at him and the way that he "almost wags his tail." The dog is good at waiting, at sitting, and at being gentle and affectionate. The boy cherishes the old dog, valuing him for what he can do and enjoying his company.

Another story of old age that presents a somewhat positive resolution of the problem of no longer being active is Rose Blue's *Grandma Didn't Wave Back*. Debbie's grandmother, of whom the child is very fond, has been living with the family for more than five years. Debbie and her friends have always enjoyed Grandma's cooking and her company. But now the old woman lapses in and out of senility: she has forgetful episodes, even beginning to do things that are potentially harmful to herself. The solution is her placement in a very carefully selected old-age home overlooking the ocean. At first Debbie is resentful of her parents for "sending her grandmother away," but the old woman reassures her granddaughter. She will be comfortable there, and she will look forward to occasional visits from her family. She tells Debbie to visit her when she can, but not to think of her all the time because Debbie's life is still ahead of her. The family in this book does not have to worry about the financial cost of the facility. The care about the feelings of everyone involved and can select the most appropriate arrangement. The story represents a good model for this kind of solution to the problem of the aged and senile, provided that material resources and physical facilities are available. Older children may raise more questions about this story than younger ones do. It can be used to stimulate comparisons and discussions of what constitutes a good institution.

A class visit to a local nursing home could be used as a follow-up to this sort of discussion or even as an introduction to the topic. Often a holiday provides a good excuse for a visit from children. If a child in the class has a grandparent in a nearby home or housing development for old people, the class can adopt that grandparent. The more comfortable children begin to feel about old people and the more contact that they have with them, the more prepared they will be to deal with the issues surrounding old age when they arise. Another useful practice is to invite old people who belong to a golden age club or who attend a local old people's meeting place to come to the classroom to read stories to the children, help them with projects, and perhaps, even, just to sit and be available for some loving. This kind of practice permits children who live far away from their grandparents to experience some of the attention that old people often enjoy giving children. It also provides a service to the elderly community by valuing them for what they can do and by demonstrating that there is a place and a function for them.

One of these projects (visiting a "retirement ranch") is described in *Just like a Real Family,* by Kristi Holl. June, one of the sixth graders involved in the activity, is assigned to a cranky, laconic old man named Franklin Cooper. After a period of time, June, her mother, and Mr. Cooper become very closely involved with each other.

•TRY THIS

Invent some scenarios about problems of aging for you to solve. Try these with children, and compare your solutions. The following is an example of one you might tackle: Your grandfather is very old. He lives in his own apartment. He forgets where he puts things. He forgets what you told him yesterday. Sometimes he forgets your name. You and he have always been fond of each other; he says you're his favorite. Your parents are afraid he will fall and hurt himself, or that he will set his place on fire. Your parents both work all day. They have decided to place him in a nursing home. They want your opinion. What will you say?

Norma Farber's *How Does It Feel to Be Old?* can be read to younger children. Older readers can benefit from the insights and wry humor of this beautifully crafted poetic reflection by a complex old woman.

A Figure of Speech, by Norma Fox Mazer, deals with old age in a painful but forthright manner. The grandfather is full of aches and pains. He is forgetful, his apartment is messy, and he slobbers over his food. Most of the members of his family treat him with disrespect. He has an apartment set up in the basement of his daughter's house, and this arrangement is all right until one day his college-age grandson comes home newly married, requiring a place for himself and his wife. Eventually the old man is moved out. The family is worried about their lack of privacy, their added responsibilities, their economic burdens—a not uncommon situation in today's world. Only Jenny understands, respects, and responds warmly to the old man.

The old man and Jenny run away from home when they discover that the family is about to put him into an institution that regards old people as worthless and helpless. This sort of institution is, perhaps, not the rule, but the description is believable. The grandfather tries to dissuade Jenny from running away with him, but she insists on going. He carefully prepares for the venture, with the knowledge that he will be on his own helping to strengthen him. Here the author is clearly saying that many problems of old age could be alleviated if old people were permitted to be functionally self-reliant and independent.

Mazer includes some excellent dialogue in this book concerning the words that people use to describe old age and death. The grandfather tolerates no ameliorating phrases referring to his age or to his eventual death. He leaves notes taped to the refrigerator indicating his displeasure at such phrases. He announces that he has no intention of "passing away"—he will die. *A Figure of Speech* does not mince words and raises questions about old age, suicide, and death that have no easy answers. The issues of morality and responsibility are important ones for adults as well as for children to consider. Children may benefit from telling the story from the perspective of each of the characters, including the parents.

The old man in Jean Robinson's *The Secret Life of T. K. Dearing* also is independent and resistant to coddling, though his family is far more understanding and far less pressured than the one in *A Figure of Speech*. Nevertheless, the elder daughter no longer wants to take care of her father, while the younger daughter, T. K.'s mother, is overly protective of her father. The old man has a distinct personality, with idiosyncracies that become annoying. He snores loudly, and even in the hottest weather he refuses to take off his suit jacket. He also invades the privacy of the boys' clubhouse. The boy and he finally manage to get along very well. T. K.'s friends enjoy what the old man contributes to their club, and they all get involved in a project to save another old man's home. A positive element of this book is that there are several old men in it, each with a personality of his own. One old man is a recluse until the boys and T. K.'s grandfather befriend him. Another is a shop owner. The old grandfather in this story demonstrates his stubbornness and independence several times. It is pointed out that he is not perfect and that his independence is not always for his own good. But none of the characters in this book is one-sided. They all make compromises in the end so that a happy arrangement can be reached.

In *LeRoy and the Old Man*, by W. E. Butterworth, there are also a number of functioning, valued old people. LeRoy's grandfather, a fisherman, is extraordinarily self-sufficient and inventive. He has a strong sense of values, is sometimes perceived as rigid, but he has the admiration and respect of the whole community. He is black and his friends are from a variety of backgrounds. His personal life has not been as rewarding as he would have wanted, but with LeRoy and his mother there is now hope for a renewed and mutually beneficial family relationship.

In books as well as life, there are no easy answers and no absolutes. Each old person is different from every other one. Each situation is also different. In one case, a nursing home is an excellent solution to a difficult situations; in another instance, it could be the worst option. The purpose of accumulating a variety of books is to find several alternative solutions for a given situation. Children should question, argue, design several possible approaches for handling a dilemma, and seek out more books and articles confirming or debating their ideas.

REFERENCES: OLD AGE

ANSELLO, EDWARD F. "How Older People Are Stereotyped," *Bulletin of the Council on Interracial Books for Children,* Vol. 7, No. 6, 1976, pp. 4–10.
Discusses how picture books treat aged characters, provides a format for critiquing books, and generally decries the negative image conveyed. This article is in two parts, in an issue that is devoted entirely to the topic of aging.

BAGGETT, MARY CAROLYN. "Ageism in Contemporary Young Adult Fiction," *Top of the News,* Vol. 37, Spring 1981, pp. 259–263.
Advocates the reading of literature containing values and philosophy of old people in order to enhance readers' personal development.

MAVROGENES, NANCY A. "Positive Images of Grandparents in Children's Picture Books," *Reading Teacher,* Vol. 35, No. 8, May 1982, pp. 896–901.
Acknowledges the presence of stereotypes in some books for young children, but points out that recent books include many positive images. Provides a list of such books.

ROCKLAND PUBLIC SCHOOLS, PROJECT CLASP. *Aging Education Annotated Bibliography.* Rockland, Mass.: Rockland Public Schools 02370, 1982.
An excellent selection of print and audiovisual resources compiled for the project on Children Learning About Aging in a Structured Program (CLASP)

RUTHERFORD, WILMA MARIE. *An Exploratory Study of Ageism in Children's Literature.* Unpublished doctoral dissertation, University of the Pacific, 1981.
Eighty books for children were analyzed for stereotyping. The test instrument and coding procedure are useful for future studies of this sort.

SKINNER, B. F., and VAUGHAN, M. *Enjoy Old Age.* New York: Norton, 1983.
Practical suggestions for how to live fully and happily every year of one's life. Advice is given to prepare for old age in the same way that one would get ready for a vacation trip. Informed, pleasurable anticipation leads to a fulfilling experience.

TAYLOR, GAIL COHEN. "Images of the Elderly in Children's Literature," *Reading Teacher,* Vol. 34, No. 3, pp. 344–347.
A review of 10 ERIC studies of children's literature with references to old people.

WATSON, JERRY. "A Positive Image of the Elderly in Literature for Children," *Reading Teacher*, Vol. 34, No. 7, April 1981, pp. 792–798.
Provides an extensive list of books, prefaced by a useful discussion, that can be used with young readers to help them acquire a positive attitude toward old people.

SOURCES FOR MATERIALS ON OLD AGE

AMERICAN ASSOCIATION OF RETARDED PERSONS (AARP). 1909 K St., N.W., Washington, D.C. 20036

AMERICAN OCCUPATIONAL THERAPY FOUNDATIONS, 6000 Executive Blvd., Rockville, Maryland 20852

GRAY PANTHERS, 3700 Chestnut St., Philadelphia, Pennsylvania 19104

NATIONAL COUNCIL ON AGING, 1828 L St., N.W., Washington D.C. 20036

BIBLIOGRAPHY: OLD AGE

ADLER, C.S. *The Silver Coach.* New York: Coward, McCann, 1979. (Ages 10–12.)
Twelve-year-old Chris and her six-year-old sister Jackie spend the summer with their paternal grandmother. Their parents are divorced, and this summer marks their acceptance of the situation.

ADLER, DAVID A. *A Little at a Time.* Illustrated by N.M. Bodecker. New York: Random House, 1976. (Ages 4–7.)
David and his grandfather spend a happy day together in New York City. The illustrations and gentle text provide a loving look at a mutually respectful relationship.

ALIKI. *The Two of Them.* New York: Greenwillow Books, 1979. (Ages 4–10.)
Sensitively written story about a young girl and her grandfather. We see the child from babyhood deeply loved and lovingly cared for by her grandfather. She cares for him when he is sick, and fondly remembers him after his death.

ANCONA, GEORGE. *Growing Older.* Photographs by the author. New York: Dutton, 1978. (Ages 10–up.)
An excellent book of biographies, illustrating the beauty and energy of the lives of people who have now grown old. Biographies draw on different heritages.

BAKER, JEANNIE. *Grandfather.* London: Andre Deutsch, 1977. (Ages 4–7.)
About the special relationship between an elderly grandparent and his granddaughter. A wonderful story for young children, showing love, learning and acceptance.

BAKER, JEANNIE. *Millicent.* Illustrated by the author. London: Andre Deutsch, 1980. (Ages 5–12.)
Remarkable, vivid illustrations accompany a text that leads the reader into the mind of a wonderful old woman who comes to the park every day to feed the pigeons.

BAYLOR, BYRD. *The Other Way to Listen.* New York: Scribner, 1978. (Ages 5–8.)
A young boy learns from his friend, an old man, how to take the time to listen to what few people can hear: seed pods bursting open, and all of the other wonders of nature. A special relationship between the two friends.

BLUE, ROSE. *Grandma Didn't Wave Back.* Illustrated by Ted Lewin. New York: Franklin Watts, 1972. (Ages 7–10.)
It is difficult for Debbie, who loves her dearly, to understand why her grandmother must go to live in a nursing home. In the end all agree that it is the best solution.

BRENNER, BARBARA. *A Year in the Life of Rosie Bernard.* New York: Harper & Row, 1971. Also in paper. (Ages 8–12.)
Rosie's mother has died, and her father, despite his promise to keep Rosie with him, must, because of the pressures of the Depression, take an acting job that keeps him on the road. He therefore brings Rosie to her maternal grandparents' house in Brooklyn. Rosie, a spunky, bright, sensitive, and engaging girl, spends the year with this family, and grows to love and appreciate them. Many issues are found in this well-crafted book: reaction to death, foster care, old age (the grandparents emerge as strong characters) and certainly a heroine who defies stereotyping.

BUTTERWORTH, W.E. *LeRoy and the Old Man.* New York: Four Winds Press, 1980. Also in paper. (Ages 12–up.)
LeRoy first meets his grandfather under difficult circumstances: running away from being forced to testify in a homicide case. LeRoy's grandfather is a self-sufficient, multi-talented man with strong feelings about proper behavior. He is respected by the community and communicates his values to LeRoy. In the end, LeRoy and his mother make a home with the grandfather.

CAINES, JEANNETTE. *Window Wishing.* Illustrated by Kevin Brooks. New York: Harper & Row, 1980. (Ages 5–8.)
Grandma Meg is not old, but she is a grandmother, and it is important for children to encounter a variety of women who are grandmothers. Grandma Meg is a wonderful character. She wears sneakers all the time, and leads a very active life. When the two children visit her she takes them fishing, and "window wishing" (her name for looking in the windows of shops and wishing for what they can one day have). Unconventional in many ways, Grandma Meg demonstrates her love and provides her grandchildren with memories they will cherish. As with all of the author's books, the characters are black.

CALMENSON, STEPHANIE. *Where Is Grandma Potamus?* Illustrated by Susan Gantner. New York: Grosset and Dunlap, 1983. (Ages 4–7.)
Grandma Potamus takes Stanley and Bebe to Playland, despite the fact that she's very sleepy, due to her having been out very late dancing the night before. After an adventure at the amusement park, Grandma Potamus goes dancing late into the night with the pilot she meets at the park.

CARROLL, LEWIS. "Father William," in *The Arrow Book of Funny Poems,* collected by Eleanor Clymer. Illustrated by Doug Anderson. New York: Scholastic, 1961. (Ages 8–up.)
The old man can do all sorts of unlikely things, like stand on his head and turn somersaults. He disturbs the young man's sense of the aged stereotype.

COONEY, BARBARA. *Miss Rumphius.* Illustrated by the author. New York: Viking, 1982. (Ages 5–9.)
Alice's grandfather is an artist. He impresses upon her that she must do something to make the world more beautiful. Alice lives a very active and adventure-filled life. When she becomes old, she plants lupus seeds in many places, and in so doing, beautifies her world. As a very very old woman, she passes on her legacy to her niece, who also promises to make the world more beautiful.

DELTON, JULIE. *My Uncle Nikos.* Illustrated by Marc Simont. New York: Crowell, 1983. (Ages 5–8.)
Both in its illustrations and gentle text, this book shows a warm relationship between a young girl and her uncle, a productive, accepting, happy, older Greek man.

DEPAOLA, TOMIE. *Nana Upstairs and Nana Downstairs.* New York: Putnam, 1973. (Ages 3–8.)
Tommy's great-grandmother gradually grows very old and dies. His mother tells him that a falling star is the grandmother's good-bye kiss.

DEPAOLA, TOMIE. *Now One Foot, Now Other Foot.* Illustrated by the author. New York: Putnam, 1981. (Ages 5–8.)
When his grandfather suffers a stroke, Bobby helps him to walk again, just as his grandfather had once helped him.

FARBER, NORMA. *How Does It Feel to Be Old?* Illustrated by Trina Schart Hyman. New York: Dutton, 1979. (Ages 7–12.)
A sensitive, joyous and often humorous poetic book. The grandmother speaks frankly about her feelings. Never maudlin or self-pitying, independence and the "right to be me" are themes throughout the poem.

GERAS, ADELE. *Apricots at Midnight and Other Stories from a Patchwork Quilt.* Illustrated by Doreen Caldwell. New York: Atheneum, 1982. (Ages 8–12.)
Aunt Pinny is a story teller. She is also an old woman who has never married, but who, nevertheless, has lived a rich and passionate life because of her understanding of others' needs, her imagination, and her zest for living.

GERAS, ADELE. *Voyage.* New York: Atheneum, 1983. (Ages 10–up.)
Mina takes charge of her brother and mother on their long journey to America. She also manages to buoy up the spirits of most of the passengers in steerage. She is an exuberant, self-assured, artistic character whose energy enlivens the voyage. Another passenger on the ship, Clara Zussmann, an old woman, is an elderly version of Mina. Her provision of small luxuries in the midst of deprivation adds a quality to the voyage that enriches all of the passengers. Geras' prose is elegant and moving. Each vignette is a piece of the tapestry woven by the author.

GAUCH, PATRICIA. *Grandpa and Me.* Illustrated by Symeon Shimin. New York: Coward, McCann and Geoghegan, 1972. (Ages 5–8.)
A vigorous grandfather and his grandson spend a wonderful summer together.

GOFFSTEIN, M. B. *Fish For Supper.* New York: Dial Press, 1976. (Ages 3–8.)
Grandmother is active, gets up early and likes to fish. The language and line drawings are simple and appealing.

GOLDMAN, SUSAN. *Grandma Is Somebody Special.* Illustrated by the author. Chicago: Whitman, 1976. (Ages 4–7.)
Grandma goes to school, works, and lives in the city. She tells stories about her life and relationships that indicate that she is not afraid to show emotions such as anger, but that she harbors no grudges. She is an attractive, lively old woman.

GREEN, PHYLLIS. *The Fastest Quitter in Town.* Illustrated by Lorenzo Lynch. Reading, Massachusetts: Young Scott Books, 1972. (Ages 6–9.)
Johnny is a quitter; he loses his temper and quits when he cannot have his way. But with the help of his aged great-grandfather, he learns the value of patience and sticking to a task till it is done. The relationship between Johnny and his grandfather is a beautiful one.

GREENFIELD, ELOISE. *Grandmama's Joy.* Illustrated by Carole Byard. New York: William Collins Publishers, 1980. (Ages 6–8.)
Rhondy has lived with her grandmother since she was a baby. Grandma calls Rhondy her "Joy" and always says everything will be all right as long as she has her joy. But when Grandma finds out they have to move not even Rhondy can make her happy until she reminds Grandma that they still have each other.

HOFF, SYD. *Barkley.* New York: Harper & Row, 1975. (Ages 4–8.)
Barkley, an old circus dog, finds a way to be useful and valued even though he is old. The problems of old age are recognized, and a happy solution is proposed in this "Early I Can Read" book.

HOLL, KRISTI. *Just like a Real Family.* New York: Atheneum, 1983. (Ages 9–12.)
Mr. Cooper, an old man, angry and bitter about being forced to live in an institutionalized setting, at first rejects June's efforts to befriend him. June is lonely and worried about her mother, who is a single parent and in ill health. A happy resolution to everyone's problems is finally effected.

IRWIN, HADLEY. *The Lilith Summer.* Old Westbury, New York: Feminist Press, 1979. (Ages 10–up.)
Twelve-year-old Eller and seventy-seven year-old Lilith don't like each other very much, but each has been tricked into thinking she is "sitting" for the other. They discover the ruse, continue to collect their sitter's pay, and begin to enjoy each other's company. Ellen learns much about the depth and breadth of a number of old people. Lilith has a companion with whom to read, write poetry, go on outings, and birdwatch. This book has much to offer.

IRWIN, HADLEY. *What About Grandma?* New York: Atheneum, 1982. (Ages 12–up.)
Eighty-year-old Wyn is a grandmother. She is also a mother, dear friend, and attractive woman. She is so full of life and energy that the reader is shocked, along

with the other characters, to learn that Wyn has a terminal illness and will die soon. She and the family and friends prepare together for her death, and, in so doing, are the wiser for it.

ISADORA, RACHEL. *Jesse and Abe.* Illustrated by the author. New York: Greenwillow Books, 1981. (Ages 4–8.)
Jesse enjoys visiting his grandfather, Abe, at work. Abe works backstage at a Broadway theater. Jesse learns how much his grandfather is valued one night when Abe is late for work. Jesse also becomes aware of how much he loves Abe.

KANTROWITZ, MILDRED. *Maxie.* Illustrated by Emily A. McCully. New York: Parents Magazine Press, 1970. (Ages 4–8.)
Maxie is an old woman who decides that she is unnoticed, unloved, and unnecessary. She remains in bed instead of adhering to her regular routine. The concerned reactions of her neighbors and the other people with whom she comes into daily contact are gratifying.

KESSELMAN, WENDY. *Emma.* Garden City, New York: Doubleday, 1980. (Ages 5–10.)
Emma is based on the life of artist Emma Stern. Emma was old and lonely and unappreciated by her family. When she started to paint, she became contented and appreciated. Deals with the need to be valued and shows that old people can learn new things and be creative.

KIRK, BARBARA. *Grandpa, Me and Our House in the Tree.* New York: Macmillan, 1978. (Ages 5–8.)
Nico and his grandfather have shared many joyful times. After the grandfather's stroke Nico learns to adjust to his grandfather's limitations, but their pleasures are not entirely wiped out.

KNOX-WAGNER, ELAINE. *My Grandpa Retired Today.* Illustrated by Charles Robinson. Niles, Illinois: Whitman, 1982. (Ages 5–9.)
The young boy and his grandfather clearly share a loving and reciprocal relationship. When the grandfather retires, the boy reassures him and helps him to overcome his depression.

LASKY, KATHRYN. *I Have Four Names for My Grandfather.* Photographs by Christopher G. Knight. Boston: Little, Brown, 1976. Photographs beautifully illustrate this loving book about a young boy and the special relationship he has with his grandfather.

LASKY, KATHRYN. *My Island Grandma.* New York: Frederick Warne, 1979. (Ages 5–8.)
A story of the close relationship between a strong, dynamic, creative grandma and her young granddaughter. The setting is a Maine island in summer.

LASKY, KATHRYN. *The Night Journey.* Illustrated by Trina Schart Hyman. New York: Frederick Warne, 1981. (Ages 11–up.)
Rachel's great-grandmother tells her stories about life long ago in czarist Russia, and how Jews were treated in those times. The book is full of flavorful language and customs of Jewish families. The old great-grandmother is greatly valued in the family, but particularly so by Rachel.

LEVOY, MYRON. *A Shadow like a Leopard.* New York: Harper & Row, 1981. (Ages 11–up.)
In order to prove his worth to a street gang, fourteen-year-old Ramon Santiago robs an old man, Arnold Glasser, at knife-point. Glasser is an artist; Ramon is a poet. The two characters form a surprising alliance, and help each other to find a way out of their problems. Both are unforgettable characters: feisty, intelligent, talented, and unwilling to conform to what others want to force them to be.

LOBEL, ARNOLD. *Uncle Elephant.* Illustrated by the author. New York: Harper & Row, 1981. Also in paper. (Ages. 4–8.)
Uncle Elephant adopts his unknown nephew when his parents are lost at sea. The two develop a tender, loving relationship while they are together and the book illustrates the sense of loss each feels when their time together is over.

MACGREGOR, ELLEN. *Miss Pickerell Goes to Mars.* Illustrated by Paul Galdone. New York: McGraw-Hill, 1951. Also in paper. (Ages 9–12.)
Miss Pickerell is an old woman who travels from one exciting adventure to another, all over the universe. She is much brighter than most of the males, and accomplishes more than most people. There is a long series of Miss Pickerell books.

MACLACHLAN, PATRICIA. *Cassie Binegar.* New York: Harper & Row, 1982. (Ages 9–12.)
No character in any of this author's books is stereotypic. In this story of changes, interactions, and, above all, love, Cassie, the young protagonist, learns to accept herself and her world. The story is remarkable for its evocation of strong feelings, lightened by an overlay of wit. The grandmother, despite her age, is a passionate lover of life and people, and understands Cassie's feelings. She is an admirable model, as are all of the male characters, who are permitted poetic and gentle thoughts, dreams and actions, without any loss of strength or dignity.

MACLACHLAN, PATRICIA. *Through Grandpa's Eyes.* Illustrated by Deborah Ray. New York: Harper & Row, 1979. (Ages 6–9.)
John spends time with his blind grandfather and learns to appreciate nature while discovering how to use all of his senses. The author's prose creates an atmosphere of caring which is augmented by Ray's soft drawings. Both grandparents are seen as productive, creative people; the grandmother sculpts, the grandfather plays the cello. Males are seen performing domestic tasks. The grandparents love each other and enjoy their lives.

MATHIS, SHARON BELL. *The Hundred Penny Box.* Illustrated by Leo and Diane Dillon. New York: Viking, 1975. (Ages 6–9.)
Michael loves his Aunt Dew. He understands her feelings. She is one hundred years old but still communicates and remembers. Michael is protective of Aunt Dew's feelings and is distressed by his mother's seeming lack of understanding.

MAZER, NORMA FOX. *A Figure of Speech.* New York: Delacorte Press, 1973. Also in paper. (Ages 12–up.)
Jenny's parents, unable to deal with her grandfather's old age and senility, want to put him in a home. Jenny objects, and so does her grandfather, who kills himself instead. This is a powerful but upsetting story. Its realism leaves the reader reeling.

MILES, MISKA. *Annie and the Old One.* Illustrated by Peter Parnell. Boston: Little, Brown, 1971. (Ages 6–8.)
A Navajo girl futilely tries to prevent the predicted death of her grandmother. But in the end, she accepts death as a necessary part of life.

O'NEILL, MARY. "Old Fingers," in *Fingers Are Always Bringing Me News.* Illustrated by Don Bolognese. New York: Doubleday, 1969. The poem explores the fragile but sure touch of the fingers of the elderly.

RABIN, GIL. *Changes.* New York: Harper & Row, 1973. (Ages 10–up.)
After Chris's father dies, his mother, grandfather, and he move in with his aunt, who is not at all pleased to have them. The grandfather's health deteriorates to the point of blindness and senility. He is placed in a nursing home which apparently maintains less than marginal standards of cleanliness and care. Chris cannot bring himself to visit his grandfather there. The author helps readers to understand the feelings of all the characters involved. The issue of the unfairness of the infirmities of old age is clearly exposed.

ROBINSON, JEAN. *The Secret Life of T.K. Dearing.* Illustrated by Charles Robinson. New York: Seabury Press, 1973. (Ages 8–11.)
T.K.'s grandfather feels useless at home. He wants to play with T.K. and his friends in this story about an independent old man and a basically understanding family.

SCHWARTZ, LYNNE SHARON. *Balancing Acts.* New York: Harper & Row, 1981. (Ages 11–up.)
Max, age 76, and Alison, age 13, mutually benefit from each other's friendship.

SECHAN, EDMOND. *The String Bean.* Illustrated with photographs. New York: Doubleday, 1982. (Ages 7–12.)
Like *The Red Balloon,* this book is based on a film. The story tells of an old woman whose life is drab until she discovers a flowerpot and plants a seed. Although her first attempt ends in disappointment, she learns a lesson and will continue to plant seeds. Next time she will succeed.

SHULEVITZ, URI. *Dawn.* New York: Farrar, Straus & Giroux, 1974. (Ages 5–8.)
A subtle but moving communication of the relationship between a young child and a grandfather. The illustrations beautifully convey the message.

SILVERSTEIN, SHEL. "The Little Boy and the Old Man," in *A Light in the Attic.* New York: Harper & Row, 1981.
The poem explores the painful similarities between an elderly man and a young child. Both drop spoons, wet their pants, and are ignored by adults.

SKOLSKY, MINDY. *Carnival and Kopeck.* Illustrated by Karen Ann Weinhaus. New York: Harper & Row, 1979. (Ages 7–10.)
Hannah and her grandmother share a special kind of relationship. Hannah helps her grandmother learn to read and write in English, and Hannah's grandmother plays with her, tells her stories, and cooks delicious food. As both of them have strong personalities, they sometimes clash; when that happens, they are very unhappy until the problem is resolved. One of a series of four books.

SKORPEN, LIESEL MOAK. *Old Arthur*. Illustrated by Wallace Tripp. New York: Harper & Row, 1972. (Ages 3–8.)
Arthur is too old to be a good farm dog anymore, so he runs away from the farmer who wants to kill him, gets put in a dog pound, and finally ends up a valued pet for a little boy. A beautiful story about the positive values of old age.

SNYDER, CAROL. *The Great Condominium Rebellion*. Illustrated by Anthony Kramer. New York: Delacorte Press, 1981. (Ages 9–12.)
Stacy and Marc visit their newly-retired grandparents in Florida. The vacation is not all that they had hoped for, mostly because of the restrictions imposed upon them by the condominium's Board of Directors, and partly because of their grandparents' uneasiness about retirement. The story introduces issues of aging that need to be confronted, such as lack of substantive, satisfying activities, preoccupation with the everyday routines of eating and shopping, isolation from younger age groups, and feelings of being unwanted and unvalued. It also contains elderly characters who are alert, contributing, and diverse. The book would have been even more successful without its occasionally condescending tone. Although the author depicts a few old people as activists, it is largely the children who show everyone the solution to their problems. Ms Snyder is part of the Judy Blume "School of Writing" and tells an amusing story that will appeal to young readers.

SOBOL, HARRIET LANGSTON. *Grandpa: A Young Man Grown Old*. Illustrated by Patricia Agre. New York: Coward, McCann and Geoghegan, 1980. (Ages 10–up.)
The life of Morris Kaye, a Jewish immigrant—a modest, dignified, "young man grown old"—described in words and actual family photographs from two vantage points: Morris's, as he looks back on seventy-eight years, and that of his seventeen-year-old granddaughter Karen, who loves and respects him for what he has accomplished and for the part he has played in her own growing up.

STOLZ, MARY. *Lands End*. Illustrated by Dennis Hermanson. New York: Harper & Row, 1973. (Ages 12–up.)
This story includes a family's warm and loving treatment of a senile old grandfather, although it is not the main focus of the book.

TATE, JOAN. *Gramp*. New York: Harper & Row, 1979. (Ages 9–12.) Simon understands that his grandfather needs to feel useful and keep busy in order to preserve his health and vitality. Through extraordinary perseverance, Simon manages to provide for his grandfather. A loving story.

UDRY, JANICE MAY. *Mary Jo's Grandmother*. Illustrated by Eleanor Mill. Chicago: Whitman, 1970. (Ages 5–8.)
One snowy Christmas Mary Jo visits her old but independent grandmother, who lives alone in the country. When her grandmother has an accident, Mary Jo gets help and cares for the old woman.

VOIGT, CYNTHIA. *Dicey's Song*. New York: Atheneum, 1982. (Ages 9–up.)
Dicey has protected and tended her younger siblings throughout a difficult year; their mother has been hospitalized for mental illness, and they are now living with their maternal grandmother, a very strong and seemingly eccentric woman. The

relationship between Dicey and her grandmother constitutes the major portion of this sensitive and intricate book.

WALKER, MARGARET. "Lineage," in *Black Out Loud,* ed. Arnold Adoff. Illustrated by Alvin Hollingsworth. New York: Macmillan, 1970. (Ages 10–up.)
The poet's "strong grandmothers" are filled with memories of "sturdiness and singing." Using their bodies to sow seed and provide labor on farms, their strong souls are too resilient to be broken. The poet wishes she were able to be like them.

WEIL, LISL. *The Funny Old Bag.* New York: Parents Magazine Press, 1974. (Ages 5–8.)
Howie and his friends make fun of an old couple in the park who carry a funny old bag; but when Howie hurts himself badly, the old people are there to help him.

WERSBA, BARBARA. *The Dream Watcher.* New York: Atheneum, 1968. (Ages 11–up.)
Albert Scully feels that he is a failure. He just doesn't seem to fit in. He can't meet his mother's expectations and his father doesn't seem to care about him. He meets Mrs. Woodson, a lonely old woman, who seems to know how to get right to Albert's heart. His life begins to turn around and a beautiful friendship develops. Everything is fine until Mrs. Woodson has a heart attack. Albert has to deal with her eventual death.

WITTMAN, SALLY. *The Wonderful Mrs. Trumbly.* Illustrated by Margot Apple. New York: Harper & Row, 1982. (Ages 5–9.)
Mrs. Trumbly is a vibrant, energetic teacher who is clearly portrayed in the illustrations as a senior citizen. Not only does she lead a productive professional life, she enjoys a romantic relationship with Mr. Klein, the music teacher, much to the chagrin of her adoring student, Martin. The story presents a well-rounded picture of two older people with enjoyable, active lives.

WRIGHT, BETTY REN. *Getting Rid of Marjorie.* New York: Holiday, 1981. (Ages 9–12.)
Emily is devastated when she learns of her grandfather's sudden marriage to a stranger named Marjorie. Emily schemes to get rid of Marjorie so that Emily and her grandfather can regain their special close relationship. Never bordering on the sentimental, this story helps destroy some stereotypes about old people and their needs.

YARBROUGH, CAMILLE. *Cornrows.* Illustrated by Carole Byard. New York: Coward, McCann and Geoghegan, 1979. (Ages 5–9.)
As Mama and Great-Grammaw braid the children's hair into cornrows, they tell of the meaning of the designs of the cornrows, and they present some of the tradition and richness of Afro-American history.

YEP, LAWRENCE. *Child of the Owl.* New York: Harper & Row, 1977. (Ages 11–up.)
Casey moves in with his grandmother who lives in Chinatown and learns to cope with the generation gap.

•EIGHT•

DEATH

UNTIL VERY RECENTLY, BOOKS DEALING REALISTICALLY with the topic of death were categorized almost in the same realm as pornography. Americans, enamored of youth and trying to remain young forever, like to pretend that death does not exist. We have shunned dying people as though dying itself were a contagious disease. We value beauty, comfort, boundless productivity, and control over our lives. We have preferred not to confront death, which is associated with pain and fear of the unknown. For some people death appears to be a punishment; for some it is an ever-present threat. Even to those for whom death has compensations as a valid end to earthly life or as a transcendental episode in the balance of the universe, there are negative aspects.

We miss our loved ones, our great ones, our kind ones. But more and more we have come to realize that, even if we do not talk about it, death will not go away. Courses concentrating on questions, concerns, and issues associated with death and dying are being offered on campuses across the country. Parents and teachers find themselves increasingly called upon to answer children's questions, prompted not only by the children's actual experiences with death and dying but also by their having encountered these concepts in books.

Before deciding to work with children on the facts, attitudes, and problems surrounding the themes of death and dying, it is useful for an adult to decide how he or she feels about these topics. Helping others to cope with or to understand a situation is difficult unless we are conscious of our own feelings. Once we know what our attitudes are, we can more easily go beyond our own views and accept the ideas of others. It is important to view this understanding as an ongoing growth process. Just because we have a strong opinion today does not mean that we will have the same idea tomorrow. As we progress, we receive and assimilate more and more information that either confirms or changes our attitudes. We must recognize this potential in children as well as in adults, taking it into consideration whenever we are dealing with a topic of any significance.

•TRY THIS

Design a questionnaire to discover what your attitudes are toward dying and death. After you have answered these questions, try to think of others that you can ask. Compare your questionnaire with one a friend has devised. Are there any questions that appear on both lists? If so, do your friend's answers differ from yours? Are there any questions either of you cannot and will not answer? Talk about your differences and your similarities. Now consider how you would handle these questions with children.

Some sample questions might be these:

How do I feel about dying? (fearful? resigned? unconcerned? panicked?. . .)

What are my beliefs about an afterlife?

Which comes closest to my perception of death? accidental? fated? under our control?

Who should teach children about death?

If I were dying, what would I want people to tell me?

Given that I must, how do I prefer to die?

What sort of funeral do I want?

How do I want my body disposed of?

What is my definition of death?

At what stage of development does an unborn child become a living person?

Who should decide that death has occurred?

What conditions should be set for defining death?

When is it right to kill?

When, if ever, is suicide an appropriate act?

Your exploration of your own attitude might take the form of a string of statements rather than a questionnaire.

•TRY THIS

Respond *yes, no,* or *I don't know* to each statement:

Death is final. Death is unjust. Death comes at the right time for each person. Death is usually peaceful. People are powerless to prevent their own death. Dying people know that they are dying. Heaven is a reward for the virtuous. Mostly very old people die. Death is necessary for the balance of nature. People should accept death gracefully. Children should be included in the rituals of death. It is natural to feel angry when someone that we love dies. Everyone is afraid to die. Only parents or ministers should talk about death to children. Children should be protected from the facts of death. I know all I want to about death.

Read some of the materials suggested in References at the end of this chapter to see how they answer these questions. With which do you agree?

After you have begun to explore your own feelings, start to exchange ideas with children. Sometimes they will ask you questions that you cannot answer, just as you have asked yourself very difficult questions. Often all that they want is confirmation that others feel as they do and can accept those feelings, even when they are unpleasant. On occasion the conversation will reveal misconceptions and contradictions ("My grandma died yesterday, but she'll come back in time for my birthday, if I'm good.") Accept all statements without judgment, waiting to comment until you have a fairly coherent idea of how the child perceives death. Then you can decide on whether or not to use this information to build curriculum, reassure the child, correct erroneous information, or refer to another professional for further handling. Several excellent sources of advice on how to talk to children about death can be found in libraries and bookstores.

It is useful for adults to be aware of the development stages through which children progress in their perception of death. It is also important to know what the usual universal responses are to the death of a loved one. It is believed that even infants are attempting to cope with and understand the concept of loss when they play games such as peek-a-boo and drop-the-object. According to psychologists, the babies are trying to control their world and they are reassured whenever the "lost" object or person reappears.

Until children are about five years old, they cannot conceive of death as permanent. They imagine that dead people are still alive, and perhaps can be found somewhere else. Because children are so self-centered at this stage, they think of everything and everyone in the light of their own desires and experiences. When they reach the age of five or six they still consider the world through their own needs, but they have begun to acknowledge the weight of their experiences. In this stage, until they are approximately nine years old, they personify death, and believe that they can control it through magic, trickery, or just the force of their wishes.

By the time they get to be nine years old, they are usually able to acknowledge that death is permanent, universal, and inevitable. In short, they have reached the stage that most adults achieve. It has been found that those children who have had the opportunity to talk about and deal with the idea of death reach this adult stage of thinking at a somewhat earlier age. What is more, they seem to be able to handle the idea of loss and death in a more stable and constructive manner than those children who have been "shielded" from any exposure to the issue.

Adults and children, react to death in an almost universal fashion, all the while thinking that each is the only one to ever feel this way. The first response is usually denial. "You're joking!" "I don't believe it!" "Tell me it isn't so." As with most areas where stages are involved, we are rarely cleanly out of one before we enter the next. Thus, even years after someone has died we may think we see him or her walking down the street. Or we may think to ourselves, "I must tell Mother about this" even when Mother has been dead for a long time.

The next stage is anger—at God, at the person who has died, at the world, and finally, at oneself. The self-anger can turn into guilt. "If I had been better, or behaved differently, she wouldn't have died. Sometimes the guilt becomes a self-castigation: "Why am I alive when he is dead? He was a much better person than I." Understandably, the sense of guilt leads to grief and depression, the last stage necessary in order to be able to achieve acceptance. The length of the stages varies from person to person, and situation to situation. Some of us never arrive at the acceptance stage.

SOME QUESTIONS TO EXPLORE

How can we help children accept their feelings about the death of people they love? What do we want children to know about death? How much realism can they tolerate? How much detail should we present about the act of dying? Do we want them to believe that it is a painless process? How much should we dwell on pain? How involved should they become in the issues of abortion, suicide, euthanasia, the controversies surrounding the definition of death, customs of mourning, funerals, the hereafter, and all the religious teachings concerning death? How protected should they be from the fact that we do not usually know in advance when we will die, and that the oldest people do not always die first? There are no right answers to any of these questions, and this list is by no means exhaustive. How can we approach the topic using books to help ourselves and children?

•TRY THIS

Read some of the factual books about death, along with the articles listed at the end of this chapter and any others that you find listed in *Library Literature* or *Education Index* concerning death and children's books, or death and children. Then draw up a list of categories suggested by these readings.The categories might include a list of issues or attitudes as headings. Genre classes, such as myth, fantasy, folk tales, picture books, poetry, and biography could serve. After determining your categories, find children's books that contain death as an important factor; list the books under each category. Then subdivide the categories so that you can differentiate the treatment of death in each of the classifications. Some poems, for example, focus on the permanence of death and some point up death as a part of the natural cycle. If permanence and natural cycle were your original categories, further subdivide those by genre, or age level, or point of view. Once you have worked extensively with the categories and books that fit them, you will have a better idea of how you can use these books further with children.

SUGGESTED CRITERIA

Storybooks for children include such topics as coming to terms with suicide, and the deaths of very young people, parents, grandparents, and animals. They describe feelings of rage, sorrow, loneliness, helplessness, and resignation. They include a look at how upper-, lower-, and middle-class families handle death. There are books containing Native American rituals and customs, Jewish and Christian procedures and beliefs, and glimpses into countries other than America. One can read about the responses of adults and children, males and females, blacks and whites. There are books aimed at the very young, the intermediate ages, and the older child. They contain a wide range of information and attitudes about death— the diversity is enormous. Children, perhaps with the help of a knowledgeable adult, can utilize the books most nearly corresponding to their level and needs.

The reading of these books invites many activities. Children can locate contradictory ideas and set up a debate. One controversy might revolve around funerals: What purpose do they serve? Evidence supporting different positions can be located in the literature. Children may enjoy writing stories stemming from their reading, adopting the same or an opposing position from the one expressed in the book. It is always an excellent practice to accumulate a class or personal library containing books that together present a balancing of the many different aspects and facts about death. Be certain that the library includes picture books, folk tales, modern fiction, nonfiction, poetry, literary fantasy, and realistic fiction so as to reach the widest audience and present the greatest diversity. Books directly concerned with death are very useful. Also important are books that contribute to the building of an outlook on the subject even when death is not the major theme.

Books should exhibit an understanding of a developmental point of view. Adults should be prepared to explain books that convey too much abstract information to young children or attempt to mask the reality of death for older children. Books are useful when they include realistic explorations into some of the major issues surrounding the theme of death. Even picture books and stories can acknowledge that most of the ideas, feelings, and questions expressed by very young children evolve from their personal experiences with death. It is not uncommon for them to have to cope with the death of a pet or a grandparent. Sometimes they must face the untimely death of a parent or sibling or friend. They do not usually ask abstract or impersonal questions. Books written for children at this stage, therefore, should take this developmental factor into consideration, and should deal with their feelings and responses. Books are more useful when they describe the characters' mourning process rather than pretending that death is easily handled.

Less than helpful are books that substitute euphemisms for accurate terminology. Readers should try to find books in which children are informed about what is happening and are invited to participate actively in the rituals and mourning process.

RESOURCES FOR ADULTS

Earl Grollman has written a pamphlet for parents entitled *Talking about Death*. Its aim is to help children to accept the reality of death. The conversations detailed in the text are also helpful in preventing harmful fantasizing. The pamphlet acknowledges the child's negative feelings and accepts them, while at the same time reassuring the child with positive statements. Edgar N. Jackson's *Telling a Child about Death* also contains direct advice for adults in handling this topic. Jackson points out differences among children of different ages in terms of their readiness to deal with concepts. Very young children can recognize the obvious differences between life and death; older children can understand the abstract idea of the balance of nature and a universal pattern. The author recommends, as does every authority on this subject, that children be told the truth as simply and as directly as possible. Euphemisms such as "went to sleep" or "went away" are frowned upon. Jackson suggests that discussions of death are often prompted by something that has occurred in the children's experience, perhaps not directly related to the death of a loved one. A tree stump might prompt a conversation about death. The death of an animal, stories that people tell or read, a grandparent's death, or an accident may serve to stimulate questions and discussion. Strong feelings are healthy, and a display of emotion should be encouraged rather than squelched.

Anna W.M. Wolf's book *Helping Your Child to Understand Death* echoes Jackson's advice. She explains that, when we evade children's questions, we are probably trying to postpone our own confrontation with the idea of death. She points out that in our country modern science has successfully removed the act of dying from our homes. Nowadays, not many young children die; and when people are terminally ill, they are usually cared for in an "appropriate" institution. We no longer automatically invite an aged relative to live out his or her last years with us; our family is more the nuclear version than it is the extended family of years ago. Wolf's suggestions include sample answers to children's questions. She stresses inclusion of the children in funeral rituals and in all the procedures surrounding the death of a relative.

She recommends taking a step-by-step approach to helping children discover the truth without fear.

Death of parents is often seen by children as abandonment. Wolf provides some possible avenues for handling these anxieties. She stresses the advisability of recognizing the content of each question that a child asks. One child, for example, because of a semantic confusion thought that "body" referred only to the trunk of a person, and wanted to know why people get their arms and legs cut off when they are dead. Once the source of the questions is recognized, it is relatively easy to answer.

Earl Grollman has also edited a comprehensive text, *Explaining Death to Children*, which is intended for adult readers. The book contains chapters devoted to Protestant, Catholic, and Jewish rituals, each written by a member of the clergy. One chapter contains a cross-cultural analysis of how death is handled. The book as a whole adopts a developmental approach; that is, it describes the different behaviors that children manifest at different age levels and hypothesizes that children go through similar stages in thinking about, and responding to, death. The chapters most specifically describing these stages are clearly written. Teachers, parents, and other concerned adults can take these developmental factors into consideration.

DISCUSSION OF CHILDREN'S BOOKS

FACTUAL BOOKS

Herbert S. Zim and Sonia Bleeker have written a book called *Life and Death*, which briefly includes some of the life processes but concentrates on death. The authors describe the scientific process of maturation and dying. The book contains much anthropological and other scientific information. The writing, straightforward and clear, is directed at children nine years of age and older.

The book clarifies some misconceptions, such as the equating of death with sleep. It states: "With death, all of the life processes, such as growth, movement, awareness, and reaction, stop—finally and permanently" (p. 19). Details, including a description of a death certificate, health officers who verify and report a death, funeral arrangements and costs, different kinds of burial (historic and contemporary), and mourning customs are provided in a nonjudgmental, dispassionate style. The authors express their point of view in several instances, hoping that readers will accept death as part of life and in its larger context in terms of the rest of the world. Many readers may find this to be a valuable book for explaining death to children who have recently experienced the death of someone close to them. The book can also serve to prepare children for understanding death when they hear about it or ask about it. It can be a tool for generating questions.

Another book that speaks directly to children about the facts of death is *Death Is a Noun*, by John Langone. The author includes discussions of critical contemporary issues. He comments on suicide; euthanasia; the problem of when to declare a person legally dead; and questions of capital punishment, murder, and abortion. He also talks about personal dilemmas of how to face death, ideas about life after death, and the weighty implications whenever a decision about life and death is made.

Langone presents several viewpoints in each chapter. He includes an impressive amount of information, usually leaving it to the reader to decide on the answer. He contends: "About all one can do is affirm the right of all to speak, to listen to the opposing views, consider both society as a whole and the individual, and then make a decision based on one's own conscience" (p. 106). The author does not abdicate responsibility; he does interject his own ideas and his sense of morality. He wants people to make life as mutually beneficial and as productive as possible. He selects his quotes and uses facts judiciously and persuasively. Young people would have to attain a fair degree of maturity to appreciate this book thoroughly. Children approaching their teen-age years can benefit from reading it, while younger children, depending on their precocity, may have more difficulty but may, nevertheless, be able to handle the content.

BOOKS FOR YOUNG CHILDREN

Funerals

The death of an animal is probably the death most frequently encountered by a young child. Authors use this experience to help children cope with, and learn about, some of the rituals, practices, and beliefs surrounding death. Following the experts' advice about including children in the ceremonial aspects of death, several authors have written stories in which a funeral service is conducted by the children for a dead animal. In 1958 Margaret Wise Brown's book *The Dead Bird* was published. The first book of its kind to be accepted for young audiences, it specifically describes the physiological manifestations of death as well as the burial service the children accord the dead bird. The story is somewhat impersonal; the bird is not a pet but simply a dead bird found in the path. But the illustrations by Remy Charlip convey the emotions of the children in a way that the simple text does not attempt. The language is at the level of the early grades in school, or even preschool, but describes clearly what is happening. It also communicates that part of the process of mourning is also being glad to be alive. As the children conduct a funeral, they sing to the bird. They cry because it is dead, but they are glad that they can participate in this ceremony. Their tears are as much in response to the beauty of their own singing and the fragrance of the flowers as they are for the death of the bird.

Joanne E. Bernstein's books on helping children to handle separation and loss are among the best sources for children and adults alike. One of her children's books, *Loss and How to Cope with It,* not only explains the stages of mourning, assuring children that they are normal to feel the way they do, but also adds reassuring advice about how to handle these feelings. Information is presented in a readable, anecdotal format, and is directed not only at people who have experienced the death of a loved one, but also to their friends, and to those who might want to know how to react to mourners.

When Violet Died, by Mildred Kantrowitz, also describes a funeral for a bird. But this bird has been a beloved pet, and the ritual of the funeral is not the same satisfying experience for these children as it is for those in *The Dead Bird.* After the funeral, when the two girls return home, they are reminded of their dead bird by the empty cage. The older sister is aware that nothing can last forever, and this knowledge saddens her. This funeral is a more realistic one for children who have had the actual experience with a loved one's death. *The Dead Bird* serves better for children who have not been intimately involved with death.

The Tenth Good Thing about Barney, by Judith Viorst, is another book in which a pet dies and a funeral is held. The child reacts to the death of his cat, Barney, by losing his appetite and by refusing to do anything but go to bed and cry. The mother, empathic, suggests a funeral service, which the child's parents and his friend, Annie, attend. The mother tells the child to think of ten good things about Barney to recite at the funeral. He can think of only nine, he tells those nine. In this book the mourning period is portrayed realistically, with the funeral helping somewhat to relieve the acuteness of the loss, but with some of the hurt remaining afterward until the boy realizes that the tenth good thing is that Barney has become a part of nature.

John, the young boy in *Scat,* by Arnold Dobrin, feels that he must remain at the cemetery after the funeral to say good-by to his grandmother in his own way. An appropriate funeral for his grandmother, complete with the kind of music she enjoyed, fails to accomplish a settled feeling for him. He needs to play a jazz tribute to her on his harmonica, even though he knows that she disliked jazz. One of the useful messages in this book is that it is acceptable to differ from someone you love in the outward show of your emotions. In the end the feelings themselves are what matter.

A surprisingly large number of books include descriptions of funerals, stressing their usefulness in helping children cope with emotions. For the families in Coburn's *Anne and the Sand Dobbies* and Lee's *The Magic Moth,* the funeral helps to focus their grief over the death of a young child. Ministers also help the families in these two books, both of which concentrate on how siblings react to a sister's death. Smith's *A Taste of Blackberries* also describes the death and funeral of a child and the reactions of his closest friend. Funerals represent the most commonly described ritual in children's books.

Some stories recount practices such as the covering of mirrors in Jewish homes, as in Fassler's *My Grandpa Died Today*. Ann Turner's *Houses for the Dead* describes the customs of many cultures, ancient and contemporary. Children can benefit from learning about the universality of ritual associated with death.

Immortality

Most of the experts advising us about how to talk about death with children recommend that we avoid definite statements about heaven or an afterlife; they suggest that we should say we do not know. Some books follow this advice and others do not. Discretion is needed here so that all views are respected, and none imposed.

In *Anne and the Sand Dobbies*, the children are told that their sister is alive and well in another world and that they will all join her some day. An older brother informs the youngest child in *The Magic Moth* that their sister is "going to a nice place, heaven." Another intimation of immortality occurs in this book when the child, Maryanne, dies: at the very moment of her death a white moth bursts from its cocoon. The family agrees that it is a magic moth. A similar idea occurs in dePaola's *Nana Upstairs and Nana Downstairs,* when a falling star is equated to a kiss from the dead great-grandmother. In most of the other books, however, the idea of a life after death is acknowledged to be a mystery.

In Warburg's *Growing Time* and Miles's *Annie and the Old One,* as well as in Viorst's *The Tenth Good Thing about Barney*, the cyclical nature of the universe and the concept of death's being necessary for the sustenance of new life is presented so that young children can understand and accept it.

The younger sister in *When Violet Died* creates her own system of immortality. she decides to name one kitten in each generation the same name as its mother, insuring that she will always have a cat with that name. She is excited by her invention, knowing all the while that nothing lasts forever, but telling herself that she has almost granted her cat eternal life. For some readers this will be a technique for softening a loss.

It is very useful for children to recognize as early as possible that books, just because they are in print, are not gospel. They must accept the challenge of disagreeing with an author whose ideas conflict with theirs. Adults should reward this kind of critical thinking, teaching children to evaluate authors' suggestions, investigate "facts," and use their own experience and judgment. If a child accepts the idea of acquiring immortality through the carrying on of a name, that is fine. But if a child refutes this idea, then the child should be encouraged to consider the issue further and to contribute his or her own point of view. The child who wishes to write to the author or publisher with a list of questions or comments is sure to receive a response.

In life as well as in books, the attempt is sometimes made by well-meaning friends or family to replace the dead loved one. For example, when a child's pet dies, the parents may buy another animal immediately, hoping to assuage the child's grief and perhaps attempting to demonstrate that though death is final, life goes on. Sometimes this is an attempt to pretend, "Your dog didn't really die; you still have a dog." In *The Old Dog*, by Sarah Abbott, the boy accepts the new puppy, but not as a substitute. He is wiser than his parents. He regrets that the old dog is not there to welcome the new one, and although he will nurture the puppy, he is still thinking about the old dog.

In *Growing Time* the young boy at first rejects a new puppy given to him to replace his dead dog. He recognizes that the puppy is meant to be a substitute, and he knows that this is impossible. His father wisely leaves it up to the boy to decide whether or not he will keep the puppy. At last the boy decides to let the puppy stay because it needs him. In *A Taste of Blackberries* the child offers himself as a substitute to his best friend's mother, and he is comforted by this act. The mother is touched by the offer. At the moment of bereavement it provides a measure of solace.

A different view of immortality is presented in a book that might be somewhat difficult for younger children to read to themselves, but it could be read to them, and certainly children aged nine and up could handle the prose themselves. The book is a gem that is worth the effort for the younger ones. It is *Tuck Everlasting*, by Natalie Babbitt. The story tells of a family that has discovered and drunk from a spring containing the water of eternal life. Many questions are raised about the value of life and death, all in the context of an exciting and well-written adventure story. Each of the characters displays a different perspective for the reader to explore and ponder.

Reacting to Death

Most books for young children stress tolerance of the reactions that children display when someone or something they love dies. Anger, withdrawal, refusal to eat, tears, confusion—all are acceptable behavior in the stories. *Growing Time* beautifully demonstrates how adults can be supportive of a young child when death has occurred. Each adult adds another perspective and another piece of information to help the boy cope with the death of his dog. The boy is permitted resentful feelings and grief. He is finally ready to accept the finality of death and the responsibility of caring for another dog.

In *A Taste of Blackberries* the boy at first denies the fact of his friend's death; he cannot face it. Gradually, with the help of supportive adults, he begins to believe and then to accept the idea. This death is a very difficult one because it is sudden, violent, and occurs while the child's friends are present. The child, Jamie, dies of bee stings. The idea of being unable to prevent an accident is a difficult one for even an adult to handle. This cause of death leaves an aftermath with which the survivors must cope for a long time to come.

Most of the story of *The Magic Moth* focuses on the responses of the youngest child, Mark-o. He creeps into his dying sister's room to see if she looks different from normal and if he can tell from her appearance that she is about to die. He tries to imagine a replacement for her, recalling a guinea pig that took the place of one that had died. He takes comfort in the myth of Proserpine, thinking that perhaps his sister, too, will be permitted to return. He asks many questions about heaven, how it feels to be buried in the earth, and what to do with his feelings after his sister does die. The entire family is involved in the preparations for responding to her death. It is a loving family and copes well. Elements of magic or mysticism intrude somewhat, but not damagingly. The point is made that describing death as "going away" is confusing. It is better to say it directly.

The boy, Ben, in *The Old Dog*, reacts in a typical young child's fashion. He misses all the functions that the dog performed for him. He misses the company of the dog and all the happiness that the dog gave him. For many young children it is the permanence of death that is incomprehensible, and their immediate reactions do not necessarily reflect their true feelings. The boy in *My Grandpa Died Today* is encouraged to play and behave in his normally cheerful fashion after the death of his grandfather, even though his parents are mourning the death at home. The grandfather in this book dies painlessly in his rocking chair after having forewarned his grandson. The grandfather has told the child that he is not afraid to die and that he knows the grandson is not afraid to live. Although the story does not provide us with enough substance for empathy, and despite its obvious didactics, the reactions to death are effectively portrayed. The father and mother both cry. The child is encouraged not to feel guilty about wanting to play. The child, in his playing, knows that his grandfather's spirit is with him. The intent of the book seems to be more protective of a child's feelings than informative. But this, too, is useful in considering the materials to use for helping children understand and manage the problem of death.

A parent's grief gets in the way of appropriate mourning in *Nadia the Willful* by Sue Alexander. In this beautifully told story, Nadia's brother, Hamed, has died, and their father has proclaimed that no one must speak his dead son's name. Wiser than her father, Nadia realizes that remembering and talking about her brother eases her grief. She finally manages to persuade her father, and helps him to accept Hamed's death. In Charlotte Zolotow's *My Grandson Lew*, a young boy misses his dead grandfather, and calls for him in the middle of the night. Lew and his mother share their loving memories and comfort each other through their conversation. This tender portrait can serve as a model to people who are afraid to talk about deceased loved ones to their young children.

Another book that accomplishes this same modeling is *Time for Uncle Joe*, by Nancy Jewell. In this gentle recollection, a little girl mourns for her beloved uncle but keeps his memory active and alive. She recalls his jokes, the details of his appearance, and the activities they shared. She also feels comforted by the fact that she has retained some of his possessions, and is able to touch them and look at them, and in so doing, to have him with her in spirit even though it is clear that she knows he is never coming back. The book is a loving tribute to the man at the same time that it affirms the love and sensitivity of the child.

BOOKS FOR OLDER CHILDREN

Death is not an easy topic about which to write or talk. Many of us, even though we are in our adult years, have yet to resolve for ourselves the questions and anxieties surrounding this issue. Death in the abstract is difficult enough, but real, immediate death can be so traumatic as to defy our ability to cope with our feelings and thoughts. Our religion, upbringing, personal experiences, and the opinions and help of those whom we respect have a great deal to do with our own attitudes and methods of handling the situation. There are many books directly concerning this topic which are helpful in different ways. Some of these books are more suitable for the much older child because of the specificity and the magnitude of the issue involved.

Reacting to Death

Julie, in *Julie of the Wolves,* by Jean Craighead George, is not very much affected at age four by the death of her mother. When she hears of the death of her adored father, she behaves with courage and a sense of independence because of what he had taught her when they were together. She responds differently to the death of the leader of the wolf pack that has adopted her. This death enrages her and prompts her to action. She averts the danger of her own death, knowing full well that its prospect is imminent, by using all of her intelligence and ability to survive with dignity. This remarkable Newbery medal winner contains substance for discussion on almost any theme. The heroine is reminiscent of the girl in Scott O'Dell's *Island of the Blue Dolphins*, another Newbery Award winner, in the way that death affects her and in how she handles it. Each of these young women is stoic, heroic, and competent to manage alone, against all odds.

In some books the characters do not respond heroically or admirably to death. One of the characters in *Meet the Austins*, by Madeleine L'Engle, is a girl who behaves unpleasantly after the death of her father. She capitalizes on the fact that she is an orphan, using this as an excuse to throw temper tantrums, disregard the feelings of others, and make people miserable when they are near her. The Austin family, who invite her to live with them, teach her to relate to other people in a less selfish and obnoxious fashion. The parents are absolutely perfect—wise, understanding, and knowledgeable at all times. They always respond sympathetically and appropriately. However, they confess to not knowing the answer to why loved ones must die and what the plan is that governs life and death. The responses of the children in this book to the death of their close family friend and to the intrusion of the orphan are presented well. Readers will probably find at least one character with whom they can empathize in this book.

Jess, the protagonist in Katherine Paterson's *Bridge to Terabithia,* is stunned by the death of his dearest friend, Leslie. The two of them have constructed an imaginary kingdom which they investigate quite regularly. Jess's feelings of guilt are compounded by the fact that on the day Leslie died, he was not with her, but was away on a pleasure trip with his art teacher. After Jess passes through all of the stages of mourning, he emerges from the experience much more attuned to other people's feelings.

Jenny, in Jean Little's *Home from Far,* finds it difficult to recover from the traumatic death of her twin brother, Michael, in a car accident. Her parents become foster parents to a little girl and her older brother. The foster boy's name, coincidentally, is Michael. Jenny, who resents him bitterly, suspects that her parents are trying to replace her dead brother. She is angry with her mother for disposing of all of her twin Michael's possessions. At last Jenny and her mother talk about their feelings. They realize they have both been missing Michael and that the mother has simply been trying to spare Jenny pain. The mother talks about the way that the mourning of a dead child was mishandled when she was a little girl, and she has tried not to make the same mistake with Jenny. The mother uncovers all of their mementos of Michael so that she and Jenny can now begin to remember him with love and joy. Jenny can also participate in a positive relationship with the living Michael.

Where the Lilies Bloom, by the Cleavers, describes an Appalachian family, tenant farmers, whose mother has died and whose father is in the process of dying. The fourteen-year-old sister determines that she and her younger brother will bury their father secretly so that the family can remain together. Her response to death and her behavior during the time that her father is dying can be the subject of much discussion. Children can discuss what they would have done in her place.

The central character of *Admission to the Feast,* by Gunnel Beckman, must cope with her own impending death. She has just been informed that she has leukemia. An independent young woman whose mother, a physician, is away in India, she writes a letter to a friend describing her feelings. *Hang Tough, Paul Mather,* by Alfred Slote, is another book in which the protagonist, this time a boy, is afflicted with leukemia. He must deal with the likelihood of his own death.

It is important to convey different styles of living and dying in as many varied kinds of books as possible. The inclusion of these books in a class or school library will help young readers to recognize that different people follow different, acceptable patterns, but may react in whatever way is most positive and appropriate for themselves. Two young women whose reactions are detrimental to themselves may be found in Windsor's *The Summer Before,* in which Alexandra literally goes mad over the death of her dear friend; and in Arundel's *The Blanket Word,* in which Jan is immature and selfish, making everyone around her suffer because of her behavior. The authors hold out hope for both characters at the end of each book; young readers thus may be assured that, even if they behave badly, there will still be another chance for them.

Global attitudes toward death on the part of different cultures may also be found in books for young readers. *The Big Wave,* by Pearl S. Buck, describes how two Japanese villages face death caused by natural disasters. Buck's aim in writing this book is to help young people learn not to fear death. She wants them to recognize that life is stronger than death.

Maia Wojciechowska tries to present the perspective of a bullfight aficionado in two of her books, *Shadow of a Bull*, winner of a Newbery medal, and *The Life and Death of a Brave Bull.* She asserts that the bullfight is the Spaniard's way of defeating death. The books in some measure try to explain the wish to fight, kill, and die gloriously. A noble death defeats death, according to the message in these books. In another Newbery medal book, *The Cat Who Went to heaven,* by Elizabeth Coatsworth, the author attempts to express a Buddhist point of view. The cat in this story dies of pure joy because her owner, an artist, has defied tradition and has painted her into a picture of Buddha going to heaven. The idea of dying in ecstasy is a particularly Eastern one that may be of interest to Western readers. Research into Buddhism and other non-Western cultures can profitably ensue from a reading of this book.

Some authors present a resigned, accepting response to death. Others recognize the appropriateness of strong emotion even if that emotion is rage. Some people admire stoic silence. Edna St. Vincent Millay clearly advocates anger and resentment. In "Dirge Without Music," in response to the pattern of the dead enriching the earth, making it possible for other things to grow, she says: "I know, But I do not approve. And I am not resigned." All these approaches provide the opportunity for demonstrating that, given the same information, and similar circumstances, we do not necessarily respond in the same way. This must be seen as valid and valuable.

Suicide

Suicide is a form of dying that affects the living in a way different from "natural" death. *Grover,* by Vera and Bill Cleaver, concerns the death of a boy's mother. Knowing she has a terminal illness, she shoots herself, because she cannot bear the thought of going through all the changes she knows will occur if she permits the illness to take its natural course. There is no attempt made in the book to mask or to ameliorate the situation. The authors do an excellent job of describing how adults try to shield children from the truth and, in the process, sometimes harm them more than they help. Grover, the boy, initially displays little external emotional reaction to his mother's death, but in his dealings with his friends he exhibits his grief and pain. He explodes into blind rage when a nasty, somewhat demented woman taunts him with the fact of his mother's suicide. He seems to be able, partially because of the support of his friends and somewhat because of an understanding housekeeper, to rebuild his own life and continue normally. His father, however, cannot cope, grieves constantly, and resents the boy's normalcy. The situation is realistic and disturbing.

Suicide is the result of a long series of painful events in Norma Fox Mazer's *A Figure of Speech*. The eighty-three-year-old grandfather decides to kill himself rather than be sent to a home for the aged. Some of the people in this story are extremely insensitive to each other's feelings. They are especially cruel, without meaning to be, to the old man and his granddaughter, Jenny. Her love for her grandfather almost saves him, but in the end it becomes apparent that they are both powerless to prevent his being taken away to live in a place that would destroy his dignity and his sense of self. This story and *Grover* may help readers to examine their feelings and raise some questions about the absolute right or wrong of the desperate act of suicide.

Books in Which Death Is Incidental

Most books for young readers concentrate on elements other than death. Death does, nevertheless, occur in many books and is important to their plots. It is usually used either as an incidental happening or as a plot strategy in all genres of literature, including folk tales, classics, romantic novels, and poetry. Sometimes death is seen in a religious light. Sometimes it occurs almost as an author's afterthought. It often conforms to some literary expectation or proves a literary truism; for example, the virtuous characters die young in many romances.

In some classics the young heroes or heroines are angels on earth while alive, carry out their mission of tenderness and virture, and are "gathered back to God" while they are still very young. The writing is usually sentimental and has the quaintness of a period piece. The attempt is made to teach children to emulate and admire this good and kind soul who was lent to us mortals for a brief period of time. One logical conclusion a child could reach, however, would be quite the opposite from the one intended—to vow never to be that good in order not to die so young. The idea is not so far-fetched as it first may seem; forced didacticism often backfires. "Goodness" can be presented in such a saccharine and exaggerated fashion as to discourage its practice.

Hans Christian Andersen's stories, which almost always display a strong moralistic tone, sometimes pound home an obvious lesson. His characters often die as a reward for a good life. Andersen's characters go to a specific place after they die; there is no question about life after death in his stories.

Religion plays a very important part in his tales and, of course, figures heavily in the messages that he conveys about death. Children may be interested in studying Hans Christian Andersen's life in order to see the effect that it had on his writing.

Teachers may find it difficult to deal with this approach if they are uneasy about either offending or supporting any given religious attitude about the hereafter. One way of handling the dilemma is to suggest that students make a study of the different religious approaches to death. Additional research can include a comparision of modern and ancient beliefs. Other extensions of this sort of study would lead to comparative mythology, an examination of fairy tales and folk tales from around the world, an inquiry into anthropological aspects of societies and their customs surrounding death. It is always a fruitful educational experience to acquire information about beliefs and customs other than one's own, since this knowledge makes us more inquisitive and less judgmental or narrow.

Death as punishment is even more common than death as reward. The fear of death is often used in literature as a deterrent to wickedness. In literature, as in real life, this threat is usually ineffectual: the wicked continue to be evil and continue to be "justly" killed. All witches and dragons and ogres and giants die. So, too, do most if not all of the hero's enemies. The death is often violent and described in gory detail.

Villains, unless they repent, must die. What sort of attitude does this rule create in us? How can we help our students to move from the "eye for an eye" morality expressed so convincingly in our folklore? How much does this philosophy actually seep into our sense of social and political justice? For instance, why is it that in "oldtime" cowboy films we know that if a person has committed a crime belonging to a certain category, that person will die in the end? We not only anticipate this ending; we require it. Questioning this accepted pattern may lead us to discussions of capital punishment, justice, and the cause and nature of crime. The teacher can begin asking this kind of question in order to work with the level of moral and social development the students have acquired.

Although it is but one of the many components, death is a factor in the modern classic *Charlotte's Web,* by E. B. White. Wilbur is threatened with death during the first part of the book, and Charlotte dies near the end, but the book emphasizes the idea that life goes on. Grief is temporary. Wilbur never forgets Charlotte. Her children remain as her legacy, along with memories of her special characteristics and talents. Friendship, love, and tolerance of those with different lifestyles are strong themes in this beautifully written book. The handling of death is done so sensitively that it would probably provide a measure of comfort to readers who are trying to deal with the death of someone dear to them. It also can provide the basis of an interesting discussion about life cycles as well as the function of death and its aftermath for the living.

There are hundreds more books containing mention of, concentration upon, and implications of death. Some of these would be useful in helping readers cope with their own fears and problems surrounding this topic. Some may aid readers in uncovering attitudes and thoughts of which they had been unaware. Some books may, if the reader is not careful, convey ideas that may potentially be a detriment. The alert teacher will be ready to guide and respond to the child who is ready to deal with the many aspects of this theme by making available as much as the literature can provide.

REFERENCES: DEATH

ARNSTEIN, HELEN S. *What to Tell Your Child about Birth, Death....* Indianapolis: Bobbs-Merrill, 1960.
Arnstein does an excellent job discussing attitudes about death and the harmful effects that can result if well-meaning parents hide death from their children. Arnstein explores how children react to the death of an animal, sibling, parent, and so on. The main point running throughout the entire article is that the subject of death should be dealt with truthfully and simply.

BERMAN, DIANE B. "The Facilitation of Mourning: A Preventive Mental Health Approach." Unpublished doctoral dissertation, University of Massachussetts, 1977.
Presents a curriculum based on research and experience with young children to help them develop a concept of death and the ability to mourn. Helps teachers and other concerned adults to address children's questions on the subject of death. Provides suggestions for activities as well as books to use with preschool children.

BERNSTEIN, JOANNE E. *Books to Help Children Cope with Separation and Loss,* 2d. ed. New York: Bowker, 1983.
Valuable guide to selecting books for use in bibliotherapy. All categories of loss are included in this comprehensive reference tool. Criteria for judgment are provided as well as more than 600 annotations.

BUTLER, FRANCELIA. "Death in Children's Literature," in *The Great Excluded: Critical Essays on Children's Literature,* Vol. 1. *Journal of the Modern Language Association Seminar on Children's Literature and the Children's Literature Association,* 1972, pp. 104–124.
Reviews historically the treatment of death in literature for children. Recommends folk literature as the medium for introducing children through literature to the idea of death. Approves of the attitudes of acceptance and belief that death is not final, because resurrection will occur.

CARR, ROBIN L. "Death as Presented in Children's Books," *Elementary English.* Vol. 50, No. 5, May 1973, pp. 701–705.
Quotes a poem by Merrill Moore on death. Presents a brief history, but an excellent one, of the treatment of death in children's books. Describes twenty books dealing with death in a variety of ways.

COLE, SHEILA R. "Reviews," *New York Times Book Review.* 26 September 1971, p. 8.
Reviews six books for children on the topic of death. Suggests that in modern books adults try to find easy answers for children; she criticizes this approach.

FASSLER, JOAN. *Helping Children Cope: Mastering Stress through Books and Stories.* New York: Free Press, 1978.
Discusses issues of death, separation, hospitalization, illness, lifestyle changes and other potentially stress-causing situations as they are presented in books for children ages four to eight.

GROLLMAN, EARL A., ed. *Explaining Death to Children.* Boston: Beacon Press, 1967.
This book contains chapters written by experts on various aspects of death. Religions are represented. Psychologists explain and describe children's reactions to death and their perceptions of the phenomenon. Grollman suggests how parents can talk to their children about this topic.

GROLLMAN, EARL A., ed. *Talking about Death.* Boston: Beacon Press, 1971.
A short book written for parents to help them talk to their children about death. Inside back cover is a guide to how to use it. The book is a long conversation including children's questions and the answers an understanding parent provides.

HOYT, HOWARD. "For Young Readers: Introducing Death," *New York Times Book Review,* 26 September 1971, p. 8.
Satiric rap at books that pretty the process and avoid the unpleasantness of death.

JACKSON, EDGAR N. *Telling a Child about Death.* New York: Hawthorn, 1965.
Talks about children's misinterpretations of the process of death, and what parents can say to help clear these up. Recommends that each reader develop a sound philosophy of life in order to know how to deal with death.

JEWETT, CLAUDIA. *Helping Children Cope with Separation and Loss.* Cambridge, Massachusetts: Harvard University Press, 1982.
Psychological advice and some common sense as well.

KOBY, IRIS M. "And the Leaves That Are Green Turn To . . .?" *English Journal,* Vol. 64, No. 7, October 1975.
Recommends the exploration of life and death through poetry. Describes such a project with her students, and reports on its success.

KÜBLER-ROSS, ELIZABETH. *On Death and Dying.* New York: Macmillan, 1969.
This book explores the stages that a terminally ill person goes through when (s)he learns of impending death. Kübler-Ross identifies these stages as follows: denial; anger; bargaining; depression; acceptance; and hope. The book is full of warmth and understanding. Kübler-Ross learned the value of confronting and talking with the dying, old and young.

LANGONE, JOHN. *Death is a Noun: A View of the End of Life.* Boston: Little, Brown, 1972.
This book can be found in the science section of the library. It treats the subject objectively and at great length. Included in the book is an examination of each of the pressing issues we now must face concerning all aspects of death.

LOCKE, LINDA A. "A Descriptive Bibliography of Selected Children's Books That Treat Death's Effect on the Child Hero (with an Essay on Death as a Theme in Children's Books)." Unpublished Master's report, Palmer Graduate Library School, Long Island University, Brookville, New York, 1969.
A historical account is given as to how death has been handled in children's books. Analyzes twenty books presenting a variety of ways of dealing with death. Categorizes the books well. A useful reference.

MOORE, DAVID W.: MOORE; SHARON ARTHUR, AND READENCE, JOHN E. "Understanding Characters' Reactions to Death," *Journal of Reading,* Vol. 26, No. 6, March 1983, pp. 540–544.
Presents an approach to help students respond to literature that contains death as a theme. Outlines the five Kubler-Ross stages of response to death and invites student to analyze characters' reactions according to those stages.

MORRIS, BARBARA. "Young Children and Books on Death," *Elementary English,* Vol. 49, No. 4, pp. 530–532; Vol. 51, No. 3, pp. 395–398.
Describes the developmental stages that a child goes through in facing the reality of death. Cites Gesell and Ilg, Russell, Piaget, and Chukovsky. Questions the appropriateness of realistic fiction about death.

MOSS, JUDITH. "Death in Children's Literature," *Elementary English,* Vol. 49, No. 4, April 1972, pp. 530–532.
Comments on the need for treatment of death in children's books. Discusses seven books insightfully,

NILSEN, AILEEN PACE. "Death and Dying: Facts, Fiction, Folklore," *English Journal,* Vol. 62, No. 8, November 1973, pp. 1187–1189.
Discussion and reviews of books for adolescents dealing with death.

SCHAUMBERG, JUDITH B. "The Adolescent and Grief: Fiction and Nonfiction," *Signal,* Vol. 4, 1983.
Discusses several books in the light of Kubler-Ross's stages, and recommends that books be used to help adolescents cope with their own grief.

SWENSON, EVELYN J. "The Treatment of Death in Children's Literature," *Elementary English.* Vol. 49, No. 3, March 1972, pp. 401–404.
Contends that contemporary literature for children ignores death. Traces a history of treatment of death in children's books. Suggests four contemporary books that do a good job: *The High Pasture,* by Ruth Harnden; *The Big Wave*, by Pearl S. Buck; *Up a Road Slowly,* by Irene Hunt; and *Meet the Austins,* by Madeleine L'Engle.

WOLF, ANNA W. M. *Helping Your Child to Understand Death.* New York: Child Study Press, revised ed. 1973.
Many sound suggestions for telling children about death. Gives sample answers to children's questions. Also a section on parents' questions, which the author answers.

ZIM, HERBERT S., AND BLEEKER, SONIA. *Life and Death.* Illustrated by Rene Martin. New York: Morrow, 1970.
Extremely factual, objective explanation of the physical facts of death. Includes

burial practices of different cultures as well as our own. Death is presented as final and inevitable. The accent in this book is on informed understanding.

BIBLIOGRAPHY: DEATH

ABBOTT, SARAH. *The Old Dog.* Illustrated by George Mocniak. New York: Coward, McCann and Geoghegan, 1972. (Ages 7–10.)
When a boy's dog dies, the little boy misses him. His father gives him a puppy, which does not replace the old dog, but which the boy accepts as a new responsibility.

AGEE, JAMES. *A Death in the Family.* New York: Grosset and Dunlap, 1967. Also in paper. (Ages 12–up.)
A portrayal of the effects of a man's death on the rest of his family, with tremendous insights into the world and emotions of children.

ALCOTT, LOUISA MAY. *Little Women.* Boston: Little, Brown, 1868. Also in paper. (Ages 8–up.)
Beth, one of four sisters in a loving family, dies after a long illness. Saddened, but not shocked, the family is accepting of Beth's death.

ALEXANDER, SUE. *Nadia the Willful.* Illustrated by Lloyd Bloom. New York: Pantheon, 1983. (Ages 6–9.)
Nadia, a feisty Bedouin girl, disobeys her father's command that the name of his dead son, Hamed, must not be spoken. Nadia, realizing that remembering her brother eases her grief, ultimately helps her father to accept Hamed's death.

ALIKI. *The Two of Them.* New York: Greenwillow Books, 1979. (Ages 5–8.)
A young child lovingly remembers her dead grandfather and all of the happy times they shared.

ALLEN, TERRY, ed. *The Whispering Wind—Poetry by Young American Indians.* Garden City, New York: Doubleday, 1968. Also in paper. (Ages 10–up.)
This volume of poetry contains many kinds of responses to death.

ANDERSON, LEONE CASTELL. *It's O.K. to Cry.* Chicago: Children's Press, 1979. (Ages 5–8.)
After the death of a favorite uncle, a nine-year-old tries to explain death to his five-year-old brother who cannot understand the finality of death. Included in the book is a discussion of death in terms that can easily be understood.

ANDERSON, LYDIA. *Death.* New York: Franklin Watts, 1980. (Ages 12–up.)
Discusses the cycle of life, longevity, death, burial customs, and mourning. Offers factual answers to questions concerning death; does not deal with emotional responses.

ARMSTRONG, WILLIAM. *Sounder.* New York: Harper & Row, 1969. Also in paper. (Ages 11–up.)
The death of Sounder and the father of the family are presented as symbolic of the destructive nature of white society. The family members accept the deaths stoically.

ARMSTRONG, WILLIAM. *Sour Land*. New York: Harper & Row, 1971. (Ages 12–up.)
A black teacher, Moses Waters, is murdered by whites in a southern town, yet he leaves behind him, in the hearts of a few people, the hope that love will eventually overcome racial hatred.

ARUNDEL, HONOR. *The Blanket Word*. Nashville: Nelson, 1973. (Ages 12–up.)
Jan begins to grow up after returning from school to observe her mother's painful death from cancer, the funeral, and the rest of her family's reaction to the whole situation.

BARTOLI, JENNIFER. *Nonna*. Illustrated by Joan E. Drescher. New York: Harvey House, 1975. (Ages 5–8.)
When grandmother dies, everyone in the family, including father and mother cries. The funeral is described; the extended family arrives, and everyone mourns together. The family then resumes life but remembers lovingly the happy times and pleasant feelings about both grandparents.

BECKMAN, GUNNEL. *Admission to the Feast*. Translated from the Swedish by Joan Tate. New York: Holt, Rinehart and Winston, 1971. (Ages 12–up.)
Taking the form of a letter to a friend by a girl who has accidentally discovered that she is dying of leukemia, the book takes the reader through the different emotions that the young woman experiences, from terror to rejection to acceptance.

BERNSTEIN, JOANNE E. *Loss and How to Cope with It*. New York: Clarion Books, 1977. Paperback (Ages 10–up.)
An excellent resource for people of any age though it is directed at children. Contains anecdotes of personal experiences through which the reader becomes informed. Reassures people that their reactions are normal, and helps them to handle their emotions. The necessity of the mourning process is affirmed. Further reading resources are provided at the end.

BERNSTEIN, JOANNE E., AND GULLO, STEPHEN V. *When People Die*. Illustrated by Rosemarie Hausherr. New York: Dutton, 1977. (Ages 6–10.)
One woman's death, coming at the end of a productive life, is portrayed as an example of the aging process, mourning, and beliefs about an afterlife. The photographs help convey the messages.

BLERHORST, JOHN, ed. *The Fire Plume: Legends of the American Indians*. Illustrated by Aland E. Cober. New York: Dial Press, 1969. (Ages 9–up.)
Death is a major concern of many of these tales from the Algonquin family of tribes.

BLUME, JUDY. *Tiger Eyes*. New York: Bradbury Press, 1977. Also in paper. (Ages 11–up.)
Davey is fifteen years old. Her father has been killed by a thief. The family is in dire economic straits. They go to visit their father's sister, in the Southwest, and while they are there, their store in Atlantic City again is vandalized. The book deals with the issues of loss and security, and with the problem of coping with irrational tragedy. A mature novel, with some sensitive portrayals.

BOLTON, CAROLE. *Reunion in December*. New York: Morrow, 1962. (Ages 12–up.)

A fifteen-year-old girl has a hard time adjusting to the sudden death of her father and to the actions of the rest of her family after his death.

BONTEMPS, ARNA, ed. *American Negro Poetry*. New York: Hill and Wang, 1963. Also in paper (All ages.)
A book of poetry with several kinds of responses toward death. Sensitive, moving poetry.

BRIDGERS, SUE ELLEN. *Home Before Dark*. New York: Knopf, 1976. (Ages 10–up.)
Stella Mae resents her father's apparent easy forgetting of her dead mother. She is anxious about her impending move to her step-mother's house. She eventually learns to accept the fact of her mother's death.

BROWN, MARGARET WISE. *The Dead Bird*. Illustrated by Remy Charlip. New York: Young Scott Books, 1958. (Ages 3–8.)
Some children find a dead bird, conduct an elaborate funeral for it and visit the grave every day until they forget. One of the first books for young children on this topic.

BUCK, PEARL S. *The Big Wave*. Illustrated with prints by Hiroshige and Hakusai. New York: John Day, 1948. Also in paper. (Ages 8–12.)
When a Japanese boy's family dies in a tidal wave, his friend's family helps him to deal with death (and fear of death) through an affirmation of life.

BUNTING, EVE. *The Empty Window*. Illustrated by Judy Clifford. New York: Frederick Warne, 1980. (Ages 7–10.)
Joe, a young boy, is dying. He loves to look out his window at some wild parrots. When he receives one of the parrots as a gift, he sets it free, in a symbolic acceptance of his own life and death. The response of his friends to his condition is well handled in this sensitive book.

BUNTING, EVE *The Happy Funeral*. Illustrated by Vo-Dinh Mai. New York: Harper & Row, 1982. (Ages 5–8.)
Contains descriptions of Chinese-American funeral rituals, and tells of a perspective on life that accepts death as a fitting conclusion.

BURCH, ROBERT. *Simon and the Game of Chance*. Illustrated by Fermin Rocher. New York: Viking, 1970. (Ages 12–up.)
Simon, living in the Depression era, learns that life is a game of chance, when his mother is placed in an institution to recover from the death of her newborn baby, and his sister's fiance is accidentally killed on the day before the wedding.

BYARS, BETSY. *Goodbye Chicken Little*. New York: Harper & Row, 1979. (Ages 9–12.)
Jimmie feels guilty becuase he couldn't stop his uncle from taking a dare and drowning as a result of it. He is helped to overcome his guilt, and his negative feelings about himself, when his unconventional family celebrates his Uncle Pete's life with a huge party, rather than morosely mourning his death. An unusual story.

CARRICK, CAROL. *The Accident*. Illustrated by Donald Carrick. New York: Seabury Press, 1976. (Ages 6–10.)

After his dog, Bodger, is run over and killed, Christopher must deal with his feelings of depression and guilt. Christopher blames himself as much as the truck driver for the accident because he called the dog across the road. The boy finally finds a way to deal with his feelings when he and his father look for the right stone to mark the dog's grave.

CLEAVER, VERA AND BILL. *Grover*. Illustrated by Frederick Martin. Philadelphia: Lippincott, 1970. (Ages 9–11.)
Grover's mother, who knows that she is dying of cancer, shoots herself. Grover understands and accepts his mother's action better than his father does and is able to cope with his loneliness with the help of his friends and a sympathetic housekeeper.

CLEAVER, VERA AND BILL. *Where the Lilies Bloom*. Illustrated by Jim Spanfeller. Philadelphia: Lippincott, 1969. Also in paper. (Ages 9–up.)
Set in Appalachia. A fourteen-year-old girl cares for her family after the sickness and death of their father, whom they bury and pretend is still alive. Her strength is impressive but is insufficient without the help of her siblings and outside circumstances.

CLIFFORD, ETH. *The Killer Swan*. Boston: Houghton Mifflin, 1980. (Ages 10–up.)
Lex's father has committed suicide, and Lex tries to understand why it happened. He blames himself and his mother, and feels angry and confused. He finally realizes, through a symbolic encounter with a pair of swans, that he can never know the whole answer, but he must resume his own life.

CLIFTON, LUCILLE. *Everett Anderson's Goodbye*. Illustrated by Ann Grifalconi. New York: Holt, Rinehart and Winston, 1983. (Ages 5–8.)
Everett Anderson passes through the stages of grief and mourning after his father's death. He is at last able to accept the fact that his memory of his father's love for him and his reciprocation of that love will never die.

COATSWORTH, ELIZABETH. *The Cat Who Went to Heaven*. Illustrated by Lynd Ward. New York: Macmillan, 1958. Also in paper. (Ages 9–11.)
Mythical Japanese story about an artist who paints the legend of Buddha in which he is spurned by a cat and the cat does not go to heaven. The artist, however, taking pity on his cat, paints it into the picture of Buddha; then the cat dies in ecstasy.

COBURN, JOHN B. *Anne and the Sand Dobbies*. New York: Seabury Press, 1964. (Ages 11-up.)
Written by a minister, this story is about the deaths of a very young girl and a dog, and about the family's explanation to the girl's eleven-year-old brother of what has happened. Religious character of the book may make it most useful to readers who are religiously inclined.

CORNFORD, FRANCES. "A Recollection," in *Pick Me Up*, ed. William Cole. New York: Macmillan, 1972. (Ages 6–up.)
The unreality of death hits home in this poem about a child who suddenly realizes that she knows "a person who has died."

CORSO, GREGORY. "Italian Extravaganza," in *On City Streets*, selected by Nancy

Larrick. Illustrated with photographs by David Sagarin. New York: Lippincott, 1968. (Ages 7–up.)
The death of an infant and the elaborate trappings of the funeral impress the child narrator in this poem.

COUTANT, HELEN. *First Snow*. Illustrated by Vo-Dinh Mai. New York: Knopf. 1974. (Ages 5–8.)
Lien and her family moved from Vietnam to New England. It is winter, and Lien's grandmother is dying. Lien asks her grandmother to explain what dying means. She understands when her grandmother directs her to experience the snow. Recognizing the cyclical nature of life, she is content.

DIXON, PAIGE. *May I Cross Your Golden River?* New York: Atheneum, 1975. Also in paper, new title, *A Time to Love, A Time to Mourn*. (Ages 12–up.)
Jordan learns, just after his eighteenth birthday, that he will die. The book describes his and his family's reactions. It includes many details of his illness, his interaction with family and friends, and his thoughts. The loving support of his family helps him to prepare himself and them for his death. The story provides one model for readers faced with the same problem.

DOBRIN, ARNOLD. *Scat*. New York: Four Winds Press, 1971. Also in paper. (Ages 5–8.)
An eight-year-old boy says good-bye to his dead grandmother by playing his harmonica at the cemetery. This makes him feel better even though he knows that his grandmother hated jazz. He knows that she would understand and approve.

DONNELLY, ELFIE. *So Long, Grandpa*. Translated by Althea Bell. New York: Crown, 1981. (Ages 8–11).
Mike's grandfather dies after a long and painful battle with cancer. The grandfather prepares his grandson for his death. They go through a kind of rehearsal together when the grandfather takes Michael to the funeral of an old friend. Each of the family members reacts in a different way.

DRAGONWAGON, CRESCENT. *Will It Be Okay?* Illustrated by Ben Shecter. New York: Harper & Row, 1977. (Ages 3–7.)
The little girl asks her mother to assuage her fears about all sorts of things, and finally asks, what will happen if her mother dies. Her mother assures her that her love will never die, and that her memories of their time together will keep her content.

DUNCAN, LOIS. *Killing Mr. Griffin*. Boston: Little, Brown, 1978. (Ages 12–up.)
A chilling story of a group of high-school students who inadvertently cause the death of their English teacher. The major portion of the book explores their reactions to his death, and builds a picture of each of the characters, including Mr. Griffin.

ENRIGHT, D. J. "Along the River," in *Don't Forget to Fly*, collected by Paul Janeczko. New York: Bradbury Press, 1981. (Ages 10–up.)
A comparison of two suicides found in the river from the perspective of the poet as a child and as a young man.

ERWIN, JOHN. "Death," in *Miracles: Poems by Children of the English-Speaking World,* collected by Richard Lewis. New York: Simon and Schuster, 1966. (Ages 8–up.)
Relating death to the "growing of people which cannot be stopped," the poet accepts the finality of death in this five-line poem.

EYERLY, JEANNETTE. *The Girl Inside.* Philadelphia: Lippincott, 1968. (Ages 12–up.)
Three deaths come as blows to Christina. First her mother dies; then her father's death leaves her distraught and guilt-ridden. At last, after her her guardian dies, his young son's need jolts her out of her self-pity and stimulates her to cope with life.

FAIRLESS, CAROLINE. *Hambone.* Illustrated by Wendy Edelson. New York: Tundra Books, 1980. (Ages 5–8.)
Hambone, Jeremy's pet pig, must be slaughtered. Jeremy's sister, Stoner, helps him deal with Hambone's death. They construct a living memorial, a special plot where all the pig's favorite items are buried and they plant what turn out to be prize winning tomatoes.

FARLEY, CAROL. *The Garden Is Doing Fine.* Illustrated by Lynn Siveat. New York: Atheneum, 1975. (Ages 10–up.)
Corrie's father is dying of cancer. She cannot accept the fact until just before his death. Then, at last, with the help of an elderly friend, she realizes that her father's life has between an important factor in her and others' lives. She understands that his spirit and memory will be retained and that he leaves a legacy of joy and love. Corrie's feelings of selfishness, hope, superstition, despair and anger provide much food for discussion.

FASSLER, JOAN. *My Grandpa Died Today.* Illustrated by Stewart Kranz. New York: Behavorial Publications, 1971. (Ages 3–8.)
A boy's grandfather dies, and he feels sad and empty until after the funeral, when his parents encourage him to go outside and play. At first he feels guilty about resuming his normal activities, but then he realizes that this is what his grandfather would have wanted for him. The grandfather has tried to prepare the boy for this circumstance. Jewish mourning customs are alluded to in this book, and might provide a context for the discussion of other cultures' rituals.

GARDNER, JOHN. *In the Suicide Mountains.* Boston: Houghton Mifflin, 1977. (Ages 12–up.)
Three people who feel that society has short-changed them set out to commit suicide, but before they reach their destination, many things occur to make them change their minds. The tale, a reworking of traditional German and Russian folk tales, is intended to reach some of the many American adolescents who attempt suicide.

GEORGE, JEAN CRAIGHEAD. *Julie of the Wolves.* Illustrated by John Schoenherr. New York: Harper & Row, 1972. (Ages 12–up.)
Julie, an Eskimo girl, thinks that her father is dead and runs away from an unhappy situation. Living in the frozen wilderness, she courageously makes friends with the wolves and learns their ways. She must face problems not only of individual survival but also of the changing ways of her people.

GIPSON, FRED. *Old Yeller*. New York: Harper & Row, 1956. Also in paper. (Ages 12–up.)
A boy learns to deal with his grief over his devoted dog's death as a part of growing up.

GIRION, BARBARA. *A Tangle of Roots*. New York: Scribner, 1979. Also in paper. (Ages 11–up.)
Beth's mother dies suddenly, of a cerebral hemorrhage. The story details all of Beth's reactions, the Jewish ritual of the funeral and mourning, and the way that the family tries to readjust their lives afterward. Beth's relationships with her friends and family change after her mother's death. All of the responses are believable and the pace of the book is appropriate to the topic. Many details of Jewish family life are unobtrusively included. Beth's disbelief when she is told of her mother's death , her grief and reassessment of her own life, her fear of desertion, and her gradual recovery are well developed in the book.

GRAEBER, CHARLOTTE. *Mustard*. Illustrated by Donna Diamond. New York: Macmillan, 1982. (Ages 6–9.)
Alex does not want to accept the fact that his cat, Mustard, is not only old, but is seriously ill. Finally, when the cat is in extreme pain and medicine does not seem to help him, Alex's parents take the cat to the veterinarian so that the cat can "die in peace." Alex sees Mustard's dead body, and the cat is buried. Alex's father weeps, and the family agrees that they are not yet ready for another cat. A well-constructed and informative book as well as a moving story.

GREENE, CONSTANCE C. *Beat the Turtle Drum*. Illustrated by Donna Diamond. New York: Viking, 1976. (Ages 7–10.)
Joss and Kate are sisters. Joss is everyone's favorite, but Kate doesn't mind because she and Joss love each other dearly. Joss is a warm, vibrant, active person. One terrible day, in a freak accident, Joss is killed. The author writes sensitively and movingly of the impact Joss's death has on Kate, the family, and on all of Joss's friends.

GREENFIELD, ELOISE. "Keepsake," in *Honey I Love*. Illustrated by Diane and Leo Dillon. New York: Crowell, 1978. (Ages 6–up.)
Before she died, Mrs. Wiliams gave a nickel to the young girl who narrates the poem. She remembers this as an act of generosity.

GUNTHER, JOHN. *Death Be Not Proud*. New York: Harper & Row, 1949. Also in paper. (Ages 12–up.)
The true story of a young man's hopeless but courageous fight against a brain tumor. Written by his father. A very moving story for adolescents.

HARRIS, AUDREY. *Why Did He Die?* Illustrated by Susan Sallade Dalke. Minneapolis: Lerner Publications, 1965. (Ages 5–8.)
Told in verse. A child's mother explains death to her son, using several analogies to illustrate the process of growing old and dying. Although some euphemisms are used, the comparison of people to motors is a helpful one, and the tone is generally constructive.

HAY, SARA HENDERSON. "For a Dead Kitten," in *Reflections upon a Gift of Watermelon Pickle,* ed. Stephen Dunning, Edward Lueders, and Hugh Smith. New York: Scholastic, 1966. Paperback. (Ages 9–up.)
Wondering how the soft tiny body of a kitten could "hold so immense a thing as death," the poet speaks of putting away things that belonged to the cat. The reaction of bewilderment is a natural stage in mourning.

HEIDE, FLORENCE PARRY. *Growing Anyway Up.* Philadelphia: Lippincott, 1976. (Ages 10–up.)
Florence's guilt over what she feels is her responsibility for her father's death destroys her emotional health. She devises an elaborate protective system of rituals for herself. There is hope that she will recover at the end of the book; her Aunt Nina enters her life and changes her perspective. Together they recall Florence's father and the happy times they had together.

HOOPES, LYN LITTLEFIELD. *Nana.* Illustrated by Arieh Zeldich. New York: Harper & Row, 1981. (Ages 4–8.)
The little girl's grandmother has just died. Recalling her lessons on how to observe and be a part of Nature, the little girl feels that she has found a way to keep her grandmother with her at all times.

HUNT, IRENE. *The Lottery Rose.* New York: Scribner 1976. (Ages 11–up.)
A remarkably moving story about a young boy who has been a victim of child abuse, and a woman mourning her dead husband and child. The two slowly help each other to overcome their pain.

HUNTER, MOLLY. *A Sound of Chariots.* New York: Harper & Row, 1972. (Ages 12–up.)
When a young girl's father dies, she learns to cope and to rechannel her grief into creative energy.

JEWELL, NANCY. *Time for Uncle Joe.* Illustrated by Joan Sandin. New York: Harper & Row, 1981. (Ages 5–9.)
An evocative, loving memorial to the child's uncle, the book takes the reader through all of the activities and habits Uncle Joe had. The smells, sounds and sights he enjoyed, his personal objects, all are woven into the book so that by the end, the reader mourns and lovingly remembers Uncle Joe.

JUSTICE, DONALD. "Sonnet for My Father," in *Don't Forget to Fly,* collected by Paul Janeczko. New York: Bradbury Press, 1981 (Ages 10–up.)
Spoken by the poet to his dying father, this sonnet deals with the pain and understanding between the two men as death approaches. The poet recognizes the continuity of life and the finality of death.

KANTROWITZ, MILDRED. *When Violet Died.* Illustrated by Emily A. McCully. New York: Parents Magazine Press, 1973. (Ages 5–8.)
After their bird dies, the children have a funeral, realizing that living creatures do not last forever.

KIDD, RONALD. *That's What Friends Are For.* New York: Elsevier/Nelson, 1978. (Ages 10–up.)

Gary and Scott are best friends. They play chess together, do science projects, and enjoy each other's company. Neither of them cares much for sports, even though Scott is big and muscular. When Scott becomes ill with leukemia, his family tries to keep it a secret, especially from him. This book could be a manual for what *not* to do when faced with the fact of a loved one's dying. Gary finds out about Scott's condition, and doesn't know how to handle the information. After Scott dies, Gary is guilt-ridden because he didn't visit him enough in the hospital, and he's sickened when he is forced to view Scott's remains at the funeral. In the end he is depressed because he is less and less able to remember his friend. The book can serve as a discussion-starter for "What would you do if...?." It's clear that the author disapproves of the way the whole issue is handled, and is trying to spark a response from his readers.

KLAGSBRUN, FRANCINE. *Too Young to Die: Youth and Suicide.* Boston: Houghton Mifflin, 1976. (Ages 12–up.)
Examines the problem suicide in the adolescent population. By means of case histories the author analyzes different forms and causes of suicide. She assuages some fears, assures readers that it is not a hereditary factor, and warns people of its symptoms. She also appends useful lists of resources.

KREMENTZ, JILL. *How It Feels When a Parent Dies.* Photographs by the author. New York: Knopf, 1981. (Ages 8–12.)
The author taped interviews with a number of young people ranging in age from seven to sixteen to gather their responses to the death of a parent. The children's reactions are moving and comforting in their universality.

KÜBLER-ROSS, ELIZABETH. *Questions and Answers on Death and Dying.* New York: Macmillan, 1974. (Ages 14–up.)
Series of questions concerning family feelings, staff (hospital) involvement, the dying patient, funerals, etc. A good book to help with the discussions of death or the preparation for the death of a friend or family member.

LANGONE, JOHN. *Death Is a Noun: A View of the End of Life.* Boston: Little, Brown, 1973.
A hard-hitting, nonfictional survey of all forms of death—natural, euthanasia, abortion, capital punishment, murder, and suicide. How to face death, whether of a loved one or one's own are explicitly dealt with. A book only for the mature reader.

LEE, MILDRED. *Fog.* New York: Seabury Press, 1972. Also in paper. (Ages 12–up.)
As a result of his father's death from a heart attack, Luke grows up, leaving his old life and his teenage gang behind.

LEE, VIRGINIA. *The Magic Moth.* Illustrated by Richard Cuffari. New York: Seabury Press, 1972. (Ages 8–up.)
Mark-o comes to accept his sister's long illness and death from a heart defect. He preserves her memory, after the funeral, in the symbol of a moth that comes out of its cocoon when his sister dies.

L'ENGLE, MADELEINE. *Meet the Austins.* New York: Vanguard, 1960. (Ages 8–12.)
A friend of the family is killed in a plane accident, and the orphan daughter comes to live with the Austins, making them realize the difficulties of dealing with the

aftermath of death. The orphan is a spoiled brat, changing the conventional stereotype.

L'ENGLE, MADELEINE. *A Ring of Endless Light*. New York: Farrar, Straus, Giroux, 1980. (Ages 11–up.)
The fourth in the Austin family series, this book focuses on Vicky. Her family is staying on the island where her grandfather lives. He is dying. Vicky and her brother John become close friends in this story. Vicky's rivalry with her sister and her loving and protective relationship with her younger brother Bob also figure in the plot. In the story Vicky discovers that she has the gift of communicating with dolphins. The book is an investigation of love, life, and coming to terms with death.

LESHAN, EDA. *Learning to Say Good-By*. New York: Macmillan, 1976. (Ages 7–up.)
The author is a noted educator and family counselor. The book is clearly, concisely, sensitively, and beautifully written. It answers a child's questions, and discusses a child's fears and fantasies regarding the death of a parent. Excellent resource for the family.

LEWIS, C. S. *The Lion, the Witch and the Wardrobe*. New York: Macmillan, 1961. Also in paper. (Ages 9–11.)
This fantasy tale, like all the others in the Narnia series, is an allegory of Christian religious beliefs about death, life after death, and heaven.

LITTLE, JEAN. *Home from Far*. Illustrated by Jerry Lazare. Boston: Little, Brown, 1965. (Ages 10–up.)
Jenny's parents take two foster children into their home after her brother Michael is killed in a car accident. Jenny has to deal with her sadness and her resentment of her foster siblings.

LITTLEDALE, FREYA. *Ghosts and Spirits of Many Lands*. Illustrated by Stefan Martin. Garden City, New York: Doubleday, 1970. (Ages 12–up.)
These tales from around the world examine different centuries' beliefs about death and life after death.

LOWRY, LOIS. *A Summer to Die*. Illustrated by Jenni Oliver. Boston: Houghton Mifflin, 1977.
Thirteen-year-old Meg sees her beautiful, popular sister, Molly, enter the hospital at Christmas time and soon after, die of cancer. Meg has been kept uninformed of her sister's condition and is shocked by the death. She has always been jealous of her sister, and now must come to terms with her feelings. Her friends help her to overcome her guilt, and begin to accept herself for what she is.

MACLACHLAN, PATRICIA. *Cassie Binegar*. New York: Harper & Row, 1982. (Ages 9–12.)
Cassie mourns for her grandfather, and dreams about him all the time. She bitterly regrets the last time she saw him, because she yelled at him, and didn't apologize when he asked her to. She thinks that had she apologized, he might not have died. She keeps this as a bitter secret to herself until she admits it to her grandmother, who lovingly and wisely helps her to let go of her guilt.

MADISON, ARNOLD. *Suicide and Young People.* New York: Clarion Books, 1978. Also in paper. (Ages 12–up.)
Investigates the causes of suicide in young people. Is not alarmist, but presents the seriousness of the situation. Provides sources for help if young readers feel that they are suicidal.

MADLER, TRUDY. *Why Did Grandma Die?* Milwaukee: Raintree Books, 1980. (Ages 5–8.)
When Heidi's grandmother dies, Heidi is angry and worried. She is sure that by wishing hard she can get her grandmother back. Heidi's supportive family finally persuades her that it is all right to grieve. They share her tears and help her to deal with the finality of death. They also permit her to participate in the funeral proceedings.

MANN, PEGGY. *There Are Two Kinds of Terrible.* New York: Doubleday, 1977. (Ages 11–up.)
The first kind of terrible is breaking your arm on the first day of summer. The other kind, for Robbie, is having your mother enter the hospital for tests, never to return. Robbie severely feels his mother's death, and while trying to cope with it, realizes that his father feels it even more. Robbie recovers by building a new relationship between him and his father.

MAZER, NORMA FOX. *A Figure of Speech.* New York: Delacorte Press, 1973. Also in paper. (Ages 12–up.)
Jenny's parents, unable to deal with her grandfather's old age and senility, want to put him in a home. Jenny objects, and so does her grandfather, who kills himself instead. This is a powerful but upsetting story. Its realism leaves the reader reeling.

McLEAN, SUSAN. *Pennies for the Piper.* New York: Farrar, Straus & Giroux, 1981. (Ages 10–up.)
Ten-year-old Victoria and her mother have tried to plan adequately for what they know is inevitable: the mother's approaching death from heart disease. Victoria knows that she will be placed in the care of an aunt, but has really not thought through what her mother's death will mean to her. Also in the story is a young boy whose mother has neglected, abused, and finally rejected him. The book provides readers with a remarkable view of the human spirit.

MELLONIE, BRYAN, AND INGPEN, ROBERT. *Lifetimes: The Beautiful Way to Explain Death to Children.* New York: Bantam, 1983. Paperback. (Ages 5–8.)
A beautifully illustrated and poetically written book explaining the idea of comparative lifetimes appropriate for all creatures.

MENDOZA, GEORGE. *The Hunter I Might Have Been.* New York: Astor Honor, 1968. (Ages 8–10.)
A young boy shoots and buries a sparrow. He is so affected by the death that he never touches a gun again.

MILES, MISKA. *Annie and the Old One.* Illustrated by Peter Parnell. Boston: Little, Brown, 1971. (Ages 6–8).
A Navajor girl futilely tries to prevent the predicted death of her grandmother. But in the end, she accepts death as a necessary part of life.

NESS, EVALINE. *Sam Bangs and Moonshine*. New York: Holt, Rinehart and Winston, 1966. Also in paper. (Ages 7–10.)
Samantha fantasizes a mermaid mother for her real mother, who has died; but her father wants Sam to face reality instead of talking "moonshine."

NICLEODHAS, SORCHE. *Gaelic Ghosts*. New York: Holt, Rinehart and Winston, 1963. (Ages 9–11.)
Tales about chilling, scary ghosts and friendly, helpful ghosts who return from the dead in Scotland.

O'DELL, SCOTT. *Island of the Blue Dolphins*. New York: Houghton Mifflin, 1960. Also in paper. (Ages 9–up.)
Karana, a young Native American girl, is alone on her home island after her tribe has left and her brother has been killed by wild dogs. She tames two of the dogs, and manages her own survival courageously for many years until, at last, she is rescued by missionaries. She must cope with her brother's death, and the probability of her own death. Essentially, however, she must face the fact of her own isolated existence.

ORGEL, DORIS. *The Mulberry Music*. Illustrated by Dale Payson. New York: Harper & Row, 1971. (Ages 9–12.)
Libby is comforted by the music at the funeral, as she remembers the death of her beloved grandmother. An extraordinary, moving story, demonstrating how effectively children can participate in the healthy response to the death of a loved one. Also demonstrates the harm of not informing children about what is happening.

PATERSON, KATHERINE. *Bridge to Terabithia*. New York: Crowell, 1977. (Ages 9–12.)
A beautifully written story about the friendship of a boy, Jess, and a girl, Leslie, neither of whom is a conventional character. Leslie runs as swiftly as Jess, and is bold, and willing to take chances. Jess is sensitive and artistic. When Leslie dies, suddenly and unexpectedly, Jess goes through each of the stages of mourning, from denial to guilt, anger, and grief. In the end he decides to give to others of the "magic" Leslie taught him in their imaginative play, and he begins with his little sister.

PEAVY, LINDA. *Allison's Grandfather*. Illustrated by Ronald Himler. New York: Scribner, 1981. (Ages 6–8.)
Erica is afraid to ask the many questions she has about Allison's dying grandfather. She prefers to remember him the way she used to know him. This book is a good model of the fact that just because children don't openly ask questions, they don't have concerns. Sometimes adults have to answer questions that go unasked.

PECK, RICHARD. *Father Figure*. New York: Signet, 1978. Paperback. (Ages 12–up.)
When Jim and Byron's mother kills herself, their grandmother decides it's time they see their father, who many years before had left them. The boys come to terms with their father, after going through the pain of mourning, and the additional pain of accepting themselves and their father for who they all are.

PLATT, KIN. *Chloris and the Creeps.* Philadelphia: Chilton, 1973. Also in paper. (Ages 12–up.)
Chloris cannot accept her parents' divorce or her father's subsequent suicide. She is hateful and destructive to her mother, her mother's new husband, and their home because she thinks of her father as a kind of superman. She is finally helped to remember her father realistically and to build a positive relationship with her stepfather.

PRINGLE, LAURENCE. *Death Is Natural.* Illustrated by the author. New York: Four Winds Press, 1977. (Ages 9–12.)
Photographs illustrate a scientific investigation of the topic of death, showing how it fits into the natural order of the world. Not concerned with emotions, or particularly with humans, the book places death in a context of inevitability, even of the end of our earth.

RHODIN, ERIC. *The Good Greenwood.* Philadelphia: Westminster Press, 1971. Also in paper. (Ages 12–up.)
Louis dies in an accident with a gun. Mike, his best friend, does not like what the townspeople do to destroy the memory of Louis and to make him into somebody he was not.

SAINT-EXUPÉRY, ANTOINE DE. *The Little Prince.* New York: Harcourt, Brace, 1943. (Ages 8–up.)
A little prince from another planet comes down to earth to explore and, in the end, "returns to his planet" after being bitten by a poisonous snake. A mystical allegory about life and death.

SCHOTTER, RONI. *A Matter of Time.* New York: Philomel Books, 1979. (Ages 11–up.)
Focusing on the preparation for the death of sixteen-year-old Lisa Gilbert's mother, the book provides a model for how a family can helpfully anticipate death and its attendant feelings afterward. While the grieving must occur, it is made more bearable when it has been worked through ahead of time.

SHARMAT, MARJORIE WEINMAN. *I Don't Care.* Illustrated by Lillian Hoban. New York: Macmillan, 1977. (Ages 4–7.)
Jonathan loses his beautiful balloon. At first he tries to make the balloon return. Then he "doesn't care." He refuses a replacement. At last he grieves. He cries and vents his sorrow. Although this sensitive and endearing book deals only with the loss of a toy, it helps children to recognize the validity of their feelings about any loss.

SHREVE, SUSAN. *Family Secrets.* New York: Knopf, 1979. (Ages 9–12.)
The death of a pet and suicide are but two of the issues included in the stories in this collection. Seen through ten-year-old Sammy's eyes, the events are described with sensitivity and humor. Sammy goes through the stages of mourning when his dog dies, and his parents wisely aid him in the process.

SIMON, NORMA. *We Remember Philip.* Illustrated by Ruth Sanderson. Chicago: Whitman, 1979. (Ages 7–12.)
Mr. Hall's son Philip has died in a mountain-climbing accident. His class feels very sad for their teacher and they try to help him through his grief. They ask Mr. Hall to

bring in slide pictures of Philip and they decide to do something special to show Mr. Hall they care. The class plants a tree in the school yard and they dedicate it to Philip's memory. Mr. Hall feels strengthened by this gesture of love.

SLOTE, ALFRED. *Hang Tough, Paul Mather.* Philadelphia: Lippincott, 1973. (Ages 9–12.)
Paul is twelve years old and has leukemia. The descriptions of his reactions to his medication are graphic, but the book essentially conveys a hopeful message. The boy's devotion to baseball carries him through some of the bad times with his illness.

SMITH, DORIS BUCHANAN. *A Taste of Blackberries.* Illustrated by Charles Robinson. New York: Crowell, 1973. (Ages 7–10.)
Jamie dies of an allergic reaction to a bee sting, and his friend feels guilty, lonely and cannot believe it happened, until after the funeral, when he offers himself as a substitute son to Jamie's mother when and if she wants one.

STEIN, SARA BONNETT. *About Dying.* Illustrated by Dick Frank. New York: Walker, 1974. (Ages 4–10.)
One of the "Open Family" series. Physical description is given of the death of a pet bird. The mother factually and supportively deals with the child's questions and needs. Then the grandfather dies, and again the child is helped by ritual, family support, and answers to questions. An excellent resource for adults and children, discussing reactions and stressing keeping pleasant memories alive.

STEVENS, MARGARET. *When Grandpa Died.* Chicago: Children's Press, 1979. (Ages 5–8.)
Grandpa knows a lot about living things. He knows that they change and eventually die. Death is natural. When Grandpa gets sick and dies, the child feels hurt and angry. But she has good memories about her grandfather and learns to accept his death. In the end she shares these memories with a younger sister.

STOLZ, MARY. *The Edge of Next Year.* New York: Harper & Row, 1974. (Ages 12–up.)
A moving story of the devastating effects of a mother's death on her family. The husband becomes an alcoholic, and the two boys must try to fend for themselves. In the end there is hope that the father will recover.

STULL, EDITH G. *My Turtle Died Today.* New York: Holt, Rinehart and Winston, 1964. (Ages 5–8.)
About a boy's sadness over the death of his turtle and how he copes with it.

TALBOT, TOBY. *Away Is So Far.* Illustrated by Dominique Michele Strandquest. New York: Four Winds Press, 1974. (Ages 8–12.)
The setting is Spain. Pedro's mother has died, leaving him and his father totally forlorn. They leave their home to wander all over Spain and France. Pedro's father needs the time to pull himself together. He canot tolerate the physical daily reminders of his wife's death. At last, with Pedro's loving support, he recovers, and the two of them return to their home. A gentle, well-written story.

TOLAN, STEPHANIE, *Grandpa—and Me*. New York: Scribner 1978. (Ages 9–12.)
Kerry's grandfather has become embarrassingly and dangerously senile. In a remarkably mature fashion, Kerry tries to protect him, but she cannot. In his last lucid act, the grandfather decides to commit suicide rather than lose total control. A thought-provoking book.

TURNER, ANN. *Houses for the Dead*. New York: David McKay, 1976. (Ages 10–up.)
Ten separate cultures, from prehistoric to contemporary times, are described in terms of how they mourn their dead. By means of personalized stories in each of the settings, the author presents the myths, rituals, and practices surrounding the death of the particular member of that culture. A fascinating and comforting book.

TURNER, ANN. *A Hunter Comes Home*. New York: Crown, 1980. (Ages 11–up.)
Several deaths occur in this story of a boy becoming a man. Jonas's father and brother die prematurely in a blizzard, and their death is bitterly mourned. His grandfather drowns while he is in the process of teaching Jonas how to become a fisherman, but his death comes at the end of a long, active life, and his life is celebrated at his death. The book tells of the difficulty of the decisions Jonas must make about his identity as an Inuit, and as an individual.

VIORST, JUDITH. *The Tenth Good Thing about Barney*. Illustrated by Erik Blegvad. New York: Atheneum, 1971. (Ages 5–9.)
Barney, a boy's pet cat, dies. The boy's parents encourage him to have a funeral and to think of ten good things about the cat, so that he will not feel so bad about its death. He finally recognizes that the death of the cat contributes to the cycle of life.

WALLACE-BRODEUR, RUTH. *The Kenton Year*. New York: Atheneum, 1980. (Ages 7–11.)
Nine-year-old Mandy learns to accept the death of her father and gradually adjusts to a new style of life in a different locale.

WARBURG, SANDOL STODDARD. *Growing Time*. Illustrated by Leonard Weisgard. Boston: Houghton Mifflin, 1969. Also in paper. (Ages 5–8.)
A little boy's beloved dog dies, and the boy's family help him to understand and accept the pet's death. Each adult that he questions adds to his store of knowledge and comfort.

WHITE, E.B. *Charlotte's Web*. Illustrated by Garth Williams. New York: Harper & Row, 1952. Also in paper. (Ages 9–up.)
Charlotte, the spider, saves the life of Wilbur, the pig, and they become loving friends. When Charlotte finally dies, Wilbur treasures her memory, and cares for her children, grandchildren, and great-grandchildren.

WHITEHEAD, RUTH. *The Mother Tree*. Illustrated by Charles Robinson. New York: Seabury Press, 1971. (Ages 8–11.)
Temple's mother has died, and, at ten years old, she must care for her father, her dependent sister, and her headstrong brother. After a time of inward rebellion and resentment, Temple accepts her responsibilities.

WIER, ESTER. *The Loner.* Illustrated by Christine Price. New York: David McKay, 1963. (Ages 12–up.)
An orphan who experiences the death of one of his only close friends is found, helped, given a name, and befriended by a strong woman. He realizes that he is no longer a loner. Her grief over the death of her son is also resolved in a constructive manner.

WINDSOR, PATRICIA. *The Summer Before.* New York: Harper & Row, 1973. Also in paper. (Ages 12–up.)
The accidental death of her boy friend causes Alexandra to have an emotional breakdown. The shock is so severe that the potential for her recovery seems slight.

WOJCIECHOWSKA, MAIA. *The Life and Death of a Brave Bull.* Illustrated by John Groth. New York: Harcourt, Brace & World, 1972. (Ages 8–up.)
Written from the perspective of a bullfight aficionado, this book stresses the aim of achieving reputation and glory through fighting and killing, and the idea of defeating death by dying nobly.

WOJCIECHOWSKA, MAIA. *Shadow of a Bull.* Illustrated by Alvin Smith. New York: Atheneum, 1964. (Ages 9–12.)
Although death is feared in this book, "brave" death invites admiration. Manolo fears that he is a coward because he does not want to be a bullfighter. The plot's resolution creates a happy ending for Manolo, and maintains the concept of the "noble" death.

YOUNG, JIM. *When the Whale Came to My Town.* Photographs by Dan Bernstein. New York: Knopf, 1974. (Ages 6–10.)
A whale washes up on the shore to die. A boy discovering the whale begins to think about life and death. Despite the Coast Guard's efforts and the presence of several doctors, the whale at last dies.

ZINDEL, PAUL. *Pigman.* New York: Harper & Row, 1968. Also in paper. (Ages 12–up.)
The story of two teenagers who discover an unhappy, lonely old man who cannot accept his wife's death; they mistreat and exploit him and then regret it after he dies of a heart attack.

ZOLOTOW, CHARLOTTE. *My Grandson Lew.* Illustrated by William Pène duBois. New York: Harper & Row, 1974. (Ages 3–8.)
A little boy and his mother share loving memories of the boy's dead grandfather. The mother helps the child to cope with this grief through these positive reflections.

•NINE•

WAR

MOST PEOPLE AGREE THAT WAR IS UGLY, destructive, and frightening. War in the abstract is relatively easy to deal with; it is simply dismissed as evil. Some people think that there are no controversial issues within the topic of war in children's books. Their reasoning is logical: We want to construct a peaceful society; therefore we must instruct our children about the negative aspects of war.

Complications arise when we consider specific wars and when we move beyond the generalized realm of war as a concept. It is then that we encounter a complex set of issues including causes, individual concerns, ethical decisions, and conduct during war. Today's children, living in the era of so many controversial armed conflicts, probably have been exposed to a wider variety of responses to war than were children who were growing up during the time of the Second World War, when there was widespread support of our participation. Those who dissented were more often than not labeled as traitors, fascists, or, at the very least, unpatriotic.

Feelings about a specific war run very high, particularly at the time when the conflict is raging. National response is greatest when our own soldiers are involved, but we also react emotionally when people with whom we are concerned, even indirectly, are engaged in war. The issues become very complex, depending on the level of the relationship between us and the warring nations. During the Biafran War, even within black communities opinion was divided about who was in the right. Nonblack populations were also divided in their opinions and recommendations. Similarly, during the Israeli–Arab confrontations, Jews have been split in their sympathy, as have non-Jews. So it is with every war. Sides are drawn; action is proposed. Arguments are presented for and against the combatants as well as the issues.

SUGGESTED CRITERIA

In order to encourage the kind of constructive decision-making necessary for a healthy society, children should be exposed to the complexities of moral and political issues. Very young children may not be able to comprehend all the ramifications of specific situations, but they can understand the processes of escalation and competition. They can perceive the ambiguity of what is "right" or "fair." They must daily make decisions for themselves that, on a scaled-down level, are the same sorts of decisions political leaders must handle for their countries. Therefore, an effective book dealing with war should present some indication of the difficulty of viewing any conflict in absolute terms. When only one side is right, the story becomes a piece of propaganda that is usually less effective than its author intended. Teachers can instruct children how to recognize and deal with propaganda, but it is a detrimental factor in a literary work.

•TRY THIS

Examine three books about a specific war, such as the American Civil War or the Second World War. How does the author treat the "enemy"? How human are the characters? What are set forth as the causes of the war? How many causes are given? How unanimous are the opinions of all the "good" characters? Compare your reactions to each of the three books. How much more insight or information do you think that you now have about the war?

Some authors fear that young children cannot understand complexity. They therefore write in oversimplified terms rather than risk confusing the young readers. Unfortunately, they use children's inability to deal with abstractions as an excuse to omit detail. Children can handle many ideas at one time. They can follow subplots and can sort out several characters. Another criterion, therefore, for a book about war is that it contain enough detail and depth so as to convey a sense of the many facets of war, and of history.

•TRY THIS

Find several picture books about war. Read them to a four-, five-, or six-year-old child. Ask the child to tell you the reasons for the war, then to describe the events of the war. Judge for yourself from which books the child has gained understanding and perspective.

As has been stated before, a well-written book is always more powerful than is a poorly constructed work. A book about war that has an unlikely ending is less memorable than one that is constructed so as to convince the reader of its accuracy. The same is true for a presentation of the causes of the war. In some books that will be discussed in this chapter, it is apparent that the authors were so concerned with discussing the war's impact that it did not seem to matter what initiated the war. Similarly, many fictitious wars end in so contrived a fashion that even four-year-olds say, "That couldn't be."

•TRY THIS

Find a book telling a story about war whose ending or beginning dissatisfies you. Rewrite the portion that you question. Encourage a child to perform this exercise but do it orally. How easy is it for the child to do this?

DISCUSSION OF CHILDREN'S BOOKS

BOOKS FOR YOUNG CHILDREN

General Books

Almost all the books written for young children concentrating on the theme of war are attempts at allegory. Their universal intent is to prove that war is meaningless, wrong, and hurtful. Unfortunately, in a preponderance of these books the construction of the plot is so absurd or untenable that the reader, no matter how young, is tempted to relegate the lesson to the ranks of often heard but seldom heeded proverbs and wise sayings. Recognizing the truism, they divorce it from real-life behavior.

In some picture books the authors portray the pain and discomfort of war, and the illustrations may be very well executed, but there is no apparent reason for the war to have begun. Sometimes peace comes through a simplistic solution. This sort of presentation needs to be talked about, and compared to reality.

Some picture books present a balanced view, depicting neither army as more in the right than the other. They show the land to be devastated by the battles. Plot and character should carry the message. Even in these books for young children, details should be accurate and story lines should be logical.

The well-intentioned failures can be effective in the classroom as vehicles of criticism for the students. It would be healthy for the children to recognize that conveying a socially acceptable message does not guarantee that a book is good. If the story appeals to some children and not to others, the teacher can help them to set up a debate or panel discussion. There should be no class vote or decision on whether or not the book is good or who is right. Some readers may appreciate the illustrations; some may be ready for the moral that a particular book conveys. There should, therefore, be no derision of anyone for a difference of opinion. All substantive opinions should be respected.

One book that lends itself to debate and investigation is *Drummer Hoff,* by Barbara Emberley. The colorful, bold illustrations by her husband, Ed, are essential to the book, which won the Caldecott Award in 1968. There are details and subtleties both within the illustrations and in the plot that bear repeated examination. The story is simple: A band of soldiers assembles and fires a cannon; the refrain "But Drummer Hoff fired it off" is repeated. The text describes the military preparations carried on by each of the soldiers, starting with the general. A double-page spread of the actual firing is impressive. At the end the cannon is left in a field of grass and flowers, a haven for grasshoppers, spiders, and birds.

The refrain seems to indicate that the firing of the cannon is a glorious event and that Drummer Hoff is to be envied. But a close inspection of the soldiers reveals that the powder man has a wooden leg and that one soldier has only one eye. The text, coming as it does from an old folk rhyme, could be interpreted as nonsense, as pro-war in the glorifying of the act of the drummer, or as antiwar in that all of the upper-echelon soldiers pass the burden of responsibility for the act of destruction onto the drummer.

Very young children may need help noticing some of the details of this intricate book. They can be invited to discuss why the cannon is all by itself in the field, without any people around it at the end. They might be asked how they would feel if they were the drummer. Those readers particularly interested in things military can assemble a hierarchical listing of ranks and analyze the importance of the task according to rank.

An allegory that avoids many of the traps of oversimplification is Jane Yolen's *The Minstrel and the Mountain.* The story is told poetically. The cause of the war, although obviously not one that real nations would respond to, translates into one of jealousy, resentment, and ignorance. The solution is a happily-ever-after fantasy, but, in this case, the intervention of the magical minstrel moves the action in a satisfactory fashion. If, in reality, and despite the talents of "minstrels," lasting peace is not as readily achieved, at least this book conjures up the possibility of unusual solutions to seemingly hopeless conflicts.

Kjell Ringi has designed an allegory that works well. The book *The Winner* has no text whatsoever; the story and lesson are told entirely through the illustrations. The plot, in which two characters trying to outdo each other finally get destroyed, communicates the dangers of escalation and competition. It demonstrates that the acquisition of powerful weapons destroys everyone. In this case, a dragon is the ultimate weapon that eventually eats its "master." Children of any age, and adults as well, can "read" this book and learn from it. The illustrations are colorful and amusingly graphic. The arms race begins harmlessly enough and ends in disaster. Perhaps the absence of words is one of the greatest advantages of the book; it insures that each reader will insert vocabulary appropriate and manageable at that reader's level. The ending is not a happy one, even for the dragon, because now there is no one left to eat. The people do not spring magically back to life. They are dead. This book could be used as the starter for many discussions, providing the stimulus for some extensive thought and investigation of the problems inherent in waging war. Children can write their own text or dictate the words to an adult. They can construct puppets and perform the story in front of an audience.

Another interesting and somewhat complicated book, which was named as one of *The New York Times's* Best Illustrated Children's Books of 1969, is *Bang Bang You're Dead,* by Louise Fitzhugh and Sandra Scoppettone. Designed for the five-to eight-year-old, the book's text and illustrations are controversial in their explicitness and violence. The authors are unmistakably attempting to discourage physical conflict, to introduce the concept of war to young children, and to teach the lesson that negotiation and friendly behavior are better. The story relates how the game of war for one group of little boys no longer remains a game when an invading group of bigger and rougher boys challenges them. They call each other names such as "puke-face" and "freak-out" and graphically inflict pain upon each other. One illustration shows the conflict, with one combatant sustaining a gushing bloody nose.

The fight ends with both sides losing. This is somewhat of a surprise because of the superior strength and size of the attackers, but all the boys are lying on the hill in various attitudes of pain after the fighting is done. At this point, after agreeing that no one had much fun, they decide to share the hill for playing make-believe war together. The controversies raised by the book go beyond the language and illustrations. Questions can be asked about the usefulness of the "happy" ending if the boys are indeed going to continue to play at war. If one side had won, what would have happened? How often does the logical or peaceful solution occur to groups of mutually angry children? For some readers the humor will be remembered without the intended moral.

Questions should be raised not only for purposes of criticism but also for purposes of analysis. If readers of all ages acquire the habit of actively questioning what they read and of having that process valued by people they respect, then one of the more important goals of responsible education will be accomplished.

Several authors have attempted, as Fitzhugh and Scoppetone have, to explain war to children by equating it with children's arguments. Crosby Bonsall's *Mine's the Best* is a very easy-to-read book describing an argument between two boys who are carrying identical balloons. Each believes his balloon is best and, in the process of arguing, destroys it. At that point, a girl walks by with a balloon identical to theirs. Quickly, the former enemies align with each other and say, "Ours was the best." The analogy is not unlike countries at war becoming allies when new adversaries appear. The book attempts to demonstrate realistic child behavior rather than to be a more ambitious attempt at symbolizing war, but the extensions are possible.

Three other books—*The Hating Book,* by Charlotte Zolotow, *Let's Be Enemies,* by Janice May Udry, and *I Am Better Than You,* by Robert Lopshire —describe arguments between friends and their eventual reconciliation. These books may not have been designed to carry a message beyond that of children and their disagreements. But if a group of children and a teacher are talking about war and conflict among nations, then this sort of book is perfect as an introduction or even as a case in point for use when analyzing the more complex international situations. Children may even assign names of countries to the characters for the purpose of carrying out the analogy.

The Hating Book is about a misunderstanding. One child mistakes what she hears her friend say. Until the error is cleared up the friendship is on rocky ground. The child's mother keeps suggesting that her daughter ask her friend directly why she is behaving in such an an unfriendly way. When, at last, the girl takes her mother's advice, the whole misunderstanding dissolves. It would be wonderful if nations could function so directly and happily, but at least this serves as a model for unwarlike behavior for children. *Let's Be Enemies* is somewhat different. Two boys are friends, but one is angry with the other because of his constant bossy behavior. John becomes so angry upon thinking of James's behavior that he goes to the other's house to declare that he is no longer James's friend, whereupon James also declares his enmity for John. Strangely enough, and with no seeming intervention, John invites James to go roller-skating, and James offers John a pretzel. Perhaps this does happen when children quarrel, but they should be encouraged to exercise judgment and recognize rational behavior. Why should they be friends if they mistreat each other?

I Am Better Than You involves two lizards who appear exactly alike to the reader. One of them, Sam, is determined to prove that he is the best lizard there is. He is very competitive and very quarrelsome. Pete, the other lizard, is a pefect model of excellent temperament and good fellowship. Finally, after it is shown that Sam is not the better lizard, but is, in fact, somewhat silly, Pete and Sam resume their friendship. Sam promises henceforth to be quiet. Again, this book could be used as a jumping-off point for analyzing the behavior of countries engaging in competition of various sorts. Pete's behavior could be used as an example of how to avoid wars, or at least arguments.

Historical Books

There are fewer books for younger children that relate to actual wars than there are books that deal with war in general. Nathaniel Benchley has contributed an easy-to-read book about the American Revolutionary War called *Sam the Minuteman.* The young boy, Sam, helps his father fight at the Battle of Lexington. Benchley does an excellent job of communicating the fear and anger caused by the incidents of the battle. By graphically portraying Sam's reactions to his friend's being wounded, he personalizes the experience of war for young children. Sam's ideals take second place to his immediate responses. Although bravery is valued, Benchley makes it clear that raw survival sometimes has nothing to do with heroism. The book manages an excellent balance between recognizing that the war had a cause and that war itself is a gruesome experience. Nothing much is said about the British side, but there is enough in this book to start some thoughtful inquiry about the different shades of justification for warfare.

The Revolutionary War, the Civil War, and the Second World War are well represented in literature, especially for older children. But one war this author had never heard of is the subject of a book by Betty Baker called *The Pig War,* a Harper and Row "I Can Read History" book. It describes a real war that took place in 1859 off the coast of the state of Washington, where there was a small island whose rightful ownership was disputed. Both the British and the Americans claimed possession. American farmers lived there, as did a small detachment of British soldiers. The conflict erupted when a small display of patriotism escalated into a grand display of power. In the end, the armies sent to do the fighting ate up so much of the island's products that the regular inhabitants were disgusted with the intervention and sent everyone else away. They decided to live in peace with each other until at last ownership was given to the United States. The story sounds too good to be true, but the author assures us of its authenticity. Children can begin a correspondence with her through the publisher, and can send to the State Historical Society of the state of Washington to investigate the Pig War. Research skills could be practiced to good advantage by using this book as a starter.

Poetry

Nursery rhymes and nonsense verses for young children mention war more often than is at first apparent. Usually the pageantry and excitement of war in general are mentioned in these verses. One collection compiled by Leonard Clark, called *Drums and Trumpets,* titles its first section, "Here Come Processions." Martial poems of glory comprise most of the selections, but there is a Thomas Hardy poem, "Men Who March Away," that hints at the futility of war and the lack of comprehension on the part of the people who fight the war as to why they are there.

A deeply moving book of poetry was selected from the archives of the State Jewish Museum in Prague by Hana Volavkova. *I Never Saw Another Butterfly* contains children's drawings and poems from the Terezin concentration camp. All the young poets represented in this book were destroyed by the war. Their camp was a way station to extermination centers, and they knew this; but their poetry speaks more to the joy of life than to a fear of, or preoccupation with, death. They express hope, love, and determination to survive. This powerful antiwar book does not preach against war and does not moralize. It conveys its strong message because of the information that the reader brings to the poetry. It is therefore a book that knowledgeable adults should share with others and should encourage children to read so that the strength of the message can be reinforced.

BOOKS FOR OLDER CHILDREN

In contrast to books written for the very young, most of the books written for older children about war are specific and based on fact. The bulk of the work falls under the category of historical fiction. But the entire Narnia series, by C. S. Lewis, contains descriptions of battles and wars that symbolize the conflict between good and evil. The message contained in the works is that violence and bloodshed are justified when the cause is a virtuous one. Lewis does not guarantee that good will triumph, but he avers that the fight is worth it.

History

For older children, most of the books about war involve young heroes or heroines so as to arouse interest and empathy in the readers. Some stories, such as Anne Frank's *Diary,* are true accounts, told in the first person. These books, which carry enormous impact, are generally the ones that readers remember best after a long period of time. If the intent in dealing with these books is to affect future attitudes and behavior, then teachers and librarians should follow through on the children's reading with questions, discussions, and recommendations for further readings. For the purposes of this chapter, only a representative sampling of the books available on this topic will be discussed; others will be included in the annotated Bibliography. Although there are books written about every war, not every war will be mentioned here. The intent is to recognize that although certain elements of war are universal, each war has its own individual complexities and issues.

Revolutionary War

Esther Forbes's *Johnny Tremain* has become a classic read by many children ages ten and up. This book, which won the Newbery medal in 1944, is more the story of Johnny and his life than it is of the Revolutionary War. Yet, as with all good historical fiction, a sense of the times comes through clearly; more is learned about the war and its beginnings than from a purely factual text. The Whigs and Tories, as well as the British soldiers, are described as real people with several dimensions, rather than as flat characters dwelling only in history.

The Colliers' *My Brother Sam Is Dead,* a Newbery honor book and a finalist for the National Book Award, leaves the reader with the intriguing question of whether this war was absolutely necessary for the founding of our country as an independent nation. The authors help readers to view the

American Revolution as a personal tragedy for some people, communicating that perhaps it was not the glorious and patriotic event depicted in many books and films.

The Civil War

Most of the books about the Civil War take a stance that the North was totally virtuous and that the South had no redeeming arguments. The war is usually described as a wrenching one for our country, but it is seldom explained that both sides had their villains as well as their heroes. Most of the many books in print for children telling about the Civil War describe the battles and their effect on the participants.

Irene Hunt's *Across Five Aprils* handles the rarely considered issue of what happens to the people who are not actively involved with the war but who nevertheless suffer. This war story—more about people than it is about war—concerns a family, the Creightons, living in southern Illinois at the time of the Civil War. They have suffered much hardship. Several children have died of fever, and one daughter was killed by a drunken neighbor in an accident. One of the sons, Bill, is considered "odd" in the somewhat narrow-minded community where the Creightons live. He loves to read, dislikes drinking, carousing, and roughhousing, and is gentle and soft-spoken; moreover, he is strong and a hard worker. He is clearly meant to be an admirable character.

As the book progresses, there is conversation about the impending war and its causes. Discussions and arguments are mounted for and against all of the sides. Slavery is brought out as only one of the issues of the war; industrialization is also thought of as a great threat to the country. Two of the brothers—Bill, the kind one, and John, the unfriendly, somewhat distant one—argue about the war. Surprisingly enough, it is John who is for the Union, while Bill sides with the Southern cause. Here the "good guys" are not always on the "right" side. The author has presented us with a dilemma. Students may enjoy arguing about these two characters and the logic of their stances.

For Jethro, another son, who is nine years old, war is an exciting idea. He believes that it will solve all problems and demonstrate the validity of the Union. He recognizes the thrill of battle and the satisfaction of overcoming an enemy. Bill is his favorite brother, and this causes him to be confused by what he had assumed were clear issues. Bill explains to Jethro that he, too, is confused. He hates slavery and the thought of the dissolution of the Union, but he cannot see how the war will settle the differences between two parts of the country. He cannot agree with the overwhelming prejudice against the entire southern part of the nation.

At last, Bill and his brother John, despite their love for each other, have a violent fistfight. Bill decides that he must leave to fight, not so much for the South, but against Northern arrogance and hypocrisy. He goes unhappily, but believing that he must, even though he knows that no side is in the right. His reflections help the reader understand that what the history books depict as a clear-cut cause is not, after all, that simple.

Across Five Aprils won the Follett Award and was a Newbery honor book in 1965. Very well written, it uncovers many levels of emotion and behavior in wartime. Some of the community people who are ostensibly on the "right" side of the war persecute the Creightons because of Bill's actions. The Creightons' nineteen-year-old son, Tom, is killed in the war. Eb, a boy whom they have brought up since he was ten and who was Tom's best friend, deserts. The father has a heart attack and remains in feeble health. Through each of these disasters the family endures, as the nation endures. The events of the war are interwoven with the happenings at the farm. The book ends with the death of Lincoln and the agony and anxiety over the fate of the nation. The book helps students to compare different accounts of battles, causes of war, and issues in order to begin to construct a balanced, informed view.

World War II

This war, almost above others, had the support of most of the country, though it was a war that touched America less directly than other nations. It is no surprise, therefore, that most of the books written about the Second World War focus on the experiences of people in other countries. One, however, *The Summer of My German Soldier,* by Bette Greene, centers on a girl in a small town in Arkansas. When German prisoners of war are brought to the town, Patty becomes very much attracted to one of them. The book shatters many stereotypes. Patty is a desperately unhappy and lonely twelve-year-old Jewish girl living in a small southern town. Hers is the only Jewish family in the town. The parents are emotionally abusive to Patty, who is considered a misfit. Ruth, the maid, cook, and housekeeper, who is black, is Patty's only friend. The story is tragic in its implications of what happens to people, not only in time of war but in any time of stress.

The German soldier is a likable, intelligent, nonviolent young man. The reader hopes that he will escape, but he is caught, despite Patty's help, and is killed. He does not fit the pattern of the bestial German that Americans were taught to recognize, and the Jewish family does not fit the pattern (except for the storekeepers) that most stories design for them. The book adds to the readers' thinking about the consequences and complexities of war.

Holocaust

It is difficult for children to conceive of as monumentally evil a concept as the planned elimination of an entire people. The Second World War was, perhaps, only accidentally the context for the Nazis' design for the destruction of the Jews. Gypsies and other "undesirables" also were marked for extermination, but the Jewish population was the prime target. Adults, too, have difficulty believing that such an event in history was permitted to occur. It is all the more important, therefore, that Holocaust curricula and books be provided for children to read and understand.

One exemplary planned curriculum on genocide focuses on the Holocaust. Designed for adolescents, the materials of Strom and Parsons's *Facing History and Ourselves: Holocaust and Human Behavior* can be adapted to other age levels. Books are recommended; information is provided for a variety of sessions, probing historical, psychological, economic, and political factors.

Some books on this topic deal specifically with children and their lives. Judith Kerr's *When Hitler Stole Pink Rabbit* describes a family who escaped from Germany just before Hitler's election. Their father is an anti-Nazi journalist. The family is Jewish, although they have not practiced the religion actively. They go to Switzerland, where they are physically safe, but where they unhappily encounter anti-Semitism. They then move to France and, ultimately, to England. Not a horror story, this book details the everyday small discomforts and large fears occasioned by Hitler's takeover. It provides an interesting perspective for readers who have been exposed only to the tragic Anne Frank.

A story quite similar to Anne Frank's *Diary,* and also based on fact, is Johanna Reiss's *The Upstairs Room.* It has a happy ending, as the people hidden away from the Germans emerge alive at the end of the war. This book describes the individual actions of people who risk their own lives to save other people, not in active combat, but through acts of quiet courage. Ordinary people—uncomfortable, but nevertheless believing that they have responsibility for others—become the important heroes of this war. At Yad Vashem, the institution in Jerusalem dedicated to the study and documentation of the Holocaust, there is a beautiful tree-lined path called "The Path of the Righteous." Each of the trees represents a non-Jewish person or family who risked their lives to protect Jews.

One of the most devastatingly effective books on the Holocaust is *Friedrich,* by Hans Peter Richter, written from the perspective of a non-Jewish German boy. Perhaps the most powerful part of the book is the unadorned chronology appended to the text, recounting the regulations put into effect against the Jews. Young readers are horrified by the detailed sadistic thoroughness of Nazi oppression, as exemplified by such regulations as those forbidding Jews to keep pets, go to barbershops, or use public phones. This story does not have a happy ending; few stories about the Holocaust do. But children become involved in the action and with the characters, and think about the implications of the message long after they close the book.

Another story that does not end happily, but that keeps the reader glued to its pages, is *Alan and Naomi,* by Myron Levoy. In this story, Naomi is a victim of the Holocaust: She has witnessed her father's death by beating at the hands of the Gestapo. For a while it seems that Alan will help her to adjust to normal living. But a vicious anti-Semitic remark causes Alan to become involved in a fistfight, and Naomi lapses into hysteria because of the blood. The book ends with questions about the meaning of life as well as the causes of hatred.

Some books help to offset the stereotype that all of the Jews were passive victims. *Uncle Misha's Partisans*, by Yuri Suhl, tells of an actual band of Jewish guerrillas who wrought much damage on the German army. One of the partisans is a young boy named Mottele. He is also the subject of a book by Gertrude Samuels, called *Mottele*. Both books are designed for students no younger than ten or eleven years of age. The stories are not pretty ones, but they are true, and their message is important for young people to learn.

Children of the Resistance, by Lore Cowan, also tells of young people who actively aided in the resistance in Nazi-occupied countries. These heroic girls and boys were involved in death, violence, and destruction. While the book does not glorify war per se, it does value resistance and support the necessity for retribution. Each chapter describes a young person from a different country. Ms. Cowan collected the material from many European countries after the war. The stories, told as great adventures, occasionally take the form of simulated diaries. Germany is included among the countries in which children were active in the resistance.

The book concentrates on the "rightness" of the Allied side and the bestiality of the Nazis, with no conflicting issues raised. It does not address any of the abstract questions that pertain to war in general. When is it right to kill or maim? When both sides believe that they are right, who can say where crimes lie? World War II, in particular, seems to invite only one answer. Even if, after much discussion, readers determine that there was no right on Hitler's side, what of the actions of the Allied defenders in the process of fighting the war? No matter what the conclusions, the process of inquiry and investigation contributes to greater clarity of thought and deeper moral perspective.

Korean War

Pearl S. Buck's book *Matthew, Mark, Luke and John* tells of the plight of abandoned children after the Korean War. These children are all illegitimate offspring of G.I.'s and Korean women. The author explains in the book that Koreans consider children to belong to the father and his family; therefore these children are outcasts. Unable to withstand the social pressure, some of the mothers desert the children.

This book tells of four of these children—each with a distinctive personality—who fortuitously band together for survival. It does not deal with causes or take sides but recounts the effects that every war has on the people after the war is over. The story has a somewhat pat happy ending, for the children are all adopted. If students wish to explore further the delicate problems resulting from the impact of American military presence in foreign countries, they can research newspaper and magazine accounts to supplement this book.

Vietnam War

In contrast to the Second World War, the conflict in Vietnam was probably the least popular of any American foreign involvement. Unfortunately, most books written about it have neglected a balance of views and thus do not prepare children to make their own decisions about this or any war. *Children of Vietnam,* by Betty Jean Lifton and Thomas C. Fox, provides photographs of children who survived the conflict in Vietnam. Interviews with these children convey a sense of the suffering they endured.

Poetry

The poems included in the section for young readers are appropriate for older ones as well. The writing of the doomed children of the concentration camp invokes an even deeper response when understood by more mature readers. Some preteens can even handle Kenneth Patchen's bitter war poetry. Henry Wadsworth Longfellow wrote many poems dealing with different feelings about war; indeed, many of our most renowned poets have written several poems about war. Some of them pointing to the eventual glory of battle. Thomas Moore's "Minstrel Boy" is one such poem, the gist of which is that the minstrel boy is courageous and proud and dies gloriously. The manner of his death seems to justify it for the poet. Julia Ward Howe's "Battle Hymn of the Republic" grew to be the most popular marching song of the Civil War.

Interestingly enough, it is in our popular music that many poems, set to song, decry war and bemoan its effect. Several describe war as bloody and meaningless. Folk songs such as "Johnny Has Gone for a Soldier" and many modern ballads speak to the agonies of war and its aftermath. A reading of *The Judy Collins Songbook* will unearth many antiwar songs, as will *The Joan Baez Songbook.* "Where Have All the Flowers Gone?" by Pete Seeger is based on a traditional Russian folk song. The protests and the glorifications are available in verse as well as in longer works of fiction and nonfiction. How the teacher or librarian uses them can be of utmost importance.

Nonfiction

An investigation of *Subject Guide to Children's Books in Print* reveals many books of both fiction and nonfiction written about each war. Albert Carr, in *A Matter of Life and Death,* addresses himself to the minds of young people as well as their emotions. He makes a distinction between "death patriotism" and "life patriotism." The first requires the death of one's enemies; the other aims at improving one's country. Using the Spanish-American War as an example of how our country has dealt with war, he describes several ways in which the war could have been averted. He also details several other wars. Although he offers no concrete ideas for avoiding war in the future, he does recommend that young people make their own opinions known to their representatives. He also suggests that they evaluate advice carefully and with an understanding of the many implications that any course of action carries. *A Matter of Life and Death* is a clearly written book, useful for the purpose of making readers aware of the complexities of international relationships and of the necessity for responsible personal and public behavior.

In looking at any factual accounts of wars, the reader is cautioned to read more than one point of view. Besides examining and evaluating history texts, students should read and compare accounts of a war from the perspective of different countries. As they watch for the author's attitude toward war in general they should try to determine if and where that point of view intrudes. Is war considered a patriotic, glorious enterprise? Is it considered to be only evil, never with just and ample cause? Are wars differentiated one from the other? What sort of advice, if any, is given to the reader in terms of responding to the information? In short, how is the reader's decision-making ability enhanced as a result of reading the book?

War is indeed ugly; it does kill. There may always be another way—a better way—of solving the world's problems. But as long as war continues to be a phenomenon of our time, we must try to learn as much as we can about its causes and its effects, using information rather than propaganda. Perhaps one day we will have the ability to avoid it and to resolve our conflicts in less disastrous fashion.

REFERENCES: WAR

BAUER, YEHUDA. *They Chose Life: Jewish Resistance in the Holocaust.* New York: American Jewish Committee, 1973.
A pamphlet tracing the various forms of Jewish resistance and explaining the conditions under which it operated.

BOSTICK, CHRISTINA. "The Individual and War Resistance," *School Library Journal,* Vol. 18, No. 7, March 1972, pp. 96–97.
Reviews books with a bias toward war resistance. More than fifty books are listed. These are not children's books, but are suitable for high school students and older.

COUNCIL ON INTERRACIAL BOOKS FOR CHILDREN. *Bulletin,* Vol. 13, Nos. 6 and 7, 1982. (Special issue on Militarism and Education.)
Contains a number of articles critiquing materials, including children's books and textbooks, that deal with the topic of war.

DAWIDOWICZ, LUCY S. *The War against the Jews: 1933–1945.* New York: Bantam, 1976. Paperback.
A comprehensive history showing how large the destruction of the Jews figured in Hitler's goals, and with what demonic energy his policies carried out that aim.

FRIEDLANDER, ALBERT H., ed. *Out of the Whirlwind: A Reader of Holocaust Literature.* New York: Schocken, 1976.
Thirty-two fiction and nonfiction selections from other books and articles, with an excellent discussion guide.

GAILLARD, T. L., JR., AND GREW, J. C. "War in the Classroom," *English Journal,* Vol. 62, No. 2, February 1973, pp. 215–218.
Describes a high school course on war, using literature from far in the past to contemporary times. Evaluates the effectiveness of the books used and makes recommendations for further reading.

GERHARDT, LILLIAN N. "Peace, a Publishers for Peace Bibliography," *School Library Journal,* Vol. 17, No. 2, October 1970, pp. 104–105.
An annotated bibliography of fifty books about war and peace. The annotations were compiled by a committee chaired by Gerhardt. A useful list, although the annotations refrain from debating the relative usefulness of each entry.

HOPKINS, LEE BENNETT, AND ARENSTEIN, MISHA. "Nervose of the Thought: War and Peace in Children's Books," *Elementary English,* Vol. 48, No. 4, May 1971, pp. 460–462.
Reviews of seven children's books about war. Brief discussion of children's responses to the topic.

JUDSON, STEPHANIE. *A Manual on Nonviolence and Children.* American Friends Committee, 1977.
The methods of conflict resolution that are discussed extend beyond the classroom to the family and community.

LANE, JOAN T., ed. "Resources in Educating for Conflict Resolution," *Childhood Education,* Vol. 49, No. 5, February 1973, pp. 251–252.
A listing of resources for adults interested in designing a curriculum for peace. Includes resources for children's books.

McALPINE, JULIE CARLSON, AND SULLIVAN, STEPHANIE CARLSON. "Seventy-five Recommended Teenage Books on War," *School Library Journal,* Vol. 20, No. 5, January 1974, pp. 222–223.
Annotated list of books about different wars.

MORSE, ARTHUR D. *While Six Million Died.* New York: Ballantine, 1977. Paperback.
A chronicle of apathy, documenting the deliberate obstructions placed in the way of attempts to rescue European Jews from the Holocaust.

ORLICK, TERRY. *The Cooperative Sports and Games Book.* New York: Pantheon, 1980.
This book and its companion, *The Second Cooperative Sports and Game Book,* include games from many cultures to help teach young people cooperation rather than competition.

PRUTZMAN, BURGES, BODENHAMER AND STERN. *The Friendly Classroom for a Small Planet.* Garden City Park, New York: Avery, 1978.
Methods of conflict resolution, building a positive classroom environment, and creative problem solving.

ROTH, ROSLYN. "A Comparative Analysis of the Depiction of War in Selected Juvenile Fiction Published prior to and since 1960." Unpublished Master's report, Palmer Graduate Library School, Long Island University, Brookville, New York, 1969.
Purpose of study is to determine whether changes have occurred in depicting war in books for children since 1960. It was found there is essentially little difference, although a few more recent books introduce questions of conscience and morality.

SCHELL, JONATHAN. *The Fate of the Earth.* New York: Knopf, 1982.
A fervent plea for concerted action to avoid nuclear confrontation.

STROM, MARGOT STERN, AND PARSONS, WILLIAM S. *Facing History and Ourselves: Holocaust and Human Behavior.* Watertown, Massachusetts: Intentional Educations, 1982.
An extensive, well-designed curriculum for teacher to use with adolescents to investigate and learn from a study of the Holocaust. The Armenians as well as the Jews are included in this book.

WELCH, ELIZABETH H. "What Did You Write about the War, Daddy?" *Wilson Library Bulletin,* Vol. 46, No. 10, June 1972, pp. 912–917.
Reviews works of nonfiction about the Vietnamese War. Each book is described in great detail.

SOURCES FOR MATERIALS

ANTI-DEFAMATION LEAGUE OF B'NAI B'RITH. 823 U.N. Plaza, New York, New York 10017
(Selected and annotated resource lists of materials on the Holocaust.)

CENTER FOR DEFENSE INFORMATION (CDI). 122 Maryland Ave., N.E., Washington, D.C. 20002
(Publishes monthly newsletter.)

CENTER FOR PEACE STUDIES. University of Akron, Akron, Ohio 44325
(Spring 1979 newsletter is for the elementary and secondary level.)

CHILDREN'S CREATIVE RESPONSE TO CONFLICT (CCRC). Box 271, Nyack, New York 10960
(Publishes a newsletter, *Sharing Peace.*)

CONSORTIUM ON PEACE RESEARCH EDUCATION AND DEVELOPMENT (COPRED). Center for Peaceful Change, Kent State University, Kent, Ohio 44242

GLOBAL EDUCATION ASSOCIATES. 522 Park Ave., East Orange, New Jersey 07017
(International education network for peace and social justice.)

NUCLEAR INFORMATION AND RESOURCE SERVICE (NIRS). 1536 16th St., N.W., Washington, D.C. 20036
(Center and coordinating office for individuals and groups actively organizing for a non-nuclear future.)

PEACE EDUCATION NETWORK (PEN). Center for Peaceful Change, Kent State University, Kent, Ohio 44242

SANE (Citizens' Organization for a Sane World). 711 G St., S.E., Washington, D.C. 20003

UNITED NATIONS CHILDREN'S FUND. 866 UN Plaza, New York, New York 10011

YAD VASHEM. Sifri, 31 Jabotinsky St., Ramat Gan 42511, Israel.
(Archives for study of the Holocaust; English publications available.)

BIBLIOGRAPHY: WAR

Because of the particular interest in Holocaust curriculum, those books that contain material on the Holocaust are specially noted with a [Holocaust] notation after the age level.

AARON, CHESTER. *Gideon*. Philadelphia: Lippincott, 1982. (Ages 11–up.) [Holocaust]
Although this is classified as fiction, the story, told in autobiographical narrative, rings so true that it persuades the reader of its authenticity. Gideon becomes a member of the resistance both in the Warsaw ghetto and in Treblinka concentration camp. He survives because of his fighting spirit, and his willingness to go outside the law, as well as to sometimes deny his identity. This story, as others of the Holocaust, affirms the human ability to endure.

ARMSTRONG, LOUISE. *How to Turn War into Peace*. Illustrated by Bill Basso. New York: Harcourt Brace Jovanovich, 1979. (Ages 5–8.)
A child's guide to resolving conflict. A little girl and her friend resolve their argument without loss of either one's dignity or sense of self-worth.

ARNOTHY, CHRISTINE. *I Am Fifteen and I Don't Want to Die*. New York: Dutton, 1956. Also in paper. (Ages 12–up.) [Holocaust]
An autobiographical diary of a 15-year-old Jewish girl who lives in Germany during World War II, afraid of both the Nazis and the Russians. Her parents are unable to protect her from the constant reminders of death all around her. She feels terror and unhappiness, but most of all anger, even at her parents who must leave a loved dog behind and are powerless.

BAKER, BETTY. *The Pig War*. Illustrated by Robert Lopshire. New York: Harper & Row, 1969. (Ages 5–8.)
Takes place on an island off the state of Washington in 1859. Both Americans and British are stationed there because neither country knows to whom the island belongs. Some trespassing pigs throw the island into a minor turmoil, which is then nonviolently settled. A very practical and peaceful solution is reached. This story is based on a historical incident.

BENCHLEY, NATHANIEL. *Sam the Minuteman*. New York: Harper & Row, 1969. (Ages 3–8.)

Sam fights with his father in the Battle of Lexington and is frightened of the war until his friend is wounded. Sam then fights wildly to avenge his friend, remembering only afterward the humane ideals he supposedly believes in.

BONSALL, CROSBY. *Mine's the Best*. New York: Harper & Row, 1973. (Ages 3–7.)
Two boys have identical balloons. In the process of the boys arguing over whose balloon is the best, both balloons are destroyed. While arguing, they do not notice that there has been a special sale on balloons like theirs—until a girl walks by with one. Then the boys align with each other saying "Ours was the best!" A commentary on the subjective causes of conflict.

BRUCKNER, KARL. *The Day of the Bomb*. Eau Claire, Wisconsin: E.M. Hale, 1962. (Ages 12–up.)
An account of the bombing of Hiroshima through the eyes and words of a fictionalized Japanese family. Sadako, the daughter of the family, dying of radiation poisoning, tries to fold a thousand paper birds as a good-luck charm to ward off death. Her story has been told in several books and she has become a symbol of anti-nuclear activity.

BUCK, PEARL S. *Matthew, Mark, Luke and John*. New York: John Day, 1967. (Ages 8–12.)
The story of four illegitimate Korean-born boys who have American fathers. They have been abandoned by the Koreans and fend for themselves until they meet a kindly American. A somewhat romanticized ending, but a compelling story of the aftermath of war.

BUNTING, EVE. *Terrible Things*. Illustrated by Stephen Gammell. New York: Harper & Row, 1980. (Ages 5–8.)
In fable format, the story tells of the dangers of selfishness. Because the forest creatures do not protect each other they are all destroyed by the "Terrible Thing" that wipes them out, species by species.

BURKE, KENNETH. "If All the Thermo-Nuclear Warheads," in *Of Quarks, Quasars, and Other Quirks: Quizzical Poems for the Supersonic Age*, collected by Sara and John E. Brewton and John Brewton Blackburn. Illustrated by Quentin Blake. New York: Crowell, 1977. (Ages 10–up.)
A parody on "If All the Seas Were One," describes what might happen if thermo-nuclear warheads were dropped, in the name of "progress."

CARR, ALBERT. *A Matter of Life and Death*. New York: Viking, 1966. (Ages 12–up.)
A history of many American wars, their possible prevention, and their individual and social implications. Also included is a discussion of patriotism and the necessity of careful consideration of alternatives to war.

CLARK, LEONARD, ed. *Drums and Trumpets*. Illustrated by Heather Copley. Philadelphia: Dufour Editions, 1962. (Ages 10–up.)
Poetry for young people dealing with war—some of its glories, some of its despairs.

CLIFTON, LUCILLE. *Amifika*. New York: Dutton, 1977. (Ages 5–8.)
Amifika's father is coming home from the army after a long time. Amifika overhears his mother and cousin making preparations for the father's return, and discussing all

of the things they need to throw away. He's afraid that they'll get rid of him, too, because he can't remember his father. He hides in the yard, falls asleep, and wakens to a remembered loving embrace: his father is home.

COERR, ELEANOR. *Sadako and the Thousand Paper Cranes.* Illustrated by Ronald Himler. New York: Putnam, 1977. (Ages 10–up.)
Sadako Sasaki was twelve years old when she died of leukemia as a result of the atomic bombing of Hiroshima. This story tells of her struggle for life as she folds the complicated origami paper cranes, an ancient symbol of peace and hope in Japanese tradition. Since her death she has become a folk-hero for Japanese children, and there is now a monument to her in Peace Park, in Japan.

COLLIER, JAMES LINCOLN AND CHRISTOPHER. *My Brother Sam Is Dead.* New York: Four Winds Press, 1974. (Ages 12–up.)
Tim is the narrator of the story. His brother Sam and his father (as well as other characters in the story) are killed in the Revolutionary War. The war is presented here as neither right nor wrong; neither the Americans nor the British are favored. The authors suggest at the end that readers should consider whether or not the war was necessary. The ugliness and hardship of war are clearly presented.

COWAN, LORE. *Children of the Resistance.* New York: Hawthorn, 1969. (Ages 12–up.)
Collection of stories about young people in eight different Nazi-occupied countries who actively aided the resistance during World War II.

CRANE, STEPHEN. "War Is Kind," in *Poetry, U.S.A.,* ed. Paul Molloy. New York: Scholastic, 1968. (Ages 10–up.)
The poet asks the maiden, babe, and mother not to weep despite the horrors of war which have afflicted them. Invites a discussion on the futility as well as the ravages of war.

DANK, MILTON. *The Dangerous Game.* New York: Lippincott, 1977. Also in paper (Ages 12–up.)
Charles Marceau, fifteen years old and alone in Paris, joins the underground resistance movement. Readers learn about the work of the movement as the adventure proceeds.

DANK, MILTON. *Red Flight Two.* New York: Delacorte, 1981. (Ages 12–up.)
This well-written adventure tale presents the dilemmas of leadership in war. Who should be exposed to the most risk to save the most lives? And what is the responsibility of people not in command to do when they feel that their superior officers are making incorrect judgments?

DEGENS, T. *The Game on Thatcher Island.* New York: Viking, 1977. (Ages 11–up.)
Harry is flattered when a group of older boys invite him to participate in their game of war on Thatcher Island. His pleasure disappears when the game takes a terrifying turn. This well-written adventure story helps young readers think about the implications of war games.

DEGENS, T. *Transport 7–41–R.* New York: Viking, 1974. Also in paper. (Ages 12–up.)
A thirteen-year-old girl travels from the Russian sector of defeated Germany to

Cologne on a transport carrying returning refugees in 1946. As the adventure unfolds, readers become involved with other passengers and their suspenseful journey. The ravages of war are communicated well.

DUNNING, STEPHEN; LEUDERS, EDWARD; AND SMITH, HUGH. *Reflections on a Gift of Watermelon Pickle and Other Modern Verses.* Glenview, Illinois: Scott, Foresman, 1967. (Ages 12–up.)
Excellent collection of poetry particularly appropriate for young adolescents, some of which pertain directly to war.

EMBERLEY, BARBARA. *Drummer Hoff.* Illustrated by Ed Emberley. Englewood Cliffs, New Jersey: Prentice-Hall, 1967. (Ages 3–8.)
A folk rhyme about the loading and firing of a cannon. After the cannon blast, flowers gradually surround it and birds come to nest in the gun. The illustrations depict the deformed and maimed victims of war in bright, cartoon-like images. The book conveys an antiwar message, but adults will need to help children to analyze this book in order to come to the intended conclusion.

FISHER, AILEEN. *Jeanne D'Arc.* New York: Crowell, 1970. (Ages 8–10.)
A biography of Jeanne D'Arc, the woman who led the French into victorious battle, was captured by the enemy, and was eventually burned at the stake.

FITZHUGH, LOUISE, AND SCOPPETONE, SANDRA. *Bang Bang You're Dead.* New York: Harper & Row, 1969. (Ages 5–8.)
Two groups of boys battle for possession of a hill as a playground for make-believe wars. They mutually agree that real violence is no fun, and settle their dispute cooperatively.

FLINKER, MOSHE. *Young Moshe's Diary: The Spiritual Torment of a Jewish Boy in Nazi Europe.* Yad Vashem, Jerusalem: Sivan Press, 1965. (Ages 12–up.) [Holocaust]
Like Anne Frank, Moshe Flinker hid in Holland until his capture and death in a Nazi concentration camp. His journal, however, deals more with Jewishness and his relation to God than the day-to-day events of life. Not an easy book to read, it is, nevertheless, a worthwhile challenge for young adolescents who may also be in the throes of self-questioning and wondering about the sense of the universe.

FORBES, ESTHER. *Johnny Tremain.* Illustrated by Lynd Ward. Boston: Houghton Mifflin, 1943. Also in paper. (Ages 12–up.)
The romanticized but well-written story of a boy living at the time of the American Revolution. Johnny's story is the main focus of the book, set against the background of the war.

FORMAN, JAMES. *My Enemy, My Brother.* Boston: Meredith Press, 1969. Also in paper. (Ages 12–up.) [Holocaust]
Four young Jews who have managed to survive the Holocaust make their way to Israel. Each of them has reacted differently to the experience, and we see, through their behavior and attitudes, the complex moral issues society now faces.

FORMAN, JAMES. *The Survivor.* New York: Farrar, Straus & Giroux, 1976. (Ages 12-up.) [Holocaust]
The story of a Jewish family from Holland who undergo the tortures of the Holocaust, and emerge with only one family member surviving.

FRANK, ANNE. *Diary of a Young Girl.* New York: Modern Library, 1952. Also in paper. (Ages 12-up.) [Holocaust]
The diary of a thirteen-year-old Jewish girl who spent two years with her family hiding from the Nazis during the occupation of Holland. She describes the fear and horror of the times, before she herself is killed in a concentration camp.

FRIESEL, UWE. *Tim, the Peacemaker.* Illustrated by Jozef Wilkon. New York: Scroll Press, 1971. (Ages 3-8.)
Tim plays a flute so beautifully that all who hear him stop whatever they are doing to listen. At first Tim stops constructive work from going on, and he regrets this. Then he stops soldiers from fighting and is glad. A pleasant fantasy. The illustrations are impressive.

FRITZ, JEAN. *And Then What Happened, Paul Revere?* Illustrated by Margot Tomes. New York: Coward, McCann and Geoghegan, 1973. Also in paper. (Ages 6-10.)
One of a series of American History books by the author, each illustrated by a notable artist such as Margaret Tomes, Tomi de Paula, or Trina Schart Hyman. The books extend and personalize the events so that young readers understand and appreciate their significance. Amusing incidents are included, all meticulously researched. All of the books help children to understand better what war really is, in its everyday progress. The other titles in the series are *Can't You Make Them Behave, King George?, What's the Big Idea, Ben Franklin?, Where Was Patrick Henry on the 29th of May?, Why Don't You Get a Horse, Sam Adams?,* and *Will You Sign Here, John Hancock?*

GAUCH, PATRICIA LEE. *This Time, Tempe Wick?* Illustrated by Margot Tomes. New York: Coward, McCann and Geoghegan, 1974. (Ages 7-11.)
Another story of the Revolutionary War. The young heroine is unusual in size, strength, and behavior. Tempe outwits some disgruntled soldiers by hiding her horse in her bedroom.

GLENN, MEL. "Song Vu Chin," in *Class Dismissed! High School Poems.* Illustrated by Michael Bernstein. New York: Clarion Books, 1982. (Ages 11-up.)
The young Vietnamese immigrant vividly remembers the horrors of war he witnessed in his native land, and sardonically refers to his current schoolmates as belonging to "America, home of the ignorant."

GOOD, MICHAEL. "Addition Problem," in *The Voice of the Children,* ed. June Jordan and Terri Bush. New York: Holt, Rinehart and Winston, 1970. (Ages 8-up.)
Words such as "dying", "gone", and "Hell" are arranged in columns in the format of an arithmetic problem. They add up to the one word, WAR, in this evocative poem.

GREEN, DIANA HUSS. *The Lonely War of William Pinto.* Boston: Little, Brown, 1968. (Ages 10–up.)
Despite the patriotic fervor of his father and brothers, William, a Jewish boy in Connecticut, cannot feel loyal to the Revolution. The book describes the vicious anti-Semitism of that time, and shows how some Jews tried to dispel it by becoming super-American.

GREENE, BETTE. *The Summer of My German Soldier.* New York: Dial Press, 1973. Also in paper, (Ages 12–up.)
Twelve-year-old Patty helps a German POW to escape. She does not have many friends, and she and the POW befriend each other. He is caught and killed; Patty is questioned and sent to reform school. The setting is Arkansas during the second world war. Patty's family are the only Jews in town, a fact that compounds her problems.

GREGORY, HORACE, AND ZATURENSKA, MARIA. *The Crystal Cabinet: An Invitation to Poetry.* New York: Holt, Rinehart and Winston, 1962. (Ages 12–up.)
Excellent selection of poetry, some decrying the ugliness of war.

HABENSTREIT, BARBARA. *Men against War.* Garden City, New York: Doubleday, 1973. (Ages 12–up.)
The history of pacifism in the United States through all its wars to the present time.

HARDY, THOMAS. "The Man He Killed," in *Cavalcade of Poems.* ed. George Bennett and Paul Molloy. New York: Scholastic, 1968. (Ages 10–up.)
The poet reflects on the irony of having in battle to kill a person whom, under any other circumstances, he would have befriended. Raises the issue of the dehumanization of war.

HASKINS, JAMES. *Resistance: Profiles in Nonviolence.* Garden City, New York: Doubleday, 1970. (Ages 11–up.)
A series of biographical sketches of people such as Martin Luther King, Gandhi, William Penn, and Henry David Thoreau follow an introduction that discusses the precepts of nonviolence.

HAUTZIG, ESTHER. *The Endless Steppe.* New York: Crowell, 1968. Also in paper. (Ages 11–up.) [Holocaust]
Many readers will learn for the first time from this fictionalized autobiography about the exile of Jews from Poland to Siberia, during the period before the Nazis invaded Poland. A gripping story, the details of one family's survival despite dehumanizing conditions help readers to empathize with victims of any oppression.

HEYMAN, EVA. *The Diary of Eva Heyman.* Translated by Moshe M. Kohn. Yad Vashem, Jerusalem: Alpha Press, 1974. (Ages 12–up.) [Holocaust]
Written by a Hungarian girl from the day of her thirteenth birthday until three months later, just before she was deported to Auschwitz, where she died, the journal describes Eva's thoughts and feelings as well as giving the reader a sense of the society and events in Hungary in 1944.

HOEHLING, MARY UTSEHLING. *Girl Soldier and Spy.* New York: Judian Messner, 1960. (Ages 12–up.)

The biography of a courageous young woman who disguises herself as a male and joins the Union Army during the Civil War. It describes her struggle to survive despite the horrors of war.

HOLLANDER, JOHN, AND BLOOM, HAROLD. *The Wind and the Rain: An Anthology of Poems for Young People*. Garden City, New York: Doubleday, 1961. (All ages.)
Some moving and impressive images are contained in these poems.

HOLM, ANNE. *North to Freedom*. New York: Harcourt Brace Jovanovich, 1965. Also in paper. (Ages 12–up.) [Holocaust]
David is permitted to escape from a concentration camp. He remembers nothing aside from trhe camp, but he knows there is a mystery about his past. The story is less about war and its aftermath than one of David's survival and the unraveling of his mystery. The message of the illogical and cruel effects of war comes through.

HOWARD, VANESSA. "The Last Riot," in *The Voice of the Children*, ed. June Jordan and Terri Bush. New York: Holt, Rinehart and Winston, 1970. (Ages 10–up.)
The poet speaks of atrocities, pain, and blood. She believes that all wars would end if people, particularly those of different races, would be kind to one another.

HUNT, IRENE. *Across Five Aprils*. Chicago: Follett, 1964. Paperback: Grosset and Dunlap. (Ages 12–up.)
The story of the hardships of a family living in a border state during the Civil War helps readers to understand that war is not simple. There are no easy answers to the question of which side is right. The author makes it clear that people as individuals have good and bad characteristics, which add to the complexity of the issues.

THE JOAN BAEZ SONGBOOK. New York: Ryerson Music Publishers, 1971. (All ages.)
Songs such as "Where Have All the Flowers Gone?" demonstrate the popular feeling about war.

JONES, CORDELIA. *Nobody's Garden*. Illustrated by Victor Ambrus. New York: Scribner 1966. (Ages 10–up.)
Bridget, a new girl in school, is living with an aunt and uncle in London, having been orphaned in the war. The story describes postwar London in a very personal and vivid way. It also helps readers to understand the serious emotional aftermath of war.

THE JUDY COLLINS SONGBOOK. New York: Grosset and Dunlap, 1969. (All ages.)
Several of the songs tell of the sorrows of war.

KAY, MARA. *In Face of Danger*. New York: Crown, 1977. (Ages 11–up.) [Holocaust]
Ann, visiting Germany from England just before the outbreak of World War II, discovers that her German hostess, whose son is a member of the Hitler Youth, is hiding two Jewish girls in her attic. The story is well told, and an interesting addition to the other stories, based on true experiences, of Christian people's braving extreme danger in order to save Jewish lives.

KERR, JUDITH. *When Hitler Stole Pink Rabbit*. New York: Coward, McCann and Geoghegan, 1972. Also in paper. (Ages 8–up.) [Holocaust]
Autobiographical story of a German Jewish family who escape just before Hitler

comes to power. They go first to Switzerland, then France, then England. The impact is somewhat softened because, although the family are refugees, they seem not to suffer unduly.

KERR, M.E. *Gentlehands*. New York: Harper & Row, 1978. (Ages 11–up.) [Holocaust]
Buddy's mother has been estranged from her father for many years; Buddy does not know why. Buddy learn to know and love his grandfather, who loves music and art, lives in a cultured, almost aristocratic setting, and is kind and gentle to animals. To Buddy's horror, it is discovered that his grandfather was once a hated and feared concentration camp torturer, and is still involved with other Nazi war criminals.

KJERDIAN, DAVID. *The Road from Home: The Story of an Armenian Girl*. New York: Greenwillow Press, 1979. (Ages 12–up.)
A fictionalized biography of the author's mother, the book deals with the persecution and destruction of Armenian Christians by the Turkish Moslems. It is essentially a story of survival.

KNIGHT, CLAYTON. *We Were There at the Normandy Invasion*. New York: Grosset and Dunlap, 1956. (Ages 12–up.)
An objectively told historical account of the Normandy invasion of World War II.

KOHN, BERNICE. *One Sad Day*. Illustrated by Barbara Kohn Isaac. New York: Third Press–Joseph Okpaku, 1971. (All ages.)
The Stripes live in one place; the Spots, in another. Stripes make war on the Spots, everything and everyone on earth is killed. An allegory demonstrating the total devastation of war as well as its lack of appropriate cause.

LEICHMAN, SEYMOUR. *The Boy Who Could Sing Pictures*. Garden City, New York: Doubleday, 1968. (Ages 6–9.)
The king is at war, so the court jester takes his son traveling around the country to cheer people up. The boy sings happiness to the sad faces; back at the court, he sings the sadness of what he has seen to the blank faces. The king, realizing the truth, stops the war.

LEVITIN, SONIA. *Journey to America*. Illustrated by Charles Robinson. New York: Atheneum, 1970. (Ages 9–12.) [Holocaust]
Lisa's family decides to escape the Nazis by emigrating to America. Their decision is a difficult one, complicated by the fact that the father must go first. The children and their mother stay for a while in Switzerland, where two of them are subjected to terrible treatment in a foster care facility. Finally, they are reunited in America.

LEVOY, MYRON. *Alan and Naomi*. New York: Harper & Row, 1977. Also in paper. (Ages 10–up.) [Holocaust]
A beautifully written tragic, yet heroic story of the attempts of a young boy, Alan, to help his friend, Naomi, recover from the horror of the Holocaust. Anti-Semitism, friendship, and family love are but a few of the many issues explored in this book.

LEWIS, C.S. *The Last Battle*. New York: Macmillan, 1956. Also in paper. (Ages 10–up.)
The ending to the Narnia Chronicles, this book finishes the battle between the forces

of Good and Evil, the theme throughout the series. It is an allegorical account of the end of the world, Judgment Day, and the entrance into heaven.

LIFTON, BETTY JEAN. *Children of Vietnam*. Photographs by Thomas Fox. New York: Atheneum, 1972. (Ages 10–up.)
Interviews and pictures of children who survived the battles and massacres in Vietnam. A powerful description of individual suffering, confusion, fear, and sorrow.

LIFTON, BETTY JEAN. *Return to Hiroshima*. Photographs by Eikoh Hosoe. New York: Atheneum, 1970. (Ages 10–up.)
A pictorial view of the damage and destruction of Hiroshima by the A-bomb during World War II as well as the consequent rebuilding of the city.

LOPSHIRE, ROBERT. *I Am Better Than You*. New York: Harper & Row, 1968. (Ages 5–8.)
A competition between two lizards who really are identical. One of them declines the battle; thus war is averted. A very useful book to teach the problems of competition, escalation, and boasts. Solutions other than violent ones are suggested here.

MARKS, SHIRLEY. "Early Warning," in *Of Quarks, Quasars, and Other Quirks: Quizzical Poems for the Supersonic Age*. Illustrated by Quentin Blake. Collected by Sara and John E. Brewton and John Brewton Blackburn. New York: Crowell, 1977. (Ages 10–up.)
The poem is a parody on Paul Revere's ride, and presents the probability of annihilation if a missile hits our country.

MARUKI, TOSHI. *Hiroshima No Pika*. Illustrated by Toshi Maruki. New York: Lothrop, Lee and Shepherd, 1982. (Ages 10–up.)
Although illustrations make it appear that this is a picture book, it is not directed at very young readers. The story and pictures graphically detail the effects of the nuclear bomb. The translation of the title is "Hiroshima's Flash." A powerful antiwar statement.

MAZER, HARRY. *The Last Mission*. New York: Delacorte, 1979. Also in paper. (Ages 11–up.)
Jack Raab falsifies his papers and joins the air force at age fifteen. After the trauma of battle and capture he acknowledges the futility of war and confesses his age. After he returns home he tells his peers and his family what he has learned about the insanity and ugliness of war.

MELTZER, MILTON. *Never to Forget: The Jews of the Holocaust*. New York: Harper & Row, 1976. Also in paper. (Ages 11–up.) [Holocaust]
Based on careful research and documentation, this excellent and very readable book provides a comprehensive and specific history of the persecution of the Jews by the Nazis. Included are excerpts from diaries, letters and poems of the concentration camp prisoners. Arranged in order from "A History of Hatred" to "Spirit of Resistance," the book demands that the reader ponder the moral issues of war and persecution.

MERRILL, JEAN. *The Pushcart War*. Illustrated by Ronni Solbert. New York: William R. Scott, 1964. Also in paper. (Ages 9–12.)
An allegory of how wars begin, are escalated, and are ultimately resolved. The story colorfully and imaginatively told, is about a war (told as if it were history) between the trucks and the pushcarts in New York City. Causes, strategies, and battles are described in this humorous but thoughtful book.

MONJO, F.N. *The Vicksburg Veteran*. New York: Simon and Schuster, 1971. (Ages 6–10.)
Acount of the capture of Vicksburg, Mississippi, by Ulysses S. Grant through the eyes of his twelve-year-old son.

MOSKIN, MARIETTA. *I Am Rosemarie*. New York: Harper & Row, 1972. (Ages 10–up.) [Holocaust]
A fictionalized autobiography set in a concentration camp during the second world war. Details of the attempts to live a semblance of a normal existence make the story an unusual one.

MURRAY, MICHELE. *The Crystal Nights*. New York: Seabury Press, 1973. Also in paper. (Ages 11–up.) [Holocaust]
An unusual story of the effects of war, not only on its direct victims, but also on their family in the United States. Most of the characters are unpleasant and selfish. The backdrop of the war serves to complicate their reactions and helps the reader to recognize that no easy judgments can be made.

NAVON, YITZHAK. *The Six Days and the Seven Gates*. Illustrated with photographs. Translated by Misha Louvish. Jerusalem: Shikmona Publishing Company, 1978. (Ages 9–up.)
A modern legend of the recapture of Jerusalem by the Israeli army. Each of the gates to the city begs to have the honor of being the gate by which the city will be reclaimed. The one gate that is concerned with the lives of the people is the one selected.

OFEK, URIEL. *Smoke over Golan: A Novel of the 1973 Yom Kippur War in Israel*. Illustrated by Lloyd Bloom. New York: Harper & Row, 1979. (Ages 10–up.)
Written in the form of memoirs of a ten-year-old Israeli boy, this account of the twelve days of the war focuses mostly on the need for people to live together peacefully, and to build, rather than destroy. Saleem, a Syrian boy, and the narrator of the story are friends who manage, despite the war, to retain their friendship.

ORGEL, DORIS. *The Devil in Vienna*. New York: Dial Press, 1978. Also in paper. (Ages 11–up.) [Holocaust]
Inge, a thirteen-year-old Jewish girl, narrates the story in the form of a diary. Lieselotte, whose father is a violent man and a Nazi, is Inge's best friend, and despite her forced membership in the Hitler Youth, remains loyal to Inge. The story tells of how Inge and her family must submit to the ritual of baptism in order to escape destruction. They finally get to Yugoslavia and eventual safety.

PATCHEN, KENNETH. *First Will and Testament*. Forrest Hills, New York: Padell, 1948. (Ages 12–up.)
Passionate and angry poetry, much of it concerning war.

PRINGLE, LAWRENCE. *Nuclear Power: From Physics to Politics*. New York: Macmillan, 1979. (Ages 12–up.)
Traces the development of nuclear power to the present. Explores and explains the facts as well as the controversies surrounding this topic.

REISS, JOHANNA. *The Upstairs Room*. New York: Crowell, 1972, Also in paper. (Ages 10–12.) [Holocaust]
Annie is six years old at the beginning of the book, which spans seven years in Holland. She and her family are Jews. The story is similar to Anne Frank's, but most of the family survive. The story tells of the courage not only of the Jews but also of the Dutch people who risked their lives to help the Jews.

REMARQUE, ERICH MARIA. *All Quiet on the Western Front*. Boston: Little, Brown, 1929. Also in paper. (Ages 12–up.)
A story of the battles of World War I through the eyes of a group of German soldiers. A classic story about the senselessness of war.

RICHARDS, ALLAN. "A War Game," in *I Heard a Scream in the Street*, ed. Nancy Larrick. New York: Dell, 1970. Paperback. (Ages 11–up.)
Calling war "uniformed murder," the poet mourns the killing of children.

RICHTER, HANS P. *Friedrich*. New York: Holt, Rinehart and Winston, 1970. Also in paper. (Ages 10–up.) [Holocaust]
A novel dealing with the effect of war on the friendship between a Jewish family and a non-Jewish family in Germany during World War II. The book is unusual because it is told from the perspective of the German, non-Jewish boy. The chronology at the end of the book is chilling in its specificity of government-sponsored atrocities.

RICHTER, HANS P. *I Was There*. New York: Holt, Rinehart and Winston, 1962. Also in paper. (Ages 10–up.)
An autobiographical story of the induction of two boys into the youth corps in Germany in World War II. The book deals with children's confusion over many issues of war.

RINGI, KJELL. *The Stranger*. New York: Random House, 1968. (Ages 3–7.)
A giant stranger causes uneasiness in a land of tiny people. When the people make war on the giant he cries, flooding the land until the people float to his face level. There they talk easily and make friends. One would wish that face-to-face communications such as these could result in real-life happy endings.

RINGI, KJELL. *The Winner*. New York: Harper & Row, 1969. (Ages 3–9.)
A story about escalation and competition. The story deals with the ultimate absurdity of war. Although there are no words in this book, the message is powerful and could extend to readers well beyond age nine.

ROBERTS, MARGARET. *Stephanie's Children*. London: Victor Gollancz, 1969. (Ages 12–up.)
A book dealing with the effect of the Reign of Terror on individuals and families in France during the Revolution.

ROSS, ALAN. "Radar," in *Don't Forget to Fly*, collected by Paul Janeczko. New York: Bradbury Press, 1981. (Ages 11–up.)

The devastation of an unseen enemy is a by-product of the acutely sensitive instruments, inviting the question of responsibility on the part of the operator.

ROTHMAN, LARRY; BAMY, JAN; and PAQUET, BASIL T. *Winning Hearts and Minds: War Poems by Vietnam Veterans*. Brooklyn, New York: First Casualty Press, 1972. (Ages 12–up.)
Uneven quality, but food for discussion.

RUBIN, ARNOLD P. *The Evil That Men Do: The Story of the Nazis*. New York: Julian Messner, 1977. (Ages 11–up.) [Holocaust]
A factual account of the Holocaust, including a discussion of anti-semitism, the lack of world response to the plight of the Jews, and Jewish-Christian relations.

RYAN, CHELI DURAN. *Paz*. Illustrated by Nonny Hogrogian. New York: Macmillan, 1971. (Ages 6–8.)
Paz and his family are pacifists who own a house on the French and Spanish border. If one country is at war, they move to the other side of the house. When France and Spain fight each other, Paz declares his family independent. Many problems arise from this pacifist stance, but all ends well.

SACHS, MARILYN. *A Pocket Full of Seeds*. Illustrated by Ben F. Stahl. Garden City, New York: Doubleday, 1973. (Ages 9–12.) [Holocaust]
Nicole and her family are French Jews. She is the only one of her family to escape capture by the Nazis. Readers are left knowing that Nicole will survive, but sharing her anxiety, uncertainty, and grief over the rest of her family.

SAMUELS, GERTRUDE. *Mottele*. New York: New American Library, 1977. Paperback. (Ages 12–up.) [Holocaust]
For mature readers, the gripping story of Mottele, a young Jewish boy who joins the Partisans fighting the Nazis.

SEREDY, KATE. *The White Stag*. New York: Viking, 1937. (Ages 12–up.)
A historical Hungarian tale about the journeys and exploits of many great leaders, including Attila the Hun. War is seen as inevitable.

SIEGAL, ARANKA. *Upon the Head of the Goat: A Childhood in Hungary, 1939–1944*. New York: Farrar, Straus & Giroux, 1981. Also in paper. (Ages 12–up.) [Holocaust]
Based on the author's experiences as a child in Hungary, the books adds to the chronicles of the Holocaust with its descriptions of how ordinary people were called upon to survive with extraordinary abilities.

SINGER, ISAAC BASHEVIS. "The Power of Light," in *The Power of Light*. Illustrated by Irene Lieblich. New York: Farrar, Straus & Giroux, 1980. Also in paper. (Ages 9–up.) [Holocaust]
David and Rebecca, young survivors of the Nazis' destruction of the Warsaw ghetto, take courage from the light of a Hannukah candle, and escape from the ruins of the ghetto into the forest to join the Partisans. Eventually they settle in Israel and marry. This story is the only factual one in Singer's book of miraculous Hanukkah tales, but the story certainly tells of a miracle.

Historical fiction dealing with the courage and determination of soldiers in all the American wars.

TUNIS, JOHN R. *His Enemy His Friend*. New York: Morrow, 1967. Also in paper. (Ages 12–up.)
A German soldier stationed in France is friendly with the French. He must decide between loyalty to country and friendship. Hope is expressed at the end when the countries begin to have peaceful dealings with each other again. This book is more than a surface examination of the conflict arising out of war.

TUNIS, JOHN R. *Silence over Dunkerque*. New York: Morrow, 1962. (Ages 12–up.)
Adventure story of a British sergeant in France who fights courageously to lead his troops through Dunkerque during World War II.

UCHIDA, YOSHIKO. *Journey Home*. Illustrated by Charles Robinson. New York: Atheneum, 1978. Also in paper. (Ages 9–12.)
The sequel to *Journey to Topaz*. A Japanese-American girl and her family attempt to reconstruct their lives after their release from an internment camp. Readers may be motivated to investigate this shameful period in American treatment of Japanese-Americans.

UCHIDA, YOSHIKO. *Journey to Topaz: A Story of Japanese-American Evacuation*. New York: Scribner, 1971. (Ages 9–12.)
After Pearl Harbor is attacked, a Japanese-American girl and her family, along with many other Japanese-Americans, are forced to go to an "aliens" camp in Utah. The story tells of their internment, their maintenance of dignity and their family ties.

UDRY, JANICE MAY. *Let's Be Enemies*. Illustrated by Maurice Sendak. New York: Harper & Row, 1961. Also in paper. (Ages 5–8.)
Two boys, who were once close friends, fight and become enemies. They each think the other is wrong. They never resolve their conflict but resume their friendship, nevertheless. Discussions of this book can lead to suggestions for resolving personal conflicts.

VAN STOCKUM, HILDA. *The Borrowed House*. New York: Farrar, Straus & Giroux, 1975. (Ages 12–up.) [Holocaust]
Janna is a member of the Hitler Youth. Her parents, German actors, are in Holland. When she is required to join them, she begins to learn that there are other, conflicting ideas from the ones she has been trained to believe in the Hitler Youth. A somewhat oversimplified and melodramatic story, but one that presents an interesting perspective.

VOLAVKOVA, HANA. *I Never Saw Another Butterfly (Children's Drawings and Poems from Terezin Concentration Camp, 1942–44)*. New York: McGraw-Hill, 1962. Also in paper. (All ages.)
Though Terezin was a way station to an extermination center, these poems deal with life, happiness, love, and freedom. A powerful indictment of war.

WHITTIER, JOHN GREENLEAF. "Barbara Frietchie," in *The Charge of the Light Brigade and Other Story Poems*. New York: Scholastic, 1969. Paperback. (Ages 9–up.)
One person's view of history. Very useful for discussion.

WONDRISKA, WILLIAM. *John John Twilliger*. New York: Holt, Rinehart and Winston, 1966. Also in paper. (Ages 7–9.)

A terrible dictator rules the town, forbidding any dancing, friendship, or pets. John John, through kindness and cleverness, changes the situation for the better. The assumption in this book is that even villains and dictators are human and potentially reachable.

YOLEN, JANE. *The Ministrel and the Mountain*. Illustrated by Anne Rockwell. Cleveland: World, 1967. (Ages 5–9.)

The story of two foolish kings who are jealous of each other because one can see the sunset from his kingdom and the other can see the sunrise. A wise, peace-loving minstrel solves the problem and prevents a war.

ZOLOTOW, CHARLOTTE. *The Hating Book*. Illustrated by Ben Shecter. New York: Harper & Row, 1969. Also in paper. (Ages 3–8.)

Two girls who are friends have a misunderstanding but settle it in a peaceful fashion. This story makes a good discussion starter on the topic of personal conflict.

TEN

METHODOLOGY

TEACHING CHILDREN TO READ can be the most rewarding of all teaching experiences. To see the "aha" of discovery as they make the connection between the written symbols and the language they speak and hear is worth all the planning and time that the teacher must expend. Many workable, effective systems and approaches are available for helping children acquire reading ability. All are potentially successful, but there are some that make a lot more sense than others, and these will be described below.

The reading act includes such abilities as comprehension, recall of detail, recall of sequence, ascertaining the author's intent, evaluating information, appreciating style, classifying, predicting outcomes, telling the difference between opinion and fact, and inference. A good reader also appreciates a variety of kinds of books.

When reading is taught in a conventional manner, three "ability" groups are probably formed at the beginning of the semester, each group using a different level book from the same publisher's series, each group progressing at a given pace, answering the same questions, using the same vocabulary, and filling in the same workbook pages. The procedure is essentially the same for every reading period. All the groups do reading at the same time. The teacher divides his or her time equally among all the groups each day. While the teacher works with one group, the other two groups are occupied with workbooks, answering the questions predetermined by the teacher's manual for that text, or with performing the exercises recommended by the same manual. At the end of a unit, the publisher often provides a test to see whether or not the children have successfully completed that section of the text. If the students do not pass the test, they generally repeat all of the reading that they have just completed. Sometimes they must move to the lower group when they fail the test, because they cannot be placed in a special group and obviously cannot keep up with the group in which they were originally placed. Or else, if a number of children have failed the test, those children who have passed it must either wait until their group-mates catch up with them again or, less frequently, leap to the more advanced group.

The standard procedure for a reading lesson in such a program includes guided silent reading. The children read an assigned portion of an assigned story in order to answer assigned questions. For those children who complete both the reading and the questions before the teacher is ready for them, there may be extra work in the form of more questions; or they may play a game, do their homework, or be permitted to read books other than their texts. The implication is that after their "real" work, they may do extra, less educational activities.

The assumptions underlying this conventional approach include a reliance upon the expertise of a publisher's staff to diagnose and prescribe for the reading needs of any given group of children. It is also assumed that the stories in the books are appropriate for all the children using the texts. The stories are usually read in the sequence in which they occur in the book, leading to the expectation that a collection of stories must be read in order. While timing is not specifically prescribed, all the children are expected to complete at least one full book—ideally the one on their grade level—during the semester.

Indifference or outright dislike of a story can cause a child to read it badly. A story that is unappealing to a child can lead to that child's being perceived as a poor reader. Sometimes the fact that the child has been called away from an attractive activity to "do reading" leads to a poor performance of that particular reading lesson.

In some conventional approaches, comprehension skills are generally equated with simple recall and with locational skills. When a question is asked about a reader's opinion, there is usually an expected right answer. Rarely is there a question in the manual that does not have a correct answer supplied to the teacher; open-ended questions are not regularly included. Children are discouraged from expressing their honest opinions about anything, because they risk being chastised or penalized for a wrong or unexpected answer. A criticism or an expressed dislike of a story is sometimes viewed as an attack upon the whole reading program, rather than as an exercise of critical reading ability. In this way these well-intentioned texts can discourage the very skills that they purport to teach.

Word attack skills are sometimes handled in a fashion that blocks their acquisition. Most publishers' series rely on a particular sequence and style of word analysis, some advocating a strongly phonic approach, some devoting their attention to a patterning (linguistic) approach. Others recommend a combination of sight-word memorization, useful for certain children at some point, but the prescribed sequence and required focus can be inappropriate for a substantial number of children.

Conforming to the expectations of any given series can create problems—the child who cannot keep up with the rest of the class, or the children who become discipline problems because of their reading difficulties. Some concerned teachers become increasingly more frustrated by the illogic of treating every child in the same fashion, despite each child's obvious differences, and may respond by forming more and more ability groups composed of children who do not fit into any of the three already established groups.

In any given classroom, if only one series is used and if it used in a rigid, narrowly structured fashion, it too often occurs that children learn to dislike, and to be bored by, reading. They also learn to view reading as a time of day and a set of unpleasant practices, rather than as a challenge, and a possible source of pleasure. They become dependent upon directions from the teacher, rather than upon themselves as independent readers. Many classroom teachers, also bored by the procedure, recognize that the children are not acquiring the skills appropriate to good reading. But this scenario need not occur. Many of the readers have good stories in them; they can comfortably be used as resources and options for children to select, in the same way that library books are. The skills can be learned from them when these stories are self-selected by the children.

•TRY THIS

Select two different sets of materials, produced by different publishers. Examine one teacher's manual and accompanying child's text from each publisher at the same grade level. Use the following questions as a guideline for examining the texts. The purpose of this exercise is to demonstrate that there is more than one single correct way to teach skills. It is also to help you analyze the procedures for teaching reading.

1. What does the manual say is the purpose of the series? (You can usually find the intent in the first chapter of the teacher's edition.)
2. Search for evidence in the lesson plans that the publisher is accomplishing his stated purpose. How well do you believe this has been done?
3. What are the skills stressed in this series?
4. How do the lessons accomplish the teaching of the skills?
5. How comfortable is the format of the teacher's manual? How specific are the instructions to the teacher? How convenient is the organization for you? How easy is it for you to locate the skills, expectations, and the recommendations for teaching them?
6. How does the publisher recommend that the series be geared to individual differences?
7. What kind of content does the book present? Are there several authors, or one? How varied are the literary forms? Are there poems, plays, folk tales, biography, fiction, etc.?
8. How varied are the characters in the stories? What kinds of representations are there of lower classes, rural and urban children, minority cultures, unusual life-styles, and foreign cultures?

9. How well does the text handle racism, sexism, violence, war, and other important social issues?
10. Compare the series that you have examined, giving your opinion of their advantages and disadvantages.

Publishers have begun in recent years to recognize and acknowledge the competence of classroom teachers. They also are recognizing the importance of using a diversity of materials. These publishers are, therefore, producing programs that use many different books rather than relying on the basic text. Some of the more widely used of these new series are the Scholastic and Random House Individualized programs, and the James Moffett *Interaction* series, published by Houghton Mifflin. These series encourage teacher and student self-evaluation and selection. National conventions of such organizations as the International Reading Association and the National Council of Teachers of English reinforce the approval of the efficacy of this approach. It is becoming more and more accepted that an effective reading program must be personalized and individualized.

PRINCIPLES OF THIS READING PROGRAM

Two principles govern an effective individualized or personalized reading program. *Self-selection* and *self-evaluation* are necessary ingredients of any approach that aims to meet the skills and interest needs of the students. Self-selection involves the students' choosing whatever reading they wish to use to help themselves learn to read better. Teachers help the students to recognize that the program is aimed at continuous growth in reading ability and that each of them is responsible for aiding in that process. The fact that they choose their own reading materials insures that they are motivated. Their responses to what they have selected are encouraged, taking the form of critical and analytic evaluation. If a student dislikes a book and provides arguments for that opinion, it is seen as valid and, therefore, to be respected. Not an attack on the system, rather, it is an indication that the system is working.

Choice of reading material implies a different book for almost every child; it therefore follows that there is no expectation of uniformity of reading rate. Each child, reading at her or his own pace, finishes a different number of books from the other children. The act of reading therefore becomes a question of individual interest rather than of group conformity or competition.

All kinds of skills come into use when the students must exercise their own judgment about their reading material. Of course, the teacher remains the final arbiter and is usually an influence on the child, but the goal is to have the children assume the greatest responsibility possible. The students in this sort of program recognize that reading is necessary, not only as a school goal but as a life tool as well.

SELF-SELECTION

Each child selects the materials for learning to read better. One of the potential discomforts for teachers in a program in which the students and teachers engage in a learning partnership is that teachers feel the need to have read everything first. They wonder how else they will know if the student is giving the "right" answer to a comprehension question. After the experience of having had a manual supply them with all of the correct answers, it is sometimes difficult to move immediately to a system that has no visible keys to the answers. They soon recognize, however, that the questions they ask deal with a thinking process; the answer can be right even if the details are wrong. For example, when a teacher asks a child to tell about the story, and the plot sounds coherent, sequenced, and logical, the teacher can assume that the child has no problems in sequencing or in retelling a story. If, perhaps, another child reading the same story relates an entirely different accounting of the plot, a logical activity would then be for the teacher to have the two children come together to talk about what they have read. The teacher may be motivated to read the book as a result of the discrepancy, and a three-way conversation can ensue. A group of additional children may become interested in the story, with several substantive conversations as a result. Even if one of the original readers of the story had at first totally misunderstood it, the potential learning is far more valuable than the initial right answer. After all, if a person is asked to summarize a story, it is the procedure of recalling the story, assessing the situations, and culling from this what the major theme is (according to the understanding of the reader) that is evidence of important skills acquisition. Any reasonable answer demonstrating this process can be accepted and discussed. There are many ideas contained within any work of any complexity. If the answer that the child gives does not sound reasonable, the teacher can always ask the student to elaborate, and can note a need for future lessons on the particular skill, such as sequencing, inference or main idea.

•TRY THIS

Go to a children's library and ask three children to relate to you the plots of books they have recently completed. Read the books; then compare the children's answers with the ones that you would have given.

One of the values of this sort of program is that it encourages children to teach each other by stimulating interest, raising questions, and interacting in a lively fashion. (How often in a conventional reading program does this kind of discussion take place?) Further, the questions and ideas raised by the books published for children today are far more challenging than the questions suggested by the designers of the teachers' manuals. Teachers would do well to encourage the sort of thinking these books foster.

Another question raised by the practice of permitting children to select their own reading is that of accumulating enough printed matter so that children will have sufficient options to choose from. This is one of the most easily accomplished aspects of the program. A teacher might ask the entire class, "What can you bring in to school that we can use to improve our reading?" The children will volunteer such suggestions as magazines, library books, newspapers, catalogs, comic books, cereal boxes, signs, telephone books, instructions for games, paperbacks, cookbooks, manuals, social studies texts, reference books, and others. All these suggestion can be very productive in a reading program but the bulk of the reading will probably be done with books that the children select from the library, their collections at home, or from the numerous paperback book clubs available to school children. Even in communities that have a very low economic level, the libraries can supply a sufficient variety in order to meet the needs of the children. Regular class trips to the library can yield six books per child. This provides enough of a supply for the class to share.

Teachers initiating the individualized program worry about the students' appropriate acquisition of skills. They wonder how they can manage to mount a skills program without the benefit of a manual. The first task of a teacher, in this case, is to compile a list of skills; these can be gleaned from texts aimed at the teaching of reading, curriculum guides, manuals, or from lists circulated by the publishers. Once this list has been secured, the teacher can duplicate it for all of the children; then, as the skills are encountered and acquired, the teacher and children can check them off. The children can practice (at their own pace) word attack, comprehension, and oral interpretation skills using materials that they enjoy.

The key competence for the teacher to develop here is that of informal diagnosis. The teacher must learn to listen to a child read, observe his or her general reading behavior, and make diagnoses. Then the teacher and child together can suggest prescriptions to satisfy the child's reading needs. The informal reading inventory familiar to many teachers is useful in this program: it involves a simple set of procedures. After the child selects any passage of approximately one hundred words, the teacher listens to the child read the passage aloud. During the reading, the teacher records the positive features as well as the errors that the child makes. After the reading, the teacher and child as partners compile a list of the strengths and needs the child has exhibited. Then together they work out a program for responding to the reading needs. (For those teachers who are uneasy about their competence in this area, this author has included in References several specific "how-to" resources. Eldon

E. Ekwall's *Locating and Correcting Reading Difficulties* is an excellent guide for this process.) Teachers should become comfortable about postponing direct instruction until several children exhibit the same need, so that instruction is for small groups rather than isolated individuals.

•TRY THIS

Armed with a portable tape recorder, find a child (a visit to the children's library or a classroom should prove fruitful). Ask the child to select a book and to choose a passage of approximately one hundred words. Tape-record the child's reading of this passage. After the child has finished, both of you read the passage again while listening to the tape. Then analyze the reading: Mark the errors; note the strengths; list the needs. Ask the child what next steps may be feasible. Make some suggestions yourself. Decide what questions may be useful to determine the meaning of the story.

One of the temptations a teacher should resist in this sort of program is to ask the child to select a more difficult book if there seems to be no problem in word recognition. *There is no such thing as a book that is too easy!* It is up to the teacher to help the child practice the more complex reading skills if there seems to be no immediate need for word analysis practice. Skills of comprehension, oral performance, writing, and interpretation may be recommended. How many of us as adults always read something that is mechanically difficult for us to manage? The mechanical aspects of reading are important, of course, but they are not the only skills needed. It must be noted here that there are books that may be too *empty* because of their lack of substance. This is not to be confused with the ease with which the words can be read, but has to do with the complexity and depth of the content.

However, there *is* such a thing as a book that is too difficult. If a child selects a book that is too arduous mechanically, the frustration encountered will impede any learning. Children should, therefore, be taught how to assess whether or not a book will be frustrating for them. Teach them to find a passage of one hundred words in any book they plan to select, and count on the fingers of one hand the errors they make when reading this passage silently. They know they have made an error if a word doesn't make sense to them, or if they are stumped by a word and find it difficult to proceed. They can be taught to recognize that a book is likely to be too hard if they make more than five errors (the fingers of one hand). If they encounter five or fewer errors, the book will probably be manageable. If they count more than five errors, they should be strongly encouraged to return the book for the time being and to select another, more readable book.

SELF-EVALUATION

From the start, when a child is doing self-selection for a reading program and participating in the diagnostic procedure, that child is also doing self-evaluation. In a good individualized program, the child is aware of the necessity for self-evaluation. The children must be informed about reading skills, the questions raised in books, and the procedures useful for carrying out a program responding to reading needs. Children in this program have the responsibility of maintaining some records of their progress. They usually have some say in what sorts of records they will keep, what form they will take, and how the records will be used. The children not only help to evaluate their own progress, they also work with each other, sharing their reading and their reactions with each other and with the teacher. It is this taking of responsibility that is one of the most important features of the program.

IMPLEMENTING THE PROGRAM

The teacher would do well to gather the entire class together and involve the children in each new step. The accumulation of materials should be done only after the children have suggested what materials would be appropriate. The teacher should also lead the children in a discussion of the purposes of reading. Once the class knows that the reading program will be tailored to their ideas and needs, they participate in it actively and enthusiastically. Engaging in discussions about the books they are reading, they recommend books to each other. The organization of the program can vary; but it is useful if certain activities, such as teacher/student conferences, small-group instruction, and sharing, are built in.

KINDS OF GROUPS

An individualized reading program involves more kinds of groupings than does a conventional one. There is no need, however, for any permanent groups. The reasons for grouping are varied in this program. Sometimes a temporary group is formed because it has been established that all the children in this particular group share a next step. The teacher and the children may decide that it would be useful to practice initial consonant blends. Or a group may meet together because they have all been reading stories about war, for example, and would like to compare their reading. Perhaps a group will meet in order to write, practice, and present a play on a book that all have read. Another may meet regularly to design and to paint a mural depicting a segment of a story that they all have read and wish to share with the rest of the class.

The teacher may feel that it is sometimes necessary to call together the entire class. Perhaps methods of book selection will be the topic of the discussion, or the whole class may have exhibited the need for a session on record-keeping and its uses. Or the whole class may want to view a presentation that a small group has prepared. It is also likely that one or two children may want to perform some sort of reading in front of the entire group. The decisions are made jointly by the teacher and the children.

The kinds of groupings include not only small instructional groups, interest groups, whole class groups, teacher-led groups, and child-led groups, but also the grouping of one child and reading material, one child teaching another, two children sharing an activity, and teacher and one child. Each of the groups is formed for a specific reason and lasts only as long as there is necessity for that particular structure. The teacher and one child usually meet together for a regularly scheduled conference, generally for the purpose of diagnosis. It is less efficient to teach one child when there is the likelihood that other children are ready for the same next step. Therefore, it is useful for the teacher and student to assess what next step may be appropriate and then, in subsequent conferences, to locate other children who are also ready. In this way, the conference serves as the primary diagnostic situation. The child comes to the conference with his or her records in hand; together, the teacher and child review the child's progress. Perhaps the teacher will have the child read aloud, or they may discuss the book. A recommendation for further work should come from the conference.

SCHEDULING

The children can participate actively in the management of a schedule by signing up for activities, by suggesting activities, by reminding each other of the time, and by maintaining the writing of the schedule. The schedule, which varies daily, is usually posted on a bulletin board or on the chalkboard. Sometimes it may be comfortable for the schedule to be somewhat set; for example, the class may decide to have reading every day from 9:30 to 11:00. Then they may want to divide that time into a half-hour for conferences, a half-hour for small-group instruction, and a half-hour for sharing. The conferences probably will require no more than five to ten minutes each if they are confined to diagnosis. The small groups will probably need ten to fifteen minutes of instruction each, and the sharing could include several presentations to the entire class. Another possible arrangement could include a general schedule posted for the entire day, with children and teacher inserting activities and signing up for times that are flexible and arranged on a day-to-day basis. However the schedule is managed, the purpose is to respond most closely to the needs of the children. The sharing of time can also continue informally throughout the day. Discussions of issues, arguments, and mutual recommendations become general practices.

ROOM ARRANGEMENT

Once the teacher and the children have brought in all of the materials that they wish to use for the reading program, they can plan together how to arrange it in the room. Any sort of room is appropriate for this kind of program. A self-contained or open space, large or small room can be arranged conveniently to house the materials of an individualized reading approach. The children can establish the system as a permanent one or can change it every month. When the children are in charge, they care more about the maintenance of the area. What sort of arrangement they make is not important as long as the other children can locate materials; it is helpful if they post some charts indicating the arrangement. Sometimes the children place the books in order of size; sometimes they arrange them by color. More often, they choose to place them in order of difficulty or in interest categories. The process of categorizing is a valuable one, no matter what the ultimate arrangement. The students acquire a knowledge of the books available and expand their own reading interests in the process.

RECORD KEEPING

Both the teacher and the children should maintain and use records. Records should serve as reporting devices to parents and interested observers, but they can also be used as the substance for designing lessons for the participants and as evaluative devices for the program. Records need not be uniform; they can vary throughout the semester according to the interests and needs of the participants. Everyone should be given the opportunity to decide what to include in her or his record. Most people want to include the date, the name of the reading, and some comments, while others want more specific indications of strengths, needs, and activities accomplished. Students usually find it interesting to reserve a section of their records for special vocabulary work; they also may want to include a section on favorite books or characters or ideas. Whatever their records look like, they should be used whenever they have a conference with the teacher. Both teacher and children could attach a list of the reading skills as suggested by a manual, and they could regularly check off the skills accomplished the week before.

ACTIVITIES

The activities suitable for an individualized reading program are varied. The children read independently after having selected books that they are interested in. They maintain records, participate in diagnosis, engage in small-group instruction, help to teach some small groups, and share their reading with their classmates in as many interesting ways as they can think of. The following ideas are only a few of the hundreds that teachers and children may select from.

Appropriate Music for Story Theme	Many famous pieces of music have been inspired by children's stories, especially fairy tales. Children can select music that they feel reflects the mood of whatever they are reading. By creating a multiarts experience themselves, they are in effect enhancing their own appreciation of both reading and music.
Arrangement of Bookshelf of Similar Books	This can be done by an individual or by a group that has read the same book. Posters and pictures can be added.
Autobiography	The student rewrites or tells the story from the viewpoint of one of the characters.
Blurbs	These should be interest-arousers and not reveal too much of the plot. A collection of these can form a bulletin board display to serve as motivation for the class.
Book for a Day	The entire class or a group of children may wish to dress as characters in a book. They can portray the characters not only in dress but in actions and typical speech habits as well.
Book Jackets	A child can design a jacket to reflect the message of the book.
Book Seller	A child tries to "sell" a book to another child or group of children. This is a good exercise in being persuasive and in analyzing people's interests.
Bulletin Boards	Reviews, three-dimensional titles, eye-catching titles may attract students' attention, leading them to read.
Cartoons	Use ideas from the story to make a set of cartoon drawings to retell the story. Be sure to put the events in order.
Crossword Puzzle	A crossword puzzle using new words learned in a story can be constructed.
Character Analysis	Which characters would the student like to have as a friend? Who has behaved most admirably? etc.

Dear Author	Letters to the author in care of the publisher (see Appendix A) telling what aspects of the book impressed them, its value to them, a comparison with other books by the same author, or other comments inviting a response.
Dear Diary	Students take on the identity of one of the characters and write three entries of one hundred words each in the diary of that person.
Diorama	This is a three-dimensional representation of a scene. It usually is made in a box, such as a shoe box. The figures and scenery are placed inside.
Dolls Dressed As Characters	A child can make costumes for small dolls to represent a character.
Dramatization	Informal or rehearsed—this could be done by an individual or a group. It could be combined with murals, puppets, shadow plays.
Exhibits or Collections	May be used with books that are of informational nature, or books that are concerned with a particular issue may be placed on display, with comments written by students.
Happy Holidays	Books are located that describe different holidays, and displays are made of each holiday.
Headlines or Captions for a Newspaper Account	They should be short and to the point. The chapter titles can be changed to headlines or may be used to transform the story into a newspaper account.
History Mystery	If a book describes a historical incident, other descriptions of that same event may be found, either in fact or in other works of fiction. When students compare the different versions, they may try to unravel the mystery of which is the most accurate.
Interview (Simulated) with an Author	If two students have read the same books, one can answer questions as the author, while the other poses as an interviewer. Or real authors may be invited to answer the questions (in person or on the phone).

Library Acquisitions	Students who have read a book give advice on whether or not the book should be purchased for the classroom or school library.
Making Slides	Incidents of stories may be shown on student-made slides. As the slides are shown, accompanying parts may be read or explanations given. The oral parts may be taped for more effectiveness.
Map or Diagram	Books about treasure hunts and mysteries lend themselves especially to this type of sharing.
Mobiles	A mobile can be made with a coat-hanger and pictures of scenes in a book. They could be the child's own work or from magazines.
Movie Roll	The child can take a roll of paper and draw a series of events from a book. These pictures can be shown individually through an opening in a box. It should look like a T.V. screen and can be of any size.
Mural	This can be a group or class activity. The scene can be drawn or pasted on mural paper, or it can be done on a board with colored chalk.
Opaque Projector	The illustrations or original drawings may be flashed on the wall and used as a background while parts of the story are narrated.
Oral Reading	The student reads aloud an interesting portion of the book. This helps develop oral reading proficiency as well as interest in the book.
Outline of the Story	Choices in the area are a five-sentence outline; a series of ideas; an arrangement of questions or pictures in sequence; or movie scenes. These activities can be aided by murals, movie rolls, slides, or posters.
Out of Whose Mouth?	Find some comments or flavorful quotes; write them on index cards, and see if other people who read the same book can identify the speaker.
Panel Discussion or Debates	Useful for evaluating plot, characters, and solutions, and for accepting and evaluating differences of opinion.

Pantomime	The character is shown in action. The audience is urged to take part by telling what action is being performed and by whom.
Photographs	Student-taken photographs of situations or scenes to illustrate the story can be used to arouse interest and to personalize the book.
Poems	The student writes a comment, summary, or impression of the book in the form of a limerick or poem. Poems may also be written to laud or describe a character in the book.
Point of View	Rewrite the story from one of the other characters' perspective.
Portraits	A portrait of a favorite character may be drawn and framed. The author's description may be used as a guide. A gallery of portraits may be set up.
Posters	May be used to advertise the book, the characters or the theme. Students promote the reading of the book by combining a twenty-five- to fifty-word review with illustrations, lettering, and other eye-catching details, in an effective visual arrangement.
Predictions	Students read a part of a book, then try to predict what will happen, how a problem will be solved, or the kind of ending the author may write. They then complete their reading and compare endings with the author's. (You may like the students' solutions better than the author's!)
Puppets	Incidents may be portrayed, characters impersonated, or the story reported.
Quotable quotes	Particularly colorful or descriptive quotes are located and put into an appropriate order, then displayed.
Radio Scripts	Transformation of a story into a script for television or radio. Friends may be invited to perform the script complete with sound effects and commercial breaks.
Reading Log	Notes, pictures, and impressions that are related

SONE, MONICA ITOI. *Nisei Daughter*. Seattle: University of Washington Press, 1979. (Ages 12–up.)
A moving and authentic personal account of a Japanese-American family's internment during World War II.

STEELE, WILLIAM O. *The Perilous Road*. New York: Harcourt, Brace & World, 1958. Also in paper. (Ages 8–12.)
Chris learns a powerful lesson about right and wrong and the ugliness of war. Although this story takes no sides in the Civil War, it is told from the point of view of Chris, a young Southern boy who feels that the Confederate side is the right one.

STEICHEN, EDWARD. *The Family of Man*. New York: Simon and Schuster, 1956. (All ages.)
A photographic essay on human emotion and humanity. The section on war and its aftermath is particularly effective.

STEIG, WILLIAM. *The Bad Island*. New York: Simon and Schuster, 1969. (Ages 6–10.)
Violent and ugly creatures who inhabit a violent and ugly island are constantly at war with one another. When, suddenly, flowers start growing on the island, the creatures go totally berserk; then they annihilate each other. Eventually, the flowers take over and the island becomes an uninhabited paradise.

SUHL, YURI. *On the Other Side of the Gate*. New York: Franklin Watts, 1975. (Ages 12–up.) [Holocaust]
A young Jewish woman gives birth to a baby in the Warsaw ghetto after the Nazis have outlawed pregnancy. She and her family are helped to safety by Christians after a harrowing ordeal.

SUHL, YURI. *Uncle Misha's Partisans*. New York: Four Winds Press, 1973. (Ages 10–up.) [Holocaust]
The story, which was inspired by an actual event, describes Jewish partisans in the Ukraine. The hero is Mottele, who has been orphaned by the Nazis. He plays his violin well enough to use it as as weapon for sabotage. Although the book glorifies revenge and violence, it also portrays the ugliness of war. It presents a little-known fact of war—that of the active resistance of bands of Jews.

SZAMBELAN-STRAVINSKY, CHRISTINE. *Dark Hour of Noon*. New York: Lippincott, 1982. (Ages 11–up.)
Set in Poland, in World War II, Trina is sent to an internment camp with her family, and then to a small apartment, shared by two families. She becomes involved with a children's underground resistance movement, and helps in the Polish uprising of 1944.

TAKASHIMA, SHICHAN. *A Child in Prison Camp*. New York: Morrow, 1974. (Ages 8–12.)
A fictionalized, but factual autobiography of the internment of Japanese-Canadians during the second world war. Important information for young readers to have, the book is a readable contribution both to historical and literary study.

TIBBETS, ALFRED B. *American Heroes All*. Boston: Little, Brown, 1966. (Ages 12–up.)

to the story or stories that a child has read may be organized creatively in a notebook or log.

Souvenirs — Any items that are connected with the topic or period dealt with in the book are an aid to reporting.

Story Changes — Students add a chapter to the story or rewrite the first or last chapter. They can also add new characters, present and solve new problems, or change key incidents.

Tableau — Effective in presenting a story in which action is important. A series of "frozen" actions can convey many messages.

Tests — Students write a brief test on the book. Five to ten questions are sufficient. Duplicate the tests, and let each child who reads the book take the test "for fun."

This is Your Life — Personal events from the life of a character in the book can be interestingly reviewed in this manner. The author can also be the subject of this sort of presentation.

Title Changes — Students write other titles for the book, make new dust jackets for each new title, and display them with the original on a bulletin board.

T.V. Games — Games based upon "What's My Line?," "I've Got a Secret," "Concentration," etc. Groups of students enjoy this and can write very entertaining commercials to amuse the audience.

Twenty Questions — The sharer answers *yes* or *no* to the questions of the group. The children can try, in twenty questions, to guess the character's identity, the title of the book or the topic it deals with.

Vocabulary Lists — This technique may be employed for books that present entertaining dialogue, unusual terminology, or simply colorful words.

Where in the World? — If the book takes place in an interesting real or imagined location, a travel brochure may be designed to entice others to visit it.

A child who enjoys and is interested in reading books becomes a better reader. Children can usually influence and motivate each other more effectively than adults can; they will probably add other ideas to the list given above. Inventive teachers can adapt these ideas to their own class interests and abilities and invariably add many more.

This sort of approach to the teaching of reading attends to the goals of a wholesome, constructive educational process. In addition, it supports the lively exchange of opinions generated by the reading of varied books and engenders the reading and thinking habit for life.

REFERENCES: METHODOLOGY

ABBOTT, JERRY L. "Fifteen Reasons Why Personalized Reading Instruction Does Not Work," *Elementary English*, Vol. 49, No. 1, January 1972.
Urges readers to try a personalized program and demonstrates that it can and does work.

AUKERMAN, ROBERT C. *Approaches to Beginning Reading*. New York: Wiley, 1971.
An encyclopedia of beginning reading approaches. This book describes the published and informal methods and materials of teaching beginning reading. Materials are described; research is summarized; methodology is presented. An excellent reference.

BAILY, A. V., and HOUSEKEEPER, G. "Does Individualized Reading Affect Other Subject Areas?" *Elementary English*, Vol. 49, No. 1, January 1972, pp. 37–43.
Bases research on a questionnaire aimed at getting teachers' day-by-day observations. Results summarized—the question the title asks is answered "yes—favorably."

BETTELHEIM, BRUNO, and ZELAN, KAREN. *On Learning to Read: The Child's Fascination with Meaning*. New York: Knopf, 1982.
An extensive analysis and criticism of the basal approach to the teaching of reading. Makes a case for meaning and emotional content in primers.

BETTELHEIM, BRUNO, and ZELAN, KAREN. "Why Children Don't Like to Read," *Atlantic Monthly*, November 1981, pp. 25–31.
Discusses the importance of making reading interesting and enjoyable rather than mechanical and dull. Criticizes American reading texts, and compares them unfavorably to Swiss primers.

BROGAN, PEGGY, and FOX, LORENE K. *Helping Children Read: A Practical Approach to Individualized Reading*. New York: Holt, Rinehart and Winston, 1961.
An excellent and practical text. Includes instructions on how to manage an individualized reading program from first grade through eighth. Useful for incorporating skills, management, and methodology.

CARLSEN, G. ROBERT. *Books and the Teenage Reader,* rev. ed. New York: Bantam, 1980. Paperback. Books are organized into categories, and each category is explored, with recommended discussion-starters.

CARLSON, RUTH KEARNEY. *Literature for Children: Enrichment Ideas.* Dubuque, Iowa: William C. Brown, 1970.
Contains hundreds of activities that can be done with children to extend the impact of books.

DARROW, HELEN F., and HOWES, VIRGIL M. *Approaches to Individualized Reading.* New York: Appleton-Century-Croffs, 1960.
An excellent overview of the different approaches to individualized reading. Includes record-keeping techniques.

DECKER, ISABELLE M. *100 Novel Ways with Book Reports.* New York: Citation Press, 1969.
Includes a hundred ideas, complete with instructions, materials needed, suggestions to the teacher, for sharing books. also has bibliographies of writing aids, book lists, critical books.

DOLCH, E.W. "Getting Started with Individualized Reading," *Elementary English*, Vol. 37, No. 2, February 1960, pp. 105–112.
Step-by-step procedures. Useful bibliography.

DORAN, SYLVIA, and CAMPBELL, DIANE. *Beginning Program of Independent Reading and Writing Activities.* Woburn, Massachusetts: Curriculum Associates, 1977.
A year-long program for primary students, including initial teaching lessons to introduce the activities and a series of activities for students to do on their own.

DUKER, SAM. *Individualized Reading.* Springfield, Illinois: Charles C. Thomas, 1971.
An extensive annotated bibliography of many aspects of individualized reading.

DUNN, KENNETH and RITA. "Kids Must Learn How to Learn Alone," *Learning Magazine,* Vol. 1, No. 6, April 1973, p. 17.
Describes seven steps for individualizing instruction. Provides information on strengthening teachers' and children's diagnostic skills.

EKWALL, ELDON E. *Locating and Correcting Reading Difficulties.* Columbus: Merrill, 1981. Paperback.
Presents an excellent format for diagnosing children's reading needs in an informal setting. Suggests several options for activities to help children overcome their reading difficulties. Describes the process of reading.

FADER, DANIEL N. *The New Hooked On Books.* New York: Berkley, 1976. Paperback.
A forceful presentation of the value of teaching reading through the use of trade books, and, in this case, paperbacks. Fader's style of writing is entertaining and informative. Older students are the clients here, but the principles apply to any age level. Extensive listing of books, by category, in the appendix.

GOODMAN, YETTA M., and BURKE, CAROLYN. *Reading Strategies: Focus on Comprehension.* New York: Holt Rinehart and Winston 1980.
A practical guide for teachers in the appropriate use of reading materials to aid in children's comprehension.

HARRIS, LARRY A., and SMITH, CARL B., eds. *Individualizing Reading Instruction: A Reader.* New York: Holt, Rinehart and Winston, 1972. Paperback.
Many articles by experts in the field describing different aspects of reading instruction. All phases of instruction are included.

HELLRIEGEL, DIANE. *Fifty Ways to Use Paperbacks in the Middle Grades.* New York: Scholastic, 1980.
A compilation of projects and ideas contributed by elementary school teachers, based on successful practices.

HOPKINS, LEE BENNETT. *The Best of Book Bonanza.* New York: Holt, Rinehart and Winston, 1980. Paperback.
Originally published as articles in a regular column in *Teacher* Magazine, this compilation of information and ideas about how best to involve children with reading and books is an invaluable aid to the classroom teacher.

HOWES, VIRGIL M. *Individualization of Instruction: A Teaching Strategy.* New York: Macmillan, 1970.
Clearly written, useful techniques for individualizing instruction.

HOWES, VIRGIL M. *Informal Teaching in the Open Classroom.* New York: Macmillan, 1974.
An excellent step-by-step guide to aid teachers in setting up and implementing a classroom where children take responsibility for their own learning.

KIMMEL, MARGARET MARY, and SEGEL, ELIZABETH. *For Reading Out Loud!* New York: Delacorte, 1983.
A valuable guide to the values, process and procedures of reading aloud. Includes useful lists of books, arranged in several categories.

KOHL, HERBERT. *Reading, How To.* New York: Dutton, 1973. Also in paper.
A very clearly written account of how to teach reading in an open classroom. The philosophy and methodology of an open classroom are well described.

LEE, BARBARA, and RUDMAN, MASHA KABAKOW. *Mind over Media: New Ways to Improve Your Child's Reading and Writing Skills.* New York: Seaview, 1982. Also in paper, titled *Leading to Reading!* New York: Berkley, 1983.
A compendium of practical suggestions and activities for helping children enjoy and learn from reading. Everyday materials and experiences as well as TV, books, and travel are used to motivate and instruct young readers and writers.

LOGAN, JOHN W. "Developing Children's Love of Literature," *Language Arts,* Vol. 60, No. 4, April 1983. pp. 518–521.
Motivation is an important factor in the reading process. This report lists a number of materials available through the Educational Resources Information Center for stimulating children's interest in books.

MILLER, WILMA H. "Organizing a First Grade Classroom for Individualized Reading Instruction," *Reading Teacher,* Vol. 24, No. 8, May 1971, pp. 748–752.
A nicely organized and practical article suggesting specific ideas for implementing individualized reading in the first grade.

MONSON, DIANE L., and McCLENATHAN, DAYANN K. eds. *Developing Active Readers: Ideas for Parents, Teachers and Librarians*. Newark, Delyware: International Reading Association, 1979. A collection of eleven articles by various authors on book selection, reading programs, and suggestions for activities and discussion techniques for application in the classroom.

MUESER, ANNE MARIE. *Reading Aids through the Grades*, 4th ed. New York: Teacher's College Press, 1981.
In addition to the many ideas for activities to use with children and books, the appendix contains an annotated list of references for individualizing a reading program.

NEW YORK CITY BOARD OF EDUCATION. *A Practical Guide to Individualized Reading*. (Publication No. 40). New York: New York City Board of Education, Bureau of Educational Research, 1960. (110 Livingston St., Brooklyn, New York 11201.)
Exactly what the title says—an invaluable guide on how to establish and maintain an individualized reading program.

POVEY, GAIL, and FRYER, JEANNE. *Personalized Reading*. Encino, California: International Center for Educational Development, 1972. Practical introduction to the methodology of individualized reading. Games, techniques, record-keeping ideas, and an open philosophy are conveyed.

REASONER, CHARLES. *Bringing Children and Books Together: A Teacher's Guide to Early Childhood Literature*. New York: Dell, 1979. Paperback.
Modeled on the popular and useful guides to the Yearling books for older children, this book informs teachers how to successfully introduce and work with books in the lower grades.

REASONER, CHARLES F. *Releasing Children to Literature*. New York: Dell, 1968. Paperback.
Interesting and open-ended ideas for encouraging critical reading. This book specifically pertains to the Dell Yearling books, but the activities are imaginative and pertinent to any books. Thirty specific books are included, many of which are concerned with topics such as death, siblings, females, and war.

REASONER, CHARLES F. *When Children Read*. New York: Dell, 1975. Paperback.
The third in the series of activities and helpful synopses of Yearling books. Teachers may use these as guides for designing their own questions and activities for any books that they wish to use in a reading program.

REASONER, CHARLES F. *Where the Readers Are*. New York: Dell, 1972. Paperback.
Another invaluable teacher's guide to imaginative and stimulating activities to accompany the reading of books. Reasoner specifically discusses thirty-four Dell Yearling books, but the ideas extend far beyond the particular books.

ROWELL, ELIZABETH H., and GOODKIND, THOMAS B. *Teaching the Pleasures of Reading*. Illustrated by Beverly Armstrong. Englewood Cliffs, New Jersey: Prentice-Hall, 1982.
The authors encourage teachers to motivate the joy and love of reading at the same

time that they are reinforcing reading skills. Using such features as humor, music and the out-of-doors, the book includes a variety of activities to incorporate into an existing reading program.

RUDMAN, MASHA KABAKOW. "Helping Readers to Find Themselves and Each Other in Books," in *Integrating the Language Arts in the Elementary School,* ed. Beverly A. Busching and Judith I. Schwartz. Urbana. Illinois: National Council of Teachers of English, 1984.

Discusses how to integrate children's literature into all of the areas of the curriculum. Provides examples of books to use and questions and activities for classroom application.

SARTAIN, HARRY W. "What Are the Advantages and Disadvantages of Individualized Instruction?" *International Reading Association Conference Proceedings*, Vol. 13, Part 2, 1969, pp. 328–356.

An excellent analysis of individualized reading, with advice for turning disadvantages into advantages.

SPACHE, EVELYN B. *Reading Activities for Child Involvement,* revised ed. Boston: Allyn and Bacon, 1982.

Hundreds of activities, classified according to skills, that children can engage in with a minimal amount of intervention by the teacher, in order to enhance their reading ability.

TRELEASE, JIM. *The Read-Aloud Handbook.* New York: Penguin, 1982. Paperback.

A practical guide to the craft of reading aloud to children, written by a lover of books and a masterful story teller. Lists of recommended books are included.

VEATCH, JEANNETTE. *How to Teach Reading with Children's Books.* New York: Bureau of Publications, Teachers College, Columbia University, 1964.

An excellent book describing in great detail how to manage an individualized reading program.

VEATCH, JEANNETTE, *Reading in the Elementary School,* 2d. ed. New York: Wiley, 1978.

The most comprehensive text of its kind. All phases of individualized reading are discussed and explained. Many activities, practical suggestions, and information are included.

WIBERG, JOHN L., and TROST, MARION. "A Comparison between the Content of First Grade Primers and the Free Choice Library Selections Made by First Grade Students," *Elementary English*, Vol. 47, No. 6, October 1970, pp. 792–798.

Demonstrates that there is a marked disparity between the content of primers and the books that children select from the library.

YEAGER, ALLAN. *Using Picture Books with Children.* New York: Holt, Rinehart and Winston, 1973.

This is a guide to Holt's Owlet books. Yeager recommends using picture books with children of all ages and suggests how to adapt activities to different levels.

•APPENDIX•

PUBLISHERS' ADDRESSES

ABC (Americans Before Columbus). National Indian Youth Council, 201 Hermosa, Albuquerque, N.E. New Mexico 87108

ABINGDON PRESS. 201 Eighth Ave. S., Nashville, Tennessee 37202

ADDISON-WESLEY. Facob Way, Reading, Massachusetts

AFRO-AM PUBLISHING CO. 910 S. Michigan Ave., Rm., 5561, Chicago, Illinois 60605

ALLYN AND BACON, INC. 7 Wells Ave., Newton, Massachusetts 02159

AMERICAN ASSOCIATION OF SEX EDUCATORS AND COUNSELORS. 600 Maryland Ave., S.W. Washington, D.C. 20024

AMERICAN FEDERATION OF TEACHERS (AFT). 11 Dupont Circle, N.W. Washington, D.C. 20036

AMERICAN JEWISH COMMITTEE. Institute of Human Relations, 165 E. 56th St., New York, New York 10022

ARCHON BOOKS. P.O. Box 4327, 995 Sherman St., Hamden, Connecticut 06514

ASTOR HONOR, INC. 48 E. 43rd St., New York, New York 10017

ATHENEUM PUBLISHERS. 597 Fifth Ave., New York, New York 10017

AVON BOOK DIVISION. The Hearst Corporation, 959 Eighth Ave., New York. New York 10019

BANTAM BOOKS, INC. 666 Fifth Ave., New York, New York 10019

THE BEACON PRESS. 25 Beacon St., Boston, Massachusetts 02108

BEHAVIORAL PUBLICATIONS, INC. 72 Fifth Ave., New York. New York 10011

BERKLEY PUBLISHING. 200 Madison Ave., New York, New York 10016

BETHANY PRESS. 2320 Pine Blvd., P.O. Box 179, St. Louis, Missouri 63166

BOOKSTORE PRESS. Box 191, R.F.D. 1, Freeport, Maine 04032

R.R. BOWKER CO. 1180 Avenue of the Americas, New York. New York 10036

BRADBURY PRESS. 2 Overhill Rd., Scarsdale, New York 10583

BROADSIDE PRESS. 74 Glendale Ave., Highland Park, Michigan 48203

CAMPBELL AND HALL. Box 350, Boston, Massachusetts. 02117

CAROLRHODA BOOKS, INC. 241 First Ave., North Minneapolis, Minnesota 55401

CHILTON BOOK COMPANY. Chilton Way, Radnor, Pennsylvania 14089

COUNCIL ON INTERRACIAL BOOKS FOR CHILDREN. 1841 Broadway, New York, New York 10023

COWARD, MCCANN & GEOGHEGAN, INC. 200 Madison Ave., New York, New York 10016

DELACORTE PRESS. 1 Dag Hammarskjold Plaza, New York, New York 10017

DELL PUBLISHING COMPANY. 1 Dag Hammarskjold Plaza, New York, New York 10017

THE DIAL PRESS. 1 Dag Hammarskjold Plaza, 245 E. 47th St., New York, New York 10017

DODD, MEAD & COMPANY, INC. 79 Madison Ave. New York, New York 10016

DOUBLEDAY AND COMPANY, INC. 501 Franklin Ave. Garden City, New York 11530

E.P. DUTTON & COMPANY, INC. 2 Park Ave., New York, New York 10016

PAUL S. ERIKSSON, INC. Battell Bldg. Middlebury, Vermont 05753

EVANS AND COMPANY. 216 East 49th St., New York, New York 10017

FARRAR, STRAUS & GIROUX. 19 Union Square W., New York, New York 10003

FEMINIST PRESS. SUNY College at Old Westbury, P.O. Box 334, Old Westbury, New York 11568.

FOLLETT PUBLISHING COMPANY. 1010 W. Washington Blvd. Chicago, Illinois 60607

FOUR WINDS PRESS. 730 Broadway, New York, New York 10003

GARRARD PUBLISHING COMPANY. 1607 N. Market St. Champaign, Illinois 61820

GINN AND COMPANY. 191 Spring St., Lexington, Massachusetts 02173

GOLDEN PRESS. GREENWILLOW BOOKS. 105 Madison Ave., New York, New York 10016

GROSSETT AND DUNLAP, INC. 200 Madison Ave., New York, New York 10016

GROVE PRESS, INC. 196 West Houston St., New York, New York 10014

HARCOURT BRACE JOVANOVICH. 757 Third Ave. New York, New York 10017

HARPER & ROW PUBLISHERS, INC., 10 E. 53rd St. New York, New York 10022

HARVEY HOUSE. (E. M. Hale & Co.) 20 Waterside Plaza, New York, New York 10010

HAYDEN BOOK COMPANY. 50 Essex St., Rochelle Park, New Jersey 07662

HILL AND WANG, INC. 19 Union Square West, New York, New York 10003

HOLIDAY HOUSE. 18 E. 53rd. St. New York, New York 10022

HOLT, RINEHART & WINSTON GENERAL BOOKS. 521 Fifth Ave. New York, New York 10175

HOUGHTON MIFFLIN COMPANY. 1 Beacon St. Boston, Massachusetts 02108

HUMAN SCIENCE PRESS. 72 Fifth Ave., New York, New York 10011

INDEPENDENT PUBLISHERS GROUP. 1 Pleasant Ave., Port Washington, New York 11050

INDIAN HISTORIAN PRESS. 1451 Masonic Ave., San Francisco, California 94117

ALFRED A. KNOPF, INC. 201 E. 50th, St. New York, New York 10022

LERNER PUBLICATIONS CO. 241 First Ave. N., Minneapolis, Minnesota 55401
LION PRESS, SAYRE PUBLISHING CO., INC., 111 E. 39th St. New York, New York 10016
J.B. LIPPINCOTT COMPANY. E. Washington Square, Philadelphia, Pennsylvania 19105
LITTLE, BROWN AND COMPANY, INC. 34 Beacon St., Boston, Massachusetta 02106
LOLLIPOP POWER. INC. P.O. Box 1171, Chapel Hill, North Carolina, 27514
LONGMAN, INC. 19 W. 44th St., New York, New York 10036
LOTHROP, LEE AND SHEPARD. Division of William Morrow, 105 Madison Ave., New York, New York 10016

MCGRAW-HILL, INC. 1221 Avenue of the Americas, New York, New York 10020
DAVID MCKAY COMPANY, INC. 2 Park Ave., New York, New York 10016
MACMILLAN PUBLISHING COMPANY. 866 Third Ave. New York, New York 10022
MACRAE SMITH. Rtes. 547 and Old 147, Turbotville, Pennsylvania 17772
MADRONA PUBLISHERS. 2116 Western Ave., Seattle, Washington 98121
CHARLES E. MERRILL PUBLISHING COMPANY. 1300 Alum Creek Dr., Columbus, Ohio 43216
JULIAN MESSNER, INC. Division of Simon and Schuster, Inc. 1230 Avenue of the Americas, New York, New York 10020
WILLIAM MORROW & COMPANY, INC. 105 Madison Avenue, New York, New York 10016

NEW DAY PRESS. c/o Karamu House, 2355 E 89 St., Cleveland, Ohio 44106
W.W. NORTON & CO., INC. 500 Fifth Ave. New York, New York 10110

ODYSSEY PRESS. 4300 W 62nd. St., P.O. Box 7080, Indianapolis, Indiana 46206
OFFICE OF EDUCATION. U.S. Department of Health and Human Services, Washington, D.C. 20202
OVER THE RAINBOW PRESS. P.O. Box 7072, Berkeley, California 94707
OXFORD UNIVERSITY PRESS, INC. 200 Madison Ave., New York, New York 10016

PANTHEON BOOKS, INC. 201 E. 50th. St., New York, New York 10022
PARENTS MAGAZINE PRESS. 685 Third Ave. New York, New York 10017
PHILOSOPHICAL LIBRARY, INC. 200 W 57th St. New York, New York 10019
PLATT AND MUNK PUBLICATIONS. 51 Madison Ave., New York, New York 10010
POCKET BOOKS, INC. 1230 Avenue of the Americas, New York, New York 10020
G.P. PUTNAM'S SONS. 200 Madison Ave., New York, New York 10016

RAND MCNALLY AND COMPANY. 8255 Central Park Ave., Chicago, Illinois 60680

RAINTREE PUBS. 305 W. Highland Ave., Milwaukee, Wisconsin 53203
THE RONALD PRESS. 605 Third Ave., New York, New York 10158

ST. MARTIN'S PRESS, INC. 175 Fifth Ave., New York, New York 10010
SCARECROW PRESS. P.O. Box 656, Metuchen, New Jersey 08840
SCHOLASTIC, INC. 730 Broadway, New York, New York 10003
SCOTT, FORESMAN, & CO. 1900 E Lake Ave. Glenview, Illinois 60025
THE SCRIBNER BOOK COMPANY, INC. 597 Fifth Ave., New York, New York 10017
SEABURY PRESS. 815 Second Ave., New York, New York 10017
STIPES PUBLISHING COMPANY. P.O. Box 526, Champaign, Illinois 61820.

THIRD WORLD PRESS. 7524 So. Cottage Grove Ave., Chicago, Illinois 60619
TIME-LIFE BOOKS. 777 Duke St., Alexandria, Virginia 222314

VAN NOSTRAND REINHOLD CO., INC. 135 W 50th St., New York, New York 10020
VANGUARD PRESS, INC. 424 Madison Ave., New York, New York 10017
THE VIKING PRESS, INC. 625 Madison Ave., New York, New York 10022

WADSWORTH PUBLISHING CO., INC. 10 Davis Drive, Belmont, California 94002
WALKER AND COMPANY. 720 Fifth Ave., New York, New York 10019
FRANKLIN WATTS, INC. 387 Park Ave. Smith, New York, New York 10019
THE WESTMINSTER PRESS. 925 Chestnut St., Philadelphia, Pennsylvania 19107
JOHN WILEY & SONS, INC. 605 Third Ave., New York, New York 10158
H.W. WILSON CO. 950 University Ave., Bronx, New York 10452
WINDMILL BOOKS. SIMON AND SCHUSTER, INC., 1230 Avenue of the Americas, New York, New York 10020
THE WRITER, INC. 8 Arlington St. Boston, Massachusetts 02116

XEROX EDUCATIONAL PUBLICATIONS. 245 Long Hill Road, Middletown, Connecticut 06457

APPENDIX B

SELECTED LIST OF CHILDREN'S BOOK AWARDS

American Book Awards (formerly National Book Awards)

Awarded each year by a specially selected panel of judges—generally consisting of children's book authors—this award is given to a book published the preceding year in the United States, written by an American citizen. The book is judged for its literary excellence.

1969 *Journey From Peppermint Street*, by Meindert DeJong
      Finalists: *Constance*, by Patricia Clapp
              The Endless Steppe, by Esther Hautzig
              The High King, by Lloyd Alexander
              Langston Hughes, by Milton Meltzer

1970 *A Day of Pleasure: Stories of a Boy Growing Up in Warsaw*, by Isaac Bashevis Singer
      Finalists: *Pop Corn & Ma Goodness*, by Edna Mitchell Preston
              Sylvester and the Magic Pebble, by William Steig
              Where the Lilies Bloom, by Vera and Bill Cleaver
              The Young United States, by Edwin Tunis

1971 *The Marvelous Misadventures of Sebastian*, by Lloyd Alexander
      Finalists: *Blowfish Live in the Sea*, by Paula Fox
              Frog and Toad Are Friends, by Arnold Lobel
              Grover, by Vera and Bill Cleaver
              Trumpet of the Swan, by E. B. White

1972 *The Slightly Irregular Fire Engine*, by Donald Barthelme
      Finalists: *Amos and Boris*, by William Steig
              The Art and Industry of Sandcastles, by Jan Adkins
              The Bears' House, by Marilyn Sachs
              Father Fox's Pennyrhymes, by Clyde Watson
              Hildilid's Night, by Cheli Durán Ryan
              His Own Where, by June Jordan
              Mrs. Frisby and the Rats of NIMH, by Robert C. O'Brien
              The Planet of Junior Brown, by Virginia Hamilton

The Tombs of Atuan, by Ursula K. LeGuin
Wild in the World, by John Donovan

1973 *The Farthest Shore*, by Ursula K. LeGuin
    Finalists: *Children of Vietnam*, by Betty Jean Lifton and Thomas C. Fox
    Dominic, by William Steig
    The House of Wings, by Betsy Byars
    The Impossible People, by Georgess McHargue
    Julie of the Wolves, by Jean Craighead George
    Long Journey Home, by Julius Lester
    Trolls, by Ingri and Edgar Parin d'Aulaire
    The Witches of Worm, by Zilpha Keatley Snyder

1974 *The Court of the Stone Children*, by Eleanor Cameron
    Finalists: *Duffy and the Devil*, by Harve Zemach
    A Figure of Speech, by Norma Fox Mazer
    Guests in the Promised Land, by Kristin Hunter
    A Hero Ain't Nothin' But a Sandwich, by Alice Childress
    Poor Richard in France, by F. N. Monjo
    A Proud Taste for Scarlet and Miniver, by E. L. Konigsburg
    Summer of My German Soldier, by Bette Greene
    The Treasure Is the Rose, by Julia Cunningham
    The Whys and Wherefores of Littabelle Lee, by Vera and Bill Cleaver

1975 *M. C. Higgins, the Great*, by Virginia Hamilton
    Finalists: *My Brother Sam Is Dead*, by James Lincoln Collier and Christopher
    Collier
    The Devil's Storybook, by Natalie Babbitt
    Doctor in the Zoo, by Bruce Buchenholz
    The Edge of Next Year, by Mary Stolz
    The Girl Who Cried Flowers and Other Tales, by Jane Yolen
    Joi Bangla! The Children of Bangladesh, by Jason and Ettagale Laure
    Remember the Days: A Short History of the Jewish American, by
    Milton Meltzer
    I Tell a Lie Every So Often, by Bruce Clements
    Wings, by Adrienne Richard
    World of Our Fathers: The Jews of Eastern Europe, by Milton Meltzer

1976 *Bert Breen's Barn*, by Walter D. Edmonds
    Finalists: *As I Was Crossing Boston Common*, by Norma Farber
    El Bronx Remembered, by Nicholasa Mohr
    Ludell, by Brenda Wilkinson
    Of Love and Death and Other Journeys, by Isabelle Holland
    The Star in the Pail, by David McCord
    To the Green Mountains, by Eleanor Cameron

1977 *The Master Puppeteer*, by Katherine Paterson
    Finalists: *Never to Forget: The Jews of the Holocaust*, by Milton Meltzer
    Ox Under Pressure, by John Ney
    Roll of Thunder, Hear My Cry, by Mildred D. Taylor
    Tunes for a Small Harmonica, by Barbara Wersba

1978 *The View from the Oak,* by Judith and Herbert Kohl
Finalists: *Caleb and Kate,* by William Steig
Hew Against the Grain, by Betty Sue Cummings
Mischling, Second Degree: My Childhood in Nazi Germany, by Ilse Koehn
One at a Time, by David McCord

1979 *The Great Gilly Hopkins,* by Katherine Paterson
Finalists: *The First Two Lives of Lukas-Kasha,* by Lloyd Alexander
Humbug Mountain, by Sid Fleischman
The Little Swineherd and Other Tales, by Paula Fox
Queen of Hearts, by Vera and Bill Cleaver

1980 *A Gathering of Days: A New England Girl's Journal, 1830–32,* by Joan W. Blos
A Swiftly Tilting Planet, by Madeleine L'Engle
Finalists: *The Road from Home: The Story of an Armenian Girl,* by David Kherdian
Throwing Shadows, by Elaine Konigsburg
Words by Heart, by Ouica Sebestyen
Alan and Naomi, by Myron Levoy
Frog and Toad Are Friends, by Arnold Lobel
The Great Gilly Hopkins, by Katherine Paterson
Higglety Pigglety Pop! Or There Must Be More to Life, by Maurice Sendak

1981 *The Night Swimmers,* by Betsy Byars
Oh, Boy! Babies, by Alison Cragin Herzig and Jane Lawrence Mall
Ramona and Her Mother, by Beverly Cleary
Finalists: *The Alfred Summer,* by Jan Slepian
Far from Home, by Ouida Sebestyen
Jacob Have I Loved, by Katherine Paterson
A Place Apart, by Paula Fox
All Together Now, by Sue Ellen Bridgers
The High King, by Lloyd Alexander
Tex, by S. E. Hinton
The Westing Game, by Ellen Raskin
All Times, All Peoples: A World History of Slavery, by Milton Meltzer
The Ballpark, by William Jasperjohn
People, by Peter Spier
Where Do You Think You're Going, Christopher Columbus?, by Jean Fritz

1982 *Westmark,* by Lloyd Alexander
Words by Heart, by Ouida Sebestyen
A Penguin Year, by Susan Bonners
Outside Over There, by Maurice Sendak
Noah's Ark, by Peter Spier

1983 *Homesick: My Own Story,* by Jean Fritz
A Place Apart, by Paula Fox
Marked by Fire, by Joyce Carol Thomas

Chimney Sweeps, by James Cross Goslin, illus. Margot Tomes
Miss Rumphius, by Barbara Cooney
Dr. DeSoto, by William Steig
A House Is a House for Me, by Mary Ann Hoberman, illus. Betty Fraser

Randolph J. Caldecott Medal

Determined each year by a special committee of the American Library Association Children's Services Division, this award is given to the illustrator of the picture book judged to be the most distinguished of the previous year. The book must be published in the United States, and the illustrator must be a citizen or resident of the United States.

1938 *Animals of the Bible,* by Helen Dean Fish, illus. Dorothy P. Lathrop
Honor Books: *Seven Simeons,* by Boris Artzybasheff
Four and Twenty Blackbirds, by Helen Dean Fish, illus. Robert Lawson

1939 *Mei Li,* by Thomas Handforth
Honor Books: *The Forest Pool,* by Laura Adams Armer
Wee Gillis, by Munro Leaf, illus. Robert Lawson
Snow White and the Seven Dwarfs, by Wanda Gág
Barkis, by Clare Newberry
Andy and the Lion, by James Daugherty

1940 *Abraham Lincoln,* by Ingri and Edgar d'Aulaire
Honor Books: *Cock-a-Doodle Doo,* by Berta and Elmer Hader
Madeline, by Ludwig Bemelmans
The Ageless Story, by Lauren Ford

1941 *They Were Strong and Good,* by Robert Lawson
Honor Book: *April's Kittens,* by Clare Newberry

1942 *Make Way for Ducklings,* by Robert McCloskey
Honor Books: *An American ABC,* by Maud and Miska Petersham
In My Mother's House, by Ann Nolan Clark
Paddle-To-The-Sea, by Holling C. Holling
Nothing At All, by Wanda Gág

1943 *The Little House,* by Virginia Lee Burton
Honor Books: *Dash and Dart,* by Mary and Conrad Buff
Marshmallow, by Clare Newberry

1944 *Many Moons,* by James Thurber, illus. Louis Slobodkin
Honor Books: *Small Rain: Verses from the Bible,* selected by Jessie Orton Jones, illus. Elizabeth Orton Jones
Pierre Pigeon, by Lee Kingman, illus. Arnold E. Bare
The Mighty Hunter, by Berta and Elmer Hader
A Child's Good Night Book, by Margaret Wise Brown, illus. Jean Charlot
Good Luck Horse, by Chin-Yi Chan, illus. Plao Chan

1945 *Prayer for a Child,* by Rachel Field, illus. Elizabeth Orton Jones
Honor Books: *Mother Goose,* illus. Tasha Tudor

In the Forest, by Marie Hall Ets
Yonie Wondernose, by Marguerite de Angeli
The Christmas Anna Angel, by Ruth Sawyer, illus. Kate Seredy

1946 *The Rooster Crows,* illus. Maud and Miska Petersham
Honor Books: *Little Lost Lamb,* by Golden MacDonald, illus. Leonard Weisgard
Sing Mother Goose, by Opal Wheeler, illus. Marjorie Torrey
My Mother Is the Most Beautiful Woman in the World, by Becky Reyher, illus. Ruth Gannett
You Can Write Chinese, by Kurt Wiese

1947 *The Little Island,* by Golden MacDonald, illus. Leonard Weisgard
Honor Books: *Rain Drop Splash,* by Alvin Tresselt, illus. Leonard Weisgard
Boats on the River, by Marjorie Flack, illus. Jay Hyde Barnum
Timothy Turtle, by Al Graham, illus. Tony Palazzo
Pedro, The Angel of Alvera Street, by Leo Politi
Sing in Praise: A Collection of the Best Loved Hymns, by Opal Wheeler, illus. Marjorie Torrey

1948 *White Snow, Bright Snow,* by Alvin Tresselt, illus. Roger Duvoisin
Honor Books: *Stone Soup,* by Marcia Brown
McElligot's Pool, by Dr. Seuss
Bambino the Clown, by George Schreiber
Roger and the Fox, by Lavinia Davis, illus. Hildegard Woodward
Song of Robin Hood, ed. Anne Malcolmson, illus. Virginia Lee Burton

1949 *The Big Snow,* by Berta and Elmer Hader
Honor Books: *Blueberries for Sal,* by Robert McCloskey
All Around the Town, by Phyllis McGinley, illus. Helen Stone
Juanita, by Leo Politi
Fish in the Air, by Kurt Wiese

1950 *Song of the Swallows,* by Leo Politi
Honor Books: *America's Ethan Allen,* by Stewart Holbrook, illus. Lynd Ward
The Wild Birthday Cake, by Lavinia Davis, illus. Hildegard Woodward
The Happy Day, by Ruth Krauss, illus. Marc Simont
Bartholomew and the Oobleck, by Dr. Seuss
Henry Fisherman, by Marcia Brown

1951 *The Egg Tree,* by Katherine Milhous
Honor Books: *Dick Whittington and His Cat,* by Marcia Brown
The Two Reds, by Will, illus. Nicolas
If I Ran the Zoo, by Dr. Seuss
The Most Wonderful Doll in the World, by Phyllis McGinley, illus. Helen Stone
T-Bone the Baby Sitter, by Clare Newberry

1952 *Finders Keepers,* by Will, illus. Nicolas
Honor Books: *Mr. T. W. Anthony Woo,* by Marie Hall Ets

Skipper John's Cook, by Marcia Brown
All Falling Down, by Gene Zion, illus. Margaret Bloy Graham
Bear Party, by William Pène duBois
Feather Mountain, by Elizabeth Olds

1953 *The Biggest Bear,* by Lynd Ward
Honor Books: *Puss in Boots,* by Charles Perrault, illus. and trans. Marcia Brown
One Morning in Maine, by Robert McCloskey
Ape in a Cape, by Fritz Eichenberg
The Storm Book, by Charlotte Zolotow, illus. Margaret Bloy Graham
Five Little Monkeys, by Juliet Kepes

1954 *Madeline's Rescue,* by Ludwig Bemelmans
Honor Books: *Journey Cake, Ho!,* by Ruth Sawyer, illus. Robert McCloskey
When Will the World Be Mine?, by Mariam Schlein, illus. Jean Charlot
The Steadfast Tin Soldier, by Hans Christian Andersen, illus. Marcia Brown
A Very Special House, by Ruth Krauss, illus. Maurice Sendak
Green Eyes, by A. Birnbaum

1955 *Cinderella, or the Little Glass Slipper,* by Charles Perrault, trans. and illus. Marcia Brown
Honor Books: *Book of Nursery and Mother Goose Rhymes,* illus. Marguerite de Angeli
Wheel on the Chimney, by Margaret Wise Brown, illus. Tibor Gergely
The Thanksgiving Story, by Alice Dalgliesh, illus. Helen Sewell

1956 *Frog Went A-Courtin',* ed. John Langstaff, illus. Feodor Rojankovsky
Honor Books: *Play with Me,* by Marie Hall Ets
Crow Boy, by Taro Yashima

1957 *A Tree Is Nice,* by Janice May Udry, illus. Marc Simont
Honor Books: *Mr. Penny's Race Horse,* by Marie Hall Ets
1 is One, by Tasha Tudor
Anatole, by Eve Titus, illus. Paul Galdone
Gillespie and the Guards, by Benjamin Elkin, illus. James Daugherty
Lion, by William Pène duBois

1958 *Time of Wonder,* by Robert McCloskey
Honor Books: *Fly High, Fly Low,* by Don Freeman
Anatole and the Cat, by Eve Titus, illus. Paul Galdone

1959 *Chanticleer and the Fox,* adapted from Chaucer, illus. Barbara Cooney
Honor Books: *The House That Jack Built,* by Antonio Frasconi
What Do You Say, Dear?, by Sesyle Joslin, illus. Maurice Sendak
Umbrella, by Taro Yashima

1960 *Nine Days to Christmas,* by Marie Hall Ets and Aurora Labastida, illus. Marie Hall Ets

Honor Books: *Houses From the Sea,* by Alice E. Goudey, illus. Adrienne Adams
The Moon Jumpers, by Janice May Udry, illus. Maurice Sendak

1961 *Baboushka and the Three Kings,* by Ruth Robbins, illus. Nicholas Sidjakov
Honor Book: *Inch By Inch,* by Leo Lionni

1962 *Once a Mouse,* by Marcia Brown
Honor Books: *The Fox Went Out On a Chilly Night,* illus. Peter Spier
Little Bear's Visit, by Else Holmelund Minarik, illus. Maurice Sendak
The Day We Saw the Sun Come Up, by Alice E. Goudey, illus. Adrienne Adams

1963 *The Snowy Day,* by Ezra Jack Keats
Honor Books: *The Sun Is a Golden Earring,* by Natalia M. Belting, illus. Bernarda Bryson
Mr. Rabbit and the Lovely Present, by Charlotte Zolotow, illus. Maurice Sendak

1964 *Where the Wild Things Are,* by Maurice Sendak
Honor Books: *Swimmy,* by Leo Lionni
All in the Morning Early, by Sorche Nic Leodhas, illus. Evaline Ness
Mother Goose and Nursery Rhymes, illus. Philip Reed

1965 *May I Bring a Friend?,* by Beatrice Schenk de Regniers, illus. Beni Montresor
Honor Books: *Rain Makes Applesauce,* by Julian Scheer, illus. Marvin Bileck
The Wave, by Margaret Hodges, illus. Blair Lent
A Pocketful of Cricket, by Rebecca Caudill, illus. Evaline Ness

1966 *Always Room for One More,* by Sorche Nic Leodhas, illus. Noony Hogrogian
Honor Books: *Hide and Seek Fog,* by Alvin Tresselt, illus. Roger Duvoisin
Just Me, by Marie Hall Ets
Tom Tit Tot, by Evaline Ness

1967 *Sam, Bangs and Moonshine,* by Evaline Ness
Honor Book: *One Wide River to Cross,* by Barbara Emberley, illus. Ed Emberley

1968 *Drummer Hoff,* by Barbara Emberley, illus. Ed Emberley
Honor Books: *Frederick,* by Leo Lionni
Seashore Story, by Taro Yashima
The Emperor and the Kite, by Jane Yolen, illus. Ed Young

1969 *The Fool of the World and the Flying Ship,* by Arthur Ransome, illus. Uri Shulevitz
Honor Book: *Why the Sun and the Moon Live in the Sky,* by Elphinstone Dayrell, illus. Blair Lent

1970 *Sylvester and the Magic Pebble,* by William Steig
Honor Books: *Goggles,* by Ezra Jack Keats
Alexander and the Wind-up Mouse, by Leo Lionni
Pop Corn & Ma Goodness, by Edna Mitchell Preston, illus. Robert Andrew Parker

Thy Friend, Obadiah, by Brinton Turkle
The Judge, by Harve Zemach, illus. Margot Zemach

1971 *A Story—A Story,* by Gail E. Haley
Honor Books: *The Angry Moon,* by William Sleator, illus. Blair Lent
Frog and Toad Are Friends, by Arnold Lobel
In the Night Kitchen, by Maurice Sendak

1972 *One Fine Day,* by Nonny Hogrogian
Honor Books: *Hildilid's Night,* by Cheli Durán Ryan, illus. Arnold Lobel
If All the Seas Were One Sea, by Janina Domanska
Moja Means One, by Muriel Feelings, illus. Tom Feelings

1973 *The Funny Little Women,* retold by Arlene Mosel, illus. Blair Lent
Honor Books: *Anasi the Spider,* adapted and illus. Gerald McDermott
Hosie's Alphabet, by Hosea, Tobias, and Lisa Baskin, illus.
Leonard Baskin
Snow White and the Seven Dwarfs, trans. Randall Jarrell, illus.
Nancy Ekholm Burkert
When Clay Sings, by Byrd Baylor, illus. Tom Bahti

1974 *Duffy and the Devil,* retold by Harve Zemach, illus. Margot Zemach
Honor Books: *Three Jovial Huntsmen: A Mother Goose Rhyme,* adapted and
illus. Susan Jeffers
Cathedral: The Story of Its Construction, written and illus. David
Macaulay

1975 *Arrow to the Sun, A Pueblo Indian Tale,* by Gerald McDermott
Honor Book: *Jambo Means Hello, Swahili Alphabet Book,* by Muriel Feelings,
illus. Tom Feelings

1977 *Ashanti To Zulu: African Traditions,* by Margaret Musgrove, illus. Leo and
Diane Dillon
Honor Books: *Fish for Supper,* by M. B. Goffstein
The Contest, retold and illus. by Nonny Hogrogian.
The Golem: A Jewish Legend by Beverly Brodsky McDermott
Hawk, I'm Your Brother, by Byrd Baylor, illus. Peter Parnall
The Amazing Bone, by William Steig

1978 *Noah's Ark,* illustrated by Peter Spier
Honor Books: *Castle,* by David Macaulay
It Could Always Be Worse, retold and illus. by Margot Zemach

1979 *The Girl Who Loved Wild Horses,* by Paul Goble
Honor Books: *Freight Train,* by Donald Crew
The Way to Start a Day, by Byrd Baylor, illus. Peter Parnall

1980 *Ox-Cart Man,* Donald Hall, illus. Barbara Cooney
Honor Books: *Ben's Trumpet,* by Rachel Isadora
The Treasure, by Uri Shulevitz
The Garden of Abdul Gasazi, by Chris Van Allsburg

1981 *Fables,* by Arnold Lobel
Honor Books: *The Grey Lady and the Strawberry Snatcher,* by Molly Bang

Truck, by Donald Crews
Mice Twice, by Joseph Low
The Bremen-town Musicians, retold and illus. by Ilse Plume

1982 *Jumanli*, by Chris Van Allsburg
Honor Books: *A Visit to William Blake's Inn: Poem for Innocent and Experienced Travelers*, by Nancy Willard
Where the Buffaloes Begin, by Olaf Baker
On Market Street, by Arnold Lobel
Outside, Over There, by Maurice Sendak

1983 *Shadow*, Marcia Brown, trans. illus.
Honor Books: *A Chair for My Mother*, by Vera B. Williams
When I Was Young in the Mountains, by Cynthia Rylant, illus. Diane Goode

1984 *The Glorious Flight across the Channel with Louis Bleriot*, by Alice and Martin Provenson
Honor Books: *Ten, Nine, Eight*, by Molly Bang
Little Red Riding Hood, by Trina Schart Hyman

Child Study Children's Book Committee (Formerly Child Study Association of America/Wei-Met Children's Book Award)

Awarded each year by the Child Study Association, this award is given to a book published in the preceding year that relates to problems and realities in children's lives.

1944 *Keystone Kids*, by John R. Tunis

1945 *The House*, by Marjorie Allee

1946 *The Moved-Outers*, by Florence Crannel Means

1947 *Heart of Danger*, by Howard Pease

1948 *Judy's Journey*, by Lois Lenski

1949 *The Big Wave*, by Pearl Buck

1950 *Paul Tiber*, by Maria Gleit

1951 *The United Nations and Youth*, by Eleanor Roosevelt and Helen Ferris

1952 No Award

1953 *Twenty and Ten*, by Claire Huchet Bishop
Jareb, by Miriam Powell

1954 *In a Mirror*, by Mary Stolz

1955 *High Road Home*, by William Corbin
The Ordeal of the Young Hunter, by Jonreed Lauritzen

1956 *Crow Boy*, by Taro Yashima
Plain Girl, by Virginia Sorensen

1957 *The House of Sixty Fathers*, by Meindert DeJong

1958 *Shadow Across the Campus*, by Helen R. Sattley

1959 *South Town*, by Lorenz Graham

1960 *Jennifer*, by Zoa Sherburne

1961 *Janine*, by Robin McKown

1962 *The Road to Agra*, by Aimee Sommerfelt
The Girl From Puerto Rico, by Hila Colman

1963 *The Trouble with Terry*, by Joan Lexau

1964 *The Rock and the Willow*, by Mildred Lee
The Peaceable Revolution, by Betty Schechter

1965 *The High Pastures*, by Ruth Harnden

1966 *The Empty Schoolhouse*, by Natalie S. Carlson

1967 *Queenie Peavy*, by Robert Burch
Curious George Goes to the Hospital, by Margaret and H. A. Rey

1968 *The Contender*, by Robert Lipsyte

1969 *What It's All About*, by Vadim Frolov
Where Is Daddy? The Story of a Divorce, by Beth Goff

1970 *The Empty Moat*, by Margaretha Shemin

1971 *Migrant Girl*, by Carli Laklan
Rock Star, by James Lincoln Collier

1972 *John Henry McCoy*, by Lillie D. Chaffin
The Pair of Shoes, by Aline Glasgow

1973 *A Sound of Chariots*, by Mollie Hunter

1974 *A Taste of Blackberries*, by Doris Buchanan Smith

1975 *Luke Was There*, by Eleanor Clymer

1976 *The Garden Is Doing Fine*, by Carol Farley

1977 *Somebody Else's Child*, by Roberta Silman

1978 *The Pinballs*, by Betsy Byars

1979 *The Devil in Vienna*, by Doris Orgel

1980 *The Whipman Is Watching*, by T. A. Dyer

1981 *A Boat to Nowhere*, by Maureen Crane Wartski

Council on Interracial Books for Children Award

Awarded each year by the Council to minority authors whose unpublished manuscripts are judged to be outstanding.

1968 *Where Does the Day Go?,* by Walter N. Myers
The Soul Brothers and Sister Lou, by Kristin Hunter

1969 *ABC: The Story of the Alphabet,* by Virginia Cox
Sidewalk Story, by Sharon Bell Mathis
Letters from Uncle David: Underground Hero, by Margot S. Webb

1970 *Jimmy Yellow Hawk,* by Virginia Driving Hawk Sneve
Sneakers, by Ray Anthony Shepard
I Am Magic, by Juan Valenzuela

1971–1972 *Morning Song,* by Minfong Ho
The Rock Cried Out, by Florenz Webbe Maxwell
The Unusual Puerto Rican, by Theodore Laquer-Franceschi

1973 *Morning Arrow,* by Nanabah Chee Dodge
Grandfather's Bridge, by Michele O. Robinson
Eyak, by Dorothy Tomiye Okamoto
Song of the Trees, by Mildred D. Taylor
El Pito De Plata De Pito, by Jack Agueros

1974 *Simba, Midnight (The Stallion of the Night) and Mweusi,* by Aishah S. Abdullah
My Father Hijacked a Plane, by Abelardo B. Delgado
Yari, by Antonia A. Hernandez

1975 *Letters to a Friend on a Brown Paper Bag,* by Emily R. Moore.

1976 *El Mundo Maravilloso de Macu,* by Lydia Milagros Gonzalez
(Award discontinued after 1976)

The Golden Kite

Awards presented to children's book authors and artists by their fellow authors and artists. (Year indicated is year of award—one year after publication.)

1974 *Summer of My German Soldier,* by Bette Greene
Honor Books: *Red Rock over the River,* by Patricia Beatty
McBroom the Rainmaker, by Sid Fleischman

1975 *The Girl Who Cried Flowers,* Jane Yolen
Honor Books: *The Way Things Are,* by Myra Cohn Livingston
Meaning Well, by Sheila Cole

1976 *The Garden Is Doing Fine,* by Carol Farley
Honor Books: *The Transfigured Hart,* by Jane Yolen
Naomi, by Berniece Rabe

1977 *One More Flight,* by Eve Bunting
Honor Books: *Growing Anyway Up,* by Florence Parry Heide
The Moon Ribbon, by Jane Yolen

1978 *The Girl Who Had No Name,* by Berniece Rabe
Honor Book: *Foster Child,* by Marion Dane Bauer
Peeper, First Voice of Spring, by Robert McClung
Honor Book: *Evolution Goes on Every Day,* by Dorothy Hinshaw Patent

1979 *And You Give Me a Pain, Elaine,* by Stella Pevsner
Honor Book: *The Devil in Vienna,* by Doris Orgel
How I Came To Be a Writer, by Phyllis Reynolds Naylor
Honor Book: *Bionic Parts for People,* by Gloria Skurzynski

1980 *The Magic of the Glits,* by Carole S. Adler
Honor Book: *Cross Country Cat,* by Mary Calhoun
Runaway Teens, by Arnold Madison
Honor Book: *America's Endangered Birds,* by Robert McClung

1981 *Arthur, For the Very First Time,* by Patricia MacLachlan
Honor Book: *The Half-a-Moon Inn,* by Paul Fleischman
The Lives of Spiders, by Dorothy Hinshaw Patent
Honor Book: *Finding Your First Job,* by Sue Alexander

1982 *Little, Little,* by M. E. Kerr
Honor Book: *A Visit to William Blake's Inn: Poems for Innocent and Experi-*
enced Travelers, by Nancy Willard
Blissymbolics, by Elizabeth Helfman
Honor Book: *Dinosaurs of North America,* by Helen Roney Sattler

1983 *Ralph S. Mouse,* by Beverly Cleary
Honor Book: *Class Dismissed,* by Mel Glenn
Chimney Sweeps, by James Cross Giblin
Honor Book: *The Brooklyn Bridge,* by Judith St. George
Giorgio's Village, by Tomie dePaola

John Newbery Medal

The most coveted children's book award, this prize is given annually to the book judged by a special committee selected by the American Library Association Children's Services Division to be the most outstanding work of children's literature published during the preceding year. The award is given only to those authors who are American citizens, and the book must be published in the United States.

1922 *The Story of Mankind,* by Hendrik Willem van Loon
Honor Books: *The Great Quest,* by Charles Hawes
Cedric the Forester, by Bernard Marshall
The Old Tobacco Shop, by William Bowen
The Golden Fleece and the Heroes Who Lived Before Achilles,
by Padraic Colum
Windy Hill, by Cornelia Meigs

1923 *The Voyages of Doctor Dolittle,* by Hugh Lofting

1924 *The Dark Frigate,* by Charles Hawes

1925 *Tales From Silver Lands,* by Charles Finger
Honor Books: *Nicholas,* by Anne Carroll Moore
Dream Coach, by Anne Parrish

1926 *Shen of the Sea,* by Arthur Bowie Chrisman
Honor Books: *Voyagers,* by Padraic Colum

1927 *Smoky, The Cowhorse,* by Will James

1928 *Gayneck, the Story of a Pigeon,* by Dhan Gopal Mukerji
　　Honor Books: *The Wonder Smith and His Son,* by Ella Young
　　　　　　　　Downright Dencey, by Caroline Snedeker

1929 *The Trumpeter of Krakow,* by Eric P. Kelly
　　Honor Books: *Pigtail of Ah Lee Ben Loo,* by John Bennett
　　　　　　　　Millions of Cats, by Wanda Gág
　　　　　　　　The Boy Who Was, by Grace Hallock
　　　　　　　　Clearing Weather, by Cornelia Meigs
　　　　　　　　Runaway Papoose, by Grace Moon
　　　　　　　　Tod of the Fens, by Elinor Whitney

1930 *Hitty, Her First Hundred Years,* by Rachel Field
　　Honor Books: *Daughter of the Seine,* by Jeanette Eaton
　　　　　　　　Pran of Albania, by Elizabeth Miller
　　　　　　　　Jumping-Off Place, by Marian Hurd McNeely
　　　　　　　　Tangle-Coated Horse and Other Tales, by Ella Young
　　　　　　　　Vaino, by Julia Davis Adams
　　　　　　　　Little Blacknose, by Hildegarde Swift

1931 *The Cat Who Went to Heaven,* by Elizabeth Coatsworth
　　Honor Books: *Floating Island,* by Anne Parrish
　　　　　　　　The Dark Star of Itza, by Alida Malkus
　　　　　　　　Queer Person, by Ralph Hubbard
　　　　　　　　Mountains Are Free, by Julia Davis Adams
　　　　　　　　Spice and the Devil's Cave, by Agnes Hewes
　　　　　　　　Meggy Macintosh, by Elizabeth Janet Gray
　　　　　　　　Garram the Hunter, by Herbert Best
　　　　　　　　Ood-le-uk the Wanderer, by Alice Lide and Margaret Johansen

1932 *Waterless Mountain,* by Laura Adams Armer
　　Honor Books: *The Fairy Circus,* by Dorothy P. Lathrop
　　　　　　　　Calico Bush, by Rachel Field
　　　　　　　　Boy of the South Seas, by Eunice Tietjens
　　　　　　　　Out of the Flame, by Eloise Lownsbery
　　　　　　　　Jane's Island, by Marjorie Allee
　　　　　　　　Truce of the Wolf and Other Tales of Old Italy, by Mary Gould
　　　　　　　　　Davis

1933 *Young Fu of the Upper Yangtze,* by Elizabeth Lewis
　　Honor Books: *Swift Rivers,* by Cornelia Meigs
　　　　　　　　The Railroad to Freedom, by Hildegarde Swift
　　　　　　　　Children of the Soil, by Nora Burglon

1934 *Invincible Louisa,* by Cornelia Meigs
　　Honor Books: *The Forgotten Daughter,* by Caroline Snedeker
　　　　　　　　Swords of Steel, by Elsie Singmaster
　　　　　　　　ABC Bunny, by Wanda Gág
　　　　　　　　Winged Girl of Knossos, by Erik Berry
　　　　　　　　New Land, by Sarah Schmidt
　　　　　　　　Big Tree of Bunlahy, by Padraic Colum
　　　　　　　　Glory of the Seas, by Agnes Hewes
　　　　　　　　Apprentice of Florence, by Anne Kyle

1935 *Dobry,* by Monica Shannon
  Honor Books: *Pageant of Chinese History,* by Elizabeth Seeger
        Davy Crockett, by Constance Rourke
        Day on Skates, by Hilda Van Stockum

1936 *Caddie Woodlawn,* by Carol Ryrie Brink
  Honor Books: *Honk, the Moose,* by Phil Stong
        The Good Master, by Kate Seredy
        Young Walter Scott, by Elizabeth Janet Gray
        All Sail Set, by Armstrong Sperry

1937 *Roller Skates,* by Ruth Sawyer
  Honor Books: *Phoebe Fairchild: Her Book,* by Lois Lenski
        Whistler's Van, by Idwal Jones
        Golden Basket, by Ludwig Bemelmans
        Winterbound, by Margery Bianco
        Audubon, by Constance Rourke
        The Codfish Musket, by Agnes Hewes

1938 *The White Stag,* by Kat Seredy
  Honor Books: *Pecos Bill,* by James Cloyd Bowman
        Bright Island, by Mabel Robinson
        On the Banks of Plum Creek, by Laura Ingalls Wilder

1939 *Thimble Summer,* by Elizabeth Enright
  Honor Books: *Nino,* by Valenti Angelo
        Mr. Popper's Penguins, by Richard and Florence Atwater
        Hello the Boat!, by Phyllis Crawford
        Leader by Destiny: George Washington, Man and Patriot, by
          Jeanette Eaton
        Penn, by Elizabeth Janet Gray

1940 *Daniel Boone,* by James Daugherty
  Honor Books: *The Singing Tree,* by Kate Seredy
        Runner of the Mountain Tops, by Mabel Robinson
        By the Shores of Silver Lake, by Laura Ingalls Wilder
        Boy with a Pack, by Stephen W. Meader

1941 *Call It Courage,* by Armstrong Sperry
  Honor Books: *Blue Willow,* by Doris Gates
        Young Mac of Fort Vancouver, by Mary Jane Carr
        The Long Winter, by Laura Ingalls Wilder
        Nansen, by Anna Gertrude Hall

1942 *The Matchlock Gun,* by Walter D. Edmonds
  Honor Books: *Little Town on the Prairie,* by Laura Ingalls Wilder
        George Washington's World, by Genevieve Foster
        Indian Captive: The Story of Mary Jemison, by Lois Lenski
        Down Ryton Water, by Eva Roe Gaggin

1943 *Adam of the Road,* by Elizabeth Janet Gray
  Honor Books: *The Middle Moffat,* by Eleanor Estes
        Have You Seen Tom Thumb?, by Mabel Leigh Hunt

1944 *Johnny Tremain,* by Esther Forbes
  Honor Books: *These Happy Golden Years,* by Laura Ingalls Wilder
  Fog Magic, by Julia Sauer
  Rufus M., by Eleanor Estes
  Mountain Born, by Elizabeth Yates

1945 *Rabbit Hill,* by Robert Lawson
  Honor Books: *The Hundred Dresses,* by Eleanor Estes
  The Silver Pencil, by Alice Dalgliesh
  Abraham Lincoln's World, by Genevieve Foster
  Lone Journey: The Life of Roger Williams, by Jeanette Eaton

1946 *Strawberry Girl,* by Lois Lenski
  Honor Books: *Justin Morgan Had a Horse,* by Marguerite Henry
  The Moved-Outers, by Florence Crannell Means
  Bhimsa, The Dancing Bear, by Christine Weston
  New Found World, by Katherine Shippen

1947 *Miss Hickory,* by Carolyn Sherwin Bailey
  Honor Books: *Wonderful Year,* by Nancy Barnes
  Big Tree, by Mary and Conrad Buff
  The Heavenly Tenants, by William Maxwell
  The Avion My Uncle Flew, by Cyrus Fisher
  The Hidden Treasure of Glaston, by Eleanore Jewett

1948 *The Twenty-One Balloons,* by William Pène duBois
  Honor Books: *Pancakes-Paris,* by Claire Huchet Bishop
  Li Lun, Lad of Courage, by Carolyn Treffinger
  The Quaint and Curious Quest of Johnny Longfoot, by Catherine Besterman
  The Cow-Tail Switch, And Other West African Stories, by Harold Courlander
  Misty of Chincoteague, by Marguerite Henry

1949 *King of the Wind,* by Marguerite Henry
  Honor Books: *Seabird,* by Holling C. Holling
  Daughter of the Mountains, by Louise Rankin
  My Father's Dragon, by Ruth S. Gannett
  Story of the Negro, by Arna Bontemps

1950 *The Door in the Wall,* by Marguerite de Angeli
  Honor Books: *Tree of Freedom,* by Rebecca Caudill
  The Blue Cat of Castle Town, by Catherine Coblentz
  Kildee House, by Rutherford Montgomery
  George Washington, by Genevieve Foster
  Song of the Pines, by Walter and Marion Havighurst

1951 *Amos Fortune, Free Man,* by Elizabeth Yates
  Honor Books: *Better Known as Johnny Appleseed,* by Mabel Leigh Hunt
  Gandhi, Fighter Without a Sword, by Jeanette Eaton
  Abraham Lincoln, Friend of the People, by Clara Ingram Judson
  The Story of Appleby Capple, by Anne Parrish

1952 *Ginger Pye,* by Eleanor Estes
    Honor Books: *Americans Before Columbus,* by Elizabeth Baity
                    Minn of the Mississippi, by Holling C. Holling
                      The Defender, by Nicholas Kalashnikoff
                      The Light at Tern Rocks, by Julia Sauer
                      The Apple and the Arrow, by Mary and Conrad Buff

1953 *Secret of the Andes,* by Ann Nolan Clark
    Honor Books: *Charlotte's Web,* by E. B. White
                      Moccasin Trail, by Eloise McGraw
                      Red Sails to Capri, by Ann Weil
                      The Bears on Hemlock Mountain, by Alice Dalgliesh
                      Birthdays of Freedom, Vol. 1, by Genevieve Foster

1954 *... And Now Miguel,* by Joseph Krumgold
    Honor Books: *All Alone,* by Claire Huchet Bishop
                      Shadrach, by Meindert DeJong
                      Hurry Home Candy, by Meindert DeJong
                      Theodore Roosevelt, Fighting Patriot, by Clara Ingram Judson
                      Magic Maize, by Mary and Conrad Buff

1955 *The Wheel on the School,* by Meindert DeJong
    Honor Books: *Courage of Sarah Noble,* by Alice Dalgliesh
                      Banner in the Sky, by James Ullman

1956 *Carry On, Mr. Bowditch,* by Jean Lee Latham
    Honor Books: *The Secret River,* by Marjorie Kinnan Rawlings
                      The Golden Name Day, by Jennie Lindquist
                      Men, Microscopes, and Living Things, by Katherine Shippen

1957 *Miracles on Maple Hill,* by Virginia Sorensen
    Honor Books: *Old Yeller,* by Fred Gipson
                      The House of Sixty Fathers, by Meindert DeJong
                      Mr. Justice Holmes, by Clara Ingram Judson
                      The Corn Grows Ripe, by Dorothy Rhoads
                      Black Fox of Lorne, by Marguerite de Angeli

1958 *Rifles for Watie,* by Harold Keith
    Honor Books: *The Horsecatcher,* by Mari Sandoz
                      Gone-Away Lake, by Elizabeth Enright
                      The Great Wheel, by Robert Lawson
                      Tom Paine, Freedom's Apostle, by Leo Gurko

1959 *The Witch of Blackbird Pond,* by Elizabeth George Speare
    Honor Books: *The Family Under the Bridge,* by Natalie S. Carlson
                      Along Came a Dog, by Meindert DeJong
                      Chucaro: Wild Pony of the Pampa, by Francis Kalnay
                      The Perilous Road, by William O. Steele

1960 *Onion John,* by Joseph Krumgold
    Honor Books: *My Side of the Mountain,* by Jean George
                      America Is Born, by Gerald W. Johnson
                      The Gammage Cup, by Carol Kendall

1961 *Island of the Blue Dolphins,* by Scott O'Dell
Honor Books: *America Moves Forward,* by Gerald W. Johnson
Old Ramon, by Jack Schaefer
The Cricket in Times Square, by George Seldon

1962 *The Bronze Bow,* by Elizabeth George Speare
Honor Books: *Frontier Living,* by Edwin Tunis
The Golden Goblet, by Eloise McGraw
Belling the Tiger, by Mary Stolz

1963 *A Wrinkle in Time,* by Madeleine L'Engle
Honor Books: *Thistle and Thyme,* by Sorche Nic Leodhas
Men of Athens, by Olivia Coolidge

1964 *It's Like This, Cat,* by Emily Cheney Neville
Honor Books: *Rascal,* by Sterling North
The Loner, by Ester Wier

1965 *Shadow of a Bull,* by Maia Wojciechowska
Honor Book: *Across Five Aprils,* by Irene Hunt

1966 *I, Juan De Pareja,* by Elizabeth Borten de Treviño
Honor Books: *The Black Cauldron,* by Lloyd Alexander
The Animal Family, by Randall Jarrell
The Noonday Friends, by Mary Stolz

1967 *Up a Road Slowly,* by Irene Hunt
Honor Books: *The King's Fifth,* by Scott O'Dell
Zlateh the Goat and Other Stories, by Isaac Bashevis Singer
The Jazz Man, by Mary H. Weik

1968 *From the Mixed-Up Files of Mrs. Basil E. Frankweiler,* by E. L. Konigsburg
Honor Books: *Jennifer, Hecate, Macbeth, William McKinley, and Me, Elizabeth,* by E. L. Konigsburg
The Black Pearl, by Scott O'Dell
The Fearsome Inn, by Isaac Bashevis Singer
The Egypt Game, by Zilpha Keatley Snyder

1969 *The High King,* by Lloyd Alexander
Honor Books: *To Be a Slave,* by Julius Lester
When Shlemiel Went to Warsaw and Other Stories, by Isaac Bashevis Singer

1970 *Sounder,* by William H. Armstrong
Honor Books: *Our Eddie,* by Sulamith Ish-Kishor
The Many Ways of Seeing: An Introduction to the Pleasures of Art, by Janet Gaylord Moore
Journey Outside, by Mary Q. Steele

1971 *Summer of the Swans,* by Betsy Byars
Honor Books: *Knee-Knock Rise,* by Natalie Babbitt
Enchantress from the Stars, by Sylvia Louise Engdahl
Sing Down the Moon, by Scott O'Dell

1972 *Mrs. Frisby and the Rats of NIMH,* by Robert C. O'Brien
  Honor Books: *Annie and the Old One,* by Miska Miles
        The Headless Cupid, by Zilpha Keatley Snyder
        Incident at Hawk's Hill, by Allan W. Eckert
        The Planet of Junior Brown, by Virginia Hamilton
        The Tombs of Atuan, by Ursula K. LeGuin

1973 *Julie of the Wolves,* by Jean Craighead George
  Honor Books: *Frog and Toad Together,* by Arnold Lobel
        The Upstairs Room, by Johanna Reiss
        The Witches of Worm, by Zilpha Keatley Snyder

1974 *The Slave Dancer,* by Paula Fox
  Honor Book: *The Dark Is Rising,* by Susan Cooper

1975 *M. C. Higgins, the Great,* by Virginia Hamilton
  Honor Books: *My Brother Sam Is Dead,* by James Lincoln Collier and
        Christopher Collier
        The Perilous Gard, by Elizabeth Marie Pope
        Phillip Hall Likes Me. I Reckon Maybe, by Bette Greene
        Figgs & Phantoms, by Ellen Raskin

1976 *The Grey King,* by Susan Cooper
  Honor Books: *Dragonwings,* by Lawrence Yep
        The Hundred Penny Box, by Sharon Bell Mathis

1977 *Roll of Thunder, Hear My Cry,* by Mildred D. Taylor
  Honor Books: *Abel's Island,* by William Steig
        A String in the Harp, by Nancy Bond

1978 *Bridge to Terabithia,* by Katherine Paterson
  Honor Books: *Anpao: An American Indian Odyssey,* by Jamake Highwater
        Ramona and Her Father, by Beverly Cleary

1979 *The Westing Game,* by Ellen Raskin
  Honor Book: *The Great Gilly Hopkins,* by Katherine Paterson

1980 *A Gathering of Days,* by Joan W. Elos
  Honor Book: *The Road from Home: The Story of an Armenian Girl,* by
        David Khercian

1981 *Jacob Have I Loved,* by Katherine Paterson
  Honor Books: *The Fledgling,* by Jane Langton
        A Ring of Endless Light, by Madeleine L'Engle

1982 *A Visit to William Blake's Inn: Poems for Innocent and Experienced
    Travelers,* by Nancy Willard
  Honor Books: *Ramona Quinby, Age 8,* by Beverly Cleary
        Upon the Head of the Goat, by Aranka Siegal

1983 *Dicey's Song,* by Cynthia Voight
  Honor Books: *The Blue Sword,* by Robin McKinley
        Dr. DeSoto, by William Steig
        Graven Images, by Paul Fleischman, illus. Andrew Glass

Homesick: My Own Story, by Jean Fritz, illus. by Margot Tomes

Sweet Whispers, Brother Rush, by Virginia Hamilton

1984 *Dear Mr. Henshaw,* by Beverly Cleary

Honor Books: *The Wish Game,* by Bill Brittain

Sugaring Time, by Kathryn Lasky

A Solitary Blue, by Cynthia Voight

Sign of the Beaver, by Elizabeth George Speare

For other children's book awards see *Awards and Prizes,* a paperback published by the Children's Book Council, 175 Fifth Ave., New York, N.Y. 10010.

•APPENDIX•

OTHER REFERENCES FOR CHILDREN'S LITERATURE

ANDERSON, WILLIAM, AND GROFF, PATRICK. *A New Look at Children's Literature*. Belmont, California: Wadsworth, 1972.
Provides a methodology for literary analysis of children's stories. Also examines and discusses the different types of children's literature. Presents a stimulating and intelligent set of recommendations for teaching literature to children. Contains an annotated bibliography of children's books corresponding to the different types of books examined in the text. Interesting and informative book.

BROOKS, PETER, ed. *The Child's Part*. Boston: Beacon Press, 1969.
Provides a scholarly and historical approach to children's literature. Focuses on French critics and sources but concerns itself with children's literature in general.

CAMERON, ELEANOR. *The Green and Burning Tree*. Boston: Little, Brown, 1969. Also in paper.
A collection of essays written by the author about children's books. Sensitive analyses of the feelings and intentions of authors. The book includes discussions of fantasy, as well as on how to write for children.

CARLSEN, G. ROBERT. *Books and the Teenage Reader,* 2d ed. New York: Harper & Row, 1980. Also in paper.
Useful discussion of literary genres for readers age twelve and up. But extremely out-of-date. Does not acknowledge any of the social issues handled by contemporary books. Bibliographies are briefly annotated.

CARLSON, RUTH KEARNEY. *Emerging Humanity, Multi-Ethnic Literature for Children and Adolescents*. Dubuque, Iowa: William C. Brown, 1972.
Descriptions and suggestions for using children's books containing characters of different ethnic and cultural backgrounds. Very practical and classroom-oriented.

CARLSON, RUTH KEARNEY. *Enrichment Ideas*. Dubuque Iowa: William C. Brown, 1976.

Each chapter contains a brief discussion of the topic, the history of language, vocabulary expansion, poetry, and books using loneliness as a theme. Selected references are listed, but not annotated. Hundreds of activities are described for children to do as an extension of their reading about and studying the above topics. A treasure chest of a book.

CATTERSON, JANE H., ed. *Children and Literature.* Newark, Delaware: International Reading Association, 1970. Paperback.
Articles representing an overview of children's literature. Includes theory as well as practice for classroom teachers.

CIANCIOLO, PATRICIA JEAN, ed. *Picture Books for Children.* 2d ed. Chicago: American Library Association, 1981.
An excellent resource and guide. The annotations of the books are useful and informational. The categories overlap somewhat, but the book is, in general, easy to use.

CULLINAN, BERNICE E. *Literature and the Child.* New York: Harcourt Brace Jovanovich, 1981.
Advocates that critical reading of literature be taught to elementary school children. Presents literary analyses of children's narrative fiction. Suggests activities for teachers and students to extend their critical abilities further.

EGOFF, SHEILA; STUBBS, G.T.; AND ASHLEY, L.F., eds. *Only Connect: Readings on Children's Literature.* Toronto: Oxford University Press, 1980.
A highly literate and stimulating collection of essays critically analyzing and discussing different aspects of children's literature.

GEORGIOU, CONSTANTINE. *Children and Their Literature.* Englewood Cliffs, New Jersey: Prentice-Hall, 1969.
This book presents a genre approach to the study of children's literature. Its uniqueness lies in the lushness of its illustrations and its focus on the aesthetic quality of books. The extra-wide blocks of text are difficult to read, but the text itself is interesting. Not enough books are described for a text that aims at being used as a reference.

GILLESPIE, MARGARET C. *History and Trends.* Dubuque, Iowa: William C. Brown, 1970.
A fascinating and thorough account of the history of children's literature, including several little-known names and interesting bits of information. Little attention is paid to contemporary times, but the book as a whole is entertaining and informative.

HAVILAND, VIRGINIA. *Children's Literature: A Guide to Reference Sources.* Washington, D.C.: Library of Congress, 1966. *Third Supplement,* 1982.
Two books containing an enormous number of annotated references covering the entire field of children's literature. The format is somewhat difficult to use. There are some important references omitted, but the two volumes are extensive resources.

HOPKINS, LEE BENNETT. *Books Are by People.* New York: Citation Press, 1969. Also in paper.
Interesting accounts of authors and illustrators of children's books. Hopkins interviewed one hundred and four people for this book. The information is presented in a personal, informal style. *More Books by More People,* by the same author, published in 1974, adds sixty-five additional authors and illustrators to the list. The interviews in the second book are longer and contain longer comments by the people interviewed.

HUCK, CHARLOTTE S. *Children's Literature in the Elementary School,* 3rd ed. New York: Holt, Rinehart and Winston, 1979.
Soon to be revised, this edition of the text is, nevertheless, valuable, extensive, and informative. Although the book emphasizes a genre and historical approach to children's literature, it also includes a substantial section on practical and creative methods for the classroom. Descriptions of children's books are sensitively and interestingly written. An awareness is expressed of the issues in children's books.

ISSUES IN CHILDREN'S BOOK SELECTION: A SCHOOL LIBRARY JOURNAL/ LIBRARY JOURNAL ANTHOLOGY. New York: Bowker. 1973.
A collection of articles presenting perspective on selecting children's books. Such topics as censorship, moral values, sex, self-image, and feminism are briefly but usefully presented. All of the articles are reprinted from the *School Library Journal.*

LARRICK, NANCY. *A Parent's Guide to Children's Reading,* 5th ed. New York: Bantam, 1982. Paperback.
Extensive, practical information and advice for parents and other concerned adults on how to encourage children to read. Many books are annotated in useful, contemporary categories.

LICKTEIG, MARY J. *An Introduction to Children's Literature.* Columbus: Merrill, 1975.
An overview of all of children's literature. Every topic is lightly touched on with indications for further study. The bibliographies, unfortunately, are not annotated. The author maintains an objectivity about all the topics and all the books. The appendixes and suggested references are useful. The author also contributes some practical suggestions for working with children.

LONSDALE, BERNARD J., AND MACKINTOSH, HELEN. *Children Experience Literature.* New York: Random House, 1973.
Combines a genre approach with a practical, classroom approach. Includes a chapter on literature and personal growth. Somewhat uncritical but useful reference.

LUECKE, FRITZ J., ed.. *Children's Books, Views and Values.* Middletown, Connecticut: Xerox Education Publications, 1973. Paperback. Eight excellent articles reprinted from several scholarly journals concerning issues in children's literature. Issues included are death, violence, feminism, and multiethnic books.

MEEKER, ALICE M. *Enjoying Literature with Children.* New York: Odyssey Press, 1969. Paperback.
Practical but somewhat traditional ideas for incorporating children's books into the elementary school curriculum.

REASONER, CHARLES F. *Releasing Children to Literature.* New York: Dell, 1968. Paperback.
Interesting and open-ended ideas for encouraging critical reading. This book specifically pertains to the Dell Yearling books, but the activities are imaginative and pertinent to any books. Thirty specific books are included, many of which are concerned with topics such as death, siblings, females, and war.

REASONER, CHARLES F. *Where the Readers Are.* New York: Dell, 1972. Paperback.
Another invaluable teachers' guide to imaginative and stimulating activities to accompany the reading of books. Reasoner specifically discusses thirty-four Dell Yearling books, but the ideas extend far beyond the particular books.

ROBINSON, EVELYN R., ed. *Readings about Children's Literature.* New York: David McKay, 1966.
A book of readings relating to a genre and pedagogic approach to children's literature. The articles are interesting and provide different perspectives on books for children.

SMITH, DORA V. *Fifty Years of Children's Books.* Champaign, Illinois: National Council of Teachers of English, 1963. Paperback.
A beautifully written, extremely informative, though traditional book on the history of children's literature. No mention is made of any contemporary issues.

SMITH, JAMES A. *Creative Teaching of Reading and Literature in the Elementary School.* Boston: Allyn and Bacon, 1970. Paperback.
Lesson plans, suggestions, and a discussion of the philosophy of creative teaching make this book a very useful one for teachers.

SMITH, JAMES STEEL. *A Critical Approach to Children's Literature.* New York: McGraw-Hill, 1967.
A scholarly literary approach to children's books. The author presents a methodology for critical analysis of children's literature.

SMITH, LILLIAN H. *The Unreluctant Years.* New York: Viking, 1971. Paperback.
A highly literate series of discussions of the different genres of children's literature. Smith presents her critical approach.

SUTHERLAND, ZENA ET AL. *Children and Books,* 6th ed. Glenview, Illinois: Scott, Foresman, 1981.
Revised considerably from the 1964 edition, this valuable reference provides discussions of books based on a genre approach. One chapter takes surface

recognition of issues. The appendixes provide the reader with book-selection aids, references, publishers' addresses, children's book awards, and a pronunciation guide. The book also recommends criteria for judging children's books. This text is one of the most comprehensive references published in the field of children's literature.

TWAY, EILEEN, ed. *Reading Ladders for Human Relations,* 6th ed. Washington, D.C.: American Council on Education, 1981. Paperback. Excellent resource for books and how to extend their use with young readers. This book includes many themes pertaining to personal and emotional guidance. Creating a positive self-image and coping with change are among these themes.

VIGUERS, RUTH HILL. *Margin for Surprise.* Boston: Little, Brown, 1964. Essays reflecting on the author's love of books and her respect for their impact on children. Viguers presents her opinions, her recollections, and her observations.

WHITE, MARY LOU. *Adventuring with Books: A Booklist for Pre-K–Grade 6,* rev. ed. Urbana, Illinois: National Council of Teachers of English, 1981. Approximately 2,500 children's books, published from 1977–1980. Brief but informative annotations.

WHITEHEAD, ROBERT. *Children's Literature: Strategies of Teaching.* Englewood Cliffs, New Jersey: Prentice-Hall, 1968. Paperback. Hundreds of practical ideas for using books in the classroom. No mention is made of the impact or issues involved in books, but the intent is to provide a cookbook of ideas for activities.

YOLEN, JANE. *Writing Books for Children.* Boston: The Writer, 1976. Yolen advocates that books for children be written so that the writer and reader can "take joy." The book includes an awareness of the social issues involved in books but also advises authors to refrain from heavy didacticism. A well-written, interesting book.

ZACCARIA, JOSEPH S., AND MOSES, HAROLD A. *Facilitating Human Development Through Reading: The Use of Bibliotherapy in Teaching and Counseling.* Champaign, Illinois: Stipes, 1968. Paperback. An extensive annotated bibliography follows a theoretical section on how to use books in a therapeutic manner with young readers.

AUTHOR AND ILLUSTRATOR INDEX

TITLE INDEX

SUBJECT INDEX